INTRODUCTION
TO
ENGLISH LAW

First Edition	.	.	.	December, 1950
Second Impression	.		.	January, 1952
Second Edition		.	.	August, 1953
Second Impression	.		.	September, 1954
Third Impression	.		.	November, 1954
Third Edition	.	.	.	June, 1955
Second Impression	.		.	July, 1956
Third Impression	.		.	January, 1957
Fourth Impression	.		.	February, 1958
Fifth Impression	.		.	January, 1959
Fourth Edition.		.	.	September, 1959
Second Impression	.		.	February, 1961
Third Impression	.		.	August, 1961
Fifth Edition	.	.	.	June, 1962
Second Impression	.		.	December, 1963
Third Impression	.		.	August, 1965
Sixth Edition		.	.	June, 1966
Second Impression	.		.	April, 1968
Seventh Edition		.	.	April, 1969
Second Impression	.		.	October, 1969
Third Impression	.		.	May, 1970
Eighth Edition.		.	.	July, 1972
Second Impression	.		.	July, 1973
Third Impression	.		.	May, 1974
Ninth Edition	.	.	.	June, 1976

INTRODUCTION

TO

ENGLISH LAW

NINTH EDITION

By

PHILIP S. JAMES, M.A.

Of the Inner Temple, Barrister;
Senior Fellow and Consultant Professor of English Law
in the University College at Buckingham;
formerly a Fellow of Exeter College, Oxford, and
Head of the Department of Law at Leeds University

Chapter on Revenue Law

by

G. N. GLOVER, LL.B.

Solicitor; Senior Lecturer in Law at Leeds University

LONDON
BUTTERWORTHS
1976

ENGLAND: BUTTERWORTH & CO. (PUBLISHERS) LTD.
               LONDON: 88 KINGSWAY, WC2B 6AB

AUSTRALIA: BUTTERWORTHS PTY. LTD.
               SYDNEY: 586 PACIFIC HIGHWAY, CHATSWOOD, NSW
               2067
               MELBOURNE: 343 LITTLE COLLINS STREET, 3000
               BRISBANE: 240 QUEEN STREET, 4000

CANADA: BUTTERWORTH & CO. (CANADA) LTD.
               TORONTO: 2265 MIDLAND AVENUE, SCARBOROUGH
               M1P 4S1

NEW ZEALAND: BUTTERWORTHS OF NEW ZEALAND LTD.
               WELLINGTON: 26/28 WARING TAYLOR STREET, 1

SOUTH
AFRICA: BUTTERWORTH & CO. (SOUTH AFRICA) (PTY.)
               LTD.
               DURBAN: 152/154 GALE STREET

U.S.A.:   BUTTERWORTH & CO. (PUBLISHERS) INC.
               BOSTON: 19 CUMMINGS PARK, WOBURN, MASS. 01801

©

BUTTERWORTH & CO. (PUBLISHERS) LTD.

1976

ISBN—Casebound: 0 406 60496 7
Limp: 0 406 60497 5

To
W. J.-G.

PREFACE TO THE NINTH EDITION

The publication of this edition prompts two salient thoughts.

In the first place I reflect that when in years gone by I became a soldier for the "duration" I was told by a bemedalled veteran of World War I to observe the golden rule: "You should only", he told me, "give orders to troops when it is necessary to do so, and then they should be as few and as simple as possible. If you issue more commands than are completely essential, or worse, if you give a series of commands and counter commands, you will make a fool of yourself and (more important) you will ruin your men's morale." My fellow "durationers" will, I feel sure, agree that that was the best of advice. And yet, if one concludes with Bentham and Austin that law is a "command" and, with Professor Lon Fuller, that the attainment of certainty is a part of its "inner morality" – something seems wrong. One can only surmise that our parliament-men (and to avoid the charge of "discrimination" parliament-ladies too) were not "durationers" or that, if they were, they are bent upon destroying the national morale. For they cast down upon us a torrent of ill-digested, ill-drafted, contradictory, unknowable, arbitrary, meaningless, redundant (and at times impractical) enactments and orders which are the despair of the writer of a book such as this: and which – more cogently – engender disrespect for law.

My second thought is that the overweening intrusion of the State into almost every corner of our lives leads one to question whether the (traditional) treatment which I have hitherto followed needs to be changed. Ought I to reveal the law as what it now very largely *is*, primarily "public"; a complex of enactments, orders, rules and exercises of arbitrary discretion? Perhaps I ought; and should another edition be needed perhaps I may have to consider a pioneer remoulding of the treatment. For the present I am content to save myself the exertion by reflecting that, whatever the *truth* may be, pride of place in our seminaries is still accorded to the traditional law which relates mainly to the Man rather than the State – contract, tort, property, and the rest.

This edition does, however, introduce an important innovation which will, I hope, please the reader as much as it gratifies me. Being averse to embarking upon the dismal science of *Revenue Law*, yet, knowing it to be of central importance in this taxridden age, I have prevailed upon my old friend Mr. G. N. Glover of the Faculty of Law, Leeds University, to produce a chapter on it. If I may venture my ignorant opinion, I would highly commend his work: such is his exposition, as it seems to me, that I *think* even I understand the substance of the subject matter.

Finally, my thanks are due to Miss Claudine Lévy of the Faculty of Law, Leeds University, to Mrs. Doris Jones of that Faculty, to Mrs. Jane Edwards of the University College at Buckingham, to my wife and to the publishers. The first was kind enough to read the passages in this edition which refer to the European Communities. To the second I owe a long-standing debt for doing the typing for this book through a number of editions (or was it indeed *all* but one?); and for embarking yet again upon similar drudgery. The third I must thank for taking over from the second in mid-stream. The fourth – to whom this edition is dedicated – has earned the dedication by helping with the typing too. Of my many friends at Butterworths I can only say that I am deeply grateful for their help, their encouragement – and their olympian patience.

P. S. J.

The University College at Buckingham,
March 1st, 1976.

PREFACE TO THE FIRST EDITION

Some years ago, when I first started to teach at Oxford, I suggested to certain of my colleagues in the Law Faculty that we should collaborate in the writing of a new institutional book, designed, after the Roman fashion, to give first-year students a general view of the law. After a few desultory conversations I dropped the idea, but it returned to me like a "boomerang" last autumn when my present publishers approached me with the proposal that I should undertake that very task *alone*. I did undertake it, and this book is the result of my labour. I am thankful that it is completed and I am deeply sensible of its short-comings, for I have learnt that there is nothing harder than the creation of a "miniature".

The book, in its present form, is intended primarily for the serious student of the law in the early stages of his study, whether he be a university student or a candidate for a legal or other professional examination, but I also hope that it will prove digestible to the "man in the street". The student should appreciate that what he will find here is no more than a general conspectus. A book of this sort is like a map: it sets out only the main features of the country to be explored; it is intended to give an idea of the general lie of the land, so that when the "explorer" later finds himself immersed in the detail of the "valleys", he will retain in his mind a picture of his general whereabouts. No "miniature" can ever do more than this.

I should like to address a few words to teachers who may wish to use this book as a basis for exposition. They will appreciate that, in such a vast field, it has been difficult for me to make the right selections – to know what to stress, what to omit entirely, and what to compress. No doubt many teachers will consider that my choice has often been wrong; but I console myself with the reflection that, after all, an introductory book can never be a self-sufficient "manual", it *can* only form a starting point for discussion.

I have only three specific points to make.

In the first place, certain wise critics have already objected to my treatment of the fundamental theories of Parliamentary Sovereignty and the Separation of Powers independently of the rest of Constitutional Law. I have remained unconvinced of the soundness of this criticism:

ix

these matters are, in my opinion, of such cardinal importance that mention of them cannot properly be postponed until the chapter on Constitutional Law, which I have placed in the second Part of the book.

In the second place, I am well aware that my treatment of certain subjects is all too short. In particular, I have elected to sacrifice the treatment of the Law of Torts to the need for brevity. The reason for this choice is that, as I apprehend, the main principles which underlie this branch of the law are general, few, and simple; it gains its richness and complexity from case law alone, and this is not the place for a protracted discussion of cases. I am aware, also, that I shall be criticized for failing to devote a full chapter to Evidence and Procedure: my lame excuse for this failure is that some things *had* to be sacrificed, and I would challenge the critic to find some choicer sacrificial lamb.

In the third place, I must crave indulgence for my constant resort to a device which is, to me at any rate, an irritating one. It will be seen that I have made copious use of cross-references. This has been forced upon me by the nature of my mandate. My publishers and I were agreed from the first that I should eschew all resort to footnotes: yet, when one is writing for beginners, one must take care to explain the very simplest propositions – hence the cross-references. I may perhaps be permitted to suggest that it would be well for students to be encouraged, as far as possible, to read the book at first *as a whole*: this will to some extent obviate the necessity for making constant use of the cross-references.

3, *Dr. Johnson's Buildings,*   P. S. J.
    Temple.

October, 1950.

ADDENDUM: NEW LEGISLATION

Five new statutes need mention at proof stage: the Inheritance (Provision for Family and Dependants) Act 1975, The Sex Discrimination Act 1975, the Employment Protection Act 1975, The Children Act 1975, the Community Land Act 1975. Of these I have managed to incorporate the first (Inheritance) and the fourth (Children) into the text. Since it was not feasible to do the same with the others I will give a brief account of them here.

The Sex Discrimination Act 1975. This Act to some extent supplements and amends the Equal Pay Act 1970 (below, p. 192). It is already substantially in operation. The design of it is to eliminate sex discrimination, and the essence of it lies in s. 1 (1) "A person discriminates against a woman... if... *on the ground of sex* he treats her less favourably than he treats or would treat a man...." Though the statute is the child of feminist agitation this provision is balanced in favour of men by s. 2 (1) which enacts that "the provisions... relating to sex discrimination against women are to be applied equally to the treatment of *men*...": a measure prudently balanced by s. 2 (2) "In the application of subsection (1) no account shall be taken of special treatment afforded to women in connection with pregnancy and childbirth." (The position of hermaphrodites appears to have been overlooked.)

Part II of the Act encompasses discrimination in the field of *employment*, while Part III provides for other fields including *education*, supply of goods, facilities and services (an incomprehensible exception being made by s. 33 (1) in favour of politicians). Part IV embraces other kinds of discrimination, including the already celebrated s. 38 (3) concerning discriminatory *advertisements* "use of a job [*sic*] description with a sexual connotation (such as 'waiter', 'salesgirl', 'postman' or 'stewardess') shall be taken to indicate an intention to discriminate, unless the advertisement contains an indication to the contrary". [The use of the word "job", for "employment" or "work" may lead to the suspicion that journalists are invading the draftsman's office. It has, however, "caught on" in legislation: see the Employment Protection Act 1975, s. 48 (1), which parades it proudly.] Part V includes general *exceptions*; particularly in favour of charities. Part VI creates yet another patronizing body, the *Equal Opportunities Commission*, which it empowers to conduct

xi

formal investigations and to make reports in connexion with alleged discrimination. Part VII provides for *enforcement* by means of complaint and compensation or damages; the hard-worked *industrial tribunals* being the relevant forum in the *employment* field, the *county courts* in other fields.

The Employment Protection Act 1975. This Act, which assumes a state of economic prosperity unlikely to be reached for some time to come is likely, for that reason, to remain largely a paper dragon. It boasts 129 sections and 18 schedules. Some of its main provisions will effect the following: s. 1 creates an *Advisory, Conciliation* and *Arbitration Service* charged with "the general duty of promoting the improvement of industrial relations". As its name implies that body will have the duty of initiating conciliation and arranging for arbitration in the field of industrial disputes; it will also be responsible for drawing up Codes of Practice for the purpose of improving industrial relations. Part II is concerned with employees' rights: it provides (*inter alia*) for *guarantee payments* to be made by employers to employees in respect of "workless days" (s. 22), and it makes (ss. 34–52) provision to safeguard employment and pay for female workers in case of *maternity* – including provisions to outlaw dismissal upon the ground of pregnancy, to ensure maternity pay and to safeguard the right to return to work after confinement. Sections 53–63 contain provisions designed to guarantee *trade union* rights, including the right to join a union and the rights of employees to indulge in union activities. It ensures that employees shall be entitled to *written notice* giving reasons for dismissal (s. 70). It empowers *industrial tribunals* to order *reinstatement* after unfair dismissal and, in lieu thereof, to make *compensation* orders (ss. 71–80). It enjoins employers to supply *itemized pay statements* (ss. 81–83). It sets up (ss. 87–88) an *Employment Appeal Tribunal*, consisting of a High Court judge and experts in industrial relations, with the function of hearing *appeals* on *questions of law* from industrial tribunals in cases arising under this Act and a number of others (including the Equal Pay Act 1970). Part IV regulates the handling of *redundancies* (ss. 99–107). Part V contains miscellaneous and supplementary provisions.

The Community Land Act 1975. If not previously repealed, this statute, too, is unlikely (on account both of expense and of the difficulties attending its operation) to come into effect for some time yet. It is as awesome as it is controversial: for it sanctions a land grab which would have excited the envy of King Henry VIII. Section I sets up "*Authorities*" for the purposes of the Act, and these include (for England) *local authorities* and for Wales *The Land Authority for Wales* (s. 1 (c): Part II). Section 3 (1) defines "*development land*" as "land . . . which, in the opinion of the authority concerned, is needed for relevant development within

ten years . . .". Section 3 (2) defines *"relevant development"* as *any* development: though there are certain excluded kinds – *e.g.* the building of a
single dwelling-house, development for which general planning permission has been granted and certain kinds of development connected with
agricultural land (Schedule 1). Section 15 (1) contains what might be
called the "Henry VIII clause": "An authority shall have power to
acquire by agreement . . . or *compulsorily any land* which, in their opinion,
is suitable for development." The "land", moreover, includes certain
adjacent land (s. 15 (3)). Part IV adds to the list of permissible acquisitions
certain kinds of unoccupied office premises. There are general provisions
concerning compensation.

Perhaps the reader should finally be reminded that the White Paper
on "Devolution" (see below p. 110) proved no more helpful than the
Report of the Royal Commission on the Constitution.

CONTENTS

PART I.– INTRODUCTORY

CHAPTER 1. – THE NATURE, CLASSIFICATION AND SOURCES OF LAW

CHAPTER 2. – THE ADMINISTRATION OF THE LAW

CHAPTER 9. – THE LAW OF TORTS

TABLE OF STATUTES

TABLE OF CASES

LIST OF ABBREVIATIONS

A.C. (preceded by date) ..	Law Reports, Appeal Cases, House of Lords, since 1890 (e.g., [1891] A C.).
A.E.A.★	Administration of Estates Act 1925.
A.J.A.★	Administration of Justice Act 1925.
All E.R. (preceded by date)	All England Law Reports, 1936–(current).
B.A.★	Bankruptcy Act 1914.
B. & Ad.	Barnewall and Adolphus' Reports, King's Bench, 5 vols., 1830–1834.
B. & S.	Best and Smith's Reports, Queen's Bench, 10 vols., 1861–1870.
B.E.A.★	Bills of Exchange Act 1882.
Beav.	Beavan's Reports, Rolls Court, 36 vols., 1838–1866
Bing.	Bingham's Reports, Commons Pleas, 10 vols., 1822–1834.
C. & P.	Carrington and Payne's Reports, Nisi Prius, 9. vols., 1823–1841.
C.A.★	Charities Act 1960.
C.B.	Common Bench Reports, 18 vols., 1845–1856.
C.B.(N.S.)	Common Bench Reports, New Series, 20 vols., 1856–1865.
C.J.A.★	Criminal Justice Act 1967.
C.L.A.★	Criminal Law Act 1967.
C.P.A.★	Crown Proceedings Act 1947.
C.P.D.	Law Reports, Common Pleas Division, 5 vols., 1875–1880.
Camp...	Campbell's Reports, Nisi Prius, 4 vols., 1807–1816.
Ch. (preceded by date) ..	Law Reports, Chancery Division, since 1890 (e.g., [1891] 1 Ch.).
Ch.D.	Law Reports, Chancery Division, 45 vols., 1875–1890.
Cha. Ca.	Select Cases in Chancery, fol., 1 vol., 1685–1689 (Pt. III of Cas. in Ch.).
Cl. & Fin.	Clark and Finnelly's Reports, House of Lords, 12 vols., 1831–1846.

★Author's own abbreviations.

Co. Rep.	Coke's Reports, 13 parts, 1572–1616.
Cox, C.C.	E. W. Cox's Criminal Law Cases, 1843–1945.
De G. M. & G.	De Gex, Macnaghten and Gordon's Reports, Chancery, 8 vols., 1851–1857.
Ex.	Exchequer Reports (Welsby, Hurlstone, and Gordon), 11 vols., 1847–1856.
Ex. D...	Law Reports, Exchequer Division, 5 vols., 1875–1880.
Foster ..	Foster's Crown Cases, 1 vol., 1708–1760.
H. & C.	Hurlstone and Coltman's Reports, Exchequer, 4 vols., 1862–1866.
H.L.C.	Clarke's Reports, House of Lords, 11 vols., 1847–1866.
H.P.A.★	Hire-Purchase Act 1965.
K.B. (preceded by date)	Law Reports, King's Bench Division, 1900–1952 (*e.g.*, [1901] 2 K.B.).
Kel.	Sir John Kelyng's Reports, Crown Cases, fol., 1 vol., 1662–1707.
L.C.A.★	Land Charges Act 1925.
L.J. Ex.	Law Journal, Exchequer, 1831–1875.
L.P.A.★	Law of Property Act 1925.
L.R.A.★	Land Registration Act 1925.
L.R. App. Cas.	Law Reports, Appeal Cases, House of Lords, 15 vols., 1875–1890.
L.R.C.C.R. ..	Law Reports, Crown Cases Reserved, 2 vols., 1865–1875.
L.R.C.P.	Law Reports, Common Pleas, 10 vols. 1865–1875.
L.R. Ex.	Law Reports, Exchequer, 10 vols., 1865–1875.
L.R.H.L.	Law Reports, English and Irish Appeals and Peerage Claims, House of Lords, 7 vols., 1866–1875.
L.T. ..	Law Times Reports, 1859–1947.
Leach ..	Leach's Crown Cases, 2 vols., 1730–1814.
Lloyd's Rep. (preceded by date) [from 1951]	Lloyd's List Law Reports, 1919–(current).
M. & W.	Meeson and Welsby's Reports, Exchequer, 16 vols., 1836–1847.
M.H.A.★	Mental Health Act 1959.
O.L.A.★	Occupiers' Liability Act 1957.
P.A.★ ..	Patents Act 1949.
P.D. ..	Law Reports, Probate, Divorce, and Admiralty Division, 15 vols., 1875–1890.
Ph.	Phillips' Reports, Chancery, 2 vols., 1841–1849.
Q.B. ..	Queen's Bench Reports (Adolphus and Ellis, New Series), 18 vols., 1841–1852.

★ Author's own abbreviations.

Q.B. (preceded by date) ..	Law Reports, Queen's Bench Division, 1891–1901 (*e.g.,* [1891] 1 Q.B.); 1952–(current).
Q.B.D.	Law Reports, Queen's Bench Division, 25 vols., 1875–1890.
R.R.A.★	Race Relations Acts 1965 and 1968.
S.G.A.★	Sale of Goods Act 1893.
S.L.A.★	Settled Land Act 1925.
S.T.	State Trials, 34 vols., 1163–1820.
Str.	Strange's Reports, 2 vols., 1716–1747.
T.A.★	Theft Act 1968.
Tr. A.★	Trustee Act 1925.
T.I.A.★	Trustee Investments Act 1961.
T.L.R.	The Times Law Reports, 1884–1950.
Term Rep.	Term Reports (Durnford and East), fol., 8 vols., 1785–1800.
Wall.	Wallace Reports (U.S.A.).

★ Author's own abbreviations.

PART I
INTRODUCTORY

SUMMARY OF PART I

CHAPTER 1

THE NATURE, CLASSIFICATION AND SOURCES OF LAW

This book is intended for beginners. It has therefore been thought appropriate to open with a discussion of the elementary topics indicated in the title to this chapter. Some mention should however be made before embarking upon the first of these topics, of a matter which is even more elementary – namely the aim and purpose of legal study itself.

Most people, when they first decide to study "law", probably imagine that what they are going to do is to learn as many as possible of the existing laws of the land, so that they will in due course, without need for research, be in the happy position of being able to advise others as to their exact legal rights in every possible situation. Those who do imagine this are, in a sense, right, but in a wider sense, they are wrong, and they are wrong for the following reasons.

First – although of necessity the law insists that "*ignorantia juris hand excusat*" ("Ignorance of law is no excuse") – it is in fact impossible for anyone to know all the rules of law in force at any given time, for they are far too numerous. A glance at the shelves of any law library, or even a casual look at the backs of the serried volumes of Halsbury's "*Laws of England*" will at once convince the prospective student of the truth of this proposition.

In the second place, even if some genius were to know all the existing legal rules at any given time he would not be properly equipped either for the practice or for the teaching of law. The reason for this is, as will be explained below, that much of our law is judge-made, not imposed as an abstract series of rules, but propounded in the form of decisions in actual cases and built up from precedent to precedent. These precedents are not arbitrary rulings but reasoned judgments, and any given series of them will be found to enshrine certain rational principles (see below, p. 15). It is therefore of cardinal importance for the lawyer not merely to know as much as he can of the existing rules of law, but also to acquire a knowledge of these principles. By this means only will he be able to advise his clients how the courts are likely to decide in any

3

given case; however many and complex may be the rules of the existing law, they cannot cover every possible contingency, and new facts call for fresh decisions in the light of existing principles.

In the third place legal study is a "social science", for legal rules govern people living in society; they have therefore developed with society, and it follows that the causes which brought many of them into being are only to be explained in the light of history. A knowledge of legal history, and of English history as a whole, is therefore often essential for an understanding of modern legal rules.

There are therefore three aspects of legal study. The student must seek to gain a knowledge of general principles; he must learn something of the detail of the existing legal rules, statutory or otherwise; and finally he must know something of the development and historical background of the law.

Let us now consider the nature of "law".

1 THE NATURE OF LAW

Many books have been written and continue to be written about the nature of law; here we must be brief. All will agree that it is a set of rules which form the pattern of behaviour in a given society. And they will agree, too, that the laws with which we have to deal differ from the "laws" of nature which are "rules" derived from observation of the physical universe (*e.g.* the rule that the tides ebb and flow): for "law" in our sense is normative (pattern-setting), a *prescription* rather than a *description* of behaviour. Go further than this, however, and there is perennial disagreement, dictated much, perhaps, by the predilections of each particular jurist.

One school of thought which has persisted through the ages, and which was epitomized by the work of John Austin (1790–1859) – a follower of Jeremy Bentham (1748–1832) –, has it that law has nothing to do with justice or morality because it is a *command* of political superiors ultimately backed by a "sanction", an unpleasant consequence (such as imprisonment), in case of disobedience. This theory is attractive, if only on account of its simplicity: it derives ultimately from the image of imperial Rome and is connected with the work of Jean Bodin (1530–1596) who saw in the emergent structure of the nation states and absolute monarchies of the post-Reformation a social structure based upon the "*sovereignty*" of the monarch, whose word was law – "L'état", said Louis XIV, "c'est moi": and that was very true. But this was an inadequate picture: for not only may laws be broken without anything in the nature of punishment (as, for instance, the rules which prescribe the forms for making a will) but in a complex modern State, with its political checks and balances, it is by no means easy to detect a "sovereign" in anything more than a formal sense. We shall return to the concept of sovereignty when the nature of legislation is examined.

Another school of thought, equally old, is the school which seeks to identify law with "justice". This has great fascination for some: and was reflected in the writings of Saint Thomas Aquinas (1224–1273) who saw law as the ultimate inspiration of divine reason. This school is not, however, easy to subscribe to when one recalls that "justice" is so hard to define – and so much a matter of subjective judgment – that Plato spent much of the *Republic* trying to define it without reaching a satisfactory conclusion.

Others, whose views it is simplest here to endorse, are content to omit the question "Why is law obeyed?" and to accept the *fact* that it *is* obeyed in political societies and that, like the rules of a club, *it is the rules upon which those societies are grounded* and which persist as long as, but only as long as, each particular society endures. This is all that can be attempted upon this metaphysical subject here; but it may be of interest to add that if the reader starts to think about the phenomenon of obedience to law he may find it strange that a nation can accept that as "law" which emanates from a tiny parliamentary majority which does not reflect the will of the majority of people. This is, perhaps, peculiar; and it may suggest that obedience to law is a convention – something like the rules of a game – resting only upon the *custom* (or habit) of conformity.

2 THE CLASSIFICATION OF LAW

Municipal law, *i.e.* state law, as opposed to international law, is commonly divided into categories. The chief of these categories is the distinction between public law on the one hand, and private law on the other.

Public law consists of those fields of law which are primarily concerned with the State itself. Thus constitutional law, which regulates the functioning of the organs of the central government, and the relationship of the individual to them, is a branch of public law. Criminal law is also "public" law because crimes, as we shall see below, are wrongs which the State is concerned to prevent and punish; and so is most of the law created by the modern statutes designed to promote social security, for these statutes cast special duties upon the State.

Private law is that part of the law which is primarily concerned with the rights and duties of individuals. Thus the branches of the law which govern private obligations – that is to say, the law of contract, of quasi-contract and of torts – are all aspects of private law. So too, is the law of property, which determines the nature and extent of the rights which people may enjoy over land and other property, and the law of succession which governs the devolution of property upon death, and in certain other events.

These are only examples of sub-divisions of public and private law; many others might be given. Here it must suffice to explain that both the main division, and the sub-divisions are, to some extent, arbitrary and that they are made primarily for the purposes of convenient exposition; each field of law tends to overlap with that of its neighbours and no one field can be fully understood in isolation from the rest. Further the sub-divisions may themselves often be sub-divided; for example, the law of agency and the law relating to insurance are branches of the law of contract, but they are commonly subjected to independent treatment; constitutional law also, in its wildest sense, includes many special branches, such as the law of local government, electoral law and administrative law.

Mention should here be made of a special subject which cannot receive further notice in this book; this is private international law (also called the "conflict of laws"). The "international" law referred to above, which governs the mutual relationship of states, is "public international law". "Private" international law governs a different field; its rules are primarily concerned with determining what system of state law should properly be applied by our courts in cases which contain some "foreign" element. Suppose, for instance, that A, in England, makes a contract by correspondence with B, a Frenchman, in France and that by the terms of this contract B is to perform certain services for A in America. Suppose that B breaks his contract and that A sues him in England. It will be clear that *English* law is not necessarily the correct law to be applied to *all*, at any rate, of the facts of this case. In order to determine which is the correct system to apply, the court will consult the rules of private international law.

Another important division of the law, the difference between "Substantive" and "Adjective" (*i.e.* procedural) law, will be mentioned at a later stage (below, p. 54).

3 THE SOURCES OF ENGLISH LAW

The courts are the interpreters and declarers of the law; the "sources" of law are therefore the sources to which the courts turn in order to determine what it is. Considered from the aspect of their sources laws are traditionally divided into two main categories according to the solemnity of the form in which they are made. They may be either *written* or *unwritten*. These traditional terms are misleading, since the expression "written" law signifies any law that is formally *enacted*, whether reduced to writing or not, and the expression "unwritten" law signifies all *unenacted* law. For example, as we shall see, judicial decisions are often reduced to writing in the form of law reports, but because they are not formal enactments they are "unwritten" law.

Since the fashion was set by the *Code Napoléon* many continental countries have codified much of their law, public and private; on the Continent, therefore, the volume of written law tends to preponderate over the volume of unwritten. But in England unwritten law is predominant, for more of our law derives from judicial precedents than from legislative enactment. This does not, of course, mean that none of our law is codified, for many parts of it are; such as the law relating to the sale of goods (Sale of Goods Act 1893) and the law relating to partnership (Partnership Act 1890). All that is meant is that we have not adopted the system of wholesale codification which prevails in many continental countries. Yet in modern England legislation is by no means a rare phenomenon: far from it! A point which the reader who perseveres with this book will learn to appreciate.

Two principal and two subsidiary sources of English law require description. These principal sources are Legislation, and Judicial Precedent; the subsidiary sources are Custom and Books of Authority.

The Principal Sources

1 LEGISLATION

Legislation is enacted law. In England, as has already been pointed out, the sole ultimate legislator is Parliament, for in our *traditional* constitutional theory Parliament is sovereign. The composition of Parliament and the nature of the legislative process will be discussed below (Chapter 5); here we are only concerned to explain the signficance of the doctrine of *"parliamentary sovereignty"*. It means first, that all legislative power within the realm is vested in Parliament, or is derived from the authority of Parliament – Parliament thus has no rival within the legislative sphere – and it means secondly that there is no legal limit to the power of Parliament. Parliament may therefore, and constantly does, by Act delegate legislative powers to other bodies and even to individuals (see below, p. 126), but it may also, by Act, remove these powers as simply as it has conferred them. By Act, moreover, Parliament may make any laws it pleases however perverse or "wrong" and the courts are bound to apply them. The enactments of Parliament are not subject to question, for our constitution knows no entrenched rights similar to the fundamental liberties guaranteed by the Constitution of the United States and safeguarded by the Supreme Court. It will have been noted that we have referred to the "traditional" theory. This is intended to serve as a warning to the reader that when constitutional law falls to be discussed the effect of "Common Market" membership upon that theory will have to be considered. It is proper to add that when we speak of Her Majesty as "Sovereign" we use the word in a different, and symbolic, sense: whatever may have been the position of Henry VIII the Queen is not now the supreme law-maker. Her Majesty is "sovereign" only in the affection of her people and as the embodiment of national unity.

In the legislative sphere Parliament is thus legally "sovereign" and master, but this does not mean that the courts have no influence upon the development of enacted law; for every enactment, however it be promulgated, has to be interpreted (or *construed*) in order to be applied, and the courts are the recognized interpreters of the law. The meaning of words is seldom self-evident; they will often bear two, or even more, possible interpretations and hence the courts must always exercise a considerable degree of control over the practical application of statutes (enactments of Parliament). The difficulty of interpretation may be illustrated by a simple example. Suppose that Old King Cole, who is an absolute despot, commands that all "dogs" in his kingdom are to be killed. Suppose that Jack Sprat, one of his subjects, who has an alsatian wolf hound, applies to the courts for a decree that it shall be spared, alleging that it is a "hound" and that the royal command is only concerned with "dogs". The court will have to decide whether the word "dogs" is to be taken to embrace "hounds": whichever way it decides, it will influence the practical application of the King's command.

The task of interpreting enactments is primarily a task of seeking to find the intention of the legislator. This "intention" may, in theory, though not in law, be discovered in at least three ways. First, the legislator himself may be consulted. This method is impracticable in modern times and it is, in any case, undesirable: it is impracticable because modern legislatures are usually large bodies which cannot easily be consulted; it is undesirable because it would give the legislature an opportunity of applying its own enactments to particular cases – and justice requires that laws shall be rules of *general* application. Second, the interpreter may look to the wording of the enactment and consider it broadly in the light of the whole setting and circumstances of its promulgation, taking account of its general purpose and the declared intentions of the legislator at or about the time that it was passed. In the third place, the wording of the enactment may be strictly construed according to its literal and grammatical meaning, upon the assumption that the legislator has given perfect expression to his intention.

In the main, our courts adopt the third of the above methods of approach. But they have developed certain rules (or "canons") of construction which – though they are now as much honoured by judicial disregard as by judicial acceptance – every lawyer ought to know if he is to be able to advise a client about the relevance of an enactment in his particular case. Some of the more important of these *rules of construction* must therefore now receive notice.

i The literal rule – The cardinal rule is that the words of an enactment must *prima facie* be interpreted in their *ordinary, literal or grammatical* sense. And provided that so to interpret them does not give rise to some absurdity, repugnancy or inconsistency the court is not entitled to construe them loosely or fancifully, even if a strict construction appears to it to lead to an undesirable result.

ii The golden rule – Here we may cite Lord Wensleydale in *Grey v. Pearson* (1857), 6 H.L. Cas. 61, at p. 106: "In construing statutes", he said, "the grammatical and ordinary sense of the words is to be adhered to"; in other words, the Literal Rule is to be applied. This is how a lawyer takes his first look at an enactment; but perforce, for such is often the case, Lord Wensleydale went on to say that if this approach proves useless as leading to "some *absurdity*, or some *repugnancy* or *inconsistency* with the rest of (the statute)" then "the grammatical and ordinary sense of the words may be modified *so as to avoid that absurdity and inconsistency, but no further*". This is the so-called "Golden Rule": be strict in interpretation, but modify the construction where essential so as to avoid absurdity or inconsistency. How, then, is such modification to be approached?

iii Consider the whole enactment – If the use of the "Golden Rule" leads to the conclusion that the words under consideration produce absurdity, repetitiveness, inconsistency or redundancy the next thing the lawyer must do is to look at the whole of the enactment in question. (How often have students been advised that if they think their answers to Question 1 or 2 are likely to lead to absurdity they must look at the paper as a whole; for there may be at least one question in the ten which they feel they can answer!) For what seems absurd or redundant as it stands may take on meaning in the light of the total context. And in considering the statute as a whole certain matters have to be borne in mind.

a The Preamble. It is legitimate to consult not only the body of the

Act, but where there is one, also the Preamble. Statutes used commonly (though they now rarely do) to be preceded by a preamble, similar to "recitals" in a deed, setting out the background and purpose of the enactment: and this may be of assistance in understanding the meaning of any part of it. For instance, the Preamble to the famous Statute of Uses (1535) gives a valuable guide to its general intent.

b Punctuation. No attention should be paid to punctuation: for in parliamentary, as in other, draftsmanship punctuation is a matter of personal preference.

c Marginal notes. These are common in modern enactments but – though some find them helpful – they are not, according to the prevailing opinion, to be relied upon as guides. The reason for this appears to be that since they are inserted at the draftsman's discretion, and are not subject to parliamentary debate, they should not be taken to indicate Parliament's intention so much as the *draftsman's* interpretation of it; which is a matter of no legal weight.

iv   The history of the enactment – The word "history" is here used in a double sense. In the first sense it signifies the *genesis* of the enactment itself: its progress through Parliament and the debates and discussions which produced it. Nothing would, perhaps, seem more sensible than that the courts should consider these things in order to discover the true intention of the legislators; and, indeed, not only do some other legal systems permit such consultation but even in the House of Lords itself it has recently been suggested that it should be permitted here. In due course it may be. But the law at present is that the "history" in this sense may *not* be referred to; and the main argument in favour of this is that debates are two or many-sided affairs from which no sure indication can be gained.

A second sense of the word "history" in this context signifies the *background* against which the statute is passed. This may include, for instance, a previous series of enactments in the same field as the Act to be interpreted (often, misleadingly, called the "parliamentary history" of the enactment) and it may also include such matters as the general social, political and legal background prevailing at the time of the passing of the Act. It *is* permissible and generally desirable for the court to consider the "history" in these senses.

v   The rule in Heydon's case – Although perhaps it is no more than a particular illustration of (iv) this rule is sufficiently important to receive special mention. It is as follows. "That for the sure and true interpretation of all statutes . . . four things are to be . . . considered: (1) What was the *common law before the Act*; (2) what was the *mischief* . . . for which the common law did not provide; (3) what remedy the Parliament hath resolved ... to cure the disease of the commonwealth; (4) the true reason of the remedy." (*Heydon's Case* (1584), 3 Co. Rep. 7a.) This Rule is also called the "Mischief" Rule; and it applies today as much as it did four hundred years ago. For example, in *Gorris* v. *Scott* (1874), L.R. 9 Exch. 125 the plaintiff claimed against the defendant in respect of the loss of his sheep which were washed overboard and drowned while the defendant was engaged in carrying them by sea. The loss was due to the fact that no pens had been provided for the sheep: and this was in breach of a duty imposed by a certain enactment to provide pens for animals carried by sea. The plaintiff asserted that since the loss followed upon the breach of this duty he ought to succeed; but it was held that the purpose of the relevant rule was not to prevent loss overboard but to minimize the spread of contagious disease, and it therefore followed that the claim did not fall within the "mischief" of the Act.

There are numerous other rules of interpretation of statutes which there is not space to mention: but it is thought essential to refer to the following.

vi Ut res magis valeat quam pereat – ("Let the thing stand rather than fall"). – It must be presumed that the draftsman intends every word to bear a meaning: to be something which "stands", so as to be neither repetitious nor redundant. And if a particular clause appears on the face of it to be either of these things then the court must seek to give it a meaning which avoids such a conclusion.

vii Expressum facit cessare tacitum – ("If something is expressed there is no room for implication.") – This may also be rendered: "*expressio unius, exclusio alterius*" ("If something is expressed it must be taken to exclude something else"). Thus where an Act imposed rates upon "houses, buildings, works, tenements and hereditaments" but expressly exempted "land" it was held that the word "land" (which in normal legal terminology would include "houses ... etc.") must here mean land alone (in the layman's sense) unencumbered by "houses ... etc." In other words, the express mention of "Houses ... etc." excluded the legal implication, which would normally have tacitly arisen, that "land" would include land bearing "houses ... etc.".

viii The ejusdem generis – ("Of the same genus") rule. – Frequently enactments refer to a class of things (genus) to which their provisions are to apply, and after the class there follow some general words which imply that other "like" things are intended to be included. Then the question may arise in the course of litigation whether something which is not one of the specified genus falls within the general words. The issue then becomes whether the thing in question is or is not *ejusdem generis* with the class specified. Let us suppose a statute to embrace "Any motor car, van, motor cycle or other such thing." And let us suppose the issue to be (a) whether a motor cycle combination (side car), (b) whether a pedal cycle, comes within the intent of the statute. It may be guessed that (a) would be held to be included but that (b) would not. (a) is clearly of similar genus, (b) is not. Though as to (b) the reader must be reminded that the court must have regard to the Act as a whole; and it is therefore possible, that a review of the whole purpose of the Act might lead it, as it were to open the gate, and conclude that (b) is intended to be included: such a conclusion might, for example, be reached if it were plain that the Act as a whole was intended to govern road traffic of any kind.

NOTE—Now that the United Kingdom has become a member of the European Communities questions arise as to the true interpretation of *Community* enactments, including the Treaties and secondary legislation of the Council and the Commission of the Community. The European Communities Act 1972, s. 3 (1) provides that ". . . any question as to the meaning and effect of any Community instrument shall be treated as a question of law and, (if not referred to the European Court), be for determination as such in accordance with the *principles laid down by any relevant decision of the European Court*", *i.e.* the Court of Justice of the European Communities. What these "principles" are, or may in the course of time become, is by no means clear but it seems that the Court seeks to synthesize the approaches to interpretation of all the member States and to seek to follow the "spirit" of the Communities as a whole as enshrined in the Treaties. There is little doubt that the general intention of the Court is that all matters of interpretation should be determined by the Court *itself*, and that they ought to be referred to it by national courts in which they arise. On the other hand, under art. 177 of the EEC Treaty it is permissible for a national court—provided that it is *not* a final court of appeal (such as the House of Lords) – to undertake the interpretation itself. Where an English court avails itself of this right it will not follow the English rules of interpretation we have just discussed but will, as s. 3 (1) of the European Communities Act provides, be guided by the interpretative practice of the Court of Justice of the European Communities (situated at Luxembourg).

2 JUDICIAL PRECEDENT

In all countries, at all times, the decisions of courts made in the course of litigation, are treated with respect, and they tend to be regarded as "precedents", which subsequent courts will follow when they are called upon to determine issues of a similar nature.

There are probably two reasons for this phenomenon, the one psychological, the other practical. The psychological reason is that anyone who is called upon to decide a dispute will prefer to justify his decision, if he can, by reference to what has been done in the past rather than to take the entire responsibility of decision upon his own shoulders. The practical reason is that it is clearly desirable that decisions shall be uniform, for it is often asserted that it is more important that the law shall be certain than that it shall always promote justice in individual cases.

In England, by way of contrast with our European neighbours who, following the tradition of codification set by Justinian's *Corpus Juris Civilis* (A.D. 534), derived their law primarily from enacted codes, the law has traditionally been built up, like an ever-mounting coral reef, from court decisions. Thus, to us, the precedents which such decisions embody are of especial importance; and Her Majesty's judges, who, through these decisions, give direction to the law, have an exceptionally important place in our society.

Judicial precedents thus play a singularly important role in the administration of justice in England. But they do even more than this, for not only are they regarded as authoritative pronouncements of the law, but certain classes of them are treated as *binding* upon courts which are subsequently called upon to try similar issues. "Binding" precedents are not merely "persuasive" authorities which *may* be followed if they appear to be correct; they are precedents which *must* be followed.

This doctrine of the binding case forms one of the distinctive characteristics of English law. The system by which it operates may be illustrated by reference to the rules which apply among our civil courts. It will be explained in the next chapter that there is a hierarchy of courts. The House of Lords is the ultimate appeal court, the highest court in the land. All decisions of the House are absolutely binding upon all other courts; this means that they must be followed by courts called upon to determine similar issues, whether they appear to be correct or not. Below the House of Lords comes the Court of Appeal; the decisions of the Court of Appeal bind the courts inferior to it, and, generally speaking, it is also bound by its own previous decisions. Below the Court of Appeal comes the High Court of Justice. Here there is a slight, but not very important, departure from the general rule. A judge of the High Court is, of course, absolutely bound by decisions of the House of Lords and of the Court of Appeal, but he is not *absolutely* bound to follow previous decisions of other High Court judges. In practice, however, he will nearly always do so unless he sees some very good reason for departing from the rule previously enunciated. Beneath the High Court come the County Courts; circuit judges are bound by the decisions of all superior courts; and, of course, on the criminal side, magistrates' courts are similarly bound by all higher authority.

Until recently the House of Lords treated its *own* previous decisions as binding upon *itself*. This produced a situation by which a point of law might, as it were, become tied at the top without hope of change unless the Legislature intervened (as in practice it sometimes does) to annul the House's decision. Hence, legislative intervention being a ponderous method of effecting change on particular points, rulings of the House could become outmoded with the passing of time. On July 26th, 1966, the Lord Chancellor therefore announced that from that date though normally – having regard to the danger of disturbing settled principles which have been relied upon as the basis of legal rights – the House *should* continue to follow its own rulings, it should yet for the future *permit* itself to *"depart from a previous decision when it appears right to do so"*. It must however be understood that it is only the House of Lords itself that has been accorded this freedom of action, and that all other courts still remain strictly bound by the hierarchy of precedent. It must also be appreciated that previous decisions will not lightly be overturned.

Precedents have thus far been described as "decisions", but this bald statement requires to be amplified. Not everything which a judge says in the course of his judgment creates a precedent, but only his pronouncement of law in relation to the *particular facts before him*. This pronouncement is called the *"ratio decidendi"* of the case. Judges may, of course, and often do, let fall *"obiter dicta"* (pronouncements "by the way"), in the course of their judgments, upon points of law which are not directly relevant to the issue before them. These *dicta* may be of great assistance to subsequent courts, especially if they are pronounced by judges of high repute, but they are *never binding*; subsequent courts are under no *duty* to follow them.

The precedents formed by decided cases are, thus, as Bacon wrote of the Reports of Sir Edward Coke, the "anchors of the laws". A practitioner who is asked to consider a legal matter will therefore look to the reported decisions of the courts; and he will do this even though the point in issue is regulated by a statute, for, as we have seen, statutes are interpreted by the courts, and a decision which is concerned with the interpretation of a statute is just as binding as any other decision. When this much has been said, it must not, however, be imagined that the law is always discoverable by the simple process of looking up, and finding, the right precedent. For facts are infinitely various and by no means all cases are exactly covered by previous authority. Quite the reverse, the facts in issue often resemble two or more divergent authorities. In these circumstances the courts therefore have freedom of choice in deciding what previous authority to "follow", and much of the ingenuity of counsel is directed to "distinguishing" the facts of precedents which appear to bind the court to decide against him. Further, even today, cases of "first impression" sometimes arise; cases which bear no direct resemblance to any previous authority.

The administration of justice is not therefore a slot-machine process of matching precedents. The judges exercise discretion in making their decisions. But they do not exercise this discretion in an arbitrary way, for they rest their judgments upon the general *principles* enshrined in case-law as a whole. Case-law does not consist of a blind series of decisions, "A will succeed", or "B will fail", but of reasoned judgments based upon rational principles. These principles have been evolved by the courts through the centuries; and, building precedent upon precedent, they have framed them with two ends in view. First, they have sought so to formulate them that their application may be capable of effecting substantial justice in particular cases; second they have sought to make them sufficiently general in scope to serve as sure guides to lawyers faced with the task of giving advice in future legal disputes. Thus in a sense the history of the common law (as opposed to statute law — for statutes are sometimes arbitrary and they have often wrought injustice) is the story of the evolution of the judges' conception of justice realized in the form of rules of law intended to be general in their application and as easily ascertainable as possible. The task of attempting to distribute *justice*, while satisfying the essential need for *certainty*, has not been an easy one; in fact the attempt can never achieve more than a compromise; but, on the whole, it has been so well performed that the common law may justly be compared with the Roman Law, its mighty rival.

It is the duty of the judges to know and to apply the principles which emerge from the case-law of the past, to adapt them to the conditions of the present, and so to mould them that they may be fit to serve for the future. It is also, as was pointed out above, not so much a knowledge of cases, as a knowledge of principle that the student should seek to acquire.

Law Reports — It will readily be appreciated that the system of case-law calls for accurate reporting and publication of all the more important decisions of the superior courts. Consequently there has been *law reporting* of some kind from as early as the thirteenth century. The history of the law reports falls into three main periods: the period of the "Year Books", the period of private reporting, and the modern period.

The *Year Books*, many of which have from time to time, been printed with varying degrees of accuracy, and some of which are now available in translation, appear to have been notes, taken by counsel or students upon cases which they considered to be of interest. They were originally written in Anglo-French (the court language of the Middle Ages) and they cover the period from 1283 to 1535. They are seldom cited today, partly because there is now seldom need to refer to decisions of these early times and partly because, on the whole, they are not, and apparently were not intended to be, accurate records of the decisions of the courts. Although some rulings upon important points of law appear in them, they are more often concerned with matters which seem irrelevant to the modern lawyer, such as arguments between judge and counsel, arguments conducted out of court and occasionally even remarks about the weather. They are, nevertheless, invaluable documents to the mediaeval historian.

Law reporting proper began with the era of *"private"* reporting. About the second quarter of the sixteenth-century practitioners (one of the earliest of them was Sir James Dyer, a Chief Justice of the Court of Common Pleas, whose Reports begin in 1537) began to compile reports of cases which, for various reasons, they or their successors found it convenient to publish. These reports were intended for practical use; hence in the course of time they came to contain the essential matters which practitioners required to know; that is to say, a statement of the facts in issue, the general nature of the pleadings on either side, a brief statement of the arguments of counsel and, above all, the judgment of the court. The technique of these "private" reports tended to improve as time went on, and by the close of the eighteenth century they had attained a degree of relevance and accuracy approximating to that of the modern reports. The most renowned reports of this type are those of Sir Edward Coke, the greatest of our judges (1552–1634); they cover the years 1572–1616 and are to this day accorded the distinction of being referred to as "*The* Reports" by reason of their author's unrivalled eminence. Sir George Burrow's *Reports* (1756–1772) are also held in high esteem. At about the close of the eighteenth century certain of the reporters became "authorized"; this meant that the judges who decided the cases noted by these reporters themselves examined and, where necessary, amended the reports before publication. Many of the "private" reports are still in use, and most of them have been reprinted in a series of a hundred and seventy-six volumes, called the *English Reports*.

The *modern* period of law reporting began after 1865, when, as the result of a general demand from the legal profession, the General Council of Law Reporting was set up. This body is constituted as a self-supporting commercial enterprise and it had, and still has, the function of issuing a series of *Law Reports* which are "authorized" in the sense just explained. The old private reporting ceased soon after this Council came into being.

The Law Reports continue to be issued at the present time and they are now supplemented by a series of *Weekly Law Reports*. But this does not mean that the Council enjoys a monopoly in the field of reporting; for numerous other reports are issued by commercial concerns. The *All England Reports*, a most useful series, first issued in 1936, afford an outstanding example.

The names of most of the Reports, past and current, are commonly abbreviated when they are referred to in legal literature, and the usual abbreviations will be used in this book. A complete key to them is to be found in Halsbury's *Laws of England*, but even without consulting this or any other key, the student who cares to spend some of his time in a law library will find it quite a simple matter to familiarize himself with all of the more important of them.

The Subsidiary Sources

1 CUSTOM

Customs are social habits, patterns of behaviour, which all societies tend to evolve without express formulation or conscious creation. In a sense custom should be accorded pride of place as one of the principal sources of law for much, if not most, law was originally based upon it. Moreover custom is not solely important as a source of *law*, for even today some customary rules are observed in their own right and they command almost as much obedience as rules of law proper; they only differ from rules of law in that their observance is not *enforced* by the organs of the State. Thus, we shall see (below, p. 106) that many of the fundamental rules governing the Constitution are "conventional" (*i.e.* customary), rather than legal, rules.

But in modern times most general customs (*i.e.* customs universally observed throughout the realm) have either fallen into desuetude or become absorbed in rules of law. For example many of the early rules of the common law were general customs which the courts adopted, and by this very act of adoption made into law. So too, much of our modern mercantile law owes its origin to the general customs of merchants which the courts assimilated during the course of the seventeenth and eighteenth centuries. So also many of the rules of the law relating to the sale of goods originated as customs, were adopted by the courts, and eventually moulded into a statutory code by the Sale of Goods Act 1893. General custom has therefore now ceased to operate as an important source of law. For law, whether enacted or judicially declared, has in most fields superseded custom.

On the other hand customs, prevailing among particular groups of people living in particular localities, are sometimes still recognized by the courts as capable of creating a special "law" for the locality in question at variance with the general law of the land. For instance in a well-known case the fishermen of Walmer were held entitled, by reason of a local custom, to a special right to dry their nets upon a particular beach. But recognition of such variants upon the general law will only be accorded if certain conditions are satisfied. The following are among the more important of those conditions: – The custom sought to be established must, (1) not be unreasonable, (2) be "certain", that is to say the right which is claimed must be proved to adhere to a defined group of people, (3) must have existed since "time immemorial". Literally this means that it must go back to 1189 (by historical accident the terminal date of "legal memory") – see below, p. 350. But in practice the burden upon a plaintiff to establish such a custom – for example a customary duty in his neighbour to fence against a common upon which he has grazing rights – is not so formidable. For if he can prove that such a usage has in fact existed in the locality for a reasonable time a lawful origin for the usage will be *presumed*, provided, of course, that such an origin was possible; and custom itself is such a lawful origin.

2   BOOKS OF AUTHORITY

On the Continent the writings of legal authors form an important source of law. In England, in accordance with our ancient tradition that the law is to be sought in *judicial decisions*, their writings have in the past been treated with comparatively little respect. They have been cited in court, if cited at all, rather by way of evidence of what the correct interpretation of the law is than as independent sources from which it may be derived.

This general rule has, however, always been subject to certain recognized exceptions; for there are certain "books of authority", written by authors of outstanding eminence, which may not only be cited as independent sources in themselves for the law of their times but which also carry a weight of authority almost equal to that of precedents. Among the most important of these works are Bracton's *De Legibus et Consuetudinibus Angliæ* (thirteenth century), Coke's *Institutes* (1628–1641) and Blackstone's *Commentaries* (1765).

When this much has been explained, it must nevertheless be admitted that in modern times the established tradition appears to have been breaking down, because many text-books are now in practice constantly cited in the courts, though only the best of them are likely to command attention. The reason for this departure from the established tradition is probably that in comparatively recent years a large increase in the popularity of the study of English law in all our major universities has done much to improve the quality of legal writing and to increase the volume of legal literature. Thus, today Salmond's *Law of Torts* is commonly referred to in court and even works of living authors, such as Cheshire's *Private International Law*, are now often cited, though by a rule of etiquette, counsel who refers to works of the latter category should not cite them directly as authorities, but should request the leave of the court to "adopt" the arguments which they contain as part of his own. In practice, however, even this latter etiquette is now seldom observed.

4 LAW REFORM

This is perhaps the most suitable place to mention the machinery of law reform. Traditionally, as has been seen, the development of the law has depended upon parliamentary action in the form of legislation wherever change was desired and upon the slow evolution of rules by the accretion of case-law. Change and reform did therefore take place, but very much by fits and starts: as for instance, in the case of the great legislative reforms of Henry II or of Edward I and, in the nineteenth century, of the Judicature Acts 1873–1875. During the present century it has come to be realized that more direction is required in the matter of law reform than the traditional agencies of change could supply. Special committees therefore came into being such as the *Law Reform Commmittee* and the *Criminal Law Revision Committee* to which specific areas of the law are from time to time referred for reconsideration and suggested amendment by legislative action. Even these have, however, not been successful in giving full impetus to the desire for reform. Consequently the Law Commissions Act 1965 inaugurated a new departure by setting up a full-time *Law Commission*. This Commission is appointed by the Lord Chancellor and it consists of a Chairman and four commissioners drawn from the profession and – refreshingly – also from university law teachers. The functions of the Commission include, *inter alia*, the keeping "under review all the law ... with a view to its systematic development and reform, including in particular the codification of such law, the elimination of anomalies, the repeal of obsolete and unnecessary enactments and generally the simplification and modernization of the law". Various kinds of reports have to be made to the Lord Chancellor and annual reports have to be made to Parliament.

The Commission has already sponsored a number of reforms and it may prove to be an enduring factor in the struggle of the law to keep pace with change, though signs are not lacking that since all change is not necessarily change for the better there may, before long, be a demand that the activities of this and of the other agencies of "reform" should be relaxed.

CHAPTER 2

THE ADMINISTRATION OF THE LAW

In this Chapter we shall first discuss the legal system, its background and the present-day court system, and then describe the organization of the legal profession.

A THE BACKGROUND

1 The Common Law

Our "common law" consists of a body of principles built up from the precedents of the old courts of common law. These courts, consisting of the Court of Exchequer, the Court of Common Pleas (or "Common Bench") – both dating from the twelfth century – and the Court of King's (or as appropriate "Queen's" Bench) were royal courts set up by the Crown and they superseded a network of local courts which had existed since Anglo-Saxon times. The law which these latter courts administered was local customary law which varied in content in different parts of the country.

Naturally, when the Royal Courts, which were centralized and had jurisdiction over all of the country, came into being they evolved and applied a uniform system of law, common throughout the land: hence this law came to be called "*common*" in contradistinction to the older local laws.

The term "common law" is, however, now used in several different senses as marking special contrasts. For instance, we say that England, the United States (with the exception of Louisiana) and most of the Commonwealth countries are "common law" countries when we wish to contrast the Anglo-American systems as a whole with countries like France whose law ultimately derives from the Roman law: and we call these "*civil* law" countries. The expression "common law" can also be used to denote our own "case" law as a whole contrasted with our statute law. And in another sense, as we shall see, "common law" is contrasted with *"equity"*.

Having thus explained the primary meaning of "common law", as that system of principles which was built up by the common law courts we must now explain the basis upon which those principles were evolved. And this means that we must give a brief description of the "Forms of Action" (the reader should consult F. W. Maitland, *The Forms of Action at Common Law*) or "Writ System" as they, or it, were called.

In these days a civil action starts with the serving of a *writ of summons* (below, p. 56): this is a formal document and the purpose of serving it is to give notice to the *defendant* (person sued) upon whom it is served that the *plaintiff* (complainant) intends to bring proceedings against him, and to warn him to defend the action. The formulation of the grounds of the plaintiff's case comes substantially, through the pleadings, at a later stage.

Under the old law the system was different. The standard machinery for starting an action at common law in any of the three common law courts was the *original writ* ("original" because it originated, or started, the action). There was nothing mysterious about a *"writ"*: writs were simply concise written orders emanating from higher authority – in the case of a royal writ from the King, through the Chancery, the secretarial department of State. The use of writs for administrative purposes goes back to Anglo-Saxon times and was probably a borrowing from Frankish court practice. It echoes the "mandates" of ancient Rome.

The "original writs" with which we are here concerned were documents obtained on payment from the administrative offices of the Chancery. There were many variations in form according to what sort of matter was involved, but the general purpose for which most of them were designed was to secure the presence of the defendant before the King's courts, usually through the agency of the Sheriff (as the principal royal official) of the county in which the dispute arose. Further, and this is a vital point, each writ contained a brief statement of the plaintiff's ground of claim. If the position had invariably been that the plaintiff set out the specific facts of his case, had then complained of injury, and if it had invariably been for the chancery clerks or for the judge at the trial to decide whether these facts (if proved) disclosed a cause of action against the defendant the content of the writs would have been of no general importance. We shall see that writs could be of such a nature and that that fact was fundamental in the development of the law, but the first thing to stress is that – as is natural in any administrative system – writs rapidly became stylized. Claims concerning certain types of misconduct came to be recognized and each type of misconduct came to have its own appropriate writ.

Bringing an action at common law thus came generally to consist in selecting the writ appropriate (as he hoped to prove in court) to the facts of a plaintiff's case. For instance, there was the ancient writ of Right by which the "demandant" (plaintiff) claimed from the tenant (defendant) that the latter "unjustly" and without a "claim of right" deprived him of his land. There was the ancient writ of Debt (below, p. 203), alleging that the defendant owed (*debet*) him so much money, and the writ of Detinue (below, p. 203) stating that the defendant detained (*detinet*) something which was the plaintiff's from him. Into one or other of the accepted forms, such as these, the facts of the case had to fit; if they did not fit however just the claim, the plaintiff must fail.

But though writs thus became stereotyped clearly there were means of creating new ones, otherwise the law could not have developed. The agencies of evolution varied. Sometimes Parliament would recognize a new form of action (writ), sometimes the creation would be administrative – as by the Chancery clerks – sometimes, as in the case of the all-important writ of Trespass (see below, p. 278) we think we can trace it to an innovator: in that case said to be William Raleigh, thirteenth century judge, and Master of Bracton. But by the fourteenth century, after much hesitation and political obstruction, a practice emerged by which the *courts* upon the facts stated, and upon proof by the plaintiff of actual damage at the hands of the defendant, allowed actions "*on the Case*" to succeed: in other words the courts were authorized in such circumstances to grant *new* writs. It must not be thought that this task was lightly undertaken, for the mediaeval judges never forgot that, in Francis Bacon's words, they were "Lions" *under* "the Throne" and innovation might displease the Crown. Indeed, cautiously and lawyerlike, the development of new writs through actions on the Case was, at first, at least, slow and a matter of development by strict *analogy* from pre-existing writs. Yet, in this way our common law grew. The Register of Writs expanded in the course of time and, of course, at any given time the Register containing the sum total of available writs *contained* the *common law*. Within the ambit of the writs lay people's rights: no writ, no right – unless the court *would* grant a new writ.

Thus the stream of the evolution of the common law can be traced in the proliferation of the Forms of Action (writs). This evolution is a long one, extending over more than seven hundred years; and there were times of stagnation, as after the Barons' war in the thirteenth century; and there were times of change, as, strangely perhaps, in the early Tudor Period. The recognition of a new right might well be a political matter: there are times of social peace and times of social ferment. Legal conservatism also tells: the fear of departing from the rulings of one's forbears. There were experiments: new forms replaced old. But the story *was* one of expansion: at first few writs and few rights that could be asserted in the royal courts – though it may be that they could, in mediaeval times, be vindicated in the local courts or in the Church (Ecclesiastical) courts. But by the time the Writ System was abolished by the Common Law Procedure Act 1852 (and, indeed, not entirely until the Judicature Acts 1873–1875) there were many forms of action which, in sum, contained the common law.

The modern procedure based upon the Judicature Acts now prevails and, as we shall see, the ancient system has gone. Legal innovation (especially legislative) during the past hundred years has been prolific, so that we have cut away from the roots created by the Writs, yet the framework of our civil actions is still based upon them. And it is unwise to forget Maitland's warning that "the Forms of Action we have buried, but they rule us from their graves". The common law, as opposed to statute law with its fits and starts, is still a thing of continuous creation from its ancient fountain-heads.

It may, perhaps, be added that the principal defect of the Writ System was its formalism – a besetting sin of early law paralleled by the *legis actiones* of ancient Rome. While the Forms of Action ruled it was not only true that the plaintiff had normally to find a writ to suit his case but also that if he chose the *wrong* writ his claim must fail. There was no changing of horses in mid-stream (no "amendment" as we now know it): one rode one's writ to judgment, and if it then turned out to be the wrong one one could only go back and try another "horse" – assuming that one had the time, the money and the patience.

2 Equity

Before the Royal Courts of Justice were housed at their present place (in the Strand) they used to sit in Westminster Hall. The three common law courts were on one side of the Hall and the Court of Chancery was on the other. In this Court *equity* was administered, and litigants who could not obtain justice in the common law courts would cross the Hall to seek the Chancellor's aid.

The office of Chancellor (more recently "Lord Chancellor") has an ancient history. Originally the *"cancellarius"* (from Latin *"cancellus"*: a bar or lattice) was an usher who served at the bar of a Roman court. In its more distinguished form the office goes back to the court of Charlemagne and had been translated to England by the time of Edward the Confessor. In this form the Chancellor became the King's right-hand man ("Secretary of State for all Departments", as the historian, Bishop Stubbs, put it) and the most powerful official in the realm. He headed the "Chancery", the royal Secretariat, and he was responsible for the use and custody of the Great Seal of the Realm. He was, moreover, closely associated with the administration of justice, for, as has been remarked, the original writs were issued from the Chancery: further, he was an important member of the *King's Council* whose duty it became to consider and adjudicate upon petitions addressed to the Council by subjects who sought justice from it as the body most close to the King himself. Petitions might be presented for various reasons. In particular, they were often presented by people who had, in one way or another, failed to obtain justice in the common law courts. This failure was usually due to one of three causes. First, the common law was in some ways *defective*: for example, the early common law in respect of breaches of contract was grossly inadequate (see below, p. 203). Second, the only *remedy* which the common law courts would usually supply was the remedy of damages (below, p. 256), and damages are by no means always a satisfactory form of relief. Third, although the law was adequate to meet the case, *justice might not always be obtainable* in the common law courts because of the greatness of one of the parties, who might, in mediaeval times, often be in a position to over-awe the court itself. The Chancellor could remedy these defects; he was one of the chief royal officials, and being closely associated with the king, he was bound by neither the rules nor the procedure of the common law courts; nor was he likely to be over-awed by any man.

In hearing these petitions (or "bills" as they came later to be called when the Chancery had become a court) the Chancellors slowly began to evolve a set of rules which remedied the defects in the common law, and to grant new forms of remedies different from, and more effective than, the common law remedies. Thus they redressed breaches of contract, for they regarded them as morally reprehensible breaches of faith; and it must be remembered that the early Chancellors were ecclesiastics. They also decreed *specific performance* and granted *injunctions* (below, pp. 261–263). Moreover, in the course of time, they made use of a special writ of *subpoena*, by which they could compel the attendance of parties or witnesses under threat of fine or imprisonment, should they fail to attend.

The Chancellors therefore came to administer justice, but at first they had no independent court; they often acted in consultation with the Council and even with the judges themselves. But by the close of the fifteenth century the Chancellor was acting in a judicial capacity upon his own initiative; so that the history of the *Court of Chancery*, as opposed to the more ancient Chancery itself, really begins then. This court continued to exist until the Judicature Acts abolished it, retaining the memory of its name in the "Chancery" Division of the High Court of Justice.

The new rules which were thus administered in the Court of Chancery came to be known as the rules of *"Equity"* (derived from the Latin *aequitas* ▬ levelling). There will be further discussion of equity later in this work; especially in the chapters on the Land Law and Trusts – the latter being the greatest contribution of equity to our legal system. At present only four points need be noted.

First, it was only gradually that equity developed into a systematic body of rules; indeed, it was not fully developed until systematized under the ponderous chancellorship of Lord Eldon (Lord Chancellor 1801–1806; 1807–1827). The early Chancellors administered it according to discretion (Cardinal Wolsey's administration of it seems to have been conspicuously fair); so much so that John Selden (1548–1554: lawyer, populist and antiquarian) once remarked that early equity varied "according to the length of the Chancellor's foot". From the chancellorship of Sir Thomas Moore (1529–1532), however, it became usual to appoint *legally* trained Chancellors and this, by the nineteenth century, had led the Court of Chancery to rely upon precedent almost as much as the common law. *But* even today the administration of equity rests upon discretion; and specific performance of a contract, for example, will not be decreed in a case in which it would be unjust to do so.

In the second place, and conversely, before Sir Thomas Moore's chancellorship the Chancellors were usually not only administrative officials but also ecclesiastics and chief of the royal chaplains: it followed that in exercising their discretion, and laying the foundations of the rules of equity, they borrowed, and built into the structure of equity, many rules of the canon (church) and civil (Roman) law.

In the third place, it is often not appreciated – and it must be appreciated – that by the very nature of its origin equity *assumes the law*: it did not come to defeat the common law but to supplement it and to *"fulfil"* it. It is not a rival, but an ancillary system of rules: as Maitland put it, it is a "gloss or appendix" to the law. [Sometimes examinees who prefer to rely upon lectures rather than reading repeat this statement as "Equity is a glossy appendix on the common law"]. Moreover, as another maxim of equity has it, "Equity *follows* the law", and yet another, that it *"acts in personam"*, upon the conscience (not surprisingly in view of its ecclesiastical origin) of a defendant. These considerations lead to the result that a person who has an *equitable right* to property has something of less validity than one who acquires a *legal right* to the same property. The position is that an equitable right will be destroyed if the property be acquired under a legal title by a *bona fide purchaser for value* of the legal right to the property *without notice* of the right of the person entitled in equity. This important limitation upon the validity of the equitable right will appear when the Law of Property falls to be considered. For the present let us just give a simple illustration of the distinction between the (weaker) "*equitable*" and the (universally valid) "*legal*" right. Suppose that Λ is a beneficiary in respect of certain property which is held by X in trust for him. Trusts are the creation of equity and the position therefore is that A's right is *equitable*: X, the trustee, has the *legal* title to the property which in conscience (enforceable by imprisonment if necessary) he is bound to hold for A, so that A has full use and enjoyment of it – in the old law X was said to hold "to the use" (or "*ad opus*") of A. Suppose that X, perhaps for his own profit, sells the entrusted property to B. Then, *prima facie* B has a legal title to that property, and his title *defeats* A's; so that all A will have is a right of action (for what it may be worth) against X. We assume by this that B is a *bona fide* purchaser for value of what is of course the *legal* title to the property *without notice of* the trust. Thus law defeats equity. But change the facts and A's equitable right will acquire a strength of its own. It is *only* the *bona fide* purchaser for value of the legal title to the property who will prevail. So that let B have *reason to know* of the existence of the trust or let him fail to give value for the property: then, in either case his right will cede to A's. In the one case A's conscience will be affected, and the Chancellors would force him to act conscionably and yield to A; in the other equity, as another maxim has it, "will not assist a volunteer", so that B's gratuitously acquired right (even though he has no notice) gives way to A's equitable title.

It is important at the start to understand this difference between legal and equitable rights.

B THE MODERN LEGAL SYSTEM

The Superior Courts

1 NINETEENTH CENTURY REFORMS

The eighteenth century was an age of stagnation in legal affairs, complacently described and accurately mirrored in Blackstone's *Commentaries on the Laws of England* (1765). By contrast, the nineteenth century was an age of reform. The reform movement was largely due to the exertions of one man, Jeremy Bentham (1748–1832) who, throughout his long life, set himself the task of publicly criticizing legal institutions and of writing books suggesting the means for their reform. His work was enthusiastically assisted during his life, and carried on after his death, by a host of "Benthamite" followers; and it eventually bore fruit in a series of reforming enactments.

There were five main defects in the English legal system in the early part of the nineteenth century.

First, law and equity were, as we have seen, administered in separate courts. This meant that *a litigant who felt himself aggrieved by the decision of one of the common law courts, and wished to seek the assistance of equity, had to institute separate proceedings in the Chancery*; this system was both time-wasting and costly.

Second, although, as has been seen, equity was originally evolved as a subsidiary system to mitigate the rigour of the common law, some of its rules had by this time come to conflict directly with the common law.

Third, the Ecclesiastical Courts (matrimonial causes and probate – see below, p. 43) and the Court of Admiralty, having developed independently of the other courts, had a special and peculiar procedure and practice of their own.

Fourth, the system of appeals against wrong decisions was both intricate and unsatisfactory.

Fifth, procedure, especially in the common law courts, was cumbersome and antiquated.

An extreme instance of the unhappy state of affairs which prevailed is provided by the case of *Knight* v. *The Marquis of Waterford* (1844), 11 Cl. & Fin. 653 where it took an unfortunate litigant fourteen years to carry an appeal to the House of Lords only to discover then that, since he had originally started his action in the Court of Chancery when he ought properly to have started it in a common law court, he must go back and start all over again.

The reformers were therefore faced with a threefold problem. First, the system of courts required to be simplified. Second, the administration of law and equity needed to be harmonized. Finally, the system of procedure was ripe for recasting.

We are not here concerned with the third of these problems and the methods by which it was solved.

Apart from the all-important changes effected by the Judicature Acts (below), the first problem was initially tackled by the passing of the Court of Probate Act 1857, which abolished the probate jurisdiction of the Ecclesiastical Courts (see below, p. 43) and set up a new *Court of Probate*. The Matrimonial Causes Act of the same year, also transferred the matrimonial jurisdiction of the Ecclesiastical Courts to a new *Divorce Court*; at the same time so altering the law as to make divorce by judicial decree for the first time possible in certain cases.

The second problem was initially solved by the passing of the Common Law Procedure Act 1854 which gave the common law courts the following powers – (i) To take into account certain defences upon which a defendant would have been entitled to rely had the action been tried in a court of equity; thus in certain defined cases obviating the need for application to be made to two separate courts. (ii) To grant injunctions (see below, p. 262) in certain cases. Further, by the Chancery Procedure Act 1852, the Court of Chancery was empowered to decide points of common law which arose in the course of Chancery proceedings. Finally, by the Chancery Amendment Act 1858 (Lord Cairns' Act), the Court of Chancery was empowered to grant the common law remedy of damages in lieu of, or in addition to, its own remedies of specific performance (see below, p. 261) and injunction.

All these reforms were far less important than the radical changes made by the Supreme Court of Judicature Act 1873–1875, passed upon the recommendation of the Judicature Commission set up in 1867 (hereafter the "Judicature Acts").

By these Acts the superior courts were reorganized and were placed substantially upon their present-day footing. One *Supreme Court of Judicature* was set up; this consisted, as it now consists, of two branches, the *Court of Appeal* and a lower branch, the *High Court of Justice*. The new organization came into being on November 1st, 1875, and at that time the High Court was made to consist of the following Divisions: –

(i) The Queen's Bench Division;
(ii) The Chancery Division;
(iii) The Common Pleas Division;
(iv) The Exchequer Division;
(v) The Probate, Divorce and Admiralty Division.

The Acts empowered the Crown to make further reorganizations by Order in Council. This power was exercised in 1881 when the Common Pleas Division and the Exchequer Division were merged in the Queen's Bench Division.

Thus today the Supreme Court of Judicature is composed of the Court of Appeal and the High Court of Justice; and until the Administration of Justice Act 1970 the latter was subdivided into the *Queen's Bench Division*, the *Chancery Division*, and the *Probate, Divorce and Admiralty Division*.

When the Acts came into force, the old courts – the three Common Law Courts, the Court of Chancery, the Court of Probate, the Divorce Court, the Court of Admiralty and certain appellate courts were abolished.

Having set up this new and simplified system of courts, the Acts further provided that for the future all branches of the Supreme Court should be empowered to *administer both law and equity*, and to grant both legal and equitable remedies. Further, all Divisions of the High Court were given competence to try any actions; though certain specific matters were reserved for each Division, roughly corresponding with the matters falling within the jurisdiction of the courts they had replaced. Finally, by section 25 of the Act of 1873, points of conflict between law and equity were resolved. This section set out a series of specific rules to govern certain specific points for the future; and in its final subsection, (11), it enacted that for the future "in all matters not hereinbefore particularly mentioned, in which there is any conflict or variance between the rules of equity and the rules of common law with reference to the same subject-matter, the rules of *equity shall prevail*" (italics ours).

It cannot be over-stressed that the Acts did *not* purport to *fuse* law and equity into a single system of rules; they only provided that the two systems should for the future be *administered* in the same courts. Nothing short of codifying the whole law could fuse the two systems into one: each set of rules has a different history, they are based upon different principles; and to this day they are separate and independent.

The Judicature Acts were subsequently amended by and consolidated in the Judicature Act 1925, and the structure just described remained intact until the coming into force of two statutes, the Administration of Justice Act 1970 (hereafter "A.J.A. 1970") and the Courts Act 1971 (hereafter "C.A."), which were mainly inspired by the Report of the Beeching Commission (1969 Cmnd. 4153). The effect of this legislation and the present structure (since January 1st, 1972) of the superior courts must therefore now be considered.

2 THE SUPREME COURT OF JUDICATURE

This is now divided into the *High Court of Justice* (Civil) and the *Crown Court* (Criminal) from both of which appeals may lie to the *Court of Appeal*.

i The High Court of Justice – It will be remembered that the High Court was formerly divided into the *Queen's Bench*, the *Chancery* and the *Probate, Divorce and Admiralty* Divisions. The A.J.A. 1970 abolished the last of these divisions and transferred its jurisdiction partly to the newly created *Family Division* and partly to the other two Divisions. Moreover, the C.A. (s. 1 (2)) effected a radical change by abolishing the time-hallowed "Assize" system and making it possible (s. 2) for sittings of the High Court to take place anywhere in England or Wales according to convenience.

Although *any* matter *may* be determined in *any* Division of the High Court (even though it be assigned by any enactment to some other Division) and the conception of the unity of the High Court is thus preserved, normally each Division keeps to its special business, so that the three Divisions require separate consideration.

The *Queen's Bench Division* has for its president the Lord Chief Justice of England (abbreviated " – L.C.J."), with a staff of 46 "puisne" judges at the present time. Its jurisdiction is mostly original (*i.e.* devoted to "first instance" hearings of cases initially tried by it), but it does also have some appellate jurisdiction.

The *original* jurisdiction is for all practical purposes purely civil today. Unlike the County Courts which, as we shall see, have only limited powers, the jurisdiction of the Queen's Bench Division (in common with the other Divisions of the High Court) is subject to no limitation in respect of the amount at stake or otherwise; though minor causes within the jurisdictional competence of the County Courts will not normally be tried in the Queen's Bench Division.

In the exercise of its original jurisdiction the court consists of a single judge, whether sitting at the Royal Courts of Justice in London or elsewhere. Juries are now rare in civil actions, so the judge is *usually* judge of both law and fact, but where technical issues are involved he may be assisted by "lay" (non-lawyer) "assessors".

The classes of actions tried in the Division are still mainly those that used to be tried by the old common law courts which it replaced. For instance, breaches of contract, actions for the recovery of land and claims (*e.g.* "running-down" cases) founded upon tort or breach of statutory duty are usually Queen's Bench matters.

In hearing *appeals* the Queen's Bench Division sits as a *"divisional court"* of three, or sometimes two judges. Its *civil* jurisdiction in this respect is not large; it mainly consists in the hearing of appeals by way of case stated (see below) in certain civil matters heard before magistrates' courts and of appeals from a number of tribunals, such as rent assessment committees and the Pensions Appeal Tribunal. On the *criminal* side the appellate jurisdiction is more important, consisting of hearing appeals by way of case stated from magistrates' courts and the Crown Court. From these hearings appeal lies to the House of Lords, subject to certain conditions (see below, p. 36).

Like the old Court of King's Bench, the Queen's Bench Division exercises an important *"supervisory"* jurisdiction in respect of the prerogative orders (see below, p. 133); in this capacity it also takes the form of a divisional court.

The above are what we may perhaps be permitted to call the regular functions of the Queen's Bench Division. Two specialized courts which now also form part of it must, however, also be mentioned. These are the *Admiralty Court* and the *Commercial Court*.

The Admiralty Court is the creation of the A.J.A. 1970, s. 2 which transferred the jurisdiction formerly exercised by the admiralty side of the Probate, Divorce and Admiralty Division to the Queen's Bench Division in the form of a specialized court. This Court has both "*instance*" and "*prize*" jurisdiction. The first concerns civil cases connected with ships and shipping; in particular with collisions at sea. The second requires explanation. International law has always permitted belligerents to authorize the seizure of enemy or, in certain circumstances, neutral ships and cargoes by way of "prize". When a foreign ship is thus captured it must be taken to a port in the captor's country for "adjudication" before a *Prize Court*. The business of that court is, amongst other things, to decide whether the capture has been a lawful one by the rules of international law. In admiralty matters the judge is usually advised by nautical assessors (Elder Brethren of Trinity House). The Admiralty Court is not a very active court, since many shipping cases are settled by insurers and they also tend to go to arbitration. Naturally prize jurisdiction only relates to times of war.

The Commercial Court is new only in the sense that the A.J.A. 1970, s. 3 gave recognition to a long standing practice by which specialist judges have been assigned to commercial cases and by which a special "commercial list" has been drawn up. Here the aim has always been to conduct commercial business as simply and as speedily as possible by means of unelaborate procedure (a method which might well be adopted by all the higher courts). This aim is, however, so far from being realized that commercial disputes are in practice normally settled by arbitration.

The *Chancery Division* is in theory headed by the Lord Chancellor, but in practice (since the A.J.A. 1970) its president is the *Vice-Chancellor* (in legal writings abbreviated " – V.-C.") at present assisted by a staff of 10 puisne judges. This Division also has both original and appellate jurisdiction. In its exercise of its original jurisdiction it is the successor of the old Court of Chancery and although, since the Judicature Acts, all divisions of the High Court are competent to administer both law and equity it is nevertheless still the fact that as a general rule matters which used to lie within the province of the Court of Chancery remain primarily the business of the Chancery Division. Certain matters are, however, expressly assigned to it by the Judicature Act 1925, s. 56: amongst these are the execution of trusts, the administration of estates and partnership and company matters. Since the A.J.A. 1970 the Chancery Division (in succession to the probate side of the former Probate, Divorce and Admiralty Division) also deals with all contentious probate (see below, p. 458) business – non-contentious probate is assigned to the Family Division.

A divisional court of the Chancery Division hears, amongst other kinds of appeals, *appeals* in bankruptcy matters.

The *Family Division* has a *President* (in legal writings abbreviated " – P."), at present assisted by a staff of 16 puisne judges. As befits its name, it has original jurisdiction in respect of all matrimonial matters (formerly exercised by the divorce side of the Probate, Divorce and Admiralty Division), proceedings in respect of the wardship of minors, adoption and guardianship proceedings, claims connected with s. 17 of the Married Women's Property Act 1882 (see below, p. 412) and (*inter alia*) proceedings under the Matrimonial Homes Act 1967 (see below, p. 412).

This Division also has *appellate* jurisdiction in respect of certain classes of appeals from magistrates' courts, including a number of matters connected with matrimonial disputes and with minors.

Appeals – Appeal from all Divisions of the High Court normally lies to the Civil Division of the *Court of Appeal*, but in order to save cost and delay, the Administration of Justice Act 1969 introduced what is often called "leap-frogging" procedure by which in most kinds of *civil* cases appeal may be made *direct* from the High Court to the *House of Lords*. This procedure may be used only where both parties agree and where the trial judge grants a certificate to sanction it; but the judge may do so only if he is satisfied that a point of law is involved which is of general public importance and which either relates to a matter of construction of an Act or of a statutory instrument *or* else is one in respect of which he considers that he is "bound" by a previous decision of the Court of Appeal or of the House of Lords. No appeal lies against a grant or refusal by the judge of such a certificate. If it is granted, however, the appellant must then apply direct to the House of Lords for leave to appeal.

ii The Crown Court – This is the creation of the C.A. 1971. Like the High Court, this court may conduct its business either in London or in any part of England or Wales; for this purpose the country is divided into "circuits", groups of centres to be visited. Each circuit has a "circuit administrator" with a permanent staff whose duty it is to make arrangements for sittings of the Crown Court within the circuit areas, under the general direction of a High Court judge or judges appointed by the Lord Chancellor as "presiding judges" of the circuit.

The Court has some minor civil jurisdiction, but its main business concerns all criminal proceedings upon *indictment* (see below, p. 59). Its structure is complicated by the fact that it has three kinds of judges; *High Court* judges, *Circuit* judges and *Recorders*. Which of these judges will sit will normally depend upon the gravity of the offence involved according to a classification of offences which will shortly be mentioned. The difference between the Circuit judge and the Recorder (a new office unconnected with the Recorders of former times) is not one of jurisdiction but of employment; Circuit judges being full-time judges, Recorders only part-time. Circuit judges are appointed by the Queen on the recommendation of the Lord Chancellor, and they must have been barristers of at least ten years' standing or have been Recorders for at least five years. Recorders may be appointed to their part-time office from among barristers or solicitors of ten years' standing. It should be added that in most cases, and always upon the hearing of appeals, not more than four or less than two justices of the peace sit with a Circuit judge or Recorder.

The *original* jurisdiction of this court consists, as we have seen, of jurisdiction over all *indictable* offences and the work is apportioned according to the following general scheme.

Offences are divided into four classes. *Class 1* offences include very serious crimes, such as murder and offences under the Official Secrets Act 1911, s. 1: these are reserved for trial by a High Court judge. *Class 2* offences, such as manslaughter, child destruction, infanticide and rape must be tried by a High Court judge unless released by or on the authority of a presiding judge for trial by a Circuit judge or a Recorder. *Class 3* offences: these consist of indictable offences other than those falling within the other classes. They will usually be listed for trial by a High Court judge, but they may, with leave of a presiding judge, be tried by a Circuit judge or a Recorder. *Class 4* offences include, *inter alia*, all offences which may, in appropriate circumstances, be tried either upon indictment or summarily. They will normally be listed for trial by a Circuit judge or a Recorder – as opposed to a High Court judge.

From the Crown Court appeal against *conviction* or *sentence* lies to the Criminal Division of the Court of Appeal.

The appellate jurisdiction of the Crown Court consists in the hearing of appeals from magistrates' courts either against conviction or against sentence and it also tries cases of committal for sentence from those courts (see below, p. 42). In respect of this appellate jurisdiction there is a further right of appeal from the Crown Court to a divisional court of the Queen's Bench Division by way of "case stated" (see below, p. 42).

A useful innovation was made by the Criminal Justice Act 1972, s. 36; namely that where a trial upon indictment has resulted in an *acquittal* the Attorney-General (the chief law officer of the Crown) may refer any point of law which has arisen in the case to the Criminal Division of the Court of Appeal for its opinion. The latter may then refer the matter to the House of Lords.

The Crown Court for London is the *Central Criminal Court* (the "Old Bailey").

Locations for sittings of the Crown Court have been arranged upon a three-tier system. Major centres are "first-tier" centres served by High Court judges, Circuit judges and Recorders, and which have both civil and criminal jurisdiction; "second-tier" centres are similarly served, but they are only concerned with criminal cases; "third-tier" centres are served only by Circuit judges and Recorders, also having criminal, but no civil jurisdiction.

iii The Court of Appeal – Although certain other high-judicial officers, including the Lord Chancellor, are *ex-officio* members of the Court of Appeal, its president on the *civil side* is in practice the *Master of the Rolls* (in legal writings referred to as " – M.R."). His office dates from the Middle Ages when the Master of the Rolls was chief deputy to the Chancellor in his judicial capacity. The M.R. is therefore a judge, though the strange title derives from the fact that he was keeper of the Royal Records; and he still has duties in connexion with the Record Office. In the Court of Appeal he has a staff of *Lords Justices of Appeal* (in legal writings abbreviated " – L.J.": plural " – L.JJ." – in the same way that puisne judges are "Mr. Justice", abbreviated "J.": plural "JJ."). Lords Justices must not be confused with their seniors, the Lords of Appeal in Ordinary. Any High Court judge may, however, be required by the Lord Chancellor to sit in the Court of Appeal should an addition of strength be necessary. The quorum for a sitting of either division of the court is normally three and any number of courts may sit in either division at any given time. On the *criminal side* the Lord Chief Justice presides.

Formerly this Court exercised jurisdiction in civil matters only, but since the Criminal Appeal Act 1966 it has entertained appeals in

a   *The Civil Division* – In its civil aspect the jurisdiction of the court includes power to hear appeals from the decisions in *civil* matters (*i.e.* non-criminal matters) of all three divisions of the High Court. The court also hears appeals from the County Courts. *Bankruptcy* appeals from the County Courts form an exception, for they lie, as we have seen, not to the Court of Appeal, but to a Divisional Court of the Chancery Division. Appeals from the Prize Court (as opposed to appeals from the "instance" jurisdiction of the Admiralty Court of the Queen's Bench Division) also form an exception, for they lie to the Judicial Committee of the Privy Council.

The method of appeal is now by way of rehearing; the method which always prevailed in the case of appeals from the Court of Chancery.

This does not mean that the Court recalls the witnesses heard in the Court below, nor that it will normally admit fresh evidence, not taken at the trial; but that it reviews the whole case from the shorthand notes of the trial and from the judge's notes.

b *The Criminal Division* – The Criminal Appeal Act 1966 transferred the powers formerly exercised by the *Court of Criminal Appeal* (set up by the Criminal Appeal Act 1907) to this division of the *Court of Appeal*; and much of this criminal jurisdiction of the Court of Appeal is now defined by the Criminal Appeal Act 1968.

The division entertains appeals from the Crown Court. In respect of *convictions* appeal lies as of right on a question of law alone, and by leave of the Court of Appeal (*i.e.* in this context the criminal division) on questions of fact or of mixed law and fact; though in the latter cases appeal will also be as of right if the trial judge certifies that an appeal is justified. Appeal will be allowed if the court think (i) that the jury's decision was under all the circumstances "unsafe or unsatisfactory" or (ii) that the decision was wrong in point of law, or (iii) that there was a "material irregularity" in the course of the trial: but an appeal may be dismissed if the court consider that "no miscarriage of justice has actually occurred". Further, if the court are of opinion that the proper verdict would have been one of not guilty by reason of insanity or a finding that the appellant was under disability, they may order him to be admitted to a hospital. In certain circumstances a retrial may be ordered.

Appeal against *sentence* lies only with leave of the Court of Appeal; and whereas formerly – in order to discourage frivolous appeals – the Court of Criminal Appeal had power to increase the sentence, the court may now only so vary it that in the result the appellant is not dealt with more severely than he was dealt with in the court below.

The 1968 Act also contains detailed provisions relating to appeals against findings of insanity or of unfitness to stand trial. If the Court of Appeal consider it necessary or expedient in the interests of justice they *may* hear fresh evidence not given at the trial if, *inter alia*, it appears that there is a reasonable explanation for failure to adduce it then. Orders for costs may be made; and in particular an order that an unsuccessful appellant shall pay the costs of the appeal – in some cases at least, a safeguard against hopeless appeals. No judge may hear an appeal in any case in which he was a member of the court of first instance. The decision of the court must be given in a *single* judgment except where the presiding judge states that the question is one of law on which it is convenient that separate judgments should be pronounced. A salutary rule for those who seek to discover the meaning of decisions.

There is a further right of appeal from either division to the House of Lords, as will now appear.

3   THE HOUSE OF LORDS

Most people would think of the House of Lords as the Upper House of Parliament; that is, of course, correct and we shall discuss the Upper Chamber later. But if we go back in time we find that in the early mediaeval period what we now think of as the House of Lords in the normally accepted sense was the *Curia Regis* (King's Court), a central governing body which existed before Parliament evolved. And this body exercised all the powers of government, including judicial functions. Thus when Parliament became established the Upper House retained *judicial* powers. At times, indeed, these powers were wide: they included the right to adjudicate impeachments made against individuals by the Commons (as in the case of Warren Hastings) and, until quite recently, the right to try peers accused of serious offences. Now the House itself – though there are some left, such as the right to try disputed claims to peerages – retains few of these functions, and when a *lawyer* thinks of the "House of Lords" he will normally have in mind not the Upper Chamber, but the *Court* of that name which, though technically a Committee of the House, is really separate from it.

The "House of Lords" in this sense, properly called the "Appellate Committee" of the House of Lords is the highest court in the land. The ultimate court of appeal. It was created by the Appellate Jurisdiction Act 1876 and it consists of a number (at present 9) of life peers ("Lords of Appeal in Ordinary") appointed from people who have held high judicial office, or from eminent barristers, presided over by the Lord Chancellor for the time being (abbreviated "L.C.") and also attended by any ex-Lord Chancellors available.

On the *civil* side the House, subject also to the leap-frog procedure already mentioned (above, p. 32), hears appeals from the Civil Division of the Court of Appeal; though only if leave of that Court or of the House itself has been granted. The jurisdiction on the *criminal* side consists of the hearing of appeals from the Criminal Division of the Court of Appeal and from the Courts-Martial Appeal Court (below, p. 45): but in either case there is no right of appeal unless the lower Court grants a certificate that a point of law of general public importance is involved, and either that Court or the House grants leave. Subject to similar restrictions there is also a right of appeal to the "Lords" from divisional courts of the Queen's Bench Division in criminal matters.

The House also entertains appeals from the appellate courts of Scotland and Northern Ireland. The quorum of Law Lords for the hearing of an appeal is three, but in practice more usually sit. Since in theory the

Appellate Committee is part of the House of Lords (*i.e.* the legislative body) itself judgments are delivered as "speeches" and the decision is formally put to the vote.

It has been explained that House of Lords' decisions are absolutely binding on all lower courts though now it may exceptionally refuse to follow its *own*.

4   THE JUDICIAL COMMITTEE OF THE PRIVY COUNCIL

The importance of the Judicial Committee of the Privy Council is one of rise with the expansion of the Commonwealth and fall with its decline. Originally this jurisdiction sprang from the right of the King's Council (an inner body of the *Curia Regis*) to exercise jurisdiction under the royal prerogative – including an ancient right, which still exists, of hearing appeals from the Channel Islands and from the Isle of Man. With the fall of the Star Chamber in 1641 no jurisdiction could be exercised by the Council over cases arising within the realm, but as the Empire grew the Privy Council (as it came to be called) became the ultimate court of appeal from the whole of the expanding Commonwealth. Originally this massive power was exercised by lay members of the Council, but since an Act of 1833 the jurisdiction was placed in the hands of a "*Judicial Committee*" of professional judges; and it now consists of such Privy Councillors as hold, or have held, high judicial office in the United Kingdom and of certain other members (who must also be Privy Councillors) such as commonwealth judges. In practice a sitting of the "Judicial Committee" will normally consist of Lords of Appeal in Ordinary assisted by a commonwealth judge or eminent practitioner.

The Statute of Westminster 1931 empowered the countries of the Commonwealth to abolish appeals to the "Judicial Committee"; and most of them have done so. Consequently this court is now of little importance, although a few countries have retained the right of appeal.

The Judicial Committee does, however, retain some miscellaneous functions (connected with its origin as a committee of the Council) such as the ancient right in respect of the Channel Islands and the Isle of Man, the hearing of appeals from the ecclesiastical courts in respect of faculties (below, p. 44) and of appeals from the Prize Court. As final repository of the powers of the mediaeval Council it may also determine any disputed question of law referred to it by the Crown. The Judicial Committee is not bound by its own previous decisions. Moreover its decisions do not *bind* lower courts in the United Kingdom; their authority is only "*persuasive*"; though, naturally since the judicial staff of the Committee is very similar to that of the House of Lords its rulings are treated with great respect.

Since the Judicial Committee is still in *theory* a Committee of the Privy Council (though the two bodies are in practice distinct) its decisions are delivered in the form of advice to Her Majesty; only one opinion is usually given (since advice, to be effective, must be unanimous); though since 1966 it has been made possible (a retrograde step?) for dissentient opinions to be recorded. This is in contrast to the practice in other appellate courts: in the House of Lords, for instance, all speeches, "majority" and "dissenting", are delivered and reported; so also are all the judgments given in the civil division of the Court of Appeal.

The Inferior Courts

Chief among the inferior courts are the County Courts, which exercise civil jurisdiction, and the magistrates' courts exercising powers which are in the main criminal.

1   THE COUNTY COURTS

There has always been, and there always will be, a need for local courts to determine minor civil disputes. This need was originally supplied by the old County ("Shire") Courts and the Hundred Courts which existed in Anglo-Saxon times but fell into desuetude by the close of the Middle Ages. From the Reformation until 1846 there was no national system of civil courts for minor causes. The County Courts Act of that year, however, set up a new system of County Courts, which is still substantially in operation today. The name "County" Court is misleading, for these comparatively new courts have no connexion with the old communal "County" (Shire) Courts and their organization is not based upon the geographical division of the country into counties.

For the purpose of the county court system England and Wales are divided into districts and judges' "circuits" in such a way as to ensure that local courts for minor civil causes are readily available throughout the country according to the needs of population. These courts were formerly served by County Court judges, but the Courts Act 1971 abolished that office and replaced the holders of it by *Circuit Judges* (see above, p. 32) who, as has been seen, may also sit in the Crown Court; many of them being at present former County Court judges, with only a change of title. There is moreover a County Court *Registrar* who has jurisdiction in matters involving less than £75. Recorders (above, p. 32) may also deputize for the judge.

Under the provisions of the County Courts Act 1959 (as amended by subsequent enactments) the County Courts have a very wide jurisdiction including – (i) Jurisdiction over most actions in contract or tort, or for money recoverable by statute where the debt or damages claimed do not exceed £750; (ii) Jurisdiction over actions for the recovery of land where the net annual value of the land for rating does not exceed £1,000; (iii) An equity jurisdiction up to £5,000; (iv) Probate jurisdiction where the net value of the estate is less than £1,000; (v) A jurisdiction involving any amount where either the parties agree to accept the jurisdiction of the court or the case is remitted to it from the High Court.

It should be added that *some* county courts also have a limited jurisdiction in admiralty matters and that certain of them designated as *divorce* county courts have jurisdiction in undefended divorce cases: though defended suits must be transferred to the High Court. In order to discourage the conducting of minor litigation in the High Court, which could have been brought in a county court, a party who succeeds in the High Court upon a matter falling within the county court limits may in certain circumstances be awarded no costs or only awarded costs on the county court, as opposed to the High Court, scale.

Beside the types of jurisdiction already mentioned, numerous nineteenth and twentieth century statutes have conferred further duties upon the county courts. Thus, for example, they have been accorded very important powers under the Landlord and Tenant Acts (below, Chapter 10) and in matters arising under the Housing Acts and most of them now have an unlimited jurisdiction in bankruptcy matters.

Procedure is simpler in the county courts, and litigation less costly, than in the High Court. The judge almost invariably sits without a jury; and solicitors as well as barristers have a right of audience.

If the importance of a court is to be assessed from the standpoint of the amount of work it does, rather than from the importance of the issues it tries, the County Courts, in the civil sphere, like the magistrates' courts in the criminal, must be regarded as the most important tribunals in the land; for the amount of litigation conducted in them far exceeds the amount conducted in the High Court. It is well for the student to remember this, because in the course of his studies he will become familiar almost entirely with decisions of the superior courts and will tend to forget the enormous *practical* importance of the work of the county courts.

There is a right of appeal, as we have seen, from the county courts to the Court of Appeal.

2 MAGISTRATES' COURTS

The office of justice of the peace is an ancient one; it goes right back to the creation of "conservators of the peace" in the thirteenth century – gentlemen appointed in the counties to assist the sheriffs in keeping the peace – a "policing", rather than a judicial, function. The name "*justice* of the peace", however, appears about 1363 when similar people came to be given the function of trying cases of minor crime at quarterly sessions and this practice developed into the "Quarter Sessions" which remained with us until, in the name of efficiency, they were abolished (together with the much older and more important institution of the Assizes) by the Courts Act 1971. In this way a considerable amount of criminal justice in minor indictable offences came to be done by the voluntary services of laymen (non-lawyers). The memory of Quarter Sessions is preserved in the fact that, as has been seen, lay justices now sit with circuit judges and recorders to hear cases coming to them on appeal to the Crown Court and in most other cases the latter try. It should be added that in modern times Quarter Sessions did usually have legally qualified chairmen.

More to the present purpose, numerous statutes from the sixteenth century onwards empowered these lay "justices" to try petty offences (less serious than the minor indictable offences triable at Quarter Sessions) *summarily* (*i.e.* sitting without a jury). These more frequent and less formal sessions came to be known as "Petty Sessions". Further, from 1554 justices were empowered to conduct *preliminary examinations* (or enquiries) of people charged with indictable offences in order to determine whether there were a sufficiently strong *prima facie* case to commit them for jury trial at Quarter Sessions or (in the most serious cases) before the Royal Justices of Assize.

Both the *summary* jurisdiction of the magistrates and the duty of holding *preliminary examinations* ("committal" proceedings) still survive.

Summary jurisdiction – trial without jury – has always, through distorted historical memories of the clause in Magna Carta which demanded trial by "peers", been regarded with suspicion in our law. Its scope is therefore restricted to offences of a minor sort and the power of magistrates' courts is circumscribed – six months' imprisonment and a fine of £400 are the usual limits of the penalties imposable. This ensures that more serious cases are sent to the Crown Court.

Although summary offences are "non-indictable" offences (see below, p. 58) a person who is accused of one may, nevertheless, elect to be tried by jury upon indictment where the offence charged is one which carries a maximum penalty of more than three months' imprisonment. On the other hand, in order to relieve the pressure of work in the higher criminal courts, *certain* indictable offences (often called "hybrid" offences) have also by contrast, been made subject to summary trial; though where the accused is an adult, his consent to be so tried for an indictable offence, must always be obtained. Generally speaking, however, "children" (*i.e.* persons under fourteen) must, except in cases of homicide, *always* be tried summarily, and "young persons" (*i.e.*

minors between fourteen and seventeen) *may*, subject to similar exceptions, *always* be tried summarily provided that they consent.

When trying people under seventeen the court sits as a "Juvenile Court", consisting of three lay magistrates (both sexes being represented) drawn from a special panel. Juvenile Courts must sit in a separate place from, or at separate times from, the ordinary sessions and they must not sit in a room that has been or will be used by another court within an hour before or after their sitting ; the parents must normally be present and the public are excluded.

The justices also have a limited civil jurisdiction ; and they have power, in certain circumstances, to make affiliation orders, orders for judicial separation, and for maintenance.

In certain urban areas there are full-time paid *"stipendiary" magistrates* appointed by the Crown, upon the recommendation of the Lord Chancellor, from among barristers or solicitors of a certain standing. Stipendiary magistrates *may*, and usually do, sit alone. In London there are petty sessional courts known as "Metropolitan Stipendiary Courts". Their judges are full-time paid professional magistrates called "Metropolitan Stipendiary Magistrates" who are the sole judges of the court.

The clerk of a Magistrates' Court is the "Clerk to the Justices" or, colloquially, "Justices' Clerk". Clerks are usually solicitors (though barristers may be appointed) and, as such, they properly have considerable influence over the "lay" bench.

The other judicial function of the justices is, as has been explained, to conduct *preliminary examinations* in the case of indictable offences, in order to determine whether a *prima facie* case has been made against an accused person and, if so, to decide upon the appropriate court of trial. The nature of the procedure at a preliminary examination will be discussed below (p. 59).

To complete this brief account of the justices of the peace it is, perhaps, proper to add that in bye-gone days they were much more important than they are now. From the Black Death (1348–1349) when, by the Statutes of Labourers (1349–1360), they were given the task of enforcing the law governing labour relations, what Lambard (who wrote a classic treatise on the justices in the reign of Elizabeth I) called "stacks and shoals of statutes" imposed innumerable administrative duties upon them – *e.g.* upkeep of highways, rating, licensing of ale houses and administration of the poor law. All these and more, under the general supervision of the Council. When the latter, with the abolition of the Star Chamber (1641), lost its power the great age of the justices began, as mirrored in the activities of the country squires of eighteenth century literature : they were the rulers of the countryside. This state of affairs terminated with the Industrial Revolution, whereafter administration passed to other hands, and ultimately to local authorities. Today the chief surviving administrative powers are the issuing of warrants and licensing.

There are two classes of appeals from courts of summary jurisdiction. First, appeal lies to a Divisional Court of the Queen's Bench Division by way of "case stated". Either the *prosecution* or the *defence*, may, under this form of procedure, require the justices to set out their findings of fact, and may then apply to a Divisional Court of the Queen's Bench Division for a re-determination of any question of law which they dispute. Secondly, the *defence* has a right of appeal to the Crown Court. This is a true right of "appeal", for the evidence is re-heard and questions both of law and of fact may be reviewed. The Crown Court also hears appeals against sentence, but has power to *increase* the sentence, upon hearing such appeals. There is a further right of appeal from the Crown Court to the divisional court of the Queen's Bench Division by way of "case stated". As has already been noted (above, p. 32), subject to strict safeguards there is now a final appeal from the divisional court to the House of Lords.

In connexion with the inferior criminal courts bare mention should also be made of the *Coroners' Courts*. The office of "coroner" is very ancient and the Coroners' Court equally so, but its jurisdiction is now small. The chief functions of this court are to hold inquests upon the finding of "treasure trove" and in cases of unexplained death or death in prison. The latter powers are important, because the finding of a coroner's jury may sometimes (though in practice rarely) be used to support the preferment of an indictment in homicide cases, without the prior necessity for a preliminary inquiry before justices. Every inquest must be opened, adjourned, and closed in a formal manner; but, apart from this provision, proceedings at inquests are largely informal. The public are admitted, but the coroner may exclude them if he considers it to be in the national interest. Coroners are appointed from among barristers, solicitors, and legally qualified medical practitioners. Most of their duties are now prescribed by statute (the Coroners Acts 1887 to 1954) and Rules made under statutory authority.

If the Report of the Committee on Death Certificates and Coroners ("Brodrick" Report: 1971 Cmnd. 4810) is acted upon coroners will in future always be lawyers and their functions in respect of deaths will be confined to making findings as to the cause of death without the existing power of making findings of guilt.

C SPECIAL COURTS

The courts which have been discussed so far are the "ordinary" courts, institutions which have grown from the origins of the common law. Some mention must now be made of the numerous tribunals which fall outside this category.

For the purpose of exposition (but for this purpose only; for there are in practice no clear distinctions in this matter) these tribunals may be divided into three categories. First, there is the huge company of "*administrative*" tribunals, such as the wide powers of certain Ministers to determine disputed issues within their own executive province, or local tribunals under the Social Security Act 1975 (below, pp. 196–7), rent assessment committees (below, p. 343), rent tribunals (below, p. 344), or the powers of the Special Commissioners of Income Tax; these tribunals assume great importance today, but their nature and the constitutional difficulties which their prevalence creates will best be discussed below (below, p. 131). In the second place, there are what we may call courts of "*special jurisdiction*"; these are similar to the ordinary courts but they are constituted to exercise jurisdiction within specialized fields or among certain classes of people only, and consequently their staff and procedure often differ from the standard model of the ordinary courts. Finally, there are "*domestic*" tribunals; these are courts of a special nature set up among groups of people engaged in some common pursuit with the aim of regulating the behaviour of the members of the group.

Examples of *courts of special jurisdiction* and of *domestic tribunals* will now be given; but it must be stressed that they are examples and no more, many others might be given under each head.

Courts of Special Jurisdiction

Three of these courts will be considered: The Ecclesiastical Courts, Courts-Martial and the Restrictive Practices Court.

1 THE ECCLESIASTICAL COURTS

In mediaeval times the jurisdiction of the ecclesiastical courts was as ample as the power of the mediaeval Church itself – as the quarrel between Henry II and Becket displayed. Not only were the ecclesiastical courts special tribunals for the clergy as a class – a very numerous class at that – but they also held sway over the laity, especially in matters of morality (*e.g.* swearing, defamation, drunkenness) marriage and death (wills and intestacy). The court structure was correspondingly complex and until the Reformation, as Henry VIII's matrimonial troubles bore witness, there was a final right of appeal, in consonance with the universality of the mediaeval Church, to the *Papal Curia* at Rome.

Except for the abolition of the latter right of appeal the court structure was little affected by the Reformation and practice in the ecclesiastical courts continued to be an important and specialized business. The law administered was not common law; it was based, like the law of the admiralty courts, upon the romanized civil law of Europe and the "canon" law of the Church. There was thus a separate Bar for these courts, consisting not of barristers but of "doctors" ("civilians") who had their own special habitat at "Doctors' Commons" rather than the ordinary Inns of Court.

In 1857 the matrimonial and probate (wills) jurisdiction of the ecclesiastical courts was transferred to the then-created Divorce and Probate Courts, and the doctors and their "Commons" ceased to be. As we have seen these two courts, in their turn, were merged by the Judicature Acts into the Probate, Divorce and Admiralty Division of the High Court of Justice which was only recently abolished.

In keeping with the decline in the Church's authority, the jurisdiction of the ecclesiastical courts has diminished, but they still exist. The usual court of first instance in matters which are *not* concerned with doctrine, ritual or ceremonial is the *Consistory Court* of the bishop's disocese which is presided over by a legally qualified "Chancellor" who is appointed by the Bishop. His jurisdiction includes the granting of "faculties" (the right to alter the ornamentation or fabric of churches) and the adjudication of *clerical offences* committed by priests or deacons which do not involve doctrine, ritual or ceremonial. Appeal lies to the one or the other of the two *Provincial Courts*, the "*Court of the Arches*" (Canterbury: so named because it used to be situated in the old church of St. Mary-le-bow, built upon arches) and the *Chancery Court* of York: these are presided over respectively by the "Dean of the Arches" and the "Auditor", both being eminent barristers or judges. A further appeal lies to the Judicial Committee of the Privy Council. *Offences by bishops or archbishops* (not involving doctrine, ritual or ceremonial) are tried by *Commissions of Convocation*, whence appeal lies to a *Commission of Review*, consisting of three Lords of Appeal in Ordinary and two Lords Spiritual.

Matters concerning *doctrine, ritual or ceremonial* are differently treated, whether in relation to the granting of faculties or to clerical offences; they are tried by the *Court of Ecclesiastical Causes Reserved* which consists of two persons who hold or have held high judicial office, and three diocesan bishops. Thence appeal lies to a *Commission of Review*. Orders of *Certiorari* (see below, p. 136) do not lie to ecclesiastical courts, but orders of prohibition and mandamus do.

2 COURTS-MARTIAL

In order to secure the high degree of discipline essential in an army, soldiers (although they are in general also amenable to the ordinary law) have always been to some extent subjected to special rules of *"military law"*, which apply to them and not to people generally. These rules are to be found in the Army Act 1955 (as amended by the Armed Forces Act 1971), which is itself renewable annually by Order in Council until 1976. Special rules governing soldiers are also made by Queen's Regulations and by regulations issued under Royal Warrant. This law is administered by special courts, called *Courts-Martial*, which consist of military officers assisted in serious cases by members of the Department of an official called the *Judge-Advocate General* who are civilians in full-time employment recruited from barristers of standing. The Courts-Martial (Appeals) Act 1951 set up a special court, called the *Courts-Martial Appeal Court* to hear appeals from courts-martial. The composition and jurisdiction of this Court are now regulated by the Courts-Martial (Appeals) Act 1968. It is composed of the judges of the Court of Appeal, of such judges of the Queen's Bench Division of the High Court as the Lord Chief Justice (after consultation with the Master of the Rolls) may nominate, and of certain high judicial officers of Scotland and of Northern Ireland. The quorum is three, but a larger number of judges may sit provided that the number is uneven. The jurisdiction is similar to that of the Court of Appeal (see above, p. 35), except that appeal only lies with leave of the Appeal Court itself, and then only after a petition to the Defence Council (the co-ordinating organ of the combined services) has been unsuccessful. Appeal from the Appeal Court to the House of Lords (see above, p. 36) lies at the instance of either the appellant or the Defence Council.

Members of the Navy and of the Air Force are similarly subject to special rules of discipline and to court-martial procedure, and they also have similar rights of appeal.

3 INDUSTRIAL TRIBUNALS

These tribunals were first set up by the Industrial Training Act 1964 to determine certain matters arising under that Act. They are regionally organized and they consist of a legally qualified chairman who sits with a representative of employers and a representative of employees. Since 1964 the powers of these tribunals have repeatedly been increased: for instance, they now hear cases under the Contracts of Employment Act (below, p. 252), the Redundancy Payments Act (below, p. 192), the Equal Pay Act (below, p. 192) and, when it comes into operation, they will also have a considerable jurisdiction under the Employment Protection Act 1975. Even the Health and Safety at Work etc. Act 1974 adds to their duties by giving them jurisdiction in respect of enforcement notices served upon employers in respect of safety regulations.

4   THE RESTRICTIVE PRACTICES COURT

This court was set up by the Restrictive Trade Practices Act 1956. A sitting of it consists of a High Court judge with two lay members having "knowledge or experience in industry, commerce or public affairs". Appeal on questions of law lies to the Court of Appeal.

The Act, as amended by the Restrictive Trade Practices Act 1968 and the Fair Trading Act 1973, sets out certain classes of trading agreements which are presumed to be objectionable. These include, for instance, "any agreement between two or more persons carrying on business within the United Kingdom in the production or supply of goods ... being an agreement under which restrictions are accepted by two or more persons in respect of: (*i*) prices to be charged ... for goods supplied": (*ii*) "the prices to be recommended ... as the prices to be charged ... in respect of the resale of goods supplied" (*iii*) "the quantities or descriptions of goods to be produced, supplied or acquired". Moreover, by the 1973 Act the Secretary of State for Trade and Industry may by statutory instrument bring under control certain classes of agreements relating to the supply of *services*, as well as of goods. Certain kinds of agreements are, however, exempted by the statutes and others may be exempted by the Department of Trade and Industry – *e.g.* "agreements calculated to promote projects of importance to the national economy or to promote industrial or commercial efficiency".

All agreements within the defined classes must be registered in the register of restrictive trading agreements kept by the *Director General of Fair Trading* (who has an overall responsibility for fair trading, including control of monopolies and mergers – see below, p. 191); and it is the duty of this official to bring such agreements before the Restrictive Trade Practices Court for adjudication. The *presumption* is that any such restrictions as those mentioned are *contrary to public policy* and are therefore void; but on certain grounds specified in the Acts (*e.g.* that the restriction is reasonably necessary to protect the public against injury and that it is not unreasonable, or that it does not discourage competition within a trade or industry to any material degree) even restrictions falling within the Act may be upheld by the Court.

Trading agreements, of course, affect the economy. It follows that they fall within the law of the European Communities; and that that law may have a bearing upon the decisions of the Restrictive Practices Court. This matter is controlled by the European Communities Act 1972, s. 10 (1) which provides that the Court may exercise its jurisdiction in respect of an agreement even though it is one which (under art. 85 of the EEC Treaty) falls under European control and may be void under the (overriding) community law: but both the Court and the Director General are given discretions – the one may postpone or decline jurisdiction if it appears right to do so in order to keep in line with community law, the other, for similar reasons, may refrain from bringing an agreement before the Court. It must, however, be stressed that only agreements affecting trade *between* member states normally fall within community control; so that purely internal agreements will not usually conflict with community law. By s. 10 (2) of the European Communities Act (as amended by s. 99 of the Fair Trading Act) agreements between coal and steel undertakings – controlled under art. 80 of the ECSC Treaty – will normally be exempt from registration, and will be controlled only by community law. (For discussion of the European Treaties, see below, pp. 107–109.)

Domestic Tribunals

There are many domestic tribunals governing the conduct of particular groups of people; and this is natural, for, as Pollock and Maitland wrote in their *History of English Law*, "there can hardly exist a body of men permanently united by any common interest that will not make for itself a court of justice if it be left for a few years to its own devices". One could instance as an example constantly before the public eye the disciplinary powers which trade unions exercise over their members by means of district and other committees; or as an example banned by the Restrictive Trade Practices Act 1956, the powers formerly exercised among themselves by traders who combined to form what were in effect domestic courts to ensure that conditions as to resale prices collectively agreed upon should be enforced.

But here we must confine ourselves to three instances: the Solicitors' Disciplinary Tribunals under the Solicitors Acts, the Disciplinary Tribunals of the Bar, and the Medical Disciplinary Committee of the General Medical Council. (As to the legal powers of domestic tribunals see further below, p. 47.)

1 THE SOLICITORS' DISCIPLINARY TRIBUNAL

This tribunal was created (in succession to the "Disciplinary Committee under the Solicitors Acts") by the Solicitors Act 1974, s. 46. It consists of solicitors and lay (*i.e.* non-lawyer) members appointed by the Master of the Rolls. Its function is to hear applications to strike the name of a solicitor off the roll or applications by solicitors who have been struck off to have their names restored. The quorum for a hearing is three, though there may be more members. There must always be at least one lay member, but the number of solicitors sitting must exceed the number of laymen (*i.e.* non-lawyers). Appeal lies from the decisions of the Tribunal to the High Court – or, in certain circumstances, to the Master of the Rolls.

Complaints against solicitors are in the first instance investigated by a committee of the Law Society which decides whether there is a case to go to the Tribunal. The 1974 Act has made an innovation (s. 45) by empowering the Lord Chancellor to appoint "*lay observers*" whose duty it is to examine any written allegation made by a member of the public concerning the Law Society's treatment of a complaint against a solicitor: in other words, to ensure that the investigation is impartial.

2 DISCIPLINARY TRIBUNALS OF THE BAR

Ultimately the control of the conduct of barristers lies with the higher judiciary, who are themselves appointed from the Bar, but this power of control has long been delegated. It used to be exercised by the Benches of the Inns of Court, but in 1966 the duty of investigating charges of professional misconduct at the Bar was passed to a new body, the "Senate of the Four Inns of Court": in 1974 this, in turn, was replaced by the *Senate of the Inns of Court and Bar* which consists of representatives of the Inns and of the Bar as a whole. If satisfied that there is a *prima facie* case the Senate must set up a *disciplinary tribunal* to hear the complaint, and if it is satisfied that there has been misconduct the tribunal will report the offender to his Inn with directions, *e.g.* to reprimand, suspend or disbar him. Against the tribunal's decision there is an appeal to the Lord Chancellor who may appoint five judges to act as "visitors" to the Inn concerned and review the case.

3 THE MEDICAL DISCIPLINARY COMMITTEE OF THE GENERAL MEDICAL COUNCIL

This Committee is empowered by the Medical Act 1956 to order the erasure from the Register of the name of any fully registered medical practitioner who has been convicted of any crime or offence, or who after due inquiry is adjudged by the Committee itself to have been guilty of "infamous conduct" in any professional respect. But the Committee may, after a certain period, also order the restoration of a name so erased. A qualified lawyer must attend the meetings of this Committee as a legal assessor to give advice upon points of law arising in the case. There is a right of appeal to the Judicial Committee of the Privy Council. There is also a Penal Committee of the G.M.C. which investigates charges in order to determine whether there is a *prima facie* case to go to the Disciplinary Committee.

The Dentists Act 1957 contains similar provisions as to dentists; the General Dental Council having a Preliminary Proceedings Committee and a Disciplinary Committee: here again, appeal lies to the Judicial Committee of the Privy Council. And the system was further extended by the Professions Supplementary to Medicine Act 1960 to other allied bodies such as the chiropodists' and dietitians' professions.

D THE LEGAL PROFESSION

1 The Bar

In the manner of the mediaeval guilds the Bar was, by the fourteenth century, organized as an association of members of the *Inns of Court*. Although today there are only four of the Inns left (the Inner and Middle Temples, Lincoln's Inn and Gray's Inn) there were originally more of them, including Inns of Chancery and Sergeants' Inns – the latter being associations of *sergeants* (*"servientes"* – the King's servants) who were the most senior barristers, having the monopoly of audience in the Court of Common Pleas, and from whose ranks the judiciary were created. Even to this day no one can practise at the Bar unless he has been "called to the Bar" and become a member of an Inn. Originally the Inns were like colleges, centres of legal learning and education and, by Shakespeare's time, fashionable training places for young men. Vestigially the remaining Inns still retain something of the atmosphere of colleges, with powers of control over their members, libraries and halls in which the members lunch and dine: and each Inn has its "Bench" of senior members and judges who are the "Masters" or "Benchers" of the Inn. But much of the central control of the profession has now passed to the *Senate of the Inns of Court and Bar* and the education of barristers, under the ultimate surveillance of the Senate, is now a matter for the *Council of Legal Education* and the *Inns of Court School of Law*, situated in Gray's Inn. Moreover, the *General Council of the Bar* ("Bar Council"), created in 1895, now represents the Bar as a profession.

The best way of explaining the functions of a barrister is to call him a "trial" lawyer and to compare his position *vis-à-vis* a solicitor with that of a consultant as opposed to a general practitioner in the medical profession. The barrister's principal work therefore lies in the oral presentation of cases, for the most part in the higher courts where barristers enjoy a practically exclusive right of audience; he is employed not directly by his client but almost always through the medium of a solicitor. This duality of function between barristers and solicitors is peculiar

to the English common law system and, indeed, is even not followed
in the United States. It is said to be desirable in that it ensures that the
barrister does not become personally involved with the parties to the
action and can thus present the case impartially: it also has the advantage
that the barrister, being (as opposed to the solicitor) the specialist in
"law", can be used by the solicitor, like a general practitioner uses a
consultant, as someone whose opinion can be sought in matters of doubt
or difficulty.

Although the barrister is primarily an advocate, of necessity he does
a certain amount of "paper" work, such as giving written opinions
is founded. Barristers do their work, when not engaged in court, in
"chambers": sets of rooms in common occupation headed by a senior
barrister and managed by a chief clerk. By tradition they may not
enter into partnerships. Since the days of James I, after the example of
Francis Bacon, barristers of standing have "taken silk" become "Queen's
(or Kings's) Counsel", become entitled to occupy the front bench
in court and to wear a silken gown. "Silk" is obtained on application
and the advantage of becoming a "Q.C." is that it means almost exclusive concentration upon advocacy: a "silk" cannot usually appear in
court without a "junior" who will prepare the pleadings. "Juniors" are
barristers who are not "silks"; and by no means every barrister does
take silk, so that the grade is not necessarily an inferior one: for although
before the "Order of the Coif" (the degree of Sergeant) was abolished
in the nineteenth century one had to be a sergeant – if only, as in the case
of Sir Edward Coke (1552–1634) our greatest judge, for the occasion –
before one could be made a judge, it is not necessary to take silk in order
to be elevated to the Bench.

Before leaving the subject of barristers three special offices need mention. The *Attorney-General* is the Head of the Bar and the Chief Law
Officer of the Crown: his appointment is political and "attornies" come
and go with governments. He is responsible for answering questions in
Parliament and – with the help of junior counsel to the Treasury – for
advising Government Departments which either he or the latter may
represent in civil litigation. He will always represent the Crown in any
matter of constitutional importance which has to be litigated, and he has
considerable power in criminal matters – such as the power to "enter
a *nolle prosequi*", to withdraw proceedings upon indictment by virtue
of the royal prerogative.

The *Solicitor-General* is also a political officer who effectually acts
as the Attorney-General's deputy. He is a barrister, not a solicitor. Like
the Attorney he is a Law Officer of the Crown.

The *Director of Public Prosecutions* is a lawyer (barrister or solicitor)
appointed by the Home Secretary who works under the general

control of the Attorney-General. He is, amongst other things, responsible for the investigation and prosecution of serious crimes.

2 Solicitors

The solicitor may be colloquially described as the "front of house" man: the person who, like the general practitioner, deals directly with the client and, where litigation is involved, instructs the barrister. The origins of this side of the profession go back to the mediaeval *"attornatus"* (attorney) who was – as the solicitor still is, but the barrister is not – an officer of the court. The attorney's business was originally to help the client in the preparatory stages of cases. In the course of time a similar class of people practising in the Court of Chancery came to be called "solicitors". By the close of the Middle Ages neither class was admitted to the Inns of Court, and the two sub-professions became merged. This meant that inevitably they sought to form a separate organization of their own and by the eighteenth century such an organization had appeared, though it was not until 1845 that the *Law Society* as the representative organization of the solicitor's profession came into being. The "attorney" disappeared.

The work of a solicitor is too diverse to classify. Everyone knows that solicitors act as personal and family advisers to their clients, that they manage conveyances of property, that they prepare wills, advise on matrimonial matters and handle the defences of accused people. What is not, perhaps, so well known is that many solicitors are active advocates in the lower courts, such as the magistrates' courts and county courts, in which (as opposed to the superior courts) they have right of audience. However, as we have seen, in High Court cases the solicitor must "instruct counsel", *i.e.* employ a barrister. But this does not mean that the solicitor takes no further interest in the case, for it is his function, acting upon the barrister's "advice on evidence" to prepare the witnesses and get the case ready for trial: in particular he must take written "proofs" of evidence from his witnesses so that at the trial counsel knows (or *hopes* he knows) what they will say.

As has been explained, the *Law Society* is responsible for the solicitors' branch of the profession. It is centred at the Law Society's Hall in Chancery Lane, and it works through a Secretary-General and a permanent staff under the ultimate control of its *Council* of representative solicitors and its (annual) President. It has very wide powers under the Solicitors Acts: the latest of which is the Solicitors Act 1974 (hereafter "S.A."). Thus no one is qualified to act as a solicitor unless he has been admitted by the Society, his name is on the Roll kept by the Society, and he has in force a practising certificate issued by the Society (S.A., s. 1). The Society (S.A., s. 2) is also responsible for the examining and training of entrants to the profession; the latter responsibility is in practice, through its Education Committee, undertaken by its own institution, the *College of Law*. Moreover, as we have seen (above, p. 47), the Society is responsible for the professional conduct of its members and must investigate charges against them and, if necessary, refer them to the Solicitors' Disciplinary Tribunal.

One further matter of importance should be noted. We remarked that the original *attornatus* was an officer of the Court and solicitors still are officers of the Supreme Court. The effect of this is that, whatever the powers of the Law Society or of the Tribunal, the Supreme Court of Judicature or any judge thereof still has disciplinary powers over solicitors, and applications for striking off may be made to the High Court.

3 Legal Executives

With the increase in the volume of legislation in recent years, the need for able and well-qualified legal assistants in solicitors' offices has become very great. This need is being met by members of the Institute of Legal Executives. The Institute, which developed out of the old Solicitors' Managing Clerks' Association, was found in 1963 with the object of providing an independent, self-contained educational and professional structure for persons working in solicitors' offices in both private and public practice. The Institute's training scheme emphasizes the value of practical experience allied to a sound theoretical knowledge of the underlying law. Members of the Institute, who are designated Fellows, must have completed eight years in employment with a solicitor and must also have passed all of the Institute's examinations. The Institute's final, Fellowship, examinations are of a very high standard and the Law Society accepts passes in these as exempting candidates from the equivalent papers of the Solicitors Qualifying Examination.

The aim of the Institute of Legal Executives is to encourage the emergence of a body of highly qualified legal specialists who, whilst working under the ultimate authority of their principals, possess a high degree of expertise within their chosen field and who act on their own initiative and, to a great extent, under their own responsibility.

CHAPTER 3

PROCEDURE AND EVIDENCE

THE FUNCTION OF THE COURTS

Adjudication is the principal and proper function of the courts, and the judges are thus known collectively as the *Judiciary*. There are, however, two other aspects of government beside the judicial, namely the *legislative*, by which laws are made, and the *executive* (or "administrative") by which they are put into operation. The French jurist de Montesquieu in his great book *"L'Esprit des Lois"* (1748) is usually credited with the distinction of being the first to put forward the idea that it is politically desirable that these three aspects, or, as he called them, "powers", of government should be kept distinct and exercised by separate persons or bodies. The logic of this proposition could not and cannot be denied; for division of power is a shield against despotism.

This doctrine of "Separation of Powers", as it came to be called, enjoyed a great vogue among eighteenth and nineteenth century theorists and many constitutional lawyers still consider that separation should be maintained as far as possible. But time and experience have shown that strict adherence to the theory is, for at least two reasons, impracticable. First, rigorous separation hampers effective government; thus, as we shall see later, our whole system of responsible government, which controls the relationship between the Legislature and the Executive, has been developed in defiance of the doctrine. In the second place, it is not always theoretically easy or practically convenient to assign any particular activity to any one of the three categories of "powers". Thus the Legislature, the Executive and the Judiciary, although they are each primarily concerned with their own special functions, often in practice perform acts which ought in strict theory to fall within the province of one or other of their neighbours. The student of law should not therefore be surprised to learn that officials of the Executive often have to make decisions which border upon the "judicial" and that the courts have some "administrative" duties to perform. In respect of the courts this divergence of function is most apparent in relation to such matters as the administration of the estates of deceased persons and the supervision of the guardianship of minors, but it should be realized that, in almost every case which comes to be tried, some matters have to be settled which might strictly be assigned to the category of "administration"; for instance in divorce cases orders have to be made to ensure the future welfare of the children of the family. Absolute separation of powers is a theoretical ideal and no more.

The cases which the courts have to try may roughly be divided into two main types, civil cases and criminal cases. In a civil action one party (generally called the *Plaintiff*) makes a claim against, or seeks a determination of his rights in respect of, another party (generally called the *Defendant*); the duty of the court is to determine and declare the rights of the parties and where necessary to grant remedies for securing them. The aim of criminal process is, on the other hand, not to give relief to an injured party (though many crimes, such as theft may give rise to an independent civil suit), but to determine whether an *offence* has been committed and to make such order as may be necessary for the punishment or reformation of the offender.

THE METHODS OF LEGAL PROCESS

If C undertakes to decide a quarrel between A and B he may act in one of two ways: either *he* may take the initiative and examine the parties and their evidence himself, or he may call upon *them* to take the initiative and present their cases to him. Anglo-American law has traditionally adopted the latter method of proceeding, which we may perhaps be permitted to call the "contentious" or "adversary" method, as opposed to the former, which is "inquisitorial". Clearly the difference between these two methods of proceeding lies only in the degree of initiative taken by the court, and, provided that the court is impartial, the "contentious" method has no great advantage over the "inquisitorial". It is, however, essential to bear in mind that most English trials represent a drama in which the parties, through their champions (counsel), fight a forensic battle against each other: the court decides who has the better cause. This method of proceeding is adopted in criminal, as well as in civil trials; the prosecutor, although etiquette forbids him to press for a conviction, appears not as an inquisitor, but as an adversary of the defence.

SUBSTANTIVE LAW AND PROCEDURE

The rules of substantive law are legal rules which guide the courts in making decisions, and a discussion of these will form the main subject-matter of this book. Rules of procedure or "adjective" law, as it is sometimes called, are the rules which determine the course of an action; they govern such matters as how the case is to be presented, in what court it shall lie, or when it is to be tried. Procedural rules are, in other words, the rules which govern the machinery as opposed to the subject-matter of litigation. It is a striking fact, much remarked upon by historians, that in the earlier stages of legal development these rules assume paramount importance; form is better understood than substance, and in early law formal requirements, rather than abstract principles, usually determine the nature of legal rights. Since the development of the common law has been continuous this early dominance of procedure has had a lasting influence upon many of the doctrines of the modern substantive law. Generally speaking, however, procedure, though it is of great importance to the practitioner, is today treated as the servant and not the master of substance, and the rules of procedure are now fewer and more flexible than once they were. They derive from various sources. Most proceedings in the Supreme Court (that is, most of the more important civil proceedings) are now governed by a code of rules known as the Rules of the Supreme Court ("R.S.C."). These rules, which were originally authorized by the Judicature Acts, 1873–1875, are amended from time to time, under powers first conferred by those Acts, by a committee known as the "Rule Committee" which is headed by the Lord Chancellor. The R.S.C. are set out in the *Annual Practice* (The "White book"). Similar rules are laid down for the County Courts. these appear in the *County Court Practice*. With some exceptions – such as the Magistrates' Courts Rules – the rules of criminal procedure have not been codified; they are to be found in works such as Archbold's *Criminal Pleading, Evidence and Practice* and Stone's *Justices' Manual*, which treats of the work of the magistrates' courts.

OUTLINE OF CIVIL AND CRIMINAL PROCEEDINGS

Civil Proceedings

It is of course impossible to outline all the different varieties of procedure in a very short space; actions, for instance, in the Chancery Division or the Family Division and proceedings in bankruptcy have special rules of their own. The following is a bare sketch of the course of proceedings in an action in the Queen's Bench Division; a type of action which may, up to a point, be regarded as 'standard'.

The plaintiff (usually through his legal representative) starts the action by obtaining a *writ of summons:* the writ is a printed document containing blank spaces for the inclusion of appropriate particulars. It must be presented at the Central Office of the Supreme Court (or, outside London, at a District Registry) from whence it is said to "issue", and it marks the commencement of an action. In form it is a command in the Queen's name to the defendant to enter an "appearance" within eight days and it must, in order to warn the defendant of the substance of the claim, be endorsed with a concise statement of the latter – just sufficient to give the defendant notice of the nature of it; but it is in no sense an irrevocable formulation like the original writ in the days of the Forms of Action (above, pp. 21–23). Upon presentation at the appropriate office it is stamped and filed and a copy of it must then be served upon the defendant or his solicitor. An appearance must be entered on his behalf within the eight days or he may suffer judgment by default. "Appearance" does not mean appearance in person before the court; it is effected by completing a formal memorandum of appearance and taking or sending it to the office of issue.

After appearance come the *Pleadings.* Pleadings are documents, usually drafted by counsel, which (R.S.C., O. 18, r. 7(1)) must contain, and contain only, a statement in summary form of the material facts on which the party pleading relies . . . and the statement must be as brief as the nature of the case admits. They are thus documents which, by stating the facts as seen by each party, define the issues to which at the trial the evidence will be directed. The first of the pleadings to be delivered is the *Statement of Claim*: this is delivered to the defendant or his representative on behalf of the plaintiff; it is a summary statement of the material facts upon which the plaintiff proposes to base his case. Within a limited time the defendant must, in turn, deliver his *Defence,* together with any *Counterclaim* which he may have. Further pleadings, *Reply* (plaintiff), *Rejoinder* (defendant), *Surrejoinder* (plaintiff), and sometimes even more, may follow if they are necessary for the clear formulation of the issue; though, in practice, pleadings now seldom go beyond the Reply stage. Where one of the parties does not make his meaning clear in his pleadings the other party is, subject to certain limitations, entitled to demand what are known as *Further and Better Particulars*; that is to say written explanations or amplifications of any of the statements made.

At the close of pleadings there follow the "*interlocutory*" stages *i.e.* proceedings between pleadings and trial. Applications to the court in interlocutory matters must be made to *Masters* of the Supreme Court in London or to *District Registrars* in the provinces. These officials have many kinds of powers. Among the more important may be mentioned the power to order one party at the instance of the other to answer upon oath written questions called *interrogatories*: these answers may help to shorten the evidence required at the trial. The Master may also order *discovery of documents*; that is, he may at the instance of one party order the other to set out in an affidavit (a sworn and written statement) a list of relevant documents which he has in his possession; the other party may then, unless his opponent gives reason for objection, inspect and take copies of those documents. Again, the Master may be asked to sanction *amendments* of the pleadings or to order dismissal of the case for *want of prosecution*; *i.e.* undue delay by the plaintiff in prosecuting the claim. The interlocutory proceedings conclude with the taking out by the plaintiff of a *Summons for Directions* before the Master. The latter will then, if previous applications have not been made, make various orders of the kinds already mentioned and will give directions for the trial. The directions will include the determination of the place and mode of trial, whether, for example in London or elsewhere, or whether before a judge alone (more normal) or before a judge and jury. Finally, the plaintiff will be ordered to set the action down for trial within a specified time.

In a High Court trial the parties usually appear by counsel, though they may appear in person: solicitors, however, have no right of audience in the High Court. The plaintiff's counsel opens with a speech in which he outlines his case and lays the issues before the court; he then calls his witnesses and examines them "*in chief*". Each witness may be "cross-examined" by the defence and, if necessary, be "re-examined" by the plaintiff. The principal object of *cross-examination* is to test the accuracy of the evidence given in chief by the witness; the object of *re-examination* is to re-establish belief in that evidence where it has been seriously challenged in cross-examination. After the plaintiff's witnesses have been heard, in the normal case in which there is oral evidence for the defendant, his counsel may open the defence (outline his case) and in any event he will call his witnesses, whose evidence is tested in the same way as the plaintiff's: defence counsel then makes a closing address followed finally by a closing address on behalf of the plaintiff. Where the defence calls no oral evidence this procedure varies in that the plaintiff's counsel makes his closing address after calling his witnesses and then the defendant (thus having the advantage of the "last word") states his case. These orders of proceedings may, however, be varied if the judge so directs. Finally the judge (unless he wishes to reserve it for consideration) gives judgment; though if (as it is now rare) there be a jury he will sum up the evidence to them and direct them upon the relevant law, the actual decision upon the facts being theirs.

Such, in outline, is the procedure in a civil action in the Queen's Bench

Division. County Court actions follow very similar lines; though they are, in most respects, less formal than High Court actions. Appeals have already been discussed. It should be noted that the expense and delay of a High Court action is in practice often avoided by resort to the special procedure authorized by Order 14 of the R.S.C.; by the provisions of this Order, if a plaintiff swears an affidavit to the effect that the defendant has no good defence on the merits, and if the defendant is unable to oppose this affidavit by demonstrating that there is some ground of defence, the Master may enter judgment for the plaintiff without sending the case for trial; though there is, of course, a right of appeal from the Master's decision to a Judge.

Criminal Proceedings

Criminal proceedings normally arise either with the arrest of the offender without a warrant or with the laying of an information. Powers of arrest without warrant will be discussed below, pp. 141–143. An *information* is a statement made, usually by the police, to a *justice of the peace* accusing some person of a crime: this statement is generally reduced to writing. After the information has been laid the justice must, if he decides to act upon it, determine how the presence of the offender is to be secured for trial. He may decide to issue either a summons or a warrant. A *summons* is issued in cases where the offence is not serious and the offender is likely to appear if required. A *warrant* is a written command, usually addressed to the police, ordering the person to whom it is addressed to secure the offender.

When the trial is due to take place there are two possibilities: either the case is one which the justices may or must try *summarily*, or it is one which may or must be sent for trial *upon indictment*: we have already considered the extent of the magistrates' jurisdiction in this matter. The procedure in a *summary* trial is as follows. The Clerk to the Justices reads out the charge and calls upon the accused to plead to it: if the plea is one of not guilty, or if the accused refuses to answer, the trial will proceed. Normally, after addressing the court the prosecutor calls his evidence which is tested by cross-examination, as in a civil case. The accused (or his representative) may then, if he wishes, address the court. The defence evidence, if any, is then called and similarly tested; after this the prosecutor may, if he is in a position to do so, call evidence to rebut the defence. The accused may then (either himself or by his representative) address the court but, if he has already done so at the opening of his case, he will only be permitted this second opportunity of addressing the court if he and any other witnesses have given evidence; and even then, only with the leave of the court. If the accused has thus addressed the court twice the prosecutor has a final right of reply.

The court then considers its decision. If it finds the accused guilty it will have to consider the question of punishment; to assist it in this task the prosecution may call evidence as to previous convictions and the defence may call evidence as to good character and make a speech in mitigation. If the offence is an indictable offence which has been tried summarily and if, on obtaining information as to the accused's character and antecedents, the court is of opinion that they are such that greater punishment should be inflicted than it has power to order, the accused may be remanded in custody so that the case may be considered by the Crown Court which may then sentence him to any punishment to which he would have been liable had he been convicted upon indictment. If the accused pleads guilty at the outset, the proceedings are similar to the proceedings after conviction just explained, except that in this event it is normal for the prosecution to summarize the facts of the case for the benefit of the court. Finally, at any time in the course of the proceedings the court may accept a change of plea of guilty to one of not guilty if justice so requires, and the case will then proceed as upon a plea of not guilty.

Formerly even in the case of a summary trial the accused had always to appear in person, but now in the case of *summary* offences carrying a maximum penalty of three months or less (and not also triable upon indictment) he may avoid appearance by sending the court a written notification that he wishes to plead *guilty*. But provided that the accused has been notified of the prosecution's intention to refer to it, a previous conviction of a summary offence may then be given in evidence and taken into account in awarding punishment. These rules do not apply to juvenile courts.

The procedure in a trial upon *indictment* is different. Here it is necessary, as a first step in the proceedings to determine whether there is sufficient evidence against the accused to justify a trial. This is the task of magistrates, sitting as *examining justices*, and traditionally the preliminary examination proceeded (and may sometimes still proceed) thus. The prosecutor outlines the prosecution case and calls his witnesses who give their evidence and may be cross-examined in the usual way; this evidence is written down, signed by the witness, and counter-signed by one of the justices. The records of the evidence thus obtained are known as the *depositions*; they are used amongst other things for checking the witnesses' evidence at the trial. Unless the court then decides that the prosecution has failed to establish a *prima facie* case, it will (unless this has already been done) cause the charge to be read to the accused; and, after advising him that he is under no compulsion to do so, will ask him if he wishes to make a statement. If he does, the statement will be taken down in writing and may be given in evidence at the trial. The accused may then himself give evidence and may call witnesses. Most of this evidence is also reduced to writing. Where the accused is legally represented his counsel or solicitor may then address the court; and they may also do so, with leave of the court, where the accused gives evidence and calls witnesses, *before* the defence evidence; but if they thus address the court *twice* the prosecution will have a final right of reply.

The Criminal Justice Act 1967 (s. 1), however, made an important change by introducing what is often referred to as "instant committal"; and this is now the usual procedure. The effect of it is that where *all* the evidence submitted is written the court may commit the defendant for trial *without consideration of the contents of the statements.* But this may be done only if the defendant is *legally represented* and *if no submission has been made that the statements disclose insufficient evidence to put him on trial.* Further (though less important in practice), under s. 2 of the Act, written statements of witnesses are – even though the older oral procedure be employed – admissible in evidence, thus dispensing with the need for attendance of the witness. In order to be admitted the statement must be signed by the witness and it must contain a declaration (*inter alia*) that it is true to the best of his knowledge and belief; a copy of it must be tendered to the defence, and the latter must not object to its admission.

This Act also (s. 3) restricts the reporting or broadcasting of committal proceedings except where, on application by the *defendant*, the court orders otherwise. Further, s. 6 enjoins examining justices to sit in open court *except where* any enactment contains an express provision to the contrary (*e.g.* the Official Secrets Act, 1920, s. 8 – which empowers the court to exclude the public on application by the prosecution) *or where* it appears to the court that the ends of justice would not be served by sitting in open court.

After the committal proceedings the justices must send the accused to the Crown Court for trial and they must decide whether he is to be detained in custody pending trial or whether to release him on bail; in making this decision they must take into account his character, the whole circumstances, and the nature of the offence. The composition of the Crown Court to which the accused is to be committed will, it will be recalled, vary according to the nature of the offence, but it must here be pointed out that if the justices form the view, in the case of an offence in class 4 (see above, p. 33), that the trial should be before a High Court judge they must indicate that view, giving their reasons for holding it. It has, moreover, been ruled that a number of specific considerations should influence them in reaching such a decision: these include, *inter alia*, the fact that the case involves death or serious risk of life, that it involves widespread public concern, or that a novel or difficult question of law is raised.

Between committal and trial the *indictment* must be drawn. The indictment is a document which contains a concise statement of the nature of the offence or offences charged; it is usually drawn by counsel who is assisted in the task by having access to the depositions, or the written statements, of the prosecution witnesses. At the start of the trial the accused is *arraigned*, that is to say the clerk reads the indictment and asks him whether he pleads guilty or not guilty. Upon a plea of guilty the proceedings are similar to summary proceedings (above, p. 58). If the plea is one of not guilty the jury must be called and sworn. Thereafter the procedure is again similar to summary procedure; but with two exceptions. First, under the Criminal Procedure (Right of Reply) Act 1964, the prosecutor's right of reply must be exercised at the close of the evidence for the defence and before the closing speech (if any) by or on behalf of the accused. Second, the judge, circuit judge or recorder must sum up the evidence to the jury and direct them upon the law. The jury then consider their verdict. After verdict the proceedings are, again, similar to summary proceedings.

The time-honoured rule of the common law in favour of liberty was that jury verdicts had to be unanimous. This rule has now been modified, and the relevant enactment is the Juries Act 1974, s. 17. This section provides (s. 17 (1)) that in the Crown Court or the High Court (where there are juries of twelve) a verdict of a *majority of ten* may now be accepted; though if, through illness or otherwise, the number of jurors has dropped to ten (below which number it must never fall) then a majority verdict of *nine* may be accepted. In a county court it will suffice if *seven* agree (s. 17 (2)). By s. 17 (3), however, no *Crown Court* must accept a majority (as opposed to a unanimous) verdict unless the foreman of the jury has stated in open court what the *numbers* of jurors were who respectively agreed and dissented: failure to conform with this provision will render the majority verdict invalid. But despite these reforms the statute agrees with the common law that unanimity is the golden rule; and accordingly s. 17 (4) enacts that no court shall accept a majority verdict unless it appears to it that, in all the circumstances of the case, there has been reasonable time for deliberation, and in Crown Court proceedings that the jury have retired for at least two hours. In *civil* proceedings the rules may be relaxed (s. 17 (5)): for the parties may consent to accept any majority verdict and may even agree to proceed with a case in which the jury has fallen below the minimum number.

EVIDENCE

Evidence is the means by which facts are proved, and the rules of legal evidence are rules of law concerned with the proof of facts in courts of law. These rules are designed to determine four main problems. First, who is to assume the burden of proving facts. Second, what facts must be proved. Third, what facts must be excluded from the cognizance of the court. Fourth, how proof is to be effected. Let us consider these points in order.

(i) Generally speaking, apart from certain statutory exceptions, the burden of proving any facts which are advanced in support of any proposition lies upon the person who advances it. Thus if X alleges that Y has stolen his motor car he must, amongst other things, prove facts which substantiate the claim that Y deprived him of the car. Any other rule than this would work injustice; for it is easier to establish an affirmative proposition than a negative one.

Naturally, just as it is impossible to demonstrate that there is any such thing as "absolute" truth, so it is equally impossible to establish any proposition by "absolute" proof. The "burden of proof" is therefore always taken to have been discharged where the facts adduced demonstrate the truth of an allegation beyond *reasonable doubt*, and in civil cases it will suffice if they demonstrate it upon the *balance of probabilities*. Thus in criminal cases, out of fairness to the accused, the burden which is cast upon the prosecution is more onerous than the burden which is cast upon parties to civil actions. In this context it has been authoritatively said that proof beyond "reasonable doubt" means proof to such a degree of certainty as a man would seek to reach before making an important decision in the affairs of his own life. Moreover, the prosecution must establish every material allegation in its case to this high degree of certainty; if it fails to do so at *any point*, the accused is usually entitled to an acquittal (see below, p. 151); for, by our law, *every man is presumed to be innocent until he is proved to have been guilty.*

(ii) As a general rule a party must give proof of all material facts upon which he relies to establish his case, but there are certain exceptions to this rule. Three of them may be noted.

First, there are certain classes of facts which need not be proved because the court is entitled to take "judicial notice" of them. This means that they are facts which are too notorious to require proof. Examples are, events which happen in the ordinary course of nature, Acts of Parliament passed since 1850 (unless there is a special provision in the Act in question that it shall require to be proved), and public matters affecting the government of the country. Thus, for example, if A alleges that B is the father of her child, and it is proved that B was in some remote part of the world at the time when conception must have taken place, the court will not require proof of the fact that B could not have been the father; for the period of gestation is a notorious fact.

Second, when certain facts are proved the court will in some cases *presume* the existence of other facts which naturally follow from them until their existence is *disproved* by the other side. Thus, for instance, there is a presumption that a child of over ten and under fourteen is incapable of forming a criminal intent; there is a presumption that where one person advances money (otherwise than by way of loan) to another to make a purchase, the intention of the parties is that the second person is to hold the article purchased as a trustee for the benefit of the first (see below, p. 397); there is a presumption that a person who holds a bill of exchange "in due course" has taken it in good faith and given value for it (see below, p. 384).

In the third place, in civil proceedings in order to obviate the necessity of proving facts which are not in dispute, formal *admissions* may be (and often are) made by the parties, prior to or during the trial. These admissions may be made in the pleadings, or orally in court and in various other ways. At common law admissions, other than "confessions" (see below, p. 1), could not be made in criminal cases; but the Criminal Justice Act 1967, s. 10, authorized the making of them either during or before the proceedings; though in the latter case they must be in writing and approved by the legal advisers of the party concerned. They may be made by either prosecution or defence; and here again, as in the case of civil proceedings, this machinery for admitting non-contentious evidence is useful in saving time and expense.

(iii) It might be supposed that proof would be permitted of any facts which *might* tend to support any proposition advanced. But this is not the case. Partly in order to prevent waste of time, and partly in order to prevent certain classes of facts from being put before juries which might tend to lead them to unwarranted conclusions, English law only permits proof of facts which are *in issue* and of facts which are *relevant* to the issue.

The expression "facts in issue" requires little explanation: the facts in issue are the facts which are in dispute upon the pleadings of a civil action, or the facts averred in an indictment, and denied by a plea of "not guilty". Thus, upon a charge of burglary the fact that X, at a certain time and in a certain building took Y's watch is clearly likely to be a fact in issue.

"Relevancy," in its legal signification, is a difficult term to define. Broadly speaking any fact which is logically probative of, or which serves to explain, a fact in issue will be treated as relevant to the issue and will therefore be admissible. This is, however, only a very broad and general rule, for evidence of certain classes of facts is, for the reasons explained above, treated as legally "irrelevant" – and therefore inadmissible – even though it might be considered logically probative of the issue. Facts which are thus inadmissible fall into certain well-known classes. Here there is only sufficient space to make brief mention of two of these classes.

First, in civil actions parties are normally not permitted to give *evidence of their good character*, *i.e.* of their general reputation for good character. The reason for this is that evidence of good character might give rise to prejudice. If Tom Jones demonstrates that he is a really good fellow unwarrantable conclusions may be drawn in his favour; if Peter Smith, his opponent, does the same attention may be diverted from a critical examination of the facts as given by the witnesses on either side to a hypothetical counter-balancing of the supposed merits of the parties.

Second, it might at first sight appear relevant, where a certain course of conduct is alleged, to prove that the person so alleged to have conducted himself *had* in fact so conducted himself upon other occasions. For example, where W alleges that X has obtained his ring from him by deception, proof that X had previously obtained Y's chickens and Z's bicycle in a similar way might appear to support W's case. In logic it clearly might; but in law evidence of *conduct on other occasions* is not, as a general rule, admissible (though this rule is subject to recognized exceptions). The object of a trial is as far as possible to ascertain the truth or falsity of the allegations made, and the fact that a man can be proved to have done other acts at other times, similar to those alleged against him at the trial, may well tend to show that he is the kind of person who is *likely* to do the acts alleged, but it affords no proof whatever that he actually has done them.

(iv) The law recognizes three kinds of proof; proof by oral evidence, proof by documentary evidence, and proof by real evidence.

Oral evidence is evidence which is given by witnesses – usually upon oath or affirmation. Each side to a dispute will normally call one or more witnesses to support with their evidence the truth of the story which that side has to tell. The function of a witness is to inform the court or the jury of *the facts* as he actually perceived them, and clearly, unless he is an expert whose opinion on a technical point it may be essential to ascertain, his *opinions* as to how the facts ought to be interpreted are of little value: for, given the facts, the court or jury are the judges and it is for them to assess and interpret. Thus at common law a witness of a street accident might testify that the "car was driven fast" (an observable fact) but strictly speaking his observation that "X was driving *too* fast" was inadmissible. And, indeed, at discretion, the court may still exclude such a statement; but because it was found that it is often difficult for a witness to give a truthful account of what he actually did observe without including an element of interpretation (opinion) of it the Civil Evidence Act 1972, s. 3 (2) provided that in *civil* proceedings a statement of opinion by such a witness of facts may be admitted "if made as a way of conveying relevant facts personally perceived by him". This relaxation only applies to civil cases and leaves room for the court to rule against admissibility of such a statement.

But as Lord Mansfield (1705–1793) once put it, "The opinion of scientific men upon proven facts may be given by men of science within their own science." Such people are *expert* witnesses, and in our "adversary" system of procedure they play a leading rôle – as where the cause of disease is in dispute and doctors are called by either side to given their diagnoses. But there are, or have been, two limitations upon this expert function. First, evidence by an expert on matters within the knowledge of the judge or jury is, strictly, inadmissible: for expert opinion must not usurp the function of the court itself. Thus a psychiatrist may be called to testify about the existence of mental disturbance, but he should not give evidence that a man whose wife has confessed adultery is likely to behave hysterically: a matter of common knowledge. In the second place, at common law an expert witness was not allowed to give his opinion about the main issue in the case – *e.g.* "Was the designer of the aircraft negligent?" Again, that is the issue for the court *itself.* However, here again, the Civil Evidence Act 1972, s. 3 (1), (3) has relaxed the rule in *civil* cases: for now (subject to the court's discretion) an expert may express his opinion "on *any relevant matter* on which he is qualified to give expert evidence".

It is, perhaps, germane to add that, in a case in which it is necessary to ascertain the law of a foreign country, expert evidence of it must be called: formerly only people qualified to practise in the country in question could be called as experts, but the 1972 Act (s. 4) makes it also possible to call people (such as teachers of law) not necessarily qualified to practise.

As a general rule in our law, unlike the law of many other systems where written evidence is preferred, evidence is *oral* rather than written (though affidavit evidence is common in the Chancery Division). But, by way of exception, in order to save time and expense the Criminal Justice Act 1967, s. 9, subject to safeguards, made it possible for the court in criminal proceedings (other than committal proceedings) for the court to accept a signed and written statement from an absent witness.

Witnesses may give evidence about what they have heard, just as they may give evidence about what they have seen; but this proposition is subject to a very important exception. "*Hearsay*" evidence is, in general, not admissible where it is sought to be introduced to prove the *truth* of any matter in dispute. This means that, in general, where it is desired to prove the truth of some disputed fact, evidence of what was said by some person *not called as a witness*, or of what was stated in some document executed by such person, will not be admitted. For example, in a murder case a witness would not generally be permitted to testify that, "Percy Jones (some third person not called as a witness) said that he had seen (the accused) do it". The reason for this rule is said to be that if such evidence were admitted there would be no way of testing its veracity, for the speaker or the writer of the statement was not necessarily upon oath when he made it, and there is no way of testing the credibility of a person who is not present for cross-examination.

Moreover, anyone who has ever participated in any kind of inquiry will realize that such evidence must necessarily often be of little weight and to admit it wholesale would be to introduce much irrelevant matter. Another example may perhaps help to illustrate this: suppose the issue to be what is a fair rent (see below, p. 343) for a house and that a witness seeks to establish this fact by saying that "Mrs X, my neighbour's cousin who lives two houses away, told me that she pays £2 rent." If this fact were proved it would plainly be relevant to the issue; but the statement is suspect, since there is no check that the witness heard or remembered aright nor that Mrs. X was telling the truth. Yet the exclusion of "hearsay" is said to be peculiar to the common law and it must be confessed that, since there is no smoke without fire, a lot of hearsay pointing in one direction may lead a reasonable man to judge that the cumulative effect of it is true; further, if all evidence had to be direct then it would be hopelessly confined. Hence, for a long time past a number of exceptions (too complicated to be examined in detail here) have been engrafted upon the general rule which excludes "hearsay".

Thus "hearsay" will be admitted where it is plainly necessary that it should; but in most, at least, of the instances where it is thus exceptionally admitted, it will be found that there is some particular reason for supposing that the statement was one which the maker really believed to be true. Thus for example statements made by parties to an action, or by their agents, which are *against their interest* may be given in evidence as "*admissions*" (not to be confused with the formal "admissions" above referred to) – for there is every reason to suppose that when a person makes a statement which is against his interest it will be true: and this rule is confirmed by s. 9 (2) (a) of the Civil Evidence Act 1968 (below). So also, where a person has *died* before the time of the trial, it is sometimes essential to permit "hearsay" evidence of what he said, for he can no longer be called as a witness. A large category of "declarations" of deceased persons are thus permitted to be given in evidence, but in each instance falling within this category it will be found that there is some special reason to believe that the permitted "hearsay" statement was true. For example, declarations made by deceased persons in the "course of duty" may sometimes be admitted to prove the truth of the facts stated; for when people are acting in the course of some duty which is imposed upon them they generally have no incentive to tell lies. Thus if it is the duty of a clerk to receive payments for his employer and to make entries in a cash book, and he makes an entry "Mr. Thomas paid Smith (the clerk's employer)" such and such a sum upon such and such a day, and if the clerk later dies, and Smith denies the payment, the entry, if proved to be authentic, may be adduced to prove the fact of payment. Further, beside preserving the common law as to admissions (and also various other kinds of evidence too numerous for mention here) the Civil Evidence Act 1968 (hereafter "C.E.A."), by s. 9 preserves the common law rules which – in the words of the section – make "admissible as evidence of facts of a public nature stated therein" *published works* dealing with matters of a public nature (*e.g.* histories, scientific works, dictionaries and maps), and, as "evidence of facts stated therein" *public documents* (*e.g.* public registers) and *records* (*e.g.* court records and treaties). So, should the question be, say, whether a certain object is a crystal, dictionaries and scientific works may be consulted even though their authors be alive and reasonably available as witnesses.

The C.E.A. itself must now be considered. Superficially at least it makes a large inroad into the rule which excludes hearsay; though it must be noted that it applies only to *civil* proceedings. Subject to important reservations shortly to be mentioned, s. 1 (1) of the Act permits "a statement other than one made by a person while giving oral evidence" to be admissible as evidence of any fact stated therein. And this is confirmed by s. 2 (1) which in effect only adds the obvious proviso that such evidence must be otherwise – *i.e.* apart from the fact that it is hearsay – admissible; *e.g.* it must be relevant. Section 2 (3), however, excludes *oral* evidence which is what is sometimes called "second-hand" hearsay. The effect of this is that if, for example, a witness seeks to testify that "B said that (C told him) that the elephant was pink" evidence of C's statement is inadmissible; whereas the statement "B said to me that the elephant was pink" is admissible *under the Act*.

Section 4 of the Act (confirming and enlarging upon the Evidence Act 1938, which the C.E.A. for the most part repeals) makes special provision for the admission of hearsay contained in private documentary records. Assuming that it would be otherwise admissible (*e.g.* that it is relevant), it is enacted that "a statement contained in a document shall ... be admissible as evidence of any statement made therein ... if the document is ... a *record* compiled by a person *acting under a duty* from information which was supplied by a person ... who had ... *personal knowledge* of the matters dealt with in that information and which, if not supplied by that person ... directly, was supplied by him ... indirectly through one or more *intermediaries each acting under a duty*." Acting "under a duty" includes (s. 4 (3)) "a reference to a person acting in the course of any trade, business, profession or other occupation in which he is engaged or employed or for the purposes of any paid or unpaid office held by him". Thus, in the case of such records, subject to the *restrictions* (shortly to be mentioned) which the C.E.A. itself imposes upon its admission, hearsay is allowed with a vengeance. By s. 5, the provisions of which are complex, certain kinds of evidence contained in documents produced by computers are also admissible in contravention of the hearsay rule.

Thus far it may appear that the floodgates were opened wide for the admission of hearsay under the Act; but the restrictions which are imposed are formidable. Section 1 provides that unless the parties *agree* to the admission of the hearsay it may only be admitted "to the extent that it is ... admissible by virtue of any provision ... in ... this or any other Act". And the provisions "in this ... Act" are highly restrictive. By s. 8 of the Act (as implemented by Rules of Court) it is provided that a party who wishes to adduce any of the kinds of hearsay evidence mentioned above must, within a limited period (usually twenty-one days of setting down for hearing) give *notice*, with particulars of the evidence, to *every other party* to the proceedings. The party so served may then serve (within a further period) a *counter-notice* requiring the first party to call the maker of the statement as a witness unless (as is self-evident) he "is dead" or unless he is "unfit by reason of his bodily or mental condition to attend as a witness, or cannot reasonably be expected to have any recollection of matters relevant to the accuracy of the statement". It must, however, be added that the court is given a general discretion to *allow* the statement where the rules as to notice have *not* been complied with; whereas, though there is power to order *exclusion* of the evidence where the rules *have* been complied with, it is narrowly confined. Section 6 (3) contains a reminder that hearsay, if admitted, cannot be given the same weight as first-hand evidence by providing that in assessing it "regard must be had to all the circumstances from which any inference can reasonably be drawn as to the accuracy or otherwise of the statement". Thus, for instance, the question whether the statement was made contemporaneously with an occurrence in issue or whether it was made some time after must be pertinent in assessing how much weight is to be attached to it. It will be appreciated that the rules as to notice etc. apply only to hearsay evidence received *under the Act* and not to the kinds of hearsay exceptionally admissible – whether confirmed by s. 9 of the Act or not – at common law. This is important since in practice hearsay usually enters the picture during the trial when a witness unexpectedly introduces it : a situation with which the C.E.A. is not concerned.

The Civil Evidence Act 1972, s. 1 has, in general, permitted hearsay statements of *opinion* to be given in evidence upon the same grounds on which hearsay statements of fact were permitted to be adduced under the C.E.A.

It is worth repeating that the C.E.A. applies only to *civil* cases; but it should be mentioned that the Criminal Evidence Act 1965, in criminal cases, permits the introduction of documents containing business records made by people having knowledge of the facts stated in them as evidence of those facts, provided that the person who made the record is unavailable on account of death, sickness etc. to give oral evidence.

It must be stressed that the "hearsay" rule only operates where the evidence in question is sought to be introduced as proof of the *truth* of the facts stated. There is no objection to its introduction for any other purpose, provided that it is otherwise relevant; as, for instance, to prove the fact that a debated statement was *made*. Thus if in an action for slander A claims that X called him a thief, it will be in order for a witness to testify that he heard X say this: since what is in issue is *not* whether A is a thief, but whether X made the remark: a fact to which, of course, the witness can testify at first hand.

Documentary evidence is, as its name suggests, evidence which is contained in documents. Five points require notice with regard to evidence of this class.

First, as has already been indicated documents fall into two classes; "public" and "private". Public documents consist of publications made for public reference, such as public statutes, public registers, and maps. Private documents are documents made for private purposes.

Second, all private documents must as a general rule be "proved" before their contents may be given in evidence; that is to say, they must be shown to be genuine – any other rule would put a premium upon forgery. This "proof" is effected by showing that the documents were duly executed by the person by whom they purport to be made. Either the maker of the document, or, if it is attested, an attesting witness, or even a person who merely saw it executed, may testify as to the authenticity of the writing or signature. If no such person is available the maker's handwriting may be proved by anyone who can show that he had reason to be acquainted with it. The authenticity of handwriting may also be proved by comparing the disputed document with one which has been proved to have been written by the person concerned; but in this case a handwriting expert should normally be called to make the comparison. This rule as to strict "proof" is, however, subject to exceptions. (*a*) In most civil actions documents which are not required by law to be attested are usually "agreed" and admitted as genuine by the opposing party; this dispenses with the need for proof. (*b*) "Ancient" documents, *i.e.* documents twenty years old or more, are presumed to be genuine provided that they are produced from proper custody, that is, from the custody of some person who would naturally be expected to keep them. (*c*) By the C.E.A., s. 6 (1) documents tendered under the provisions of that Act may be proved either by production of the document itself or by a copy of it "authenticated in such manner as the court may approve".

Third, in *civil* actions no document which is required by law to be stamped should be allowed to be produced in evidence unless and until it has been properly stamped.

In the fourth place, private documents must *usually* be produced *in the original*. This is an example of what is called the "best evidence" rule, which insists that proof must always be made by the *best* means possible, for where reliable evidence is available and a party seeks to rely upon less reliable proof, his motive becomes suspect; he is likely to be doing so because the production of the best evidence will show something inimical to his case. "Secondary" evidence (*i.e.* something other than the production of the original) of a document, either in the form of a copy, or even in the form of oral evidence as to the contents, may, however, be given where it can be shown that for some reason the original cannot be produced, *e.g.* where it can be proved to have been lost. And, as has just been remarked, the C.E.A., s. 6 (1) makes an important exception to the "best evidence" rule in relation to documents. Moreover, since originals of *public documents* are seldom available, for they are usually too valuable to be released, authenticated copies of them are allowed. It should be added that tape recordings of conversations may (provided that the voices of those concerned are properly identified), subject to considerable caution on the part of the court, be admitted in evidence.

Real evidence is afforded by the inspection of physical objects by the court or the jury. The court may, for instance, view the site of an accident or objects of importance in the trial may be produced for its inspection – such as the knife which is alleged to have caused the wound – and where a plaintiff alleges that he has suffered physical injuries, the court will often wish to inspect the injuries in order to obtain an estimate of their severity for the purpose of assessing damages. So also, photographs, tape recordings and radio recordings are admissible as real evidence, and rent tribunals and rent assessment committees (below, p. 343) are in practice required to inspect premises under review. Contrary to the "best evidence" rule relating to documentary evidence, "secondary" oral testimony may always be given as to the nature of physical objects other than documents; there is no rule which demands their production.

This seems the place to explain the expression "*circumstantial evidence*". It is evidence, whether oral, documentary or real, of surrounding circumstances from which the existence of facts in issue or of facts relevant to the issue may reasonably be inferred. If the only admissible evidence were direct evidence of those facts themselves the arm of the law would be blunt; for a killing not actually perceived would always go unpunished. Hence evidence of circumstances which *argue* the fact of the deed must be allowed; for instance that a knife bearing the finger prints of the accused was found beside the corpse immediately after the death. The cogency of circumstantial evidence must of course vary according to the closeness of its connexion with the fact in issue: thus such a knife found ten days later twenty miles from the scene of the crime provides but weak evidence, requiring much more explanation to connect it with the murder.

Before leaving the subject of evidence, very brief mention must be made of some of the special rules which apply in *criminal*, as opposed to civil cases. Some points of difference have already been noted, but the following are of particular importance.

In the first place, there are strict rules as to the admission of *confessions* of guilt, other of course than a plea of guilty at the trial. Confessions made in previous *judicial* proceedings are admissible; though generally only if they were made on oath and the accused did not object to making them. No confession made in other circumstances will be admissible unless the *prosecution establishes* that it was made "voluntarily". The word "voluntary" has in this connexion a special meaning; it denotes that the confession must *not*, in the words of a very eminent judge, have "*been obtained from (the accused) either by fear of prejudice or hope of advantage exercised or held out by a person in authority*". For this purpose a "person in authority" is anyone who occupies a special and superior relationship to the accused, such as a police officer, or an employer, or even a teacher, parent or, in the case of theft, an owner of the stolen property who has power to instigate a prosecution; but a person is not "in authority" just because he is someone who may be called as a witness. "Fear of prejudice" means fear of some actual temporal disadvantage, such as fear introduced by a threat that, "It will go badly for you if you don't own up" – even if the threat relates to some other offence than the offence being investigated or to the well-being of some other person. But if the confession is to be inadmissible *threat* there must be: if the statement is voluntarily made because the suspect is in a "tizz" when questioned by a policeman the mere fact of the "tizz" will be no reason for refusing to admit it. "Hope of advantage" means hope of some temporal, as opposed to merely moral, advantage. Thus where the person in authority says, "If you confess I will see that you get bail" the accused's statement will not be admissible; but it will be if all that is said is, "Come, confess for the good of your soul". However, it makes no difference to the inadmissibility of the confession in the former kind of circumstances that the offer of advantage was made at the accused's own request – as where a suspect says to a policeman, "Will you see that I get bail if I confess?" and the latter agrees to this. It is for the judge to rule whether a confession is to be admitted and for the jury to decide what weight should be given to it if admitted.

It should be stressed that the *mere* fact that a confession is made to a person "in authority" does not render it inadmissible, even if it is made to a policeman; but under what are known as the Judges' Rules (revised in 1964) the police are enjoined to *caution* suspected persons whom they question. The formula is well-known – "You are not obliged to say anything unless you wish to do so but what you say may be put in writing and given in evidence" (this is commonly misquoted as "in evidence against you"; of course in fact the statement he made need not necessarily tell *against* the suspect). The caution is not, however, absolutely obligatory in the sense that the confession cannot be admitted in its absence; for the matter is one in which the judge always has a discretion. Further, there is no need of the "caution" unless the questioning policeman has at the time *some* evidence of guilt: if he has no more than suspicion he knows of no evidence that *could* incriminate the person being questioned, so that he has no reason to warn him of the danger of making a statement. A confession made to persons *other* than "persons in authority" will not cease to be "voluntary" because *they* hold out a hope of advantage etc., for they are presumed to exercise no special influence over the accused. Akin to the subject of confessions is the matter of statements made by people in custody. If these are overheard by police or others there is no *prima facie* objection to their admissibility. But if there is a trap – as where a prison officer is disguised as a prisoner in order to elicit information – the court may at discretion reject the statement, and it will be likely to do so unless the gravity of the case otherwise demands.

Mention must also be made of certain rules governing evidence as to the character and previous record of accused persons. It is obviously just that a criminal charge should be tried upon its own merits, and there is much to be said for excluding all evidence tending to show that the accused is a bad character or has a criminal record from the knowledge of the court or jury until after conviction – when the previous record naturally becomes a vital factor in the court's determination of the appropriate *sentence* to award. The general rule is therefore that no evidence which reflects upon the character of the accused may be advanced by the prosecution *during the trial*. This rule is, however, subject to certain exceptions, of which the following are the most important. (*a*) We have seen that, as a general rule, the parties to a civil action cannot tender evidence as to their good character, *i.e.* as to their general reputation for good character. In a criminal case the accused may always do so; but, if he does, the prosecution will then be entitled to seek to rebut this evidence by calling counter-balancing evidence as to his bad character. (*b*) Before the passing of the Criminal Evidence Act 1898, an accused could not be called to give evidence on his own behalf. That Act altered the law and permitted him to do so (though he *need* not) and it further provided by s. 1 (*f*) that if he does choose to do so he may not in general be asked any question, when cross-examined by the prosecution, "tending to show that he has committed or been convicted of or been charged with any offence ... or is of bad character". But this prohibition is subject to important provisos; for questions of the forbidden class may be put at the discretion of the trial judge in the following events: (i) If (as is sometimes the case) evidence of a previous offence, or of previous offences, is admissible to show that the accused is guilty of the offence charged. (ii) If the accused or his counsel have asked questions of the witnesses for the prosecution with a view to establishing his own good character: if the accused has given evidence of his own good character: if the nature or conduct of the defence is such as to involve imputations upon the character of the prosecutor, or of the witnesses for the prosecution, even though these imputations form a necessary part of his own defence and even though they impute moral obiquity rather than criminal behaviour. (iii) If the accused has given evidence against any other person charged with the same offence as himself. In the two last-mentioned cases, (ii) and (iii), the accused is said to have put his own character "in issue" by his conduct.

CHAPTER 4

PERSONALITY, STATUS AND CAPACITY

1 LEGAL PERSONALITY

In everyday life when one speaks of a "person" one means an individual human being, but in the terminology of the law the word has a different and, as it happens, an older signification. *"Person"* is derived from the Latin *per* ("through") and *sonare* ("to sound"); for in ancient times *"persona"* signified an actor's mask through which the sound of his voice came to the audience.

It has already been suggested that a lawsuit is like a drama, and this is no new idea, for, by a gradual transference, *"persona"* came to mean first the actor himself, as identified with his part, then in a legal sense it came to signify the subjects of legal rights and duties. In the course of this transference the word lost nothing of its original force because it came to denote, not an individual litigant as a *human being* but anybody or anything permitted to assert legal claims or subjected to legal duties: on the legal "stage" the mask of personality does not therefore necessarily have to be worn by human beings. Thus in its legal sense the word has come to mean something a great deal wider than simply a human individual; it means any individual, group, or even thing which the law will recognize as a bearer of legal rights and duties.

For different reasons at different times different systems of law have thus accorded legal personality (sometimes distinguished from "ordinary" personality as "artifical" personality) to many other things beside people and it has sometimes denied "personality" to human beings. Thus in early Roman Law slaves had no rights which the law would directly enforce; hence although they were "people" in the ordinary modern sense, just as much as their masters were, they had no legal standing, no legal "personality". At various times also non-human entities have been made subject to legal rights and duties and have thus become artificial legal "persons". Animals were, for example, tried for crimes in the Middle Ages and in an Indian appeal to the Privy Council it was recognized that, in keeping with the existing customs of India, rights could be accorded to an idol and that it could thus be regarded as a legal "person".

Even modern English law which, of course, gives legal "personality" to human beings also accords it to certain entities that are not human; these entities are known as "corporations" and they are said to be endowed with "corporate personality".

The various classes of corporations known to the law must now be considered. It will be seen that most, though by no means all, of them are composed of groups of individuals (associations). Thus, for the sake of completeness it is proposed first to discuss corporations and then to deal briefly with certain other associations which receive some degree of legal recognition without being endowed with independent legal "personality".

Corporations

It is essential to stress at the start that once a corporation comes into being, it acquires, in the eye of the law, a separate existence from the individual members who compose it. The members all continue to have their own private rights and duties, but the corporation also comes to have *its* "own", apart from theirs. Moreover, corporations differ from their members in one essential way; they are endowed with "perpetual succession", that is to say, until they are legally dissolved, they never die; they continue to exist regardless of the entrances and exits (by death or otherwise) of the humans who compose them.

There are two main classes of corporations – corporations "*sole*" and corporations "*aggregate*". A corporation *sole* is composed of one person (*i.e.* one human individual) *and his successors*: examples are, the Monarch in her public capacity, symbolized by the "Crown" and all bishops and parsons. The people who occupy these offices are, of course, in their *private* capacity, with the exception of the Monarch, ordinary individuals, and they are recognized as such in the courts. Thus, for instance, as an individual, a bishop may own land or other property and is entitled to deal with it in every way that other people deal with theirs, and the courts will protect his rights. But in their public capacity, in the performance of their offices, the members of a corporation sole are regarded as one with their predecessors and with their successors, for the corporate office never dies until it is legally dissolved; thus the property which the members hold by virtue of their offices devolves rather upon their *public* than their personal successors; or, to put the matter in its true perspective, the property which they hold in their corporate capacity never really "devolves" at all, since the office, which is deathless, transcends its holders.

Corporations *"aggregate"* consist of groups of people, such as the mayor, aldermen and burgesses of a borough, the dean and chapter of a cathedral, the chairmen and members of public boards (such as the National Coal Board) or the members of a trading company.

Since corporate personality is an artificial legal concept a corporation can come into existence in a manner which only the law prescribes. It provides three principal methods. First, corporations may be created *by the Crown*, by virtue of the prerogative (see below, p. 123), by royal charter; in the past it was in this way that the East India Company and the Hudson's Bay Company were formed, and, as a modern example, universities are generally created by charter. Second, corporations may be created *by a particular statute*. The familiar modern public corporations such as, for example, British Airways and the National Coal Board thus respectively owe their existence to the Civil Aviation Act 1971 and the Coal Industry Nationalization Act 1946. Third, certain classes of corporations may come into existence *by compliance with statutory formalities* which regulate their creation as a *class*. Corporations created by either of the last two methods are called "statutory" corporations, by way of contrast with chartered corporations, which are a species of "common law" corporations. Corporations of the third class are now far more numerous than the others; amongst them are included trading and other companies incorporated under the provisions of the Companies Acts, of which the most recent is the Companies Act 1948 (as amended by the Companies Act 1967).

Incorporation in general has the following, amongst other, results:

(*a*) Since the corporation becomes a legal "person", it may sue and be sued, and may sometimes even be criminally prosecuted, under its corporate name. One of the main objects in according "personality" to corporations is to effect this result; since it is clearly simpler to treat an undying "office" or an aggregate group as a single artificial individual, than it is to treat them as a series or group of distinct members.

(*b*) Once a corporation has come into being, it forms a separate entity from the individuals who compose it. This proposition is usually, and aptly, illustrated by reference to the leading case of *Salomon* v. *Salomon & Co., Ltd.*, [1897] A.C. 22, where S, a boot manufacturer, incorporated his business as a limited company under the Companies Acts. He held practically all the shares in this company and he acted as its managing director. The company borrowed money from him (S) in his private capacity and issued debentures to him. This, as we shall see, meant that he became entitled to a first charge upon the company's assets. The company became insolvent and went into liquidation. S claimed to be treated as a "secured" creditor and to have his claim satisfied in priority to the company's ordinary creditors. The House of Lords held that his claim was justified. The company was an artificial person, with a *legal* existence of its own, independent of S, and the relationship between it and him was one of debtor and creditor. In *Lee v. Lee's Air Farming, Ltd.*, [1961] A.C. 12, like reasoning was applied to permit the wife of a man killed in an air crash to succeed against a company formed by him on a very similar basis to Salomon's company, upon the ground that at the time of his death he was acting as an "employee" of the company. It must, however, be understood that the courts will not allow the fiction of corporate personality to be carried so far as to create absurdity or bring about substantial injustice. Thus, for instance, it was held by the House of Lords in *Daimler Co., Ltd. v. Continental Tyre and Rubber Co. (Great Britain) Ltd.*, [1916] 2 A.C. 307 that in time of war a company incorporated in the United Kingdom but almost wholly owned by alien enemies must be treated as alien; and more recently the Court of Appeal held that where a company gained a tax advantage by the employment of a wholly-owned subsidiary the theoretical independence of the corporate personality of the subsidiary must be disregarded: as Lord Denning, M.R. remarked: "The doctrine of *Salomon v. Salomon & Co., Ltd.* has to be watched very carefully . . . The courts can and do often draw aside the veil (of corporate personality). They can, and often do, pull off the mask." The fact is that this is a field in which theory must at times yield to expedience: probably the decision in *Salomon's Case* goes as far as theory is ever likely to go in this respect.

(*c*) Since corporations are recognized as "persons" they are entitled, within their powers, to carry on activities, such as trading, just like an ordinary person. In doing this, however, they can only act through their properly constituted agents, since they are themselves abstractions, devoid of mind and body.

(*d*) Because corporations are distinct from their members, the common law rule was that they could only make contracts under their corporate seal, which symbolizes their independent existence; but for reasons of practical convenience, this rule was abolished in the case of companies incorporated under the Companies Acts as long ago as 1867 (see further below, p. 211).

(*e*) Since corporations are legal "persons" one would expect them to have the same legal rights and powers, and to be subject to the same liabilities as ordinary individuals. Chartered corporations are treated in this way: generally speaking, subject to any special reservations in their charters of incorporation, they may through their agents do much the same things as adult people. Statutory corporations on the other hand derive their whole being, and with it their rights and powers, from the statute which creates them, and statutes on the whole refrain from creating leviathans with unlimited powers. Every act done on behalf of a statutory corporation must thus be justifiable by reference to the powers which its parent Act (or, in the case of a company incorporated under the Companies Acts, its memorandum of association) has conferred, and any act which its agents do in excess of these powers ("*ultra vires*") will be ineffective to bind it; it exists only for the purpose of exercising them; once step beyond these, fictitious personality disappears, and the wraith which the law has created fades into the air. Thus if the directors of a company empowered to run motor buses were to contract to buy aircraft on the company's behalf, whatever the directors' liability, the company itself could not be bound by the contract. This principle is often referred to as the rule in the "Ashbury Carriage Case" (*Ashbury Railway Carriage and Iron Co., Ltd.* v. *Riche* (1875), L.R. 7 H.L. 653, the leading case on the subject.

This "*ultra vires*" doctrine is one which runs all through the law; it has particular reference to excess of statutory powers, and is of especial importance, as we shall see, in constitutional law. It must be noted, however, that in respect of corporations the doctrine is subject to a number of limitations in favour of people who deal with them. In particular, the European Communities Act (hereafter E.C.A.) 1972, s. 9 (1) provides that in the case of companies incorporated under the Companies Acts any transaction "*decided on by the directors*" shall, "in favour of a person dealing with a company in good faith … be *deemed to be one which it is within the capacity of the company to enter.*" This means that the company may, under these conditions, be bound by a transaction effected after a decision "by the directors" though it is outside the objects clause of its memorandum of association: so that if the directors of our bus company were now to decide to deal in aircraft a person who contracted to sell aircraft parts to the company would be able (as formerly he would not have been) to enforce the contract against the company. This relaxation of the *Ashbury* rule is, however, *confined* to companies incorporated under the Acts *and* it depends upon good faith on the part of the person contracting with the company – which would mean, presumably, that such a person could not claim in respect of the aircraft transaction if he *knew* that it was *ultra vires* the company's objects. "Decided upon by the directors" is a loose phrase which awaits judicial interpretation.

(*f*) Corporations may in general hold and dispose of land and of other property as if they were ordinary individuals.

Reference will be made to the contractual, tortious, and criminal liability of corporations in the appropriate chapters below.

Corporations, as we have explained, continue to exist until they are "dissolved". The dissolution of a chartered corporation may be effected in a number of ways: amongst the most important are dissolution by Act of Parliament and dissolution by the Sovereign, who may repeal the charter at will or to whom the charter may be surrendered. The method of dissolving a statutory corporation is usually prescribed in the statute which creates it. Trading companies incorporated under the Companies Acts 1948–1967 are, as we shall see, dissolved by a process called "winding up".

These latter corporations are of such importance that they must be separately described.

The Companies Acts – The 1948 Act introduced no great innovation, though it made certain changes in the law: it is mainly a consolidating Act which re-affirms principles established by a long series of Companies Acts, originating in the nineteenth century. The following represents, in briefest outline, the scheme which it enshrines.

Any seven or more people (or, in the case of a "private" company, any two or more people) may form a company by subscribing their names to a *memorandum of association*, and also, where these are required, to *articles of association*. These documents must be delivered to an official called the "Registrar of Companies" whose duty it is, upon examining them, and satifying himself that they are in order, to retain them and register them, and to certify that the company has become incorporated. This act of certification therefore represents the birth of a new legal "person".

The *memorandum of association* contains matters of interest to people who may wish to have dealings with the company; for it sets out the objects of the company and the sort of business which it is empowered to carry on; it states its corporate name and the part of the United Kingdom in which its registered office is to be situated, and it also states the nature of the liability of its members and the amount of its capital. Thus, people who have dealings with the company's agents can ascertain, since the memorandum is registered, what sort of a company it is and the *limits of its powers*. The Act provides that companies may, by *special resolution*, alter their memoranda in certain particulars after they have been incorporated: for example, they may change them to a certain extent in order to enlarge their "objects"; in order, for instance, to extend the purposes of their business. The resolution must be registered.

The *articles of association* regulate the internal organization and method of management of the company.

The E.C.A., s. 9 (5) and (6) provides that where any alteration is made in the memorandum or articles the relevant document must be reprinted and forwarded to the Registrar of Companies.

The Companies Act authorizes three classes of companies; companies *limited by shares*, companies *limited by guarantee*, and *unlimited companies*. Companies *limited by shares* are the commonest class; in companies of this sort the liability of shareholders for the corporate debts is expressed in the memorandum of association to be limited, and is limited, to the amount, if any, unpaid on their shares. The capital of such companies may consist of different classes of shares; a common distinction being a distinction between *preference* and *ordinary* shares. Preference shares carry fixed rights to dividend, and in many cases to the return of capital when the company is wound up. The rights of ordinary shareholders, on the other hand, are not fixed but depend for dividend upon such part of the profits of the company as is set aside by the directors for distribution, and, for the return of capital, upon what assets are available when the liabilities of the company have been met. A company *limited by guarantee* is one in which the liability of members is limited to the amount which they each undertake to pay. An *unlimited company* is a company in which the liability of members is unlimited. A company limited by shares *need* not have special articles of association; the other types of companies *must* always have them. But a company limited by shares which does not have special articles will automatically be governed by certain standard articles set out in what is called "Table A", which will be found in the First Schedule to the 1948 Act.

The Act also permits the formation of *"private"* companies: like other companies, these may be registered with limited liability. They are endowed with special advantages, but they are also subject to certain restrictions – for example, their total membership must not generally exceed fifty persons, no invitation must be issued to the general public to take shares in them, and the right to transfer shares in them must be restricted.

The signatories of the memorandum of association are the original "members" of a company, but other people may, and, of course, usually do, become members subsequently by taking up shares and having their names entered in the *register of members* which a company must keep.

Once in each year every company must hold an *annual general meeting* which all members are entitled to attend. The company's affairs are usually reviewed at this meeting and, unless the articles make some other provision, the directors are normally elected or re-elected at it. Companies *may* also hold "extraordinary" meetings at other times.

The *directors* are the people responsible for the general control and management of the company's affairs: they are, as has sometimes been said, the "head and brains" of its artificial personality, and through them the more important of its activities are carried on.

Debenture holders must be distinguished from shareholders; they are creditors of the company who have advanced it loans in return for the payment of interest and they are entitled to hold a document, commonly called a "debenture", certifying the company's indebtedness. This indebtedness is generally secured by a mortgage or a charge upon the company's property which entitles the debenture holders, should the company become insolvent, to receive payment in priority to the other ordinary creditors. This security may take one of two forms; it may either be effected (usually in the case of a series of debentures by means of a trust deed) in the form of a "*fixed charge*" by way of legal mortgage (see below, p. 367), or by some other means, over some specific part of the company's property; or it may be effected by an equitable "*floating charge*". The floating charge is a most useful and practical device. It has been judicially defined as a "charge on the assets for the time being of a going concern (which) attaches to the subject charged in the varying condition it happens to be from time to time". Suppose that X & Co. is a shipping company and that it wishes to borrow money. If it can find lenders they may be issued with debentures. Suppose that these debenture holders are given a "fixed" charge over one of the company's vessels. Until the loan has been repaid the charge will attach to the vessel. This may clearly become inconvenient, since the company might wish to sell the vessel in order to make replacements in its fleet, and it might not be easy to find a buyer for a ship which is subject to a charge. Hence the usefulness of the "floating charge". If the lenders are given such a charge, their rights do not attach to any particular part of the company's property, but only "crystallize" upon the whole of the undertaking at the time when they seek to enforce their security – that will of course normally be when, the debt remaining unpaid, the company becomes insolvent. Thus, unless and until such enforcement occurs the company can deal freely with its property.

Companies incorporated under the Act are dissolved by a process called "*winding up*". There are three sorts of winding up; "compulsory", "voluntary" and winding up "under supervision".

A company may be wound up compulsorily upon the happening of certain prescribed events, the most important and usual of these events being that it is unable to pay its debts. Proceedings are commenced by the presentation of a petition to the court, generally, in practice, at the instance of an unpaid creditor. Upon the presentation of a successful petition the company's assets fall provisionally into the custody of an officer called the "official receiver" who becomes provisional "*liquidator*". Normally the court will, in due course, appoint some other person as permanent liquidator; though it may sometimes cast that duty upon the official receiver. The liquidator has control and custody of the company's property, though it is not normally actually vested in him. His duty is, under the general direction of the court, to do everything which may be necessary for winding up the company's affairs, including the realization (where necessary) and the distribution of its assets. He may, where necessary, bring or defend actions on the company's behalf. He must as far as possible, satisfy the company's liabilities and divide any surplus assets among the shareholders. When, and not until, the entire affairs of the company have thus been settled the court will make an order for its dissolution. The "court", in this context, will normally be the Chancery Division or, in the case of companies having small assets, a county court.

A "voluntary" winding up is effected by resolution of the company itself. In this case it appoints (subject in some circumstances to the approval of the creditors) its own liquidator whose duties are similar to those of a liquidator appointed by the court in a compulsory winding up. The only important difference between the two classes of liquidators is that the liquidator in a voluntary winding up is to some extent independent of the court.

Where a resolution to wind up voluntarily has been passed by a company the court may in certain circumstances make an order that the voluntary winding up shall continue "under supervision". The general effect of such an order is that the liquidator becomes in some respects subject to the court's supervision, though he is not entirely under its control as is a liquidator in a compulsory winding up.

Two further provisions of the E.C.A. require mention. In the first place s. 9 (3) and (4) enacts that the Registrar of Companies must cause *official notification* to be made in the *London Gazette* of the receipt of certain specified documents including, *inter alia*, any certificate of incorporation and any copy of a winding-up order. The effect of failure so to notify the documents in question is that the company cannot rely as against other persons on the happening of certain stated events including any alteration of the memorandum or articles and the appointment of a liquidator. In the second place, under s. 9 (7) all business letters of a company must mention "in legible characters" the place of registration of the company and the address of its registered office.

Unincorporated associations

Unlike incorporated associations, unincorporated associations are endowed with no independent legal "personality": in the eye of the law they are simply groups of separate individuals.

There is an enormous variety of unincorporated associations; they range from small informal groups of people united together for the enjoyment of some sport or pastime, such as bird-watching societies, through the more important and formal cricket, golf and social clubs, to vast and highly influential groups, such as trade unions and unincorporated employers' associations.

Subject to certain important reservations shortly to be made the general rule is that the law simply disregards the existence of these associations as independent groups. It treats their property as the joint property of all their members, it treats contracts made on their behalf as the contracts of the particular individuals who make them, or authorize their making, and it holds their members *individually* responsible only for such torts as they may themselves have committed – or authorized – in the course of the combined activities of the group. Thus, for example, in *Brown* v. *Lewis* (1896), 12 T.L.R. 455 the committee of a football club employed a person to repair a public stand; this person repaired the stand so ineffectively that it collapsed and a member of the public was injured. The committee who had authorized the work, not the members of the club generally, were held responsible.

To this general rule there are four important exceptions which, nevertheless, in no way affect the general theory that unincorporated bodies themselves have no independent legal existence.

The first exception is this: Order 15, rule 12 of the Rules of the Supreme Court provides that: "Where numerous persons have the same interest in any proceedings . . . the proceedings may be begun, and, unless the Court otherwise orders, continued, by or against any one or more of them as representing all. . . ." Thus, for example the fruit vendors of Covent Garden were once held entitled to be represented by certain of their number in an action to vindicate preferential rights which they enjoyed in respect of their stalls.

The second exception is that although they are not recognized as legal "persons", the courts and Parliament have for reasons of convenience in some instances allowed unincorporated associations to sue and be sued. Thus at common law Trustee Savings Banks may (particularly because the relevant statutes governing these institutions contain implications to this effect) be sued as such.

The third exception is that in some cases where unincorporated groups of people have interests in property it is sometimes held by trustees on their behalf. The nature of trusteeship will be explained in a later chapter; here all that need be noted is that the trustees are, as such, the legal owners of the property; actions in respect of it may therefore be brought by and against them.

The fourth exception is that the law recognizes that unincorporated associations may make rules binding upon their members and may confer powers of governance upon some of their number; for example powers of expulsion are often conferred upon committees, such as the Stewards of the Jockey Club. Such committees and similar bodies therefore form a species of *domestic tribunal* and the law accepts their powers and it will not usually interfere with their exercise. But abuse will be restrained, and the decisions of these tribunals may be successfully attacked in the ordinary courts, where the tribunal has acted ("*ultra vires*") in excess of the powers conferred upon it – as by delegating a decision where no power to delegate exists – or has made a decision which contravenes the rules of natural justice (see below, p. 133); even though the decision be an administrative rather than a judicial one. Further, the rules which bind these associations and their tribunals may sometimes be challenged. For instance a rule that the members of the committee "shall be the sole interpreters of the rules" and that the committee's decision "shall be final" has been held to be contrary to public policy and void in so far as it constituted an attempt to oust the jurisdiction of the courts by making the committee final arbiter between itself and its members upon a point of law; which can never be done. Again, a rule giving a union an unfettered discretion to exclude a member so as to make it possible to exclude him capriciously has been held to be invalid.

Unincorporated associations may cease to exist – rendering the joint property distributable among those who are members at the time of cessation – in a number of ways. Thus its rules may provide for dissolution in certain events; all the members may agree to its termination; the court may make an order that it shall cease to exist; and it may also be dissolved when the purpose for which it came into being – the "substratum" of its existence – has gone. A good illustration of a dissolution of the latter kind is to be found in the Irish case of *Feeney and Shannon* v. *MacManus*, [1937] I.R. 23, where it was held that a dining club which met in the building of the Dublin General Post Office automatically ceased to be when that building was destroyed.

So much for the general rules relating to unincorporated associations. It must now be explained that there are certain classes of unincorporated associations which, for one reason or another, are so important and common that the law has been forced, without according them full legal "personality", to make some special rules in relation to them. Two classes of associations of this type are, indeed, so important that they must be mentioned here: these are trade unions and unincorporated employers' associations on the one hand and partnerships on the other.

TRADE UNIONS AND UNINCORPORATED EMPLOYERS' ASSOCIATIONS

Originally regarded as common law conspiracies, *trade unions* now enjoy a special status. This is governed by the Trade Union and Labour Relations Act 1974. Unions are not corporate bodies, but s. 2 of the 1974 Act provides that they shall be capable of making contracts, that their property shall be vested in trustees to hold on their behalf, that they shall be capable of suing and being sued in their own name and that they shall not be treated as unlawful by reason of being in restraint of trade. Section 3 of the Act grants similar status to unincorporated *employers' associations*. Section 14 (1), however, provides both unions and employers' associations with a wide *immunity* which was originally conferred by the Trade Disputes Act 1906. Under this section no action in *tort* may lie in respect of any act alleged to have been done, threatened or intended to be done, by or on behalf of a trade union or of an employers' association. And this protects not only the union or association itself but also its trustees and its members or officials acting on behalf of themselves and of all other members. By s. 14 (2), however, this special protection is – *provided that* it does not arise from an act done "in contemplation or furtherance of a trade dispute" – withdrawn from any act done by way of negligence, nuisance or breach of statutory duty which results in *personal injury* to any person (*e.g.* injuries arising from highway accidents); and the subsection also withdraws protection from breach of any duty owed in connexion with the ownership occupation, possession, control or use of any property. Outside the hallowed freedom attaching to "trade disputes" (below, p. 312) the immunity is thus not so sweeping as at first appears. But it does mean that, although a union may sue for libel in its union name, it cannot be sued.

PARTNERSHIPS

The law relating to partnership is codified in the Partnership Act 1890. A partnership is there defined as the "relationship which subsists between persons carrying on a business in common with a view of profit". Thus, a partnership is a "relationship", and it may therefore come into existence without a formal agreement though, in practice, it will usually be constituted by the conclusion of formal "articles of partnership". Such a relationship will not, however, exist unless partnership is the common intention; so that where two people are working together with the aim of forming a company as yet not formed their relationship is not one of partnership.

Although a partnership is not a legal "person", because it is a joint enterprise all partners are taken to be each others' agents in respect of all acts done in or about the partnership business, and for convenience they may sue and be sued in the name of the "firm". Thus as a general rule, any act done in furtherance of the business by one partner binds the rest, even though he has done it without their authority. This rule is in the nature of things subject to certain exceptions: for example, where the partners have agreed that none of them shall alone have power to bind the firm in relation to certain matters, if one of them purports to do so *and the person with whom he deals knows of the agreement*, the firm will not be bound.

A further important rule of the law of partnership, which derives from a general rule of law and of common sense, must also be noted. In order to protect strangers to the firm, wherever a man "holds himself out" as a partner by acting as if he were one, although he is not – for example by permitting his name to appear upon the firm's note-paper – he may generally be held liable to anyone who gives the firm credit in reliance upon this false representation, just as though he really were a partner.

A partnership firm may be made liable for torts committed, as well as for debts incurred, by any partner acting in actual or apparent furtherance of the business.

In their mutual dealings, the law requires all partners to observe the utmost good faith; they must disclose all profits they make in relation to the business, so that they can be shared in common by their fellows according to their respective rights. Should one partner compete with the firm upon his own account he may be compelled to disclose, and to share, his profits.

Unlike the liability of the members of companies, the liability of partners for the partnership debts is generally unlimited. It is, however, possible to create a "limited" partnership under the provisions of the Limited Partnerships Act 1907: in these (uncommon) partnerships the liability of some of the partners may be limited to the amount of the capital which they supply; but at least one of the partners must be a "general" (as opposed to a "limited") partner and as such his, or their, liability will be unlimited.

The number of persons associating in a partnership must never exceed *twenty*, and in the case of a banking business it must never exceed *ten*. *Any association for business purposes which exceeds this number* will be illegal unless it be incorporated under the Companies Acts or in some other way. The Sex Discrimination Act 1975, s. 11, renders it unlawful for a firm consisting of *six* or more partners to discriminate on the ground of sex against any person wishing to join the firm or against any member of it. So that six becomes the permitted limit for birds of a feather.

2 STATUS AND CAPACITY

"Status" signifies membership of a particular class or group to which special legal capacities, liabilities, or immunities adhere. It will be found that in all societies at all times some people have been endowed with special powers and capacities peculiar to themselves or to their class, while others have been subjected to special incapacities. Thus the Head of the State invariably has certain pre-eminent privileges and immunities which, in the eyes of the law, place him or her upon a different standing ("*status*") from ordinary citizens: with us, for example, the Queen cannot be tried in her own courts for any crime, nor, in her private capacity, may she be sued in tort. Foreign sovereigns, too, and their ambassadors are entitled to certain legal immunities. On the other hand, some sorts of people, such as minors and persons of unsound mind are for their own good subjected as a class to legal *incapacities* which make their rights and duties different from those of the sane adult.

It is interesting to note that in the laws of early societies differences of status were greater than they are in most civilized countries today. Anyone who cares to glance at the institutional books on Roman Law will quickly be able to assure himself of this; he will find that a large amount of space is devoted to discussion of the Law of Persons, which describes the different classes of society, such as the slave, the son under his father's "power", the freedman, and the married woman. In England also in mediaeval times the status of an overlord differed greatly from that of a villein, and even the fact that a man was a craftsman belonging to a particular gild might give him special rights.

The course of history in the West has, under the influence of Christianity and humanism, shown a general decline in the importance of status; for it has gradually come to be felt that it is right that everyone should as far as possible receive equal treatment at the hands of the law. Nevertheless, some kinds of special status still remain and they almost certainly always will remain; it is therefore still necessary for some reference to be made to the legal position of certain classes of persons, and to examine their special rights and duties, capacities and immunities.

Here we must content ourselves with a very brief discussion of three matters affecting status: nationality (to which we will append mention of immigration and of race relations), minority and unsoundness of mind.

1 Nationality

It need hardly be explained that nationality is a matter which affects a person's relations with the outside world, and that it is not usually of much concern in municipal law; for municipal law normally has to deal only with its own nationals. But nationality is clearly a matter of such importance that it must be discussed, and this seems the most suitable place to consider it. In any event, as we shall see, even as regards municipal law, "nationals" may in a sense be regarded as having a special status by way of contrast with non-nationals, who are subject to special incapacities.

The law relating to British nationality is now governed by the British Nationality Acts 1948–1965 (as amended), and regulations made thereunder. In respect of their political status people are divided into three main classes: "*British subjects*", "*British protected persons*", and "*aliens*". Let us consider these three classes of persons.

BRITISH SUBJECTS

"British subjects" are divided into two main classes, *Commonwealth citizens* (citizens of the independent nations of the Commonwealth) and citizens of the "*United Kingdom and Colonies*". The status of citizens of the independent countries is governed by the laws in force in the countries concerned; the modes of its acquisition and loss need not therefore concern us here. Citizenship of the *United Kingdom and Colonies* may be acquired in the following ways:

(*a*) *By birth* – As a general rule anyone born within the United Kingdom or the Colonies automatically acquires citizenship, *whatever* the nationality of his or of her parents.

(*b*) *By descent* – Anyone *wherever born* whose *father* is, at the date of his or her birth, a citizen of the United Kingdom and Colonies, will acquire citizenship (by "descent") at birth. Further, anyone whose *father* is thus a citizen by *descent may* also acquire citizenship (by "descent") at birth, but only under certain circumstances and subject to certain conditions prescribed in the Act.

(*c*) *By registration* – A citizen of one of the independent States of the Commonwealth, or of the Republic of Ireland, if of full age and capacity, may apply to the Secretary of State for registration as a citizen of the United Kingdom and Colonies. Registration will, however, only be permitted if the applicant has been resident in the United Kingdom or employed there in certain specified kinds of employment (*e.g.* Crown service) for five years immediately preceding the date of registration and if he is of good character, has a sufficient knowledge of English or Welsh, and intends to continue to reside or to be employed in the United Kingdom or in a colony or protectorate. It should, however, be noted that a *"patrial"* within the meaning of the Immigration Act 1971, s. 2 (1) (*d*) below – need only satisfy the residence (or employment) condition in order to be registered.

(*d*) *By naturalization* – Aliens and British protected persons may apply to the Secretary of State for a certificate of naturalization. This may be granted, upon their taking the oath of allegiance, provided that they are of full age and capacity and provided that they satisfy certain conditions as to residence, character, knowledge of the language, and certain other matters.

(*e*) *Citizenship by incorporation of territory* – When any new territory becomes a part of the United Kingdom and Colonies the Queen may by Order in Council provide that all, or specific classes of, persons within that territory shall for the future enjoy citizenship of the United Kingdom and Colonies.

NOTE – Citizenship of the United Kingdom and Colonies need not necessarily be an exclusive status. Suppose, for example, that X is born in England, of Ruritanian parents. He will, as we have seen, become a citizen by birth. This will not, however, necessarily mean that he will not also be a Ruritanian national according to Ruritanian law.

The 1948 Act made certain important changes with regard to the status of married women. Formerly, when a female British national married an alien under whose national law she acquired his nationality she lost her British nationality. She now retains United Kingdom citizenship in all circumstances unless and until she renounces it. By contrast, formerly when an alien woman married a British national she automatically acquired British nationality: she will now only acquire United Kingdom and Colonial citizenship, if she chooses to do so, by *registration*.

Citizenship of the United Kingdom and Colonies may be lost by renunciation and deprivation. Renunciation applies to citizens who are also citizens of the independent Commonwealth States or citizens of the Republic of Ireland, or foreign nationals. They may renounce their citizenship by making a declaration of renunciation, which will become operative when registered by authority of the Secretary of State. Deprivation applies mainly to citizens who have acquired their citizenship by naturalization or by registration. They may be deprived by order of the Secretary of State (in some circumstances by order of a colonial Governor) upon certain specified grounds; but only subject to the overriding proviso that no such order may be made unless the Secretary is satisfied that it is not conducive to the public good that they should continue to be citizens.

British protected persons are neither British subjects nor aliens. The status embraces any members of a class of persons declared by Order in Council to be British protected persons by virtue of their connexion with any protectorate, protected state, or mandated or trust territory.

Citizens of the Republic of Ireland occupy a peculiar position: they are not as a *general rule* British subjects, though they may become such by registration.

IMMIGRATION

Formerly the law relating to immigration differed according to whether an immigrant was a member of the Commonwealth or whether he was an alien, unconnected with Britain or the Commonwealth. It has now been remodelled by the Immigration Act 1971 (hereafter "I.A."). Section 1 of this Act provides that anyone who has the "right of abode" in the United Kingdom shall be free to come to, live in, and come and go from it without let or hindrance (this, of course, has no reference to customs regulations). Anyone who lacks this right may only live, work and settle here subject to permission and control. For immigration purposes the "Islands"—*i.e.* the Isle of Man and the Channel Islands—and the Republic of Ireland are treated as a "common travel area" so that immigration restrictions do not apply as between them.

Having thus distinguished two classes of persons (with reservations in favour of Commonwealth citizens settled in the United Kingdom at the time of coming into force of the Act) it is then enacted that the first class ("*patrials*") shall consist of the following: *First*, (s. 2 (1) (*a*)), any citizen of the United Kingdom and Colonies who is himself such by reason of birth, adoption or (in general) registration *in the United Kingdom* or the Islands. *Second*, (s. 2 (1) (*b*)), any citizen of the United Kingdom and Colonies whose *parent* had such citizenship at the time of his birth or adoption *and* who had *either* at that time already obtained it by birth, adoption, naturalization or registration *in the United Kingdom* or the Islands *or* had himself (the parent) been born of or adopted by a parent who, at the time of his (the parent's) birth or adoption, had acquired such citizenship by similar means. This is, perhaps, a little complicated; but the effect of it is that a person can be a "patrial" by reference back to the acquisition of British citizenship *in the United Kingdom* by a parent or grandparent. *Third*, (s. 2 (1) (*c*)), any citizen of the United Kingdom and Colonies who has at any time been settled in the United Kingdom or the Islands after at least five preceding years of residence. *Fourth*, (s. 2 (1) (*d*)), any *Commonwealth* citizen born or adopted by a *parent* who had at the time of birth or adoption citizenship of the United Kingdom and Colonies by *birth in the United Kingdom* or the Islands. By s. 2 (2) *women* who are *Commonwealth citizens* are also patrials by dint of marriage to any of the kinds of patrials described in s. 2 (1).

"Patrials" thus being defined, we must now consider the position in respect of immigration of a person who is *not* a patrial. By s. 3 of the I.A. such a person must have leave to enter the United Kingdom; and this leave may be granted conditionally, *e.g.* as to time of stay, or employment, or registration with the police. Non-patrials are, moreover, liable to *deportation* if they outstay the period of leave or break some condition of it, or if the Secretary of State deems their deportation to be conducive to the public good (s. 3 (5)). They may also be deported by court order if, being over seventeen, they are convicted of an offence punishable with imprisonment (s. 3 (6)). Moreover, members of the family – a husband, wife (or wives) or children under eighteen – of the deportee may also be deported with him (or her).

The power to *refuse* leave to enter the United Kingdom lies with immigration officers and the power to give leave to remain in it rests with the Secretary of State (s. 4).

The Immigration Appeals Act 1969 (now repealed and largely re-enacted by the I.A.) set up a system of appeals against decisions of immigration officers and of the Secretary of State in respect of immigrants. Briefly, there are two kinds of tribunal: *"adjudicators"* and the *Immigration Appeals Tribunal.* The former are appointed by the Secretary of State – together with a chief adjudicator – ; the latter consists of a number of members appointed by the Lord Chancellor, and it sits with a legally qualified chairman and two lay members. Appeals in some matters (such as refusal of leave to enter) are reserved for adjudicators and in others (such as a deportation order made in respect of a member of a family) are reserved for the Tribunal; and a further appeal against any decision of an adjudicator lies to the Tribunal.

It should finally be noted that the Secretary of State (s. 29) has wide powers (subject to Treasury consent) to pay expenses in respect of the removal from the country of non-patrials, and that (ss. 24–28) the Act creates a number of *offences* – such as being "knowingly concerned in making . . . arrangements . . . for facilitating the entry . . . of . . . an illegal entrant" (s. 25 (1)) – in connexion with deportation and illegal entry.

RACE RELATIONS

This seems the proper place to mention this much-debated subject. It is governed by the Race Relations Acts 1965 and 1968 (hereafter "R.R.A.").

The R.R.A. 1965 amongst other things (below, p. 146) made it unlawful (s. 1) for the proprietor or manager of any place of public resort – *e.g.* a restaurant or a theatre – to refuse access to anyone on *"the ground of colour, race or ethnic or national origins".* The *Race Relations Board* with ancillary local *"conciliation committees"* was set up (s. 2), and these bodies in conjunction were empowered to receive complaints against contraventions of s. 1 and to seek to settle the differences of the parties which are the subject-matter of complaint. If the differences cannot be so ironed out the Board is ultimately empowered to report the case to the Attorney-General who may, where proper, bring proceedings in a county court for the grant of an injunction to stop the contravention.

This Act was thought to be too narrow in scope, with the result that the R.R.A. 1968 was passed. It includes detailed provisions and we can only select the more important of them. It makes it unlawful *on the grounds* (above mentioned) specified in the R.R.A. 1965 for anyone or for anyone aiding or abetting him *to discriminate*: – (i) (if he is concerned with the provision to the public or a section of the public of such things) against any person seeking the supply of goods, facilities or services – such as hotel accommodation, loans, banking, insurance, education, transport or business or professional services (s. 2); (ii) against any person in the matter of employment or terms or conditions of service (s. 3); (iii) against any person in the matter of admission to, enjoyment of the benefits of, or expulsion from any organization of employers or workers – such as trade unions (s. 4); (iv) against anyone seeking to obtain housing accommodation, business premises or land (s. 5).

The most debatable point which this legislation has so far raised is what is meant by providing facilities, etc. "to the public". It is not to be assumed that it was the intention of the legislature to ban discrimination within the *private* (as opposed to the public) sphere. And clearly, as the House of Lords have seen it, there was no intention of preventing people from discriminating in respect of private guests. But it has been held that if a person who agrees to take children under care were to refuse, say, coloured (as opposed to non-coloured) children that would be discrimination – for the service such a person offers is a service to the public in general. Clubs also cause difficulty. A club is essentially a world of special people, a private institution discriminatory in essence since it is a clubbing together of mutually congenial people: thus it is like a private home; and it cannot therefore be assumed that Parliament intended to place a ban upon the right of clubs to select their own members. This principle has been upheld by the House of Lords; and indeed in *Dockers' Labour Club and Institute, Ltd.* v. *Race Relations Board*, [1974] 3 All E.R. 592 it was even held that a club could lawfully discriminate upon grounds of colour despite the fact that the person discriminated against was a member of an "associated" club.

To these provisions there are, however, many and detailed *exceptions* which include: (a) In the case of accommodation – discrimination in respect of residential accommodation in "small premises" (as defined by s. 7 (2)), in the disposal of owned and wholly occupied premises *otherwise than* through the medium of an estate agent *or* by means of public notice or advertisement (s. 7 (7)), and in the allocation of sleeping cabins for passengers on a ship (s. 7 (5)); (*b*) In the case of employment (s. 8) – discrimination by employers of not more than twenty-five persons (though this figure will eventually be reduced) as regards those employed; discrimination in respect of employment in an undertaking, made in good faith, to secure or preserve a reasonable balance of racial groups; discrimination designed to ensure that work especially suited to the attributes of people of a particular nationality should be employed for that work. Moreover, discrimination in favour of charitable benefactions and in respect of acts done to safeguard national security is exempted. The Act binds the Crown. "*Discrimination*" is defined (s. 1) as treating people on any of the grounds above set out, and for any of the purposes above defined, "less favourably" than other people would be treated.

The R.R.A. 1968 continued in existence the Race Relations Board and the local conciliation committees; but it enlarged their powers to include investigation of complaints (which must be in writing and made within two months of the act complained of) in respect of all matters rendered unlawful under its own provisions. Though to this there is one partial exception concerning complaints in respect of employers' or workers' organizations, for these must in various ways be channelled through the Department of Employment. Where conciliation fails the Board may, in respect of acts made unlawful by the 1968 Act, initiate civil proceedings for *injunction* or *damages* in a county court.

This Act also brought into being the *Community Relations Commission*, a body concerned to encourage and assist others in securing "harmonious community relations" and to advise the Home Secretary on matters connected with race relations.

ALIENS

The expression "alien" comprises all persons who are neither British subjects nor British protected persons: aliens are, therefore, foreigners. They are subject to certain incapacities under English law: for instance, they cannot own British ships, nor can they normally act as masters of British ships, nor can they be Members of Parliament, nor vote at elections.

2 Minors

Formerly "infants" were people under the age of twenty-one, but the age of majority was altered to eighteen by the Family Law Reform Act 1969, s. 1; and although this section does not apply retrospectively in respect of references to "majority" in private documents, such as wills executed before 1970, it does so apply to such references in statutes, *e.g.*

the Infants Relief Act 1874 (see below, p. 209). The effects of minority insofar as it affects the family will be considered in Chapter 13 and its effect upon criminal and civil liability will receive mention in the appropriate places. Here it is proposed to mention only certain general matters.

Broadly speaking, it may be stated that a minor may hold *property* in the same way as an adult; but this principle is subject to such important exceptions and reservations that, as a matter of practice, it might perhaps be better left unstated. In the first place, although a minor may own personal property, such as money, a car or a pony, which is given or sold to him by some living person, he may, in general repudiate any disposition he makes of it. This right to repudiate is, however, subject to the limitation that if the minor has received something (as by way of sale or exchange) in return for the disposition, he will not be entitled to exercise the right unless it is possible to restore the parties to their original position at the time when he seeks to do so. In the second place, no minor may now hold a legal estate in land (Law of Property Act 1925, s. 1 (6)). The meaning of this will be explained later in the chapter on the Law of Property. Third, any property which comes to a minor by way of settlement, or *upon the death* of some other person, will now usually be held on his behalf by trustees or by personal representatives until he attains his majority. A minor can therefore only enjoy an *equitable interest* in land, or in any property which comes to him upon the death of another person. The meaning of this will also be explained later in this book.

Although the matter was formerly in doubt, it has now been decided that a minor may be made *bankrupt*; but it must, however, be realized that the circumstances in which this may occur will necessarily be rare.

The Children and Young Persons Acts 1933 to 1969 provide an extensive and amorphous code of legislation giving protection and assistance – for the most part under local government control – to "children" (for most, but not all, purposes people under fourteen years of age) and "young persons" (people between fourteen and seventeen years of age). It would be neither profitable nor possible to describe this legislation here; but it should be mentioned that the scope of the enactments is both considerable and detailed, and that much of their purpose is to secure special protection for juveniles in respect of such matters as cruelty, exposure to danger and to harsh terms of employment, and to ensure for them special forms of trial and treatment. The Children Act 1973 provides that no one may be employed under the age of thirteen.

Minors may not conduct *litigation* in person. Plaintiff minors must always be represented by their "*next friend*", and defendant minors by their "*guardian ad litem*". These representatives will usually be one of the minor's parents or his or her guardian.

3 Mentally Disordered Persons

Insanity is a thing which affects a person's legal capacity in many ways and the law has always had to take account of it. Such aspects of it as concern contractual capacity (below, p. 211), matrimonial law (below, Chapter 12) and criminal law (below, p. 156) are discussed in the appropriate places. Here, after some general remarks about unsoundness of mind, it is proposed to confine attention to the provisions of the Mental Health Act 1959 (M.H.A.) concerning the care and treatment of mentally disordered persons and the protection of their property.

Unsoundness of mind affects a person's power to understand the nature of his dealings with others, and the law must therefore give recognition to this fact and make allowance for it. It follows that, for instance, deeds executed or gifts made by people found by a court to be incapable through unsoundness of mind of understanding their nature or effect will be void, and the wills of such people will only be valid if it can be proved that the testator was capable of appreciating their import at the time of executing them. Further, in equity, transactions of people of low intelligence (though not necessarily amounting to unsoundness of mind) may be set aside by the court where there is evidence that the other party to the transaction has taken advantage of their weakness. Moreover, a person who by reason of mental disorder is incapable of managing his property or affairs must as a general rule be represented in a civil action by a next friend or guardian *ad litem*.

Passing now to the M.H.A., it must be stressed that its object is only to make "provision with respect to the treatment and care of mentally disordered persons and with respect to their property and affairs". It thus seeks to achieve only this and provides only for "*mentally disordered persons*", a class which for its own purposes it defines. It therefore replaces the common law rules as to insanity *only* within this field and in respect of this particular kind of mentally afflicted people. In summarizing the law which falls under this Act we must first ascertain the nature of this special class, then consider first the provisions as to their care and treatment and next those relating to their property and affairs.

Section 4 of the M.H.A. defines "mental disorder" as "*mental illness, arrested or incomplete development of mind, psychopathic disorder, and any other disorder or disability of mind*". Of these categories the two middle are further defined. "*Arrested or incomplete development of mind*" may be of two kinds – (i) "*severe abnormality*" when the state of the patient is such as to include "subnormality of intelligence and is of such a nature or degree that the patient is incapable of living an independent life or guarding himself against serious exploitation"; (ii) "*subnormality*" when the state is one "(not amounting to severe subnormality) which includes subnormality of intelligence and is of a nature or degree which requires or is susceptible to medical treatment or other special care or training of the patient". "*Psychopathic disorder*" means "a persistent disorder or disability of mind (whether or not including subnormality of intelligence) which results in abnormally aggressive or seriously irresponsible conduct on the part of the patient, and requires or is susceptible to medical treatment".

The special class being thus defined, we may turn to the provisions concerning care and treatment.

The Act is concerned with regulating the compulsory admission to hospitals of mentally disordered people and providing compulsory guardianship for them; but it must be noted that it also envisages that a "patient" (*i.e.* a person "suffering or appearing to be suffering, from mental disorder") may wish to be admitted to hospital voluntarily and informally, and it places no obstacle in the way of his obtaining such admission.

Compulsory admission may be required for two purposes: for observation or for treatment. Whichever of these two reasons for admission is in view the admission must be founded upon an application to the hospital managers by the patient's nearest relative or by a mental welfare officer of a local health authority, and this application must be supported by written recommendations of two medical practitioners made in specified form.

Where a patient has been admitted for observation he must usually be discharged from hospital after twenty-eight days of admission unless some further application or order has been made within that time. Where the admission is for treatment the patient may be detained for one year, but authority for his detention may then be renewed for a further year and thereafter for two-year periods. No one may, however, by application be compulsorily admitted for treatment as a subnormal or psychopathic patient after he has attained the age of twenty-one, and all patients in these two categories admitted for treatment by application must be released upon reaching the age of twenty-five; though this latter rule is subject to certain safeguards.

The Act sets up *Area Mental Health Review Tribunals*, and it is the main function of these tribunals – consisting of lawyers, doctors and certain other people – to protect the liberty of the subject by considering applications by the patient and others, such as his nearest relative, for his discharge. Subject to certain limitations these applications may be made at any time during the patient's detention.

It is now generally believed that it is in the best interests of the mentally infirm that they should be permitted, as much as possible, to live in the community like other people; consequently compulsory admission to hospital is a last resort. In many cases the mentally afflicted may reasonably be left free to mix with their fellows provided that they seek the help and advice which is now available to them; as through the services of mental welfare officers. But there are intermediate cases in which neither hospital treatment nor entire freedom are indicated. For these cases the Act provides machinery for *compulsory guardianship*.

The implementation of the provisions of the M.H.A. as to compulsory guardianship, like the provisions as to hospital detention, is under the ultimate control of the Department of Health, but in practice future responsibility in relation to guardianship falls upon local health authorities. These authorities have the duty, through their appropriate officers, of considering applications in respect of people suffering from mental illness or severe subnormality or in respect of people under twenty-one who are suffering from any form of mental illness. The formalities governing such applications are in most respects similar to those which govern applications for hospital admission. The effect of successful application for guardianship is that the patient will be placed by the local health authority under the supervision of a guardian who must then act towards him as though he were his father and the patient himself were under fourteen years of age. In most respects the rules governing renewal of and discharge from guardianship are similar to the hospital treatment rules appertaining to the same matters, and mental health review tribunals also exercise powers of review over guardianship.

Another way in which compulsory admission and compulsory guardianship may be brought about is by *court order*. The Crown Court and, within limits, magistrates' courts may, in lieu of sentencing accused persons make "hospital orders" or "guardianship orders" in respect of them, if they are satisfied upon specified medical evidence that they are mentally disordered. In general the rules governing the duration of treatment or guardianship thus imposed are similar to the rules relating to treatment or guardianship arising as the result of application, and resort may be had to mental health tribunals. But it is important to note that court orders are not confined in the case of subnormal or psychopathic people to those under twenty-one, nor is there any upper limit to the age at which they may be imposed in such cases.

The Crown Court also possesses another special power: where it is satisfied that it is necessary for the protection of the public so to do it may, upon making a hospital order, make a further order in respect of an *offender* containing special statutory restrictions; and in particular restricting the time of his discharge either to such time as may be ordered or without limit as to time. The general effect of these orders is that the patient will remain in hospital detention until the specified time or indefinitely and applications for discharge, and the ordinary powers of review of mental health tribunals, are excluded. But where the court thus authorizes this special kind of detention, power of review and discharge passes to the Home Secretary who may exercise his discretion irrespective of the court's directions; and there is special machinery by which he may be forced to consider the advice of a mental health tribunal. Magistrates' courts have no power to impose restrictions, but they are authorized to commit offenders found to be suffering from mental disorder to the Crown Court which may then impose restrictions.

It must also be added that where, upon a plea of insanity (see below, p. 156), a jury find that an accused person was insane at the time when he committed the crime alleged he must be ordered by the court to be detained during Her Majesty's pleasure. It is then the duty of the Home Secretary to direct that he be detained in a hospital. Under the M.H.A. this direction has similar effect to a hospital order restricting discharge without limitation of time. The same applies in the case of a like direction made by the Home Secretary in respect of a person who is found unfit to plead on account of insanity at the time of trial.

We now come to the last matter that needs mention. Mentally disordered people are sometimes *incapable of managing their own property and affairs* whether or no their condition is such that they need special care and treatment. In such cases the law must provide a method by which other people can do these things on their behalf. This is the second main concern of the M.H.A.

The Act reconstituted the *Court of Protection* which now consists of a master, a deputy master and other officers. It is the business of this court to supervise control over the property and affairs of mentally disordered people who have been found after consideration of medical evidence to be incapable of managing these things for themselves. (It will be noted that this court is in fact rather an administrative body than a "court" in the strict modern sense.) In practice, under the powers of the Act, the court delegates the actual control exercisable over the patient's property, business dealings, and other affairs, to a person called a "receiver" who may be a near relative of the patient. The receiver then acts as the patient's agent under the general direction of the court.

There are, however, certain powers of supervision which can only be exercised by special judges of the Chancery Division; these include such important matters as authorizing proceedings for divorce or judicial separation on the patient's behalf and the power (provided that the patient is adult) to authorize someone to make a will for him where there is reason to believe that he is incapable of making one for himself. Such wills must be in special form and their validity is subject to special rules (Administration of Justice Act 1969, Part III). Moreover in theory the M.H.A. places ultimate responsibility for the control of the patient's property and affairs upon the Lord Chancellor, although the only function that he is in practice required to perform is that of exercising the right of patronage on behalf of patients who happen to be patrons of ecclesiastical benefices.

PART II
PUBLIC LAW

SUMMARY OF PART II

CHAPTER 5

THE LAW OF THE CONSTITUTION

Constitutional law defines the principal organs of government and determines their relationship to one another and to the individual. It thus embraces a wide field which can only be outlined here in bare essentials. We will consider it under six heads: (1) The development of the constitution; (2) The nature of the constitution; (3) The conventions of the constitution; (4) Europe and the future; (5) The institutions of government; (6) The individual and the State.

1 THE DEVELOPMENT OF THE CONSTITUTION

The Norman and Plantagenet kings ruled through the *Curia Regis* (the "King's Council"); this was the grand council of the realm consisting of the great feudal vassals, the earls, the bishops and the barons. This Council (which is today represented in Parliament by the House of Lords) was in origin the king's "feudal" court, though this description is misleading if one thinks of it as a "court" in the modern sense; for it was not purely a judicial institution, but a governing body for the nation in which any kind of business might be transacted; though it should be added in deference to modern historical research that those meetings of the Great Council which were first given the name of "Parliaments" were probably principally meetings of a judicial nature. In the course of time a momentous development occurred. The king's ordinary revenues were "feudal" revenues (below, p. 327) which his vassals were bound to pay him as such, but he often needed more money than these revenues sufficed to supply. When he thus required "extraordinary" revenue it was clearly impolitic to attempt to raise it without obtaining some semblance of assent from the nation as a whole, upon whom the burden of payment fell. For this reason it slowly became customary for the king to summon to his great assemblies, in addition to the magnates of the realm, representatives of the shires and boroughs of England. The object of these meetings then became, on the king's part, to obtain money, on the part of the representatives of the nation (the "Commons") who now attended, to obtain redress of grievances in the form of legislation. The king, with the consent of the magnates, granted rights and liberties to his people by means of solemn enactments; in return the Commons granted him the money he needed. Thus gradually *Parliament* as we know it emerged, consisting of Queen, Lords and Commons. But it must not be imagined that this development was a sudden one; for the "Model Parliament" (1295) of Edward I is now regarded by historians as a myth and it is thought that Parliament did not begin to emerge in something akin to its modern form until the latter part of the fourteenth century.

The rise of Parliament brought about a fundamental change in the constitution, for in the course of time it became settled that Parliament was the sole "sovereign" Legislature (see above, p. 8). But this change was not effected quickly or without a struggle. The kings did not lightly relinquish their powers. Indeed, it was not until after the physical victory of the Parliamentarians over the king in the civil war of the seventeenth century that the royal claim to legislate without Parliament was dropped. With the flight of James II and the Glorious Revolution (1688) which set William and Mary upon the throne, Parliament finally triumphed and the king lost the power to legislate alone in England.

The victory of Parliament did not, however, mean that the sovereign had lost *all* power. If it was for Parliament (or rather the "King in Parliament", for the Legislature is a trinity of Monarch, Lords and Commons) to legislate and for the courts to adjudicate, someone still had to *govern*, and that someone was clearly the king, acting through his Ministers. It was only in the course of the eighteenth and early nineteenth centuries that the king lost this, the last of his powers and the English monarchy became a "constitutional" one in which the monarch, though nominally head of the State, is shorn of most *actual* power.

We have seen (above, Chapter 2) that the Act of 1641 destroyed the judicial functions of the Council within the realm. Nevertheless, the Council (by then the "Privy Council") continued to exist for the purpose of advising the king on matters of government. By the Restoration (1660) this body had, however, become too large to be an effective advisory body; so Charles II selected a small group of able men to advise him in matters of policy and to carry on the business of government: the famous "Cabal" typifies this new institution. These men were both in theory and in practice the king's servants and so, to the close of the eighteenth century, the situation remained. But it was soon apparent that no government could rule unless it enjoyed the confidence of Parliament which, as we have seen, had already become the ultimate and sovereign source of power. Thus it became the normal practice for these advisers – the king's Ministers – to be members of one or other House of Parliament, and, as such, to be responsible to Parliament for the administration of the Departments of State, which many of them controlled, and for the policies pursued by the government. Nevertheless, at first the monarch continued to be in fact, as well as in name, head of this group of ministers (which soon came to be called the "*Cabinet*": a name derived from the fact that it customarily met in a small room) and hence of the Executive. But the whole course of constitutional development was against the monarch's retaining the actual power of governing in any of its aspects. In the first place, due to the historical accident that the first two Georges were foreign to England and had little taste for politics, they absented themselves from Cabinet meetings (a convention that has been followed by subsequent monarchs). In the second place – and more important – probably as much as the result of the new wealth born of the Industrial Revolution as from any other cause, the increased political awareness of the nation as a whole and, after the great Reform Act of 1832, the widening of the electorate – it became inevitable that the country should be governed by its elected representatives rather than by an hereditary king. Even in the eighteenth century George III's surreptitious attempts at personal government were an anachronism. Thus in due course, especially under the impetus of the growth of the modern party system, the actual work of government came to be done by the king's ministers, and the monarch lost all actual power and responsibility for the control of the nation's affairs.

2 THE NATURE OF THE CONSTITUTION

Since the rules of a constitution are laws of fundamental importance, it is not surprising that they are often embodied in a single written document. Thus, for example, the Constitution of the United States was reduced to writing in 1787 and the document which comprises it (as subsequently amended) lays down the fundamental law of America today. Further the U.S. Constitution, like many other written constitutions, cannot be altered easily; a constitutional amendment can only be carried if a very substantial majority, both in Congress and in the individual States, approve it.

Our Constitution is just as important to us as the U.S. Constitution is to the Americans. Nevertheless, it is not "written"; that is to say, it has never been wholly reduced to writing. Further, since Parliament is "sovereign" it can, without any special procedure, and by simple Act, alter any law at any time, however fundamental it may seem to be.

Although, therefore, our courts have always been astute to safeguard the rights of the subject and although certain legal remedies, such as *Habeas Corpus*, are designed to protect him, yet, under our Constitution, there are no guaranteed rights similar to the fundamental liberties safeguarded by the U.S. Constitution.

The statement that our Constitution is not "written" does not mean that we possess no important constitutional documents; it merely means that the Constitution is not embodied in any single document, or series of documents, containing our essential constitutional laws. Thus we have many enactments which either have been or still are, of great importance. One need only cite as examples Magna Carta (1215), the Bill of Rights (1688) – which sets out the principal rights gained by Parliament and the nation as the result of the seventeenth century constitutional struggles – the Act of Settlement (1700), and the Parliament Acts 1911 and 1949.

3   THE CONVENTIONS OF THE CONSTITUTION

Many constitutional rules, such for example as the provisions of the Act of Settlement (below), are "laws" in the ordinary sense, that is to say, they will be recognized and enforced by the courts. But there are certain other rules which govern the working of the Constitution, which are not laws in this sense. They are called "*conventions*". They arise from usage, or agreement, tacit or express, and they are adhered to, once they have developed, not because the courts will enforce them, but because political expedience and respect for tradition demand their observance.

Many of the rules which govern the functioning of the central government and the relationship of the Executive to the Legislature are thus conventional. The conventions relating to Ministerial Responsibility and certain other conventions, will be mentioned below; here it must suffice to give only a few general examples.

The Cabinet came into being purely by convention: no statute created it. The kings' practice of abstaining from attending Cabinet meetings started, as we have seen, as an historical accident and became a convention; no monarch would now claim the right to attend. By convention, when it becomes necessary to form a new Government, the monarch must invite the leader of the party or group commanding a majority in the House of Commons to form it; the Queen will not in practice invite any other person, though "legally" she could do so. The person so invited will become *Prime Minister* of the new Government; this, the most important of all political offices, grew up entirely by convention, and it was not until the present century that it received recognition in any statute. The Queen *could* refuse her assent to an Act of Parliament, but there is now a long established convention that she will not do so.

By convention, a Ministry which is defeated on a major issue in the House of Commons should (though whether in fact a modern government *will* is quite another question) either resign or advise the Queen to grant a dissolution. If it advises a dissolution and is then defeated at the ensuing general election it should, by convention, resign either at once or upon its first defeat in the House of Commons. By convention Parliament must be summoned at least once a year, though *legally* it need only meet once in three years (Meeting of Parliament Act 1694 – generally known as the "Triennial Act"); this convention is, as we have seen, grounded firmly upon political expedience; for Parliament alone can grant the Government the funds it requires annually for the public administration. Finally, although it is not usually treated in works on constitutional law as such, the fact that the courts treat themselves as bound to apply Acts of Parliament is conventional, and so is the doctrine of judicial precedent itself.

Beside conventions, there are certain other important constitutional rules which are not "laws" in the sense that the courts will enforce them. These are the rules which regulate the internal affairs of Parliament, such as the rules governing the procedure of legislation and the conduct of debates. Many, but not all, of these "customs" of Parliament are now contained in the Standing Orders of the two Houses.

4   EUROPE AND THE FUTURE

In this part we shall consider the impact of the European Communities Act 1972 (hereafter "E.C.A.") and its likely effect on future constitutional development. We shall also mention the possibility of change raised by the Report of the Royal Commission on the Constitution.

The European Communities and the Constitution

The coming into force of the E.C.A. started a radical new departure in our constitutional affairs. Without attempting to embark upon the specialized subject of European "community" law we must try to give some indication of the scope of this change.

Section 1 of the E.C.A. defines the European "Communities". They are: (i) *The European Economic Community* (EEC). This was established by the Treaty of Rome (1957). Its far-reaching "task" (EEC Treaty, arts. 2 and 3) is, *inter alia*, "the establishing (of) a *common market* and *progressively* approximating the economic policies of member states". Its "activities" include, *inter alia*, the elimination of customs duties, the establishment of a common customs tariff, the abolition of obstacles to freedom of movement within the Community for persons, services and capital, common agricultural and transport policies, the ensuring that competition within the common market is not "distorted" and "*the approximation of the law of Member States to the extent required for the proper functioning of the common market*". (*ii*) *The European Coal and Steel Community* (ECSC). This was established by the Treaty of Paris (1951). Its objects are to set up a common market in coal and steel and to harmonize the development of those industries among the member states. (*iii*) *The European Atomic Energy Community* (Euratom). This was established by a second Treaty of Rome (1957). Its main object is to foster the co-ordinated growth of nuclear industries throughout the Community.

By s. 2 (1) of the E.C.A. accession to the Treaties was signified. The effect of this is that the basic law contained in the Treaties themselves becomes a part of the law of the United Kingdom by what has been styled "self-enforcement". Further, by s. 2 (1) the laws made or to be made by the law-making agencies of the Communities – the *Council of Ministers* and the *Commission* – are also adopted or to be adopted. There are two main types of the latter: they may either be "regulations" or "directives". It used to be thought that this difference of *form* reflected a difference of effect: that *regulations*, like the "self-enforcing" provisions of the Treaties, were directly applicable within member states, and that *directives* could only become law within those states when implemented by local legislation. In *Van Duyn* v. *Home Office (No. 2)*, [1975] 3 All E.R. 190, however, the Court of Justice of the European Communities held that, whatever it is expressed to be, an enactment of the law-making agencies of the Communities which is in fact by its very nature capable, without further clarification, of becoming law within member states is directly enforceable.

Section 2 (2) of the E.C.A., which is concerned with the *methods* of implementing such community legislation as does require implementation, prescribes that it may be brought into force within the United Kingdom by *Orders in Council* or by *departmental regulations*. This subordinate legislation is, however, subject to parliamentary control and to certain limitations contained in Schedule 2 of the Act. Control is secured by requiring that they must (by positive or negative procedure) be laid before Parliament (see below, p. 126). The limits include, *inter alia*, a ban upon the imposition of taxation and upon the creation of major criminal offences. Objects such as these are thus reserved for Parliament itself. Further, in order to ensure conformity with community law, s. 2 (4) enables such subordinate legislation (subject to similar safeguards) to amend existing or future Acts of Parliament themselves. As we have seen questions of interpretation of community law are ultimately reserved (E.C.A., s. 3) for the European Court (Luxembourg).

The remaining sections of the E.C.A. are concerned with detailed provisions intended to bring United Kingdom law into line with the laws of the Communities which were already in force at the time of its enactment. It has, for example, been noted (above, p. 78) that s. 9 made certain changes in company law to that end.

The effect of this legislation is thus to bring us *under the laws of the Communities within the ambit of the Treaties* and we are now thus partially governed by a new form of law: "community" law. As a people we thus look two ways: for the most part we are at present governed, as we always have been, by common law and statute; but in matters, such as the economic ordering of the community of member states, within the scope of the Treaties we fall, whether directly or indirectly, under the general law of the Communities. Present indications are that the field of the latter is likely to increase at the expense of the former.

So the question now arises "What of parliamentary sovereignty?" Puristically, technically and theoretically the form of the E.C.A. in fact preserves it: for the Act, in the exercise of the supreme power of Parliament, *makes* community law, *our* law. Realistically, and practically, however, we now have two "sovereigns" situated at Westminster and Brussels respectively: just as the peoples of the United States look both to state law and to "federal law". Realistically therefore the traditional view of parliamentary sovereignty must be modified. And this poses the further question, "Given that (as the recent referendum suggests) the future trend is likely to be towards greater integration with the Communities, would it be possible to reverse the process and return to isolation from Europe?" Despite certain theoretical objections, this would in fact be both politically and legally possible. There is no bond with the Communities which politically we could not break, and it is to be noted that no attempt was made in the E.C.A. to limit the freedom of future parliaments – indeed, any such attempt would be futile, since present laws and present politicians have neither rights nor powers to bind their successors.

One further comment is needed. The accession effected by the E.C.A. is *unique*. As the Court of Appeal has stressed, the fact that, for example, we are party to the European Convention for the Protection of Human Rights and Fundamental Freedoms does not signify that the rights enshrined in that Convention are a part of the law of England so that a statute which made provisions repugnant to those rights would be invalid. They are only binding rights in the sense that signatory States will be in breach of the Convention if they permit anything which derogates from them. It is otherwise with community law; as long as we

continue to accede to it, it is a "higher" law than our municipal law
which our courts must obey in preference to the latter.

The Royal Commission on the Constitution

The Royal Commission which was set up in 1969 reported in 1973 (1973
Cmnd. s. 460). Its terms of reference were "to consider, having regard
to developments in local government organization and in the administrative and other relationships between the various parts of the United
Kingdom! and to the interests of the prosperity and good government
of our people under the Crown, whether any changes are desirable in
those functions or otherwise in present constitutional relationships". The
key to the Commission's work is, perhaps, to be found in their assertion
that the vast increase in the scope, scale and complexity of government
business, and in the manpower and other resources devoted to it, has
had a cumulative effect on people's lives, and is an underlying factor
in complaints about the working of the present system of government.

The Report is in two volumes; volume I contains the majority recommendations, and volume II is a minority Report. The whole is too long,
inconclusive, rambling and contradictory to summarize, but the important point is that both the majority and the minority Reports are in
favour, in one form or another (whether legislative, executive, economic
or all three) of *devolution* of governmental powers: particularly to Scotland and Wales. Regional devolution, of one kind or another, is also
recommended in England itself. One sees, perhaps with fear and trem-
bling, the future bringing into being an intermediate series of governmental institutions between Parliament and the already overweighty
local authorities. It may be feared, too, that the ultimate outcome of
the Report may be the adoption – unnecessarily as some may think –
of some complex and cumbersome form of federalism: which would
mean that we should face three ways, to the laws of a Region, to the
laws of the United Kingdom and to the laws of the Communities. It
might have been hoped that this Report might (apart from the special
cases of Scotland and Wales) have been assigned to oblivion: but at the
time of writing it is understood that a government White Paper on the
subject is impending. There seems to be no end to the appetite for
change.

5 THE INSTITUTIONS OF GOVERNMENT

The Judiciary has already been described in Chapter 2. The remaining
institutions with which we must now deal are therefore the Monarchy,
the Legislature and the Executive.

A   The Monarchy

Ours is now, as has been seen, a "constitutional" or "limited" monarchy. The Queen and the Crown (which represents not only the Queen herself, but also her Government) are symbolic of the whole might and unity of the State; but, for all practical purposes, the Queen is herself powerless. The business of government which is carried on in her name is done by her Ministers. Her Majesty only acts upon the "advice" of her Ministers and they are, as we shall see, responsible to Parliament for their acts.

The monarch's duties are thus now for the most part ceremonial, though they are innumerable: the Queen makes State visits abroad, signs endless documents, confers honours, receives foreign ambassadors, and performs many other duties. Individual monarchs may, too, exercise considerable *personal* influence in State affairs, for the Prime Minister is by convention bound to report the conclusions of Cabinet meetings to the Sovereign.

The succession to the throne is regulated by the Act of Settlement (1700). By that Act the crown was vested in Princess Sophia (Electress of Hanover – grand-daughter of James I) "and the heirs of her body, being Protestants". The rules governing this descent are, roughly, the old rules which used to govern descent to real property (below, p. 448) and the effect of this is in particular that the throne passes to the eldest son to the exclusion of older daughters. It is, however, to be noted that Roman Catholics, and those who marry Roman Catholics are barred from the succession. Further when, as at the time of the accession of our present Queen, there are two or more surviving females *only*, of equal degree, the eldest succeeds in preference to the younger.

By the Royal Marriages Act 1772 no descendant of George II may as a general rule (unless he be the issue of a princess married into a foreign family) marry without the Sovereign's formal assent.

The Regency Acts 1937 to 1953 make special provisions to cover the event of minority or incapacity. A monarch is deemed to attain majority at eighteen years of age. Should a monarch under this age succeed to the throne, then the person next entitled in line of succession who has attained the age of twenty-one will become *Regent*.

The Queen and the Royal Family are provided with annual payments to cover their personal expenses and the expenses of the Royal Household are defrayed by means of the "Civil List", a permanent charge upon the Consolidated Fund. A Civil List Act is passed at the beginning of each reign.

The Queen has private property, *e.g.* the Sandringham Estate, but "Crown lands" are not the Queen's private property; they belong to the Crown in its *public* capacity, *i.e.* to the State. In her private capacity the Queen cannot be sued in tort, though it seems that it may still be possible, as a matter of grace, for Her Majesty to consent to be sued in respect of contractual or property claims by an antiquated process known as Petition of Right procedure.

B   The Legislature

It has already been remarked that the "sovereign" Legislature is a trinity, composed of Queen, Lords and Commons. Since the monarchy has been discussed above, and it has been pointed out that the royal assent to an Act of Parliament is by convention never refused, it now remains to describe the nature and functions of Parliament as a whole. This topic will be considered under three heads: (1) The Meetings of Parliament, (2) The Composition of Parliament, (3) The Functions of Parliament, (4) The Machinery of Legislation.

THE MEETINGS OF PARLIAMENT

The period between the time when Parliament is summoned and its termination by dissolution or by lapse of time is called "*a* parliament". Parliaments are summoned and dissolved by Royal Proclamation. By convention the Queen will not dissolve Parliament upon her own initiative but will act upon the advice of the Prime Minister. In the unlikely event of a Prime Minister not seeking a dissolution before the full period has expired, a parliament will "die" when it has been in existence for five years from the date of its summoning; for the Parliament Act 1911 provides that a parliament shall not endure for more than five years. This period is, however, sometimes extended in emergencies by special Act, as in the Second World War.

Each parliament is divided into *sessions*; one or more a year. The Queen *summons* Parliament at the beginning of a session and *prorogues* it at the end. A session is thus a formal thing, and is something like a little parliament in itself; public bills in progress at the end of a session have to be introduced *anew* when the next session begins.

Prorogation affects both Houses, but either House may *adjourn* of its own motion during a session. There may thus be adjournments from day to day, or for a week, or for a month or more.

THE COMPOSITION OF PARLIAMENT

The two Houses of Parliament are the House of Lords and the House of Commons.

The members of the *House of Lords* are the Lords Spiritual and Temporal. The Lord Chancellor presides at meetings of the House. The Lords Spiritual are the two Archbishops, the Bishops of London, Durham and Winchester, and twenty-one other diocesan bishops, who are entitled to seats according to seniority of appointment. The Lords Temporal comprise the peers and peeresses in their own right of the United Kingdom and Scotland and the Law Lords (as to the latter, see above, p. 37). The Temporal Peerage is either *hereditary* or for *life*. Formerly only United Kingdom peers were entitled as such to an hereditary seat. Scottish and Irish peers being elected from the respective hereditary peerages upon a representative basis only. The representation of Irish peers has, however, now lapsed and by the Peerage Act 1963 all Scottish peers are accorded seats.

Life peerages came into being under the provisions of the Life Peerages Act 1958. That Act empowered Her Majesty to confer *life* peerages by letters patent; and appointment to a life peerage carries with it a right to attend the House of Lords and to sit and vote therein. A further important change was also made by ss. 1–3 of the Peerage Act 1963. Before that Act an hereditary peer could not disclaim his title, but he may now do so for the period of his own life, provided that he disclaims within 12 months of succeeding to the title. Disclaimer once made is irrevocable and another hereditary peerage may not later be conferred, though a life peerage may. The same rules apply to peeresses in their own right, so that by disclaimer peers and peeresses may now make themselves eligible for the Commons, being treated as commoners in every respect. During the life of a disclaimant the title is not accelerated so as to let in the next in line, but is in abeyance.

The *House of Commons* is composed of Members of Parliament who are the elected representatives of the nation. Electoral law forms a large and complicated branch of law which cannot be described here. Voting has, since the Ballot Act 1872, been by secret ballot. All adults (*i.e.* since the coming into operation of the Representation of the People Act 1969, s. 1, everyone aged *eighteen* or more), not subject to special disqualification, now possess the right to vote; but they can only exercise it if they are registered in an electoral register. The right to be registered depends, under the provisions of the Electoral Registers Act 1953, upon residence in a particular constituency upon a "qualifying" date (October 10th). Much of the machinery governing elections is to be found in the Representation of the People Act 1949 as amended by later Acts.

Most British subjects are now eligible for election to the House of Commons as Members of Parliament provided they have attained the age of twenty-one. The following classes of people amongst others, are however not eligible. (*a*) Peers, and peeresses in their own right. (*b*) Clergy of the Established Churches of England and Scotland, Roman

Catholic clergy and all episcopally ordained priests and deacons. (*c*) Full-time judges of the superior and inferior courts, including some judges of courts of special jurisdiction, such as the Chief National Insurance Commissioner. J.P.s do not come within this category. (*d*) Members of the regular armed forces of the Crown. (*e*) Convicted offenders detained in penal institutions (Representation of the People Act 1969, s. 4). (*f*) Members of the Civil Service. This is of vital importance: the essence of the Civil Service is that it is a non-political and permanent institution. Political Heads of Departments change as Governments come and go, but the civil servants who staff the Departments act as permanent advisers to all Governments, whatever their political colour.

THE FUNCTIONS OF PARLIAMENT

Parliament still retains its two original functions. In the first place, it is still generally true to say that no public money may be expended without the sanction of Parliament. In the second place, the most conspicuous of its functions is legislation.

Besides these two functions, modern parliaments have a third. They are, in theory, the "watch-dogs" of the nation, having the power and the duty of controlling the Government. This comes about as the result of the principle of "*Responsible Government*". The Government must, according to this principle, command a majority in the House of Commons and, as we have just seen, any Government which is outvoted on a major issue should resign or seek a dissolution. Hence, in theory, the Government can only continue in office as long as it retains the good-will of the House. In theory, therefore, the House is master of the Government, especially since there is a constitutionally recognized Opposition Party ready to take advantage of its mistakes. In modern practice, however, this ultimate power of control is seldom exercised. The reason for this is that modern Governments are usually able to retain their majority, once they have gained it, by means of their party organization. The Government usually represents a single party, and members will seldom vote against it – both for reasons of loyalty and because they fear a general election which will certainly put them to expense and may lose them their seats.

Parliament is thus seldom able to exercise its power of control over the Government directly, but it does exercise it indirectly in at least two ways. First, a salutary check is kept upon the doings of Ministers and Departments during the daily "question time" in the House of Commons: an unsatisfactory answer, given due publicity in the Press, may have a material effect upon the popularity of a Government. Secondly, debates, whether in the Commons or in the Lords, may show weaknesses in the administration. Debates are published – in particular in *Hansard's*

Reports – and their substance is often broadcast to the nation; it is through debates that the electorate appraises political personalities and Governments, and modern Governments generally are sensitive to feeling in the constituencies.

THE MACHINERY OF LEGISLATION

It has been explained that, in order to become law, Acts of Parliament require the threefold blessing of Queen, Lords and Commons. It has also been explained that the Royal Assent is now a formal matter, being signified by Letters Patent under the Great Seal signed by Her Majesty and pronounced either in the House of Lords in the presence of the Commons or separately in either House.

Until it has received the Royal Assent an inchoate Act is called a *"bill"*. Bills are divided into "clauses", which subsequently become "sections" in the Acts of which they form the basis. Most bills may be introduced in either House, but bills seeking to impose a charge upon the public revenue *must* be introduced in the Commons upon the responsibility of the Government.

Bills fall into two main categories, *"Public"* bills (which deal with matters of public importance) and *"Private"*, or *"Local"* and *"Personal"* bills (which deal with local matters or matters affecting individuals). The latter must not be confused with a third category, *"Private Members'"* bills, *i.e.* bills, whether Public or Private, which are introduced by ordinary members. Due to pressure of business in recent times, and to the control which the Government exercises over parliamentary time, bills of this third class now seldom succeed in passing into law unless they are adopted by the Government and accorded government time (which does sometimes happen). Since there is no substantial difference in procedure between these bills and public bills they merit no separate discussion.

Public bills may be subdivided into "ordinary" Public bills and *"money bills"*. The following, in brief outline, is the procedure for passing an ordinary Public bill through the Commons. Upon its introduction the bill receives a *formal* "first reading". It is then printed. A "second reading" follows: this raises a debate upon the general merits, but no specific amendments may be moved. After the second reading the bill reaches the "committee" stage, that is to say, it is referred to one of two classes of committees for detailed discussion and amendment. The two classes are – (*a*) *Standing Committees*. These are appointed at the beginning of each session by the Committee of Selection. Formerly there could only be five of them, but this limitation has now been abandoned. Each must consist of at least twenty members, but the Committee of Selection may add as many as an extra thirty for the consideration of a particular bill. The Committee for Scottish Bills consists of all the Scottish members and not less than ten, nor more than fifteen, other members. (*b*) *Committees of the Whole House.* Important legislation is referred to the House as a whole, sitting as a Committee. When the House "goes into Committee" the Speaker, the normal chairman of the House, vacates the Chair and an official called the Chairman of Committees (the Chairman of "Ways and Means"), or his Deputy, takes the Speaker's place. Since 1967, non-controversial bills may go straight into Committee for their second reading and report stage (see below), if ten days' notice has been given and twenty or more members do not rise to object.

After the "committee" stage the bill is "reported" to the House ("report" stage). The House reconsiders it, and may debate any amendments that have been made, or new clauses that have been inserted in committee; where necessary it may also return it to the committee for further consideration. After the report stage the bill is "read" for a third time. During the debate on the third reading only *verbal* alterations are allowed to be proposed.

Once the third reading has been completed the bill is ready to be passed to the House of Lords. Assuming that the Lords do not reject it, it passes through stages in the Upper House similar to the stages just described. If the Lords decide that amendments are required it is returned to the Commons for their concurrence in the proposed amendments.

Formerly the Lords had a general power to reject bills sent to them by the Commons, and thus to prevent them from being submitted for the royal assent and becoming law. This general power of rejection is now severely limited by the important provisions of the Parliament Act 1911, as amended by the Parliament Act 1949. These Acts give effect to the ever-growing constitutional principle that, as between the two Houses, the House of Commons, which represents the electorate, is the senior partner.

The Act of 1911 provides that any Public bill that has passed the Commons, and that has been *certified by the Speaker* as a "money" bill (*i.e.* a bill proposing financial measures) must be passed by the Lords *without amendment* within *one month* of the time when it is received by the Lords. If the Lords fail to pass such a bill without amendment within this period of time it may receive the royal assent and become law without their concurrence. For these provisions to operate the bill must not, however, be submitted to the Lords less than a month before the end of a session.

The Act of 1949 (amending similar provisions of the earlier Act) provides that, subject to an exception to be noted immediately, if *any* Public bill is passed by the Commons in two successive sessions (whether or not they are sessions of the same Parliament) and is rejected by the Lords in each session, it may be presented for the royal assent without the concurrence of the Lords. It is, however, provided that this result will only follow if *one year* has elapsed between the second reading of the bill in the Commons in the first session and the third reading in the second session. The bill must, moreover, be submitted to the Lords at least one month before the end of each of the two sessions. The Lords can therefore delay the passage of a Public bill (other than a money bill) for a maximum period of one year, but they can do no more. The one exception to this rule, contained in the 1911 Act and left unamended in the 1949 Act, relates to bills designed to extend the maximum duration of Parliament – which is fixed, as was explained above, at five years, by the 1911 Act: the Lords still have an absolute discretion to reject bills of this nature, and also Private bills.

In modern times Private bills have usually taken the form of enactments granting special powers to local authorities or other public undertakings. For example, Private Acts are often invoked by local authorities to make further provision for "the health, improvement, local government and finances" in their areas. Various stringent requirements have to be satisfied before a Private bill can be laid before Parliament, *e.g.* its purposes have to be advertised, and various plans and other documents have to be deposited in Parliament. Moreover, though Private bill procedure is similar in many respects to Public bill procedure, Private bills are allocated to special small committees, and these committees (unlike committees on Public bills) conduct an inquiry into the merits of the bill rather in the nature of a *judicial* inquiry. Both the promoters and the opposers of the bill may appear before the committee, and they will usually be represented by counsel.

C   The Executive

It is proposed, under this head, first to describe the constituent parts of the central Executive, then to explain the sources and nature of executive powers, and finally to examine the ways in which their exercise may be reviewed.

THE COMPOSITION OF THE CENTRAL EXECUTIVE

The central Executive is traditionally divided into three main groups of institutions, the Privy Council, the Ministry, and the Departments of State: to these there must now be added a fourth class of institutions which may be termed "governmental agencies" for want of a preciser name.

(i)   *The Privy Council*

Historically the Privy Council is the last remaining vestige of the *Curia Regis* from which, as we have seen, all our central institutions, the Legislature, the Executive and the Judiciary, originally sprang. It is now substantially a formal body which gives legal sanction, by *Order in Council* or *Royal Proclamation* to Government policies. The source of the Council's authority is either the Prerogative (below) or powers delegated to it by Parliament.

The responsible head of the Privy Council is a Minister called the Lord President of the Council, but the Queen herself still attends its meetings (usually four or five members).

The office of Privy Councillor is now, in the main, honorary: Privy Councillorships are conferred in the honours lists, and the rank of Privy Councillor carries with it the right to use the title "Right Honourable", a courtesy title also accorded to peers – though peers are not necessarily Privy Councillors. Certain officials are always made Privy Councillors; these include all Cabinet Ministers and the Lords Justices of Appeal.

Though the Privy Council has thus become largely a formal body certain Committees of it – such as the Judicial Committee, which has already been mentioned – still have active functions: these Committees are, however, in practice, separate from the Privy Council itself.

(ii)   *The Ministry*

The "Ministry" is the Government of the day. The head of the Ministry is the Prime Minister. It has been explained that by convention he must normally be the leader of the political party which commands a majority in the House of Commons; and it may be regarded as a twentieth century convention that he must be a member of the House of Commons, as opposed to the House of Lords. As well as being Prime Minister – an office which, as we have seen, was until recently purely "conventional" – he also holds the sinecure office of First Lord of the Treasury.

Upon accepting office the Prime Minister's first duty is to form a Government; that is to say to select (normally from his own party) a suitable *Cabinet* and *Ministry*.

The *Cabinet* is the nucleus of the Government. It is usually composed of about twenty of the principal Ministers. Cabinet Ministers are, as we have seen, always Privy Councillors and as such they take to Her Majesty an oath of secrecy. That this oath is binding there is no doubt, but the recent case of *A.-G.* v. *Jonathan Cape, Ltd.*, [1975] 3 All E.R. 484 (the "*Crossman Diaries Case*") in which it was held that information about discussions at cabinet meetings ten years back could, in the circumstances, be published indicates that the rule which prohibits disclosure of such discussions does not rest upon the oath. Nor does it, it seems, rest upon what was formerly supposed to be a rule of absolute secrecy until, after thirty years, cabinet papers become publishable. But that it does rest upon the *confidentiality* which collective responsibility (see below) requires if discussion is to be uninhibited. This doctrine seems dangerous because until it is decided by a *court* that in a particular case confidence *does* demand non-disclosure, no publisher can be sure of his ground – and publication of cabinet materials thus becomes as dangerous as publication of matters alleged to be obscene. Perhaps censorship (unpopular in our busybody times) is really best and the rule of absolute silence was to be preferred. However this may be, the courts will certainly inhibit divulgence of any cabinet matter if its publication is against the public interest. All the major decisions of the Government are taken by the Cabinet, and all policy is ultimately directed by it. Much of its work is prepared by committees – whether "cabinet" committees, consisting of Ministers, or committees consisting of other high officials – and it is assisted in its work by a Cabinet Secretariat under the control of the Secretary of the Cabinet – a civil servant.

We have seen that in constitutional theory the Government is "responsible" to Parliament because no Government that fails to maintain a majority in the Commons may remain in office. It ought to resign if it is out-voted on a major issue, and it must resign if it finds itself placed in a minority upon a vote of censure. It will be explained shortly that individual Ministers are also "responsible". The principle of "responsibility", however, goes further than this because Cabinet "solidarity" has become an established convention. This means that the Cabinet makes its decisions *as a whole*; it is thus "*collectively*" responsible to Parliament and it must face Parliament with a united front. Every Minister, whether he be present or not at a Cabinet meeting when particular decisions are made, must accept and act upon the policy of the Cabinet as a whole. If, therefore, some Minister, who is informed of the Cabinet policy, expresses views upon some important matter contrary to the expressed views of the Cabinet, he ought, at least in strict constitutional theory, to resign; for since Ministers are *jointly* responsible they cannot be permitted to remain in office while professing separate and individual policies. It must, however, be admitted that in recent times there has been a growing tendency for Ministers to flout this important convention: indeed, in the *Crossman Diaries Case*, though he upheld the convention, Lord Widgery, C.J. remarked "I find overwhelming evidence that the doctrine of joint responsibility is generally understood and practised and equally strong evidence that it is on occasion ignored" – as in the disclosure of divided opinions at the time of the EEC referendum.

When the Prime Minister has selected his Cabinet, his next duty is to select the rest of his *Ministry*. Numerous Ministers have to be appointed who are not Cabinet Ministers (though some of the more important of them are now accorded honorific "Cabinet" rank). Most of these Ministers are the political heads of important Government Departments and they are, in normal times, members of on or other of the Houses of Parliament. As members of Parliament they are individually *responsible* to Parliament, both in the sense that they are deemed to speak and act for the Government on all matters of policy within the province of their duties, whether they have previous Cabinet authority or not, and in the sense that they must be prepared to answer for the acts of their departmental and other subordinates. "*Ministerial responsibility*" has, however, another, and independent meaning. There is an old maxim that the "King can do no wrong"; both for this reason and because the Queen is now a constitutional monarch who acts only through her Ministers, Ministers can be made *legally* responsible in person for any wrongful acts which they do in her name. In order to secure this responsibility, every executive act which is done on behalf of the Crown must be authenticated by a document, either countersigned by a particular Minister or Ministers, or bearing a seal or seals for the custody of which he, or they, are responsible.

The Cabinet and the other Ministers who are not members of the Cabinet (together with certain less important office holders, such as Parliamentary Secretaries and Under-Secretaries) compose the Ministry. But there is nothing static about the nomenclature or composition of Ministries. Ministries and their functions, Departments and their titles appear, disappear and merge bewilderingly from time to time, vary from Government to Government and change even during a single parliament. It must also be added that at present there is a marked tendency to confer the rank of Secretary of State upon senior ministers who are heads of large Departments.

It should be added that most Ministers are members of the Commons rather than of the Lords, and this is particularly true of the more important Ministers such as the Home Secretary. But necessarily some Ministers must be in the Lords; this is partly because there is a statutory limit (at present 95 under the Ministers of the Crown Act 1974) to the number of Ministers who may be in the Commons, and partly because every Government must have some responsible spokesmen in the Upper House.

(iii) *The Government Departments*

Most of the Ministers of the Crown are, as we have seen, the *political* heads of the more important Departments. The Departments themselves form the real executive organs of the central government; for they, with their staffs of permanent officials (civil servants), are responsible for implementing the policy of the Government. All the more important Departments are headed, subject to the general control of a Minister, who comes and goes with the rise and fall of his Ministry, by a senior civil servant, called a Permanent Secretary, who has a staff of civil servants.

Space forbids a discussion of the names and functions of the multifarious Departments; many of them, such as the Home Office, the Department of Education and Science, the Ministry of Defence and the Department of the Environment, are, in any case, known to everyone. It can only be remarked here that the members of their permanent staffs are "servants of the Crown"; this means that they may in legal theory be dismissed at any time by the Crown (*i.e.* by their superiors acting on behalf of the Crown); for the Crown cannot be bound by contracts it makes with *its servants*, and this position is not affected by the Crown Proceedings Act 1947 (below). But in practice, as opposed to theory, as might be expected, the position of civil servants is secure; for their terms and conditions of service are regulated by Orders in Council and Treasury Minutes, and in practice they will usually only be dismissed for gross misconduct or inefficiency.

One Department, the *Treasury*, does require mention because it is the most important of all. Before 1714 there was a Lord High Treasurer, but this office was then put into "commission", that is to say, its control was vested, not in one official, but in several – the "Board of Lords Commissioners of H.M. Treasury" (a body which in practice never meets). We have seen that the *Prime Minister* invariably holds the *sinecure* office of First Lord of the Treasury. The *Chancellor of the Exchequer* (Under Treasurer – the next senior member of the Board) is the real head of the Department; he is assisted by the *Chief Secretary to the Treasury* and the *Minister of State* (who are responsible for public expenditure) and also by the *Financial Secretary to the Treasury*, who deputizes for him in the House of Commons. Beside the Prime Minister and the Chancellor of the Exchequer, the "Board" consists of five "*Junior Lords*". The functions of the "Junior Lords" are primarily political and parliamentary, since they are the principal assistant government whips, responsible for ensuring party discipline in Parliament. The Chief Government Whip is the "*Parliamentary Secretary to the Treasury*" (a Minister).

Below these *political* officers comes the *Permanent Secretary to the Treasury*. He is a civil servant, and, although the political office holders are technically his superiors, he is in fact one of the most important members of the Executive. As *permanent* head of the Treasury, he is the head of the Civil Service.

The Treasury is the Finance Department of the State; subordinate only to Parliament, it controls the economy of the nation, for, as will be explained below, all other departmental "estimates" have to be submitted for Treasury approval before they are laid before Parliament. It is this power of the purse which makes the Treasury the most important of the Departments. Formerly the Treasury was also responsible for the civil service establishment; that is for the control and management of the staff of the Civil Service as a whole. These responsibilities, however, now lie with the *Civil Service Department* which is nominally headed by the Prime Minister (as Minister for the Civil Service) and in practice by the *Lord Privy Seal*. The *Civil Service Commission*, which has existed for well over a century, is now also a part of the Civil Service Department, but it continues to carry independent responsibility for civil service recruitment.

iv   *Governmental Agencies*

The central Departments are by no means the only organs of the Executive. For example the business of local government has for a long time been carried on by local authorities. But special mention must be made of certain bodies of comparatively recent origin which may be classified as "Governmental Agencies".

During the present century there has been an enormous increase in the degree of control exercised by the State over the life of the nation. This control has come to be exercised in four main directions. First, the State has taken upon itself the duty of producing and distributing certain basic commodities, such as coal. Secondly, it has undertaken certain essential public services, such as the supply of electricity, the maintenance of the major civil airways and of the railways, and the control of atomic energy. Thirdly, it has undertaken various national "welfare" services, such as the maintenance of hospitals under the national health service scheme. In the fourth place it has assumed control of the use, planning and development of the land itself.

All these new State services require to be organized, and the organization of any human activity calls for control by an institution of some sort. It might have been expected that the new duties would have been cast directly upon Ministers, and Departments, and, to some extent, they have; but, for various reasons, the Departments have not been called upon to share the main burden of them. For one thing, the work of the Departments were already overwhelming, and for another, the Departments are not entirely suitable for exercising the functions of, at any rate, the first two classes of services classified above; these require to be conducted with business acumen and managerial ability, rather than with purely administrative skill. Consequently, a plan has been adopted which is not without counterpart in other countries; the new powers have been vested in a series of State-owned or State-controlled agencies. The names of many of these have now become familiar. The following may be instanced as examples of bodies empowered to operate "services" which fall within the first two of the above-mentioned categories of recently acquired State powers – the Post Office, the National Coal Board, the British Railways Board, the British Airways Board and the United Kingdom Atomic Energy Authority. Examples of authorities empowered to operate services of the "welfare" category are the Regional Health Authorities and the Supplementary Benefits Commission. In the planning category there is the Countryside Commission.

The actual structures and constitutions of these and numerous other governmental agencies naturally vary but a few brief general remarks may be made, which apply to the majority of them.

(i) Most of these agencies are subject to the ultimate supervision and control of one or other of the Ministers of State. (ii) The appropriate Minister is usually responsible for nominating the chairman and members of each of the central Boards of control and management. (iii) Members of Parliament must generally *not* be appointed by the Boards. (iv) The staff of the Boards, and those who are employed by them, are not civil servants – thus the agencies are independent of the ordinary hierarchy of the central government. (v) The Minister concerned is in most cases responsible to Parliament for the general policies of the agency or agencies subject to his control. (vi) In many cases there are committees, or "advisory councils", appointed by the Minister, after consultation with appropriate interests. It is the duty of these councils, which are not staffed by full-time employees, to make reports to the Minister upon any matters falling within the scope of the agency's duties which may be of interest to the public or to any section of it, and upon which they are empowered by the statute setting up the agency to report. (vii) There is, in general, a discernible difference between the constitutions of the "welfare" agencies and the agencies which supply essential commodities and organize public utilities. The former are more closely connected with "policy" than the latter, which are, in a sense, State-owned business; consequently they tend to be subject to stricter government control.

THE SOURCES AND NATURE OF EXECUTIVE POWERS

(i)   *The Sources*

Executive power derives either from the Royal Prerogative or from enabling Acts of Parliament.

i   Prerogative Powers – In his famous work, the *Law of the Constitu-*

tion, Professor Dicey defined the prerogative as the "residue of discretionary or arbitrary authority, which at any given time is legally left in the hands of the Crown". It has been explained that until the Revolution the kings of England asserted claims to wide powers: they exercised these powers by right of the royal prerogative. Their claims were not by any means unfounded, because in every State there must be some ultimate and supreme repository of power; and, as has already been remarked, until the end of the seventeenth century in England, this repository was clearly the king. The Revolution Settlement established the principle that the supreme source of legislative power for the future was to be Parliament. Nevertheless Parliament is too large a body to do the work of day-to-day administration; and this was entrusted, as we have seen, first to the king and his ministers, then, with the development of the principle of constitutional monarchy, to the king's ministers and the central government. When this change had occurred some of the royal prerogatives – for the most part in the administrative field – continued to be exercised, either by the king, acting through and by the advice of, his ministers or by the king's ministers or the central government, acting upon behalf of the Crown. Some of them continue to be exercised today.

Prerogative powers are many and varied; a few instances only can therefore be given. (*a*) By right of the prerogative, the Queen summons, prorogues and dissolves Parliament. (*b*) Because criminal proceedings are conducted in the name of the Queen, and because crimes are wrongs against the State (the Crown), the Crown has two special prerogative rights in relation to prosecutions. First, there is the royal power of pardon. Pardons may be granted by the Queen, acting upon the advice of the Home Secretary. The Crown (in practice the Home Secretary) may also remit or reduce sentences. Secondly, the Attorney-General (the chief Law Officer of the Crown), acting on behalf of the Crown, has power to enter a *nolle prosequi* in criminal proceedings, *i.e.* he has a discretion to prevent a criminal prosecution. (*c*) The Queen is the sole source of honours. She alone, generally acting upon the advice of her ministers, may create peers and confer other honours. (*d*) The Crown, though it has long since lost all legislative power in England – other than powers delegated to it by Parliament – may legislate by Order in Council for certain territories abroad, such as conquered or ceded territories, provided that they have been accorded no representative (*i.e.* elected) Legislature of their own. (*e*) The Crown has exclusive control of the disposition and equipment of the armed forces. (*f*) The Crown has exclusive power to make war or peace (though it would now be unlikely to exercise it in the face of an unwilling Parliament) and of concluding treaties with foreign states, and its exercise of this power cannot be questioned in any court of law. Thus in *Blackburn* v. *A.-G.*, [1971] 2 All E.R. 1380 it was held by the House of Lords that a declaration could not be sought to prevent the government from acceding to the Treaty of Rome even though such accession must impair the national sovereignty. (*g*) During a war or in contemplation of war the Crown may, whether at home or abroad, order the destruction of or damage to private property as a necessary warlike measure. Formerly it was thought that this prerogative right was subject to a corresponding right to compensation on the part of the subject aggrieved, and in *Burmah Oil Co.* v. *Lord Advocate*, [1965] A.C. 75 (where the Company claimed compensation in respect of oil wells destroyed by H.M. Forces in face of the Japanese advance into Burma in 1942) the House of Lords – though with some doubt – so held. The War Damage Act 1965, however, reversed the effect of that decision in respect of government action "during or in contemplation of the outbreak of war"; but the decision has since been confirmed as regards action taken in time of peace. (*h*) The Crown is also privileged to refuse disclosure of documents relevant to judicial proceedings on the ground that to disclose them would be against the national interest. But here again the courts have recently been active in vindicating private against public right: for in *Conway* v. *Rimmer*, [1968] A.C. 910 – where the Crown claimed privilege in respect of certain reports upon the conduct of a police constable in the course of a suit by him for malicious prosecution – the House of Lords held that a minister's certificate claiming privilege of non-disclosure is in general not conclusive against disclosure and that the Courts may demand it at their discretion. Much will depend, however, upon the class of document in question: for example an application for disclosure of Cabinet minutes could not be entertained. (*i*) In the absence of specific definition by Act of Parliament it is within the prerogative for the Crown to determine the limits of British territorial waters.

All these and many other powers may still be exercised by the Crown by right of the prerogative. But since prerogative power is the antithesis of the rule of law it is necessarily subject to limits; for any act of prerogative must be ascribable to a prerogative right recognized as such by the *courts*. Thus the Executive cannot generally claim that its actions are immune from question in the courts by pleading that they are "*Acts of State*", above the ordinary law; it must justify them by reference to a recognized prerogative, statute or common law. But the word "generally" is important; for although it is not permissible for the Crown to put its actions beyond question by pleading "Act of State" in respect of any act done which affects a British subject or even a subject of a foreign State resident *within the jurisdiction* (unless of course there be a state of war between this country and his) yet the plea is valid as against an alien subject in respect of acts committed abroad. Thus, in *Buron* v. *Denman* (1848), 2 Exch. 167, a British naval officer had been ordered to release some slaves detained upon foreign territory. He did release them, but in the heat of the rescue he exceeded his orders by burning a "barracoon" (shed) belonging to a Spanish slave trader. The Spaniard sued the officer for the loss; but when it was found that the Crown had ratified the excess of authority it was held that it became an "Act of State" and hence unquestionable. More than this: in *A.-G.* v. *Nissan*, [1970] A.C. 179, a case of a claim by an hotelier, who was a British subject by naturalization, in respect of British army occupation of his Cyprus hotel, the House of Lords indicated that though "Act of State" would not in general be available to the Executive as against British subjects in respect of acts done *abroad*, it did not exclude the possibility of circumstances in which it might be.

ii Statutory powers – Most of the powers of the modern Executive are derived from statutes; thus for instance most local government powers are statutory.

Statutory powers are conferred by a number of devices, some of which entail acts of "subordinate" legislation (see below). The following are examples of the ways in which they are acquired:

(*a*) Powers of subordinate legislation are often conferred upon the *Privy Council* by Act of Parliament. Thus, during the Second World War, that Council was, by the Emergency Powers (Defence) Act 1939 accorded vast powers for the making of Defence Regulations by which it could control not only the whole life of the nation but could also confer powers upon other branches of the Executive. These "statutory" Orders in Council must be distinguished from the prerogative Orders in Council which have already been mentioned; prerogative orders derive their authority from the Prerogative, statutory orders from statute.

(*b*) Acts of Parliament sometimes authorize *ministers* to make "provisional orders" in certain fields. A provisional order is an order which acquires legislative force by *subsequent* parliamentary confirmation in a Provisional Order Confirmation Act. The normal procedure is for Departments to combine numbers of these Orders in batches, so that a single Act may be used to sanction several of them at once. Provisional Order procedure is most frequently employed, under the authority of various Acts, to authorize the execution of public undertakings by local and other authorities. The minister concerned is generally under a duty to cause a public local inquiry to be held before he makes an order.

(*c*) Ministers are also authorized by many statutes to make *Statutory Instruments*, *i.e.* orders and regulations, having statutory force. These require no subsequent confirmation by Act: they need only be laid before Parliament and will usually become law if they are confirmed by a simple resolution ("affirmative" resolution) of each House. In some cases, however, they will become law after they have merely been "laid" for a prescribed period unless they are annulled by resolution of either House ("negative resolution"); and in certain cases subordinate legislation will even be valid if it is simply laid before Parliament immediately after being made.

(ii) *The Nature of Executive Powers*

In relation to the powers of the Executive, the theory of the Separation of Powers (above, p. 52) appears now to have little practical effect. It is true that the various organs of the Executive do administer the laws enacted by the Legislature, and this, according to theory, is their proper function; but it is equally true that they do much else beside. Ever-increasing powers of *subordinate legislation* and of *adjudication* are now cast upon the Executive. Let us consider these two classes of powers in turn.

Powers of Subordinate Legislation – It has just been explained that powers of legislating are often conferred by the Legislature upon the Executive. These powers which the Executive thus wields are therefore referred to as a class as powers to make "subordinate" or "delegated" legislation. Although Parliament does not delegate legislative powers *solely* to the Executive, the various organs of the Executive are undoubtedly by far the most active "subordinate" law-makers. By innumerable statutes Parliament confers powers of legislating by statutory instrument upon Ministers and Departments, and at the bottom of the scale it also permits local authorities to make bye-laws. Extreme examples of statutes thus conferring huge powers of subordinate legislation upon the Executive (effectively upon the Civil Service) are the Health and Safety at Work etc. Act 1974 and the Consumer Credit Act 1974. Further the process of delegation may extend to sub-delegation, for example, an Act may provide that Her Majesty may, by Order in Council, make regulations empowering such-and-such a Minister to make further regulations. And this process may go on indefinitely; sub-sub-delegation is quite common.

The volume of subordinate legislative activity is enormous, and in any given year the number of Statutory Instruments far exceeds the number of Acts of Parliament. This being so, many people have felt that we are in the clutches of a "New Despotism" (the title of a book written by the late Lord Chief Justice Hewart) of the Executive, as arbitrary and as serious as the Tudor despotism. This has led to demands for greater control of the legislative powers of the Executive than at present exists. Under the existing law both the courts (see below, p. 129) and Parliament do, however, have *some* degree of control. Some of the methods of *parliamentary* control may be mentioned here –

(*a*) As we have seen, Acts which confer legislative powers upon Ministers and Departments often provide that statutory instruments made by virtue of these powers shall be laid before Parliament, and where they are so laid, special rules are prescribed by the Statutory Instruments Act 1946 (as clarified by the Laying of Documents before Parliament (Interpretation) Act 1948).

(*b*) The Statutory Instruments Act 1946, also provides that all statutory instruments must be published by the Queen's Printer. This provision ensures that much of the vast mass of subordinate legislation is at least available to the public. But on the other hand the definition of a statutory instrument is unfortunately narrow: it includes, amongst other things, Orders in Council and rules made by ministers under Acts empowering them to legislate by statutory instrument, but it does not include many other forms of subordinate legislation.

(*c*) By the Statutory Orders (Special Procedure) Acts 1945 and 1965, a special parliamentary procedure is prescribed for the making and confirmation of orders declared by any future Act to be subject to "special parliamentary procedure". The object of this procedure is to secure maximum publicity and maximum control by Parliament. It *only* applies where the authorizing Act requires "special procedure" to be employed.

(*d*) Since 1944 there has been a Select Committee of the House of Commons (the "Scrutinising" Committee) charged with the duty of deciding whether subordinate legislation, required to be laid before the House, should be brought to the attention of the House upon certain specified grounds: *e.g.* that it imposes a charge upon the public revenues, or that it is made in pursuance of an Act which excludes it from challenge in the courts (see below).

> NOTE – It should be noted that we have here been concerned to discuss powers of subordinate legislation, conferred upon the *Executive*. Such powers are not, however, *only* conferred upon the Executive; they may be, and often are, conferred upon other bodies: thus British Rail is empowered to make byelaws and professional organizations, such as the Law Society and similar bodies, are empowered by statute to make rules binding upon their members.

Powers of adjudication – During the past fifty years there has been an enormous increase in the number of tribunals, falling outside the system of the ordinary courts, entrusted with exercising powers of a judicial or administrative nature and many of these tribunals are closely connected with the Executive. Indeed, many and very wide powers are entrusted to particular Ministers, as for instance the powers of a Secretary of State for the Environment to grant or refuse planning permission under the Town and Country Planning Acts; and other similar powers and tribunals have been mentioned in Part I, Chapter 2. It must now be explained that the nature of the powers exercised by these tribunals varies. Some have *"quasi-judicial"* powers, *i.e.* power to determine the facts of a case and to decide, not according to fixed rules of law, but according to the dictates of expedience; others have "judicial" powers, *i.e.* power to determine the facts of a dispute and to decide it according to law. Further, in some cases there is a full right of appeal from the tribunal concerned to the courts; in other cases there is a right of appeal upon points of law only; in other cases still, there is no right of appeal, and the only right of redress which an aggrieved party possesses is by way of challenge by Prerogative Order.

The decisions of these administrative tribunals are, of course, as important in their own sphere as are the decisions of the ordinary courts in theirs, and, together with those of the ordinary courts relating to administrative matters and the vast mass of delegated legislation, they form what is now generally called *"Administrative Law"*.

The name and number of administrative tribunals is legion, and no list of them can be given here.

REVIEW OF EXECUTIVE ACTION

It has already been mentioned that Parliament has some degree of control over the exercise of executive powers, but more effective control – though, as will appear, also limited in scope – is kept by the courts and by the Parliamentary Commissioner for Administration.

(i) *Judicial Review*

It will be convenient to divide this subject into two parts: the first we will call the "machinery" of judicial review, and the second the "limits" of judicial review. But before embarking upon a discussion of these matters, mention must first be made of the doctrine of the "Rule of Law" (sometimes called the doctrine of the "Supremacy of Law").

i **The rule of law** – This doctrine has always occupied an important position in English law, though it only came to be popularized when enunciated by Dicey in his *"Law of the Constitution"*. The origin of the doctrine is very remote: as far as Western thought is concerned it is probably to be found in the notion, taken by the Romans from the Greeks, that over and above all actual laws there is, if only it could be correctly interpreted, a sytem of "natural" law, capable of achieving absolute justice in all cases, which is deducible from fundamental and unchanging moral principles.

The first clear expression of this idea in England is to be found in the thirteenth-century work of Bracton, who wrote, "*Ipse autem rex non debet esse sub homine sed sub Deo et sub lege, quia lex facit regem.*" ("The King himself ought not to be subject to any man, but he should be subject to God and the law; for the law makes him King.") The mediaeval notion was that rulers and ruled alike were subject to the commandments of God and to "the law". When the temporal power of the Church declined no more was heard of the Divine Law in this connexion, but the notion of the ultimate supremacy of "the law" persisted. Moreover, if (though this is uncertain) what was originally meant to be denoted by "the law" was natural law this denotation did not persist in England; "the law" became identified – especially in the imagination of the redoubtable Sir Edward Coke in the early seventeenth century – with the common law of England. Parliament, it was true, became the recognized "sovereign", and it could therefore alter the law; but, apart from legislation, the common law ruled all men equally. The first two Stuarts, imbued with the concept of the divine right of kings, challenged this principle and tried to override the law without the sanction of Parliament. As everyone knows, their challenge failed.

The classic modern exposition of the doctrine is to be found in Dicey's book: he explains that it now denotes three things. First, that the regular law of the land predominates over, and excludes, the arbitrary exercise of governmental power. Second, that all classes of people are equally subjected to the ordinary law of the land, administered by the ordinary courts. Third, that the law of the constitution itself is not to be found in a code (as is the case in many foreign countries), but is derived from the rights of individuals, as declared by the *courts*. Writing, as he did, at the close of the nineteenth century, Dicey then proceeded to demonstrate the truth of these propositions. The last of them remains as true today as it was then, but though it remains a generally accepted principle that the courts will always protect the subject against arbitrary acts of the Executive, and, as we have seen, they will never listen to the plea of "Act of State" where the rights of a British subject are concerned – at least within the jurisdiction – yet the Legislature has, as we are about to see, deprived the courts of their powers of review in many fields. Moreover, the recent large increase in the number and variety of "administrative tribunals", to which we have already referred, has robbed Dicey's second proposition of much of its force.

As long ago as 1932 the Report of the Committee on Ministers' Powers (1932, Cmd. 4060) – the "Donoughmore" Committee, chaired by Lord Donoughmore – stressed the fundamental importance of the doctrine, and the members of the Committee were unanimously agreed that "no considerations of administrative convenience, or executive efficiency, should be allowed to weaken the *control of the Courts*, and that no obstacle should be placed by Parliament in the way of the subject's unimpeded access to them". (Italics ours) This is really the crux of the matter; whatever may be the modern practice, the doctrine of the Rule of Law proclaims that the subject *should* always be entitled to assert his rights in the ordinary courts, and this is especially true when he is imperilled by the acts of an overbearing Executive. It is an old doctrine and it is a sound one; nevertheless, for the reasons which have been explained, it is at a discount today, and its pride of place as a cornerstone of the Constitution is in serious jeopardy.

A further Committee (the Committee on Administrative Tribunals and Enquiries) was appointed in 1955 to consider and report, amongst other things, on the constitution and working of tribunals other than the ordinary courts; and this Committee, under the chairmanship of Sir Oliver Franks, reported in 1957 (Cmnd. 218). The result was the passing of the Tribunals and Inquiries Act 1958, and the law on the subject is now consolidated in the Tribunals and Inquiries Act 1971. First the legislation created a *Council on Tribunals* which is charged with the duty of keeping under review the constitution and working of certain specified tribunals and of other tribunals to be specified by appropriate authorities, and to make reports thereon: the Council is also empowered to consider and report upon certain administrative procedures generally, such as the holding of ministerial or statutory inquiries. Second, the Act provided for rights of *appeal* on points of law to the High Court from certain tribunals where previously no such right had existed. In the third place the Act prescribed that no provision in any previous enactment which purports to oust the jurisdiction of the High Court should have effect so as to prevent resort to *Certiorari* or *Mandamus* (below, p. 136). Lastly, the Act ensured that in general the decisions of certain tribunals, and the decisions of Ministers after the holding of statutory inquiries, must, if required, state *reasons* for the determination made.

This Act went some way towards meeting the dangers created by the conferring of arbitrary discretions upon administrative tribunals; but as will be seen, there are still very considerable limitations upon the control which the courts have power to exercise over administrative authorities generally.

ii   The machinery of judicial review – The following are among the more important of the legal remedies available to a person who claims to be aggrieved by some act or omission of a member of the central Executive, or of an agent of some other public authority.

He may proceed by what we may call the "ordinary" remedies, by bringing an action for *damages* (below, p. 256), seeking an *injunction* (below, p. 262) or *specific performance* (below, p. 261), or seeking a *declaratory judgment*; and he may also proceed by means of one of the *Prerogative Orders*.

(a)   The Ordinary Remedies

Formerly rights of action for damages against the Crown (*i.e.* for this purpose the central Executive) were very restricted and even rights against other public authorities were subject to special periods of limitation – that is to say they had to be brought within a stricter limit of time than claims against individuals. Since the Crown Proceedings Act 1947 (C.P.A.) and the Law Reform (Limitation of Actions etc.) Act 1954 these special privileges have been swept away, and now people aggrieved by unlawful acts of executive authorities may bring claims against them in much the same way as they may claim against private people or corporate bodies.

Injunctions or *specific performance* may be decreed where appropriate against public bodies, but even today neither of these remedies is available against the Crown (*i.e.* the central Executive) or bodies closely connected with the Crown. Declaratory judgments, however, may be obtained even against the Crown. A *declaratory judgment* is a judicial declaration of the rights of the party carrying with it no order for enforcement. This may seem a pointless remedy, but in practice where the courts have openly declared the existence of a right officials, such as Ministers, just as much as other people, will usually be constrained – if only by respect for public opinion – to act in accordance with the court's judgment. It should be noticed that this kind of remedy is not usually available *in vacuo*; people are not permitted to test the ruling of the court in hypothetical cases; in order for such a judgment to be invoked there must be an actual dispute on an issue of law of a substantial nature. Relief will not, however, be refused merely because the dispute – substantial at the time when the claim is instituted – has ceased to be of practical importance due to lapse of time at the time when the action comes to trial.

Actions against public authorities (*e.g.* local authorities) or governmental agencies (*e.g.* the National Coal Board) lie against the authority by its designated name; *e.g.* the Little Puddleton Rural District Council is sued as such. Actions against the Crown (*i.e.* the organs of the central Executive) are brought, under the provisions of the C.P.A., against Departments (*e.g.* the Home Office) or Ministers (*e.g.* the Secretary of State for the Environment); and in certain prescribed circumstances against the Attorney-General who acts as representative of the Crown in matters of litigation.

Even today the Queen cannot – as we have seen – normally be sued in her private capacity. Further, where the wrong complained of affects the public generally proceedings by way of *injunction* may normally only be instituted by the Attorney-General who may either act *"ex officio"* (upon his own motion) or by way of "relator action", upon information supplied by a private person. Exceptionally, however, where an individual can show that he has suffered special damage peculiar to himself, over and above that suffered or apprehended by the public at large, he may institute proceedings without the intervention of the Attorney-General.

(b) The Prerogative Orders

Before considering the nature of these orders it is necessary to make a digression into the realm of substantive law.

Judicial control by means of the prerogative orders and by means of injunctions depends primarily upon the application of two principles; the principle of "Natural Justice", and the *"Ultra Vires"* doctrine. These must now be considered.

Natural Justice – The courts have always insisted that where any person has to make a judicial decision, as opposed to exercising an administrative discretion, he must comply with the dictates of "natural justice". A great judge once stigmatized this expression as "sadly lacking in precision"; and so it is, but most people will probably agree that the rules which the courts require those who are entrusted with the duty of deciding disputes to observe in the name of "natural justice" are rules which every ordinary reasonable man would consider to be fair. For example –

(α) *No man may be a judge in his own cause.* The application of this principle was strikingly illustrated in the case of *Dimes* v. *The Proprietors of the Grand Junction Canal* (1852), 3 H.L.C. 759, where the House of Lords set aside a decree of Lord Chancellor Cottenham's – by which he had granted relief to the respondent company – upon the ground that he was a shareholder in the company. No doubt in fact his Lordship's decision was quite unbiased; but, as Lord Campbell said in his speech, it is essential that every tribunal should avoid even giving the appearance of having an interest in the subject-matter of an action before it. Although this principle will not be pressed to extremes it was recently held that a chairman of magistrates will be disqualified from hearing a case if he is a member of a local education committee and the question is whether food contracted to be supplied on the order of that committee to certain schools is short-supplied.

(β) "*Audi alteram partem.*" A tribunal charged with deciding a dispute must give a *fair hearing to both sides.*

The case of *Ridge* v. *Baldwin*, [1964] A.C. 40, illustrates this principle. There the appellant (a chief constable of police) was dismissed by his watch committee after he had been involved in certain criminal proceedings: the dismissal took place in his absence and he was given no opportunity to state his case. The House of Lords held that this procedure (even though the decision had been confirmed by the Home Secretary) was contrary to natural justice and the dismissal was therefore void.

The same principle applies where a defendant in a criminal case is denied sufficient time to prepare his defence. On the other hand, in a number of court cases concerning dismissals of teachers and students it has been stressed that a fair hearing does not necessarily involve the holding of an inquiry exactly on the lines of a formal prosecution. It is enough if the inquiry is thorough and impartial. In the case of administrative tribunals it has long been held (as in the leading case of *Local Government Board* v. *Arlidge*, [1915] A.C. 120) that there is no need for the hearing to be *oral* if a fair view can be formed from *written* representations.

(γ) It is sometimes said to be a rule of natural justice that every tribunal should make known to the parties the *reasons* for its decision. It has always been the practice of the ordinary courts to do this, and they will, as far as possible, insist that other tribunals follow suit. Further, as has just been seen, the Tribunals and Inquiries Act 1971 now makes the giving of reasons by many administrative tribunals (including Ministers) compulsory in many cases.

Ultra Vires – This doctrine has already been mentioned in respect of its application to the powers of corporations; it was, indeed, in relation to the powers of railway companies that it was first formulated. In the constitutional field it has a wide application. Since Parliament is "sovereign" and its legal competence is supreme and unlimited the courts, as we have seen, can never question the authority of a statute (however stupid or perverse it may be); but they can, and *will*, if called upon to do so, question the competence of any other person or body, and will ascertain the limits of his or its powers. All legal powers – save, perhaps, the authority of Parliament itself, which may probably be said to rest upon the greatest of all constitutional conventions, namely that Parliament must be obeyed – are derived either from the common law or from statute. They may therefore only be exercised within the limits which the common law or an enabling Act prescribe: once these limits are exceeded the courts will intervene if called upon to do so, and will adjudge any act done in excess of them unlawful and void.

The "*ultra vires*" doctrine has many applications. Thus it may apply to a special power conferred by statute upon a person or body to do some act which, apart from the statutory sanction, would be unlawful. It may apply to powers of subordinate legislation, as in the case of a Minister who is empowered by Act to make regulations for a certain purpose, and purports to make them for some other purpose in excess of the authority conferred upon him. It may apply to powers of adjudication; as where a tribunal exceeds the lawful limits of its jurisdiction, or, being empowered by statute to make certain decisions after compliance with certain prescribed formalities, it fails to comply with those formalities.

The applications of the doctrine are as various as the powers that may be conferred; but the principle which underlies it is clear and simple; no power must ever be exercised beyond the limits which the law places upon its excercise: those who claim to wield abnormal powers must be prepared to justify them by reference to the common law or statute. One simple and well-known example of the application of the doctrine must suffice. In *A.-G.* v. *Fulham Corporation*, [1929] 1 Ch. 440, the Fulham Borough Council established a municipal laundry. The Council was empowered, by certain Acts, to establish, amongst other things, baths, wash-houses and bathing places. The laundering activities were challenged by a ratepayer. The court had little difficulty in deciding to grant an injunction to restrain the Council from continuing them; they were clearly "*ultra vires*", beyond the powers conferred by the Acts.

NOTE – *Bye-laws* are subject to a further test, beside the "*ultra vires*" test. The courts insist that they must not only be "*intra vires*" (*i.e.* within the competence of those who make them) but that they must also be *reasonable*.

Prerogative Orders – The nature of the prerogative orders of *Mandamus*, *Prohibition* and *Certiorari* may now be explained. They constitute one of the main bulwarks of the rights of the subject against abuse or excess of power by individuals, courts, public authorities and, in some cases, by the central Executive itself. Jurisdiction in respect of them is vested in the High Court and under the Rules of the Supreme Court they now issue out of the Queen's Bench Division.

Like *Habeas Corpus*, these orders were originally Writs, and the procedure connected with them was archaic and complicated. They are now called "Orders" and the procedure has been simplified; but their scope remains unaltered.

Mandamus is a peremptory order commanding the performance

("mandamus" = "we command") of a public duty which will be made if no other remedy is available. It only lies to command the performance of an administrative act; it will not lie to enforce the exercise of a discretion. It has thus been obtained to force a borough council to hold an election of aldermen which it was *bound* to hold, and to compel a local authority to perform a legal duty imposed upon it to produce its accounts for inspection: for both these were positive *duties* which *had* to be performed.

Mandamus will not lie against the Crown.

The traditional rôle of *Prohibition* is to prevent excess of jurisdiction by an inferior court; but its scope has been considerably widened in modern times, and it will now lie to prevent excess of jurisdiction by any *public* body or person, exercising a *public* duty, entrusted with judicial or quasi-judicial powers. It will not, however, lie to prevent excess of *legislative* powers; nor will it lie against private or domestic tribunals, such as the committees of clubs.

Unlike Mandamus, Prohibition will lie against the Crown.

The purpose of *Certiorari* is to bring before the High Court any matter decided in, at issue in, or pending in, an inferior court in order that the High Court may "certify" itself that no excess of jurisdiction has occurred or is about to occur, or in order to ensure that the principles of natural justice have been complied with.

As in the case of Prohibition, so in the case of Certiorari, the word "court" has in modern times received an extended interpretation. The order lies to any person or body having jurisdiction to determine the rights of subjects either judicially or quasi-judicially. Certiorari has thus been granted, for example, to review an order of the London County Council (the forerunner of the Greater London Council) which licensed the opening of a cinema on a Sunday in contravention of a statute forbidding that practice.

But there are limits to the scope of the orders. Certiorari has never lain to the ecclesiastical courts; though they are subject to Prohibition. Further, neither Prohibition nor Certiorari will lie to restrain the actions of private arbitrators (though they will lie in respect of arbitrators acting under powers conferred by Parliament), nor to restrain officials in the exercise of purely disciplinary powers—such as the powers conferred upon chief fire officers and police officers in respect of their brigades and forces. Moreover, though the Courts Act 1971, s. 10 (5) provides that the three Orders may be directed to the Crown Court, just as much as to any other court or body it exempts from their scope "matters relating to *trial on indictment*".

In practice applications for Certiorari and Prohibition are often made together: by Certiorari proceedings in the lower court are brought to the High Court for review; by Prohibition the lower court is forbidden to exceed its powers.

Finally, it should be noted that the granting of prerogative remedies is *discretionary*; the court being free to take into account all the equities of the individual case. Thus, for example, in *R. v. Aston University Senate: ex parte Roffey*, [1969] 2 Q.B. 538 Certiorari was refused against the University because, although its examining body had failed to give a hearing consonant with the requirements of natural justice in dismissing the applicant student, the latter had been guilty of unjustifiable delay in seeking the assistance of the court.

iii   The limits of judicial review – The limits of judicial review are determined by Parliament in the exercise of its sovereign power of legislation. Statutes can and often do confer unchallengeable powers upon persons or bodies. This occurs chiefly in two ways. On the one hand Parliament may grant unfettered powers of *delegated legislation*, and on the other hand it may confer an *absolute administrative discretion*.

First as to *legislative powers*. Some statutes create subordinate legislative powers in such a way as virtually to exclude judicial review. Thus Ministers are sometimes empowered to make orders, rules or regulations which are, according to the Act which grants the power, when made, to have effect "as if enacted in this Act". Or again – and many similar instances might be given – a Department may be granted statutory authority to formulate some plan or scheme, and the enabling Act may provide that the confirmation of the appropriate Minister shall be "conclusive evidence" that any statutory requirements for the implementation of the plan have been complied with. In both these examples Parliament has conferred the right to legislate and practically endowed the grantee of the authority with its own omnipotence.

Secondly, as to *administrative discretions*. We have seen that the *judicial* discretion lies within the controlling power of the prerogative orders, and that now, by the Tribunals and Inquiries Act 1971, Parliament has itself enacted that no provision in any previous enactment which purports to oust the jurisdiction of the High Court shall have effect so as to prevent resort to Certiorari or Mandamus. But where Parliament confers an absolute right of discretion in a matter of administration the exercise of such a right cannot, in the absence of proved bad faith, be questioned by the courts. This proposition was illustrated in the much-discussed war-time case of *Liversidge v. Anderson*, [1942] A.C. 206. The appellant was detained by order of the respondent (the Home Secretary), under powers conferred by the Defence (General) Regulations, 1939, made under the Emergency Powers (Defence) Act 1939. The regulation in question empowered the respondent, *inter alia*, to detain people whom he had reasonable cause to believe to be of hostile origin or associations. The appellant sought leave to apply for particulars of the respondent's grounds for believing that he was of such an origin or that he had such associations. The House of Lords held that he was debarred from seeking the assistance of the courts to obtain these particulars. Provided that, in ordering the detention, the respondent had acted in good faith (which was not denied), the grounds of his belief could not be questioned by the courts. The discretion conferred upon him was absolute.

This case occurred in war-time when it was clearly necessary that the Home Secretary should be allowed a wide discretion in ordering the detention of suspected people. But a similar result will, nevertheless, always be reached where the courts decide that the wording of an enactment is so phrased as to confer an absolute discretion. For example, anyone who cares to consult recent legislation will find an abundance of phrases such as "Where the Minister is satisfied"; "If in the opinion of the Minister it appears to be 'necessary' (or 'desirable', 'expedient', etc.)"; "Where a Local Authority thinks fit". In all of these and many similar instances of what has sometimes been called "subjective" terminology – whether the enactment in question be an Act or a statutory instrument made by the Departments or other authorities themselves – the courts are often left with no alternative but to conclude that Parliament has deprived them of power to review the exercise of the particular administrative discretion involved. "Often", but *not always*. For even the conferment of a wide discretion may imply not merely a *power* to do something, or not to do it, but a *duty* to do it if the circumstances are such as to come within the general intent of the enabling legislation. Thus in *Padfield* v. *Minister of Agriculture, Fisheries and Food*, [1968] A.C. 997, where the House of Lords held that where the Minister, being charged with a statutory duty "if the Minister in any case so directs" to set up a committee of investigation to consider certain kinds of complaints, failed to set up such a committee upon political grounds unconnected with the purposes for which the statute had created the duty, *mandamus* would lie requiring the Minister to consider the complaints in question according to law.

Further, even the words "any determination" by (such-and-such) a person or body "shall not be called in question in any court of law" will not exclude judicial review where the decision in question is not a proper one in the sense that some irrelevant factor has been taken into account. Hence in *Anisminic, Ltd.* v. *Foreign Compensation Commission*, [1969] 2 A.C. 147 it was held that a clause in s. 4 (4) of the Foreign Compensation Act 1950 so framed did not prevent a determination of the Foreign Compensation Commission, upon which the power of determination had been conferred, from being questioned where the commission had so misconstrued the statute as to deprive the company of compensation upon the irrelevant ground that its successor in title (an Egyptian company) happened to be a foreign firm.

(ii) *The Parliamentary Commissioner for Administration*

The reader will doubtless know that this office was created in imitation of the Scandinavian *Ombudsman*, though the English version differs from its prototype. It was set up by the Parliamentary Commissioner Act 1967, and the function of the Commissioner is to investigate complaints by members of the public who claim to have sustained injustice in consequence of maladministration in connexion with action taken in the exercise of administrative functions by government departments and certain public authorities. Complaints must be made in writing and be addressed to a *Member of the House of Commons*; and it is then for the *Member*, and not the aggrieved person, with the consent of the latter, to forward the complaint to the Commissioner. The Commissioner then has a discretion whether or not to make an investigation; if he does decide to do so he must inform the branch of the Executive concerned, and when the investigation is complete must report both to the latter and to the Member; if he decides that no investigation is warranted he must still report to the Member giving his reasons for refusing one.

It is to be noted that this function is purely *investigatory*; the Commissioner has no executive powers; but if he considers that injustice has been done and that, despite his inquiry, it remains unremedied, he may lay before both Houses of Parliament a special report on the case.

The creation of such an office, while preserving the rôle of Members to act as the guardians of their constituents, is clearly much to the good; and injustices have been revealed and remedied. But the limitations upon the Commissioner's powers are considerable. In the first place, he is concerned with "*maladministration*", not with misguided decision (although the House of Commons Select Committee on the Parliamentary Commissioner made a useful contribution by suggesting that the term "*maladministration*" should extend to include harsh decisions based on the over-vigorous application of departmental policies, a suggestion accepted by the Commissioner). He is not a court of appeal from the exercise of administrative discretion, though he may question any administrative act if it appears biased, irrelevant, negligent, inept or dishonest. This is probably a necessary limitation since there is no reason why the Commissioner should know the business of departments better than the departments themselves; yet it has been much criticized and it seems not to be imposed upon the foreign prototypes. In the second place the areas to be investigated are seriously circumscribed: thus although most departments fall within the Commissioner's province a formidable number of public authorities and services are exempt from investigation – including the Cabinet Office, local authorities and the police (neither perhaps entirely innocent of maladministration), the hospital service and public corporations. Relief is thus often denied where the shoe pinches most. Moreover, criminal and commercial matters are excluded. Whether it would be practicable in a country of this size to enlarge the powers of a single Commissioner is, however, questionable.

6 THE INDIVIDUAL AND THE STATE

It has already been remarked that under our Constitution there are no such things as "guaranteed" rights – as there are in the U.S. Constitution – expressly safeguarded in a document of peculiar sanctity. Since Parliament is all-powerful it may do anything by a simple Act, and it may certainly deprive the individual of his rights – indeed, a Tudor Parliament once condescended to pass a special Act to sanction the boiling to death of one Richard Rose, the Bishop of Rochester's cook (alleged to have been guilty of poisoning).

This being the case, the citizen must look, for the protection of his rights, not to any constitutional document which guarantees them but to the general rules of law enforced at any given time by the courts; his rights derive from the ordinary law of the land (see above, p. 130). Through the medium of the prerogative orders, the courts will, as we have seen, protect these rights in proper cases even against interference by the Crown. The courts have, moreover, traditionally championed the individual. Thus, penal statutes have always been strictly construed, and there is a strong presumption that no statute is intended to have retrospective effect.

Let us now consider the extent of the protection which the law actually does afford people in respect of their personal freedom and of their enjoyment of property, and determine how far it permits them to say what they like and associate with whom they will.

A The Right to Personal Freedom

Everyone is entitled to personal freedom. This implies two things – first, that no one may lawfully be arrested except upon certain specified grounds; secondly, that if anyone is arrested or detained, otherwise than upon lawful grounds, the Writ of *Habeas Corpus* may be invoked to set him free and he may sue the person who detained him for assault or false imprisonment (see below, pp. 171–172; 301–302).

Lawful arrest – The following are the principal grounds of arrest and detention recognized by the law – (*a*) Arrest and detention in pursuance of the criminal law; (*b*) Detention of mentally disordered people (above, pp. 95–99); (*c*) Detention by order of the court or of either House of Parliament, upon the ground of "contempt".

Arrest and detention of course occur most commonly in furtherance of the criminal law; but those who seek to arrest criminals must always be careful to do so by the proper means.

Arrest may always be lawfully effected by anyone authorized to effect it by a *warrant* lawfully issued and signed by a justice of the peace or other judicial authority, naming the person to be arrested; though it should be noted that the person who makes the arrest must have the warrant in his possession at the time of the arrest, or at least be in a position to produce it immediately upon request. In some cases, however, people have the power, and may even be under a legal duty, to arrest other people without first obtaining a warrant.

Formerly the law relating to powers of arrest *without warrant* was detailed, obscure and complicated, built up over the ages by an amalgam of common law and statute law. It has now, however, been clarified by the Criminal Law Act 1967. For that Act, while abolishing the pre-existing distinction between felonies and misdemeanours (see below, p. 160), which gave rise to much of the complication of the previous law as to powers of arrest without warrant, classified certain offences as "arrestable" and defined the powers of arrest in respect of them.

Under the provisions of the Act (s. 2 (1)) *arrestable offences* are "offences for which the sentence is fixed by law" (*i.e.*, treason, murder, and piracy with violence) "or for which a person not previously convicted may under ... any enactment be sentenced to imprisonment for a term of five years, and attempts to commit such an offence". The section then goes on to provide that – (*a*) *Any person* may arrest without warrant anyone who *is*, or whom he with reasonable cause suspects to be, *in the act* of committing such an offence; and where such an offence has *actually been committed any person* may arrest anyone who is, or whom he, with reasonable cause suspects to be, guilty of the offence. (*b*) Where a *constable*, with reasonable cause, *suspects* that such an offence has been committed, he may also arrest anyone who, with reasonable cause he suspects to be guilty of it (even though it has not been committed by anyone); a *constable* may also arrest anyone who is, or whom he reasonably suspects to be, *about to commit* such an offence.

For the purpose of making such arrests (s. 2 (6)) a *constable* may also enter (if need be, by force) and search any place where a person liable to arrest under any of the foregoing powers is, or where the constable, with reasonable cause, suspects him to be. The Act (s. 3) also empowers *anyone* to use *"such force as is reasonable in the circumstances"* in the *"prevention of crime, or in effecting or assisting in the lawful arrest of offenders or of persons unlawfully at large"*. To a great extent this is merely confirmatory of the pre-existing law.

It must be appreciated, however, that the Act does not tell quite all of the story; since it is in effect only concerned to abolish previous rules of the law as to arrest which turned upon the former distinction between felonies and misdemeanours and s. 2 (7) makes this clear by providing that "this section shall not ... prejudice any power of arrest conferred by law apart from this section". This would appear to mean that powers of arrest without warrant which did *not* turn upon the above-mentioned distinction are still retained and these include a large and heterogeneous number of powers embracing, as it would seem, the right of *any person* to arrest anyone whom he sees committing or about to commit a *breach of the peace* for sufficient time to stop the commission of the offence; and the right of *a constable* to arrest such a person in order to secure him for trial. Further, it is probable that similar power exists in the case of anyone who sees anyone else committing or about to commit *bodily harm* to any person.

Further powers conferred by *statute* in relation to specific offences remain. There are many such. Examples are the provisions of numerous enactments which empower private individuals to arrest anyone *actually committing an indictable offence at night*, and the wide statutory powers of *constables* in *London* to arrest any person reasonably suspected of having committed, or of being about to commit, *any* indictable offence and to arrest *any* person found loitering at night who cannot give a satisfactory account of himself. What will amount to reasonable suspicion must, of course, depend upon the facts of every case but it must be noticed that it is possible to entertain a reasonable suspicion about something without being possessed of evidence which amounts to *prima facie* proof of the existence of the facts suspected.

Where a policeman makes an arrest without a warrant he must make the true cause of arrest known to the person arrested and he must, in cases where no question of resort to force arises, use such words (as "I arrest you") or make his intention to effect the arrest plain; for example, it is not enough merely to say "I propose to charge you with theft". It should also be noted that the police have power to call upon any able-bodied person to assist them in making an arrest; and it is the duty of any person so called upon to assist. In arresting a suspect a policeman need not necessarily take him immediately to a police station or before a magistrate, but may lawfully detain him in order to take such reasonable steps as are necessary to assure himself that his suspicions are well founded (for instance he may take the suspect to his home to see whether there is stolen property there). Further, it has long been established that if after arrest the constable or his superiors decide that there is insufficient cause for detaining the suspect they may lawfully release him without taking him before a magistrate and will not then – provided that the suspicion was reasonable – be liable to an action for false imprisonment.

It may be worth adding that, quite apart from the special disciplinary powers conferred upon naval commanders, a *master of a merchant vessel* has, by the common law, the power and duty of arresting and detaining anyone aboard his ship when he reasonably believes such detention to be necessary for the preservation of order, or for the safety of the ship. All in all, however, it may be thought that in view of the complexities of the law relating to arrest the ordinary citizen may be wise not to attempt to make one.

HABEAS CORPUS

It is one thing to say that the law does not countenance unlawful arrests; but it is quite another thing to prevent them from being made. Suppose, for example, that William Jones is seized by thugs and held captive in some remote place, or that Tom Taxpayer is detained by Efficiency Brown of the Inland Revenue Department, upon the unfounded allegation that he has not paid his income tax. What then? It will be cold comfort for the prisoners to be told that they will have a right to damages when, and if, they escape.

This is where the importance of the historic Writ of *Habeas Corpus* lies. The principle underlying the issue of this Writ cannot be better expressed than in the words of Blackstone: "The King", he wrote, "is at all times entitled to have an account why the liberty of his subjects is restrained". Anyone who is detained, or any person so connected with an interest in his liberty *acting on his behalf*, may apply in term time to a Divisional Court of the Queen's Bench Division or in vacation to any judge of the High Court, for the issue of the Writ. If the Court or judge order it to issue, it will be served upon the person having custody of the person detained who, upon a named day, must appear before the Court or judge to show legal cause for the detention: if he cannot do this the person detained will at once be freed. The Writ lies against the Crown as well as against private individuals, and any form of detention whether upon an alleged criminal charge or in a civil matter – as where a person seeks to challenge the right to custody of a minor – may be called in question.

The Administration of Justice Act 1960 made important amendments to *Habeas Corpus* procedure and clarified certain obscurities. The following points should be noted. Where an application is made to a single judge he may not *refuse* the order, and should he consider that it ought to be refused he must refer the case to a Divisional Court. Not more than one application may be made unless fresh evidence appears to support a second one. Applications made in respect of mentally disordered persons or the like are to be treated as applications in criminal matters.

In the case of all applications, whether civil or criminal – save an order of *release* in a criminal matter made by a single judge – there is a *right of appeal* against an order for release as well as against refusal. Appeal lies from the Divisional Court direct to the House of Lords; but as regards *criminal matters* if the Divisional Court has ordered release without requiring bail or ordering interim detention the discharged person will be entitled to remain at large whatever the final decision on appeal. Further, in criminal matters the right to appeal is subject only to leave of either the Divisional Court or the House of Lords and is not restricted by the ordinary requirements as to public importance (above, p. 00) which apply in the case of criminal appeals.

Apart from this, the general form of *Habeas Corpus* procedure, unlike the form of procedure on the other Prerogative Writs, has been little altered since ancient times; *Habeas Corpus* remains a Writ while the others have now become orders.

B   Freedom of Property

In days gone by the common law treated the right to property as sacrosanct: it was considered to be almost as inviolable as the right to personal liberty. Today this is no longer true. Although the courts will construe a statute which purports to destroy rights of property with the utmost strictness – especially if it gives no right to compensation – so many statutes have empowered public authorities and other bodies to acquire private land, and now even other property, compulsorily, that it is no longer true to say that our constitutional law safeguards the right to property.

The law relating to compulsory acquisition is complicated. Only two points can be mentioned here. First, until recently statutes have generally authorized the compulsory acquisition of *land* only; for example, nineteenth-century statutes empowered railway companies and local authorities to acquire land in various circumstances, and in modern times compulsory powers of land purchase are conferred by many Acts for many different purposes. But recent years have seen a new development; for the *assets* of many private undertakings, such as coal-mining and gas and electricity companies, have been compulsorily acquired for "nationalization" and there was once even a "capital levy". Secondly, where a statute does authorize the compulsory acquisition of *land* special procedures and measures of compensation laid down by various Acts including the Acquisition of Land (Authorisation Procedure) Act 1946 and the Land Compensation Acts 1961 and 1965 usually have to be applied. Further, all disputes as to compensation payable in relation to the compulsory acquisition of land have now to be submitted, subject to a right of appeal on points of law to the Court of Appeal, to a special tribunal, called the *"Lands Tribunal"* set up by the Lands Tribunal Act 1949. Unlike many other special tribunals, this body must be presided over by a barrister of standing or by a person who has held "high judicial office". Its members are members of the legal profession and people experienced in land valuation.

A further important enactment is the Land Compensation Act 1973 which contains detailed provisions concerning compensation in respect of the actions of public authorities which have adverse effects upon interests in land. Two important provisions may be noted.

In the first place s. 1 in general gives a right to compensation where the value of the interest *"is depreciated by physical factors caused by the use of public works"*. The *"factors"* concerned are "noise, vibration, smell, fumes, smoke, artificial lighting and the discharge on to the land of any solid or liquid substance". The *"public works"* include "(a) any highway; (b) any aerodrome; and (c) any works on land used in the exercise of statutory powers". It is to be noted that the claim is not in respect of the construction of, *e.g.* the airport, but in respect of its *use*, *e.g.* the noise arising from the aircraft or the noise, etc. of a motorway. The claimant's interest in his land must be in existence at the time when the work first comes into use (s. 2); and there are certain other provisions as to the time, etc. in which the claim must be brought. Moreover, except in the case of depreciation caused by the use of a *highway* no claim will lie if (because no special immunity has been provided in respect of it) an action in nuisance will lie against the perpetrator.

In the second place, by s. 29 and following sections of the 1973 Act provision for extra compensation is made for "persons displaced from land": these include payment for *"home loss"* – as where a house is acquired for demolition by a local authority – and a reasonable amount becomes payable simply for the injury involved in losing a home. There is similar provision in respect of certain caravan dwellers and the right to "farm loss payment" for people displaced from agricultural land.

C Freedom of Speech, Association and Assembly

The law does not prescribe what people *may* say or write or publish: the general rule is that anyone is free to express any views he likes; provided that he does not contravene the law of defamation, sedition, obscenity, or blasphemy. Since 1695 there has been no censorship of the Press, though the government has at times (as in the Second World War) been given limited powers of censorship during national emergencies.

Thus, generally speaking, people are free to say or publish whatever they like; but there are certain statutory exceptions to this rule. The following examples may be given. The Official Secrets Acts 1911–1939, amongst other things, make it an offence for anyone to divulge any official information which he has received from an officer of the Crown. The Incitement to Mutiny Act 1797, and the Incitement to Disaffection Act 1934, both create offences in connexion with words or behaviour calculated to seduce members of the Forces from their allegiance, and the Police Act 1964, s. 53, makes it an offence to act so as to cause disaffection amongst the members of any police force. The Public Meeting Act 1908 (as amended by the Public Order Act 1936), punishes disorderly behaviour designed to prevent the transaction of business at a lawful public meeting. Further, the Public Order Act 1936, s. 5 (as amended by the Race Relations Act 1965, s. 7) makes it an offence (irrespective of racial discrimination) to use threatening or abusive or insulting words or behaviour or to distribute threatening or abusive writings in any *public* place or at any *public* meeting, with intent to provoke or with the likelihood of occasioning a breach of the peace. But however much behaviour may annoy people no offence will be committed if it is *not* threatening, abusive or insulting: thus it was held in *Brutus* v. *Cozens*, [1973] A.C. 854 that where the defendant annoyed spectators by going onto No. 2 Court at Wimbledon when play was in progress and blowing a whistle and distributing anti-apartheid pamphlets – an attempt to persuade rather than to insult – this behaviour did not come within the section. Section 6 of the 1965 Act prohibits the publication of writings of a threatening or abusive nature, or the use in any *public* place or at any *public* meeting of words of a similar nature, with intent to stir up hatred against any section of the public distinguished by colour or race. (It may be of interest to note that it has been held that for this purpose "public *place*" means an open place and cannot include a building: what consists primarily of a building – such as a railway station, as opposed to a football ground – does not come within these Acts). Moreover, the Theatres Act 1968 – which abolished stage censorship – makes it an offence to give an obscene performance of a play unless the giving of such a performance can be justified as being for the public good on the ground of literary or other artistic merit. The same Act also makes it an offence to give a public performance of a play involving threatening, abusive or insulting words with intent to stir up hatred against any section of the public distinguished by colour, etc. By the Obscene Publications Act 1959 it is also an offence to publish matter tending to deprave and corrupt those who are likely to read, see or hear it.

Just as people are, in general, free to say and write what they like, so they are permitted to associate with whom they will. But there are also limits to the general right of free association. For instance, a combination of two or more persons to do any unlawful act, or to do any lawful act by unlawful means, will amount to a common law "conspiracy", which is itself an indictable offence (first made so by the Star Chamber), apart from any unlawful objects which it may actually achieve (see below, pp. 310–312).

Further, as in the case of freedom of speech, there are certain *statutory* limits to the right of free association. We shall see, for example, that a combination of twenty or more persons for the carrying on of any trade or business will be unlawful unless they become incorporated, and we have also seen that "monopolies" (below, p. 191) may now be restrained under certain circumstances. It may be added that, by the provisions of the Public Order Act 1936, s. 1 (1) it is unlawful at any public meeting or in any public place to wear a uniform signifying association with any political organization. This was framed to meet the menace of Sir Oswald Moseley's "blackshirts" but it was recently used against the Irish "Provisionals" when it was held that the wearing of a black beret specifying allegiance to that cause amounted to the wearing of a uniform. By s. 2 (1) of the same Act it is, amongst other things, an offence for anyone to take part in the control or management of any association which is trained or equipped for the purpose of enabling its members to usurp the functions of the police, or of the armed forces of the Crown.

It cannot be said that there is any such thing as a general "right" of *public* meeting. People who assemble upon the highway without permission will always be technically guilty of trespass to the owner of the highway (usually now a local authority); for the only *right* which the public have upon the highway is a right of passage. Moreover, people who assemble or process upon the highway will usually be technically guilty of causing an "obstruction": and if they create a nuisance by picketing peoples' premises (otherwise that in contemplation or furtherance of a trade dispute) they may be liable to a claim in nuisance. Under the provisions of the Public Order Act 1936, s. 3, the police are also empowered to prescribe routes for processions and to forbid them to enter specified public places; the police or the appropriate local authorities are also given power, in certain circumstances, to prohibit, subject to the consent of the Home Secretary, the holding of any procession for a period of three months.

Apart from any question of trespass or obstruction, wherever *three* or more people meet together for the accomplishment of a common design which is likely to involve violence, or the reasonable apprehension of violence, they will constitute an *unlawful assembly*; and "unlawful assembly" is an offence at common law. Once the participants in such an assembly move to accomplish their common design they will constitute a *"rout"*; and once they start to put the design into actual operation, they will be guilty of the offence of *"riot"*. The essence of a *common law* "riot" is the combination of *three* or more people, having a *common design* which they have actually started to *execute*, or are attempting to execute, with the common intention of helping each other by *force*, if necessary, should they be opposed; and their common activity must be such as to be calculated to cause *alarm* in the mind of at least one reasonable person. Thus, for example, where a football crowd, unable to get into the ground, climbed upon the roof of the garage of a neighbouring house, knocked down the gardener who tried to prevent them from doing so, and forced the owner's daughter against a wall when she tried to shut the gate, it was held that a riot had occurred. The essence of the offence lies in the sense of insecurity induced in observers of the behaviour or which would be so induced were such observers present; it does not lie in the fact that the behaviour takes place in public. Thus in *Kamara* v. *D.P.P.*, [1974] A.C. 104, where protesting students occupied the Sierra Leone Embassy and frightened the caretaker there, they were guilty of unlawful assembly; and so were youths, in *R.* v. *Button and Swain*, [1966] A.C. 591, who created a disturbance in a private hall while the annual Darts Club dance was in progress.

Mention should also be made of the common law crime of "affray". This crime will be committed where a person or people (as in the case of a street fight) so behave as to cause or to be likely to cause reasonable apprehension in others. There is no need for anyone *actually* to be frightened, but it seems that if the offence is committed in a *private*, as opposed to a public, place there must actually be observers there.

CHAPTER 6

CRIMINAL LAW

In this chapter we will first consider the general principles of criminal responsibility, then outline the elements of a number of specific crimes, and finally discuss the law relating to compensation for criminal injuries.

A THE GENERAL PRINCIPLES OF CRIMINAL RESPONSIBILITY

The Nature of a Crime

Crimes are offences against the State; in this, as we shall see, they differ from breaches of contract or of trust and from torts, which are all either solely or primarily wrongs to individuals. The object of criminal proceedings is to punish the offender or to ensure, by some means other than punishment, that he does not repeat his offence: the object of civil proceedings is to satisfy the claim of the party injured.

Since crimes are offences against the State, the State takes the initiative in prosecuting criminals: the Crown is in theory, though usually not in actual practice, always responsible for conducting prosecutions, and criminal proceedings are conducted in the name of the Queen. Thus if Jones commits a murder the ensuing trial will be called the case of R. (an abbreviation of *"Regina"* = The Queen) v. *Jones.* On the other hand if Jones merely breaks his contract with Smith, who sues him, this civil action will be called *Smith* v. *Jones,* for in this case the Crown has no interest in the matter beyond seeing that justice is done between the parties.

NOTE–"v." is short for the Latin *"versus"* = "against". As a matter of etiquette, when citing a case – to take the above example – lawyers either say Smith "versus" Jones, or Smith "against" Jones, or Smith "and" Jones; but the case should *never* be cited as Smith "v." Jones. "v" may be appropriate when one is talking about a football match, but the judges do not like to hear it used in abbreviated letter form in court.

149

It must not be imagined that because crimes differ from civil wrongs the same set of facts can never constitute both a crime and a civil wrong, for criminal law and civil law overlap at many points. Thus if X takes Y's motor car without his consent X's act may, in many kinds of circumstances, constitute both the crime of theft and the tort of conversion.

Criminal Responsibility

Since criminal proceedings may result in punishment it is only just that the mere doing of a prohibited act should not generally be held to constitute a crime. The common law always insisted that there shall be no conviction unless the accused had a "guilty mind" ("*mens rea*"). This requirement is commonly expressed in the words of the ancient maxim: "*Actus non facit reum nisi mens sit rea*" ("The mere doing of an act will not constitute guilt unless there be a guilty intent").

The term "guilty mind", or "guilty intent", when used in this context, is not capable of precise definition; for the courts have, from the earliest times, applied common sense rules in determining when such a state of mind exists. Thus, if a person does a criminal act, such as poisoning another person's food and there is evidence from the surrounding circumstances, or from his declared motives, that he *intended* to kill the other person there can be little doubt about his guilt. So too, an act in itself comparatively innocent may argue a "guilty" state of mind if it is one which is clearly calculated to lead to evil consequences. For instance where a prostitute buried her child beneath a pile of leaves and a kite soon afterwards struck at it and killed it, it was held that she was guilty of murdering the child; for kites were common in England in those days, and the risk that the child would be attacked was so great that it was clear that the woman either intended the death or else was reckless whether it occurred or not. (*The Harlot's Case* (1560) Crompton's Justice, 24.)

It cannot be pretended, however, that the formulation of a test for determining the existence of a guilty intention (as opposed to the formulation of the nature of the required intent itself) is a simple matter. For intention is a state of mind incapable of positive proof; and yet the prosecution must normally establish it. Needless to say, the delicacy of this operation has led to controversy. There are those who believe – and indeed it has, at the highest level been ruled – that it ought to suffice to establish *objectively* that what the accused brought about (*e.g.* the death of the victim) was a natural consequence of what he did, so that he must be *taken* to have intended the death. But there are also those who believe that the judgment ought to be *subjective*; that it ought to be established that the intent was actually *there*. Since of course the latter task is flatly impossible the conflict between the opposing views is really no more than one of degree of proof. However, for the present at least the argument appears to be settled by the Criminal Justice Act 1967, s. 8 in favour of the latter view. The section provides that "A court or jury, in determining whether a person has committed an offence – (*a*) shall *not* be bound in law to infer that he intended or foresaw a result of his actions by reason only of its being a natural or probable consequence of those actions: but (*b*) shall decide whether he did intend or foresee that result *by reference to all the evidence*, drawing such inferences from the evidence as appear proper in the circumstances."

This statutory pontification is calculated to engender further controversies. At present it can be celebrated with a qualification and a corrollary. The qualification (produced by a House of Lords decision) is that if *intending* only to frighten X, Y does some act – such as setting fire to a house – which he can *foresee* may probably result in the death of Z, and which does result in the latter s. 8 (*b*) will be satisfied. The corollary arises from the controversial decision in *D.P.P.* v. *Morgan*, [1975] 2 All E.R. 347 where the House held that where a belief in some state of affairs is part of the essence of the offence charged non-belief will negative the intent even if it be wholly *unreasonable*. The case was one of rape in which neither the jury nor anyone else gave the accused *credit* for the (unreasonable) non-belief in the woman's lack of consent – or, to put it positively, the unreasonable belief that she had consented: so the conviction stood and no harm was done. And it may be that the ruling should be treated as part of the peculiarities of the crime of rape in which lack of consent must be proved. But to anyone other than an academic purist determined to push the *mens rea* dogma to extremes it seems an odd one.

Wherever a specific intent forms a part of the offence charged – *i.e.* is the element of *mens rea* in relation to that offence – it must be *proved*: thus where a man dressed up in a cassock, and read through a marriage service in a church because he had been asked to do so by the "husband" who had told him falsely that he and the "wife" were already married and merely wished to re-enact the ceremony to please her mother, he was held not to have contravened a statutory provision forbidding the knowing and wilful solemnization of marriages by those pretending to be in Holy Orders. In the circumstances there was no real pretence and no real intent to act illegally.

This general rule which requires not merely an "*actus reus*" (a "guilty act") but also "*mens rea*" before a person can be convicted of a crime is, however, subject to certain qualifications.

First, every man is *presumed* to intend the natural consequences of his acts; for it is impossible to prove the existence of a state of mind conclusively. Hence, no one can escape the consequences of committing a cold-blooded murder simply by saying that he did not intend to do it; though, as has just been explained, the question of intention will be judged subjectively (Criminal Justice Act 1967, s. 8). But it must, nevertheless, be made clear that the *prosecution must normally prove its whole case beyond reasonable doubt*: hence if at the close of a case, upon review of all the evidence given on either side, the court or jury are left in reasonable doubt whether the accused really intended to commit the criminal act charged, he *must* be *acquitted*. This proposition may be illustrated by *Woolmington* v. *D.P.P.*, [1935] A.C. 462. In that case W. killed his wife by shooting her and he was charged with murder. Some of the evidence given at the trial supported the inference that the shooting was *accidental*. The trial judge directed the jury that once the prosecution had proved that the accused had killed his wife, a presumption arose that he had murdered her, and that it was the business of the defence to provide evidence capable of displacing this presumption. The House of Lords held that that direction was wrong because, since there was (*inter alia*) evidence before the court from which the inference that the shooting was in fact *accidental* might reasonably be drawn, it was the duty of the prosecution to displace this inference by adducing sufficient evidence of an intent to kill. And it should be added that a similar burden will lie upon the prosecution where the evidence as a whole leaves reasonable doubt as to the existence of other grounds of justification or mitigation, such as self defence, automatism (below, p. 158), provocation (below, p. 169) or reasonable doubt as to the validity of an alibi. Thus the harshness of the presumption that a man intends the natural consequences of his acts is often counterbalanced by the cardinal presumption of English law that a man is *presumed* to be *innocent* until the prosecution have proved him guilty beyond reasonable doubt. It must, however, be noted that where insanity is raised as a defence (below, p. 156) or a statutory defence is invoked, the burden of establishing the defence lies upon the *defendant*.

In the second place, although the common law always insisted upon the presence of *"mens rea"*, certain statutes, in creating criminal offences, have dispensed with this requirement and made some offences *"absolute"*, *i.e.* punishable in the absence of *"mens rea"*. There are many such statutes in force at the present time. The Legislature tends to dispense with the requirement of *"mens rea"* in the case of statutory offences for which the penalty is small, the damage to the public occasioned by their commission is great, and the state of mind of the accused would be exceptionally difficult to establish with any degree of certainty. Examples of statutory offences of this nature are the offence of making a false statement for the purpose of obtaining a certificate of insurance under the Road Traffic Act 1972, s. 170 (1), (6), and failure by a bankrupt to account for any substantial part of his estate under the provisions of the Bankruptcy Act 1914, s. 157 (1) (*c*). In *Sweet* v. *Parsley*, [1970] A.C. 132, however, the conviction of a schoolteacher under s. 5 (*b*) of the Dangerous Drugs Act 1965 for having been "concerned in the management of premises used for the purpose of smoking cannabis" was quashed upon the ground that the accused neither knew nor had the means of knowing of the objectionable habits of her "beatnik" tenants. The House of Lords stressed that offences must not be construed as "absolute" unless there is adequate reason to suppose that Parliament intended to make them so.

The principle that "*mens rea*" must normally exist before criminal responsibility can be imputed receives further illustration from the fact that normally, in the criminal law (as opposed to the law of torts) a person will not be held responsible for the acts of his servants or agents if they are done without his authority. This rule is, however, subject to one exception, even at common law – the case of public nuisance – and to many statutory exceptions created in the public interest or for some other sufficient reason. For example, the Licensing Act 1964, s. 161 (1) provides that if "the holder of a justices' on-licence knowingly sells or supplies intoxicating liquor to unauthorized persons he shall be guilty of an offence". It has been held, more than once under the provisions of this and similar statutes, that a licensee may be held liable where the prohibited acts are committed by his servants or agents without his knowledge; especially where he has delegated the management of the establishment to them. The reason for this strict provision has thus been pithily explained: "If this were not the rule", said an eminent judge, "a publican would never be convicted. He would take care always to be out of the way."

General Exemptions from Criminal Responsibility

Since the law generally insists upon the presence of "*mens rea*" in order to establish guilt one would expect the presence of certain factors, such as Mistake, Duress, Self-Defence, Necessity and Incapacity to affect criminal liability to a greater or less extent. The first four of these factors will be considered in this section; Incapacity will be considered in the next.

MISTAKE
It will usually be a defence to a criminal charge for the accused to prove

that he acted under the influence of a mistake of fact. But this rule is subject to three limitations – (*a*) The mistake must be such that, had the true facts been as the accused believed them to be, he would not have been guilty of the offence in question. Thus it will not be a defence for a man who is accused of stealing a gold watch to prove that he thought it was a silver one or that it was some other valuable object; but it will be a defence, as we shall see below, for him to prove that he honestly believed (contrary to the true facts) that the watch was his own. (*b*) The mistake must be reasonable. So that if a sane man were to cut off another man's ear and to plead, by way of defence, that he imagined that the knife which he used was a magic one, which would cause a new and better ear to grow in place of the old one, his ridiculous belief could afford him no defence. (*c*) Mistake can only be relied upon where the alleged error relates to some fact or facts essential to the charge. Thus in *R*. v. *Hibbert* (1869), L.R. 1 C.C.R. 184, H seduced a girl of fourteen. He was charged, under the Offences Against the Person Act 1861, s. 55, with the offence of taking an unmarried girl under the age of sixteen out of the possession of her parents. There was no evidence to show that he knew that the girl had any parents, and she was in fact at the time in the custody of her father. H was convicted, but the conviction was subsequently quashed because on the facts as he believed them to be he had committed no offence; for he did not know that the girl had any parents. In *R*. v. *Prince* (1875), L.R. 2 C.C.R. 154, on the other hand, P's conviction upon a charge under the same section was upheld : he had reasonable grounds for believing that a girl whom he seduced was over sixteen (though in fact she was not) but he did, nevertheless, know that she was in the custody of her father. His mistake as to her age had no relevance to the offence charged; he had made no mistake in relation to the crucial fact that he had taken her out of her father's care. (*d*) In the case of an "absolute" offence mistake is no defence. Thus in *R*. v. *Miller*, [1975] 2 All E.R. 974, that a person charged with driving on the road while disqualified cannot escape liability by proving that he honestly (but mistakenly) believed that he was in fact driving on private land.

Mistake of *law* is no defence: the general rule is that no man is permitted to excuse himself by asserting that he thought his unlawful act was lawful. The reason for this is similar to the reason for the rule "*ignorantia juris haud excusat*" (ignorance of law is no excuse): in either case knowledge must be presumed, for otherwise people could always escape liability by pretending to the lack of it. Nevertheless, the second rule is sometimes relaxed where ignorance is inevitable: as in a case where a deportation order is made against an individual without publication of any kind. An unpublished law is one which a person cannot possibly know.

DURESS

It is a defence to a criminal charge to prove that the offence was committed under the actual physical compulsion of some other person. Although fear induced by *threats* will probably not excuse a charge of *murder*, it has been held by the House of Lords that it may excuse an aider and abettor even of that crime: thus a man who, under threat of death, knowingly motors assassins to the scene of assassination will not be guilty of murder. Duress is an available defence in other crimes provided that real violence is threatened, proportionate to the occasion, and that the violence threatened is reasonably apprehended. It is not essential that the threat should be immediate: thus where a witness committed perjury because a ruffian in court at the time had threatened to "beat her up" afterwards if she told the truth duress was held to be a good defence. Due, perhaps, largely to historical accident a wife who commits a crime, other than treason or murder, in her husband's presence and under his "coercion" may generally escape liability by establishing the coercion. The word probably signifies something less dramatic than the kind of duress by threats just mentioned; it probably includes mere mental domination. It is to be noted that while it is for the wife to prove the coercion, once "duress" is raised it is for the prosecution to displace the presumption of innocence which it raises.

It seems uncertain how far it will afford a defence to a member of the Forces to plead "superior orders". The correct rule probably is that this defence will only avail where the act which the accused was ordered to do was not manifestly unlawful. A soldier, for example, who is ordered to shoot a prisoner, otherwise than by way of lawful execution, would therefore be ill-advised to carry out the order.

SELF-DEFENCE

The reasonable use of force in defence of oneself or of others, or in defence of one's property, may excuse a crime; even homicide. But the question will depend upon what is reasonable in all the circumstances: thus if you attack me with a pin I am not justified in retaliating by throwing vitriol at you and if, although your dog is chasing them, my sheep are in no danger of *immediate* harm I am not justified in shooting it. What is "reasonable" is a question of fact (compare the C.L.A., s. 3 – above, p. 142) and it may indeed be one which varies with the climate of contemporary opinion: for instance it is doubtful whether the proposition made in *R. v. Hussey* (1924), 18 Cr. App. Rep. 160 that a man is entitled to kill anyone seeking unlawfully to dispossess him of his home would be accepted today. It should be added that self-defence can only be raised in justification if – though actual physical *retreat* from the assailant may *not* be necessary – the accused has done something to show unwillingness to meet force with force. Once this defence is raised it is for the prosecution to prove that the accused was *not* defending himself, not for him to establish that he was.

NECESSITY

There is little English authority on the defence of "Necessity", *i.e.* compulsion arising from circumstances, as opposed to the intervention of another human being. A man who is pursued by wolves should therefore resist the temptation of killing his companion and delaying the attack upon himself by throwing the corpse behind him; especially since in the one important decision on the matter, the colourful case of *R. v. Dudley and Stephens* (1884), 14 Q.B.D. 273, starving shipwrecked sailors who killed a cabin boy in order to feed upon his body were held to be guilty of murder.

It should finally be noted that in every case where there is some extenuating factor which does not provide a recognized ground of exemption, it is always possible for the court to mitigate the punishment according to the circumstances, and in extreme cases there is always the possibility of commutation or pardon. For instance in the case last cited the sailors were sentenced to death, but this sentence was subsequently commuted to one of six months' imprisonment.

Incapacity

The following classes of special status require consideration: Persons of Unsound Mind, Drunken Persons, Infants and Corporations.

1   UNSOUNDNESS OF MIND

This may negative criminal responsibility in a number of ways. There are two main aspects to be considered; either the condition of the accused may be such that it amounts to insanity or it may be that he is suffering from such mental abnormality as to diminish his responsibility.

Insanity may excuse at three possible stages. First, during custody before trial: when this happens the Home Secretary is entitled under the provisions of the Mental Health Act 1959, provided that, amongst other things, he considers it in the public interest so to do, to have the accused detained in hospital. In which case of course, unless he recovers, he will not be tried at all. In the second place, although brought to trial the accused may be found unfit to plead. Here the issue is whether he is capable of understanding the conduct of the trial, and that question must be tried by a specially empanelled jury. If he is then found unfit the court must order his detention in a hospital designated by the Home Secretary.

In the third place insanity may be pleaded as *a defence to the crime charged*. In this sense "insanity" was defined in the well-known rules laid down by the judges in *M'Naghten's Case* (1843), 10 Cl. & Fin. 200. These rules may be summarized thus:

(*a*) Every person is presumed to be sane until the contrary is proved:

(*b*) It is a defence to prove that, at the time of the commission of the act constituting the offence charged, the accused was labouring under such a defect of reason, from disease of the mind, as not to know the nature and quality of his act, or (if he did know this) that what he was doing was wrong:

(*c*) Where a criminal act is committed by a man under some insane delusion as to the surrounding facts, which conceals from him the true nature of the act he is doing, he is under the same degree of responsibility as if the facts were as he imagined them to be.

Normally, as we have seen (above, p. 152), the burden of proof lies on the prosecution throughout a criminal trial, but the presumption of sanity creates an exception to this rule; for where insanity is pleaded the defence must establish on a balance of probabilities that the accused was insane.

When at the trial of an accused person the jury find him to have been insane within the meaning of the *M'Naghten Rules* at the time when he committed the crime charged a special verdict of "not guilty by reason of insanity" will be returned and he will be detained during Her Majesty's pleasure. Until recently, a finding of insanity being regarded as an acquittal, there was no appeal against the verdict. This was unsatisfactory because not only did the finding condemn the accused to indefinite confinement but it also precluded the possibility of his succeeding upon some other defence (*e.g.* alibi) which he might have had. For these and other reasons s. 2 of the Criminal Procedure (Insanity) Act 1964, subject to safeguards, now provides a right of appeal to the Court of Appeal and thence to the House of Lords.

Uncontrollable impulse is not recognized as a defence in English law. But proof that the accused acted under such an impulse may be a relevant matter to consider, because impulsive acts are symptomatic of some forms of insanity. Hence proof of impulsive action may sometimes be relevant to establish such disease of the mind as rendered the accused incapable of knowing the nature and quality of his acts or that they were wrong.

The defence of *diminished responsibility* was introduced in England by the Homicide Act 1957, s. 2. It is specifically a defence to a *murder* charge, and if successfully established it has the effect of reducing the conviction from one for murder to one for manslaughter.

This defence will be established where it can be proved on behalf of the accused, on a balance of probabilities, that he "was suffering from such abnormality of mind (whether arising from a condition of arrested or retarded development of mind, or any inherent causes, or induced by disease or injury) as substantially impaired his mental responsibility for his acts and omissions in doing or being a party to the killing". It is the duty of the jury to consider the issue broadly and without reference to the "legal" insanity of the *M'Naghten Rules*; in effect they must ask themselves "Is the accused without being insane, nevertheless on the borderline of insanity?" Here again, though uncontrollable impulse is no defence, proof of its existence may yet be relevant as pointing to a state of diminished responsibility. Where, in a murder trial, diminished responsibility is raised as a defence the prosecution may adduce evidence of *insanity*, and where insanity is raised, evidence of diminished responsibility (Criminal Procedure (Insanity) Act 1964, s. 6). Moreover, where upon an indictment for murder the medical evidence supports the inference of diminished responsibility a plea of guilty of manslaughter may properly be accepted.

Akin to the above defences is the plea of *automatism*. There is no doubt that when a person commits a crime while his mind is in a state of suspense he will not, at least in general, be held responsible for it. Instances are where, at any rate provided that his condition came about through no fault of his own, a man kills another while he is in an hypnotic trance or where he unwittingly assaults another person after insulin has been administered to him. But for this defence to succeed a reasonable foundation for it must be established – such as evidence that the accused was in a trance: normally obviously the mere statement by the accused that his mind was "a blank" would not be enough. But once such a foundation has been established it will rest upon the prosecution to prove that the act was in fact voluntary if a conviction is to be obtained. The difference between "automatism" and "insanity" as defences is that the latter rests upon the fact of *disease* while the former arises from some external factor, such as drugs: and whereas proof of the latter *must* excuse, proof of the former may, but need not, do so.

2   DRUNKEN PERSONS

In bye-gone days the law treated drunkenness (provided that it was self-induced) as no excuse for the commission of a crime, but rather as an aggravating circumstance: in the words of Sir Matthew Hale (1609–1676), "by the laws of England (a drunken person) shall have no privilege by this voluntary contracted madness, but shall have the same judgment as if he were in his right senses". But in modern times this harsh rule has been relaxed. In the first place, it is now recognized that excessive drunkenness may induce actual disease of the mind, as in the case of *delirium tremens*. Where actual disease is thus proved the accused will be treated in the same way as any other person of unsound mind, and the *M'Naghten Rules* will apply. In the second place, proof of drunkenness which induces a state of mind falling short of insanity may sometimes serve to negative the existence of some particular kind of intent necessary for the establishment of guilt. For instance, malice aforethought (below, p. 167) being an essential element in the definition of the crime of murder, where the accused can be proved to have been so drunk at the time of the killing as not to be able to form any of the intents necessary to establish such malice he cannot be guilty of murder; though such a state of mind induced by the voluntary taking of drink or drugs will be no excuse in the case of a charge – such as one of assault – where no specific intent need be proved. But of course he would be guilty of murder, whatever the effects of the alcohol, if he were to form the intent to kill first and then to get drunk in order to carry it out. It must be stressed that in this defence again the onus is on the prosecution under the *Woolmington* principle (above, p. 152) – it must establish that, despite the drunkenness the accused could form the necessary intent and it is not the duty of the defence to prove the reverse.

On the other hand, where the fact of drunkenness is *of itself* the essence of a charge (as in the case of "driving under the influence" under s. 5 of the Road Traffic Act 1972, or of driving with an undue proportion of alcohol in the blood under s. 6 of that Act) it is, of course, useless to call aid in the very thing that constitutes the offence in order to attempt to prove the absence of intention. Further, provided that the accused is capable, at the time of the commission of the crime charged, of forming the appropriate intent it will be no excuse for him to show that alcohol affected his powers of self-control – induced him, for example, to give way to some violent passion to which he would not normally have succumbed. Thus we shall see that in certain circumstances homicide may be reduced from murder to manslaughter where it can be proved that the accused acted under provocation; but it will not avail him to show that, being drunk, he was more easily provoked than he would have been had he been sober.

Although (unlike the taking of alcoholic liquor) the taking of drugs is often *in itself* unlawful, the rules governing the general criminal responsibility of persons affected by drugs are similar to those governing alcoholic intoxication.

3 MINORITY

Up to the age of *ten* no person can be held guilty of any criminal offence. A child of over eight and under *fourteen* is *presumed* to be incapable of forming a criminal intent; but this presumption may be rebutted by evidence which proves that he knew that what he was doing was seriously wrong. Further, no boy of under *fourteen* can be held guilty of rape, or of unlawful carnal knowledge; for there is an irrebuttable presumption that he is incapable of committing these offences. It is interesting to note that the age of complete criminal incapacity at common law was seven years: it was raised by statute to eight and then, again, subject to the rebuttability of the presumption noted above, to ten in 1963. By contrast the age of majority, was, as has been seen (above, p. 93) lowered by the Family Law Reform Act from twenty-one to eighteen. Up one end, down the other: a paradox?

The rules relating to the trial of juvenile offenders have already been mentioned (above, p. 41).

4 CORPORATIONS

In days gone by, when a very large number of crimes were punishable by death, it was generally accepted that corporations could not be held liable for crimes committed by their servants or agents; for, as it was truly said, "You cannot hang the common seal". Further, until the passing of the Criminal Justice Act 1925, corporations could not be indicted.

In recent times there has, however, been an increasing tendency to hold corporations criminally liable for the acts of their servants or agents committed in the course of their employment. Corporations have, for example, been indicted for conspiracy and for infringements of tax regulations. How far the courts will go in thus removing corporate immunity in criminal matters still remains to be seen, it is clear that there must be some limit to the relaxation of the older rules, for the artificial nature of corporations precludes their imprisonment just as much as the hanging of them – indeed, they can only be punished by fine. Moreover, it is unlikely that the intention to commit such crimes as rape or murder will ever be imputed to a corporation.

The Classification of Crimes

The distinction between *indictable* and *summary* offences has already been noted. Here it must be explained that until the coming into force of the Criminal Law Act 1967 (C.L.A.) crimes were divided historically into three categories: *treason, felonies* and *misdemeanours* – in descending order of seriousness. Each class had special rules of procedure appropriate to it and certain rules of substantive law peculiar to it.

While making, as has been seen (above, p. 141), a new distinction between "arrestable" and other offences the C.L.A. (s. 1) abolished the dichotomy between felonies and misdemeanours and made the law and practice relating to all offences (save treason) that which had previously been applicable to misdemeanours. Treason thus remains separate, but, since the Act (s. 12 (6)) also equiparated trial procedure in treason to that of murder, the only important practical distinction between treason and other forms of crime is that it still retains special rules in relation to the degrees of guilt of those who participate in it. The question of participation now falls to be considered.

The Parties to a Crime

There are a number of possible degrees of criminal participation. Let us take examples: (*i*) Suppose A and B combine jointly to commit a crime, *e.g.*, B holds C while A knifes him: clearly *both* are *guilty* as "principals" in the act. (*ii*) Suppose B, without actually committing the crime, is present at the scene of it encouraging its commission; *e.g.*, B connives while A stabs C. (*iii*) Suppose B, without actually being on the scene, assists A in the preparation of the crime; lends him the knife to do the deed. (*iv*) Suppose B, after the crime, assists A in concealing it; throws the knife into a pond after A's return. (*v*) Suppose while doing nothing active to help, and knowing nothing of the deed, B listens to A's story of his exploit after it is done and then takes no steps to expose A to the authorities. In all these cases – (*i*) Actual participation, (*ii*) Connivance, (*iii*) Assistance in preparation, (*iv*) Subsequent assistance, (*v*) Concealment of knowledge of the crime – though less obviously in the remainder than in the first, B has in one way or another been a party to the crime. A's position is clear, but what about B's in every case except the first?

Formerly the law in this field was complicated by the fact that the position varied according to the classification of the crime committed, whether treason, felony or misdemeanour. The C.L.A. having assimilated the law relating to felonies to that of misdemeanours, what we have to consider is what the rule would formerly have been had the crime in question been a misdemeanour. Treason, however, still stands apart.

1 CRIMES OTHER THAN TREASON
Referring to our examples (omitting the first) the misdemeanour rule

would have been, and the universal rule now is, that where there is connivance (*ii*) or assistance in preparation (*iii*) – *"aiding and abetting"* – B
will be treated in law, like A, as *guilty of the crime*: except that technically
B is not in these cases a "principal" criminal. Where, however, B merely
gives subsequent assistance (*iv*) or conceals his knowledge of the crime
(*v*) he will now (though this used not to be so in the case of felony)
be guilty of *no crime unless* he commits an *"arrestable offence"* (see above,
p. 141) which comes within the following provisions of the C.L.A.

In the first place the C.L.A., s. 4 (1) enacts that "Where a person has
committed an arrestable offence, any other person who, knowing or
believing him to be guilty of the offence or of some other arrestable
offence, does without lawful authority or reasonable excuse any act with
intent to *impede his apprehension or prosecution* shall be guilty of an
offence." Thus mere connivance after the act will never be a crime, but
the example of throwing away the knife would be – causing grievous
bodily harm being an arrestable offence, and the concealing of the knife
an act calculated to impede prosecution. There is, of course, no reason
why the impeder should know the identity of the criminal. In
the second place, the C.L.A., s. 5 (1) makes it a crime punishable with
not more than two years' imprisonment for a person to accept or to agree
to accept any *consideration* (other than making good any loss caused by
the offence or making reasonable compensation for that loss) for *not disclosing information* about an arrestable offence which he knows or believes
to have been committed. There may, however, be no prosecution for
either of these offences without the consent of the Director of Public
Prosecutions.

The position of the *aider and abettor* (*ii*) and (*iii*) can give rise to
subtleties. For example, the abettor may sometimes be guilty of the
offence while his principal is not. This position may be illustrated by the
case of the man who instigates a "rape" committed by another person who
believes the woman to be consenting – and who thus is *not* guilty of rape
while his abettor, who is aware of the lack of consent, is. Again, an abettor cannot be guilty of an offence graver than the offence actually committed by the principal: thus if C instigates B to assault A intending
that B shall occasion serious harm to A and B merely commits a minor
assault on A, despite C's intent he can only be convicted of unlawful
wounding rather than of the more serious offence of wounding with
intent to do grievous bodily harm. And finally, an interesting point was
raised by *Attorney-General's Reference (No. 1 of 1975)*, [1975] 2 All E.R.
684 (for this procedure see above, p. 33). Can a generous host who
"laces" the drink of a guest be convicted as abettor if the unfortunate
guest is subsequently charged under, the Road Traffic Act 1972, ss. 5 or
6 (above)? The answer was "Yes" he *may* be: but much must depend

upon the circumstances – for instance it may be relevant that the guest is unaware of the fact that the drink has been "laced" and it must be established that the guest's condition at the time of arrest was in fact the result of the lacing.

2 TREASON

In the case of treason a person present and conniving at the scene of the crime or assisting in the *preparation* or subsequent *concealment* of it is treated in the same way as the person who actually commits it: *i.e.* he is a *"principal"* to the crime. Moreover where anyone knows that treason has been committed (or, possibly, even knows of a plot to commit it) and fails to disclose his knowledge to the appropriate authorities he will be guilty of *"misprision"* of treason; an offence for which, *inter alia*, he may be imprisoned for life.

Attempts

An *attempt* to commit an *indictable* offence is in itself a crime. In order to constitute an attempt there must be an *intention* to commit an offence, and some *act* must have been done which is immediately connected with the commission of it and which cannot be regarded as having any other purpose. The intent is vital, mere negligence or recklessness is not enough. Step beyond this statement and, as perusal of the House of Lords decision in *Haughton* v. *Smith*, [1973] 3 All E.R. 1109 will convince the reader, one steps on uncertain ground. The nearest to a satisfactory statement of the law was adopted in that case: "Steps on the way to the commission of what *would be a crime*, if the acts were completed, may amount to attempts to commit that crime, to which, unless interrupted, they would have led; but steps on the way to the doing of something which is thereafter done, *and which is no crime*, cannot be regarded as attempts to commit a crime." The words italicized highlight the actual decision in the case which was that it is no attempt to handle goods which the handler *believes to be* stolen goods but which, because they have been restored to lawful possession, are *not* "stolen". But the first limb of the definition leaves open a multitude of questions. For example, it was asked in the judgment whether, in Conan Doyle's novel *The Empty Room* where Sherlock Holmes left a model of himself in the window of the famous lodgings in Baker Street and the villain shot at the model, intending to kill, the facts constituted attempted murder. Commonsense says emphatically "Yes"; but common law, in its eternal concern to protect the guilty *seems* to say "No". Yet we may be more sympathetic to the common law which also has it that the man who stabs a corpse thinking that it is alive cannot be held for an attempt. The distinction seems to be that in the first case Holmes was alive: in the second (though one could murder Holmes) one can hardly murder a corpse – a distinction which was not taken. Yet it seems plain that the man who, intending to poison, puts too little poison in the cup commits an attempt, while there may be doubt whether the pickpocket who fumbles for the wallet which is not in the pocket makes an attempt. Most people would surely say "yes" to the latter. The truth would seem to be that the meaning of "attempt" is much a question of fact, and that rules of law can only emerge in relation to particular situations.

It is enacted by the C.L.A., s. 7 (2) that a person convicted of an attempt to commit a crime for which a maximum term of imprisonment, or a maximum fine, is provided shall not be sentenced to a longer term, or to pay a larger fine, than that to which he could be sentenced for the completed offence.

Akin to "attempt" is *incitement*: as where a man offers, for payment, to give false evidence in another's favour. Here, though the latter refuse the offer, the former has incited him to prevent the course of justice – a crime.

Limitation of Time

As regards criminal prosecutions, the common law rule was expressed by the maxim *"nullum tempus occurit regi"* ("time does not run against the King"). A prosecution could be instituted at any time after the commission of the crime. In theory this is still the general rule, but there are statutory exceptions. The most important of these are that prosecutions for *summary* offences must normally be commenced within six months of commission; and, in the case of certain motoring offences unless the accused is warned at the time of detection that a prosecution may be considered, a summons or notice of prosecution must be served within fourteen days.

B SPECIFIC CRIMES

For the sake of convenience crimes may be divided into three main categories: offences against the public interest, offences against the person and offences against property.

Offences Against the Public Interest

There are a number of crimes which fall under this head. The following may be mentioned – treason, sedition, offences against the Official Secrets Acts, conspiracy (see below, p. 310), riot, unlawful assembly, and perjury. Some of these have already been discussed in the last chapter. Here space will only permit us to outline the bare essentials of the first, and most serious, of them – treason.

Originally there were two forms of treason, "high treason" and "*petit* treason". The latter was committed when a person of inferior status unlawfully killed his or her superior; such as a wife her husband (for the common law regarded wives as their husbands' inferiors) or a servant his master. Since 1828 offences of this type have been treated as ordinary murders.

High treason is the offence of breach of allegiance to the Crown. Allegiance was originally a personal matter, the bond between subject and Sovereign. Hence the Treason Act 1351, which still governs the law, defines treason in personal terms: the definition embraces, amongst other things, the following offences – (1) Compassing the death of the King, the Queen, or their eldest son and heir; (2) Violating the King's consort, his eldest daughter unmarried, or the wife of his eldest son and heir; (3) Levying war against the King in his realm; (4) Adhering to the King's enemies in his realm, giving them aid and comfort in the realm or elsewhere. (The word "King" must, of course, be taken to mean "Sovereign", so as to include reigns, such as the present, when there is a Queen regnant.)

By far the commonest types of treason have been those falling within classes (1), (3) and (4); and the words of the Statute have been subjected to extensive judicial interpretation; keeping pace with the needs of the expanding concept of the "State", which has long since ceased to be founded upon the personal relationship between sovereign and subject.

As to (1) – "*Compassing*" has been taken to include any "overt" act done in furtherance of the object of bringing about the Sovereign's death. Thus, in *Preston's Case* (1691), 12 Howell's State Trials, 646, it was held that an overt act of "compassing" had been committed when the accused was caught in the act of hiring a ship for the conveyance of treasonable papers to an enemy government. Further, the intent signified by the idea of "compassing" has been enlarged so as to include acts calculated not merely to endanger the Sovereign's own personal safety, but also the position of the Crown as an institution. As to (3) – It should be noted that the "*levying of war*" has been held to include any attack upon a general class of the Sovereign's subjects. In the eighteenth century it was, for example, once held that it was treasonable to incite a mob to destroy the meeting-houses of dissenters (*R.* v. *Damaree* (1709), Foster 213). As to (4) – "*Adherence*" or "*aid and comfort*" may be treasonable even though it is effected outside the realm. Thus, in *Joyce* v. *D.P.P.*, [1946] A.C. 347, William Joyce ("Lord Haw-Haw") was convicted on account of his anti-British war-time broadcasts in Germany.

Just as the concept of "treason" has expanded so also has the concept of allegiance. Originally allegiance was owed only by the King's "men", *i.e.* his subjects; but with the emergence of the modern State it came to be held that anyone who is under the the protection of the Crown, whether or not he be a British subject, is bound by the duty of allegiance. Hence, if a person who is not a British subject resides for a long time within the realm he will receive the Crown's protection, will owe allegiance, and can therefore be held guilty of treason. Moreover, such a person will in some circumstances continue to owe allegiance even after he leaves the realm; as, for example, where he leaves property within the realm or still continues to carry a British passport. It was upon this last ground that William Joyce, who was not a British national, broke the law.

During the eighteenth century the judges created many "constructive" treasons by construing the wording of the Statute so as to make it cover many cases which it was not originally intended to embrace. This tendency made juries loath to convict in any but the clearest cases; with the result that an Act had to be passed in 1795 to confirm the validity of certain of these "constructive" treasons. In 1848, however, a further Act was passed designating many of them "treason-felonies", punishable with life imprisonment only.

The penalty for treason is death and formerly execution was attended by certain peculiar barbarities. These barbarities have long since ceased to be practised and procedurally trials for treason and misprision (see above, p. 163) of treason are now (under the Criminal Law Act 1967, s. 12 (6)) treated in the same way as trials for murder.

Offences Against the Person

The following offences against the person will be selected for discussion – (1) Homicide, (2) Assault and Battery, (3) Rape, (4) Bigamy.

1 HOMICIDE

It should be stressed in the first place that it is not necessarily unlawful to kill a man. Thus, death may occur by "*misadventure*" even where some person is instrumental in causing it: an attacker may in certain circumstances, be lawfully killed by a person who is in the act of defending himself or his property; in extreme circumstances a constable making an arrest or preventing an escape, or someone assisting him, may lawfully kill the criminal who offers violence (but see C.L.A., s. 3 – above, p. 142) and of course the execution of the death penalty where lawfully inflicted by the judgment of a competent court is lawful.

A common example of death by misadventure occurs where it is caused during the playing of a lawful game. For instance a batsman who kills a fieldsman standing at "silly point" by driving the ball hard in his direction will not be guilty of any crime, provided that his act was neither intentional nor grossly careless.

The rules relating to self-defence, which apply to a charge of homicide as well as to charges involving non-fatal injuries, have already been mentioned (above, p. 155).

We may now briefly discuss the following unlawful homicides – murder, manslaughter, the aiding and abetting of suicide, and infanticide.

Murder – According to the classic definition, murder comprises the "*unlawful killing of a reasonable creature who is in being and under the (Queen's) peace, with malice aforethought . . . the death following within a year and a day*". Let us consider the various elements of this definition.

A "*reasonable creature*" signifies a human being, as opposed to an animal.

"*In being*" signifies that there can be no murder of an unborn person. In the eye of the law a child is not "born" until its body is fully extruded from that of its mother; and it will only then be "born" if it is extruded alive. Until these conditions are satisfied there can be no "murder" of the child, accordingly it will not be murder to *prevent* it from being born alive. Nevertheless, the Infant Life (Preservation) Act 1929, makes it an offence ("*child destruction*"), punishable with imprisonment for life, wilfully to cause the death of a child which is capable of being born alive – which it is presumed to be after 28 weeks of pregnancy – before it has acquired an existence independent of its mother. For a person to be convicted of this offence it must, however, be shown that the act which caused the death was not done in good faith for the purpose of preserving the life of the mother. And procuration of *abortion* is of course also a crime; though by the Abortion Act 1967 it will not be one where, under certain conditions, pregnancy is terminated by a registered medical practitioner; provided that two such practitioners are of the opinion that the continuance of the pregnancy would endanger the mother's life or health, or that of her children, or that the child to aborted would, if born, be seriously handicapped. A second opinion is not necessary in the case of emergency where immediate action is essential to save the life of, or to prevent grave injury to, the mother. As is well-known, this Act has led to many abuses.

"*Under the (Queen's) peace*" now signifies simply that it is not murder to kill an enemy in war. But it should be noted that, as an exception to the general rule that criminal jurisdiction is confined to crimes committed in this country, murder committed by a British subject anywhere is triable here.

"*Malice aforethought*" is important because it is the element of intent required to establish murder. It may consist of an intent to kill, whether particular or general: for instance X intends to shoot A and does so, or he intends to shoot A and in fact shoots B, or he places a bomb in an aeroplane intending to blow it up in flight with no particular malice against anyone in it, but with a general intent to kill. It may consist of an intent to cause grievous bodily harm, *i.e.* really serious bodily harm. But such an intent it must be, no less; furthermore (see above, p. 152) the test of intent is *subjective i.e.*, not what the state of mind of the accused appeared to be, but "What *was* it?" Thus if the jury consider, however serious the risk of causing death might seem to the man in the street observing the accused's behaviour when he did the deed, that the accused actually intended something less than grievous bodily harm there can be no murder.

"*The death following within a year and a day*" – The mediaeval law wisely prescribed that there could be no prosecution for homicide unless the death followed within a full year of the act alleged to have caused it. Before the development of modern medical science it would have been impossible to be certain, after a greater lapse of time, that the act was the real cause of death. In English law this rule still persists, though similar rules have now been abolished in other countries and it has never prevailed in Scotland.

Formerly the penalty for murder used to be death by hanging, but the Murder (Abolition of Death Penalty) Act 1965 has now substituted life imprisonment for death. At the time of sentencing the court may declare a minimum period which in its view should elapse before the Secretary of State orders release on licence.

People below the age of *eighteen* years at the time of committing a murder cannot be sentenced to life imprisonment, but they must instead be sentenced to be detained during Her Majesty's pleasure.

Manslaughter – Manslaughter is the offence of unlawfully causing the death of another, without malice aforethought.

There are two categories of manslaughter: "voluntary" manslaughter and "involuntary" manslaughter. *Voluntary manslaughter* is committed when a man causes the death of another in circumstances which would have amounted to *murder* had the act not been done under provocation or in pursuance of a suicide pact. *Involuntary manslaughter* may be committed in two ways. First, by causing death in the commission of an unlawful and dangerous act. Second, by causing death by an omission to perform a legal duty, or by performing a lawful act recklessly.

(*a*) *Voluntary Manslaughter* – In a trial for murder it is for the jury to consider whether there is such evidence of *provocation* either by the victim himself or by some other person as to justify a conviction for manslaughter. And where there is evidence upon which the jury could reasonably so find, the judge must draw their attention to it in his summing up; whether or not the issue of provocation has been raised by the defence. As to the degree of provocation required, the Homicide Act 1957, s. 3, provides that, whether it is provocative acts or words or both that are relied upon, the jury must consider whether they were such that a reasonable man placed in the position of the accused would have lost his self-control and acted as the accused did act. And it is, of course, further relevant (as in the case of self-defence) to ask whether the degree of force used bore a reasonable relationship to the provocation; though it must be stressed that what is "reasonable" is here solely a question of fact to be decided by the jury in relation to the actual circumstances of the case. Thus even a blackmailer who must expect and accept a degree of provocation from his victim – such as, "You b——blackmailing b——" – may yet rely upon it if the victim makes a serious physical attack upon him. This matter is further confused by the fact that the actual state of the accused's mind – as the jury may suppose it to have been – forms the ultimate criterion under s. 8 of the Criminal Justice Act 1967 (see above, p. 152). One may be permitted to wonder just how obscure the law can get in its anxiety to safeguard the criminal. Provocation may be successfully pleaded even though the accused did (though provoked) form an actual intent to kill.

The Homicide Act 1957, s. 4 (as amended by the Suicide Act 1961) enacts that "it shall be *manslaughter*, and shall not be murder, for a person acting *in pursuance of a suicide pact* between him and another to kill the other or be a party to the other being killed by a third person". (Italics ours.) The case assumed is of course where the accused has carried out the pact in respect of the other party or parties, or connived at its being carried out, but has failed to implement it in respect of himself. It will be noted that in order for the accused to escape the charge of *murder* he must have been acting "in pursuance of" the pact; and the section provides that for this to be the case he must himself have had a "settled intention of dying" at the time of the killing. A suicide pact is not therefore a painless way of committing a murder and escaping with a conviction for manslaughter by changing one's mind in respect of one's own future as soon as the pact is concluded. The section also provides that where the facts of a case do fall within its ambit a conviction for manslaughter may be entered, though the accused has been initially charged with murder.

It remains to be added that where, upon a charge of murder, a plea of *self-defence* (see above, p. 155) fails because, for instance, undue force has been used by the accused, it does not necessarily follow that there *must* be a verdict of manslaughter. The position is that, self-defence having failed to exonerate, other issues may arise – for example whether there was provocation or whether, indeed, an intent to murder was in fact present.

(b) *Involuntary Manslaughter* – It has been explained that killing by an act intended to kill or to cause grievous bodily harm amounts to murder. Where death results from an act intended, and likely, to cause some lesser degree of harm to the deceased the crime will be manslaughter. The difference between the two relevant kinds of harm is of course one of degree. It is also, as we have seen, no justification that a man who kills is under the influence of drink or drugs: hence where the accused is so intoxicated by either that he kills without knowing what he does – though conviction for murder is out of the question, there being no malice aforethought – manslaughter may be a proper verdict.

Manslaughter by neglect of duty can only arise where some legally recognized duty is broken; as where a parent or guardian neglects to maintain a child, with the result that it dies of starvation.

Causing death by the performance of an otherwise lawful act will only be manslaughter where the actor is *criminally* negligent, and criminal negligence is something more highly culpable than the kind of negligence which is required to found civil liability (see below, p. 290). It is sometimes defined as "recklessness" or "wanton disregard for the safety of others"; but it is a concept that cannot be comprehensively defined, nor can it easily be illustrated; for the existence or non-existence of this sort of negligence has to be determined in the light of the facts of each case. It must also be remembered that, here again, the test of *criminal* negligence, unlike the test of negligence in tort, is *subjective*. Thus it was held in *R. v. Lamb*, [1967] 2 Q.B. 981, that a man who killed another by playing the game of "Russian roulette" was entitled to have it put to the jury that if they thought he believed there was no danger in the game an acquittal was warranted. The foolish must thus be judged as fools, the wise, as wise. And again, in *R. v. Lowe*, [1973] 1 All E.R. 805 a man of poor intelligence whose child died because he failed to consult a doctor, though convicted of the lesser offence of wilfully neglecting the child, was held not guilty of manslaughter.

The maximum punishment for manslaughter is imprisonment for life, but this will only be imposed in the most serious cases. Manslaughter has been aptly described as the "most elastic of all crimes", for the degree of guilt of the accused may vary from something akin to "malice aforethought" to something close to innocence.

NOTE – Prosecutions for manslaughter probably occur most frequently in connexion with the criminally negligent driving of motor vehicles, but it should be noted that there are three lesser offences which may also be charged in cases of dangerous or careless driving. First, by the Road Traffic Act 1972, s. 1, any person who *causes the death of another* by driving recklessly or at a speed or in a manner which is dangerous to the public in all the circumstances may be charged on indictment and, if convicted, is punishable with a maximum of five years' imprisonment. Second, under s. 2 of the same Act, it is an offence to *drive recklessly* or at a speed, or in a manner, which is dangerous to the public: this offence is punishable with a maximum of two years' imprisonment upon indictment, and four months' imprisonment upon first conviction by a court of summary jurisdiction. In the third place, by section 3 of the Act, it is a summary offence to drive a motor car *without due care and attention or without reasonable consideration for other persons using the road.*

Aiding and abetting suicide – Since the passing of the Suicide Act 1961 suicide of itself is no longer a crime; but the Act makes it an offence punishable with a maximum of fourteen years' imprisonment to aid, abet, counsel or procure the suicide or attempted suicide or another and, where the facts warrant it, a person charged with murder or manslaughter may be convicted of this offence. The consent of the Director of Public Prosecutions is necessary for prosecutions under this Act.

Infanticide – This is a statutory crime. It is now governed by the Infanticide Act 1938, which provides that where a woman wilfully causes the death of her child, being *under the age of twelve months*, in circumstances which would amount to murder she will not be guilty of murder. Instead, she will be guilty of *"infanticide"*, if, at the time she did the act causing death, the balance of her mind was disturbed by reason either of her not having recovered from the effects of the birth, or by reason of the effect of lactation consequent upon the birth. Infanticide is punishable in the same way as manslaughter.

2 ASSAULT AND BATTERY

The word "assault" is commonly used to signify the two offences of "*assault*" *and* "battery", which are normally committed together. An assault *may*, however, be made without a battery.

A "common" assault consists in attempting, or offering, to do a corporal wrong to another person in such a way as to cause reasonable fear in the mind of that person that the wrong will actually be committed. A battery consists in the actual application of force to the person of another. Both assault and battery were misdemeanours at common law; they are now also statutory offences under the Offences Against the Person Act 1861.

Common illustrations of assault without battery are the act of shaking a stick at a person who is close enough to be hit, or of pointing a gun at him: according to the better view this latter act will constitute an assault even if the gun is not loaded, *provided* that the person threatened does not know that it is not; for it is essential to the commission of the offence that reasonable alarm should be caused. Any degree of force suffices for the commission of a battery, however trivial, even a mere touch.

Mere accidental contacts which inevitably occur in the ordinary course of everyday life, such as unintentional jostling in a crowd, are justifiable. Moreover, where there is consent there can normally be no assault or battery; hence, since the players impliedly assent to run the risks of the game, it will generally be justifiable to tackle another player in the course of a game of football. Consent will, however, be no defence to a charge of assault where the battery has been committed in the course of some unlawful activity, such as prize-fighting. As in homicide so, *a fortiori*, in the case of assault self-defence may justify (see above, p. 155). In order to obtain a conviction for an assault it is not essential to establish that the accused intended to assault the complainant; it suffices that the injury resulted from the accused's reckless behaviour.

When a person has been summarily convicted of assault or battery no civil proceedings in respect of either – for they are both civil wrongs as well as crimes – may be brought subsequently. The maximum punishment for a common assault is one year's imprisonment.

Besides "common" assault, there are various forms of aggravated assaults and certain other kindred offences prescribed by the Offences Against the Person Act 1861. All of these carry a higher maximum penalty than common assault. They include such things as unlawful and malicious wounding, and the infliction of grievous bodily harm.

The law relating to many *sexual* offences, including assaults, has now been consolidated in the Sexual Offences Act 1956. And it should be added that the Sexual Offences Act 1967, legalized homosexual practices among consenting males over twenty-one in private – though seamen serving on merchant ships of the United Kingdom are excluded from the benefit of this parliamentary indulgence.

3 RAPE

The offence of rape is committed when a man has sexual intercourse with a woman against her will. Thus there can be no rape where there is consent, and a husband cannot therefore normally be guilty of raping his wife, because, as Sir Matthew Hale put it, "by their mutual matrimonial consent and contract the wife hath given up herself in this kind unto her husband, which she cannot retract". Where, however, a husband and wife are living apart under judicial separation or a separation order, the logic ceases to apply and the husband may then be guilty of rape; so does it after decree *nisi* though before decree absolute for divorce. Further, though a husband cannot rape his wife he may, it seems, be guilty of *assault* if he uses force in order to have sexual relations with her against her will. It has already been noted that the requirement that the act must be done *without the woman's consent* is part of the offence; so that where the accused believes – even according to *Morgan's Case* (see above, p. 151) upon no reasonable grounds – that she does consent the offence is not made out.

The "consent" must, of course, be a real consent. Thus, consent induced by fraud (as where a man induces a married woman to have intercourse with him by impersonating her husband) will not form a defence; and it will also amount to rape if a man has intercourse with a woman while she is unconscious, for then she is incapable of giving or of withholding her consent.

Rape carries a maximum penalty of imprisonment for life.

4 BIGAMY

Bigamy is a statutory offence; governed by the Offences Against the Person Act 1861, s. 57. It is committed by anyone who, being married, "marries" any other person during the life of his or of her husband or wife.

The first essential is that the accused must be *married* to a living person at the time of the "marriage" which constitutes the offence. "Married" means lawfully married and, for this purpose, monogamously married; a polygamous marriage will not suffice to support the charge. Hence, if the first marriage was *null*, as for example where it was a marriage within the "prohibited degrees" (see below, p. 409) a second marriage will not be bigamous. This rule will not, however, apply in the case of a merely "*voidable*" marriage, *e.g.* a marriage which is liable to be set aside on the ground of impotence. No second marriage can lawfully be contracted until a decree *absolute* has been obtained annulling the first.

The statute further provides that a second marriage will not be bigamous if, at the time it is contracted, a previous marriage or marriages have been dissolved by a competent court. Moreover, since it has been possible, where a husband or wife has reason to believe that his or her spouse is dead, for him or her to obtain a judicial decree of "presumption of death" and dissolution of marriage, the effect of this decree will be to dissolve the marriage and enable the person concerned to contract a second marriage lawfully.

The second essential of the offence is that the accused shall *"re-marry"*. The essence of bigamy lies in the profanation of the marriage ceremony. Hence, as regards the *second* "marriage", provided that a legally recognized ceremony has been conducted, either according to our law, or, if the "marriage" is contracted abroad, according to some foreign law which we recognize, the offence will be committed even though the second "marriage" is in other respects a nullity; *e.g.* because the parties to *this* "marriage" were within the "prohibited degrees".

By the proviso to the Offences Against the Person Act 1861, s. 57, it is a defence to a charge of bigamy to show that the first husband or wife has been continually *absent* for a minimum period of seven years, and has not been known by the accused to have been alive during that period. Of course, if under these circumstances, and without having obtained a decree of presumption of death, the accused does "re-marry", although he or she cannot be charged with bigamy, the second "marriage" will be a nullity if the other spouse re-appears.

Apart from the Act, it is also a defence for the accused to show that he or she had reasonable grounds for supposing that his or her spouse was *dead* at the time when the second marriage was contracted. Thus, in *R. v. Tolson* (1889), 23 Q.B.D. 168, where Mrs. T was deserted by her husband in 1881, and she heard from reliable sources that he had been drowned, it was held that her re-marriage in January 1887 was not bigamous, though the husband re-appeared in the December of that year. Further, by parity of reasoning, it is also a defence to prove that the accused honestly believed on reasonable grounds that the previous marriage was annulled or dissolved, even though in fact it was not. This decision was left undisturbed by the decision in *Morgan's Case* (above, p. 151); as well it might be. A person who "marries" another knowing that he or she is already married will be guilty of bigamy as principal in the second degree, provided that the act of the other party is itself bigamous. Of course this act might be apparently bigamous, but not really so: for example, the man who "married" Mrs. T could not have been guilty as principal in the second degree, even if he had known that the husband was alive, for Mrs. T, the principal, was herself not guilty.

Bigamy is punishable with a maximum of seven years' imprisonment.

Offences in Relation to Property

The most important offences of this kind are offences connected with theft and offences connected with criminal damage to property.

1 THEFT AND ALLIED OFFENCES

The law concerning theft, formerly contained largely in the Larceny Act 1916, was re-fashioned by the Theft Act 1968 (hereafter "T.A."). There is space here to consider the following offences only – (*i*) Theft; (*ii*) Robbery; (*iii*) Burglary; (*iv*) Obtaining by Deception; (*v*) Blackmail; (*vi*) Handling Stolen Goods. And it will also be necessary to mention (*vii*) the law relating to restitution of stolen property.

i Theft – The old law of larceny (stealing) – a word which is now no longer used – was bedevilled by the fact that though it had been for the most part codified in a number of Larceny Acts it ultimately sprang from the common law which, in former times, was for a variety of reasons obsessed by the need to protect *possession*. Thus larceny was defined by reference to the observable fact of "taking and carrying away" the stolen goods, rather than by reference to the dishonesty of the chief's conduct.

This approach to the matter, necessary though it originally was in a loosely organized society where breaches of the peace arising from criminous taking were much to be feared, proved in the course of time to be unduly circumscribed since it meant that the law of theft did not embrace many types of dishonest dealing with property which did not involve a taking out of the owner's possession. Thus a patchwork of statute law had to be superimposed upon the law of simple larceny (theft) creating special offences of dishonest dealing with property which were not within the technical confines of larceny. For instance "embezzlement" was not larceny, but was a special offence; this was necessary because it was committed where a clerk or servant appropriated property received *by him* on behalf of his master, and this meant that the appropriation, he having himself the possession of the property until he gave it to the master, was not an attack upon the *master's possession*. Many other instances of the patchwork quality of the former law could be given.

Hence the T.A. started from the standpoint of widening the definition of stealing and focusing rather upon the dishonesty of the thief than upon the element of disturbance of possession. Section 1 (1) of that Act therefore provides that "A person is guilty of theft if he *dishonestly appropriates property belonging to another with the intention of permanently depriving the other of it . . .*" All the italicized words are significant.

"*Dishonesty*" is not defined since the intention is that all forms of "dishonesty" shall be embraced in the sense of the word familiar to the layman : thus, for instance, where someone takes money from another person and asserts that he intended to retain it, it will be for the *jury* to decide whether in the circumstances his behaviour was "dishonest". Though if he overdraws his giro account (which is not permitted) knowing that there will be no funds to meet his cheque such behaviour is clearly "dishonest". Certain kinds of appropriation are, however, specifically excluded by the definition : (*a*) appropriation by a person in the belief that *he has in law the right* to deprive the other of it" (T.A., s. 2 (1) (*a*)) – *e.g.* the case of the taker who honestly believes that the umbrella is his own : (*b*) appropriation by a person "in the belief that he would have the (owner's) *consent* if the (owner) knew of the appropriation" (T.A., s. 2 (1) (*b*)) – *e.g.* Jones tells Smith that he may take and keep his (Jones') bicycle at any time, Jones being absent Smith takes it ; Jones had in fact, however, changed his mind : (*c*) appropriation where a person appropriates property "in the belief that the person to whom the property belongs cannot be discovered by taking reasonable steps" – *e.g.* where A finds a jewel in the street and it does not appear that reasonable steps, such as informing the police, are likely to disclose an owner. Needless to say, it is "dishonest" to take property from the owner knowing that his consent is only apparent. Thus in *Lawrence* v. *Metropolis Police Commissioner*, [1972] A.C. 626 the House of Lords upheld the conviction of a taxi driver who accepted the wallet proferred by a foreign tourist and extracted from it an extortionate "fare". It was also pointed out that the accused could equally have been charged under s. 15 (1) – see below, p. 180).

"*Appropriates*" ; this is defined (T.A., s. 3 (1)) thus – "*Any assumption by a person of the rights of an owner amounts to an appropriation*, and this includes, where he has come by the property (innocently or not) without stealing it, any *later* assumption of a right to it by keeping or dealing with it as owner." This disposes of one of the defects of the former law (Larceny Act, 1916, s. 1 (11)) by which the intent to steal had to exist *at the time of the taking* : so if X's sheep were intermingled with Y's and Y drove the flock away in the belief that it was entirely his own, but later upon discovering his mistake, appropriated X's sheep, there was some doubt under the old law whether Y was guilty of larceny ; but now he certainly will in such a case be guilty of theft. (It should, perhaps, be noted that the restrictive nature of the old law, which was to some extent codified common law, was partially due to the fact that stealing being originally a capital offence unless trivial, the courts did all they could to curtail its ambit.) T.A., s. 3 (2) however contains a special safeguard for the case of a person who, having acquired an interest in property for value and in good faith later discovers that there was a defect in the title – *e.g.* a man buys a book and afterwards learns that the seller was not the owner of it but had borrowed it. Under this subsection such a person will not be a *thief* if he retains the property involved (though of course he may be open to a civil claim at the suit of the owner). Whether this accords with common morality is perhaps questionable, but it must be stressed that apart from this special exemption the new law is much wider than the old, which was concerned primarily with the act of "taking and carrying away"; for the T.A., s. 3 (1) forbids "*any* assumption by a person *of the rights of an owner*". And indeed, except for the fact that the appropriation must be *wilful*, this subsection to a large extent equiperates the law of theft to the civil law of conversion (see below, p. 301) which inhibits any dealing in the title to goods adverse to the owner's title whether or not there is any actual handling of them – *e.g.* Brown's goods are mistakenly delivered to Black and with White who is present at the time sells them to Black as his own (White's).

"*Property*". – By the T.A., s. 4 (1), this includes "*money and all other property, real or personal, including things in action and other intangible property*". The meaning of "things in action" will be explained below (p. 395): "real" property is land. Section 4 (2) provides that land *cannot be stolen* except (*i*) where a part of it is *severed* and appropriated by a person not in possession of the land – *e.g.* X takes a load of soil from Y's land; (*ii*) where a tenant appropriates a "fixture" (see below, p. 326); (*iii*) where someone in the position of a trustee or the like, being authorised to dispose of the land on behalf of another person appropriates it in breach of confidence. Again, in law vegetable matter growing on land is regarded as a part of the land (technically it is "land" not "goods") and it therefore receives the same treatment as land under s. 4 (2): *i.e.* under (*i*) above, it is stolen when wilfully severed by someone who does not possess it. But the T.A., s. 4 (3), makes some commonsense exceptions to this rule: thus the picking of *wild mushrooms* and the *flowers, fruit* and *foliage* of *wild plants, trees* and *shrubs* is not theft *unless done for commercial purposes*: but the *uprooting* of such things, as opposed to the mere picking of them is. The appropriation of untamed wild creatures (*e.g.* wild rabbits) not ordinarily kept in captivity is also excepted (T.A., s. 4 (4)) provided that they are not in the possession of another person and that he is not in the course of reducing them into possession. *E.g.* you appropriate a grouse which I have shot but not as yet retrieved. What amounts to being "in the course of reducing into possession" has given rise to factual disputes in other contexts from Roman times to ours (*e.g.* claims by rival hunters or whalers) and it will doubtless continue to do so.

"*Belonging to another*". This includes the case of a person who has possession or control of the property (such as a bailee with whom property has been deposited) on behalf of another, as well as the case of the person who has a proprietary interest in it as owner or otherwise (T.A., s. 5 (1)); and a co-owner or partner who appropriates the co-owned or partnership property is also a thief; for he takes what "belongs to another". It also embraces the case where the owner has entrusted the property to the thief to deal with it in a particular way; as where a club member entrusts property to the treasurer to be used for specified purposes (T.A., s. 5 (3)): formerly appropriation of this sort would not have been theft but "fraudulent conversion". It also includes the case of a person whose property comes into the hands of the thief by mistake, the latter being under an obligation to restore it or its value.

"*With the intention of permanently depriving*" the other of it. Intention "*permanently to deprive*" is in most circumstances essential, and it follows that a mere conditional intent is not enough – as where, for example, a person picks up a handbag and, having examined the contents, decides that they are not worth taking and leaves the bag where it was.

In general our law knows no such crime as the Roman "*furtum usus*" (the theft of the use of a thing). There are, however, important exceptions to this proposition. First, the T.A., s. 12, makes it an arrestable offence, *without consent*, to *take* anyone else's conveyance, or to drive it or drive in it *knowing that it has been taken without authority*; though the taking or riding of a pedal cycle in similar circumstances is only a summary offence. It has been held that "taking" implies movement, not just possession. Thus if I get into your car and simply sit in the driver's seat I cannot be guilty of the offence (and it seems that this is so even if I turn on the ignition) but once I get the car moving even by taking off the handbrake on a downward slope, by ever so little, I am guilty. It must be noted that in general the "consent" will be valid for the purposes of this section even though it be obtained by some degree of misrepresentation: *e.g.* that the taker wants the car to drive to a nearby destination when he really intends to take it to a distant one; though it is possible that a misrepresentation of a more fundamental nature might be held to indicate the consent. Second, by the T.A., s. 11, any person who, without authority and without believing that he has authority, removes any article (such as a picture) kept for display to the public in any building or in the grounds of any building commits an offence. And the T.A., s. 6, also contains further qualifications. First it provides that even though no such intention exists, an intent on the part of the thief to treat the thing as his "own regardless of (the owner's) rights" will be treated as an intention "permanently to deprive": thus an unauthorized borrowing or a lending of it by the thief may amount to stealing if, though only if, the period and the circumstances are such as to make the act equivalent to an outright appropriation – *e.g.* X retains a library book for such an indefinite period that the retention amounts to treating it as his own. Second, where a person having control of property parts with it under a condition as to its return which he may not be able to perform – and does this for purposes of his own and without the owner's authority – the act of parting may be held to amount to a treating of the property as his own "regardless of (the owner's) rights". Thus if B, without A's permission, pledges A's watch with C, a pawnbroker, without any serious probability that he (B) will be able to redeem the pledge he may be guilty of theft.

The maximum penalty for theft is ten years' imprisonment.

ii Robbery – By the T.A., s. 8, a person will be guilty of robbery "if he *steals*, and immediately before or at the time of doing so, and in order to do so, he *uses force on any person* or *seeks to put any person in fear of being then and there subjected to force*". Everyone of course knows that the man who points a pistol at the bank cashier and takes the money from the till is a robber; but it should be noted that the same applies to the gunman who, while using no force against the cashier, points his weapon at the security guard. The reader is reminded that, contrary to common usage – "I have been robbed!" meaning "My wallet has disappeared" – robbery and theft are different things: for robbery is *violent* theft.

The maximum penalty for this crime or for an assault with intent to rob (*e.g.* the gunman who holds up the cashier but is frustrated in his intent to steal by the emptiness of the till) is life imprisonment.

iii Burglary – By the T.A., s. 9, a person will be guilty of burglary if (*a*) he *enters any building as a trespasser and* with *intent* to steal anything in the building *or* of inflicting therein grievous *bodily harm or* of *raping* a woman therein *or* of doing *unlawful damage* to the *building*; or (*b*) *having* entered any building *as a trespasser*, he *steals* or attempts to steal anything therein *or* inflicts or attempts to inflict *grievous bodily harm* on any person therein. It will be noted that (*a*) involves various kinds of intent *at the time* of the trespassory entry and that (*b*) involves the *commission* of specified crimes *after* entry in the absence of intent at the time of entry. "Trespass" is, of course, a tort; not a crime (see below, p. 299). The trespasser, for the purposes of the crime, must be a trespasser *at the moment of entry*; so that he cannot be guilty of the offence if he is invited to enter by some authorized person who subsequently changes his mind and tells him to go.

In the public mind burglary is probably solely connected with *stealing* in a building (though sometimes one may also hear "My watch has been burgled in the street": to which our readers must of course retort, "That is impossible"); but it will be realized that it may also be connected with the other offences (such, inconsequently, as rape). By T.A., s. 9 (3), "building" in this context includes "an inhabited vehicle or vessel" and the offence may be committed "at times when the person having a habitation in it is not there ...".

Section 9 has simplified the law. Formerly there was a distinction between burglary (a nocturnal offence) and "housebreaking" (a daytime offence) and the details of these and other similar, but separate, offences was complex in the extreme.

The maximum penalty for burglary is fourteen years' imprisonment; but the T.A., s. 10, also provides for the case of *"aggravated"* burglary which will be committed if the burglar has with him any firearm, imitation firearm, weapon of offence (any article calculated to cause injury or incapacity) or explosive. The maximum penalty for the aggravated offence is life imprisonment.

iv Deception – By ss. 15 and 16 the T.A. created two offences relating to the obtaining of property by deception.

"Deception" means *"any deception (whether deliberate or reckless) ... as to fact or law, including a deception as to the present intentions of the person using the deception"* (s. 15 (4)). Thus if I order a meal at a restaurant I thereby impliedly represent that I shall pay for it, and if I do not in fact intend to do so I am guilty of deception (by obtaining a pecuniary advantage by evasion of an obligation to pay under s. 16): further it was held in *D.P.P.* v. *Ray*, [1974] A.C. 370 that where a person who intends to pay when he orders the meal, but changes his mind and, having consumed it, runs out of the restaurant, this is still "deception" because, unless the contrary is indicated, the implied representation continues to the moment of leaving. The false representation may be verbal or by means of some imposture, such as impersonation and may be express or – as has just been indicated – implied. It need not necessarily be made to the person who is disadvantaged by it: thus where B, knowing that her cheque would be dishonoured by her bank, paid a rail fare by cheque upon presentation to the *booking clerk* of her cheque card (which obliged *the bank* to pay the railway authority) she was guilty of deception, though it was the railway rather than the bank who had been deceived.

The first offence (s. 15 (1)) is committed where *"a person by any deception (whether deliberate or reckless) dishonestly obtains property belonging to another with the intention of permanently depriving the other of it"*; and (s. 15 (2)) *"a person is to be treated as obtaining property if he obtains ownership, possession or control of it"*. It will be appreciated that facts which constitute this offence may often also support a charge of *theft* under s. 1 (1). But sometimes the s. 15 (1) offence may be easier to prove than theft. For instance, suppose B borrows A's horse intending to appropriate it: the mere fact of B's acquiring control of the horse under the false pretence of borrowing it will suffice to establish the s. 15 (1) offence, whereas an "appropriation" in the sense described above (*e.g.* behaving in such a way as to pose a challenge to S's title) will be necessary before *theft* can be proved. This is the more serious of the two crimes, and it is punishable with a maximum of ten years' imprisonment. It replaced the former crime of "obtaining by false pretences".

The second offence is defined in s. 16 (1), and is committed by anyone "who by any deception dishonestly obtains for himself or another any pecuniary advantage". By s. 16 (2) – described in the last edition of this book and subsequently by the House of Lords in *D.P.P.* v. *Turner*, [1974] A.C. 357 as unsatisfactory – it is provided that "The cases in which a pecuniary advantage ... is to be regarded as obtained ... are where (*a*) any debt for which he makes himself liable is reduced or evaded or deferred; or (*b*) he is allowed to borrow by way of overdraft, or to take out any policy of insurance or annuity ... or (*c*) he is given the opportunity to earn remuneration or to win money by betting." In *Turner's Case* the House ruled that the words "is to be regarded as obtained" mean "is deemed to have been obtained"; so that the effect of the subsection is that in the circumstances it envisages the obtaining of the "pecuniary advantage" is assumed, and no *actual* advantage need be proved. Thus when the accused in *Turner's Case* employed someone to do some work and gave him a cheque by way of paying *knowing that he had no money in his account* and that the cheque would be dishonoured, the giving of the cheque was a deception; and the House resisted the argument that a man who has no money to pay a debt which he "evades" by giving a "dud" cheque gains no actual "pecuniary advantage" because he could not pay the debt in any event. The evasion of the payment itself was "deemed" under the section to constitute a pecuniary advantage.

The subsection is an egregious example of legislation which seeks to spell out too much: it needs amendment. The maximum penalty for the offence is five years' imprisonment.

v Blackmail – This offence formerly consisted of a number of separate crimes under the Larceny Act 1916, but here again the T.A. has simplified the law by making it a single offence which is committed by a person who "*with a view to gain for himself or another or with intent to cause loss to another, makes any unwarranted demand with menaces*" s. 21 (1). And such a demand is "unwarranted" unless the person making it does so in the belief – "(*a*) that he has reasonable grounds for making it *and* (b) that the use of the menaces is a proper means of enforcing the demand".

Thus if X says to Y (whether or not Y in fact has one) "I will reveal your criminal record unless you pay me £100" this will *prima facie* be a case of blackmail: but the state of X's mind is material, and if he really thinks that he is justified in demanding the money because, for example, it is money Y already owes him, *and* if he also thinks that a threat to reveal a criminal record is a proper way of extracting a debt, X will not be guilty. But it will of course be realized that it would be hard to establish such an ingenuous state of mind to the satisfaction of a jury.

The maximum penalty for blackmail is fourteen years' imprisonment.

vi Handling Stolen Goods – This was a new offence created by the T.A., s. 22 (1). Previously it had been an offence only to *receive* goods knowing them to have been stolen, but by the subsection the scope of this kind of criminality is widened, for "A person *handles* stolen goods if ... knowing *or* believing them to be stolen ... he *dishonestly receives* the goods, *or* dishonestly undertakes or assists in their *retention, removal, disposal or realization* by or for the benefit of another person ...". This of course envisages much more than actual receiving and the section would, for instance, cover the case of a person who assists a thief to convey the stolen goods to a hiding place provided that he knows or believes that it is stolen property. Here again the word "*dishonestly*" is important because an honest motive may negative a dishonest intent. Thus if Williams steals Walters' car and takes it to Wright who knows it has been stolen and accepts delivery of it, Wright will not be guilty if his purpose in doing so is in fact to restore the car to Walters. Here again the courts load the dice in favour of the criminal for the proof of guilt must be positive: it has been held that it is not enough to establish that a reasonable man would, in the circumstances, suspect that the goods in question were stolen; it must be shown that the accused did believe them to have been or that he deliberately closed his eyes to the obvious. A person "assists in realization" if he buys the property himself, so that "handling" is not confined to the normal case of the "fence" who disposes of it to others.

It should be added that by the T.A., s. 24 (3) it is enacted that "no goods shall be regarded as having continued to be stolen goods after they have been restored to the person from whom they were stolen or other lawful possession or custody". Thus where a person receives goods knowing that they were stolen he will not be guilty if in fact, unknown to him, they have passed into possession of the police.

The maximum punishment for this offence is fourteen years' imprisonment.

vii Restitution of Stolen Property – Where a person has been deprived of his property by means of a criminal act it is only right that, if possible, he should recover it. Satisfaction can, of course, always be had by resort to a civil action and it may be (and often is) effected by administrative action on the part of the police – though, in order to safeguard themselves against a civil claim for conversion the latter should apply for a court order under the Police (Property) Act 1897. This Act provides that where property has come into the possession of the police in connexion with *any criminal charge* magistrates' courts may order it to be delivered to any person appearing to be the owner and, after the expiry of six months from the delivery, claims to it by third parties are barred. Yet in some circumstances it may assist the owner to have the active help of the court which convicts the thief. The T.A., s. 28, therefore empowers any court which has convicted a person of any offence *with reference to theft* – an expression sufficiently wide to embrace, for instance, a case of handling – to order any person in possession of the stolen property to restore it to the person entitled to it. And, reasonably enough, an order may also be made in respect of any goods which represent the stolen goods – *e.g.* B steals A's horse and then exchanges it for a cow. Moreover, since in such a case B might rather sell than exchange the horse, the court may also order payment to the owner of any money taken out of the convicted person's possession at the time of his apprehension, not in excess of the value of the thing stolen.

Finally, in order to afford some protection to third parties who may suffer by reason of the theft, it is provided that where the thief has sold or pledged the goods to such people (being in good faith and ignorant of the theft) and the owner has obtained an order for the return to him of the goods, these people may themselves obtain an order for payment – up to the value of the price they paid or the loan they gave – of any moneys taken out of the possession of the miscreant at the time of his apprehension. Thus Jasper steals Tom's car and sells it to Fred (who knows nothing of the theft): Tom obtains an order against Fred for the return of the car to him; then Fred may, if by good fortune Jasper has the cash upon him at the time of his arrest, obtain an order for the repayment to him of the purchase price out of Jasper's ill-gotten gains. Such an ideal solution – Jasper behind bars, all property rightfully restored – must of course in practice seldom be achieved, since money does not adhere to the fingers of thieves; and as likely as not Jasper will at least *appear* upon arrest to be penniless.

2 CRIMINAL DAMAGE

The law in respect of damage to property was formerly mostly contained in the Malicious Damage Act 1861 – and it was fragmented, detailed and complicated. That Act has now been substantially repealed

and replaced by the Criminal Damage Act 1971 (hereafter "C.D.A.");
a statute containing sweeping generalizations which seem less complicated, but may prove to be more difficult to apply.

Under the C.D.A. there are now three main offences.

(*i*) The offence of *destroying* or *damaging property* (s. 1). This is committed (s. 1 (1)) where "a person ... *destroys* or *damages any* property
belonging to another intending to destroy or damage *any such* property or
being *reckless* as to whether *any* such property would be destroyed or
damaged". It is to be noted that the destruction of the offender's *own*
property is *not* here included; but that the intention or recklessness need
not necessarily be directed to the property *actually* affected: thus if I shoot
at your pet pigeon and hit your neighbour's by mistake the offence will
be committed. This offence (s. 1 (2)) also takes an aggravated form where
the intent (or recklessness) envisages danger to *the life of another person*;
and in this form the property destroyed *may* be the miscreant's *own* –
as for example where Ned blows up his garden shed, reckless whether
he endangers the life of Ted, his neighbour. In the case of an offence
under either s. 1 (1) or s. 1 (2) if the agent of destruction is *fire* the charge
will be one of "*arson*" (s. 1 (3)) (which, with the coming into effect of
the C.D.A. ceased to be a common law offence).

(*ii*) The offence of *threatening* to destroy or damage property (s. 2).
This will be committed by anyone who "makes to another a *threat*, intending that the other would fear it would be carried out – (*a*) to *destroy*
or *damage* any property belonging to *that other* or *a third person*; or (*b*)
to destroy or damage *his own* property in a way which he knows is likely
to *endanger the life of that other* or *a third person*".

(*iii*) The offence (s. 3) of *possessing* anything with intent to destroy or
damage property (the case of the possession of an "infernal machine"
par excellence). This crime will be committed where a person "has anything in his *custody* or *control*" intending ... to *use it* or cause or permit
another to use it – (*a*) to destroy or damage any property *belonging to some
other person*; or (*b*) to destroy or damage his *own* or the *user's* property
in a way which he knows is likely to endanger *the life of some other person*.

None of the offences under these sections will be committed
if the accused has some "*lawful excuse*" and it is, as always, for the prosecution, if doubt arises, to establish the absence of "lawful excuse". In the
case of infractions of ss. 1 (1) and 2 (*a*), however, this phrase – beside its
ordinary meaning, such as embraces, for example, Mistake or Self-
Defence – is given an extended meaning (s. 5) so as to include two special
kinds of circumstances. The first of these (s. 5 (2) (*a*)) is where the actor
believes that he has (in doing what he does) the consent of any person
who is, or whom he believes to be, entitled to *give consent* to the act.
The second is where the actor effects the destruction or damage while

using reasonable means to protect property of his own which he believes to require protection (*e.g.* the case of the shooting of the sheep-chasing dog). Whether the belief is justified or not is irrelevant provided that it is honestly held (s. 5 (3)).

For the purposes of the C.D.A. *"property"* means (s. 10) "property of a *tangible* nature whether real or personal, including *money"*: *wild* mushrooms and the *flowers, fruit* and *foliage* of wild plants, trees and shrubs are, however, excluded. Here there is no proviso as to commercial purposes (see T.A. s. 4 (3); above p. 177). Perhaps the rambler who picks a wild flower should bear in mind the judgment of Portia and refrain from taking any of the *stem.* The severing of branches of holly would certainly appear to fall foul of the T.A. s. 4 and of this section.

A person guilty of *arson* or of an offence under the C.D.A. s. 1 (2) may receive life imprisonment; offences under the C.D.A. carry a ten-year maximum.

C COMPENSATION

For a long time past, and, indeed, as early as the Criminal Law Act 1826 it has been possible for courts to award compensation to people who suffer loss as the result of the commission of crimes. By that Act, which is still in force (in an amended form) the court may order payment *out of public funds* to anyone active in the apprehension of people who have committed an arrestable offence by way of compensation to the former for his exertions and for any expenses he may have incurred in the course of them. Moreover, the Riot (Damages) Act 1886 provides for compensation for property damaged or destroyed by rioters; and the Merchant Shipping Acts contain similar provisions in respect of the plunder of wrecked ships by rioters, while modern legislation has similar provisions in respect of aircraft. More important than any of these particular statutes are, however, the provisions of the Powers of Criminal Courts Act 1973 as to compensation, and the awards made by the Criminal Injuries Compensation Board.

By the 1973 Act, s. 35 (1) it is provided that "a court by or before which a person is convicted of an offence ... may ... make an order (in this Act referred to as a "compensation order") requiring him *to pay compensation for any personal injury, loss or damage resulting from that offence* ...". Section 35 (4), however, provides that "In determining whether to make a compensation order . . . the court shall have regard to the means (of the convicted person)" and it has been held that no order should be made if it would be likely to have the result of inducing the convicted person to resort to further crime in order to discharge his obligations in respect of the order. By s. 35 (5) orders made by magistrates' courts are in general limited to a maximum of £400. Where (s. 38) an order has been made, and the aggrieved person later brings a civil action against the criminal in respect of the loss, the damages are to be assessed in the normal way, as if no order had been made; but the award itself must not exceed the amount (if any) by which the assessment exceeds the amount of the compensation order: thus the plaintiff cannot be compensated twice over – he will only obtain in all the amount assessed by the civil court.

The *Criminal Injuries Compensation Board* (composed of legally qualified members) was set up in 1964 upon a non-statutory basis for the purpose of authorizing *ex gratia* payments from *public funds* to victims of crimes of violence – not, be it noted, including injuries caused by motor vehicles unless (as is possible) they are used as weapons of offence. Applications must be made promptly by the injured party or, if he be dead, by his spouse or dependants; and claims will not be entertained unless the injury has given rise to at least three weeks' loss of earnings or unless it be one for which not less than £50 would be awarded by a civil court. The decisions of the Board are unappealable: though, in keeping with general constitutional practice (above, p. 136) *certiorari* will lie in respect of them.

CHAPTER 7

THE LAW OF THE WELFARE STATE

This short chapter will be devoted to a brief outline of welfare law. We will first consider the general development of it, then we shall examine existing social security legislation and finally discuss the legal aid system.

WELFARE LAW: GENERAL DEVELOPMENT

In early times the rights of rulers are generally more apparent than their duties. Thus, in the main, it is true to say that the duties which our earlier kings were deemed to owe to their subjects were only two: first, to protect them from external aggression, second, to maintain the "peace" within the realm through the criminal law or, if necessary, by force of arms. The State was thus in no way considered to be responsible for the *welfare* of individuals. This state of affairs might have caused great hardship if mediaeval England had not been principally an agricultural country, split into a mass of village communities controlled by lords of manors, or by ecclesiastical bodies, who were expected to assume, and usually did assume, responsibility for the welfare of the inhabitants of their own particular localities. Yet caution must add that generalization is dangerous, and it must be remembered that from early times surprisingly "modern" regulation of trading practices prevailed in the cities and boroughs, among the city guilds and at the great international fairs; such as the great fair of St. Ives in Huntingdonshire.

Poor law – The principle of local aristocratic paternalism broke down at the time of the Reformation when the lands of the dissolved monasteries were granted to a new class of landowners who treated their holdings as a source of revenue rather than as a mark of responsibility. Hence, in the Tudor period "poor relief" became for the first time a matter of concern to the central government. After much experimentation the Poor Relief Act 1601 placed the responsibility for the administration of relief upon parishes. Under the supervision of newly-created officials, called "overseers of the poor", who were subject to the control of the justices of the peace, every parish had to ensure that paupers resident (or "settled") in it were either set to work or provided with assistance from a newly-created local tax, the "poor rate". Until the decline of the Council's powers the poor law system was centrally controlled by the Council: this decline took place, as we have already seen, after 1641 when the Star Chamber was abolished.

From the latter part of the seventeenth century, therefore, until the passing of the Poor Law Amendment Act 1834 poor law administration was almost entirely in the hands of the justices – a return, in a sense, to the old system of local aristocratic government. This statute, which was largely the work of Edwin Chadwick (Bentham's secretary), re-established central control. At the head of the poor law system, which it created, it set up a body of *Poor Law Commissioners*. In 1847 these Commissioners were succeeded by a Poor Law Board, and this Board was, in turn, succeeded, in 1871, by a body called the *Local Government Board*. In 1919, there was a further change, when the *Minister of Health* became the ultimate poor law authority. All this time, however, parishes, or unions of parishes, remained the units of local administration and they continued to be mainly responsible for poor law finance. The Local Government Act 1929, however, removed this responsibility from the parishes and imposed it upon county and county borough councils. It will be explained presently that a further, and even greater, change has now taken place.

As long as England continued to be mainly agricultural there was little incentive for "welfare" legislation other than the poor law. But the industrial revolution had far-reaching effects: agricultural workers migrated to the towns to work in the new factories and new towns sprang up everywhere. The old rural England disappeared and a new industrial England took its place. Amongst other things, factory legislation, public health legislation, and housing legislation, followed inevitably in the wake of these events. And today, as if the wheel of social change had turned full cycle, agricultural workers, also, have legislation designed to promote their welfare.

Factory legislation – first "Factory" Act, the Health and Morals Act 1802, was passed after the outbreak of a serious epidemic among apprentices in the Manchester cotton mills. This Act contained various sanitary and moralistic provisions concerning the employment of apprentices in textile mills. From 1856 onwards, a series of Acts provided for the safety of factory workers and regulated the working hours, mealtimes and holidays of women and children employed in the mills. From 1867 factory legislation began to extend to other industries; and after a further series of enactments, the Factory and Workshop Act 1901 afforded a legislative code governing conditions of employment in all factories. This Act set the pattern for subsequent modern legislation.

Until very recently the law concerning the safety and welfare of industrial workers was to be found in the Factories Act 1961. This act comprises a comprehensive set of rules covering almost every conceivable aspect of factory life; and it also empowers the Secretary of State for Employment to make special regulations for the safety and welfare of workers whenever he considers such regulations to be necessary.

These developments are now, however, overshadowed by the Health and Safety at Work etc. Act 1974 which will (when it is brought into full operation) make sweeping changes. The general aim of the Act is to secure, by a unified system, the "health, safety and welfare of persons at work" and to protect others against risks arising from the activities of such people: it is also designed to control the use and keeping of dangerous substances (such as explosives) and to restrict the emission of noxious substances into the atmosphere. To this end it imposes a series of general duties upon employers both *vis-à-vis* their employees and *vis-à-vis* people other than employees who may be affected by health and safety risks arising from their undertakings, or from the state of their factory or other premises. It sets up a *Health and Safety Commission* and a *Health and Safety Executive* whose joint function is to effect the general purposes of the Act (except in respect of agriculture). This means that these bodies must recommend to the Secretary of State for Employment new regulations which will replace the existing "factory" laws; though it is for the Secretary himself, by statutory instrument under the authority of the Act to implement them. The objective is that when these regulations are completed and implemented it will *replace* much of the existing health and safety legislation *including* the Factories Act 1961. General responsibility for enforcement will lie with the central executive or, in some areas, with local authorities. Responsibility for health and safety in agriculture remains, however, the responsibility of the Ministry of Agriculture, Fisheries and Food. It should be added that at the time of writing many enactments have already been replaced by regulations including even some parts of the 1961 Act itself.

Public health – As well as creating new human problems, the increasing tendency for people to congregate in towns, which started with the industrial revolution, raised problems of general health which could not be ignored by the State. This led to public health and housing legislation.

Like the first factory legislation, the first tentative public health legislation (1848: sponsored, like the Poor Law Amendment Act, by Edwin Chadwick) was forced upon the government by circumstances. Asiatic cholera first swept England in 1831, when it is said to have carried off 30,000 people; spasmodic outbreaks continued to occur later in the nineteenth century. Each outbreak resulted in some measure of public health reform. The consequent legislation was at length consolidated in the great Public Health Act 1875, which placed the burden of public health administration upon local authorities. From that time to the pesent, the conception of the State's responsibilities in respect of public health has widened. In origin the main duty of health authorities was to attend to scavenging and sewage: now, under the provisions of the principal modern Act, the Public Health Act 1936, their duties include many other matters, such as the abatement of nuisances, the prevention of epidemics, and the prevention and treatment of venereal disease; and the Clean Air Acts 1956 and 1968 gave them power to create smoke control areas in order to combat the danger to health caused by smoke. With increasing awareness of the importance of the physical environment, moreover, the Control of Pollution Act 1973 makes far-reaching provisions in respect of control of waste, river pollution, noise abatement and many kindred matters. Further, under the provisions of the Food and Drugs Act 1955, local authorities are – subject to the general superintendence of the Ministry of Agriculture, Fisheries and Food – made responsible for safeguarding the public against the danger of buying contaminated food, and are, in particular, responsible for the inspection of foodstuffs exposed for sale.

Housing – The problem of housing was first faced in 1851, when the Labouring Classes Lodging-Houses Act was passed, but no real progress in the demolition of slums and the provision of reasonably salubrious accommodation for the working classes was made until after the first world war, when housing shortage had become really acute. Considerable progress was made between the world wars under the provisions of a series of Housing Acts, passed between 1919 and 1936; and under the Housing Acts 1957 to 1974, slum clearance, redevelopment, and the provision of "council" houses is now the responsibility of local authorities, acting under the general supervision of the Department of Environment.

Education – Until 1870 elementary education was largely conducted by charitable societies and church schools. Gladstone's Education Act of that year set up local School Boards under the supervision of a special Education Department of the Privy Council, to provide elementary schools in places where no adequate provision for elementary education existed. The education in these schools was not entirely free, but the Elementary Education Act 1891, provided for universal free elementary education. Free secondary education was inaugurated by the Education Act 1902. Meantime, the Board of Education Act 1899 had substituted a Board of Education as the central education authority in place of a committee of the Privy Council. A series of twentieth-century Acts, culminating in the Education Acts 1944–1968, extended the scope of primary and secondary education, which has, from 1902, been entrusted to the supervision of local education authorities. The twentieth century has also seen increasing extensions of the school-leaving age, which is now sixteen. The Education Act 1944 established a new Ministry of Education (now the Department of Education and Science) in place of the Board of Education.

The economic sphere – In the economic sphere numerous modern statutes, such as the Weights and Measures Act 1963, the Consumer Protection Acts 1961 and 1971 and the Trade Descriptions Acts 1968 and 1972 seek to ensure consumer protection against sharp practice and danger to life and health in our era of mass production.

In the important field of monopoly prevention the Fair Trading Act 1973 replaces the former Monopolies Commission by the *Monopolies and Mergers Commission* which, upon reference by the Secretary of State for Trade and Industry or by the Director of Fair Trading, has (*inter alia*) the duty (s. 5 of the Act) "to investigate and report on any question ... with respect to the existence of a *monopoly situation*, or with respect (*inter alia*) to the transfer of a newspaper ... or with respect to the creation ... of a *merger situation*" with a view to such action as to suppression or otherwise as the Secretary of State is empowered to make.

"Newspaper" and other "merger" references are described in detail in Part V (ss. 57–75) of the Act. Those provisions are too complex for examination here, but a very brief description of "monopoly situation" (ss. 6–11) can be given. Generally speaking, such a situation exists as to *the supply of goods or services of any description within the United Kingdom* if – (*i*) at least *one quarter* of all the goods or services of that description are supplied by or to one person or group: (*ii*) "one or more agreements are in operation, the ... result of which is that goods (or services) of that description are not supplied in the United Kingdom at all". In respect of *exports* of goods of any description a "monopoly situation" exists if – (*i*) "At least *one quarter* of the goods of that description which are produced in the United Kingdom are produced by one and the same person (or group)": (*ii*) "if one or more agreements are in operation which in any way *prevent, or restrict, or prevent, restrict or distort competition* in relation to, the export of goods of that description from the United Kingdom", and (the agreement or agreements) "are operative as to at least *one quarter* of all the goods of that description which are produced in the United Kingdom": (*iii*) where circumstances similar to (*ii*) exist in respect of exports of goods of any description from the United Kingdom to any *particular market*; with.the difference that in this case the restrictions upon competition are not confined to goods supplied from the United Kingdom.

Security of employment – Another aspect of welfare which has recently received attention from the Legislature is security of employment. In the first place the Contracts of Employment Act 1972 (see below, p. 252), is aimed at ensuring that adequate notice of termination of employment is given to employees. In the second place, the Redundancy Payments Acts 1965 to 1969 make it obligatory in certain circumstances for employers to make redundancy payments to employees who are dismissed, laid off or placed on short-time, by reason of redundancy. In particular such payments must (subject to exceptions) be made where the person dismissed is (if a man) under 65 years of age and (if a woman) under 60, provided that the person concerned has been continuously in the employment in question for at least 104 weeks. "Dismissal by reason of redundancy" means (s. 1 (2) (*a*)) that the dismissal must have been attributable to the fact that the employer has "ceased, or intends to cease, to carry on business for the *purposes* of which the employee was employed . . . or has ceased, or intends to cease, to carry on that business in the *place* where the employee was so employed", or (s. 1 (2) (*b*)) to the fact that the requirements of the business for the carrying on of the work of the particular kind involved have ceased or diminished or are expected to cease or diminish. In general no claim for redundancy payment can arise where the employment is lawfully terminated by the employer on account of the employee's misconduct. In case of dispute there is a right of appeal to an *industrial tribunal*. Contributions have to be made by employers to a Redundancy Fund from which payments will be defrayed where the employer defaults (with a right of recourse by the fund against the defaulting employer) and from which employers who have made redundancy payments are entitled to specified rebates. The Protection of Employment Bill 1975 will make important provisions in relation to security of employment [see Addendum: New Legislation].

The Equal Pay Act 1970 has now removed an age-old distinction between the status of men and women by ensuring equal pay and equal treatment for men and women in matters of employment.

Rural amenities – is, perhaps, finally worth noting that the modern State concerns itself with the amenities as well as with the necessities of life: for example the Countryside Act 1968 gives to local authorities and other bodies, such as the Forestry Commission, wide powers to preserve and open up the countryside for public recreation and enjoyment. The Act also sets up – in succession to the National Parks Commission – the *Countryside Commission* which has, in particular, in consultation with other planning authorities, the duties of providing and improving "facilities for the enjoyment of the countryside", of preserving and enhancing its "natural beauty and amenity", and of securing "public access to the countryside for the purposes of open-air recreation". The Litter Acts 1968 to 1971 which provide for the abatement of litter of all kinds should also, perhaps, be mentioned; as should the Town and Country Amenities Act 1974, which regulates the allocation of conservation areas.

SOCIAL SECURITY

It will be appreciated that until the second world war, although the State had assumed wide responsibilities for various forms of social welfare, successive governments had not welcomed the assumption of these responsibilities; they had rather had them thrust upon them – as in the case of the early factory and public health legislation – by force of events. Further, the whole development of State responsibility was haphazard and unsystematic.

Since 1940, there has been an enormous increase in public welfare legislation, for it had come to be realized by 1941 that the time was ripe for co-ordinating and reforming the various existing social services, such as the poor law, the law relating to unemployment assistance, and to industrial injuries and pensions. This work of co-ordination and reform was seriously embarked upon as the result of the recommendations of the Beveridge Report, published in 1942.

Although much of the legislation which that Report engendered has now been superseded, the present law nevertheless rests ultimately upon the basis of it from its origins in such statutes as the National Insurance and the National Insurance (Industrial Injuries) Acts 1946. We will consider in order the Social Security Acts 1975, the Family Allowances and Family Income Supplements Acts and the Supplementary Benefits Acts.

The Social Security Acts 1975

The Social Security Act 1975 (as amended by the Social Security Pensions Act 1975 – "S.S.P.A.") consolidates and amends in conjunction with relevant repeals effected by the Social Security (Consequential Provisions) Act 1975 the law formerly governed by the National Insurance Act 1965 to 1971 and the National Insurance (Industrial Injuries) Acts 1965 to 1974, together with part of the Social Security Act 1973.

The 1975 Act embraces a system of insurance in the form of specified "*benefits*" (both contributory and non-contributory) payable to all "*earners*" from school leaving age: "earners" being divided into "*employed earners*" and "*self-employed earners*". The system of contribution is set out in ss. 1–11 of the Act, and is too complicated for discussion here. Let us first consider the kinds of benefits, and then the administration of the system. Benefits may be divided into general benefits, industrial injuries benefits, and benefits relating to industrial diseases.

1   GENERAL BENEFITS
These are determined by ss. 12–49 of the 1975 Act; and they fall into two categories: contributory benefits and non-contributory benefits.

(*a*) Contributory benefits
These are:

(*i*) *Benefits for unemployment, sickness and invalidity* – Unemployment and sickness benefits are, subject to satisfaction of prescribed contribution requirements, in general payable after three days of interruption of employment; and they carry earnings-related supplement and prescribed increases in respect of dependants. *Unemployment* benefit ceases to be payable after 312 days. *Invalidity benefit* comprises *invalidity pension* (with increases in respect of dependants) and *invalidity allowance*. Both are payable after 168 days of interruption of employment due to sickness – *sickness benefit* ceasing to be payable after the 168 days. Invalidity pension is generally available, invalidity allowance is an additional allowance payable to people of more than five years below pensionable age.

(*ii*) *Maternity benefits* – These comprise – (*a*) *Maternity grant*: a prescribed payment, subject to satisfaction of contribution conditions; (*b*) *Maternity allowance* (with earnings-related supplement and increases in respect of dependants) payable during a period of 18 weeks, beginning with the eleventh week before the expected week of confinement.

(*iii*) *Widow's Benefit* – This comprises – (*a*) *Widow's allowance*: payable to widows under pensionable age for a period of 26 weeks from the husband's death (earnings-related supplement and increase for child dependants); (*b*) *Widowed mother's allowance*: payable to a widow who is not entitled to widow's allowance – *e.g.* through lapse of time – who has a child or children under 19. This ceases to be payable upon re-marriage or cohabitation as a wife; (*c*) *Widow' pension:* payable to a widow who is not entitled to (*a*) or (*b*) provided that she was over 40 at her husband's death but under 65. Re-marriage and cohabitation are bars.

(*iv*) *Retirement pensions* – These are payable from "pensionable age" (60 for women, 65 for men).

(*v*) *Child's special allowance* – This is, under certain conditions, available to a divorcée whose husband is dead where she has a child of theirs or of his to support. Re-marriage or cohabitation are again a bar.

(*vi*) *Death grant* – This is payable, in general, upon the death of a contributor or of a spouse or a child of a contributor.

(*b*)   Non-contributory benefits

(*i*) *Attendance allowance* – This is payable in the case of people so severely disabled that they need constant attendance. The fact that such attendance is requisite must be certified by the *Attendance Allowance Board*, a body consisting primarily of medical practitioners appointed by the Secretary of State.

(*ii*) *Non-contributory invalidity pension* – This is payable after not less than 196 consecutive days of incapacity for work: it is not, however, available to married women. It carries earnings-related supplement and increases in respect of dependants.

(*iii*) *Invalid care allowance* – Payable (with earnings-related supplement and dependant increases) to people who are not gainfully employed and who are substantially engaged in caring for the severely disabled.

(*iv*) *Guardian's allowance* – Payable to a guardian of a child in cases where both parents are dead, and in certain other cases.

(*v*) *Age addition* – This is an increase of pension to which people over 80 are entitled.

(*vi*) *Mobility allowance* – Payable to a person suffering "from physical disablement such that he is either unable to walk or virtually unable to do so".

N O T E – In the case of *retirement, widowhood* and *invalidity* pensions the S.S.P.A. creates a complicated structure which ensures a basic rate of pension together with an earnings-related increase and also provides safeguards against inflation.

2   BENEFITS FOR INDUSTRIAL INJURIES

These benefits are provided under ss. 50–75 of the Act. They are payable to employed earners who suffer personal injuries, caused by accidents "arising out of and in the course of" their employment; and to the spouses and relatives of people killed by such accidents.

"Accidents" here include mishaps which arise – (*a*) where the earner is at the time of the accident himself in breach of orders, regulations or statutes; (*b*) where the earner is travelling to or from work as a passenger in a vehicle provided by his employer; (c) where he is taking steps, in or about his employer's premises, to rescue someone or to avert serious danger to property; (c) where the cause is "misconduct, skylarking [*sic*] or negligence" on the part of another person, or the behaviour or presence of an animal (including even an insect), or a blow caused by an object, including lightning.

The relevant benefits are –

(i) *Injury benefit* – This is payable in respect of any day of the injury benefit period (156 days from the injury) in which, as the result of the injury, the earner is incapable of work.

(ii) *Disablement benefit* – Payable where an earner, as the result of an accident, suffers loss of physical or mental faculty amounting to not less than 1 per cent assessment. It is, in general, not payable within the first 3 days of the mishap nor after 156 days therefrom: and it will only be payable for such time as the earner is incapable of work. Where the assessment is less than 20 per cent the entitlement is to *disablement gratuity*: where the assessment is 20 per cent or more the entitlement is to *disablement pension*. There are further provisions which allow for increases of disablement pension on a number of grounds, and increases in respect of dependants.

(iii) *Industrial death benefit* – This comprises *widows'* and *widowers'* benefits. The widow is entitled to a *pension* upon the death of her spouse in an industrial accident. It ceases upon her re-marriage, when a *gratuity* becomes payable. A widower is similarly entitled to a pension if (his wife having died as the result of industrial injury) (a) he was maintained by the wife at the time of her death, (b) he is permanently incapable of self-support. There are increases in respect of children. *Parents* and *relatives* who were maintained by the deceased are also entitled in certain circumstances.

(c) Industrial diseases

Benefits modelled upon the system of industrial injuries benefits are available to earners in respect of injuries (other than injuries caused by accident) and prescribed diseases *due to the nature of the employment*. These are the occupational hazards all too common in industry; such as respiratory diseases in mines. See ss. 76–78 of the Act.

ADMINISTRATION OF THE SCHEMES

At the top the Secretary of State for Social Services has ultimate responsibility and certain special matters of dispute (such as whether the claimant is an "earner") are reserved for him: from his decision there is an appeal to the High Court on a point of law.

Claims and questions other than those specifically reserved for the Secretary of State are in the first instance determined by *national insurance officers* (civil servants): appeal from the decisions of these officers lies to *Local Appeal Tribunals*, consisting of a chairman and a representative (respectively) of employers, employed earners and earners other than employed earners. There is a further appeal to a *National Insurance Commissioner*. The Commission, headed by a *Chief National Insurance Commissioner*, consists of lawyers of high standing who form the ultimate court of appeal on social security matters other than appeals reserved for the High Court.

In industrial injuries matters questions relating to *disablement* (e.g the assessment of the degree of loss of faculty in an industrial accident) are referred to *medical boards* or *medical appeal tribunals* and further appeal lies to a Commissioner, or, at the direction of the Chief National Insurance Commissioner, to a tribunal of three Commissioners.

NOTE – The injured person may recover both damages at common law from any wrongdoer and industrial injury benefit payable out of the Industrial Injuries Fund under the industrial injuries legislation, but it is provided by the Law Reform (Personal Injuries) Act 1948, s. 2, that one half of the value of any rights which have accrued or probably will accrue to a plaintiff in respect of industrial benefit, industrial disablement benefit or sickness benefit, for five years from the time when his cause of action accrued, must, in actions for damages for personal injuries, be taken into account against any loss of earnings or profits arising as a result of the injuries. Although (even in relation to industrial injuries) the system of national insurance has not replaced the right to claim damages under the ordinary law, it has therefore, in respect of actions for personal injuries, affected the amount recoverable. It is also to be noted that under the Employers' Liability (Compulsory Insurance) Act 1969 employers – other than public bodies – are bound to insure against liability in respect of bodily injury or disease sustained by employees working under a contract of service.

Family Allowances and Income Supplements

The Family Allowances Acts 1965 to 1975 – These Acts provide for payment of an allowance in respect of every child of a family except the first. Payments are non-contributory. Disputes concerning claims come within the system which governs social security claims in general.

The Family Income Supplements Acts 1970 – This Act was designed to meet the difficulties of the very low paid. It created a *family income supplement* payable by the Department of Health and Social Security. Any family the gross normal weekly income of which falls below a prescribed amount is entitled to the supplement. The machinery for deciding disputed claims is the same as the machinery which applies to supplementary benefits.

NOTE – The *Child Benefit Act* 1975 (not fully in operation until 1977) will replace the scheme of the 1965 Act by creating a new *child benefit* which will be payable (tax-free) in respect of *all* children, including the first child.

Supplementary Benefits

These are governed by the Supplementary Benefits Acts 1966 to 1975. What was formerly "national assistance" administered by the National Assistance Board has now become a system of "non-contributory benefit" administered by a body called the *Supplementary Benefits Commission*. Under the 1966 Act the benefits include: the right of any person over 16 whose resources are insufficient to meet his requirements – subject to provisions of the Act – to a supplementary pension or, as the case may be, allowance; entitlement, at the discretion of the Commission, to single payments where expectional need is shown; entitlement in exceptional circumstances, and subject to similar discretion, to benefit in kind. As a general rule, however, school attenders and people in remunerative full-time employment, are excluded from the benefits. Moreover, the Commission may require people claiming or in receipt of a supplementary allowance, as a condition of payment, to be registered for employment or to attend a course of instruction or training; and alternatively it may determine that, in lieu of payment, they shall be entitled to be maintained in a "re-establishment centre". Such centres the Commission is required to provide for any people in need of instruction or training in order to fit them for regular employment: it is also, mainly through the instrumentality of the larger local authorities, required to provide "reception centres" for people who need assistance in helping them to lead a settled life. Claimants dissatisfied with decisions of the Commission in respect of benefits have a right of appeal to Appeal Tribunals (which sit locally) on most matters; and generally speaking, the decision of these tribunals is final.

LEGAL AID AND ADVICE

Although legal aid (*i.e.* the provision of free legal services) in relation to the conduct of cases, whether civil or criminal, has been in existence in one unsatisfactory form or another since the thirteenth century, no serious attempt was made to make it generally available in respect of civil cases until the Legal Aid and Advice Act 1949; and – though the "dock brief" by which an accused may select for himself any counsel present and robed in court to represent him for a nominal fee had long been with us – it was not until the Criminal Justice Act 1967 that aid in relation to criminal cases was rationalized.

The law in relation to legal aid is now based upon the Legal Aid Act 1974 and regulations made thereunder. We will examine the subject under three heads; legal advice and assistance, legal aid in civil cases and legal aid in criminal cases.

Legal advice and assistance – This is available (s. 1 of the 1974 Act) to any person whose *disposable income* does not exceed £24.50 a week or to any person in receipt of supplementary benefit or of family income supplement *and* (in either case) whose *disposable capital* does not exceed £250. These terminal figures must, however, be accepted with caution since there is power to increase them by regulation at any time. "*Disposable*" in either case means the person's income or capital after certain deductions "as may from time to time be prescribed" have been made in respect of "the maintenance of dependants, interest on loans, income tax, rates, rent and other matters" (s. 11). By s. 4 – and also subject to increase of the terminal amounts by regulation – people having a disposable income between £12.50 and £24.50 a week do not receive the advice and assistance entirely *free*, but must make graduated contributions.

"*Advice and assistance*" include the giving of advice on legal problems and taking steps (such as settling a claim or drafting a document or a will) to meeting the needs of the problem. But, although this part of the legal aid scheme *also covers representation* by a solicitor upon the request of a magistrates' court or county court it does *not* include representation in any case in which a legal aid certificate has been issued or a legal aid order made (these arise under the main legal aid scheme which will be discussed below).

This part of the scheme is, it must be stressed, a minor one: by s. 3 it is normally limited to circumstances in which the "value" of the services rendered does not exceed £25 (though, again, that figure may be increased by regulation).

Legal aid (civil proceedings) – Legal "aid" in the strict sense is available "for any person whose disposable income does not exceed £1,175 a year but it may be refused if – "his disposable capital exceeds £1,200, *and* it appears that he could afford to proceed without legal aid". Again these figures are subject to increase by regulation. And it must be added that the applicant may be called upon to contribute where his disposable income exceeds £375 and his disposable capital exceeds £250. (These figures, too, are subject to increase). Matters concerning contributions and the computation of disposable income and capital are determined by the Supplementary Benefits Commission.

Subject to these conditions legal aid, which in this context consists "of *representation* . . . by a solicitor, and so far as is necessary by counsel", is available in respect of most proceedings in civil courts and in respect of proceedings, such as affiliation proceedings, in magistrates' courts. Though there *are* exceptions both as to courts and as to subject-matter (*e.g.* actions for defamation are excluded) set out in Schedule I of the Act.

In order to obtain legal aid the applicant has not only to satisfy the Supplementary Benefits Commission as to the financial matters just mentioned but also to obtain a *legal aid certificate*. This he must acquire from a *local certifying committee* consisting of solicitors and barristers, whose duty it is to determine whether (as plaintiff or defendant) the applicant has a reasonable chance of success. Appeal against refusal of a certificate lies to an *area committee*.

Since 1964 (now ss. 13 and 14 of the 1974 Act) an injustice has been remedied by giving power to a court to make an order for costs out of public funds in favour of an unassisted person (*i.e.* a person not in a position to take advantage of the scheme) who succeeds in a case against an assisted person.

The administration of legal aid is ultimately the responsibility of the Lord Chancellor but its practical implementation lies with the Law Society, through its Legal Aid Committee. The cost of supporting it is defrayed from a special public fund, the "legal aid fund".

It should be added that since 1972 (now s. 16 of the 1974 Act) the Law Society has been authorized to *employ* solicitors to work in conjunction with local organizations in giving aid and advice. This is an attempt to meet the age-old reproach that assistance is least available in the less prosperous areas because few solicitors work in those areas.

Legal aid (criminal proceedings) – Under the 1974 Act almost any criminal court from a magistrates' court to the House of Lords may where "it appears to the court to be in the interests of justice" make a *legal aid order* for an accused or convicted person to receive assistance (*i.e.* to receive free representation); but the court must be satisfied that the person's means are such that assistance is really required and in making an order it may also order him to make a proper *contribution*. Questions concerning means may ultimately fall to be determined by the Supplementary Benefits Commission.

As in the case of civil proceedings, so in the case of criminal; the monies to fund legal aid derive from "monies provided by Parliament" (*i.e.* public funds) but although such monies are also paid out of the legal aid fund in relation to proceedings in magistrates' courts, in the case of other criminal proceedings they are channelled through the Home Office.

NOTE – The Litigation in Person (Costs and Expenses) Act 1975 enables litigants appearing in person to recover costs in civil proceedings.

PART III
PRIVATE LAW

SUMMARY OF PART III

CHAPTER 8

THE LAW OF CONTRACT

---

1 THE NATURE OF A CONTRACT

A contract is a legally binding agreement. This would appear to be an elementary proposition even to a person who knows nothing about law. As a matter of fact it is not so elementary as it seems; in fact the idea that contractual obligation is based upon agreement is one which has evolved slowly, and even today it is not universally true to say that all contracts are agreements.

In mediaeval times the royal courts did not enforce agreements as such. There was a writ of *covenant* by which formal promises made under seal were enforced; but the obligation to which these promises gave rise derived binding force from the solemn form of the promise, not necessarily from any agreement into which the parties had entered. There was a writ of *debt* where the plaintiff alleged that the defendant owed him money: this money claim might have arisen either as the result of some transaction by which the plaintiff had delivered something ("*quid pro quo*") to the defendant and now claimed his money in return, or simply because the defendant was in justice under an obligation to refund the plaintiff; as where A, having paid money to C at B's request, claimed reimbursement from B. There was also a writ of *detinue* which lay against anyone who wrongfully detained goods which rightly belonged to another, whether the claim of right arose from an agreement or from any other cause. But the mediaeval law had no action based upon agreement as such.

It was only in the course of the fifteenth and sixteenth centuries that a writ called "*assumpsit*" ("*quare assumpsisset*" – "because the defendant undertook") was evolved to remedy breaches of informal promises. *Assumpsit* was one of a group of actions known as actions "upon the case", and in these the plaintiff had to show that he had suffered *damage* if his claim were to succeed; hence the breach of a mere gratuitous promise would not suffice to found the claim, but the breach of an agreement would, since the essence of *assumpsit* was *loss* to A caused by his *reliance* upon B's undertaking. And thus the mere giving of the plaintiff's own promise, coupled with his performance of it, or with his readiness to perform it, was – after some hesitation – held to amount to a detriment to him.

The reader might imagine that a reference to history is redundant, but for at least two reasons this is not so. First, the modern law still enforces "covenants" (which we today call "*contracts under seal*"): these still derive validity from their form alone and need not necessarily be based upon agreement. Thus, though contracts are for most practical purposes "legally binding agreements", that definition is not quite all-embracing.

In the second place it will be seen that, though the mediaeval law did not enforce agreements as such, yet by means of the actions of *debt* and *detinue*, it did perform substantial justice to the plaintiff wherever he could show that the defendant had received a benefit at his expense, and by this oblique method a remedy was given for many broken agreements.

The modern law goes further, and enforces agreements as such, but the mediaeval law teaches us a lesson which should always be borne in mind; claims based upon "unjust enrichment", or in a wide sense, "property", overlap claims based upon *agreement* at many points, the one type of claim shades imperceptibly into the other, and it is not in ideal theory possible to classify them independently. We shall see instances of this overlap between the two fields later on when we come to consider bailments and the so-called "quasi-contractual" claims.

It should be added that agreements are of two kinds, *bilateral* (or "synallagmatic") and *unilateral*. A "bilateral" contract is one in which both parties undertake mutual duties which are enforceable by law; and these are of course the commonest kinds of contracts. "Unilateral" contracts must not be confused with gratuitous promises; for they are supported by consideration (below, p. 214) and are binding on one of the parties. They differ from bilateral contracts in that they consist of a contingent obligation by which the latter only is bound. Thus if I grant you a lease with an option for renewal, the lease during its currency is bilateral, but the option (supported by the initial consideration) is unilateral in that it binds *me*, not you. You, in due course, may take it up or not as you choose, but you are under no legal obligation either way. If you do take it up a fresh bilateral contract will come into being.

Subject to these reservations, we may now accept the general proposition that a contract is a "legally binding agreement". The sections immediately following will be devoted to an examination of this expression. It is proposed first to consider the nature of "offer" and "acceptance", the twin elements of which agreements are composed, then to explain in turn the various requirements which have to be satisfied before an agreement will be regarded as a legally binding contract. These requirements are the following. First, the agreement must be one which is both intended to create and capable of affecting legal relations. Second, the parties must be persons of full contractual capacity. Third, in those instances in which special formalities are required by law to accompany the agreement, these formalities must be complied with. Fourth, there must normally be what is technically known as "consideration". Fifth, the objects of the agreement must not be unlawful.

A Offer and Acceptance

An agreement merely to negotiate does not constitute a contract; for agreement denotes a meeting of the minds of two or more persons upon some matter – "*consensus ad idem*", as it is sometimes called. For legal purposes it will not suffice for this "consensus" to be locked up in the minds of the parties, for it must receive some outward form of expression which is susceptible of proof; and further, the question whether or no an agreement has been reached must, in practice, be judged not according to what the parties assert about their own states of mind, but according to what may reasonably be inferred from their words or actions – if it were otherwise, a person could always escape liability by denying that he intended to do what he did. All agreements are capable of analysis into an "offer" and an "acceptance", either or both of which may be made by words or conduct. But not all offers, nor all acceptances, will be permitted to initiate legal agreements, and the courts have formulated certain rules in relation to offer and acceptance some of which we must now consider.

First, as to *offers*. An offer may be made to a particular person or people or it may be made to the world in general; in neither case, however, will there be an agreement until a particular person or persons accept. Not only must the offer be made, but it must be communicated to the acceptor. What amounts to communication is always a question of fact. In the absence of revocation, an offer, not under seal and without consideration, is assumed to be open for a reasonable time, unless it is expressed to be an offer of limited duration. Nevertheless, if the acceptor delays his acceptance beyond a reasonable time he may be met by the plea that though the offer was once intended it has now lapsed. What does amount to a reasonable time for acceptance is again a question of fact. The death of either party, however, creates an automatic lapse; moreover, if the offeror himself fixes a time-limit for acceptance, it is clear that the offer lapses if no acceptance is made within that time.

Further, unless a subsidiary binding agreement to the contrary has been made, it is always open to the offeror to revoke his offer; but the rule is that *revocation must be communicated before acceptance* is made. Thus in *Byrne* v. *Van Tienhoven* (1880), 5 C.P.D. 344, B, in Cardiff, posted a letter containing an offer to A, who was in New York, asking for a reply by cable. This was on October 1st. A received the letter on October 11th and at once accepted, as requested, by cable. On October 8th B had posted a letter in which he revoked the offer; this letter of course reached New York *after A had accepted by the prescribed method*, and *the revocation was thus inoperative*. Here A did not know of the attempted revocation at the time of acceptance; had he known of it, through the medium, for instance, of some third party, there is authority for saying that, at least in equity, he would not have been able to keep B to his bargain, for his conduct would have been virtually fraudulent.

In order to become legally binding an offer must be clear and unequivocal; a statement made in the course of negotiation will thus not necessarily amount to an offer. So in the well-known decision of the Judicial Committee, *Harvey* v. *Facey*, [1893] A.C. 552, the plaintiffs were seeking to buy property called "Bumper Hall Pen"; they telegraphed to the defendant owners, "Will you sell us Bumper Hall Pen? Telegraph lowest price". The defendants replied, "Lowest cash price Bumper Hall Pen, £900". The plaintiffs then sought to clinch what they thought was a bargain by answering, "We agree to buy Bumper Hall Pen for £900 asked by you." It was held that the defendants' statement was merely a statement of price and not an offer to sell; consequently no contract had been formed. But an unequivocal statement, may in similar circumstances amount to an offer. Thus in *Bigg* v. *Boyd Gibbins, Ltd.*, [1971] 2 All E.R. 183 where one party wrote "For a quick sale I would accept £26,000" and the other replied "I accept your offer" there was a binding contract.

With regard to *acceptance*, it is clear on principle that the acceptor must know of the offer at the time he signifies acceptance; for agreement, as we have seen, denotes a meeting of the minds of the parties. This seems a truism, but it is possible to conceive of a case in which A does a certain act and only subsequently discovers that B has made an offer in respect of that act; in such a case A would, according to the better opinion, have no right to sue B upon his offer. Acceptance need not necessarily be signified in words, it may also be signified by conduct; as where X offers a reward to anyone who finds his lost dog and Y looks for it, finds it, and takes it to X. Signified, however, it *must* be: thus in the well-known case of *Felthouse* v. *Bindley* (1962), 11 C.B. (N.S.) 869 where, after some argument as to price, an uncle wrote to his nephew "If I hear no more about him, I consider the horse is mine at £30 15*s*."

there was held to be no contract because, although the nephew had intended to set the horse aside from a sale, having failed to do so he had not indicated acceptance to his uncle. Hence the title to the animal passed to the buyer rather than the uncle.

In this area difficulty has been caused by "high pressure" salesmanship. What of the case where B sends goods to A unsolicited and indicates that unless A returns them he will expect him to pay for them? In the past this has been a source of irritation to many, and the law was uncertain, especially if A appropriated the goods. It is a matter which has now received legislative attention. The Unsolicited Goods and Services Act 1971 provides that where goods are sent to a person unsolicited by him (and he having no reasonable cause to believe that they were sent with a view to his acquiring them for business purposes) they are to be considered to be an *unconditional gift* to him under certain circumstances. These circumstances are that *either* (*a*) during the period of *six months* from the day that they were received the sender did not take possession of them and the recipient did not unreasonably refuse to permit him to do so; *or* (*b*) not less than *thirty days* before the end of the six month period the recipient gave notice to the sender (in a form prescribed by s. 1 (3) of the Act) and that within thirty days from the sending of this notice the sender did not take possession of the goods, nor the recipient unreasonably refuse to permit him to.

It may sometimes be relevant, as we saw in relation to *Byrne* v. *Van Tienhoven*, to determine the exact moment at which acceptance is made. Usually the answer to this question will depend upon the facts of the case; but there are certain circumstances in respect of which the courts have been forced to lay down arbitrary rules. So in the case of contracts concluded by correspondence where the offeror designates no particular time or mode of acceptance, the rule is that acceptance is made *when the letter of acceptance is posted* (this is sometimes called the Rule in *Adams* v. *Lindsell* (1818), (B & Ald. 681); if therefore the offeror wishes to withdraw his offer he must do so before that time. Naturally, however, if it is stipulated that acceptance must be communicated in order to be effective mere posting will not be enough to conclude the contract. Auction contracts have also given rise to difficulties. Where goods are sold by auction at what time are the offer and the acceptance respectively made? It has been decided that normally, in the absence of contrary expressed intention, the highest bid constitutes the offer, the fall of the hammer constitutes the acceptance: this rule is now statutory (Sale of Goods Act 1893, s. 58 (2)). In the familiar case of the sale of articles displayed in shops – such as books in a bookshop – in the absence of special circumstances the rule is that the display is only an invitation to treat (like an advertisement) and the customer's act of selecting the article and taking it to the shop-keeper constitutes an *offer to buy*, not an acceptance of a general offer. Accordingly, until he has accepted this offer by agreeing to sell the article the shop-keeper is under no obligation to sell.

It remains to be added that if there has been both offer and acceptance a contract can only be complete if all essential terms have been agreed upon; for there can be no agreement if any such terms remain to be settled. This does not, however, mean that everything must be completely finalized; it suffices that the *essentials* are agreed. Thus for instance in *Sweet & Maxwell, Ltd.* v. *Universal News Services, Ltd.*, [1964] 3 All E.R. 30, the Court of Appeal held that an agreement for a lease was not to be treated as incomplete only because one of its clauses contained a provision that, beside certain terms specifically set out, there should be "such conditions as shall reasonably be required" by the lessor; for the court could, and courts often do, determine in this context what is or is not reasonable; and hence the agreement was not too indeterminate to be enforceable. By contrast *Courtney and Fairbairn, Ltd.* v. *Tolaini Brothers (Hotels), Ltd* [1975] 1 All E.R. 716 where one party wrote to the other that he would be happy to contract if the other would get a third party to "negotiate fair and reasonable contract sums" there was no contract. For the vital element of price remained unascertained and at the discretion of the third party.

B   The Intention to Contract

We have seen that most contracts are agreements. It should now be noted that it is by no means true to say that all agreements are contracts. Many agreements fall outside the scope of the law of contract, either because they concern matters of moral, rather than of legal, obligation or because the parties agree that they are not to be treated as enforceable contracts, or because they are not intended to be such. A familiar example is the case of a person who drives a friend somewhere in return for payment of the petrol. The courts have, moreover, repeatedly declined jurisdiction over agreements, which are expressed in a way which shows an intention to exclude their jurisdiction. On the other hand, what appears on the face of it to be a business transaction will not lightly be treated as a merely moral obligation, and it should be noted that expressed *intention* may sometimes have the effect of turning into a binding contract an agreement which might otherwise have been regarded as non-contractual. A famous example of the latter situation was provided by *Carlill* v. *Carbolic Smoke Ball Co.*, [1893] 1 Q.B. 256. The defendants manufactured "carbolic smoke balls" which they advertised as miraculous cures for influenza. The advertisement stated that £100 reward would be paid to anyone who contracted influenza after having used the ball as prescribed. It was further stated that £1,000 was deposited with a bank to show the sincerity of the Company's intention. The plaintiff, Mrs. Carlill, used one of these balls, but nevertheless contracted influenza: she sued for the promised reward. It was held that she was entitled to recover: normally such advertisements are mere "puffs" which are not intended to create legal relations, but in this instance taking into account, amongst other circumstances, the reference to the deposit at the bank, the court found that the Company had intentionally made a binding offer which the plaintiff had accepted.

C Capacity

Generally speaking any legal "person" may be a party to a contract; but there are exceptions to this rule. Thus, for reasons of policy, in time of war an enemy subject cannot sue upon a contract in our courts and, by a rule of professional etiquette, a barrister may not sue for his fees. Three classes of incapacity call for special mention.

MINORS

The common law rule was that infants' contracts were *voidable at the infant's option*: that is to say, anyone under *twenty-one* years of age might treat a contract as a nullity if he so elected. This rule was reinforced by the Infants' Relief Act 1874, which provided (s. 1) that all contracts made by infants for "*money lent or to be lent, or for goods supplied or to be supplied . . . and all accounts stated with infants*" should for the future be "*absolutely void*". Further, by the same Act (s. 2) it was provided that no one should, upon attaining his majority, be permitted to ratify (affirm) a contract made during infancy.

It has already been remarked that by s. 1 of the Family Law Reform Act 1969 the age of majority has been made *eighteen* instead of twenty-one; and it is now usual (see s. 12 of the Act) to refer to people below that age as "*minors*" rather than as "infants". These changes, however, amount to no more than this, and, subject to the substitution of "minor" for "infant" and *eighteen* for twenty-one, both the statute law and the common law regarding the capacity of minors remain unaltered.

There were, and are, three exceptions to this general rule that infants cannot be bound by their contracts. First, where under any contract (whether falling within the provisions of the Act or not) a minor receives "*necessaries*", he is bound to pay a *reasonable* price for them. "Necessaries" include anything required by the minor, not in order to keep body and soul together, but to keep him suitably provided according to his particular standard of living at the relevant time; a question to be decided upon the facts of each case. In the second place, there are certain types of contract, such as contracts to pay rent under a lease, which involve property of a *permanent nature* and require *continuous mutual relations* between the parties. Although contracts of this type are voidable during minority, a minor will become fully bound by his obligations under them upon attaining his majority unless he repudiates the contract within a reasonable time of majority. In the third place, *contracts of apprenticeship* and *service* which appear to the court *beneficial* to a minor are generally enforceable both by and against him. But this does not mean that a minor will always be liable upon a contract just because it is likely to be beneficial to him: the *general* rule is that he is not liable. For instance, if he engages in trade he cannot be sued upon contracts relating to his business.

Exceptions apart, minor contractors are therefore the pampered favourites of the law. So far is this true that the courts have refused to permit their immunity to be circumvented by allowing actions against them, which ought properly to be framed in contract, to be framed in tort: thus where a minor is guilty of fraud in inducing a person to contract with him by misrepresenting his age, he cannot be sued in the tort of deceit; for if this were permitted the minor's *contract* would be indirectly enforced (see below, p. 283).

This tenderness of the law towards minor contractors is subject to certain restrictions which justice demands. Thus where, under a contract, a minor has transferred property to the other party, he will not be allowed to recover the property unless he can show a total failure of consideration; that is, unless he can show that he has received *nothing* in return for the property. Decisions subsequent to 1874 have made it clear that this rule remains substantially unaffected even by the drastic terms of s. 1 of the Infants' Relief Act.

Moreover there are two ways in which the rules of equity mitigate the inequitable lot of those who contract with minors. In the first place, the one-sided remedy of specific performance will not be granted at the suit of a minor. In the second place, the court may sometimes force the minor, at any rate where he has acted fraudulently, to restore any ill-gotten gains which he has acquired under the contract. This equitable right to restitution is, however, a proprietary right, and it follows that the other party to the contract cannot normally recover *money* which he has paid, for in the nature of things money is not easy to earmark as one's own. Further, to paraphrase a famous dictum, "restitution stops where repayment begins"; so that if the minor sells goods which he has acquired under the contract he cannot be made to pay over the proceeds of the sale; the goods, and the goods alone are the "property" of the other party. (The rights and liabilities of minors in respect of matters other than contractual liability have already been discussed: above, p. 93.)

2 CORPORATIONS

At common law, corporations could usually contract only be means of formal contracts authenticated by the use of their corporate seal. But this rule, long since abolished in relation to companies incorporated under the Companies Acts (above, p. 79), has now been abolished in respect of all corporations by the Corporate Bodies' Contracts Act 1960; the agents of corporations may thus now make contracts on their behalf in regard to any matter within the corporate powers in whatever way similar contracts are made between individuals.

3 PERSONS OF UNSOUND MIND AND DRUNKEN PERSONS

It will be recalled that mentally disordered persons may be subject to the control of the Court of Protection (above, p. 98) and that, if they are contracts may be made by their receiver on their behalf. Apart from this, in the case both of persons of unsound mind and of drunken persons the rule is that their contracts will be voidable at their option if, and only if, it can be established that they were wholly incapable of understanding what they were doing at the time of contracting *and* that the person with whom they contracted *knew* of their condition. These two classes of persons are, nevertheless, always bound to pay a reasonable price for necessaries (Sale of Goods Act 1893, s. 2).

D Formalities

Generally speaking, no special formalities are required for the creation of a contract. But there are certain major exceptions to this rule which call for discussion.

1 CONTRACTS WHICH ARE VALID ONLY WHEN MADE IN A SPECIAL FORM

At common law two classes of contract had to be made under seal, by way of *deed* or "speciality" as it was called – that is to say, to be reduced to writing, signed by the party or parties contracting, and impressed with a seal. These were *gratuitous* promises and contracts made on behalf of *corporations*. These two matters need not detain us, for, as we have seen, gratuitous promises, *though they must still be made under seal if they are to give rise to a binding obligation*, are not really "contracts", according to modern classification, for they are not agreements. Contracts made by corporations, as we have also seen, are now freed from the common law requirement. It should, however, be noted that by the Law of Property Act 1925, s. 52 (1), "all *conveyances of land* or of any interest therein are void for the purpose of conveying or creating a *legal estate* (see below, p. 333) unless made by *deed*". Further, there are certain contractual documents, such as policies of marine insurance and bills of exchange, which are *required* by law to be *written* and, as will later appear, many credit agreements fall under statutory provisions as to writing (see below, p. 274).

2   CONTRACTS REQUIRED TO BE EVIDENCED IN A SPECIAL FORM

It will be appreciated that there is a difference between requiring a contract to be *made* in a special form and requiring it to be *evidenced* in a special form: in the one case failure to adopt the prescribed form affects the validity of the contract itself, in the other it affects only the *proof* of its existence and failure to produce that proof only renders it *unenforceable*; so that ("enforcement" meaning *actionability*) its existence may yet be used as a defence to a claim, though the required evidence be lacking.

Several classes of contracts are required to be *evidenced* in special ways, and in particular two types of contract falling under the provisions of s. 4 of the Statute of Frauds 1677. This section, as interpreted by the courts (and as drastically curtailed by the Law Reform (Enforcement of Contracts) Act 1954), renders these contracts *unenforceable by action* unless they are evidenced *in writing* and signed by the party against whom the action is brought or by his authorized agent. The contracts in question are:

  i   *Promises to answer for the debt, default, or miscarriage of another person*—
      This provision has been construed so as to cover contracts of guarantee, but not of indemnity. The distinction requires explanation. In both classes of contract one person undertakes to accept responsibility for the obligation of another, but whereas the *guarantor* only accepts responsibility *if the principal defaults*, the *indemnifier* undertakes to discharge the obligation *in any event*. Thus, to adopt a time-worn illustration, where A and B come into a shop together and A agrees to buy goods, but has no money with him, and B undertakes to pay the shop-keeper at a future time in the event of A's default, B is a guarantor of A's debt. If, on the other hand, B undertakes to be responsible whether A pays or not he is an indemnifier. In the former instance only will the contract – being one of guarantee (or "suretyship") – fall within the Statute and require written evidence. It should, however, be noted that by the Consumer Credit Act 1974 (ss. 105 and 106) regulated (see below, p. 274) suretyship *and* indemnity agreements *require*

a written "security instrument", as defined in s. 105, and unless this instrument is properly executed they can only be enforced by court order.

ii *Contracts for the sale or other disposition of land or of any interest in land* – The wording of this clause is the result of an amendment introduced by s. 40 (1) of the Law of Property Act 1925. The exact scope of the meaning of the words "or other disposition" is by no means clear, but agreements for leases certainly fall within the section.

The writing which the Statute requires is, as has been explained, purely *evidentiary*. It follows that there need be no one document containing the whole contract; it suffices if a series of documents are produced and connected the one to the other by oral evidence; though these documents, when so connected, must tell the whole story in its essentials. But the story they tell must be one of a contract; so that if, for example all they disclose is an agreement "subject to contract" or to "formal exchange of documents" (see below, p. 225) they do not constitute a sufficient memorandum. Further, the courts have gone as far as to hold that the requirements as to signature may be satisfied by an authenticating mark or even by the imposition of a rubber stamp.

The Statute (which if it is relied upon as a defence must be specially pleaded) was passed in order to prevent frauds by requiring strict evidence of the contracts to which it applied; but it was soon found that rogues could evade their obligations by ensuring that the requisite evidence was *not* supplied. Hence the courts did all in their power to prevent the Statute from thus being turned into an "engine of fraud". They attacked the problem in two ways. First, they sought to achieve justice by straining the word of each section to bring particular facts within or beyond the scope of it as the merits of the case before them might require. It is for this reason that a highly complex web of case law was woven around the interpretation of the Statute. In the second place the Court of Chancery evolved what is known as the equitable doctrine of *Part Performance*. The basis of this doctrine is that where, in the case of a contract which is rendered unenforceable by reason of non-compliance with the statutory requirements, one party has *carried out his part of the agreement*, the other party will be forced to perform his; for it would plainly be inequitable to allow him to evade his obligations by pleading the Statute in such a case.

Part performance of course constitutes a direct judicial circumvention of the Statute, and it is not therefore surprising that it has a very limited field of application. The following points must be noted.

First, the act of performance relied upon must be such as, on balance of probabilities, to indicate that it has been performed in reliance upon a contract with the defendant which is consistent with the contract alleged. Thus in the leading case of *Maddison* v. *Alderson*, (1883), 8 App. Cas. 467 where a housekeeper who had looked after an old man for a number of years alleged an oral agreement by him to convey some property to her after his death it was held that, after that event his promise could not be proved in support of her claim to the property because the mere fact of the woman having kept house was not necessarily referable to such a contract. She might have done so in a mere vague expectation of benefit. On the other hand, in *Wakeham* v. *Mackenzie*, [1968] 2 All E.R. 783 a widow who had kept house for another old man and had claimed, after his death, that he had orally agreed to leave the house to her, was held entitled to recover; since she was able to prove that, as part of the agreement, she had during the deceased's life-time paid for her own board and coal – something plainly referable to a contractual situation. The *second* requirement is that the act relied upon must be such as to render it inequitable for the defendant to take advantage of the absence of writing: in other words, the plaintiff must have altered his position irretrievably for the worse. And it was for that reason that it used formerly to be said that a money payment cannot constitute part performance, since money can always be returned. This proposition was, however, denied in *Steadman* v. *Steadman*, [1974] 2 All E.R. 997 where the House of Lords held that a man who had paid £100 as part of a settlement with his divorced wife in respect of a contract by which she was to relinquish her interest in the matrimonial home could rely upon that payment as an act of part performance. *Third*, the doctrine can only be invoked (since it was evolved by the Court of Chancery) in cases where, had the contract been in writing, the equitable remedy of specific performance would have been available. In practice, this requirement restricts the application of the doctrine almost entirely to cases concerning *land*. *Fourth*, the alleged contract, though *ex hypothesi* it cannot be proved by written evidence, must be properly proved by oral or other evidence.

E   Consideration

No contract, other than a contract under seal, will be enforced unless the plaintiff can show that he has furnished *consideration*. What is "consideration"? We have seen (above, p. 000) that English law did not start with a theory that agreements ought to be enforced, and then search about for a means of enforcing them. They came to be actionable indirectly; principally through the medium of the actions of *debt* and *assumpsit*. In order to succeed in an action of *debt* the plaintiff had to show that he had conferred a benefit upon the defendant: in order to succeed in *assumpsit* he had to show that he had suffered a "detriment", or loss.

In the course of time it came to be recognized that it is the business of the law to enforce agreements *as such*, not merely to accord them incidental validity because they were the means by which a formal promise had arisen (covenant) or by which a benefit had been conferred (debt), or a loss sustained in reliance upon the undertaking (*assumpsit*). "Contract" thus became an independent branch of the law. Nevertheless the mature law retains traces of its adolescence. Despite the dissent of the great Lord Mansfield in the eighteenth century, the courts have insisted that no contract (other than a contract under seal, the grandchild of *covenant*) shall be enforceable unless each party to it can show that, by entering into the agreement, he either confers a benefit (as in the old action of debt) upon the other, or brings some detriment (as in the old *assumpsit*) upon himself.

The benefit conferred or the loss suffered constitute "consideration" which was therefore defined in *Currie* v. *Misa*, (1875), L.R. 10 Exch. 153, thus – "*A valuable consideration in the sense of the law may consist either in some right, interest, profit, or benefit accruing to one party, or some forbearance, detriment, loss, or responsibility given, suffered or undertaken by the other.*"

Since consideration is one of the essential elements which distinguish binding contracts from unactionable promises we must now consider some of the rules concerning it.

1 THE NATURE OF CONSIDERATION

Consideration may be of two kinds: "executed" or "executory". Consideration is said to be *executed* when the plaintiff, who claims to have furnished it, can show that he has actually performed his part of the bargain. *Executory* consideration is consideration which the plaintiff has promised to furnish, and is ready and willing to furnish, if the defendant will perform his part. If you sue me for failing to take delivery of a piano which I have agreed to buy from you I clearly cannot be permitted to escape liability merely by showing that delivery has not been made: if I were allowed to do this I should be freeing myself of my obligations by taking advantage of my own wrong.

The essence of consideration is *mutuality*: it is the element which distinguishes gratuitous promises ("I will give you my watch") – which are only actionable if made by deed or are in the form of declarations of trust – from *contractual* ones. Usually, as where you and I come to an agreement, it consists of a *promise* in return for a promise; but, provided that the doer knows that a promise has been made by the promisor in respect of the doing of the act done, it may also be constituted by the doing of an *act*. And this will be so (as in the case of a promised reward in respect of a lost dog) even though the promise is made generally to no one in particular: a proposition illustrated by the *Carbolic Smoke Ball Case* (above, p. 208). Putting the matter another way, an offer may be made to the world at large.

Consideration must be *"real"*, *i.e.*, it must be something of some ascertainable value in the eye of the law. The meaning of this may best be illustrated by giving some examples of acts which have been held to be of insufficient value to form consideration. In the first place, a promise to do something which is obviously *impossible* (such as a promise to touch the sun) is clearly valueless. Second, a promise of a *vague and indefinite* nature will not constitute sufficient consideration. For example, in *White* v. *Bluett* (1853), 23 L.J. Ex. 36, a son sued his father's executors, alleging that the father had promised to pay him some money if he would cease, which he alleged he had done, from complaining to his father that he had been unfairly treated. The court held that this was no more than a promise to stop "boring" the father, and that it was therefore too vague to form a "real" consideration. Third, a promise to do something *unlawful* cannot constitute consideration.

One question has given rise to difficulty. It is this: can the performance of an existing duty be treated as consideration for a fresh promise, made by the person to whom the duty is owed, or by some third party? The law on this subject is a little uncertain, but the present position may be summarized in the following way:–

(a) Where A is already under contract to do something for B, and B makes a fresh promise on condition that A performs his duty, the performance will not amount to consideration for the fresh promise, and therefore A cannot sue upon it. For instance, where two members of a crew deserted their ship during a voyage the master promised the rest that, if they worked the ship to port, the deserters' pay would be split between them. It was held that the crewmen could not sue upon this promise. The reason was that, at the time when it was made, they were already under an obligation to work the ship to port.

(b) A promise to perform a public duty can be no consideration. Thus a policeman cannot claim a proffered reward for stolen property which he recovers *in the course of his duties*.

(c) If B contracts to do something for A, can B rely upon the doing of it as consideration for a promise made to him (B) by C? This point has been much disputed and it is one upon which the House of Lords has not as yet pronounced; but in *The New Zealand Shipping Co., Ltd.* v. *A. M. Satterthwaite & Co., Ltd.*, [1975] A.C. 154 a majority of the Judicial Committee decided that such an act was valid consideration. The simplified facts of that case were that cargo owners agreed with carriers (shipowners), who were contracting *as agents* for stevedores who, by contract with the *carriers*, were to unload the cargo that the stevedores should, *vis-à-vis* the cargo owners, be exempt from liability for damage to it during unloading. The stevedores did damage it, and it was held that the exemption clause covered them. The fact that they unloaded in consequence of their contract with the *carriers* did not prevent the act of doing so from being consideration for the promise, extracted from the cargo owners by the carriers as their (the stevedores') *agents*, to exempt them. The decision must, however, be treated with caution for, as will later appear (below, p. 245), the fact of agency was vital.

The statements under heads (*a*) and (*b*) above, are subject to the proviso that if the plaintiff does something more, in return for the promise, than he was bound by his existing duty to do, this will form a consideration, and he will be able to recover. Thus a policeman was held entitled to a reward for the supply of information where, in supplying it, he did something outside the scope of his public duty. It should also be added that, according to an extreme view, the law is that *any* pre-existing obligation (under (*a*), (*b*) or (*c*)) may be real consideration provided that it would not in a particular case be contrary to public policy to enforce it.

One very important application of rule (*a*) is the rule in *Pinnel's Case* (1602), 5 Co. Rep. 117. It was there laid down that payment of a lesser sum than the amount due, cannot normally be treated as a satisfaction for an existing debt. Thus if A owes B £100, and B promises to discharge him if he pays £50, B can break his promise and sue for the whole £100. But this rule will not apply if there is a material alteration in the mode of payment. Thus if A's debt of £100 were due in London, and B, to suit his own convenience, agreed to discharge the debt in return for a payment of £50 at York, B's promise of discharge would bind him. The discharge would also be binding if A, instead of making a part payment, were to give B some article (however small) in return for it. It would also, of course, be binding if it were made by deed.

"Composition" agreements form an exception to the rule in *Pinnel's Case*. Where a debtor, by agreement with his creditors, undertakes to pay so much in the pound none of them may sue for the full debt; for if any one of them were to do so, he would be defrauding the others.

2 THE RULES GOVERNING CONSIDERATION

Three important rules require mention:

(1) although consideration must be real, it need not be adequate;

(2)   consideration must move from the promisee;
(3)   consideration must not be "past".

(1) *Adequacy of consideration.* For the purposes of the law of contract the common law regards the ordinary man as a commercial man. He must stand on his own feet, and make his own bargains. *Caveat emptor* ("buyer beware") is a maxim of importance. Equity apart, in the absence of fraud or misrepresentation, the courts will not assist a man who complains that he has made a bad bargain. Hence, provided that the plaintiff has given some consideration, it will be no defence for the defendant to plead that it was disproportionate to the value of the promise. Consideration need not be *"adequate".*

(2) *Consideration must move from the promisee.* In order to sue upon a broken contract the promisee (the plaintiff, to whom the promise has been made) must normally show that *he* has furnished the consideration: it will not suffice for him to show that someone else has done so. This rule does not, however, apply to actions brought upon negotiable instruments. (These will be discussed below in Chapter 10.)

(3) *Consideration must not be "past".* Consideration may, as we have seen, be "executory" or "executed" but it must not be "past". The meaning of "past" consideration was illustrated by the case of *Roscorla* v. *Thomas* (1842), 3 Q.B. 234. A bought a horse from B. Some time *after* the sale, B affirmed that it was sound; it was not. A sued B upon this affirmation; the action failed. The reason was that although A had furnished consideration in the form of payment at the time of the sale he had furnished none for the affirmation. The consideration which a plaintiff alleges must normally be given *in respect* of the promise made by the defendant. Where a benefit is conferred, either gratuitously or in return for a previous promise, a subsequent promise made in respect of this past benefit is not actionable; it is unsupported by consideration. Consideration, as we have seen, is the hallmark of *mutuality*, so that it must be "present".

There is at least one exception to this rule; namely that "past" consideration may support an action upon a negotiable instrument.

NOTE. The doctrine of consideration has often been criticized. In 1937 it was the subject of a report by the Law Revision Committee (Sixth Interim Report). Amongst other recommendations, the Committee suggested that the requirement of consideration should be dispensed with in the case of written contracts, and that "past" consideration should be rendered actionable. The legislature has not, however, acted upon these recommendations.

It must now be added that modern decisions, starting with *Central London Property Trust, Ltd.* v. *High Trees House, Ltd.,* [1947] K.B. 130, have shown that equity will not permit a person who has made a promise or assurance by which he intentionally modifies his existing contractual rights against another person to resile from that promise or assurance once the other person has taken him at his word and acted upon it. For instance, suppose that X & Co. let a block of flats to Y & Co. at a ground rent of £2,500 *per annum*, and suppose that, later, X & Co. promise in writing to accept only £1,500, and suppose that Y & Co. accordingly reduce the rents due to them from the tenants in actual occupation of the flats. X & Co. will not be permitted to invoke the absence of consideration for their promise in order to support a claim for the full £2,500.

This doctrine (sometimes called "*promissory estoppel*") which is substantially novel, though it is a development from older authorities, may go some way towards mitigating the rigour of the rule in *Pinnel's Case*: but at present it is not possible to assess the full implications of it. The potentialities of the doctrine are, however, fundamental; so two further comments should be made. First, in order for it to operate, the person sued must have *acted in reliance* upon the promise made to him; if he has not done this, no injustice will have been occasioned by the plaintiff's lack of good faith. Thus in *D. & C. Builders, Ltd.* v. *Rees*, [1966] 2 Q.B. 617, the doctrine could not be invoked where a debtor offered a lesser sum in discharge of a greater debt under threat that unless the creditor accepted the offer nothing would be paid at all. In paying the lesser sum the debtor suffered no loss in reliance upon anything; for he had himself forced the transaction upon the creditor. In the second place, the doctrine has been judicially described as a "shield" and not a "sword"; it cannot be used to *found* a claim, but only to *avert* one, or to rebut a defence that might otherwise be available. Thus, in *Combe* v. *Combe*, [1951] 2 K.B. 215, where a husband, after decree *nisi* for divorce, promised gratuitously to pay his wife £100 *per annum* by way of maintenance, and the wife in consequence (though not at the husband's request), forbore to apply to the court for an order for maintenance, it was held that the wife could not invoke her voluntary forbearance in order to force the husband to keep his promise In the third place, although *obiter*, Lord Denning, M.R., the progenitor of the doctrine in the *High Trees Case*, has expressed the view that it is not confined to cases in which a contractual relationship between the parties pre-exists the statement relied upon by way of estoppel (*i.e.* by way of barring the claim).

F Illegality

No action will lie upon a contract which involves the doing of something *illegal* if the plaintiff has to rely upon illegality as a necessary part of his claim ("*ex turpi, causa non oritur actio*" – "there can be no cause of action upon a base ground"). And though it is true that where no part of the illegal purpose has at the time of action been entered upon, property conveyed under the contract may be recovered (a *locus poenitentiae*, pause for repentance, is said to be afforded), yet the presence of an illegal object is regarded as so serious that a defendant sued upon a contract involving such an object may set up his own conscious participation in the illegality as a defence to the plaintiff's claim. Yet it must be noted that the courts will not carry principle so far as to make the presence of an illegal object an excuse for confiscation. Thus, if in prusuance of an unlawful conspiracy (for instance, to evade some statutory requirement) the property in goods be transferred from A to B and these goods be then sold by C (a thief) to some fourth party, B (despite the illegal origin of his title) may sue the latter. For if he cannot who can?

Some transactions are rendered unlawful by statute, others are unlawful at common law. Examples of contracts which are illegal at common law are contracts to commit crimes, contracts contrary to public policy, and contracts which offend against the accepted rules of morality.

"Illegality" is, however, a vague and indefinite term and the effect of it varies according to the nature of the unlawful element. Some things are so clearly "wrong" that the courts will refuse to enforce contracts that have the barest connexion with them. In *Pearce* v. *Brooks* (1866), L.R. 1 Ex. 213, for example (a case which, for some reason, students always remember), the plaintiffs hired out an attractive-looking brougham to a lady (the defendant), knowing that she wished to use it in order to assist her in her profession – prostitution. It was held that the contract, although innocent on the face of it, was tainted with illegality; and that therefore the plaintiffs could not recover the hire money.

Prostitution is an extreme example of an activity of a morally reprehensible type; the effect it has upon contracts in any way connected with it is therefore extreme. There are other things which, for one reason or another, are "illegal" without being clearly "wrong". For instance, wagering contracts are rendered "void" by the provisions of the Gaming Act 1845. Normally, therefore, no action may be brought in respect of a wager. The Act does not, however, render wagering *unlawful*, nor does betting offend the general sense of public morality. Hence, in some circumstances, the courts will enforce wagers. Where, for instance, a bet is made abroad in some country where a bet of the nature concerned is entirely lawful it may sometimes be enforced here.

Contracts in contravention of *public policy* require fuller discussion. The term "public policy" is here used in a special sense. In one sense, all the principles of common law and of equity which have been evolved through the centuries are rules of public policy, for they have been created by the judges in the light of what they deem to be for the public good (see above, p. 15). But this is not the sense in which the term is used here: in relation to the law of contract it refers to certain restrictions which the courts place upon the right to make contracts which they believe to be contrary to the public interest. It has been held, for example, that an agreement made by a married person to marry a third party in contemplation of the termination of the marriage by death or dissolution is, if the facts be known to the third party, invalid; for it is in the public interest that the sanctity of marriage should be maintained. Contracts which tend to injure the State, to pervert the course of justice, or to undermine the public service, are also held to be contrary to public policy. Thus it is unlawful to make a contract with an alien enemy in time of war, or to perform such a contract during the continuance of a war, even though it was entered into before the war began. So too, agreements aimed at "stifling" prosecutions are invalid. So also, where a person in a position of influence contracts with another to use that influence in order to secure for the other some special advantage from the government, the contract will not be upheld; as, for example, where a person agrees to obtain a public honour for someone else in return for a gift to charity.

One of the most important categories of agreement that are held to be against the public interest are contracts in *"restraint of trade"*; a term which includes agreements restraining business activity and freedom to compete. The policy behind the restriction imposed upon such agreements is, of course, fundamentally economic and it has a long and fascinating history which mirrors changes in political and economic thought. We are, however, only concerned with the present day attitude of the courts to such agreements. The modern law stems from the speech of Lord Macnaghten in *Maxim-Nordenfelt Gun Co.* v. *Nordenfelt*, [1894] A.C. 535. Nordenfelt was a famous inventor and manufacturer of guns and ammunition. He sold his business to the gun company and agreed, subject to certain reservations, not to carry on business *anywhere* in competition with it for a period of twenty-five years from the sale. In breach of this agreement he did enter into business with a rival company before the stipulated period had expired. The gun company claimed the right to hold him to his contract, and the House of Lords held that although the restraint was world wide the company was entitled to have it enforced.

The importance of the decision lies in Lord Macnaghten's statement of the law which was adopted in later decisions. In summary the law is this – (*a*) All contracts in restraint of trade are to be deemed *prima facie* invalid; (*b*) it makes no difference (as was formerly thought to be the case) that the restraint sought is general or universal as opposed to partial or local; (*c*) a contract which imposes a restraint will be upheld if the party seeking to enforce it can establish that it is *reasonable* as between him and the other party (in the *Nordenfelt Case* the restraint was held in the circumstances to be reasonable in this sense); (*d*) if a contract imposing a restraint has been shown to be reasonable *as between the parties* it may still be held invalid if the party seeking to rid himself of the restraint can establish that its enforcement is against the public interest. The burden of proving this latter proposition is, however, a heavy one.

Such are the rules: but of course they tell us little in themselves, since everything depends upon what the courts regard as "reasonable": this depends upon all the circumstances involved, and the subject has attracted a large case law. The cases cannot be discussed here, though the following salient points which derive from them must be mentioned. Restraints imposed by business competitors contracting on an equal footing, such as the gun company and Mr. Nordenfelt, will be more likely to be upheld than restraints imposed by employers upon employees who are in an unequal bargaining position, or upon people such as writers, composers and artists who lack business experience. Indeed, whereas upon the sale of a business it may be reasonable for the buyer to restrain the seller against *competition*, it has constantly been held that an employer is *not entitled to impose a restraint upon an erstwhile employee* upon this ground alone. Yet the employer may reasonably impose some restrictions to protect himself; for instance, though it is not reasonable to bind a man who leaves one's employment to refrain from using elsewhere skills that he learnt while employed, it has long been held to be reasonable to restrain him from divulging *trade secrets* to others or making use of one's own *goodwill* – as by canvassing customers with a view to directing their custom to himself. So true is this that, even apart from express agreement, the law implies a term of fidelity in every contract of service itself; thus if you work for firm A you may be restrained from working at the same time on the sly for firm B, a rival firm. Then again, it *may* be reasonable to require someone like a clerk or a hairdresser's assistant who is leaving, or a partner who has retired, to refrain from engaging in business within a defined area from his former place of work; though such restraint must be confined to a reasonable area and apply only for a reasonable period of time. Yet it will not be reasonable to impose a restraint which involves arbitrary discrimination; thus the Court of Appeal found no difficulty in ruling that the Stewards of the Jockey Club were acting unreasonably in refusing a training licence to an applicant solely upon the ground of her femininity. (Indeed, in view of the feminine conquest of their own profession they could scarcely have ruled otherwise – and the Sex Discrimination Act 1975 now buttresses their position).

Where restraint seriously limits freedom of choice, freedom of action, or personal liberty it can seldom be upheld. This may be illustrated by *Eastham* v. *Newcastle United Football Club Ltd.*, [1964] Ch. 413; the facts were complex, but the short point was that by the combined rules of the Football League and the Football Association as then drawn, to which every player had by contract to subscribe, professional players were employed from year to year, and at the end of each season could, if their club so desired, be put on either a "transfer" list or a "retain" list. If a player were put on the latter list the effect was that, unless he were willing to sign on anew, he was retained at a wage by the club and was under the rules unable to obtain employment as a player elsewhere in any way unless some other League club were willing to pay a sufficiently attractive fee to induce their own club to transfer him. The player could thus be tied by his initial contract to his own club as long as he remained a professional player. The court held that these rules were invalid as being in restraint of trade. But the facts of every case govern the particular decision and it may sometimes, though seldom, even be reasonable to restrain personal liberty; thus in *Denny's Trustee* v. *Denny*, [1919] 1 K.B. 583 a settlement was upheld between father and son by which the former paid the latter's debts, and in return imposed *inter alia* an embargo upon the son's going within 80 miles of Piccadilly Circus without consent.

It will be realized that the main object of this aspect of legal policy is to ensure that enterprise shall not be fettered so as to deny to the State the economic benefit of the work or skill of the individual; and this is clearly a principle which ought to be upheld. Yet it cannot be taken too literally; for if it were, a contract by B, for example, to give his services to A would be invalid on the ground that it denied these services to everyone else. Hence a balance has to be maintained and, amongst other things, business actualities and the degree of restraint imposed have to be taken into account. As to the former, for instance, no serious doubts have ever been raised about "sole agency" agreements nor, until recently, about the familiar practice of the "tied" public house; and it has been held that a contract by a restaurateur to take all his wines from one merchant for an indefinite period of time is valid. The question of *degree* of restraint was considered by the House of Lords in *Esso Petroleum Co., Ltd.* v. *Harper's Garage (Stourport) Ltd.*, [1968] A.C. 269. The facts were that the respondents owned the M. Garage and the C. Garage. They had entered into "solus" agreements for the sole supply of petrol from the appellants in respect of both garages; the agreement as to the

M. Garage was for four years and five months and as to the C. Garage (reinforced by a mortgage see below, p. 366) for twenty-one years. In both contracts there were further clauses including, *inter alia*, terms that the garages should remain open at all reasonable hours and that, if sold, they should only be sold to a buyer who would accept the same kind of agreement. It was held that, although "solus" agreements were not necessarily to be considered as being in restraint of trade, the latter terms brought these agreements within the category and that though the M. contract was not unreasonable, the C. contract was; since twenty-one years was in the circumstances too long a period.

It should also be explained that the courts will sometimes enforce a contract although some part of it is admittedly contrary to public policy. This is done by "severing", *i.e.* cutting out, the invalid part and enforcing the rest. Such an operation will not be embarked upon where the contract as a whole is clearly unlawful, and in practice it is for the most part applied to contracts in restraint of trade. Even in relation to these, however, severance will only be permitted if the part of the contract which will remain, after the invalid part has been struck out, contains all the elements of a valid contract in itself. This may occur, for instance, where one of two alternatives may be disregarded while leaving another unaffected. Thus where an estate agent had two offices in different places some miles apart and employed an assistant in one of them, the assistant agreed that if he should leave the agent's employment he would not practise for a period of three years thereafter in *either* place. It was held that this was reasonable in respect of the place where the assistant had worked, but unreasonable in respect of the other place; yet there was no difficulty in enforcing the restriction in respect of the one place and declaring it invalid in respect of the other.

Although many restraints are *contractually* imposed this need not necessarily be so – they may, for example, be imposed within a profession by dint of a professional code – but this does not alter the right of the courts to scrutinize them if they are challenged. Indeed, it has been held that the Pharmaceutical Society are not entitled to insist that chemists sell only their "traditional" wares (*e.g.* drugs) as opposed to their more modern ones (*e.g.* wines and spirits).

Finally, it must be noted that by the provisions of Article 85 of the EEC Treaty (which is directly applicable in the United Kingdom) agreements between undertakings and concerted practices which have as their object the *prevention, restriction or distortion of competition* within the common market are *void* unless the article be declared inapplicable to the particular case by the European Commission. This *may*, in some circumstances, render certain kinds of contracts in restraint of trade void by community law.

2 THE TERMS OF A CONTRACT

The Kinds of Terms

A contract being concluded when an offer is accepted, it thereafter becomes necessary to examine the terms of the completed agreement. By tradition terms are of two kinds; they are either conditions or warranties. *Conditions* are terms of major importance which form the main basis of the contract and breach of a condition gives the party aggrieved a right to damages or (though subject to an important qualification which will be noted shortly) a right, at his option, to repudiate the contract. *Warranties* are terms of minor importance and breach of warranty gives a right only to damages. Traditionally the question whether a particular term *is* a condition *or* a warranty is referred to the intention of the parties themselves to be gleaned either from any statements they may make as to the comparative importance of the term in question or from the general tenor of the contract as a whole.

This general statement, however, requires to be qualified. In the first place, once the contract is executed, that is to say substantially entered upon, a condition becomes an "*ex post facto*" warranty; this means that it is treated as if it were a warranty and its breach gives rise only to a claim to damages. The reason for this is that repudiation is only really practical as long as the parties have not done anything under the contract to alter their position. In the second place it must be noted that the terminology is comparatively new and that until comparatively recent times the words "condition" and "warranty" were used interchangeably; further even in present day usage "condition" may be used to mean something somewhat different, namely a stipulation which either *suspends* the implementation of the contact ("suspensive" condition or condition "precedent") or *resolves* the contract after it has come into force ("resolutive" condition or condition "subsequent"). The important rule that upon a conveyance (*e.g.* of a house) where, as in *Eccles* v. *Bryant*, [1948] Ch. 93, according to the usual practice the completion of the contract is made "subject to exchange of documents" either party may withdraw until the exchange has actually been effected illustrates the operation of a condition precedent. On the other hand, if I sell you my car in March subject to a proviso that if my uncle Tom dies before April 10th you are to return the car to me, the contract is defeasible by the condition subsequent that if uncle Tom dies it will be at an end. In the third place, the dogma that the nature ("condition" or "warranty") of a particular term is determined by reference to the parties' intention is generally no more than make-believe; and this is inevitably so because people seldom do intimate the comparative importance of the terms of their agreements. As a number of recent appellate decisions have shown, the truth is that, although some terms (whether so expressed or whether implied by statute) are in their nature conditions which will give rise to a right of repudiation, yet it is for *the court at the trial* to determine, *taking into account the extent of the alleged breach*, whether that breach is sufficiently fundamental (see below, p. 230) to allow repudiation. Thus where a contract between two companies stated that it was to be a condition that stipulated frequent visits should be made on behalf of one of them to customers of the other it was held that a claim to repudiate because a few visits had been omitted could not be upheld.

Perhaps an understanding of the difference between conditions and warranties may be helped by two simple illustrations. In *Poussard* v. *Spiers and Pond* (1876), 1 Q.B.D. 410, a singer contracted with an opera company to perform in a new opera: the period of the projected run was uncertain, but at the best it was thought likely that it would not be a long one. The singer fell ill and was unable to perform for the first week. It was held that this unwelcome lapse was fundamental and that it amounted to a breach of condition which entitled the company to repudiate the contract. In *Bettini* v. *Gye* (1876), 1 Q.B.D. 183, the facts were similar; but with a distinction. There another singer was engaged by a producer for the better part of a year "to undertake the part of first tenor in the theatres, halls and drawing-rooms of the United Kingdom" (a nostalgically Victorian contract!). He also failed through illness to meet the exact requirement of the contract in that he missed all the rehearsals prior to the first night of the whole engagement, which was a theatre performance. The court saw this as a minor lapse and treated it as a breach of warranty: it was stressed that the rehearsals and the theatre engagement itself were only part of a considerably larger agreement.

Thus far it may have been assumed that terms must be express, oral or written declarations of the obligations undertaken. Though contracts may arise solely by implication from conduct, most contracts do in fact rest upon statements made by the parties and hence most contracts do contain *express* terms, however few. But terms may also be *implied*. All agreements are made in the light of circumstances known to the parties and these circumstances may bear upon the agreement as being a tacitly accepted part of it; terms that are understood but not declared.

Terms may be implied for any number of reasons, the sole basis of the implication being that the parties may be taken to have tacitly agreed to them. There are, however, certain common sources of implication. One such source is usage: where a contract is made between people of the same trade it may usually be assumed that it is to be conducted against the accepted background of that trade (for instance the "baker's dozen" = 13) or where a contract is made in a particular locality it may be assumed that it is made in the light of the customs of that locality: hence the usage may be treated as being incorporated into the contract. Further, there is a doctrine known as the rule in *The Moorcock* (1889), 14 P.D. 64, by which the courts will at times imply a term where it is necessary to do so in order to give the contract business efficacy. For example, in *The Moorcock* itself the plaintiff's ship was berthed under contract at the defendant's wharf; at low tide she settled on some rock which lay under the river bed and she was damaged. There was nothing in the contract about the safety of the berth but it was held that it must be assumed as a business proposition the parties had contracted upon the basis that it was sound. This doctrine is, within limits, clearly a reasonable one but current judicial practice is to apply it with caution, since the courts shrink from making peoples' contracts for them after the event. Hence, today it is probably true to say that *The Moorcock* doctrine will only be called into use where what has been omitted from the express terms is something which anyone would have assumed to be basic to the agreement, and which the parties themselves would clearly have expressly agreed to had they thought about it. Moreover, no such term will be implied if it contradicts the *express* terms of the contract.

Again terms may be implied *by law*, either by general rules of the common law itself or by statute. Among outstanding examples are the implied terms contained in the Sale of Goods Act 1893 (see below, p. 270) many of which were incorporated in the Act from pre-existing case law.

Exemption Clauses

It is best to discuss these separately, but the discussion follows from the fact that there is a general right to "contract out" of any terms, whether express or implied. In many business transactions (especially contracts of sufficiently frequent occurrence to necessitate the use of written or printed documents in "common form") it has long been customary for one of the parties to contract upon the basis that restrictions are to be placed upon his liabilities. There are thus many common form types of *exemption clause* by which a party offering some service – such as transport or warehousing – enters the transaction only upon the basis that he is to be exempt from liability, or that the extent of his liability is to be limited. This raises the question of policy whether the courts ought to give full effect to such clauses, thereby permitting one party – who, as for example in the case of a hire-purchase company, is often in a strong economic position *vis-à-vis* the other – to escape obligations which it may be thought he ought as a matter of fairness to honour. The principle of freedom of contract comes near to self defeat when one party is free to refuse to be bound by the very obligations which on the face of it he appears to be undertaking.

It is the duty of the courts to prevent sharp practice and to protect the weak against the strong, but it is also their duty to uphold the principle of freedom of contract. Hence a middle path has been chosen: such clauses have been allowed to operate; but the scope of their effectiveness has been kept within limits.

This curtailment has been effected both by the legislature and by the courts. For instance, as will appear the Supply of Goods (Implied Terms) Act 1973 (as amended) renders void the exclusion of certain implied terms in contracts of sale or hire-purchase, while the Transport Act 1960 makes void any attempt to "contract out" of liability to railway passengers in respect of death or personal injury, and the Road Traffic Act 1960 contains similar provisions as to passengers in public service vehicles. Further, the Misrepresentation Act 1967, s. 3, provides that any agreement which contains a provision which would exclude or restrict any liability to which a party may be subject *by reason of any misrepresentation* made by him before the contract was made shall *be of no effect* except to the extent that in any legal proceedings arising out of the contract the court may allow reliance on it *"as being fair and reasonable in the circumstances of the case"*. It is to be noted that though this provision is in general terms, and affects all kinds of contracts, it is limited to exclusion of liability in respect of *misrepresentations*; it does not apply to *terms* of the contract. It does, however, give the courts a welcome freedom of discretion to enforce such clauses where they appear to be fair.

Apart from these modern enactments the courts have tackled the problem posed by exemption clauses in two main ways. First, they have always been at pains to ensure that the party who seeks to rely upon such a clause has done *all that is reasonable to make known to the other party the nature of the conditions* he is imposing: this may be done either orally or in writing, but it must be effectively done. For example, if I hire out to you a deck chair and intend to accept no liability for any injury you may receive (*e.g.* if it collapses due to defective structure) I am at liberty to say so; but it will not be enough if I hand you a ticket which bears a printed statement of my terms, but which is in such a form that you would be justified in assuming that it is a receipt and put it in your pocket unread. And in *Thornton* v. *Shoe Lane Parking, Ltd.*, [1971] 2 Q.B. 163, where a company which owned an automatic car park caused words to be printed upon the tickets produced from their machines which referred the customer to a notice in the interior of the car park which displayed conditions exempting liability on their part in very wide terms (including exemption in respect of personal injuries to customers), it was held that they had not done enough to incorporate this exemption into the contract. Thus they could not plead it as a defence to a customer injured on the premises as the result of this negligence.

In the second place exclusion clauses are *narrowly construed and closely scrutinized*; for the courts will not lightly assume that a man has divested himself of his contractual obligations. Certainly, especially where there is no inequality between the parties, people may make whatever stipulations they will, and it is not for the courts to frame their contracts for them: thus it has been said by the highest judicial authority that – "a contractor may ... make a valid contract that he is not to be liable for any failure to perform his contract, including even wilful default" – "*but*" it was then added "*he must use very clear words to express that purpose*". Thus words which exclude liability for "all conditions, warranties and liabilities, *implied* by statute, common law or otherwise" will not exclude liability for an *express* term, such as an express statement that a car sold by B to A is a "new" one when it turns out to be second-hand.

Moreover, it has of recent years become plain that in certain kinds of circumstances this restrictive interpretation will be particularly severely applied. These circumstances include cases (*i*) where the parties are on an unequal footing – *e.g.*, hire-purchaser as against hire-purchase owner; (*ii*) where the clause relied upon is solely inserted for the benefit of the person who seeks to rely upon it; this of course need not necessarily be the case – *e.g.* I may seek to exclude liability in order to give you the advantage of a lower price than I could otherwise offer; (*iii*) where the contract in question has broken down upon some fundamental matter.

The third of these kinds of circumstances needs amplified treatment. What do we mean by "some fundamental matter?" The answer to this has been the subject of a not-too-illuminating discussion in a series of cases which include *Suisse Atlantique Société d'Armement Maritime S.A.* v. *N.V. Rotterdamsche Kolen Centrale*, [1967] A.C. 361, *Harbutt's Plasticine, Ltd.* v. *Wayne Tank and Pump Co., Ltd.*, [1970] Q.B. 407, *Farnworth Finance Facilities, Ltd*, v. *Attryde*, [1970] 2 All E.R. 774 and *Kenyon, Son and Craven, Ltd.* v. *Baxter Hoare & Co., Ltd.*, [1971] 2 All E.R. 708. It would seem, from these decisions that a breach of contract of a major kind (a "*fundamental breach*") may in legal analysis fall into one of two categories which we may consider separately.

The first category is the kind of breach which is catastrophic: which amounts to total non-implementation of the contract, as if I were offering to sell you a pig and to deliver a cow. If I were do to this, and then

to seek to rely upon my own statement to the effect that I gave you
"no guarantee as to the fundamental nature of the article delivered",
you would doubtless think the law deficient if it upheld my "exemption
clause". And this, therefore – *where the defendant's performance is totally
different from that which the contract contemplates* – the law will *not* do. The
basis of the contract disappears; and with it the protection of the exemption clause. To what kind of circumstances will this apply? We can only
give examples. In *Glynn* v. *Margetson & Co.*, [1893] A.C. 351 a ship was
chartered to carry oranges from Malaga to Liverpool under a bill of
lading containing terms wide enough to permit it to call at almost any
European or North African port. It was held that, whatever the terms
of the bill, the purport of the contract was a voyage from Malaga to
Liverpool; so that when the ship so deviated from its route as to call
at Buriana (a port further from Liverpool than Malaga), and the oranges
were damaged due to the resulting delay, it was held that the breadth
of the clause would not excuse the shipowner's default. Again, in *Lilley*
v. *Doubleday*, [1881], 7 Q.B.D. 510 a warehouseman, having contracted
to store goods in a certain warehouse, chose to store them in another:
it was held that a clause exempting him from negligence in respect of
the one would not protect him when the goods were destroyed by fire
in the other. And in *Harbutt's Case* it was held that an exemption clause
could not exempt a firm of engineers who supplied to a mill some plastic
piping which was so utterly unsuited for the stipulated purpose that it
became distorted upon overheating, and a fire ensued which burned
down the mill. In the *Farnworth Case* a motor-cycle was supplied by
way of hire-purchase which was so defective as to be entirely un-
roadworthy; and, again, an exemption clause was held not to avail the
defendants.

    There is, however, it seems, a second category of "fundamental
breach", namely, a breach which, without being so serious as the former,
will *yet entitle the aggrieved party to repudiate the contract*; as in the *Suisse
Atlantique Case*, where there were a series of delays by the shipowners
in delivering the cargo on a number of occasions – yet not as serious as
the first kind of fundamental breach. In the case of a fundamental breach
of this kind the legal dogma would seem to be that, though an exemption
clause will be strictly construed, yet the *true intent* of the parties will be
sought to be given effect to; and if upon construction it appears that
the exemption clause was intended either to exclude repudiation or to
limit or exclude liability it will be upheld. This was illustrated in
Kenyon's Case where (unlike *Lilley's Case*) goods (groundnuts) were
stored in an *agreed* warehouse, but were badly damaged by rats: it was
held that the breach of the duties of a bailee – which clearly there was –
was "fundamental" in the second, and not in the first, sense, and that

accordingly a clause which exempted the defendants from all but "*wilful*" default (which clearly there was not) was operative.

It must be added that, as in the case of distinguishing between conditions and warranties (see above, p. 225), so here, in distinguishing "fundamental" breach (of either kind) from non-fundamental breach, it is not just the quality of the act that has to be examined, but the whole circumstances including what follows upon it. For instance the supply of the defective piping in *Harbutt's Case* might have been a matter of no intrinsic importance *if* more suitable piping had been substituted before overheating or *if* someone had turned a switch off before overheating occurred. But that was not what *did* happen: what *did* happen was plainly catastrophic.

These fine distinctions with their shades of difference and metaphysical refinement, may disgust the student. But it must be borne in mind that it only constitutes an attempt to justify a holding of the balance between freedom of contract on the one hand and the protection of lawful expectation on the other. It will be tolerable only if, as usually it will be, it is justly and sensibly applied.

3   VOID AND VOIDABLE CONTRACTS

Sometimes an agreement may be legal and may apparently contain all the elements of a valid contract and yet certain factors may in reality be present which render it void or voidable. A *void* contract is a nullity, and no rights can be acquired under it. A *voidable* contract is one which may be treated as ineffective by one of the parties, subject to certain conditions. The factors which have to be considered are Mistake and Misrepresentation.

A   Mistake

This is the most difficult and controversial branch of the law of contract. Where an operative (*i.e.* legally effective) mistake is established the result is that the contract is *void*. It will be appreciated that this is a very serious consequence since, amongst other things, third party rights may be jeopardized. Thus, for instance, if we may anticipate, it will be seen that if I obtain goods from you by means of a fraudulent misrepresentation our contract is *voidable* by you as long as I have not parted with the goods to a *bona fide* purchaser; but once I have done this the goods will become his, not yours. If on the other hand, whether induced by fraud or not, you can prove that you contracted under some mistake which the law treats as operative, the contract being *void*, I can give no title to the purchaser – with the unhappy result that, however innocent he is, you will have a claim in *conversion* (see below, p. 301) against him.

Such a state of affairs, threatening (as it may) the security of completed transactions, is not therefore easily to be inferred and it will be seen that in consequence the ambit of operative mistake is restricted. Two points need notice at the start. First, in order to be legally operative a mistake must be as to some material or fundamental matter going to the *essence* of the contract. If a party makes a mistake as to some minor matter the law will not heed his complaint: for instance if I buy your cow under the mistaken impression that she answers to the name of "Daisy" and it turns out that her name is really "Primrose" I am not entitled to force you to take her back; that is, of course, provided that the mistake is only in the name and not as to the identity of the cow. In the second place, people who allege that they have contracted under the influence of a mistake must necessarily be judged rather by their actions than by reference to their innermost thoughts: thus, as Blackburn, J., said in *Smith* v. *Hughes* (1871), L.R. 6 Q.B. 597 "If whatever a man's real intention may be, he so conducts himself that a reasonable man would believe that he was assenting to the terms proposed by the other party, and that other party upon that belief enters into the contract with him, the man thus conducting himself would be equally bound as if he had intended to agree to the other party's terms." This proposition is often treated by writers as though it enshrined some mysterious dogma; but all it means – though this is important – is that no one can escape his obligations by simply stating that he was mistaken about the terms of the contract: he can only escape if he *proves* that he was mistaken, and even then, as we have seen, the mistake must be one which relates to some *material* particular. It it were not for these two rules all contractual transactions would be in danger of being set aside at the whim of a party who alleges that he did not appreciate the nature of his undertaking.

Before analysing the various kinds of operative mistake it may be helpful to revert to a matter already touched upon. Mistake and Misrepresentation have different effects in law, but the one is often induced by the other: *e.g.* my statement that I am the Prince of Richitania may induce you to give me credit for the purchase of a Rolls-Royce. True, you may sue me for damages upon my fraudulent misrepresentation; but you will also have been led to make a material *mistake*, and this is important from your point-of-view since if there were merely *fraud* and no mistake you could not claim the Rolls (or its equivalent in money) from third parties – and in practice, of course, I should take good care to go abroad so that your claim for damages from *me* would be likely to be worthless.

We may now turn to a consideration of the various kinds of operative mistake. The subject will be discussed under three heads. First, Mistake at common law; second, Mistake in equity; third, the *non est factum* plea.

1   MISTAKE AT COMMON LAW

At common law mistake may have one or the other of two effects: it may be such as to nullify what appears on the face of it to be a valid contract, or it may so operate as to destroy *consensus* by producing a situation in which the offer given does not correspond with the acceptance made; thus preventing any contract from coming into being.

i   Mistake which nullifies an apparently valid contract – Of this we may give four examples; though, as will appear, the fourth is a category of doubtful validity.

Mistake as to the existence of the subject-matter – If at the time when the contract is made, unknown *to both parties*, the subject-matter of it does not exist the contract will be void. Thus in *Couturier* v. *Hastie* (1856), 5 H.L. Cas. 673, where corn was sold while in transit by sea from Salonica to England and it transpired that at the time of the contract the ship's master had in fact (owing to its serious deterioration) disposed of the corn at Tunis, it was held that the buyer was absolved from payment of the price.

Obviously mistake as to the very existence of the subject-matter is fundamental; what appears to be a contract about something is really a contract about nothing, and such a transaction must therefore generally be void. But this will not always necessarily be so, since it is possible for a person to contract upon the terms that he will be liable whether or not the subject-matter exists. Clearly such situations are rare; but *McRae* v. *Commonwealth Disposals Commission* (1950), 84 C.L.R. 337 (an Australian case) affords an example. There the defendants, having "disposed" to the plaintiffs of a wreck believed by both parties to be lying on a named reef – when in truth not only the wreck but also the reef were non-existent – were held liable to the plaintiffs for the cost of an expedition by the latter to retrieve the "wreck"; for the situation was such that the defendants must have been taken, in view of the very nature of their business, to have warranted the existence of the thing they purported to "dispose" of.

Mistake as to physical possibility – Where *both parties* think that they are contracting about something which is physically possible the contract will be void if what is contracted for turns out to have been a physical impossibility. Thus in *Sheikh Bros., Ltd.* v. *Ochsner*, [1957] A.C. 136 a contract was held void where it was agreed that one of the parties should deliver to the other a quantity of sisal growing on a certain piece of land which, unknown to both parties, was incapable of producing the stipulated amount of sisal.

Mistake as to title – Mistake of *law* will never avoid a contract, but a common mistake as to private title may. Thus in *Cooper* v. *Phibbs* (1867), L.R. 2 H.L. 149 (a case in equity, though the result would have been similar at common law) where A took a lease of a fishery from B and it transpired, unknown to both parties, that A was really the owner of the fishery, the contract was held to be void.

Mistake as to the quality of the subject-matter – This is the doubtful case. In Roman Law there was, it seems, a doctrine of *"error in substantia"* by which – to adapt a *dictum* of Lord Atkin's in *Bell* v. *Lever Bros., Ltd.,* [1932] A.C. 161 – if the thing contracted for was *essentially* different in *quality or attributes* from the thing as it was believed by both parties to be the contract would be void. In theory this notion is sound enough since there is a world of difference between, say, a genuine diamond and a counterfeit one; but in practice it is difficult to draw the line between what is "essential" and what is "non-essential" – no one would argue, for instance, that the sale of a pig should be void because, being believed to have two ears, it only has one. Thus though some writers support the view that mistakes of this kind, if they are as to the *essence* of the subject-matter, may avoid a contract, the actual decisions appear to go the other way, and to suggest that no such category of "mistake" is accepted as operative at common law. *Bell* v. *Lever Bros., Ltd.* (above) and *Leaf* v. *International Galleries*, [1950] 2 K.B. 86, afford extreme instances in support of this conclusion. In the former case two employees of the respondent company were sued by the company for the return of certain large payments which had been made to them as compensation for terminating their service agreements. The facts were such that unknown to all parties, owing to certain previous transactions by these employees, the agreements could have been terminated without compensation; and upon discovering this the company made their claim. It was held that the mistake was *not* "essential" since the subject-matter of the contract was in essence the *service agreements* and the fact that they might have been terminated without compensation was only a side issue. Yet, if anything could have been regarded as "essential" surely it was the validity of the agreements? In the latter case a picture believed by both parties to be a Constable was sold by the one to the other; it turned out not to be a Constable and, when the buyer sued, the Court of Appeal intimated that the common mistake was not one which would avoid the contract. Surely, again, in all common *sense* the assumption that the picture was a Constable was as vital a factor in the transaction as anything could be? These decisions and others therefore lead to the conclusion that the *common law* may not treat a mistake as to the quality of the subject-matter, however essential, as operative. The decision of the Court of Appeal in *Magee* v. *Pennine Insurance Co., Ltd.*, [1969] 2 Q.B. 507, where an insurance company had paid a sum of money by way of compromising a claim which they mistakenly thought to be valid, however, supports the contrary view: but due to conflict among the judgments this is not a satisfactory case.

ii Mistake which nullifies consensus – Here the mistake produces the effect that the parties are not *ad idem* (agreed); A is making one kind of offer, B accepting another. This may occur in two sorts of situations. Either *both* parties may be mistaken (this may be called "*mutual*" mistake: though the word is not a term of art) or only *one* party may be mistaken (this may be called "*unilateral*" mistake). In the latter situation the rule is that the mistake will not be operative unless the party not mistaken *knows of the other party's mistake*. We may give three examples of mistake which thus nullifies "*consensus*".

Mistake as to the terms of the contract – Suppose (taking the facts from *Smith* v. *Hughes* – above) A and B contract for the sale of some bags of oats. A (the buyer) believes them to be old oats, B (the seller) believes or knows them to be new oats: A seeks to repudiate the contract on the ground of mistake. We have seen that even if the mistake is common – in the sense that the oats are new and both parties believe them to be old – it is one as to quality only, and therefore probably not operative. Therefore, in general, A cannot repudiate. But suppose that B knows them to be new and *also knows* that A thinks he is selling them as old, then there is room for *unilateral* mistake to operate. For B knows that he is selling A new oats, and A thinks he is buying old ones; the offer and acceptance do not therefore correspond. But as noted above, such a mistake will only avoid the contract if B also *knows* that A thinks he is selling the oats *as old*.

Mistake as to the identity of the subject-matter – Where there are two things in existence and one party is thinking of one of them while the other is thinking of the other the contract will be void for mistake. The parties are at cross-purposes: there can be no *consensus*, and in the nature of things, the mistake will be mutual. Thus in *Raffles* v. *Wichelhaus* (1864), 2 H. & C. 906, there was a contract of sale for the consignment of cotton "*ex Peerless*, Bombay" and two ships called *Peerless* were due to sail from Bombay within a short time of each other. One party had one in mind, the other had the other. The contract was held to be void.

Mistake as to personal identity – It must not be supposed that this will always go to the validity of a contract: for example, our law accepts the doctrine of the undisclosed principal (see below, p. 268), and the shop-keeper who sells me apples for cash cannot claim that the sale is void solely because in buying them I have impersonated someone else to whom he might have been equally willing to sell. The identity of a party may, however, be so relevant to the particular contract that a mistake in relation to it will avoid it.

For mistake as to personal identity to be operative the identity of the party concerned must therefore be *relevant* to the formation of the contract; moreover the position must be such that the party mistaken believes the other party to be some real person other than the person with whom he is actually contracting. For if a person is willing to contract with a non-existent entity he presumably does not regard the personality of his co-contractor as a matter of importance.

The following cases may serve to illustrate the law as to mistakes of this kind. In *Cundy* v. *Lindsay & Co.*, (1878), 3 App. Cas. 459, a fraudulent person called Blenkarn signed a letter in a way which made the signature look like "Blenkiron & Co." which was a reputable firm; in this letter he asked the plaintiffs to send him some goods at his address, which was in the same street as Blenkirons' premises. The plaintiffs thus having mistaken Blenkarn for Blenkiron & Co. sent the goods to Blenkarn on credit, and needless to say, without paying for them Blenkarn sold them to the defendants. It was held that the contract between the plaintiffs and Blenkarn was void for mistake and that the plaintiffs' claim in conversion was therefore sustainable. In *Ingram* v. *Little*, [1961] 1 Q.B. 31, the facts were rather similar; a person called at the plaintiffs' house and offered to buy their car; he proposed to pay by cheque, and upon the plaintiffs demurring, gave his name as "P. G. M. Hutchinson". Mr. Hutchinson was a real person, and upon consulting the 'phone book the plaintiffs found his name and address in it as given to them by the caller. Thus satisfied, they accepted a cheque and parted with the car: the cheque was dishonoured and the car disposed of to the defendant. Again, the mistake was operative and the defendant was here held liable to the plaintiff in conversion. In both these cases reliance had been placed upon the assumed credit of an identifiable person or firm. By contrast in *King's Norton Metal Co., Ltd.* v. *Edridge, Merrett & Co., Ltd.*, (1897), 14 T.L.R. 98, a rogue called Wallis pretended to be an imaginary firm which he called "Hallam & Co." and had pretentious notepaper bearing that name printed. He ordered goods from the plaintiffs by writing to them on this notepaper and they sent them to him; he then sold them to the defendants. It was held that the defendants were *not* here liable in conversion; for Wallis' personality could not have affected the minds of the plaintiffs – if they were willing to give credit to "Hallam & Co.", a non-existent entity, they were willing to give it to anyone. So, though there was fraud, there was no operative mistake and the defendants to whom Wallis had sold the goods were not liable in conversion. Further if the parties are present together at the time of the transaction there is a *prima facie presumption* that, whoever the rogue holds himself out to be, the person who alleges that he was mistaken did intend to contract with the actual person (the rogue) thus present to sight and hearing. So, in *Phillips* v. *Brooks*, [1919] 2 K.B. 243 it was held that a jeweller who made a sale to one North, who represented himself as "Sir George Bullough" was not in a position to recover from an innocent third party to whom the jewel was sold; and the same applied to the plaintiff in *Lewis* v. *Averay*, [1972] 1 Q.B. 198 who sold a car to a man who, in his presence, purported to be a famous actor. This being so, *Ingram's Case* must, from this angle, be regarded as a special one in which, on the facts, the presumption was displaced.

Such being the various kinds of operative mistakes recognized at common law, it remains necessary only to repeat that the effect of such mistake is to make the contract *void*; with the result that it may be repudiated entirely and no rights or liabilities can arise under it.

NOTE. It is often suggested that Mistake is a category which could, as a matter of pure analysis, be dispensed with entirely. This is because all the categories we have considered can be explained on other grounds: for instance as cases of *initial* impossibility – which was in fact the way Roman Law treated them – similar to *subsequent* frustration (see below, p. 252), or as cases turning solely upon non-correspondence of offer and acceptance. This may be true, but the fact remains that the courts, which make the law, do treat Mistake as a special legal category.

2 MISTAKE IN EQUITY

When equitable relief is sought, as by way of specific performance (see below, p. 261) or rescission (see below, p. 263) or rectification, the grant of it is discretionary and in exercising this discretion the courts will take the effect of mistake into account upon grounds wider than the grounds recognized by the common law. Thus *Solle* v. *Butcher*, [1950] 1 K.B. 671, is authority for the proposition that in *equity* a contract may be *voidable* (not void, thus leaving room for the protection of third party rights) where the mistake is one as to the attributes rather than the essence of the subject-matter. In that case the landlord and tenant wrongly thought that the house let was outside the Rent Act (see below, p. 341) limits, whereas in fact it was within them; it was held that though this mistake was not one which would operate to make the tenancy void at common law, it was nevertheless voidable in equity. Yet it was ruled in *Riverlate Properties, Ltd. v. Paul*, [1974] Ch. 133 that in the absence of knowledge of the mistake by the other contracting party even equity will not give relief in the case of a purely unilateral mistake – as where a person mistakenly states in a lease a lower rent than he had intended to demand.

This equitable jurisdiction is, however, discretionary and as such impossible to define accurately: moreover, where equity does grant relief it will do so upon its own terms. Thus, for instance, in *Cooper v. Phibbs* (above, p. 234) the plaintiff was only allowed to obtain the return of the lease from the defendants upon the terms that the latter should have a lien on the fishery for the payment of money which he had spent on making improvements during his occupation of the property. And in *Grist* v. *Bailey*, [1967] Ch. 532, A agreed to purchase a house from B: both parties thought (the converse of *Solle* v. *Butcher*) that the house was subject to rent control and in fact it was not – a circumstance seriously affecting its value. The truth having been discovered, the vendor sought to resist specific performance of the contract: this he was in the circumstances permitted to do, but only upon the terms that he would enter into a fresh agreement with the purchaser at a revised price.

3   NON EST FACTUM

"*Non est factum*" ("I did not make it") is an ancient plea. Originally it applied to a case where a man denied liability arising under a document which bore his signature upon the ground that the signature was not his. Later the defence came to be applied to people who were blind or (as used often to be the case) illiterate, and who had been persuaded to sign away things which they did not intend through misrepresentations by others as to the nature of the document. It is a defence which may still be relied upon, but in *Saunders* v. *Anglia Building Society*, [1971] A.C. 1004 the House of Lords gave broad indications as to its limits.

In that case it was made plain that a *prima facie* burden lies in such a case upon the signer to establish that in signing as he did he was not negligent, in the sense that he used all reasonable care in all the circumstances of the case to ascertain the nature of the document. Hence, those who sign things in reliance upon the statements of others *without reading* them can seldom be protected by the plea. On the other hand, the issue being one of fact, the courts will not now necessarily limit the defence to the case of blind or illiterate people. The question is, "Did the signer, having taken proper care to ascertain the purport of the transaction, know *substantially* what the effect of his signature would be?"

In many cases the issue must turn upon the latter point. "Was the document in fact *substantially*, *seriously* or *fundamentally* different in its purport from what the signer believed to be the case?" What constitutes the "substantial" etc. must again be a question of fact (a former distinction between mistake as to "content" on the one hand and "character" on the other being now discarded). Thus, for example in *Saunders' Case* it was held that where an old lady, who had broken her spectacles, was persuaded to assign the lease of her house – with the result that a companion of her nephew's was enabled to raise a loan from a building society upon the security of it – was *not* entitled to demand the lease back from the Society. Her mistake had been that she was transferring the house by way of gift to the nephew in order to help him to secure a loan; whereas in fact she had been persuaded (for the nephew's own supposed convenience) to make a purported sale to the companion who, having obtained the loan from the Society, absconded with the money. In either event, as Russell, L.J. had put the matter in the Court of Appeal, the "object of the exercise" was substantially the same: the deed was knowingly put into circulation by the signer as a security for money.

B Misrepresentation

We have seen that the terms of a contract are promises or statements which are intended to form the framework of the contract, and which define the mutual obligations of the parties. It often happens however that, at or about the time of the making of a contract, one of the parties makes a statement of fact which, though it is not intended to be a *term* of the contract, nevertheless induces the other party to contract. Statements of this sort are called *representations*.

Whether any particular statement is a term, or a representation, is technically a question to be determined by reference to the intention of the parties; but as in the case of the distinction between conditions and warranties, so here, since people do not always express their intentions, all the surrounding circumstances have to be considered. Thus such factors as whether a statement was reduced to writing, whether the situation was such that one of the parties might be expected to have placed special reliance upon it, and even the time that it was made, all have to be taken into account. The distinction may be illustrated by contrasting the case of *Harling* v. *Eddy*, [1951] 2 K.B. 739, with the old case of *Hopkins* v. *Tanqueray* (1854), 15 C.B. 130. In *Harling's Case* the defendant put up an unpromising-looking heifer for sale at an auction. There being no bids, the defendant then declared that there was nothing wrong with her. The plaintiff then bought her in reliance upon this statement made *during the auction*. The heifer's condition at once proved unsatisfactory and it died shortly afterwards. It was held that the defendant's statement formed a term of the contract, and that accordingly the plaintiff was entitled to damages. In *Hopkins' Case* the defendant was going to sell a horse at Tattersall's, and on the *day before* the sale the plaintiff was examining it when the defendant said "I assure you he is perfectly sound". The plaintiff bought it the next day in reliance upon this statement which was held to be a *representation* rather than a term.

When a representation is untrue it is called a *misrepresentation*. Just as parties are free to make whatever terms they like, so also they are not *bound* to make representations. Only *active* misrepresentations will therefore normally give rise to a cause of action; mere silence, even as to known defects, does not normally amount to misrepresentation. Thus in *Ward* v. *Hobbs* (1878), 4 App. Cas. 13, where a man sold pigs "with all faults" it was ruled that, though to his knowledge they had typhoid, he could not be held liable: he had made no misrepresentation. This rule is, of course, another application of the *caveat emptor* principle: in theory, at least, the prudent buyer should safeguard himself by exacting terms from the seller.

The effect of misrepresentation varies according to whether it is fraudulent or innocent. We must therefore first consider fraudulent and innocent misrepresentation separately, and then mention must be made of certain special contracts which do require a *positive* duty of disclosure.

1   FRAUDULENT MISREPRESENTATION

A fraudulent misrepresentation is one which constitutes the tort of *fraud* (or "deceit"). This tort is committed when a person makes a *false representation of fact, knowing it to be false, or without believing it to be true, or recklessly, careless whether it be true or false*. The false representation must, further, be made with the *intention that it is to be acted upon* by the party deceived; and if his claim is to succeed this person must prove that he actually did *act* upon it *to his detriment*. These various elements of the tort may be considered in turn.

(*i*) *The representation must be a representation of fact* – Thus a mere statement that something "*will be*", cannot form a ground for an action of deceit. For instance, if I say to you, "My car will win the Monte Carlo Rally", and you buy it in reliance upon my statement, you will have no claim against me, even though the car fails to cross the start-line. I have not deceived you as to an existing fact. It must also be noted that although it has been convenient thus far to treat representations as if they were always verbal statements, this is not always the case. Acts, as well as words, can deceive. For example, a person who, not being a member of the university, dresses up in a cap and gown in a university town, and thus obtains false credit from a shop-keeper, is guilty of deceit. Further, a mere statement of *opinion* is not a statement of fact.

(*ii*) *The representation must be made with a knowledge of its falsehood, or recklessly, without a belief in its truth* – This proposition was illustrated in the leading case of *Derry* v. *Peek* (1889), 14 App. Cas. 337. The directors of a company issued a prospectus stating that the company was empowered to run steam trams in Plymouth. This was not really true, because authorization had to be obtained from the Board of Trade which had not actually been granted. The directors, however, honestly believed that it was certain to be granted. Authorization was in fact eventually refused; but meantime the plaintiff had bought shares on the faith of the prospectus. As a result of the refusal the company had to be wound up; the plaintiff therefore suffered loss. When he sued the directors for fraud the House of Lords held that his action failed: the directors might have been stupid, but they *honestly* believed in the statement they had made.

Today, as we shall see, the duties of directors or promoters who issue company prospectuses have been made more stringent than they used to be, but the proposition of law laid down in *Derry* v. *Peek*, that an *honest* statement cannot be fraudulent, still holds good.

(*iii*) *The representation must be made with the intention that it shall be acted upon by the party deceived* – Thus the *mere* telling of a lie will not make the liar responsible to the world at large, for the liar does not always intend that people shall act upon what he says.

(*iv*) *The plaintiff must show that he acted upon the representation to his detriment* – Thus, suppose that Peter offers John a stamp and asks him for £10, asserting that it is a particularly valuable one. If Peter knows that it is not, and John is deceived into paying £10, Peter is guilty of deceit. If, on the other hand, John knows that it is really quite common, and offers Peter 50p which Peter accepts, Peter's attempted deceit has failed, it is not actionable; for John has not been induced to act upon it, and has lost nothing.

Remedies for fraudulent misrepresentation – Where a misrepresentation which is fraudulent in the sense above defined induces a person to make a contract the contract will be *void* if the effect of the fraud is to induce an operative mistake (see above, p. 232); hence no property can pass under it and the plaintiff may claim from the fraudulent person or from third parties anything that has been transferred. As has already been explained, however, by no means all frauds do induce operative mistake and the more usual effect of fraudulent (like innocent) misrepresentation is to render the contract *voidable* at the option of the person defrauded. The effect of this is that that person may –

(i) Recover damages for fraud (or deceit); *i.e.* in tort, in respect of any loss;

(ii) He may, upon discovering the fraud – and within a reasonable time he must – make an election whether to affirm or repudiate the contract; then the result will depend on his choice – (*a*) If he affirms, the contract remains valid and he may insist upon its performance; (*b*) If he repudiates within a reasonable time the contract is avoided and he may take back anything he had lost under it. Repudiation may take the form of actual notification to the other party or of taking such steps to bring it to his attention as is reasonable in the circumstances. It is essential that repudiation should be communicated as soon as possible, since delay may mean that innocent third parties may acquire rights in respect of the subject-matter of the contract (*e.g.*, by its resale by the rogue); once such rights are acquired in the absence of reasonably prompt repudiation the right to avoid is lost. It should be added that sometimes it may be advisable for the aggrieved party to institute an *action* for rescission of the contract instead of relying purely upon his extrajudicial right of repudiation.

2   INNOCENT MISREPRESENTATION

This is a matter which, as will be seen, has recently received the attention of the Legislature. Any misrepresentation which is not "fraudulent" in the sense defined above is "innocent", whether negligently made or not. The law governing such misrepresentations has much in common with fraudulent ones. First, as in the case of fraudulent misrepresentation so in the case of innocent; unless the effect of the statement is to produce operative mistake the contract is voidable at the plaintiff's option; not void. Second, the party aggrieved may affirm the contract either by words or conduct, and although mere lapse of time after knowledge of the misrepresentation will not normally amount to an affirmation in itself, it may be treated as evidence of it. Lapse of time beyond the appropriate limitation period (see below, p. 264) will of course, *per se.* form a complete bar. Third, once third parties have acquired rights (as for example in goods sold, and bought for value and in good faith) the contract cannot be avoided.

Formerly, however, in the case of innocent misrepresentation it was not possible either to obtain rescission of the contract once it was executed, *i.e.*, once performance had been entered upon, or to obtain damages for loss incurred as the result of the misrepresentation; though equity gave a limited right of compensation.

The Misrepresentation Act 1967, however, altered this position. By s. 1 it is provided that neither the fact that the misrepresentation has been incorporated into the contract and become a term of it, nor the fact that the contract has been performed, will preclude a claim for *rescission*. But rescission is an equitable remedy governed by discretion rather than by rule, and the court must therefore take all circumstances and equities into account. For instance, quite apart from the former rule which made the bare fact of execution of the contract a bar to rescission, rescission in equity must depend upon the power of the court in all the circumstances to effect *"restitutio in integrum"* – put things back where they were when the parties entered upon their bargain – and lapse of time and intervening events may make this impossible. Hence the Act (s. 2(2)) provides that the court may refuse rescission at discretion and grant *damages in lieu* of wherever it would *"be equitable to do so, having regard to the nature of the misrepresentation and the loss that would be caused by it if the contract were upheld, as well as the loss that rescission would cause to the other party"*.

Section 2 (1) of the Act provides that a person who enters into a contract as the result of innocent misrepresentation and *suffers loss* thereby may recover damages against the misrepresentor provided that damages would have been recoverable had the statement been fraudulent; *but* the defendant will *escape* liability if he *"proves that he had reasonable ground to believe and did believe up to the time the contract was made that the facts represented were true"*. Thus, in effect, damages may be obtained for *negligent*, though *not* for what might be called entirely innocent, misrepresentation. The two different grounds for awarding damages must, however, be kept clearly apart: damages *in lieu of rescission* are one thing, damages claimed for *loss suffered* are another. Thus in a particular case damages might be awarded under both heads; rescission *and* damages having been claimed. Where this happens s. 2 (3) operates: this provides that if both are awarded the court must take into account in assessing liability in respect of damages in lieu of rescission any award made (under s. 2 (1)) in respect of damages for loss arising from the negligent misstatement.

3   CONTRACTS IN WHICH DISCLOSURE IS REQUIRED

The duty which the law in general imposes upon people negotiating a contract is, as we have seen, the purely negative duty to refrain from making misrepresentations. But there are two special classes of contracts in respect of which such people are required to make positive disclosure of facts known to them, but unknown to the other party.

First, where the parties are in a confidential relationship, equity requires the person in whom confidence is reposed to make full disclosure of all material facts in respect of any contract he may make with the other party. This is a general rule, and it is not limited to particular classes of relationships. The solicitor-client relationship, however, forms a stock example.

Second, there are certain classes of contracts in respect of which one party has means of knowledge which, in the nature of things, the other party cannot be expected to possess. These contracts are called contracts *uberrimae fidei* ("of the utmost good faith"). Here the party having the special means of knowledge must make full disclosure of all material facts known to him which might influence the other party's decision to enter upon the contract or to continue to perform it once it has been entered upon. Failure to disclose such facts will give the other party an option to rescind, even though *restitutio in integrum* is no longer possible.

By far the most important of the contracts *uberrimae fidei* are contracts of insurance. A person who applies for insurance of any sort must disclose all facts known to him which would be likely to affect the decision of the insurer to undertake the risk. But it should be noted that the applicant need only disclose facts *known* to him. Thus, if an applicant for a policy of life insurance is asked, "Do you suffer from any known disease?" and he replies "No", and it subsequently appears that, without knowing it, he had cancer, he will not be guilty of non-disclosure. In practice, however, insurance companies tend to evade this rule by so framing the terms of policies that the statements of the assured become the basis of the contract; thus the knowledge of the assured becomes irrelevant.

There are several other classes of contracts in which a degree of disclosure is required; and they are therefore in some respects similar to contracts "*uberrimae fidei*". The degree of disclosure required varies, and is not usually so strict as that required in the case of contracts of insurance. Here it can only be mentioned that promoters of companies are bound, by the provisions of the Companies Act 1948 (s. 38; Sched. IV, Part I) to disclose certain specified matters in their prospectuses.

4 PRIVITY OF CONTRACT

A contract creates a kind of special law for the parties who enter upon it. It follows logically from this that *only such people as are "privy" (parties) to a contract can normally be affected by it*. This aspect of the law of contract is often epitomized in the Latin maxim "*res inter alios acta aliis neque nocere neque prodesse potest*", which may be loosely translated, "An agreement can only bind the parties; it can neither impose *obligations* upon other people, nor confer *rights* upon them."

This general rule is, however, subject to exceptions. The two branches must be considered separately.

A   A Contract Cannot Impose Obligations Upon People Who are not Privy to it

The courts have generally been disposed to uphold this principle, and have refused to countenance attempts to evade it. Thus in *Scruttons, Ltd. v. Midland Silicones, Ltd.*, [1962] A.C. 446 a firm of *stevedores* whose servants damaged some *cargo* were held not entitled (in an action by cargo owners) to rely upon a clause which limited liability for damage and was contained in the bill of lading, which of course represented the contract between cargo owners and *ship* owners. And this was so even though it had been agreed between stevedores and the shipowners that the former should "have such protection as is afforded by the terms" of the bill of lading. It would have been otherwise, as we have seen (above, p. 217), if the shipowners had contracted on behalf of and as *agents* for the stevedores: for then, through the agency of the carriers, the cargo owners would have been in a contractual relationship with the stevedores, who could thus have taken advantage of the exemption clause.

But there are exceptions to the general rule –

In the first place, in some circumstances *resale price maintenance* between manufacturer, wholesaler and dealer may now be enforced by the manufacturer directly against the dealer. This was not so at common law, since there was no privity of contract between those two parties. The enforcement was first permitted by the Restrictive Trade Practices Act 1956, but that Act now stands amended by the Resale Prices Act 1964. The result of the two Acts is that the position today is that agreements, both as between the immediate parties (manufacturer and wholesaler/wholesaler and dealer) and as between manufacturer and dealer are *void* if they fix a *minimum* price. But they will be *valid* if they relate to goods which have been *exempted* by the Restrictive Practices Court or if an application to the Court is pending in respect of them. On the other hand agreements which fix a *maximum* price are valid both as between the immediate parties and between *manufacturer* and *dealer*: this is, of course – as also in the case of an exempted minimum price agreement – an exception to the rule as to privity.

It should be added that for the sake of simplicity the only parties mentioned have been manufacturer, wholesaler and dealer: in practice of course there may be other parties (to whom the same rules will apply) in the sale "chain".

In the second place, where a contract creates an *interest of an enduring nature*, the subsistence of this interest will sometimes be permitted to have an adverse effect upon the rights of third parties. An obvious example of an interest of this sort is to be found in the case of a lease of land. Suppose that A leases land to B for seven years, and that A sells the land to C while five years of B's lease remain unexpired. At any rate since the Middle Ages, it has never been doubted that C takes the land subject to B's right under the lease. In this case C is therefore adversely affected by the contract between A and B.

Further, there is authority – though a later decision has exposed the matter to considerable doubt – for the proposition that where shipowners sell a *ship* which is subject to charter (*i.e.* is let out to a charterer) the buyer may, if he has full notice of the charter and its terms, be restrained by the charterer from using the ship in a manner inconsistent with the charter until the charter period expires.

B A Contract Cannot Confer Rights Upon People Who are not Privy to it

This rule does not mean that where Smith contracts with Jones to confer a benefit upon Brown, Brown cannot take the benefit. It means that Jones, and Jones alone, can force Smith to keep his contract. This aspect of "privity" must be clearly distinguished from the rule that consideration must "move from the promisee" (above, p. 218). The two rules sometimes produce a similar result, but they are distinct. For instance, if in the last example Smith had agreed with both Jones and Brown to confer the benefit upon Brown, and Jones alone had furnished consideration, Brown would still have been unable to sue Smith, even though he was privy to the agreement; for he would not have furnished consideration.

The rule that third parties cannot be adversely affected by contracts made between other people is both logical and practically just. The rule that strangers to a contract cannot acquire benefits under it rests upon logic alone, and it is subject to a considerable number of exceptions. The following are among the more important of them.

(*i*) Where one of the parties to a contract enters into it as trustee for a third party, the third party acquires an equitable right (see above, p. 26) which is a right practically equivalent to a right of property in the subject-matter of the contract. He may therefore force the trustee to insist upon the performance of the contract on his behalf.

(*ii*) A principal may acquire the benefit of a contract made by his agent. Agency will be discussed below.

(*iii*) Certain statutes permit third parties to acquire rights under contracts made by other people. Two of them may be mentioned. First, by s. 148 (4) of the Road Traffic Act 1972 insurers who issue a policy which covers third-party risks are in some cases made liable to people, other than the assured, for whose benefit the assured has taken out the policy. Second, by the Third Parties (Rights against Insurers) Act 1930 third parties who have claims against an assured in respect of a motor accident may claim direct against the insurers if, amongst other things, the assured becomes bankrupt. They thus receive a benefit as the result of the contract between the assured and his insurers. Perhaps more important still is the agreement of 1946 between the Minister of Transport and the Motor Insurers' Bureau whereby the latter undertakes to indemnify anyone in whose favour judgment is given in an accident claim if the judgment has not been satisfied in respect of any liability required to be covered by the Road Traffic Acts.

(*iv*) The so-called "collateral warranty" doctrine may also sometimes form an exception to the rule. This arises where A and B are considering making a contract and B, in the course of negotiation makes some statement which induces A to enter into the contract at some later stage, thereby (the assertion being misleading) suffering loss. In these circumstances the assertion is the "collateral warranty" : though what is really involved is not a single contract with a warranty attached (which might then in fact amount merely to a representation) but *two* contracts, the one a contract to enter into a contract, and the other the contract itself – the warranty being part of the former. Such warranty may be sued upon by A *even though he is not a party to the second contract* with B if he suffers loss in reliance upon it. A simple illustration may help. In *Wells (Merstham) Ltd.* v. *Buckland Sand and Silica Co.*, [1965] 2 Q.B. 170, A & Co. were chrysanthemum growers, B & Co. were owners of sandpits. A & Co. needed special sand to propagate their cuttings. A & Co.'s representative saw B & Co.'s representative and, by reference to chemical analysis, the latter assured the former that B & Co. would be able to supply just the right kind of sand, which he named by its technical name. Later A & Co. contracted with C & Co. to get them supplies of that sort of sand from B & Co. B & Co. then supplied different sand to C & Co. who delivered it to A & Co. who used it. It killed a large number of cuttings. It was held that A & Co. could sue upon the "warranty", although they were *not privy to the main contract* but merely to the prior agreement that if A & Co. were to order (as they in fact contemplated) the sand B & Co. would supply it.

(*v*) One practical way of circumventing the harshness of the rule in some cases rests upon the fact that where A contracts with B in favour of C, though C cannot sue B for breach of the obligation, A, of course, can. And if he does, he may recover damages in respect of any loss to C (see *Jackson* v. *Horizon Holidays, Ltd.* [1975] 3 All E.R. 92 – father recovered on behalf of family in respect of disappointing holiday). Moreover, where the equitable remedy of *specific performance* is available (see below, p. 261) A may obtain it in favour of C. Thus in *Beswick* v. *Beswick*, [1968] A.C. 58, a man assigned his business to his nephew (the defendant) upon condition that after his (the assignor's) death the defendant would pay an annuity to the assignor's widow. After the latter's death, the nephew failing to carry out his promise, it was held that the widow, as personal representative of the deceased, though not of course in her own right – for she was not a party to the contract – could claim specific performance in her own favour against the defendant. This exception to the rule is, however, necessarily limited to cases in which specific performance is an available remedy.

NOTE – The rule that a third party can acquire no rights under a contract has long been subject to criticism (see the Report of the Law Revision Committee: (1937) Cmd. 5449).

5 ASSIGNMENT OF CONTRACTUAL RIGHTS AND LIABILITIES

Assignment of Rights

An "assignment" of a right is a transfer of an existing right from one person to another. At common law *choses in action* were not assignable. The nature of choses in action will be explained below (Chapter 10). For the present it need only be noted that they have been authoritatively defined as "*all personal rights of property which can only be claimed or enforced by action, and not by taking physical possession*". Contract rights, such as the claim of a creditor against a debtor, are therefore "choses in action". It follows that, at common law, contract rights were not assignable. The reason for the adoption of this rule is obscure and it need not concern us here. In respect of choses in action generally, the rule as to non-assignability has long since been eaten away by exceptions. Negotiable instruments (below, Chapter 10) became freely assignable by the custom of merchants, and most other choses in action have been made expressly so by various statutes: copyright and patent rights may be instanced as examples.

The Legislature has also been active in making *contract* rights other than negotiable instruments assignable. Thus the assignment of life insurance policies is governed by the provisions of the Policies of Assurance Act 1867, and policies of marine insurance are assignable under the provisions of the Marine Insurance Act 1906. By far the most important enactment, however, in this regard, is s. 136 of the Law of Property Act 1925 : this section re-enacts s. 25 (6) of the Judicature Act 1873. It provides that : "*Any absolute assignment by writing under the hand of the assignor* [*i.e.* transferor] . . . *of any debt or other* . . . *thing in action, of which express notice in writing has been given to the debtor* . . . *is effectual in law* . . . *to pass and transfer from the date of such notice* . . . *the* . . . *right to such debt or thing in action.*"

The above enactment governs contract rights generally. Therefore, if B owes A £100 and A wishes to transfer the debt to C, he may do so by making an out and out transfer in *writing* and giving *written* notice of the transfer to B. The transfer may be either voluntary or for value.

This being so, the obvious question arises, "What happens if A wishes to make the assignment, but fails to comply with the *statutory* provisions?" Suppose for example that A fails to comply with the requirement as to writing. The answer to this question is that the assignment *may* still be valid. Although assignment of contract rights was not possible at common law, it could, from comparatively early times, be effected by the operation of the rules of equity. "Equitable" rights, *e.g.* the rights of a beneficiary to funds in the control of his trustee, were always and still are, freely assignable. Further, the Court of Chancery would support the claim of an assignee of a purely "legal" right, such as a claim to a simple money debt. This was done by forcing the assignor (the creditor) to bring an action at law against the debtor and to transfer the fruits of the action to the assignee. Since the Judicature Acts have combined the courts which administer law and equity this cumbrous procedure need no longer be adopted; but "*equitable assignments*" can still be made according to rules which are less exacting than the rules laid down in the Law of Property Act.

No particular formalities are required for an *equitable assignment*. It is sufficient for the assignor to transfer his right to the assignee by any appropriate means. It does not, however, follow that *all* purported assignments will be valid. The reason for this is that there are certain rather complicated rules which govern equitable assignments. These rules cannot be discussed here.

Two rules which govern assignments generally, whether statutory or equitable, require attention.

First, apart from the provision as to written notice in s. 136, it is always wise for an assignee to give *notice* of the assignment to the debtor. If the assignee fails to do this, the debtor will be entitled (since he knows nothing of the assignment) to discharge his liability by paying the assignor himself, or by paying any other assignee who gives him notice. For example : W, for value, assigns to Y X's debt to him. W is a rogue. He goes to Z, receives value, and re-assigns the same debt to *him*. If

Z gives notice to X before Y gives notice, Z will be entitled to payment and Y will have lost his right. Where the right assigned is an equitable right, such as the claim of a beneficiary to a trust fund, the notice to the trustee must be *written* if it is to be effective (Law of Property Act 1925, s. 137 (3)).

In the second place, an assignee always takes subject to any rights (such as rights of set-off) which the debtor may have against the assignor. *Nemo dat quod non habet* ("No one can give what he has not got"). The assignor cannot give the assignee a better right than he himself has.

Finally, even at the present time there are certain classes of contract rights which are not assignable. The most important of these are bare rights of action (*e.g.* mere claims to damages upon a *broken* contract) and rights of a personal nature (*e.g.* rights to the performance of personal services): though this statement must be qualified to the extent that, provided that the requirements of the L.P.A. s. 136 are complied with, an insurer who has paid his insured in respect of loss arising from the commission of a tort or breach of a contract may sue the wrongdoer in his own name in order to recoup himself.

Assignment of Liabilities

As a general rule liabilities are not assignable. This is common sense. If, for instance, A were to commission B to paint his portrait A would be very surprised if, without consulting him, B were to transfer his obligations to another artist.

The rule is well illustrated by *Robson & Sharpe* v. *Drummond* (1831), 2 B. & Ad. 303. D hired a carriage from S for a period of five years. S undertook to keep it painted and in good repair. Unknown to D, S was in partnership with R. When S retired from business, while there were two years of the contract still to run, R claimed to be entitled to continue with the contract. It was held that he could not, and that D could treat it as terminated by S's retirement.

There are three things which may possibly be considered to constitute exceptions to the general rule that contractual liabilities cannot be assigned.

First, the parties to a contract may *agree* that the duties of one of them shall be assignable; there is nothing to prevent this. Thus if Drummond had agreed, Sharpe might have stipulated that his duties should be transferable to Robson in certain events. Second, liabilities may be transferred by "*novation*", *i.e.* by the termination of an existing contract and the formation of a new one, under which a third person undertakes to perform the duties of one of the parties to the old contract. Third, although liabilities are not *assignable*, they may sometimes be *vicariously performed* by a third party on behalf of the person bound. For instance, if I employ a man to repair a common article, such as a table, as long as the table is repaired I cannot complain if someone else does the job. As *Robson's Case* shows, however, there are limits to this rule, and there can be no vicarious performance of a contract which requires any special personal skill.

Since "assignment" denotes the *transfer* of an *existing* obligation the last two, at any rate, of the above-mentioned "exceptions" are more apparent than real.

6 DISCHARGE OF CONTRACT

Contractual obligations may be discharged by performance, by agreement, by supervening impossibility, and by breach.

Performance

It is obvious that a party to a contract who has performed his obligations will be discharged from further liability. He will also normally be discharged if he makes a valid offer (or "tender") of performance which the other party rejects. Mere tender of a *money* debt will not, however, operate as a discharge; in order to escape liability a debtor must show, not merely that he tendered the correct sum upon the date on which it was due, but also that he was ready and willing to pay, up to the time that the creditor brought his action for the recovery of the debt. He should then pay the money into court.

Discharge by Agreement

Discharge by agreement may take four forms.

First, the contract may be discharged by "*waiver*"; that is to say, both parties may mutually agree to forgo each other's obligations. In this case the waiver by one party constitutes consideration for the waiver by the other, and the transaction is therefore binding. Where, however, one party has *performed* his own obligations, he cannot (subject to the possible exception founded upon the decision in the *High Trees Case*, above, p. 218) be bound by a mere promise to waive the obligations of the other. A waiver of this sort will only be valid if it is supported by independent consideration or made under seal. The reason for this is that the other party has given no consideration for the waiver.

In the second place, an existing contract may be mutually discharged, and a *new one substituted* in its place: this is a form of novation.

In the third place, the contract may be subject to a *condition subsequent* (see above, p. 225) in which case failure of the condition may give rise to discharge.

In the fourth place, a contract may be discharged by *accord and satisfaction* – as where B owing A £200, the latter agrees to accept a motor cycle in satisfaction of the debt. But it will be remembered that payment of a *lesser sum of money* would not discharge B (see above, p. 217) unless the doctrine of promissory estoppel (above, p. 219) were to come into play.

Further, many kinds of contracts are not intended to be of indefinite duration, and either expressly or by implication they depend upon appropriate notice for their discharge. Agreements for periodic leases afford an example (see below, p. 346), but perhaps the commonest contracts of this kind are contracts of employment. These are subject to the Contracts of Employment Act 1972. This Act governs both notice and the form of the contract. The rules are detailed and must be consulted in particular cases but, broadly, the position is that in the case of most employees who have been continuously employed in *full-time employment for 13 weeks or more* one week's notice is required to be given by the employer to the employee for the first two years of employment, two weeks' notice between two years and five years, four weeks' between five and ten years, six weeks' between ten and fifteen, and eight weeks' for any longer period. The employee for his part must give one week's notice, however long the service. Either party may, however, waive the right to notice and may accept payment in lieu of it; moreover, no notice of dismissal is required where substantial misconduct is involved. It must be noted that no penalty is imposed upon an employer who gives less than the statutory period of notice, but statutory rules will be taken into account in assessing damages for wrongful dismissal. As to the form of the contract: the Act provides that within thirteen weeks from the beginning of continuous full-time employment the employer must make known to the employee *in writing* the main terms of the employment (the details required are to be found in s. 4 of the Act): this provision does not, however, apply in the case of written contracts nor to contracts involving less than 21 hours' work weekly. [As to the effect of the Employment Protection Act 1975, see Addendum: New Legislation.]

Frustration

It sometimes happens that, in the course of the performance of a contract which is intended to last over a period of time unforeseen events occur which render further performance impracticable or impossible. Examples of such events are sickness, accident, war, the interference of third parties and legislation which renders further performance illegal.

The occurrence of such unforeseen events will now normally have the effect of *"frustrating"* the contract. That is to say, the courts will excuse further performance of it if the effect of the event has been to render such performance substantially impossible. Thus, in the leading case of *Taylor* v. *Caldwell* (1863), 3 B. & S. 826, A agreed to hire out a music hall to B. Six days before the letting was due to commence the hall was destroyed by fire. It was held that the continued existence of the hall was a basic assumption upon which the contract was founded and that it was therefore discharged when the hall was destroyed. Similarly, where war breaks out unexpectedly, commercial contracts, such as contracts for the chartering of ships, have often been held to be "frustrated" where the outbreak renders voyages to enemy or prohibited destinations impossible.

Not all supervening events will, however, operate to annul contracts. A party who seeks to avoid a contract on the ground that an event has rendered further performance impossible must show not merely that the event has rendered the contract more onerous than he had expected, but also that it has destroyed the whole foundation of it; or as it has sometimes been put in relation to commercial contracts, that it has destroyed the whole basis of the venture, made continued fulfilment something radically different from what was originally contemplated, or rendered its continuance positively unjust. (It is to be noted that here we come very close to the rationale of "fundamental breach" – above, p. 229 and, perhaps, of mistake). Thus, for example, if an artiste dies or is taken seriously ill so as to be unable to perform, of if an employee who holds a key position in a business is sentenced to a long term of imprisonment either contract may be frustrated. By contrast, where on account of a criminal charge the head of a school was suspended for a time until the charge was dismissed, it was held – especially in view of the fact that his staff continued to run the school in his absence – that the suspension did not frustrate the contracts for the education of the pupils so as to enable the latter to be withdrawn from the school without the customary term's notice. And again something which merely adds to the length of a voyage does not *necessarily* frustrate a contract the fulfilment of which depends upon the voyage. So in *Taskiroglou & Co. Ltd.* v. *Noblee & Thorl G.m.b.H.*, [1962] A.C. 93 a contract for the sale of groundnuts which was elastic in its terms as to the date of delivery in Hamburg (the port of destination) was held by the House of Lords not to have been frustrated by the closure of the Suez Canal in 1956, which forced the carrying ship to take the longer Cape route rather than the normal and shorter Suez route from Port Sudan to Hamburg. Had the delivery date been a matter of importance the result might have been different.

Further, the element in the contract which the supervening event destroys must be something which both the parties, not merely one of them, must be taken to have regarded as basic. Thus in *Blackburn Bobbin Co.* v. *Allen*, [1918] 2 K.B. 467, the seller agreed to supply the buyer with Finnish timber. Unknown to the buyer, the seller held no stocks, but customarily shipped orders direct from Finland. War broke out and the seller's supplies were cut off. It was held that this event did not frustrate the contract, since the *method* of supply was irrelevant to it. For all that the buyer knew, the seller held stocks of Finnish timber, or obtained it indirectly from some other country.

The doctrine of "frustration" is also subject to three major limitations. In order for it to operate the following conditions must be satisfied:

(*i*) The supervening event must not normally be one which the parties expressly provided against in the contract. Thus, if I contract to build a house beneath the Matterhorn and agree to do so expressly in the face of the risk of avalanches, I cannot claim to be discharged from my obligations if an avalanche destroys my work when it is all-but finished. The event was one which the contract itself envisaged. On the other hand the mere fact that a subsequent event is foreseeable or even foreseen at the time of the contract does not mean that its occurrence cannot result in frustration. Thus in *Tatem (W. J.), Ltd.* v. *Gamboa*, [1939] 1 K.B. 132, a ship was let on charter to the Republican Governmen; to evacuate refugees during the Spanish Civil War. It was clear that there was risk of capture by the Nationalists but no provision was made to cover the event: nevertheless, capture was held to frustrate the contract.

(*ii*) The frustation must not be "self-induced" by one of the parties. For example in *Ocean Tramp Tankers Corporation* v. *V/O Sovfracht: The Eugenia*, [1964] 2 Q.B. 226, it was held that when the charterers in 1956 allowed the *Eugenia* to enter the Canal Zone in face of the obvious danger of closure they could not treat her detention in the Canal as frustration, since they themselves brought it about.

(*iii*) The event relied upon must destroy the very root of the contract. It seems that the courts will not permit the doctrine to be invoked so as to allow a party to escape liability for the breach of a minor obligation. Thus it was held that where a tenant left a house without painting it as the terms of the lease provided that he should, he could not escape liability to his landlord by proving that war-time regulations had made it impossible for him to obtain a licence to paint.

Once it has been proved that a contract has been frustrated, it is automatically avoided. This rule formerly led to unhappy results, because it was held that the supervening event had the effect of leaving matters exactly as they lay at the moment it occurred. Hence money, once paid, could not be recovered even though frustration made further performance of the contract by the recipient impossible, unless there had been a total failure of consideration. The position is, however, now regulated by the Law Reform (Frustrated Contracts) Act 1943. The Act provides that, where frustration occurs, sums paid before the happening of the frustrating event are to be recoverable, subject to deduction of expenses incurred by the payee. All subsequent liabilities are extinguished. Further, if one party has conferred a benefit upon the other, as by performing services for him, he may claim the value of this benefit from the other, or, as the case may be, may set the value off against any claim which the other may have against him. Certain classes of contracts are excluded from the operation of the Act: in particular, contracts for the sale of specific goods, which are frustrated by the perishing of the goods, are not included, for they are governed by the Sale of Goods Act 1893 (see below, p. 273).

Discharge by Breach

Where one of the parties to a contract breaks his side of it entirely, the other may, if he wishes, *repudiate* it and he will then be discharged himself from further performance, and he may also claim for any loss he has suffered.

Breach may take one of two forms. It may either be constituted by substantial failure of performance, or by renunciation before or after the due time for performance arrives. Whichever of these two forms it may take, it must amount to a *substantial* failure of performance, or of refusal to perform. Further, where a breach occurs during performance, it is often a nice question whether it can be regarded as "substantial". Instalment contracts often raise difficulties. A party who claims the right to rescind will seldom succeed if he can only show a failure to deliver one of a series of instalments. He will, however, always be entitled to claim *damages* for any breach, however small.

Where, before a contract is due to be performed, one party renounces his obligations, or renders performance impossible by his own act, he is said to have committed an "*anticipatory*" breach. English law, unlike most other systems, gives effect to anticipatory breaches. Thus in the days when breach of promise of marriage was actionable, where B promised to marry Miss A when B's father should die, and B renounced the contract during his father's lifetime, it was held that Miss A could sue him. It will be noticed that this is an extreme instance of an "anticipatory" breach, for not only was the time for performance not due, but it might never have arrived at all. Either of the parties to the contract might have predeceased the father.

7　REMEDIES FOR BREACH OF CONTRACT

Having considered the circumstances in which a contract may be discharged (*i.e.* terminated) as the result of a breach, we must now consider the nature of the principal remedies which are open to the party injured by the breach. These are damages, *quantum meruit*, specific performance and injunctions, and rescission and rectification.

Damages

Damages are a common law remedy, and they may be claimed by an injured party as of right. They are money compensation for loss suffered. The object of granting them is to put the injured party, as far as money can do it, into the position in which he would have been had the loss not been suffered, *i.e.* (as far as concerns us here) had the contract not been broken. Thus, there can be no rule which will prescribe in every case what damages the plaintiff *will* obtain: the amount of damages must always depend upon the "value" of the loss. There are, however, certain general rules governing damages, some of which must now be mentioned.

(*i*) The "value" of the loss is generally assessed, not according to the price the plaintiff puts upon it, but objectively, according to the value that an ordinary, reasonable, person would put upon it. Thus, for example, where a breach of contract consists of failure by the defendant to deliver goods under a contract of sale, the general rule is that the "measure of damages is *prima facie* to be ascertained by the difference between the contract price and the market, or current, price of the goods at the time when they ought to have been delivered". (Sale of Goods Act 1893, s. 51 (3).) Note: "price" here means the "market" (*i.e.* ordinary) price, not, for instance, the price at which the plaintiff may, unknown to the defendant, have himself contracted to re-sell the goods.

(*ii*) Damages may be recovered only in respect of loss arising from the breach of contract itself. There can be no claim in respect of loss which is too "*remote*" from the breach to be regarded as a proximate result of it. The distinction between remote and proximate damage is hard to draw. The courts, however, apply a test which was first propounded by Alderson, B. in *Hadley* v. *Baxendale* (1854), 9. Ex. 341, at p. 354.

The learned Baron laid down the following rule. "*Where two parties*", he said, "*have made a contract which one of them has broken, the damages which the other party ought to receive in respect of such breach of contract should be such as may fairly and reasonably be considered either arising naturally, i.e. according to the usual course of things, from such breach of contract itself, or such as may reasonably be supposed to have been in the contemplation of both parties, at the time they made the contract, as the probable result of the breach of it.*" It will be seen that this really provides two rules. According to *Rule I* damage will be regarded as "proximate" if it is damage which arises "naturally" from the breach. Subsequent decisions have shown that, for the purposes of the law of contract, this means damage which the party in breach ought reasonably to have *foreseen*, in the light of the knowledge of the circumstances which he possessed at the time the contract was made as *likely*, in the ordinary course of things, to follow from breach of his obligations. According to *Rule II*, as appeared from later statements in Alderson, B's judgment, damage which is not "ordinary" in the above sense may give rise to a claim for damages (*i.e.* may be "proximate" and not "too remote") where though it is of an extraordinary nature, the parties did in fact contemplate that it might occur. This will happen, for example, where the plaintiff communicates the likelihood of a *peculiar kind* of loss to the defendant, and the defendant accepts the contract with that likelihood in mind. Though, according to the nature of what is contemplated, the effect of the Rule *may*, of course, be to diminish rather than increase the extent of liability if the harm they *did* both contemplate was something *less* drastic than might ordinarily have been expected.

The operation of Rule I may be illustrated by *Hadley* v. *Baxendale* itself. A crank shaft broke in the plaintiffs' mill. This meant that the mill had to stop working because it could not operate without the shaft. The plaintiffs wanted to send the shaft to the manufacturer at Greenwich as quickly as possible, so that it could be used as a pattern for a new one. Speed was essential since, while the mill was stopped, the plaintiffs lost profits which they would otherwise have made from its use. The plaintiffs' servants therefore delivered the shaft to the defendants, who were carriers (Messrs. Pickford & Co.) and who accepted it for carriage, but were guilty of serious delay in making delivery.

On the above facts, the plaintiffs brought an action for breach of contract by reason of the delay; they claimed, amongst other things, damages for loss of profits which they would have obtained by use of the mill during the period of delay and had the shaft been returned in time. The court held that this loss of profits was not a "natural" consequence of delay in delivering a crank shaft, and that the claim therefore failed; for the plaintiffs had done nothing to bring the case within the operation of Rule II (above). All that the defendants knew, when the contract was made, was that the article to be carried was a broken shaft, and that the plaintiffs were millers. There was nothing in this information to suggest that delay in delivery would cause a loss of profits – as far as the defendants knew, the plaintiffs might, for instance, have had a spare shaft.

The case of *Victoria Laundry (Windsor), Ltd.* v. *Newman Industries, Ltd.*, [1949] 2 K.B. 528, provides a contrast with *Hadley* v. *Baxendale*. The plaintiffs were launderers and dyers who required a particularly large boiler, both in order to extend their existing business and in order to provide them with a suitable plant for obtaining certain exceptionally profitable dyeing contracts. The defendants, a firm of engineers, contracted to sell them such a boiler. Through the fault of the defendants' sub-contractors, the delivery of this boiler was seriously delayed. The plaintiffs claimed as damages, first, an amount equal to the estimated loss of *the increased profits* which the use of the boiler would have acquired for them during the period of the delay, second, the amount which they would have earned from the *dyeing contracts* during the same period. Since the defendants knew, at the time of the agreement, that the plaintiffs were dyers and launderers and they were informed that the boiler was required for immediate use the Court of Appeal held that damages were recoverable under the *first head*. Whereas there is no reason to suppose that delay in delivering a mill-shaft will cause a milling business to cease, anyone would reasonably expect that a laundry which requires a boiler immediately will be likely to need it to satisfy the demands of its customers. With regard to the *second head*, the court held that the plaintiffs could not recover upon the basis of the exceptionally high figure contemplated in their contracts – this was something which the defendants could not reasonably have contemplated in the light of the facts known to them at the time of the agreement, and the plaintiffs had not informed them of the contracts: had they done this, of course, they might have recovered this exceptional amount under Rule II.

In *The Heron II, Koufos* v. *C. Czarnikow, Ltd.*, [1969] 1 A.C. 350, the House of Lords reconsidered the relationship of the rules as to remoteness of damage in contract and tort. It will be seen (below, p. 320) that the test of reasonable contemplation or foresight now in the main governs in both fields. But their Lordships stressed that the degree of foresight required under Rule I in *Hadley* v. *Baxendale* is something less than what is required in tort. In the latter, at least in some circumstances, the defendant will be held liable for consequences which are not inherently probable, but which are nevertheless "on the cards".

In contract the liability depends upon the presumed contemplation of the parties at the time when they made their agreement, and it is to be presumed that they would only contemplate liability for what is *usual, normal or not unlikely to happen*; it is therefore only for events of this kind that the defendant will be made to pay. Thus in *Hadley* v. *Baxendale* though "on the cards", the loss of profits was something far from probable; but in *The Heron II* the House had no difficulty in maintaining that delay in delivering goods at a commercial port was something which would have the *probable* effect of depreciating the re-sale value of the goods by reason of a drop in the market price of them during the period of delay. And that the owners of the goods could therefore recover their loss of profit from the defendant shipowners.

(*iii*) Parties sometimes include a clause in a contract to the effect that if one of them breaks it he shall pay a sum of money to compensate the other for the breach. If the sum agreed upon is a *genuine pre-estimate* of the value of the loss which one party suffers, he may sue to recover it by way of liquidated (*i.e.* quantified) damages from the party in breach. The sum so assessed must *not*, however, be a "*penalty*", *i.e.* an amount greatly in excess of the loss that is likely to be suffered. Thus it has been held that a clause in a hire-purchase agreement which purported to secure for the owner upon any breach of the agreement, *not merely* repayment of instalments and interest due, but also a sum representing a minimum of *two-thirds of the whole price* as "agreed compensation for depreciation of the goods" was a penalty and unenforceable. The true object of such a clause is clearly not to secure compensation – for a breach may occur after a single instalment out of many is due – but to ensure the owner a minimum unearned return.

(*iv*) *Exemplary* damages (below, p. 319) cannot be recovered in actions based upon contract.

(*v*) It is now settled that, as in tort so in contract, damages are not confirmed to items of physical loss and may be recovered in respect of inconvenience, frustration, disappointment, anxiety, etc. So that a man who took a holiday in Switzerland through a travel agency and discovered that it in no sense matched up to its description in the brochure was held entitled to damages to compensate for his disappointment.

Finally, it needs to be pointed out that in contract, as in tort (see below, p. 295) there must be a *causal* connexion between the defendant's default and the plaintiff's loss; for the former cannot by any test be held responsible for something which he did not *cause*. Thus in *Quinn* v. *Burch Bros. (Builders), Ltd.*, [1966] 2 Q.B. 370, the plaintiff was engaged upon some building work as sub-contractor for the defendants who were obliged, when necessary, to supply him with a ladder on request. This they failed to do, so the plaintiff used an unfooted trestle which was clearly dangerous in the circumstances; and he fell and was injured. It was held that, although it was true that they had broken their contract, the defendants were not liable, since the plaintiff had brought the injury upon himself.

Quantum Meruit

A claim for damages is a claim for compensation for loss. A claim upon a *"quantum meruit"* (for an amount "earned") is a claim in respect of unremunerated services.

Where, under the terms of a contract, one person performs services for another, and the other breaks or repudiates the contract, the person who has performed the services may usually, instead of claiming damages, sue upon a *quantum meruit* to recover the amount earned by his labours. Thus, in *Planché* v. *Colburn* (1831), 5 C. & P. 58, the plaintiff agreed, for £100, to write a book for the defendants, who were publishers. When he had written part of the book the defendants abandoned the project and repudiated the contract. It was held that the plaintiff could recover £50, upon a *quantum meruit*; for, though, in the circumstances, he had never completed the contract, yet, he ought not to lose the fruits of his labour upon the defendants' behalf.

It must also be explained that a *quantum meruit* may be used, not merely as a remedy for breach of contract, but also as a method of recovering a reasonable remuneration for the performance of a contract when no specific remuneration has been agreed upon. Thus, where X renders Y services which are clearly not intended to be voluntary, but in respect of which no price has been fixed, X may sue Y upon a *quantum meruit* for a reasonable sum of money. The same rule applies in respect of goods delivered; where no price is determined, the buyer must pay a reasonable price (Sale of Goods Act 1893, s. 8 (2)). But it should, perhaps, be added that the claim in this case is, strictly speaking, upon a *quantum valebat* (for the "value" of the goods). It must be appreciated, however, that where a person agrees to do something for a lump sum, for example to build a wall, he can normally only sue for payment if the work is *substantially* performed. Frustration apart, he cannot – unless at that stage the other party prevents further performance or repudiates the contract – build half the wall, and then claim upon a *quantum meruit* for half the money. The courts will not *imply* a contract in favour of a plaintiff who has made an express agreement and failed to perform it. This rule is known as the Rule in *Cutter* v. *Powell* (1795), 6 Term Rep. 320. In that case the defendant agreed to pay Cutter 30 guineas for acting as second mate aboard a vessel plying between Jamaica and Liverpool. Cutter died when the vessel was nineteen days short of Liverpool. It was held that his widow could recover nothing in respect of the work he had performed during the previous forty-nine days of the voyage.

The above rule is logical because it is based upon the principle that no one should be entitled to claim payment unless he has done what he has bargained to do: but pushed to extremes it may clearly work injustice, and its rigour is mitigated in two respects. First, as elsewhere in the law of contract, the word *"substantially"* may be subjected to common-sense construction; for example, in *Hoenig* v. *Isaacs*, [1952] 2 All E.R. 176, the plaintiff agreed to furnish and decorate the defendant's flat for £750: he completed the contract, but made some of the furniture so unsatisfactorily that it required alteration. The defendant had paid £400 by instalments in the course of the execution of the contract, but, when sued for the remaining £350, he invoked *Cutter* v. *Powell* on the ground that the plaintiff had not performed his part. The Court of Appeal held that the contract had been *substantially* completed, and upheld the plaintiff, while reducing his claim by £55 18s. 2d., the cost of making the necessary alterations. In the second place, in cases where a contract has been "frustrated", the importance of the Rule in *Cutter* v. *Powell* has now been much diminished by the provisions of the Law Reform (Frustrated Contracts) Act 1943, and, indeed, as the result of these provisions (see above, p. 255) a different result would be reached today upon the facts of the case itself.

Specific Performance and Injunctions

Specific performance and injunctions are equitable remedies. They were therefore originally only obtainable in the Court of Chancery. Since the Chancery was a court of "conscience", they were always, and since the combination of the courts administering law and equity, still are, discretionary remedies. Unlike damages, which are granted as of right, equitable remedies are only granted where, in all the circumstances of the case, it is fair and just that they should be granted. *Specific performance* is a decree of the court ordering a defendant to perform his obligations under a contract. For the purposes of the law of contract an *injunction* is an order commanding a defendant to refrain from breaking his contract.

SPECIFIC PERFORMANCE

The following rules govern the granting of a decree for specific performance –

(*a*) Specific performance will never be decreed where damages will provide an adequate remedy; for equity "*follows the law*", it is designed to supply the defects in it, not to override it. Thus, though a purchaser may obtain specific performance of a contract to purchase land, there can never be a decree for specific performance in respect of a mere money loan. But it must not be thought that this remedy is confined to land cases; for, in accordance with its purpose of supplying the defects in the law, a decree may (at discretion) be made for the return of specific goods of especial and peculiar value (though normally damages will suffice to recompense non-delivery), and in exceptional circumstances even an order to enforce the supply of non-specific goods – such as the supply of petrol – may be proper if an award of damages would be inadequate. Indeed, perhaps inconsequently, it has even been held that although a decree cannot be made to force a tenant to perform a repairing covenant it may be made to force a landlord to do so.

(*b*) Specific performance will not be granted in the absence of "mutu-ality". In order for a contract to be specifically enforceable, the parties must, in fairness, be on a footing of equality. Thus there cannot be specific performance of a gratuitous promise, even though it be made under seal – equity, as the maxim goes, "will not assist a volunteer", someone who offers no consideration. Similarly, there will be no specific performance in favour of a minor.

(*c*) There can be no specific performance of a contract for personal services.

INJUNCTIONS

For the purposes of the law of contract injunctions are in general "pro-hibitory"; that is to say, they are orders commanding a person to refrain from doing something. Thus a man who has undertaken not to do some particular thing may be forced by an injunction to refrain from doing it. Injunctions may, however, also be used as an indirect means of obtaining specific performance where, for some reason, that remedy is un-obtainable. For example, if B contracts to obtain supplies only from A the contract cannot be specifically enforced, for enforcement would require continuous supervision; but an injunction may be granted to restrain B from obtaining supplies from elsewhere.

In the case of contracts for *personal services* injunctions will only be granted in respect of *express negative* covenants. Thus, in the leading case of *Lumley* v. *Wagner* (1852), 1 De G. M. & G. 604, Miss W undertook to sing at a series of concerts organized by L, and she also undertook *not* to sing elsewhere during the period for which the concerts were to last. It was held that an injunction could be granted to restrain her from singing elsewhere. It is to be noted that in this case the effect of granting the injunction was not necessarily to force Miss W to perform the positive covenant to sing for L; it merely *encouraged* her do do so, by preventing her from singing elsewhere. If the effect of it would have been to "tie" her to L it could not have been granted; for in the case of contracts for *personal services* injunctions will not be used so as to tie someone to someone else or "starve" – as it has been said – thus enforcing specific performance by indirect means.

Rescission and Rectification

RESCISSION

Subject to the qualifications already mentioned (above, pp. 237–240) the court, in exercise of its equitable jurisdiction, may order *rescission* of a contract where it would, on account of mistake, misrepresentation or otherwise, be unreasonable to tie the parties to it.

RECTIFICATION

This equitable remedy applies where it is sought to correct, or rectify, a document which purports to embody some prior agreement, whether oral or in writing, and this prior agreement has not – due to mutual mistake – been properly reproduced in the document. It must be understood, however, that the issue is entirely whether agreement and document fail to correspond: and if they do correspond it will be useless for one of the parties to assert that he did not intend what was said or written in the agreement. This may be illustrated by *F. E. Rose (London), Ltd.* v. *William H. Pim Jnr. & Co., Ltd.*, [1953] 2 Q.B. 450, where the plaintiffs received from the Middle East an order for " 'Moroccan horsebeans' described here as *'feveroles'* ". In negotiating with the defendants for the supply to them of these articles the plaintiffs asked what they were. The defendants asserted that they were just "horsebeans"; so in the contract the plaintiffs ordered "horsebeans", then, having discovered that feveroles are in fact not horsebeans, but beans of a special kind, sought to have the contract rectified so as to read "feveroles" for "horsebeans". It was held that this could not be done (so as to entitle the plaintiffs to sue the defendants upon the contract) since agreement and document were in accord; both referred to "horsebeans" and there was therefore nothing to be rectified. This may perhaps seem formalistic; but the logic is plain. It should be added that except in cases of grave injustice the courts will seldom, in the exercise of this discretionary jurisdiction, rectify a contract where the alleged mistake is unilateral.

8 LIMITATION

Rights of action cannot be permitted to endure for ever. People must be made to press their claims with reasonable diligence. Hence rules of *limitation* have to be made, *i.e.* rules which prescribe the time within which actions are to be brought.

Most of the rules in respect of limitation are now contained in the Limitation Act 1939 as amended by the Law Reform (Limitation of Actions, &c.) Act 1954, the Limitation Act 1963 and the Limitation Act 1975. As regards contract claims the rules are that –

(*i*) An action upon a *simple* contract (*i.e.* a contract other than a contract under seal) must be brought within *six* years of the accrual of the cause of action;

(*ii*) An action upon a contract under seal must be brought within *twelve* years of the accrual;

(*iii*) An action upon a *simple* contract which consists of, or includes, a claim for damages in respect of *personal injuries* to any person must be brought within *three* years of accrual. The expression "personal injuries" includes not only actual physical injury, but also disease and any impairment of a person's physical or mental condition.

The cause of action normally "accrues" at the time when the contract is broken.

The above rules are subject to certain exceptions.

First, where a person who is liable for a liquidated (*i.e.* a quantified) sum either makes a written *acknowledgment* of his indebtedness or makes a *part-payment* of the debt, time will start to run against him afresh from the date of acknowledgment or part-payment. Hence, if X were due to pay Y £100 under the terms of a contract under seal dated January 1st, 1964, Y's claim would normally have been barred by effluxion of time on January 1st, 1976. If, however, X were to have made a written acknowledgment of his indebtedness on, say, January 1st, 1968, Y's rights to bring his action would subsist until January 1st, 1980. Moreover, an acknowledgment made *after* January 1st, 1976, would have the effect of reviving the right for the statutory period.

In the second place, there are certain *"disabilities"*, such as minority and unsoundness of mind. Where a plaintiff is under a disability, time normally begins to run against him from the moment when the disability ceases, or from his death, whichever first occurs.

Third, where the plaintiff's action is based upon *fraud*, or where his right of action is *concealed by the defendant's fraud* (or the fraud of his agent or of any person through whom he claims), or where the action is for relief from the consequences of the plaintiff's *mistake*, the period of limitation does not begin to run until the plaintiff discovers the fraud, or the mistake, or could, with reasonable diligence, have done so. "Fraud" in the *second* of the above-mentioned contexts ("concealed" fraud) does not bear the usual meaning described above (p. 000); it embraces as well what is known as "equitable" fraud, which includes any form of unconscionable concealment even though not involving moral turpitude. For example in *Applegate* v. *Moss* [1971]; 1 Q.B. 406 it was held that the employee of a builder who covered up bad foundations so that the result of his slipshod work was not discovered until the house collapsed some years later could rely upon the statute as a bar to the houseowner's claim against him until six years *after the truth had been discovered.*

In the fourth place, as regards actions for *personal injuries* the 1975 Act provides specially for injuries (*e.g.* slow developing diseases such as silicosis) which may not be discoverable until long after the event which causes them. In these cases time (*three* years) begins to run either from the date of the *accrual of the cause of action* or from the date (if later) of the plaintiff's *knowledge* of the injury: though, at discretion, and subject to exceptions, even the latter period may be extended by the court.

In general, claims to equitable remedies, such as specific performance and injunctions, are not governed by the 1939 Act (see s. 2 (7)). Instead, they are governed by the equitable doctrine of "*laches*" (the application of which is expressly preserved by s. 29 of the Act). This doctrine is based upon the principle that it is unjust to permit a person to sleep upon his rights: delay may either be evidence of acquiescence in the infringement of the right violated, or may give rise to such changes in circumstances that it may become unfair to keep the other party to his bargain. Where this doctrine applies the length of time required for it to operate is variable, depending upon the "equities" arising in each case; though in the case of the particular remedy of specific performance, the time is usually likely to be short, for even a short delay is likely to alter the circumstances of the defendant. In certain cases, however, where an equitable claim is essentially similar to a common law claim, the courts may (under the authority of s. 2 (7)) apply the statute "by analogy", disregard the doctrine of "laches", and permit the full statutory period to run. Thus, for example, a secret profit made by an agent is recoverable as an equitable debt, and yet the plaintiff is entitled to insist upon the full six-year period of limitation; further, in this particular case, time does not begin to run against the plaintiff until the facts are discovered. Moreover, the "laches" doctrine applies only to the person who sleeps on his own rights, not for instance to a successor in title who claims under him.

9 QUASI-CONTRACT

The term "quasi-contract" is a misnomer. Quasi-contractual claims are
really claims to money owed *otherwise* than upon a contract. It is hard
to draw a strict theoretical distinction between *contractual* claims, claims
to what is "owed" *otherwise* than by way of contract, and claims that
are purely "proprietary". We have seen that the action of *debt* materially
assisted in the development of the law of contract, and claims in *debt* were
not – as was explained above (p. 203) – necessarily "contractual" (at any
rate, in the sense in which we now use the word); they were claims
to money *owed*, and money may be owed for other reasons, beside the
fact that a defendant has contracted to pay it. Thus *debt* was, for instance,
the proper remedy for A to invoke where he had, by mistake, paid
money to B which he really owed to C. B clearly "owed" the money
to A, but A's claim was not contractual.

For various procedural reasons the action of *assumpsit* was more
favourable to plaintiffs than the action of *debt*. Hence, in the course of
the seventeenth and eighteenth centuries, the court allowed claims to
be brought upon an *assumpsit* in cases (such as claims for money paid
by mistake) which, in strict theory, should have been remedied by means
of an action of *debt*, since the claim was *not* based upon a breach of *undertaking*. Actions of *assumpsit* brought upon claims of this type took a
special form called *indebitatus assumpsit* ("being *indebted*, the defendant
undertook"). The allegation of "debt" in this writ was true, for the
defendant "owed" the money, but the allegation of *"assumpsit"* ("undertaking", *i.e.* promise) was false; it was a fiction, alleged in order to entitle
the plaintiff to bring his action in the advantageous form of an *assumpsit*,
rather than in *debt*.

It is unfortunate that partly due to infelicitous borrowing from
Roman Law, and partly due to the association of the false allegation
of *"assumpsit"* with the kinds of claim under discussion, such actions
came to be treated as an appendage to the law of contract. *Debt* and
assumpsit have long since been abolished, but claims to money owed
otherwise than upon a contract are still called "quasi-contractual", and
are usually discussed in relation to the law of contract.

Very brief mention may be made of some of the classes of quasi-contractual actions in the modern law; they fall, roughly, under three heads.

i Actions for money had and received – Where, for some reason,
A pays money to B to which B is not entitled, A may recover it. Thus,
money paid upon a *total failure of consideration* must be returned. This
may happen, for instance, where, under a valid contract, one party pays
money to another who *entirely* fails to honour his side of the bargain:

here the quasi-contractual remedy for the recovery of the money is alternative to an action for damages.

Money paid by mistake – as for instance, to Brown, instead of to the true creditor, Thompson – is also (as instanced above) recoverable under this head. So also, is money paid under a *void contract*, as, for instance, where it is paid in respect of some article which, unknown to the parties, has ceased to exist when the contract is made (see above, p. 233). It should be noted, however, that the mistake which the plaintiff alleges, must be a mistake of fact, *not* a mistake of *law*. *Ignorantia juris haud excusat* ("Ignorance of the law is no excuse").

ii Actions for money paid to the use of another – These actions lie, for example, in favour of an assignee of a debt against the principal debtor, or in favour of a surety against the person whose debt he has paid. Though it is to be noted that in the latter case the claim will only normally lie where the surety has been requested by the debtor to act as such : people cannot act as sureties for others without their knowledge and then claim indemnity.

iii Actions for services rendered and benefits conferred – An action upon a *quantum meruit* (above, p. 260) where the defendant has broken his contract and the plaintiff claims, not upon the contract, but for the value of the benefit he has conferred upon the defendant, falls under this head. So also, in all probability, does a claim against a minor for a reasonable price in respect of "necessaries" supplied.

From the above examples it will be plain that the notion which underlies the law of quasi-contract is that people should be entitled to recover from those who are in any way "indebted" to them by being unjustly enriched at their expense.

10 SPECIAL CONTRACTS

We can only consider agency, sale of goods and consumer credit and consumer hire contracts.

Agency

"Agency", in the strict sense of the word, is a special relationship whereby one person (agent) agrees upon behalf of another (principal) to conclude a contract between the principal and a third party.

In respect of the contract made with the third party, the agent is normally a mere conduit, or link, for establishing contractual relations between the principal and the third party : once the contract is concluded his duties are at an end and he fades, as it were, out of the transaction.

Agency is usually constituted by the principal giving the agent express directions to act for him. It sometimes happens, however, that people lead others to believe that someone is their agent, when in fact they have given him no authority; if they do this, they will be liable for the "agent's" acts. Thus, if I habitually send my servant to order goods for me at a certain shop, in such circumstances that the shop-keeper comes to look to me for credit, I am not entitled to terminate the agency by merely telling the servant that he is to stop making orders. If I do this, and he continues to make orders, ostensibly for me, but really on his own behalf, I shall be liable to the shop-keeper for the price of the goods he orders. I am "*estopped*", as it is said, from denying that I have given the servant continued authority to act on my behalf, until I inform the shop-keeper that he is no longer entitled to act as my agent. This principle of "holding out" is not limited to contracts of service; it is an important principle of general application. Anyone who permits another person to act in such a way as to justify other people in thinking that that other person is his agent, may find himself held liable as principal; a husband, for example, in respect of purchases made by his wife. This principle, moreover, goes further, so as to cover the case of such officials as company secretaries who, by the *very nature of their office*, without any actual indication by the company to the plaintiff that it will be responsible for their acts, are the ostensible agents of the company. For this form of estoppel to apply there must, however, be a "holding out": so that where at an auction the catalogue contained a statement that the auctioneers had no authority to make any representations on behalf of the vendor, and they did make a misrepresentation, it was held that the vendor could not be held liable: the purchaser had been warned not to look to the principal.

An agent is subject to certain special duties arising out of the relationship between his principal and himself. First, though he is entitled to receive a commission for his services, he must not make a profit from the position he occupies. If he does this without authority the principal may recover the profit from him. Thus where a soldier in uniform received remuneration for driving in the front of a civilian lorry in order that the police should be deterred by the sight of his uniform from examining its illicit contents it was held that the Crown was entitled to recover the remuneration from him. A soldier in uniform is an agent of the Crown.

Second, once a man has undertaken to act as agent, he must continue to act as such; he is not allowed to alter his position and step into the shoes of the other contracting party.

Third, since an agent enjoys a confidental position, he may not delegate his duties to another person without his principal's consent.

An agent may either contract with the third party as agent for a named principal, or simply "as agent" without naming his principal, or, by an anomalous rule of English law, he may, at any rate in making commercial contracts, act for an "*undisclosed principal*", while purporting to contract on his own behalf; and, unless the contract is by its terms expressly or impliedly confined to the parties to it, the undisclosed principal may both sue and be sued upon it. Where the contract is made on behalf of a named principal, or by a person acting "as agent", it does not matter if he really has no authority to act at the time that he makes the contract; as long as the principal "ratifies" (adopts) the contract subsequently. Where, however, the contract is made on behalf of an *undisclosed* principal he must have authority to act *at the time when the contract is made*.

Naturally, where the existence of the principal is undisclosed, the third party has special rights. Though an agent normally incurs no liability under the contract he makes, an agent for an undisclosed principal is in a less happy position, for the other party may not only sue the principal when he discovers his identity but also the agent himself. Election to sue the one, however, extinguishes the claim against the other. What amounts to election is a question of fact; obtaining a judgment will of course be an irrevocable election, but going even as far as issuing a writ may not be.

People sometimes purport to act as agents for others without authority. If they do this, they may either do so by mistake, thinking they have, or will obtain, authority, or dishonestly, pretending to be agents, but knowing that they are not. Where this happens an innocent person may suffer by entering into a contract with the supposed agent, and such a person clearly requires legal protection. If the agent knew he had no authority, and that he could get none, he may be sued for fraud; if, on the other hand, he acted honestly, he cannot be held liable for fraud. Accordingly it became necessary to evolve the doctrine of "warranty of authority" by which everyone who purports to act as an agent may be held liable to the other contracting party, upon an implied "warranty of authority", if in fact, however innocent he may be, it turns out that he has no authority from his principal.

Sale of Goods

The law relating to the contract of sale of goods is governed by the Sale of Goods Act 1893 – as *amended*: in particular by the Supply of Goods

(Implied Terms) Act 1973 and the Consumer Credit Act 1974. This statute has already been referred to in several places, but the subject can now be considered in greater detail. It must, however, be realized that, even at this place, only some of the salient features of the law can be set out.

It will be simplest to examine this matter under the following heads.

1 THE NATURE OF THE CONTRACT

The contract is defined as "*a contract whereby the seller transfers or agrees to transfer the property in goods to the buyer for a money consideration, called the price*" (s. 1 (1)).

Contracts of sale must be distinguished from two other types of contract –

i Exchange (barter) – Here the consideration is goods or other property in exchange for goods or other property, whereas a sale is a transaction whereby property is exchanged for *money*.

ii Contracts for work and labour and materials supplied – It is not always easy to distinguish these contracts from sales, though the distinction may be of practical importance; for if the contract is a sale special rules may apply to it which do not apply to other contracts. The test for drawing the distinction seems to be, "Was the contract *primarily* intended to result in the transfer of property?" If so, it will be a sale: if not, it will be a contract for work and materials. Thus if A contracts to make a fur coat for B, and himself supplies the fur, the contract will be a sale, even though, clearly, part of the price is determined by the work that A does in making the coat. Where, on the other hand, A contracts to paint B's portrait, it has been held that the contract will be one for work and materials. Here the element of skill is more important than the goods produced.

The expression "contract of sale" denotes two things, a "*sale*" and an "*agreement to sell*". There is a "sale" where, under the contract, the property in the goods is transferred to the buyer. The contract is an "agreement to sell" where the transfer of the property in the goods is to take place at some future time (s. 1 (3)).

2 IMPLIED TERMS

In every contract for the sale of goods the following (amongst other) terms are *implied* by the Act.

(*i*) (*a*) A *condition* on the part of the seller that in the case of a sale he has the *right to sell* the goods, and in the case of an agreement to sell, he will have the right to sell the goods, at the time when the property is to pass (s. 12 (1)); (*b*) a *warranty* that the goods are free, and will remain free until the time when the property is to pass *from charges* or *encumbances*: such, for example, as patent rights vested in a third party; (*c*) a *warranty* that the buyer will enjoy *quiet possession*.

By s. 55 (3) it is provided that any terms *exempting* the seller from *any* provision of this section is *void*: but under s. 61 (6) this rule does not apply in the case of *international* sales (s. 12 (1)).

(*ii*) Where the seller sells goods *in the course of a business*, there is an implied *condition* that the goods supplied under the contract are of *merchantable quality*, *except* that there is no such condition – (*a*) as regards defects *specially drawn to the buyer's attention* before the contract is made; or (*b*) if the buyer examines the goods before the contract is made, as regards defects which *that examination ought to reveal* (s. 14 (2)). "Merchantable quality" means merchantable in a *commercial sense*.

(*iii*) Where the seller sells goods *in the course of a business* and the buyer, expressly or by implication, *makes known to the seller any particular purpose* for which the goods are being bought, there is an implied *condition* that the goods supplied under the contract are *reasonably fit for the purpose*, whether or not that is a purpose for which such goods are commonly supplied, *except* where the circumstances show that *the buyer does not rely*, or that it is unreasonable for him to rely on the *seller's skill or judgment* (s. 14 (3)). A useful illustration of unfitness for a particular purpose was the case of a Jaguar car so unfit for the road that its engine seized up after only three weeks' use.

(*iv*) In contracts for sale by *description* there is an implied *condition* that the goods shall *correspond with the description*, and where the sale is by *sample and description* that the bulk shall correspond both with the *sample and the description*. The fact that goods *exposed for sale* are selected by the buyer does not prevent the sale from being a *sale by description* (s 13).

(*v*) In the case of contracts for sale *by sample* there are *implied conditions* that –

    (*a*) the bulk shall correspond with the sample in quality;
    (*b*) the buyer shall have a reasonable opportunity of *comparing* the bulk with the sample;
    (*c*) the goods shall be free from any defect *rendering them unmerchantable* which would not be apparent *upon reasonable examination of the sample* (s. 15).

Exemption clauses – It must be remembered that the S.G.A. was originally passed in 1893, at the height of the philosophy of commercial individualism, when freedom of contract was regarded as sacrosanct: hence, the original s. 55, as it stood unamended provided simply that "any right, duty or liability" which would arise by *implication* under a sale of goods could be *negatived* or varied by express agreement, the course of dealing between the parties or usage. In effect, agreement would oust any of the implied terms. Under the amended Act this rule still stands as s. 55 (1), but it has been greatly modified – (*a*) by s. 55 (2) it is enacted that "an express condition or warranty does *not* negative" an implied one "*unless inconsistent* therewith"; '(*b*) any term which exempts liability in respect of any of the implied terms contained in ss. 13, 14 & 15 shall be *void* in the case of a *consumer sale* and, in the case of *any other sale*, shall not be enforceable "to the extent that it is shown that it would *not be fair or reasonable* to allow reliance" on it (s. 55 (4)). "Consumer sale" means (s. 55 (7)) a sale (other than a sale by auction or by competitive tender) by a seller *in the course of business* where the goods are of a type "ordinarily bought for private use or consumption" *and* are sold to a person who is *not* buying them in the course of business. The effect of this is that if in my shop I sell you a tin of beans and seek to exclude liability in respect of their quality the attempted exclusion will be *void* if you are an ordinary customer, but that it will be *valid* if you are a fellow dealer *unless* it can be shown that it would not be fair and reasonable to allow reliance on it.

3   THE EFFECT OF THE CONTRACT

Some of the more important points may be noted.

i   The passing of property – The cardinal rule is that property passes (and the "agreement to sell" becomes a "sale") when it is *intended* to pass (s. 17 (1)). Section 18 lays down rules for ascertaining the intention of the parties where it is not made clear. These rules should be consulted in detail. The most important of them (Rule 1) is that, "Where there is an unconditional contract for the sale of specific goods, in a deliverable state, the property in the goods passes to the buyer *when the contract is made*, and it is immaterial whether the time of payment or the time of delivery, or both, be postponed". It is important to note that the goods may become the buyer's *before delivery*. But by the Misrepresentation Act 1967, s. 4 (1), (which amends the S.G.A., s. 11 (1) (c)) the passing of property in specific goods (under S.G.A., ss. 17 and 18) to the buyer is *not* to be treated as an event which in itself, as it formerly did, reduces a condition to an *ex post facto* warranty (see above, p. 225) so as to cause the buyer's right to repudiation to be reduced to a mere right to damages.

No property can pass to the buyer where the goods are still "unascertained" (s. 16). Goods are "unascertained" until they are appropriated to the contract. Thus, if I agree to sell 1,000 reels of cotton out of my stock of 50,000, no property can pass to the buyer until a particular 1,000 are singled out and appropriated to the contract.

ii Effect of the destruction of the goods – The "risk" of accidental destruction passes to the buyer when the property passes, unless it is otherwise agreed (s. 20). Hence, before *delivery*, the buyer may often both own the goods and be forced to take the risk of accidental destruction. If, of course, the goods perish, or are damaged, as a result of the seller's negligence, it is another matter. The seller is in the position of a bailee.

Where, through no fault of the buyer's or of the seller's, the goods perish before sale, but after the agreement to sell (*i.e.* before the property has passed to the buyer), the agreement is avoided (s. 7). This is, of course, a case of frustration (see above, p. 259).

iii Protection of third parties – It has been explained that the goods may sometimes be the buyer's, even though they have not been delivered; that is to say, while the seller retains possession of them. Similarly, the seller may sometimes permit the buyer to take delivery before the property has passed to him. Wherever either of these two things happen, the person in possession becomes a source of potential danger to third parties; he appears to be the owner of something that is not really his.

In order to avoid the consequences to which this situation might lead, s. 25 (re-enacting, with some modification, ss. 8 and 9 of the Factors Act 1889) enacts that the buyer or seller "in possession" may validly transfer the goods to any person who takes in good faith, without notice of the sale. "Transfer" includes a "sale, pledge, or other disposition". This important rule may appear to operate harshly upon the true owner, but he has, after all, by his conduct, by entrusting the possession of the goods to the other party, permitted him to hold himself out (see above, p. 268) to strangers as the owner. If it were not for this rule, innocent third parties might buy goods, only to find themselves subjected to an action for conversion by an owner whose very existence they had no reason to suspect.

iv Unpaid seller's rights – An unpaid seller has a right ("seller's lien") to retain possession of the goods against payment. This right subsists where – (*a*) the goods have been sold without any stipulation as to credit; (*b*) the goods have been sold on credit, but the term of credit has expired; (*c*) the buyer becomes insolvent (s. 41 (1)).

Further, an unpaid seller may stop the goods "in transit" ("stoppage *in transitu*") and resume possession of them, after he has himself parted with them, if the buyer becomes insolvent. For this purpose "transit" lasts until the goods are delivered to the buyer or his agent (s. 45 (1)). The expression "agent" here signifies "representative", not an agent in the technical sense, as described in the last section.

Suppose, for instance, that X, in London, sells goods to Y in Sydney. X delivers them to his agent, with instructions to take them to Sydney. Y sends an agent to collect them at the harbour. If X hears that Y has become insolvent, he may stop the goods *in transitu* by ordering his agent to retain them, at any time up to the moment when they are delivered to Y's agent at the quay in Sydney.

Consumer Credit and Consumer Hire Agreements

Although it must be stressed that at the time of writing the Consumer Credit Act 1974 ("C.C.A."), which emerged from the Report of the Crowther Committee on Consumer Credit ((1971) Cmd. 4596), is not yet in operation the likelihood seems to be that at the time of publication it will be. So that a brief account of the vast field of credit agreements governed by that statute is necessary, though essentially brief because the statute has no less than 192 sections and five schedules; and worse still, its implementation – it being no more than a colossal blueprint – depends upon a mass of detailed rules and regulations emanating mainly from the Department of Trade and the Director General of Fair Trading. It is thus an outstanding example of the unknowability of modern English law. Moreover, its drafting is far from felicitous.

Regulated agreements – The C.C.A. "regulates", *i.e.* contains special rules about most consumer credit and consumer hire agreements which fall within an economic range of credit or of payment for hire of not less than £30 and not more than £5,000, and which are made between an individual (or partnership, but not a corporation) and any other person (the "creditor" or "hirer") by which the latter provides credit, or, in the case of hire, hires goods, to the former (ss. 8 and 15). Certain agreements are, however, *exempt* from regulation (s. 16): notably agreements made with local authorities and with building societies.

Classification – In order to distinguish between different kinds of agreements in certain defined respects the Act contains cumbersome, and at times overlapping, classifications of them. The main, and simple, differentiation is between "*consumer credit agreements*" (s. 8) and "*consumer hire agreements*" (s. 15).

First, as to "*consumer credit agreements*". By s. 8 (1) the Act distinguishes the generic form of "*personal credit agreements*" from "consumer credit agreements" which are defined (s. 8 (2)) in terms of agreements subject to the financial limits already mentioned and these "consumer credit agreements" are thus – as opposed to agreements above that limit – "regulated" agreements. They are divided into the following categories –

(a) "*Restricted use credit*" and "*Unrestricted use credit*". The former includes transactions (such as hire-purchase and credit and conditional sale) where the credit is given for a particular purpose; the latter includes such things as bank loans and personal loans directed to no special purpose. [A "*credit sale*" agreement is an agreement, other than a conditional sale agreement, under which the purchase price is payable by instalments: a "*conditional sale*" agreement is "an agreement for the sale of goods or land under which the purchase price is payable by instalments, *and the* property is to remain in the seller (notwithstanding that the buyer is in *possession*) until such conditions as to the payment of instalments or otherwise as may be specified in the agreement are fulfilled – see C.C.A. s. 189].

(b) "*Debtor-creditor-supplier agreements*". These are typified, though not exclusively, by the common case of a "supplier" (dealer) who disposes of a car on hire-purchase through the usual medium of a finance house ("creditor") which owns the vehicle. Such agreements the Act contrasts with "*Debtor-creditor agreements*": *i.e.* all other credit agreements.

(c) *Credit-token agreements*. These may be exemplified by credit cards.

"*Credit*" includes a cash loan and any other form of financial accommodation (s. 9), and it is classified as either "*running account credit*" or "*fixed sum credit*": examples of the former are bank overdrafts and credit cards, and of the latter loans by banks, pawnbrokers, etc.

Contrasted with "consumer credit agreements" are, as we have seen, "*consumer hire agreements*". These are agreements – *other than* hire-purchase agreements – in respect of the hire of goods, which agreements are capable of subsisting for more than three months, *e.g.* hire of a tractor for 4 months, even though the agreement may be terminated in 2; but *not* a 2-month contract. The limit of regulation being, of course, again £5,000.

The total credit charge – Although its operation embraces all credit agreements, and is not limited to the regulated consumer credit agreements as above defined, the vital provision of s. 20 of the C.C.A. must be noted. The section provides that the Department of Trade are required to make regulations to ensure that the creditor makes known to the debtor the "*total credit charge*", *i.e.* the *total actual* cost of the transaction (including *e.g.* charges, fees, stamp duty, etc.) not just the amount of the loan and interest. This is plainly a beneficial provision.

General rules of regulated agreements – In general (but only in general) the following rules apply to regulated agreements:

(*i*) Certain information prescribed by the Department must be disclosed by the creditor/owner to the debtor/hirer before the agreement is made (s. 55);

(*ii*) where an agreement is only at the prospective stage either party may withdraw by giving notice, written *or oral* (s. 57);

(*iii*) A regulated agreement will not be "*properly executed*" unless it is – (*a*) made in prescribed form, (*b*) signed by *both* parties or their agents, (*c*) readily legible (s. (1)). If an agreement is "*improperly*" (*i.e.* not "*properly*") executed the result will be (s. 65) that it can only be enforced by *court order*. Which means, for example, that where the debtor defaults in such a way that the creditor would normally have a right of recaption (re-taking) of goods subject to the contract he can only exercise this right by court order;

(*iv*) There are complicated provisions concerning the supply by the creditor/owner to the debtor/hirer of prescribed ("statutory") copies of the agreement under certain conditions. These must be consulted (ss. 62 and 63);

(*v*) Regulated agreements are *cancellable* upon the giving of written notice within a defined period – in *general* fourteen days from signature by the debtor/hirer – *if* they emerged from *oral representations* by the creditor/hirer or his agent, *e.g.* the case of house-to-house canvassing. *But* two classes of agreements are not, in any event, cancellable: namely, agreements secured on *land* and agreements which are signed by the debtor/hirer at the creditor/owner's *business premises*.

It is important to note that s. 74 *exempts* (*inter alia*) *non-commercial* contracts from almost all of the above rules: purely private loans are thus, for example, not "regulated".

The currency and termination of the agreement – Parts VI and VII of the Act contain detailed provisions concerning the dealings and rights and duties of the parties during the currency of the agreement and its termination by default or otherwise. These are too complex for discussion here. But it should be noted that the Supply of Goods (Implied Terms) Act 1973, as amended by Schedule 4 of the C.C.A., imposes upon *hire-purchase* contracts implied terms, similar to the implied terms of the S.G.A., and with similar rules as to the exclusion of liability from such terms.

Hire-Purchase Act 1964, ss. 27 and 28 (motor vehicles) – These sections (as amended by the C.C.A., Schedule 4) extend to *hire-purchase* and *conditional sale* transactions similar protection to an innocent purchaser from a dishonest hirer or conditional sale purchaser (both of whom have possession, but – unlike the purchaser under a *credit sale* – not the ownership of the car involved) to that enjoyed by an innocent purchaser under the S.G.A., s. 25 (above, p. 273). Section 27 enacts that a hirer who disposes of a motor vehicle to a private purchaser (*i.e.* someone other than a motor dealer or a finance house) may give a good title to the purchaser, provided that the latter takes in good faith and without notice of the hire-purchase agreement. Those in the trade (being people who may be expected to be on their guard against that kind of fraud) do not fall within this protection, and still cannot acquire a good title from a fraudulent hire-purchaser; but the "*first private* purchaser" may acquire a good title if he takes from them. This means that if A (hirer) sells to B (dealer) and B sells to C (first *private* purchaser) who is not a dealer and who takes in good faith and without notice, then C acquires the property in the vehicle and may, of course, pass a valid title to anyone else, even to another dealer.

Liability of creditor for breaches by supplier – By the C.C.A., s. 75, in the case of a regulated debtor/creditor-supplier agreement the creditor (*e.g.* a finance house) may be held liable by the debtor in respect of any claim against the supplier (dealer) in respect of misrepresentation or breach of contract – that is, he may be held legally responsible for the default of the supplier *e.g.* in respect of the latter's breach of condition, express or implied, or misrepresentation. The creditor has, however, a right to be indemnified by the supplier. Further, the supplier is deemed by law to be the agent of the creditor for a number of purposes: *e.g.* receipt of a notice of cancellation.

Licensing of credit and hire business – Under the general control of the Director of Fair Trading, the Act brings into being a system of licensing (local authorities and certain other bodies being exempted) of consumer credit and consumer hire businesses which deal in regulated transactions.

CHAPTER 9

THE LAW OF TORTS

A   GENERAL MATTERS

It is proposed first to discuss matters affecting tortious liability in general, then to give some examples of specific torts.

The Nature of Tortious Liability

The word "tort" is derived from the French "*tort*" ("wrong"). Torts must be distinguished from crimes on the one hand, and from breaches of contract on the other.

A *crime* is, as we have seen, a wrong which, by means of punishment or otherwise, the State inhibits. A tort is a *civil* wrong which entitles a person who is injured by its commission to claim damages for his loss, whether purely by way of reparation or as a way of bringing home to the defendant the anti-social nature of his act. An injunction is also a proper remedy in some circumstances.

A breach of contract is, like a tort, a civil wrong; but it is different from a tort. Whereas *contractual duties are imposed by the parties* to the contract themselves, the duty to refrain from committing torts is *imposed by the general law* of the land, independently of the wishes of the plaintiff or of the defendant. It was only by an accident of history that breaches of contract were originally remedied by a tortious action – *assumpsit* (above, p. 203).

Historically, torts are divided into two main classes: *trespasses* and actions "*on the case*". A trespass is a "direct and forcible" injury. This is the most obvious and dramatic of all wrongs; it is not therefore surprising that, in point of time, trespasses were the earliest torts which the law recognized and remedied. Actions "on the case" were actions for damage caused otherwise than "directly and forcibly". They were called actions "on the case" primarily (although historically the matter is really somewhat more complicated than this) because they were originally

278

granted in certain cases where the plaintiff could show that, upon the facts of his case, he had suffered damage as the result of some act or omission of the defendant.

The difference between "trespass" and "case" may be illustrated. If Jones hits Brown, or walks over his land, or kicks the paint off his car, he has committed a trespass. Suppose, however, that Jones carelessly leaves a mat on a slippery floor where Brown is likely to walk over it, and suppose that Brown slips on the mat and is injured. Or suppose again, that Smith negligently permits a fire that has arisen on his own land to spread, and to damage Clark's crops. In both these two latter examples there has been no "direct and forcible" injury; in the second the injury was neither "direct" nor "forcible". Yet in both instances, the injured party could sue the other by means of an action on the Case.

For the purpose of pleading, the vital distinction between "trespass" and "case" has long since disappeared. History has, however, left this legacy, that where a plaintiff's claim is founded upon a trespass, he need – except where the trespass is one to the person and arises from negligence (see below, p. 300) – prove no actual damage, he is entitled to compensation (it may be purely nominal) as of right, upon mere proof of the trespass. In most other tortious actions a plaintiff must prove that he has suffered some *actual* ("special") damage, for damage was nearly always an essential element in the plaintiff's claim in actions on the Case.

From mediaeval times, then, trespasses have not been the only actionable torts; for injuries other than trespasses were remediable by means of Case. Indeed, most of the modern torts, such as deceit, libel, slander and negligence derive from these. It must not, however, be imagined that, because proof of damage was essential to found an action upon the Case, that therefore proof of *any sort of* damage would, or will, give rise to a claim in tort.

There always has been, and there always will be, damage ("*damnum sine injuria*") which the courts must regard as "damage without injury"; for there are necessarily some types of loss which the law cannot recognize as giving rise to legally redressible injury. Thus, some harm is too trivial to found an action, while the courts look upon other harm as part of the give and take of life in a world in which interests must often compete and conflict. Thus, for instance – in the absence of the limited redress afforded by the law relating to fraud, patents, copyright, trade marks, conspiracy, malicious falsehood, and unjustified interference with contractual relations – damage to business interests in the course of trade or industrial competition is seldom actionable, even though it be intentionally inflicted. The case of *Allen* v. *Flood*, [1898] A.C. 1 illustrates this. F and T were *shipwrights*, engaged by shipowners to repair the *woodwork* of a ship: under their contract they were liable to be discharged at any time. Some ironworkers, also employed on the ship at the same time, objected to the employment of F and T because in the past F and T had repaired *ironwork* on other ships, and this was a practice which the ironworkers' union were seeking to stop. The ironworkers therefore sent for A, a union delegate, and informed him that unless F and T were discharged they would cease work. A approached the shipowners and told them that if they would not (as lawfully they could) discharge F and T the ironworkers would strike. Under fear of this threat the owners did discharge F and T, who then sued A in respect of the loss thus wantonly inflicted upon them. The action failed, for A, however malicious his conduct might have been, had violated no legal rights of F or T.

Allen v. *Flood* may thus be used to illustrate the fact that although in general – subject, however, to exceptions, as in the case of defamation and liability under the Rule in *Rylands* v. *Fletcher* (see below, p. 308) – tortious liability can only arise if the harm complained of was caused by the *fault* of the defendant (in the sense that he acted *intentionally* or *carelessly*), the *motive* which actuates him, whether good or bad, is *in general* irrelevant to legal inquiry. For instance, if I take the Duchess' diamonds intending to sell them for the relief of the poor it would clearly be socially undesirable to allow me to plead my charitable motive by way of defence. And equally a bad motive ("malice") will not usually make that unlawful which, the motive apart, would otherwise be lawful: for instance I have, in general, as we have seen, freedom to cause harm to your business by means of my own competition, and it can normally make no difference to this fact that that competition is actuated by a desire to spite you. To these general propositions, as to most such propositions, there are, however, exceptions. For example, in tort, as in crime it will *excuse* my assaulting you if I can show that in doing so I was actuated by the respectable motive of seeking to use reasonable force in defending myself. And it will be seen below that *"malice"* may exceptionally create *liability*; as in nuisance, malicious falsehood and conspiracy, and in respect of qualified privilege in defamation.

There is some harm, too, which, though it arises from unlawful acts, is too far removed from them in point of time, space or circumstances, to be justly visited with legal sanctions: though in philosophy it may be true that *every* antecedent act is linked with *every* later consequence, the law, to be practical and just, can only make wrongdoers pay for the more *immediate* results of their misdeeds. For example, where Brown carelessly runs down and kills Smith on the highway, although, as we shall see (below, p. 289) Smith's dependant relatives will in certain circumstances be entitled to claim from Brown compensation for their loss, Smith's employees, who may be thrown out of work and suffer hardship as the result of their employer's death, will have no legal claim against the wrongdoer.

It follows that although the categories of recognized civil injuries have expanded from time to time, and doubtless will continue to expand, this expansion must nevertheless be limited by the practical consideration that not every injury of which people may complain can be regarded as a legal wrong. A tort does not consist simply in the infliction of an injury, but in the infliction of a *legally recognized* injury. Moreover, the different classes of recognized injuries (or "torts") have in the course of time each become subjected to special legal definitions, and special rules have come to apply to each of them; so that they will only be actionable within the limitations thus imposed.

General Defences to Actions in Tort

There are certain general defences to actions in tort. Inevitable accident, assumption of risk, self-defence, and statutory authority may be instanced. Of these inevitable accident and assumption of risk require mention.

1 INEVITABLE ACCIDENT

An inevitable accident is something which cannot be avoided by the taking of ordinary precautions. With some exceptions, as in the case of liability under the Rule in *Rylands* v. *Fletcher* (below, p. 308), the plea of "inevitable accident" will form a good defence to actions in tort. Thus in *National Coal Board* v. *J. E. Evans, Ltd.*, [1951] 2 K.B. 861, it was held that where, unknown to the landowners, the plaintiffs placed an electric cable under certain land, and a firm of contractors employed by the landowners to excavate a trench in the land caused damage to the cable, the latter were not liable to the plaintiffs in trespass, since they did not know of the existence of the cable and they were entirely without fault in permitting their excavator to strike it.

2 ASSUMPTION OF RISK

A person who consents to run the risk of injury cannot maintain an action in tort against the person who causes that injury. "*Volenti non fit injuria*" ("Where there is consent there is no injury").

This is a principle of general importance. It applies not only in cases where people agree to run the risk of injury, but also in cases where the law presumes that they have consented to do so.

Three points must be noticed in connexion with "assumption of risk".

(*i*) No one will be allowed to consent to run the risk of *illegal* harm.

Thus the rule would not apply in the case of a boxing-match conducted with bare fists.

(*ii*) Mere *knowledge* of a risk need not necessarily amount to *consent* to run it. So in *Smith* v. *Baker*, [1891] A.C. 325, a workman was employed to drill rock in a cutting. He knew that a crane carrying loads of stones constantly swung the loads over his head, and that there was danger that a stone might drop on him. Due to the negligent manner in which his employers allowed the crane to be operated a stone did drop, and he was injured. The House of Lords held that the man could recover against the employers. His knowledge of the danger did not, under the circumstances, imply that he consented to run the risk of injury. But it must be added that outside the master-servant relationship – where the employee tends to run inherent risks under compulsion, for fear of losing his job – knowledge of the existence of a risk coupled with a continuation of the activity to which it is incident, may sometimes be treated as equivalent to consent to incur it. Thus, if a harbour authority *notifies* shipowners that a particular anchorage is dangerous, and the owners nevertheless use it, they will not be able to substantiate a claim for damage resulting from such use.

(*iii*) Where one person creates a dangerous situation, and another tries to avert the danger, the latter is not necessarily debarred from suing the former because he knowingly took a risk. He will be debarred if he was merely meddlesome or foolhardy, but not if he acted under a clear moral duty. Thus, in *Haynes* v. *Harwood*, [1935] 1 K.B. 146, where a van was negligently left unattended in the street, and a boy threw a stone at the horses with the result that they bolted, it was held that a policeman, who rushed from a police-station to stop the horses, could recover damages from the owner of the van for injuries received in stopping them. The accident occurred in a public street and a woman and children were in grave danger from the horses.

It is not at present clear what situations the courts will regard as giving rise to sufficient moral compulsion to bring this rule into play. It has been extended to cover people who run risks in the protection of the property (as well as of the person) of others, provided, at any rate, that they bear some special relationship to the owner of the property. For instance, a servant is under a moral duty to protect his master's goods; if, therefore, he sees that they are in danger from, say, fire, he should rescue them. It follows that if the fire has been started through the master's negligence, and the servant is injured in the rescue, he is entitled to make a claim against his master. The rule has also been extended to cover the case of a doctor who was asphyxiated while trying to rescue a man from a well which had become filled with fumes due to the defendant's negligence. On the other hand it has been held that a man who is injured in attempting to stop a run-away horse *in the country*, where no one is in danger, will have no claim against the owner. The law encourages the hero, but dislikes the busy-body.

Capacity

Generally speaking anyone of full age may sue and be sued in tort. The rules which govern the rights and liabilities of the Crown have already been considered (Chapter 5) and the capacity of married women will be discussed below (Chapter 12). It therefore remains to describe the position of minors and of corporations.

(a) Minors – Although, as a general rule, minors enjoy no special exemption from tortious liability, the fact that a defendant is under age may have some effect upon it. For instance, a child who is charged with negligence, or with contributory negligence, will be judged, not according to the standards of a reasonable adult, but according to the standards of a child. Thus, for example, it was held in a Canadian appeal to the Judicial Committee that a person who negligently sold petrol to a child was liable for injuries caused to the child when the latter set light to the petrol as a part of a game of "Red Indians". It is not negligent for a *child* to set light to petrol.

In one exceptional case minors are exempted from liability in tort, and this is an incident of their strict immunity from *contractual* liability (see above, p. 209). A plaintiff will not be permitted to evade the rule which accords contractual immunity by framing his action in tort. Thus, in *Jennings* v. *Rundall* (1799), 8 Term Rep. 335, a minor hired a mare and injured her by over-riding. It was held that since his act was substantially no more than a breach of contract, the owner could not sue him in tort for the damage caused by his negligence. But it must be noted that if a wrong done is *independent of* a contract, though connected with it, the minor may be liable despite the existence of the contract. Thus in *Burnard* v. *Haggis* (1863), 14 C.B. N.S. 45, where another minor similarly hired a mare for riding, but used her for *jumping*, against the express admonition of the owner, and consequently injured the animal, it was held that the minor could be made liable in tort. The act of jumping, though connected with the contract, was beyond the ambit of its terms, and could therefore be treated, independently, as a tort.

Minors have full capacity to *sue* in tort, though (as in the case of all litigation) they require to be represented in the action by an adult acting as "next friend".

(b) Corporations – Corporations are abstractions; they are incapable of indulging in any activities; consequently they cannot commit torts. It might therefore be imagined that they cannot be held liable in tort. This is not, however, the case. A corporation is regarded in law as the employer of its agents – from director to office boy – and employers may, as we shall see, be held "vicariously" responsible for the torts of their agents acting within the course of their employment.

Joint Torts

Torts are sometimes committed, not by one person alone, but by two or more people jointly. For instance, A and B may combine together to defraud C. Moreover, for special reasons, two or more people may be held jointly liable where one of them only has in fact committed a tort; thus, as will shortly be explained, a master is jointly and severally liable with a servant for torts committed by the servant in the course of his employment.

Liability for "joint" torts is both "joint" and "several". The plaintiff may, at his option, sue *both* (or *all*) of the defendants, or he may recover the full amount of his loss from *one* of them alone. Although it was not usually so at common law, since the Law Reform (Married Women and Tortfeasors) Act 1935, one tortfeasor who is jointly liable to a plaintiff with another, or others, in respect of the same damage, may recover contribution from his fellow-tortfeasors where the plaintiff has recovered the whole amount, or more than his fair share, from him. The amount of contribution recoverable is such, in the words of the Act, "*as may be found by the Court to be just and equitable having regard to the extent of [the fellow-tortfeasor's] responsibility for the damage*".

Under the provisions of the Act, however, no contribution can be obtained where the person sued is liable to *indemnify* his co-tortfeasor, or tortfeasors. Liability to indemnify may arise, for example, where one man employs another to do something which is not obviously wrong, but which he (the employer) knows in fact to be tortious. In such a case, if someone is injured and recovers damages from the innocent dupe, the latter will have a right to be indemnified by his employer. Under the Act the employer, if sued alone, will therefore have no right to contribution from the dupe. These principles may be illustrated by *Adamson* v. *Jarvis* (1827), 4 Bing. 66, where B employed A (an auctioneer) to sell goods to which he (B) knew he was not entitled: the true owner recovered damages in conversion (see below, p. 301) from A, and A then claimed, and was accorded, complete indemnity from B. If a like situation were to arise at the present day, and if the true owner were to sue B, B could not claim contribution against A under the Act.

The same Act also abolished an old rule that judgment obtained against one joint-tortfeasor (even though unsatisfied) barred the plaintiff's right of action against the other or others.

Vicarious Liability

Masters (employers) are held "vicariously" liable for torts committed by their servants (employees) in the course of their employment, *i.e.* they are held liable for the wrong of the servant even though the tort is one which they have not ordered or authorized. This is a common-sense rule, for employees are usually people of slender means and it is fair that an injured plaintiff should be entitled to seek compensation from those who control and profit by the organization by which he is employed. But, on the other hand, in legal theory (though practice usually parts company with theory, since no one sues a "man of straw") there is nothing to prevent the master from making good his own loss by claiming against the servant-tortfeasor.

Before vicarious responsibility can be imposed upon a defendant, it has to be shown that; (*a*) the person who committed the tort was his "servant", and (*b*) that the servant was, at the time when the tort was committed, acting within the course of his employment.

1   WHO IS A "SERVANT"

According to the time-worn definition a *servant* is any person who works for another upon the terms that he is to be subject to the control of that other person as to the *manner* in which he shall do his work. Thus chauffeurs, casual labourers and apprentices are clearly servants. Skilled (self-employed) workers, such as electricians, carpenters and dressmakers, who come to work in people's houses, are *independent contractors* and not the servants of the householder; for though he may give them general directions, he cannot control the actual manner in which they are to set about their work. People who work under contracts of the former type are sometimes said to be employed under a contract of *"service"*, while people who work under contracts of the latter type are said to work under a contract *"for services"*. Generally, of course, today those classes we have instanced under the second head will be the "servants" of someone else who will then, himself, be an "independent contractor" *vis-à-vis* the householder.

It must, however, be explained that at the present time this branch of the law is being modified in the process of judicial decision. Although no new definition of a "servant" has as yet gained currency, the modern "servant" begins to look different from his prototype, the manual or domestic worker. For instance, hospital authorities have been held vicariously responsible for the negligence of nurses, radiographers, and even of whole-time assistant medical officers; and companies are regularly made liable for the torts of their executives. Both "servant" and "master" are therefore expanding categories and the policy which underlies this expansion probably springs from a feeling that it is right that large institutions and enterprises should bear the losses incidental to their activities; activities which they can only, in the nature of things, perform through the instrumentality of their staff. To which the student may reflect, "What's in a *name*?" For present purposes the "servant", "employee", "worker", call him what you will – is a person for whose torts another will at any given time be held legally responsible.

2   THE COURSE OF EMPLOYMENT

Clearly a master cannot be made liable for every wrongful act which his servant commits, but only for wrongs committed "about the master's business", and whether any particular act does thus fall within the "scope of employment" must always be largely a question of fact.

The law may be illustrated by the following example. Smith employs Jones (a "servant") to drive his lorry from A to B. While on the road, Jones negligently knocks down Thomas. Smith will be liable to Thomas. If, instead of going direct from A to B, Jones makes an unauthorized detour through C, and an accident occurs, Smith will again be liable provided that Jones has been negligent. If, however, instead of merely deviating from his course, Jones were to drive off to place D, in the opposite direction from B, upon a "frolic", as a famous judge once expressed the matter "of his own", Smith could not be held liable for any accident which might occur. The question is, "Was there a *deviation* or a *departure* from duty?" This question is equally apposite when applied to all forms of employment, not only to deviations made in the course of journeys.

It should be noted that the employer may be held liable even if he has *prohibited* the servant from doing the act in question. Though prohibition may be relevant in determining whether the act was committed in the "course of employment", it cannot, of itself, exculpate the master: if the law were otherwise masters could always escape liability by the simple expedient of prohibiting their servants from committing any torts during their service. Thus, in *Limpus* v. *London General Omnibus Co.* (1862), 1 H. & C. 526, where a driver caused an accident by drawing his bus across the road so as to obstruct a rival bus, it was held that the Company were liable; even though orders had been given that their drivers were not to race or to obstruct rivals.

It should also be mentioned that difficulty arises in cases where one employer (sometimes called the "*general* employer") lends a servant to another ("*special* employer") for some particular purpose or for a period of time. In such cases which of the two masters should be held responsible if the servant causes tortious injury to some third party? On the face of it the answer is simple: "Whichever of the two had the right of control over the servant's activities at the time the injury was caused." But the application of this principle is difficult. For instance, in the leading case of *Mersey Docks and Harbour Board* v. *Coggins and Griffiths (Liverpool), Ltd.*, [1947] A.C. 1, the facts were these. The appellants hired out a crane to the respondents (a firm of stevedores) for the purpose of unloading a ship. The appellants also provided a driver for this crane upon the terms that he should be for the duration of the contract "the servant of the hirers". In fact although the respondents supervised this man's work, they had no power of control over his actual management of his machine. Through negligent handling of it he injured someone. Which of the two masters was liable? The driver himself, little realizing that the effect would be to attract sole liability to himself, stoutly objected in evidence that he was no one's servant. But the House of Lords paid no attention to this. Nor did they heed the terms of the contract; for the parties could not by agreement between themselves affect the legal rights of the person injured. They took the view that the crucial issue was which of the masters had the ultimate control over the driver's management of the crane, and that, since this right remained in the appellants, liability was theirs.

Circumstances alter cases, and it will be appreciated that the determination of this issue must always depend upon a consideration of all relevant facts; but in the *Mersey Docks* case the House of Lords enunciated an important rule for the future guidance of the courts; namely that it lies upon the general employer to establish that the vicarious responsibility which is initially his has been shifted from his shoulders to those of the special employer; and they stressed that the onus of establishing the change is to be treated as a heavy one.

Independent contractors – As a general rule people are not liable for the torts of independent contractors, *i.e.* people whom they employ to work for them otherwise than as servants. For example, if I commission X & Co. to build a ship for me and a fire is negligently caused by one of their servants during the work, if this fire burns down Y's wharf, X & Co. will be liable, but I shall not.

This general rule is, however, subject to a number of exceptions. Instances are – (*i*) Where the contract under which the contractor works is one which, if it is to be properly implemented, is likely to involve the commission of a tort. For example, if A employs B & Co. to erect a building in a congested area he may be held liable for nuisances caused by the inevitable dust and vibration incident to the work. (*ii*) Where an especially high duty of care is imposed upon a person by law he cannot escape liability for its breach by employing an independent contractor. Thus, people who do dangerous things on or near a highway (other than acts, such as driving a car, which constitute an ordinary user of the highway), will be liable for any injuries caused to the public; even though they employ an independent contractor for the work. For instance, in *Tarry* v. *Ashton* (1876), 1 Q.B.D. 314, the occupier of a house was held liable for injuries caused to a passer-by by the falling of a lamp from a rotten bracket which projected over the pavement from his wall. It was no defence for him to show that he had employed an independent contractor to repair the bracket. (*iii*) Where liability is "strict" (independent of negligence), as in the case of liability under the Rule in *Rylands* v. *Fletcher* (below, p. 308), a defendant will be liable for the acts of an independent contractor.

The Survival of Actions

The death of either of the parties may affect rights of action in tort. At common law the general rule – although there were important exceptions to it – was expressed by the maxim "*actio personalis moritur cum persona*" ("a personal action dies with the litigant"). Whether the plaintiff or the defendant died, the right of action died with him.

Since the Law Reform (Miscellaneous Provisions) Act 1934 (as subsequently amended), the above general rule no longer exists. Rights of action in tort now survive both in favour of the estate of a deceased plaintiff and against the estate of a deceased defendant. This proposition is, however, subject, amongst others, to the following qualifications.

(*i*) Actions for defamation, do not survive.

(*ii*) Exemplary damages (see below, p. 319) cannot be awarded in favour of the estate of a deceased plaintiff.

Beside the maxim just discussed, there was another maxim enshrining a different principle which did, and to some extent still does, affect the survival of actions. This is the maxim that "*In a civil court the death of a human being cannot be complained of as an injury.*" (The "Rule in *Baker* v. *Bolton*" (1808), 1 Camp. 493.)

Suppose that Smith has a servant, Tompkins, and that Atkins negligently runs down and kills Tompkins in a street accident. Smith, however great the loss he may suffer as the result of Tompkins's death, will have no claim against Atkins, even though he might have had one if Tompkins had lived. It may be that Atkins may be prosecuted for manslaughter, but, whether he can or no, Smith will have no *action*. Thus, it is sometimes, as has often been said, "cheaper to kill than to maim".

The harshness of this rule is mitigated in two ways—

(*a*) The rule forms no bar to an action based, as sometimes happens, not merely upon tort, but also upon breach of contract. Thus, in *Jackson v. Watson & Sons*, [1909] 2 K.B. 193, J bought some tinned salmon from W. He gave it to his wife to eat and it poisoned her. In an action by J against W for breach of contract, it was held that the injury he suffered as the result of the loss of his wife's society and services might be taken into account as an element in the assessment of J's damages.

(*b*) By the provisions of the Fatal Accidents Act 1846 (as subsequently amended) the *dependants* of a deceased person can claim damages for loss arising by reason of his decease if the death was caused by some default on the part of the defendant which would, had the deceased remained alive, have entitled him to bring an action in tort.

The action should normally be brought by the personal representatives (see below, Chapter 13) of the deceased person, on behalf of the dependants. "Dependants" for this purpose include the deceased's wife, husband, parent, child, grand-parent, grandchild, step-parent and step-child. Illegitimate and adopted children are also now included.

The "loss" which the statute envisages is *pecuniary* loss, the loss of a "bread-winner"; damages will not be awarded merely for the *mental* suffering which the death causes the dependants.

Claims may be brought in respect of the same fatal accident, both under the 1934 Act (in respect of any cause of action arising before the death, see above, p. 288) and the Fatal Accidents Act, but no award may be made which would have the result of giving a dependant a benefit twice over. For instance, if an award is made under the 1934 Act in respect of a deceased husband who has, say, died without making a will and leaving his wife as his sole surviving relative, the benefit which the wife will receive from this award, as sole successor to the husband's estate, must be taken into account in assessing the amount she is to receive under the Fatal Accidents Acts.

Money spent by dependants upon funeral or mourning expenses is now recoverable, although it used not to be.

B   EXAMPLES OF SPECIFIC TORTS

There is insufficient space to attempt more than a very brief outline of some of the essential characteristics of a few of the more important torts, and the reader who wishes to make a serious study of the subject is referred to the specialized works, such as the author's *General Principles of the Law of Torts*.

Two general remarks should, however, be made. In the first place the reason for curtailing discussion of the law of torts is that it is case law *par excellence*; it might be described as a honeycomb of particular instances, albeit resting upon a delusively simple structure of principle. The study of torts can only be based upon the cases, and if we were to stray among their fascinating pastures we should be in danger of leading the reader into a large volume. Thus he must be warned that what appears here as simple in plan is in complex in realization, and little hint can be given of the wealth of this complexity. In the second place, as has been seen, tort law has been built up by the courts in what was once judicially described as "disconnected slabs": the writer therefore believes that there is no merit in choosing any particular order of treatment and would on the whole be happy to adhere to the traditional method of discussing Trespass and its immediate offshoots first, since they came first in point of time. But if Saturn devoured his children similar opprobrium falls upon the modern tort of Negligence, for it has not only over-shadowed Trespass, its grandfather, but bids fair to swallow up many of its other less illustrious tort relatives. In modern practice, therefore, most of "Torts" is Negligence. So, to mark this fact and impress it upon the reader we will discuss Negligence first.

1   NEGLIGENCE

"Negligence", for the purposes of the law of torts, is a word which is used in a dual sense. On the one hand it may signify the attitude of mind of a party committing a tort; thus, goods may be "converted" (see below, p. 301) intentionally, unintentionally, or "negligently" – the taker having made insufficient inquiries to satisfy himself as to their true ownership. On the other hand, "negligence" is today also a tort in its own right, independent of other torts; and it is with the independent tort of negligence that we are now concerned.

"Negligence" in this latter sense signifies *the breach by the defendant of a legal duty to take care not to damage the person or property of the plaintiff*; if such a duty is broken, and the plaintiff can show that he has been damaged as a result of the breach he will have a right of action against the defendant.

The first thing to be considered in relation to this tort is, therefore, *In what circumstances does a legal duty to take care exist?* There are, of course, many situations in which it is so clear that a duty is owed that this matter will require no consideration. For instance, it is clear that drivers of motor cars owe a duty to other road users to drive carefully, and there-fore if they injure people through careless driving they are guilty of negligence, and can be sued. Not all situations in which people claim that they have been injured by the carelessness of others are, however, of such a simple and familiar nature. It is thus at least desirable that there should be some general test by which the existence or non-existence of a *"duty of care"* can be determined. In the leading case of *Donoghue* v. *Stevenson*, [1932] A.C. 562, Lord Atkin attempted to propound such a test in a passage in his speech which became famous. After characterizing the duty as a wide duty "not to injure one's neighbour" and evoking the analogy of the parable of the Good Samaritan, he defined a "neighbour", for the purposes of this branch of the law, in the following words. *"Who, then,"* he said, *"in law is my neighbour? The answer seems to be – persons who are so closely and directly affected by my act that I ought reasonably to have them in contemplation as being so affected when I am directing my mind to the acts or omissions which are called in question."* In other words, according to Lord Atkin, the duty exists wherever one person is in a position to *foresee* that an act or omission of his may injure another, and by "may" is generally (but see below, p. 321) meant not "possibly might" but "is reasonably likely to".

This test, when applied by Lord Atkin to the facts of *Donoghue's Case*, resulted in a decision in favour of the plaintiff (a decision in which the majority of the House of Lords concurred). The facts were that a friend of the plaintiff at a café in Paisley bought a bottle of ginger beer from the proprietor and gave it to the plaintiff. The bottle was opaque, so that its contents could not be seen: in fact, as well as ginger beer, it contained the decomposed remains of a snail. Upon drinking part of the contents the plaintiff became ill, and sued the manufacturer of the ginger beer for negligence. The House of Lords held that the manufacturer ought to have foreseen the likelihood that a person in the position of the plaintiff would consume his wares and that he therefore owed her a duty of care to ensure that the bottle should not contain the objectionable matter it did; hence, if this duty had in fact been broken the manufacturer would be liable.

The negative aspect of the test may be illustrated by the case of *Hay* (*or Bourhill*) v. *Young*, [1943] A.C. 92. There the respondent was the personal representative of one Y who was killed in a street collision caused by his own negligent riding of a motor cycle. The appellant was at the time of the collision descending from a tram forty-five yards from the scene of the crash, and could not see what had occurred, but could hear the noise of the collision. Yet this noise so affected her nerves (she being pregnant at the time) that she became ill and was for a while unable to continue her trade. The House of Lords held that although the deceased might reasonably have expected to have foreseen injury to people in the immediate vicinity of the place of impact he could not reasonably have been expected to foresee injury to a person so far from the spot as the appellant; the respondent was not therefore liable, since the deceased owed no duty of care to the appellant.

Further negative illustration may be afforded by two striking American cases. In the *Nitro-glycerine Case* (1872), 15 Wall 524, carriers were held not liable for damage caused when their servant created an explosion by opening a case of nitro-glycerine with hammer and chisel, for at that time Nobel had only just explored the explosive quantities of that substance, and its properties were generally unknown; no ordinary person could therefore then have foreseen the unhappy results of the servant's labours. The other similar and more tragic case appears in an English report; *The Grandcamp*, [1961] 1 Lloyd's Rep. 504. This action arose out of the disaster which occurred in Texas City in 1947 when many deaths were caused, and seventy million dollars' worth of damage done to property, as the result of the explosion of a cargo of fertilizer grade ammonium nitrate following upon a fire aboard the defendant's vessel. Here again, this chemical was a new compound of ammonium nitrate, no one knew of its highly explosive qualities, and consequently the defendants, though they were negligent in permitting the fire to arise, were held not responsible for the results of the explosion which was not a thing of which they could reasonably have foreseen the likelihood.

The "foresight" test is now generally accepted as the appropriate criterion for determining whether a duty of care is owed. Yet it has often been criticized for its vagueness, and the question what a person ought to foresee in given circumstances imports, as often as not, social and moral considerations as well as quantitative judgments in terms of time and space. Moreover the test cannot be applied to all kinds of situations and in some circumstances its application needs to be modified for practical reasons. Acts and words, and the injury that may arise from them respectively, being essentially different, and a certain social freedom in respect of misstatement being generally accepted, careless *misstatement* will by no means always give rise to a claim; even though injury could have been foreseen by the maker of the statement. Indeed, until the important decision in *Hedley Byrne & Co., Ltd.* v. *Heller & Partners, Ltd.*, [1964] A.C. 463 it was thought to be the law that no claim could be brought upon a careless (as opposed to a fraudulent) misstatement (at least so long as it caused non-physical loss) under any circumstances unless the maker of the statement owed a contractual or fiduciary duty to the person injured. In *Hedley Byrne's Case* – where a firm of bankers gave a misleading reference about the affairs of one of their customers to another bank whose customer relied upon it to his loss – the House of Lords disposed of the fallacy that *no* claim will lie upon a careless misstatement, but stressed that the mere probability of injury arising from a misstatement will not always be enough to found a claim.

The exact impact of this decision at present remains to be seen and the *ratio decidendi* is by no means clear-cut, but it would appear that careless misstatement which causes injury whether in an economic or in any other form, will be actionable if the injury was foreseeable at the time when the statement was made; but *if*, and *only if*, the circumstances were such that either the defendant was someone possessed of a special skill, such as a doctor or an accountant or an architect, who made the statement in the course of his business, or *if* the statement was made by someone not possessed of such a skill but who made it in circumstances such as to mislead the plaintiff into thinking that he had it. It would follow that if in the course of a journey by train a solicitor should find himself in company with a stranger who should ask his legal advice, he would be well advised (*being* a solicitor) to warn the stranger that such counsel as he might give would be extra-professional and without liability. And it also followed that in *Mutual Life Citizens Assurance Co., Ltd.* v. *Evatt,* [1971] A.C. 793 (a Judicial Committee decision), the appellant Company was held not liable to one of its policy holders who suffered loss by investing in another company in reliance upon a misstatement as to the financial stability of that company made by one of the appellant Company's officials. For advice about investments is no part of an insurance business, nor had the officer intimated that he was purporting to exercise the functions of a stockbroker.

In order to avoid confusion it must be appreciated that the provisions of the Misrepresentation Act 1967 (see above, p. 242) in respect of negligent misrepresentation apply only to representations made in the course of the conclusion of a *contract*.

The decision that a defendant owes a duty of care does not of itself render him liable. The plaintiff must show not only that a duty was owed, *but also that the defendant broke it*. In other words, it must be shown that the defendant failed to exercise a certain "standard" of care. The standard required is the standard of an ordinary "reasonable" man, placed in the circumstances of the defendant. To revert to a familiar instance. The driver of a motor car owes a duty to avoid running into pedestrians. But this does not mean that all that has to be proved against him is that he has run down a pedestrian. He will only have broken his duty if it is clear that he could, as an ordinary prudent driver, have avoided the accident. It will not, moreover, be enough to show that the most expert of racing drivers might have avoided it, if an ordinary reasonable driver could not; nor, on the other hand, since the law requires that people be equal to the tasks they undertake, will the defendant be permitted to excuse himself upon the ground that he is an exceptionally inefficient driver.

Just as the scope of the *duty* of care falls to be defined by judicial decisions so the courts are continually being called upon to determine the appropriate *standard* of conduct to be taken to constitute reasonable *care* in all the multifarious situations which cases bring before them. Many factors have to be taken into account. For instance some kinds of activity require greater care than others because they involve *special risks*: if I give you a *hydrogen bomb* to carry I suspect that you will feel called upon to handle it with more circumspection than if I only entrust you with a *pencil*; and the law demands such circumspection. In respect of all the categories of things which fall between these two extremes such care will be required as a reasonable man would consider necessary according to the danger potential of the article: failure to act in the appropriate way will constitute negligence. Moreover, where the danger to be anticipated if insufficient care be taken is such as ought to put a man especially upon his guard, the law may demand of him a degree of *foresight*, *higher* than foresight *of the probable*. Thus in *Overseas Tankship (U.K.), Ltd.* v. *Miller Steamship Co., Pty., Ltd. (The Wagon Mound (No. 2))*., [1967] A.C. 617, the defendants' engineer permitted furnace oil to be spilt from their ship upon the waters of Sydney Harbour. The oil then floated across the harbour to a wharf where oxyacetylene equipment was in use, so that sparks fell upon the oily water. This caused a conflagration and the plaintiffs' ship was damaged. It was found that the risk of oil on water catching fire was by no means great, but was nevertheless appreciable; and it was held that the defendants were liable, since their engineer ought to have realized that what he was doing was so potentially dangerous as to put him on his guard against the contingency.

Again, the reasonable man adapts his *conduct to his company*; greater care is demanded in dealings with children than in dealings with adults, and special care is needed when one comes into contact with disabled people. In *Paris* v. *Stepney Borough Council*, [1951] A.C. 367, for example, the appellant, who was employed by the respondents as a garage hand, had to their knowledge *only one sound eye*: while he was at work beneath a vehicle a piece of metal flew off and injured this eye. The respondents were held to have been negligent in failing to provide the appellant with goggles, even though it was not usual in the trade to supply them for that sort of work; and thus the respondents might not have been held liable had the appellant not to their knowledge *been afflicted* in the way he was.

Again, *necessity* may sometimes excuse what might otherwise be lack of care. If I, a lawyer, undertake to amputate your leg and gangrene sets in through my lack of skill I shall be answerable (*imperitia culpae adnumeratur* – "lack of skill", where skill is needed, "amounts to fault" in English Law just as it did in Roman); but it would be otherwise if I were to operate in case of necessity to save your life when far from proper help.

Then again, amongst many other factors, even the *economic practicability* of a course of action is sometimes a matter to be taken into account. Thus in *Latimer* v. *A.E.C., Ltd.*, [1953] A.C. 643, due to an exceptionally heavy rainstorm, the floors of the respondents' workshops became flooded, and this flooding caused oil, normally contained in open artificial channels, to be washed over the whole of the floors, where it remained in patches. The respondents at once used all available supplies of sawdust to cover the floor, but through lack of further supplies left some areas uncovered. The appellant, an employee of the respondents, slipped upon an uncovered patch and sustained injuries. It was held that the respondents were not liable; they had done all that could reasonably be expected of them; and although it was true that the accident could not have occurred had they closed their plant and sent their workers home, this drastic step, with its accompanying economic loss, was one which could not reasonably have been demanded. And so one could go on with illustrations: and so the courts have to go on, laying down a reasonable standard of care in accordance with current ideas and in the light of existing knowledge.

Assume now that there is a duty of care and that that duty has been broken; one more factor remains, beyond proof of actual damage, before the plaintiff's case is fully established. That factor is that the injury must result from, or be *caused* by, the breach of duty. Whether or no a particular injury is the cause of a wrong done by the defendant is usually an obvious question which can be answered without thought; and in all torts the element of *causation* is usually assumed either to exist or not to exist, in which latter case there can be no liability. But sometimes, and particularly in negligence cases, the causal element creates difficulty. Thus a *"novus actus interveniens"* (an independent intervening act) or a *"nova causa interveniens"* (independent intervening cause) may, as it were, isolate the defendant's wrong from the damage suffered by the plaintiff – as where, B having carelessly lit a fire, C *intentionally* spreads it to A's land, or an earthquake *unforeseeably* occurs and brings about a similar result. And the plaintiff's *own* act or fault may similarly prove, upon examination of all the facts, to be the true cause of the injury rather than the defendant's apparent wrongdoing. Thus in *Cummings* v. *Sir William Arrol & Co., Ltd.*, [1962] 1 All E.R. 623, a man was killed by falling from a steel tower and it was alleged that the death was due to (*i.e.* caused by) the negligence of his employers in failing to supply a safety-belt; whereas examination of all the facts showed that, although it was true that they had failed to supply one, the essence of the matter really was that even if they had done so the deceased would not have worn the belt so the true situation was that it was not the negligence of the defendant employers which brought about the death but the behaviour of the deceased himself, which was the real *cause* of his death, and accordingly the employers were not liable.

Normally, therefore, in an action for negligence, the plaintiff must prove that the defendant owed a duty, that he broke the duty, and that the plaintiff was *damaged* in some way as the result of the breach. There are certain types of situation, however, where "*res ipsa loquitur*" ("the thing speaks for itself"). Here mere proof of a given set of facts argues so strongly in favour of negligence that the court may at once find in favour of the plaintiff, unless the defendant can produce some explanation which suggests that his negligence was not in fact the cause of the accident. If, however, the defendant does produce such an explanation it is then up to the plaintiff to *prove* negligence affirmatively if he can. *Byrne* v. *Boadle* (1863), 2 H. & C. 722, forms a stock example of a "*res ipsa*" situation. The plaintiff was walking along the street when a barrel of flour fell upon him from an open door in an upper floor of the defendant's warehouse. It was held that the proof of these facts raised such a strong presumption of negligence that the case could go to the jury without any evidence being adduced as to how the accident occurred.

Before the Law Reform (Contributory Negligence) Act 1945 it was a complete defence to an action of negligence for a defendant to show that the plaintiff's own negligence had *contributed* to cause the damage of which he complained. For instance, if in a collision between two cyclists it were shown that the defendant was riding with his eyes shut, but that the collision had been partially caused by the fact that the plaintiff's bicycle had defective brakes, the plaintiff could recover nothing. The Act has now altered the law on this point. It provides (s. 1 (1)) that "*Where any person suffers damage as the result partly of his own fault and partly of any other person . . . a claim in respect of that damage shall not be defeated by reason of the fault of the person suffering the damage, but the damages recoverable in respect thereof shall be reduced to such extent as the Court thinks just and equitable having regard to the claimant's share in the responsibility for the damage.*" Thus, in the example given, the plaintiff's claim might no longer fail entirely, but his damages might be reduced by, say, one third of the sum which he would have obtained had he not been at fault at all.

Having considered the more important of the principles underlying the tort of Negligence in general, mention should now be made of the special rules which govern its application in two common kinds of situation; first in relation to the *employer's obligations to his em-*

ployees and secondly in relation to the duties owed by *occupiers* of land, premises and permanent structures to other people who they permit to use them.

(*i*) *Employers* – The *employer's* duty has broadly been judicially defined as requiring him to "*take reasonable care for his servant's safety in all the circumstances of the case*". But this is a flexible definition and it really tells us no more than that he must not be negligent towards the servant. Consequently the cases show that the obligation can be expressed more specifically, by breaking it down into a threefold aspect; namely, a duty to provide *competent staff, adequate plant and material, and a safe system of work*. The employee who is injured as the result of his employer failing to make reasonable provision in any of these respects will have a right of action. This is a field in which there is prolific litigation and no attempt can be made to summarize the effect of it here – especially since the decision in every case depends upon all the circumstances. But it must be stressed that all that is required of the employer is "reasonable care"; he is not an insurer of his servant's safety, nor does he even owe him that obviously high degree of care that a teacher owes to a pupil. For instance if the employer supplies a suitable tool for a particular piece of work and an experienced employee chooses to use an unsuitable one, thereby bringing injury upon himself, he will have no claim.

It is also important to remark that in many kinds of employment special statutory duties are cast upon the employer by statute, *e.g.* the Factories Act 1961 – shortly, as we have seen (above, p. 189), to be replaced by the Health and Safety at Work Act 1974 and regulations thereunder. While some of these duties are "strict" others are based upon lack of care; and which of these things they are depends upon the construction of each enactment. In the former case proof of breach of the duty – assuming that this breach caused the injury – is all that is required to establish liability, while in the latter negligence must be proved. And it is also possible that where injury arises from a breach of duty there was also negligence under the ordinary rules of the common law; so that it is usual to plead alternatively both breach of the statutory duty and common law negligence.

(*ii*) *Occupiers* – We must now consider the obligations owed to *visitors* (and their property) by *occupiers* of land or premises or of fixed or movable structures, such as vessels, vehicles or aircraft. The law on this subject is now regulated by the Occupiers' Liability Act 1957 (O.L.A.).

"Visitors" in this context include people who come upon the property either in the occupier's interest (*e.g.*, plumbers) or in their own (*e.g.* guests) or in the exercise of some right conferred by law (*e.g.* users of public parks), and also people who enter as the result of a contract between the occupier and some third party (*e.g.* where a landlord retains a common staircase in his own control but contracts to allow his tenant's visitors to use it).

The occupier's obligation concerns "*dangers due to the state of the premises or structures or things done or omitted to be done on them*" (O.L.A. s. 1 (1)) and it is a duty to "*take such care as in all the circumstances of the case* is reasonable to see that the visitor will be reasonably safe in using the premises *for the purpose for which he is permitted by the occupier to be there*" (O.L.A. s. 2 (2) – italics ours). This duty the section terms the "*common duty of care*". The words italicized are important. In the first place what is "reasonable" may vary according to the visitor: a fence at a particular spot may be necessary to protect a child but not an adult, a warning that a rubber connexion is perished may be necessary in the case of a casual guest, but not in the case of a gas-fitter. In the second place the visitor who abuses his invitation by going where he has not been invited (as by breaking uninvited into a locked room) ceases to be a visitor and becomes a trespasser.

Further, what is required of the occupier is no more than "reasonable" care. Hence he will not be held liable for the negligence of an independent contractor (as for instance where such a contractor carelessly fixes a chandelier which falls upon a guest at dinner) provided that he has taken reasonable steps to satisfy himself that the contractor is reasonably competent and that his work has been properly executed. Moreover, the occupier may absolve himself by giving reasonably effective warning of dangers (such as low beams), and he will not be liable in respect of injuries from risks willingly accepted by the visitor – as where the visitor, seeing a rotten floor board, volunteers to take the risk of jumping on it.

Mention must also be made of a special class of people, those who enter for a purpose which *primarily envisages the use* of the premises or structures: hotel patrons, for instance, or users of racecourse stands. Such people enter under *contract* and consequently the particular contract may contain special terms. But the O.L.A. s. 5 (1) provides that in the absence of such terms the occupier will owe to such visitors the "common duty of care". There are, however, certain exceptions to this rule and the most important of them concerns contracts "*for the hire of, or the carriage for reward of persons or goods in any vehicle . . . or other means of transport*". (O.L.A. s. 5 (3)). Here, apart from special terms in the contract, the occupier's duty remains what it was at common law, namely to ensure that the vehicle is as fit for the purpose for which it is to be used as reasonable care and skill *on the part of anyone* can make it. This is a burdensome duty, for in this kind of case the occupier may, for example, be held liable for the carelessness of an independent contractor though he was himself in no way at fault.

The Act is only concerned with *lawful* visitors, not with *trespassers*; so a final word must be added about the occupier's obligations to this kind of unwanted visitor.

Before the decision in *British Railways Board* v. *Herrington*, [1972] A.C. 877 the rule was that an occupier owed to a *trespasser* no greater obligation than to refrain from injuring him by acts deliberately aimed at harming him or done with reckless disregard of his presence. That case (in which a child, due to the careless failure of the defendants' servants to fence the railway line, received serious injuries by coming into contact with a "live" rail) replaced this austere rule by a new one: namely, that though the occupier does not owe a *trespasser* the "common duty of care" yet he must act towards him with ordinary humanity. The full meaning of this exhortation remains to be clarified by case law, but in *Pannett* v. *McGuiness & Co., Ltd.*, [1972] 2 Q.B. 599 (where a child trespasser received burns from a fire carelessly left unguarded by demolition workers) Lord Denning, M.R. suggested a number of pointers. He repeated the truism that what is or is not 'negligent' must here, as elsewhere, depend upon all the circumstances, and then he added that among the factors to be considered are – (*i*) the "gravity and likelihood of probable injury": (*ii*) the character of the intrusion by the trespasser. "A wandering child or a straying adult stands in a different position from a poacher or a burglar": (*iii*) "the nature of the place (safe or dangerous) where the trespass occurs". (*iv*) the "knowledge which the defendant has . . . of the likelihood of trespassers". To these considerations we may add that in *Herrington's Case* Lord Reid was not alone in suggesting that the character of the *defendant* may also be important: thus, for example, a private person can seldom be expected to spend a large amount of money on foolproof fencing, whereas, for example, given conditions of danger, a public authority may be required to do so.

2 TRESPASS

It has already been explained that a trespass is a "direct and forcible" injury. There are three forms of trespass: trespass to the person, trespass to goods, and trespass to land.

Trespass to the person may take the form of an actual battery or of a technical assault (see above, p. 171) from whence it will be apparent that assault is a crime as well as being a tort). Until recently all trespasses to the person were, in keeping with the historical development of the law which has been described, like other trespasses, actionable *per se*, *i.e.*, without proof of *actual* damage, and the burden of proving that the trespass was justified (as by inevitable accident) lay upon the defendant. But the law on this point has become complicated since the Court of Appeal decision in *Fowler* v. *Lanning*, [1959] 1 Q.B. 426. The facts were that (no doubt unintentionally) B shot A during a shooting party and A claimed in trespass, alleging only, as under the pre-existing law he was entitled to do, the fact of the shooting and leaving it to B to *justify* his conduct – as by proof that it *was* an accident. The Court held, contrary to the previous law, that A could have no claim unless he could *establish* in B one of two things; either *intention* or *negligence*. And in a later case the new position was clarified. Where the injury is direct and *intention* is established then the claim will be in *trespass to the person*, with the result that, as before, actual damage need not be proved and the damages (as before) may be merely nominal – though of course if the circumstances so warrant they may be substantial or even aggravated (see below. p. 319). Where negligence only is established the claim *no longer lies in trespass* and the tort will be *Negligence*, not trespass at all; actual damage and *lack of care* having consequently to be *proved* by the plaintiff.

Whether this improves the law is open to doubt; for surely if I hit you, you are entitled to demand that I justify the blackness of your eye? It should be added that, at present at any rate, it is not thought that the *Fowler* v. *Lanning* ruling affects other forms of trespass; it is to be assumed that they remain actionable *per se*, without proof of special damage and that the burden of justifying them remains upon the defendant.

Trespass to goods is direct interference with goods in the possession of another. Such interference will usually be physical, as by touching, or removing, the goods; but this need not necessarily be so, for it is a trespass to drive another man's cattle out of a field, even though there is no physical touching of them. (Similarly, of course, one may commit a trespass against the *person* by setting one's dog on another person.)

Trespass to land is committeed when one person enters upon land in the possession of another without lawful justification, or remains upon it after his authority to be upon it has been revoked. It may also be committed by merely throwing or putting things upon the land. Contrary to popular belief, trespass to land is not, of itself, a crime: the familiar notice "Trespassers will be Prosecuted" is an idle threat unless the trespasser does some criminal damage (see above, p. 183).

3 FALSE IMPRISONMENT

Where one person falsely (*i.e.* unlawfully) restricts the physical freedom of another, that other person will be entitled to bring an action for damages for the tort of false imprisonment. Imprisonment, in the sense of actual incarceration, is not essential for the commission of this tort; what is required is that there should have been complete restriction of the plaintiff's liberty of action by the defendant. Thus, though arrest may sometimes be lawful, even without a warrant (see above, pp. 141–

142), where an *unlawful* arrest is made, this will amount to a false imprisonment; for while under arrest, even though no physical force be used – but, for example, mere threats or persuasion – the movements of the person arrested are under the control of his captor. But, for the purposes of this action, the control must have been complete, not merely partial; thus if I prevent you from passing along a path by placing an obstacle across it, this obstruction may be a nuisance, but I shall not be liable for false imprisonment; for, if you wish, you are free to make a detour, or to go back the way you came: your liberty is only inhibited in one direction.

A further restriction upon the competence of this action is that it lies only in respect of the active imposition of restraint. Thus if a man voluntarily submits to restraint of liberty the law will not require others – at any rate apart from a contractual or other special duty to do so – to release him upon his demand. For instance, in *Herd* v. *Weardale Steel etc. Co.*, [1915] A.C. 67, a miner sued his employers for false imprisonment. After a dispute had arisen, while the man in question was in the pit, he demanded to be taken to the surface before his shift was due to end. The employers' agents at first refused to grant him the use of the cage, and he was thus stranded, idle, in the pit for some twenty minutes. His claim for damages in respect of this detention failed; for he had entered the pit of his own accord, and his employers were under no duty to convey him to the surface until the end of the shift.

The action for false imprisonment helps to vindicate the constitutional right to personal freedom; but, of course, it is small solace to a prisoner to know that once he is released he may have a right to a civil action, and it will be remembered that everyone who is imprisoned, otherwise than by due process of law, may secure immediate release by means of the writ of *Habeas Corpus* (see above, p. 143).

Finally, it should be noted that although assault usually accompanies false imprisonment, the two causes of action are distinct; for it is possible to imprison a person without committing an assault, as where one person locks another in a room.

4   CONVERSION AND DETINUE

Conversion is in a sense (but only in a sense) the civil counterpart of the crime of theft. But it rests upon a different basis, since it is committed when a person deals with the goods of another in such a way as to show that he calls the *title* of the other in question. Clearly the most obvious form of conversion is therefore the wilful taking of another person's goods. But this is not the only form. For example, a man who innocently acquires goods from a thief (who can give him no title to them) will usually be liable in conversion if he does anything which affects the title.

Thus, in *Hollins* v. *Fowler* (1875), L.R. 7 H.L. 757, X obtained cotton from F by fraud. X sold the cotton to H (a cotton broker) who re-sold it to Y, receiving only broker's commission for the deal. It was held that H was guilty of conversion; for he had purported to deal in the title to the goods, even though he was ignorant of F's rights.

Detinue consists of the wrongful retention of the possession of goods, as where A lends B a car which B refuses to return.

It has already been seen (above, p. 203) that detinue was a very old form of action and it was, and is, essentially a claim by the plaintiff for the *return* of his property. Thus, whereas an action in conversion is purely an action for damages, an action in detinue is a claim either for the *return of the property* or for damages. Until the Common Law Procedure Act 1854 a *defendant* in an action of detinue had the choice either of making restitution, or of paying damages: since the passing of that Act the rule has been that the court may, if there is some special reason (*e.g.* where the goods detained are goods of peculiar value), *order* the defendant to return them but this is a discretion which is seldom used.

It should be noted that it is possible to commit a trespass to goods without committing either conversion or detinue. Thus, in *Bushell* v. *Miller* (1718), 1 Str. 128, where a porter at a custom house quay, in order to get to his own chest, put aside some goods belonging to someone else, and the goods were subsequently lost because he forgot to replace them, it was held that he was not guilty of conversion, since his act constituted no denial of the plaintiff's title; and clearly he did not *detain* the goods. He had, however, committed a trespass.

5 DEFAMATION

Defamation may be broadly defined as "the publication of a statement which tends to lower a person in the estimation of right-thinking members of society generally".

The tort of defamation is divided into two major categories, *libel* and *slander*. A *libel* is defamatory matter which is published in some permanent form. The usual form is writing or printing. Permanence being the essence of the matter, however, writing is not essential: for example, it has been held that the inclusion of defamatory statements upon the sound-track of a film may constitute a libel, and an effigy at Madame Tussaud's has also been held to be libellous. Further, under the provisions of the Defamation Act 1952, words and images broadcast for general reception by wireless or television are now treated as publications in a permanent form, and the Theatres Act 1968, s. 4, applies the same principle to verbal statements and gestures in the public performance of a play. *Slander* is the publication of defamatory matter in a transient form, normally in the guise of an oral statement.

It is important to distinguish the two classes of defamation because, whereas a libel is actionable (*per se*) *without proof of special damage*, slander is (subject to exceptions) only actionable if the plaintiff can show that he has actually suffered damage. Moreover, whereas libel is a crime, as well as a tort, slander (except where the words spoken tend directly to create a breach of the peace, or are blasphemous, obscene, seditious, or reflect upon the due administration of justice) is *only* a tort. (Criminal prosecutions are, however, now practically obsolete.)

For the purposes of the law of torts, in order for a defamatory statement to be actionable it must be published not merely to the person defamed, but *to some third party*. The essence of the plaintiff's claim is that he has suffered damage through loss of reputation; and there can be no loss of reputation where the *plaintiff alone* knows of the statement. In the case of the *crime* of libel it is otherwise, for the purpose of punishing libels is to prevent breaches of the peace, and the party defamed is the most likely person to commit a breach of the peace if the libellous statement is communicated to him.

At common law a defamatory statement is actionable even though it is made entirely innocently. "Liability for libel", it has been judicially declared, "does not depend upon the intention of the defamer; but on the fact of defamation". It was, at common law, enough for the plaintiff to establish that the defendant made and published the statement and that it was defamatory; if he could do this he did not need to concern himself with the defendant's state of mind. Thus in *Newstead* v. *London Express Newspaper, Ltd.*, [1940] 1 K.B. 377, it was stated in a newspaper that "Harold Newstead, thirty-year-old Camberwell man" had been convicted of bigamy. The statement was true of a certain barman in the Camberwell district, but not of the plaintiff, a hairdresser, of the same name and age, to whom the defendants were not adverting, and of whose very existence they did not know. It was held that the plaintiff could recover from the defendants.

This is a harsh rule, and it is now modied by the Defamation Act 1952, s. 4, which provides that if the person who publishes (*i.e.* makes or otherwise disseminates) an "*innocently*" defamatory statement makes an "*offer of amends*", in a prescribed form, coupled, amongst other requirements, with an offer to publish an apology, he shall be entitled to the following relief. If the offer be *accepted*, it will form a *bar to an action* by the party aggrieved, though the High Court may award him certain costs and an allowance for expenses reasonably incurred. If the offer be *refused*, provided that it was made as soon as reasonably practicable, and has not since been withdrawn, proof of the "innocence" of the statement will form a *defence* should the aggrieved party sue. Statements are to be deemed to be "*innocent*" (s. 4 (5)) if (*a*) the publisher did not intend to publish them of and concerning the plaintiff, and did not know of circumstances by which they might be understood to refer to him; or if (*b*) the words were not defamatory on the face of them, and the publisher did not know of circumstances by virtue of which they might be understood to be defamatory of the party aggrieved.

There are three special defences to an action for defamation:

(*i*) *Justification* – The defendant may escape liability if he can prove that the statement was substantially "justified" (true). No one can claim that his reputation has been damaged by the publication of the truth. Here again, the *crime* of libel differs from the tort: it is not usually a defence to a criminal prosecution for libel to prove that the statement was true.

(*ii*) *Privilege* – A defamatory statement made upon a "privileged" occasion is not actionable. The reason for this is that the occasion is one which the law regards, for some reason, as sacrosanct. There are two classes of privileged occasions; occasions when statements are *absolutely* privileged and occasions when they are subject to *qualified* privilege. Examples of statements which are absolutely privileged are statements made in either House of Parliament or in the course of judicial proceedings. Qualified privilege arises in certain cases where the maker of a statement is under a duty to make it, and the person to whom it is made has a reciprocal interest in receiving it. The best example of an occasion of this sort is where a person, upon request, gives a reference to a prospective employer. Where privilege is *absolute* the existence of ill-will, or "malice", on the part of the maker of the statement does not destroy the privilege. *Qualified* privilege will, however, be destroyed by the presence of malice; the protection it affords only covers statements honestly, if mistakenly, made.

(*iii*) *Fair comment* – Statements of opinion, as well as statements of fact, may be defamatory; yet it is clear that, in the public interest, criticism should be free as long as it is fair. Hence it is a defence to an action for defamation to show that the alleged defamatory statement was a "*fair comment*" honestly made upon a matter of *public interest*. "Public interest" is a wide term; it covers the behaviour of all public men, such as Ministers of State and local officials, or anyone who performs any public function. It also covers the works of people, such as authors and artists, who invite criticism by publication of their works. In order to acquire protection the comment must satisfy four conditions. First, it must be a statement of *opinion*, not an assertion of fact. Second, it must be "*fair*", *i.e.* something reasonably warranted by the matter commented upon: "criticism", said Collins, M.R., "cannot be used as a cloak for mere invective". Third, it must *not* be "*malicious*", *i.e.* it must not be prompted by spite or ill-will. Fourth, it must not reflect upon the *moral* character of the person criticized.

6 NUISANCE

The word "nuisance" is connected with the Latin *"nocumentum"* (harm). Nuisances are divided into two main classes: Public Nuisances and Private Nuisances.

A *public nuisance* is a *crime* indictable at common law. It may also be restrained by injunction at the suit of the Attorney-General. Examples of public nuisances are keeping a common gaming-house, obstructing highways and rendering them dangerous. If, however, any person suffers *special* damage as the result of a public nuisance, over and above the harm caused to the public at large, he may bring an action in *tort* against the person who creates the nuisance. Thus, in *Benjamin* v. *Storr* (1874), L.R. 9 C.P. 400, B kept a coffee-house in Rose Street, Covent Garden. S, for the purposes of his business, kept horses and vans standing outside the coffee-house all day long. This caused an obstruction to the highway. B complained that he suffered special damage because the vans obstructed the light to the windows of his coffee-house and he had to incur expense in keeping gas lights burning all day. He further alleged that the smell from the excreta of S's horses made the premises objectionable and deterred customers. It was held that these facts amongst others, constituted special damage which would entitle B to maintain an action against S.

A *private nuisance* is solely a *tort*. It is in essence a wrong (other than a direct act of trespass) which incommodes a person in the use and enjoyment of his land; though it also embraces certain injuries and inconveniences caused to users of the highway. There are two classes of private nuisances: (*a*) Nuisances which damage the plaintiff's enjoyment of an easement (see below, Chapter 10), such as a right of way, or his enjoyment of a natural right, such as his right to have his land supported by the land of his neighbour. Nuisances of this class are generally actionable by the plaintiff *without the necessity of proving any actual damage.* (*b*) Nuisances which arise when obnoxious things, such as smoke, water, smell, vibrations, animals or the branches or roots of trees are allowed to escape or obtrude upon the plaintiff's land. Nuisances of this class are only actionable if the plaintiff can prove that they have *actually* incommoded him in the enjoyment of his land.

These are the commonest form of nuisances, but all the causes which give rise to nuisance are so various that it would be idle to attempt to enumerate them here.

Further, the law of nuisance is a branch of the law which is preeminently governed by the rule of "give and take": we must all bear certain reasonable inconveniences from the activities of our neighbours, and the law takes this commonplace consideration into account. The cases, therefore, show that a variety of factors have to be weighed in determining the incidence of liability. The following examples may be given.

First, in nuisance (by way of exception to the general rule – above, p. 280) the presence of *"malice"*, in the sense of improper motive, such as spite or ill-will, may sometimes be a determining factor in liability. But an important distinction has to be observed. Where the law gives a person a legal *right* to do something no amount of ill-will in the doing of it will make that right into a wrong. This was the position in *The Mayor of Bradford* v. *Pickles*, [1895] A.C. 587. Water percolated in no defined channels beneath Pickles' land and flowed thence to land belonging to the appellant Corporation. The Corporation used this water for their city supply. Actuated by a desire to force the Corporation to buy his land at his own price, Pickles obstructed the flow of water by sinking shafts in his own land. The Corporation sought an injunction to restrain him from his mercenary behaviour. It was held that no injunction would lie, because a previous decision of the House of Lords had laid down that whereas it is a nuisance to obstruct the flow of water when it runs from one's own land to another's in defined channels it is no nuisance to extract merely percolating water – indeed, if this were the law it would provide a disincentive to land drainage. This kind of obstruction was therefore something which Pickles had a *right* to do; as Lord Halsbury, L.C. said, what he did was "a lawful act, however ill the motive might be" and he therefore "had a right to do it".

On the other hand the law often concedes to people the *privilege* of doing things without conferring upon them a positive right; as for example the "right" to shoot on their own land. Here the "right" is something which *may* be done, but *only* if it *is done lawfully*, and the element of "malice" may render the activity unlawful (and therefore a nuisance) where, in the absence of "malice" it would have been lawful. Thus in *Hollywood Silver Fox Farm, Ltd.* v. *Emmett*, [1936] 1 All E.R. 825, the plaintiffs were awarded damages against the defendant who had ordered his son (on account of differences between him and the plaintiffs) to fire guns on his (the defendant's) land as near as possible to the plaintiffs' land in order that, as actually occurred, the plaintiffs' vixen might miscarry. Had there been no evidence of spite, and had the damage been caused without malicious intent – merely as incidental, for example, to a shooting party – the plaintiffs would have had no claim.

In the second place, a person who is abnormally *sensitive*, or who owns property peculiarly liable to damage, must put up with inconveniences which cause harm to him by reason only of this exceptional sensitivity. Thus in *Robinson* v. *Kilvert* (1889), 41 Ch.D. 88, the plaintiff occupied the upper part of a house and the defendant the lower. For the purpose of his business the defendant had to use a furnace, and the heat thus generated damaged some brown paper which the plaintiff (a paper manufacturer) had in store. This paper was exceptionally sensitive to heat and ordinary paper would not have been damaged under the circumstances. For that reason it was held that the defendant's activities did not constitute a nuisance.

In the third place, though a single act may probably amount to a nuisance – as where I throw a banana skin onto the pavement and you slip upon it and are injured – the *duration* or *repetition* of an obnoxious activity may sometimes (upon the principle of "give and take") be relevant in determining whether that activity constitutes a nuisance. This proposition may be illustrated by contrasting the case of *Castle* v. *St. Augustine's Links* (1922), 38 T.L.R. 615, with *Stone* v. *Bolton*, [1950] 1 K.B. 201 (reversed in the House of Lords, [1951] A.C. 850, upon other grounds). In the former case the plaintiff was a taxi driver who lost his eye when a golf ball was sliced onto the road from a tee on the defendant's course. In the latter case the plaintiff was in the highway near a cricket ground when she was injured by a ball hit out of the ground. In the former case the plaintiff was held entitled to recover in nuisance because balls had *constantly* been driven onto the road at the place; the tee constituted a continuing danger. In the latter case the plaintiff failed to recover in nuisance because balls had *seldom* been known to be hit onto the road on previous occasions; the playing of cricket in the ground did not therefore constitute a continuing danger.

Private, as opposed to public, nuisance is essentially a remedy for an occupier of land, the right to sue inheres in him *qua* occupier; no one else is entitled to it, save a reversioner (see below, p. 330) who has a prospective interest in the land, and may therefore sue if the nuisance be such as to cause permanent injury. Thus, in *Malone* v. *Laskey*, [1907] 2 K.B. 141, where vibrations from an engine upon adjoining premises caused a cistern to fall upon and injure the wife of an occupier, it was held that she had no right of action in nuisance: she had no proprietary or possessory interest, actual or prospective, in the land. But it must be added that as the law *now* stands the wife might have had a claim in *negligence*.

A person will be liable in an action for nuisance if he either *creates* the nuisance, or, being in a position to abate (stop) it, he *permits it to continue* once he knows that it exists upon his premises. People will not, however, be liable for nuisances which arise upon their land in such circumstances that they could not reasonably be expected to have known of their existence. Thus, in *Caminer* v. *Northern and London Investment Trust, Ltd.*, [1951] A.C. 88, an elm tree, growing on land of which the defendants were the lessees, fell onto the highway, injuring the plaintiff and damaging his car. The tree was 130 years old and was affected by a disease of the roots, called "elm butt rot". Because while the tree was still growing the defendants could not by reasonable examination have discovered the existence of this disease, it was held that they were not liable.

7 THE RULE IN RYLANDS V. FLETCHER

Liability under the Rule in *Rylands* v. *Fletcher* (1868), L.R. 3 H.L. 330, has been selected for mention because it is an example (there are others) of what is sometimes called "*strict*" liability, *i.e.* it is an instance of the imposition of tortious liability independent of any "fault" or negligence on the part of the wrongdoer.

The facts of this case were the following. The defendant desired to construct a reservoir upon his land. He employed an independent contractor to execute the work. Unknown to the defendant there was a disused shaft of a coal mine under the site of the reservoir, which communicated with an adjoining mine belonging to the plaintiff. Through the contractor's negligence, this shaft was not discovered, and as a consequence, when the reservoir was filled, the plaintiff's mine was flooded and he suffered damage. He brought an action against the defendant. It was held that, despite the defendant's innocence, the plaintiff could succeed.

When the case (which eventually reached the House of Lords) was before the Court of Exchequer Chamber, Blackburn, J., propounded the doctrine which has now become known as the Rule in *Rylands* v. *Fletcher*; he said, "*the person who for his own purposes brings on his lands and collects and keeps there anything likely to do mischief if it escapes, must keep it in at his peril, and if he does not do so, is prima facie answerable for all the damage which is the natural consequence of its escape*" (L.R. 1 Ex. 265, 279–280).

This proposition was accepted by the House of Lords, and it has since been acted upon as a general rule of law. Lord Cairns, L.C., however added to it a rider which is now treated as a part of it. He said that, in order for the Rule to apply, the defendant's use of the land must be "*non-natural*". The courts have found some difficulty in defining what is a "non-natural" user. For example, *Rylands* v. *Fletcher* itself decides that the collection of a large quantity of water upon one's land is "non-natural"; on the other hand in *Read* v. *Lyons* (below) Viscount Simon doubted whether the making of munitions for the Government in a factory in time of war does amount to a "non-natural" user. The truth seems to be that the distinction between "natural" and "non-natural" user must be one which depends, as Lord Porter said in the same case, upon "all the circumstances of the time and place".

Two points require notice. First, the Rule applies to things "*likely to do mischief if they escape*". Whether a thing is one which is "mischievous" raises a question. The following things have, among others, been held to fall within the rule: gas, electricity, fumes, rusty wire from a fence, explosions, a flag-pole. But this list is capable of expansion as fresh circumstances arise. Second, in order to give rise to "*Rylands v. Fletcher*" liability there must be an "escape". This point was made clear in *Read v. Lyons & Co., Ltd.*, [1947] A.C. 156. The plaintiff was an inspector of munitions in the defendant's factory in wartime. While she was on the premises a shell exploded, and she was injured, and this explosion could not be attributed to negligence on the part of anybody. It was held that the plaintiff could not recover under the Rule in *Rylands v. Fletcher*, for her injury was not caused by anything that had "escaped" from the premises. (It was further indicated, though not decided, that, in any event, liability under the Rule ought not to apply in the case of claims for injuries to the *person*; though under the existing law it probably does.)

Defences – Though this liability is "strict", and exists despite the absence of intention or lack of care, there are, nevertheless, several defences to an action under the Rule in *Rylands v. Fletcher*. The following should be noted –

(*i*) Where the plaintiff has consented to permit the defendant to bring the mischievous thing upon his property there can be no liability under the Rule; though the defendant may of course be liable if he has been negligent. Thus, where a house is divided into flats and water escapes from a cistern in an upper flat, and damages a lower flat, the lower owner will normally have no action under the Rule: the cistern being kept for the mutual benefit of both parties, the lower owner will be taken to have consented to the collection of the water.

(*ii*) Where the escape is due to the plaintiff's own fault he will have no action. For instance, if a man were to remove a retaining-wall, so as to cause his neighbour's pond to overflow onto his own land, he could not invoke the Rule.

(*iii*) Where the escape is due to the wrongful act of a stranger there is no liability. Thus in *Box v. Jubb* (1879), 4 Ex.D. 76, a third party caused the defendant's reservoir to overflow onto the plaintiff's land by emptying his own reservoir into a stream which fed the defendant's. The defendant was not liable.

(*iv*) Whereas it is no defence for the defendant to plead that the escape was "accidental", it is a defence for him to show that it was due to an "Act of God" which he could not reasonably have foreseen and provided against. An "Act of God" is an event, such as a storm, which produces consequences independently of human agency. It is clear that not all Acts of God will excuse, but only such as are exceptional and cannot be guarded against. The defence has only succeeded in one reported case (and that of doubtful authority) where some artificial dams in a stream were washed away by a storm which was described by witnesses as the "heaviest in human memory".

(v) Where the mischievous substance is collected by the defendant under statutory authority he will not normally be liable under the Rule. For example, where a local authority has statutory power to carry a substance such as water or gas in a main, it will not normally be liable, in the absence of negligence, if the substance escapes and does damage.

These defences have been set out because they show that, though it is "strict", liability under the Rule can be avoided; but it must not be thought that they would not be available as defences to claims in other torts. Thus the first may be regarded as an instance of assumption of risk, the second and third as depending upon lack of causal connexion, the fourth as a case of accident and the fifth (statutory authority) as a universal excuse, since, being "sovereign", an Act of Parliament can, in law, achieve any result.

8 CONSPIRACY

Conspiracy is a *crime* of a very indeterminate nature, turning upon *agreement between* two *or more people* to commit a crime or to do some other unlawful act. There may thus be a charge against two or more people who have *combined* to (say) defraud (deceit being a crime, as well as being a tort) when the object of preferring the charge is to ensure conviction should the actual fraud, the principal charge against each individual, fail to be established at the trial. There may also be a charge of conspiracy where no crime is alleged to have been committed by the individuals concerned but the object of the combination falls within certain categories of activity deemed by the common law to be criminal *only when done in combination*. Recent examples of the latter kinds of prosecutions are *Shaw* v. *D.P.P.*, [1962] A.C. 220 (publication of "*The Ladies' Directory*", an advertising medium for prostitutes) where the charge was one of conspiracy to corrupt public morals, and *Kamara* v. *D.P.P.*, [1974] A.C. 104 (occupation of Sierra Leonian Embassy by demonstrating students) where the charge was one of conspiracy to trespass (a tort) – the House of Lords holding that the charge could only be established if the trespass involved the public domain (*e.g.* concerned a public building) or if the object of the intended trespass was to do actual damage.

The modern *tort* of conspiracy emerged later than the crime, but as early as *Gregory* v. *Duke of Brunswick* (1843), 6 Man. & G. 205 it was held to be actionable for a group of barrackers to hiss an actor off the stage. The potentialities of the tort, like those of the crime, are thus wide; but, being in origin an action on the case, not only must a combination to injure the plaintiff be proved, but also *actual* damage. It is thus in general a tort (conspiracy) for *two or more people to combine to injure another or others so as to cause them actual damage.* But in practice actions for conspiracy have been confined to cases of damage caused to business interests in the course of commercial or industrial competition; and, in this field – especially since the enlightening decision of the House of Lords in *Crofter Hand Woven Harris Tweed* v. *Veitch*, [1942]˙A.C. 435 – it is possible to be reasonably specific. In that case it was made clear, after some fifty years of judicial vacillation, that *a combination which has the predominant object of inflicting wilful injury upon the business interests of another is unlawful, and, if damage to these interests does in fact ensue, there is a cause of action in conspiracy.* But this proposition must be qualified by stressing the importance of the element of *motive*; for where it is proved that the infliction of the damage, though intentional, was merely incidental, and that the *predominant* object of the agreement was blameless (for example, an honest desire to promote the conflicting, though legitimate, interests of the parties to it), then there will be no conspiracy, and no action will lie.

It may assist the reader to grasp the implications of this branch of the law if the facts of the *Harris Tweed Case* are recited. The defendants were two trade union officials. The plaintiffs, who were producers of tweed cloth in the island of Lewis, in the Outer Hebrides, conducted their business by obtaining yarn, ready-spun, from the mainland, distributing it to crofters on the island, for weaving in their homes, and then sending the cloth back to the mainland for "finishing" and marketing. This process was cheaper than the process employed by certain rival island concerns which, while also employing the crofters to weave, spun their own yarn and also "finished" their cloth on the island. Ninety per cent of the workers in these mills were members of the defendants' union, and so were the dockers of Stornoway, the port of Lewis. The defendants, amongst other things, not here essential to relate, approached the mill owners with a request for higher pay for their mill-worker members, and this request was refused upon the ground that the plaintiffs' competition made such a course impossible. The defendants, then, in order to achieve their object by forcing the plaintiffs to agree to a general island scheme of minimum prices, by agreement between themselves, instructed the dockers to refuse to handle the plaintiffs' goods as it passed on its way to and from the island. This, without committing any legal wrong, even a breach of contract, the dockers did; thus causing financial loss to the plaintiffs by delaying the transit of their cloth. Upon these facts, the plaintiffs sued the defendants for conspiracy. The House of

Lords, after considering and explaining certain well-known, but per-
plexing, decisions of its own, held that the claim failed because the
defendants' predominant object was to improve the wage prospects of
their members by preventing unregulated competition on the island,
a legitimate object for trade union officials to pursue.

Two further points require consideration. *First*, the reader may
wonder why, in the law of conspiracy, it is necessary to prove the agreement of a minimum of *two or more*. Why two? Why not more or less?
One man may be as powerful as a host, yet, as long as he does not trans-
gress the criminal law or the law of torts, he may inflict wanton damage
upon others with impunity (see *The Mayor of Bradford* v. *Pickles*, above,
p. 306 and *Allen* v. *Flood*, above, p. 279). The answer, once again, is
that because the tort of conspiracy is allied to the crime of conspiracy,
conspiracy, in its civil form, retains the element of combination, which
originally made it an offence: it was created by the Court of Star
Chamber because *combinations* of individuals are sometimes dangerous
to the State, and a combination of two is the smallest form of combination. *Second*, ever since the Trade Disputes Act 1906 the activities of those
who indulge in trade disputes have been shielded from claims in conspiracy and certain allied torts. The relevant enactment now is the Trade
Union and Labour Relations Act 1974 which provides (s. 13 (4)) that
"An *agreement or combination* by two or more persons to do or to procure
the doing of any act *in contemplation or furtherance of a trade dispute is not
actionable* in tort if the act is one which, if done without any such agreement or combination, *would not be actionable in tort*". And since by
s. 13 (2) it is declared that "an act done by a person in contemplation
or furtherance of a trade dispute is *not actionable in tort* on the ground
only that it is *an interference* with the trade, business or employment of
another person, or *with the right of another person to dispose of his capital
or labour as he wills*" a conspiracy to injure in contemplation of furtherance of a trade dispute is not actionable unless its objective (*e.g.* to
maim) is in itself illegal. "*Trade dispute*" is defined by s. 29 (1) so as to
include (*inter alia*) disputes as to terms and conditions of employment,
allocation of work, facilities for officials of trade unions and negotiating
machinery. And by the (perhaps unfortunate) s. 29 (3) it is provided that
"There is a trade dispute ... even though it relates to matters outside
Great Britain".

9   INTERFERENCE WITH CONTRACTUAL RELATIONS

Like conspiracy, this tort is one of comparatively recent origin. It began
with *Lumley* v. *Gye* (1853), 2 E. & B. 216 where, as the reader will remember, the defendant induced Joanna Wagner, a celebrated singer, to

break her contract to sing for the plaintiff, an impresario: and it was held to be a tort *maliciously to induce a breach of contract*. Since then the tort has lost its youthful simplicity and has extended well beyond mere "*inducement*" to breach of contract.

The requirement of "malice" was dropped before the end of the nineteenth century, though *knowledge* of the existence of the contract was essential; but the element of "inducement" has been expanded to include *interference* in other ways, e.g. X will commit the modern tort if, A having a contract with B which necessitates the use of certain tools, X removes the tools so as to stop the performance of the contract.

Further, provided that "*unlawful means*" are employed to interfere with the contract the interference *need not* now *be direct*. Thus in *Daily Mirror Newspapers, Ltd.* v. *Gardner*, [1968] 2 Q.B. 768 an injunction was granted against officials of a retailers trade union in the following circumstances. In the interests of their union the officials sought to induce their members (retailers having newspaper shops) to stop taking supplies from wholesalers who were themselves under contract to buy the papers from the plaintiff newspaper proprietors. The officials' action, being *unlawful* as a breach of the Restrictive Trade Practices Act 1956, the Court of Appeal held that this *indirect* attack upon the wholesalers' contract with the plaintiffs – for the ceasing of the retailers' orders to the wholesalers would have forced the latter to break that contract – came within the ambit of the tort. The reader may think that the requirement that where the attack is indirect the "means" must be unlawful is illogical: and so it is – it in fact crept in because of the close involvement of this tort with the jungle of trade dispute law which, as we have seen, is solicitous in its protection of unions and their members.

Further, under the modern law "interference" need not amount to actual breach. This may be illustrated by *Torquay Hotel Co., Ltd.* v. *Cousins*, [1969] 2 Ch. 106 where union officials threatened to stop fuel oil supplies by Esso to the Imperial Hotel by calling upon tanker men (*in breach of their contracts* with Esso) to refuse delivery to the Imperial. It was held that, had this actually been done, the tort of interference would have been committed (indirectly by the use of "unlawful means" – breach of the tankermen/Esso contracts) even though the contract *attacked* – the Esso/Imperial contract for Esso to supply the oil – would *not* have been *broken* because there was a clause in it excusing them from delivery in the case of labour disputes, the situation which had actually arisen: but it would, of course, have been *interfered* with.

Still more, though *malice*, in the sense of spite or ill-will was, as has been explained, early discarded as an essential element of the tort, until recently it was thought that the defendant must *know* of the existence of the contract attacked; but even this requirement seems now to have been dropped and it may be enough if the interferer acts recklessly, in-different whether a breach of contract will result or not.

Where inducement is relevant – which of course it will not be where the interference takes the form of, for example, removing the tools essen-tial to performance of the contract, nor where the interferer knowingly engages the contract breaker upon some project incompatible with his performance of it – then some sort of persuasion must be used: mere *advice* is not enough. The distinction between persuasion and advice is not, however, always an easy one to make.

No action lies where the defendant acts with *lawful justification*. But what amounts to lawful justification is not at present very clear: on the one hand, by way of contrast with the law of conspiracy, it is no justifica-tion for members of an association (such as a miners' federation) to prove that they were acting in the interests of their association; but, on the other hand, in *Brimelow* v. *Casson*, [1924] 1 Ch. 302, it was held that members of an actors' protection association were justified in boycotting a theatrical manager – who persistently paid his chorus girls so little that they were forced to supplement their earnings by immorality – by in-ducing theatre proprietors not to engage him, and, in cases where they knew that contracts to do so were already in operation, to break them.

Finally, here, as in the case of conspiracy, the 1974 Act casts protection around trade disputes. It provides (s. 13 (1)) that "An act done by a person *in contemplation or furtherance of a trade dispute* shall not be actionable in tort on the ground only (*a*) that it *induces another person to break a con-tract of employment*." And s. 13 (3) declares that "an act which by reason of subsection (1) is *itself not actionable* . . . shall *not* be regarded as the doing of an *unlawful act* or the use of *unlawful means* for the purpose of establish-ing liability in tort". Thus inducement to breach and interference with performance (the *Torquay Case*) are covered. Section 13 (3) would seem to give protection in a case like the *Torquay Case*, where the "unlawful means" consisted of inducement to breach, but not in a case like *Gardner's* where the means were defiance of the 1956 Act. It is also important to note that the contract attacked need *not* be a contract *of employment*: so that if, in the course of a trade dispute, union action were to force firm A to break its contract to *supply materials* to firm B by, say, calling out A's drivers in breach of their contract with A the situation would be covered.

NOTE. If the controversial Trade Union and Labour Relations (Amendment) Bill 1976 becomes law s. 13 (1) (*a*) will be modified after "to break a contract": thus – "*or interferes or induces any other person to interfere with its performance.*"

10 INTIMIDATION

Before *Rookes* v. *Barnard*, [1964] A.C. 1129 there was some doubt whether there was such a tort as "intimidation", but it was there settled that there is. The essence of this tort is the causing of harm to another person by means of *violence* or *threats*. The kind of situation envisaged is where B by violence or threats either forces A to do or refrain from doing something to A's loss or by similar means coerces X to do or refrain from doing something which causes A loss. Where *threats*, as opposed to violence, are involved they must be threats to do something unlawful – whether a crime, a tort or a mere breach of contract. Thus in an old case the plaintiff was held entitled to claim against the defendant when the latter fired guns and thus drove African traders away from the plaintiff's ship whereby the former lost trade; and in *Rookes* v. *Barnard* the plaintiff was permitted to recover against trade union officials who caused the plaintiff to lose his employment by threatening to call their men out on strike (in breach of agreement by the men not to strike), with the consequence that the plaintiff's employers (B.O.A.C.) dismissed him.

The actual effect of *Rookes' Case* was, however, annulled by legislation which cast protection around intimidation in relation to trade disputes. The relevant provision is now the Trade Union and Labour Relations Act 1974 (as amended), s. 13 (1) (*b*): "An act done by a person in *contemplation or furtherance of a trade dispute* shall not be actionable in tort upon the ground only ... that it consists in his *threatening* that a contract of employment (whether one to which he is a party or not) *will be broken* or that he will *induce another person* to break a contract of *employment* to which that other person is a party." This protection is, of course, limited; it embraces threats, not violence, and it affects intimidation only in relation to breach of, or to interference with, contract. Here again, s. 13 (3) applies.

NOTE. If the 1976 Bill becomes law, s. 13 (1) (*b*) will be modified after the words "that a contract" thus – "(whether one to which he is a party or not) will be *broken* as its performance interfered with, or that he will *induce another person to break a contract* or to *interfere with its performance*".

11 MALICIOUS FALSEHOOD

This is a compendious term used to denote a group of torts concerned with the making of damaging imputations.

Essentially, malicious falsehood is committed when a person damages another by making false and *malicious* imputations – written, oral, or otherwise – which cause that other person damage in respect of some interest other than his reputation. The damage here envisaged is usually damage to business interests, but the tort is not entirely confined to the redress of damage of this sort: for example, in an old case, a lady succeeded in an action against the defendant who wrote to a man she was about to marry, falsely alleging that she was married to him (the defendant), with the result, in the antique phrase of the reporter, that she "lost her marriage".

Malicious falsehood differs from *fraud* (see above, pp. 240–242) in that it lies in respect of an obnoxious statement addressed not to the person complaining of the damage, but to some other person, and (in a way, perhaps, more subtle) it differs from *defamation* (see above, pp. 302–304) in that it is concerned, as has been explained, with statements calculated to damage interests other than the right to reputation. It is true that an imputation against a man in respect of his business or office *may* amount to actionable defamation – as where one alleges incompetence in a surgeon, or says of a trader that his goods are spurious – and, indeed, this kind of imputation, if oral, is actionable as slander, without proof of special damage; but in order to fall within the scope of the law of defamation, the statement must be of a kind – as the two above examples are – that is calculated not merely to damage the plaintiff in respect of the goodwill of his profession or business, but to damage his character as well. Malicious falsehood, to the contrary, is *not* concerned with *reputation*. The point may be illustrated by reference to the facts of *Ratcliffe v. Evans*, [1892] 2 Q.B. 524, the starting point of the modern law relating to this tort. B published in a newspaper a false statement to the effect that A had ceased to carry on business, and naturally A's business declined; though the statement was clearly no libel, for no one thinks the worse of a man for shutting up shop, there being evidence of malice, it was held to be actionable as *malicious falsehood*. By contrast, in *Drummond-Jackson v. British Medical Association*, [1970] 1 All E.R. 1094 it was held that an article in a journal which charged the plaintiff with having practised a dangerous dental technique was *libellous*.

Although it is possible in an action for slander of title (and probably in any action for malicious falsehood) to obtain a declaratory judgment (vindicating the plaintiff's rights without awarding either damages or an injunction, in the absence of proof of malice) *malice* is normally an essential ingredient in all forms of malicious falsehood; and "malice" here signifies some indirect or improper motive in the defendant, *e.g.* a desire to inflict injury. Further, at common law, proof of special damage (*i.e.* proof that some particular loss has been caused) was normally essential; but, by s. 3, the Defamation Act 1952 made proof of this unnecessary where either the statement complained of is both calculated to cause pecuniary damage and is published in a permanent form – including broadcast statements – or is calculated to cause damage to the plaintiff in respect of his current business or profession. Since, in modern times, most cases of malicious falsehood have concerned imputations of the latter type, it can now, therefore, be said that proof of *special damage* will *not* normally be necessary.

It remains to mention two special varieties of malicious falsehood:

slander of title and slander of goods. *Slander of title* is committed by a defendant who falsely and maliciously disparages another person's title to property in a manner calculated to cause him damage: for example, where Y falsely and maliciously alleges that X is offering certain goods for sale, in infringement of a patent vested in Z. *Slander of goods* is committed when a person falsely and maliciously disparages goods manufactured or sold by another, even though his motive be to boost his own sales; but a statement by B that his goods are better than A's will not form grounds for an action because, amongst other things, if the judges were to countenance actions upon this basis they would be encouraging the use of the court as a forum for advertising.

12 PASSING OFF

Partly because it was originally developed upon divergent lines by the common law courts, on the one hand, and by the Court of Chancery, on the other, partly because it takes many forms, and partly because its exact scope is still unsettled, this is a difficult tort to define. But its name supplies an indication of its essence: essentially it is the wrong of damaging the business interests of another by doing acts calculated to delude the public that one's own business activities are his. It will be appreciated that this may be done in many ways, and the reader must turn to larger works than this for detailed illustration; but three examples can be given. First – and this is, indeed, the field in which the tort originated – it is passing off to adopt or imitate the trade mark or trade name of another; and, although properly *registered* trade marks now have special protection under the Trade Marks Act 1938, which continues the policy of previous similar legislation, this aspect of passing off is still important to possessors of *unregistered*, or improperly registered, trade marks; for the Act, while permitting a special action for "infringement" only in respect of registered marks, expressly preserves the common law rules as to passing off. Second, it is passing off to use any device calculated to persuade the public that, in dealing with the defendant, they are really dealing with the plaintiff: a simple example of this kind of situation is to be found where Y decorates his shop premises in a way calculated to induce the public to mistake them for X's. Third, it is passing off to imitate the appearance or "get up" of another person's wares; for example, by copying the labels on his bottles. But it must be admitted that neither the definition attempted nor the examples given can furnish the reader with a full understanding of this tort: for, to take only one example of the difficulties, it is also passing off to sell the plaintiff's wares of one quality upon a misrepresentation that they are the plaintiff's wares of another quality.

This tort is essentially concerned with damage to *business interests* and although, where it is clear that the act done is one which is calculated to cause such damage, no special damage – *e.g.* loss of particular customers – need be proved, the damage complained of must, nevertheless, be damage of this kind: an action for passing off will therefore fail if the act in question is not calculated to affect the plaintiff's business interests. This may be illustrated by *McCulloch* v. *May*, [1947] 2 All E.R. 845: the plaintiff, a well-known broadcaster, known to the public as "Uncle Mac", challenged the right of the defendants to sell a cereal under the same name: the action failed, for broadcasting and the selling of cereals are poles apart, and the two activities do not clash in a business sense. So also, it has been held that where B, who lives in the same street as A, capriciously adopts for his own private house the same name as A's, A will have no claim for passing off: however much inconvenience may be caused, for B has not attacked A in respect of his *business* interests.

Although at one time a different view was held, it is now settled (to the mind of the theorist, somewhat inelegantly) that passing off is to be regarded as a species of invasion of *proprietary* right; hence the defendant's state of mind is not a determining factor to take into account, and neither fraud not malice need essentially be alleged. The remedies open to the plaintiff are an injunction to restrain further interference with his interests, damages, or, where appropriate, an order for an account of profits which have accrued from the defendant's activities: in proper cases the court will also order any offending material, such as imitative labels or devices, to be delivered up for destruction or erasure.

This tort affects economic matters and this means that it can be affected, as one decision has already shown, by EEC legislation.

C REMEDIES IN THE LAW OF TORTS

The two principal remedies available to a plaintiff in an action in tort are damages and injunctions.

i Damages – The main purpose of awarding damages in tort, as in the case of breach of contract, is to compensate the plaintiff for the loss he has suffered. The assessment of the amount due is often a simple matter; for instance in a case of conversion a correct assessment can usually be made by reference to the value of the goods of which the plaintiff has been deprived. Assessment is not, however, *always* a simple matter. For instance, where the plaintiff has sustained physical injuries, damages may be awarded him as compensation for his pain and suffering, and they may now also be awarded for loss of amenity (*i.e.* for loss of the ability to enjoy the accustomed pleasures of life) and for "loss of expectation of life" where the injuries are such that they may be proved to have shortened this "expectation". The difficulty of assessment under this latter head is obvious, and the courts experienced great difficulty in arriving at a proper sum until the House of Lords laid down certain rules in respect of it, in the case of *Benham* v. *Gambling*, [1941] A.C. 157. These rules were that, at any rate where through infancy, unconsciousness or otherwise the plaintiff was not mentally aware of the loss, the sum awarded must be moderate, and that it must be measured, not by a statistical test as to the number of days by which the plaintiff's expectation of life has been shortened, but by reference to the prospects of happiness of which he has been deprived. In any event the figure to be awarded should be less in the case of a child than in that of an adult.

Damages are classified in a number of ways. The most important distinction is between "*general*" and "*special*" damages. "General" damages are damages at large which are not susceptible of exact calculation: *e.g.* for pain and suffering or loss of a limb. It is for the court or jury to assess the amount. "Special" damages are awarded in respect of such losses (*e.g.* medical expenses or loss of earnings prior to trial) as are exactly calculable and they must be specifically set out in the pleadings.

Damages may be "*nominal*" or "*substantial*". Nominal damages are awarded when the plaintiff can prove that his rights have been infringed, but is unable to prove any *actual* damage. Thus if X walks upon Y's land, he commits a trespass, and nominal damages, say five pence or even less, may be awarded against him, even though he did no damage. Substantial damages are damages awarded, not in respect of the mere infringement of a right, but in respect of actual damage, however large or small. Where *actual* damage is the gist of the action, as in an action for negligence, nominal damages can of course never be awarded.

As has just been stated, as in contract so in tort the main aim of damages is to compensate the plaintiff for his loss, however difficult it may be to do this in money terms, so that, in general, they are *compensatory*, but they may also be *aggravated*: for instance if an act, such as slapping a man in the face, is done wilfully and publicly it may cause greater than normal injury to his feelings and hence the damages required for compensation may be larger ("aggravated") than the act complained of would normally justify. In certain special circumstances, however, the courts will depart from the compensative principle and permit the awarding of damages ("*exemplary*", "*punitive*" or "*vindictive*") based upon the principle of punishing the defendant rather than of compensating the plaintiff. These circumstances (the principle being a deviation from the normal compensatory rule) are not common and they were defined by the House of Lords in *Rookes* v. *Barnard* (above, p. 314). First such damages may be awarded where – as to John Wilkes in the great constitutional case of *Wilkes* v. *Wood* (1763), Lofft. 1 – the plaintiff has been injured by arbitrary action of government servants: second, in cases where the defendant's conduct is such as to be calculated to make a profit for himself by his tort which exceeds any compensation which he would usually have to pay the plaintiff: in the third place where statute authorizes their award.

The rules as to remoteness of damage in relation to the law of contract have been discussed above (p. 257); the reader will therefore be familiar with the meaning of "remoteness". It will be recalled that in contract damage is "proximate", or "direct", under the first Rule in *Hadley* v. *Baxendale*, if it arises "naturally" from the breach of contract; *i.e.* if it is such as the parties must be taken reasonably to have foreseen as likely to follow, in the ordinary course of things, from the breach.

In tort until quite recently it could have been asserted with reasonable certainty that the rule was different, and that the test of remoteness was one of direct *consequence*. The defendant would of course be liable for all *intended* consequences, whether direct or indirect, but he would also be liable for all consequences *directly* connected with his wrongful act or omission whether or no they were such that he ought reasonably to have foreseen the probability of their ensuing. Establish the wrong to the plaintiff, and the defendant must foot the bill for the consequent harm; what ought to have been foreseen, in the words of the late Lord Sumner, "goes to culpability" (*i.e.* in torts such as Negligence where "foresight" is a relevant element in liability) "not to compensation". It should of course be noted that even this seemingly harsh proposition does not spell compensation without limit, for the defendant would only be held responsible for such damage to the plaintiff as is causally connected with his wrong; he would not, for instance, be liable for such injury as the plaintiff avoidably brings upon himself, nor for injury due to the intervention of other people, nor for extraordinary intervening occurrences such as earthquakes; for the problem here involved is one of causation (see above, p. 295), and a person should never be held liable for what he has not caused.

The rule so stated is the law laid down by the Court of Appeal in *Re Polemis and Furness, Withy & Co.*, [1921] 3 K.B. 560. The facts of this case were that a ship was hired under charter and during the voyage some of the petrol containers which constituted her cargo leaked, and her hold became full of petrol vapour. At a port of call a stevedore in the employment of the charterers negligently let a plank fall into the hold. For some unexplained reason the fall of this plank touched off a spark; there was an explosion, and in the resulting conflagration the ship became a total loss. The owners sued the charterers for the value of the ship – nearly £200,000 (a large sum then!). It was found as a fact that "the causing of the spark could not have been reasonably anticipated from the falling of the (plank), though some damage to the ship might reasonably have been anticipated". The court held the charterers liable for the full amount. Once the stevedore (the servant of the charterers) had been proved to be negligent – as he was, for "some damage to the ship" might reasonably have been anticipated from his carelessness – all damage directly following upon his act was, under the rule as stated above, recoverable. The limits of the rule may be illustrated by adding a fanciful variation to the facts: suppose that some malevolent stranger had, unknown to the stevedore or to the charterers, placed an explosive charge beneath the plank and that this charge had been detonated by the fall, then the catastrophe would have been caused by the stranger rather than by the stevedore, and the charterers would have escaped liability for anything but a nominal sum for such harm as the actual falling of the plank might have been assumed to have caused.

In 1961, however, the Judicial Committee in *Overseas Tankship (U.K.), Ltd.* v. *Mort's Dock and Engineering Co. Ltd (The Wagon Mound (No. 1))*, [1961] A.C. 388, decided to depart from the "direct consequence" test of *Re Polemis* and to adopt in its stead a *"foresight"* rule similar to, but not the same as, the familiar "foresight" test of Rule I in *Hadley* v. *Baxendale* (see above, p. 257). This case arose out of the same occurrence as *The Wagon Mound (No. 2)* – above, p. 294 – but the plaintiffs were different, and the two cases also differed on a matter of vital evidence: for in *The Wagon Mound (No. 1)* the evidence was that no one could at that time be expected to know that furnace oil floating on water *could* be set alight. Hence, the Judicial Committee, in *The Wagon Mound (No. 1)*, having decided that "foresight" was to be the determining test rather than direct consequence, by no possible means, however long-sighted the "foresight" might be found to be, could the defendants be held liable. The *Polemis* test would, of course, have produced the opposite result, since the ship's engineer was undoubtedly initially negligent – and, indeed, even doing a criminal act by committing a public nuisance – and the damage sustained was the direct consequence of that negligence.

"Foresight" thus rules in tort as well as in contract but whereas, as will be remembered, "foresight" in contract is limited to such consequences as the parties might have been expected to contemplate as the *probable* result of the breach, in tort, by contrast, there are some kinds of circumstances (as was ruled in *The Wagon Mound (No. 2)* – in which the defendant will be expected to foresee results which are by no means probable and held liable if he fails to guard against them.

Moreover, the decision of *The Wagon Mound (No. 1)* in favour of "foresight" has to be qualified. In the first place the Judicial Committee were there solely concerned with the tort of Negligence and there was therefore some reason to suppose that the new rule was only intended

to apply to *that* tort: for one thing, since Negligence consists in the infliction of negligent harm, and the concept of negligence itself involves
the foresight element, there is logic in maintaining that the defendant's
liability ought to cease within the limits of such damage as he has foresee-
ably caused. The rule has, however, not been so confined; for in *The
Wagon Mound (No. 2)* it was held that the "foresight" test (in its tortious
guise) also governs in cases of Nuisance, whether resting upon a basis
of lack of care or not, and whether public or private. But beyond this
that decision does not go: and it is at present therefore still possible that
the *Polemis* rule governs other torts; especially torts of strict liability,
such as those within the rule in *Rylands* v. *Fletcher*. And the Court of
Appeal has held that it does apply to the tort of deceit (fraud) – as to
which see above, p. 240.

In the second place it has been ruled that where *foreseeable* injury is
caused and *unforeseeable* injury of similar *type*, or kind, ensues the defendant will be made to pay not only for the former injury but also for the
latter. Thus, for example, it was held that where a man received a slight
burn on the lip as the result of his employers' negligence and entirely
unforeseeably this burn produced lethal cancer, a claim could be had in
respect of the unfortunate man's death; for both injuries, the burn and
the cancer (or at least so the court purported to think), were similar in
"type". Thus in a wide area, even where Negligence is involved, the
direct consequence (*Polemis*) rule still prevails.

It may be wondered which of these conflicting rules is "right". To
this no answer can be given. B commits a wrong to A and unforeseeable
damage results to A. Should A's right to compensation depend upon
the limits of B's foresight of the result? Or should it depend upon
whether the consequential loss follows upon B's act, or upon some
extraneous cause? Which solution is the right one depends upon fundamental policies which, due to our case-law system which confines the
courts to the consideration of the issues immediately before them, seldom come to the fore in English judicial decisions. If the proper aim
of the law of torts is solely to compensate for injury (which many believe
to be the case) then of the two parties B is the less innocent and, hard
though it may seem to B, the *Polemis* rule would appear to be justified.
But if the aim is to inhibit socially undesirable conduct by visiting the
wrongful actor with the unpleasant consequence of having to pay
damages, frankly to punish him, then no one should be punished beyond
the limits of his foresight, and the *Wagon Mound* is right. Historically,
since crime was, at least partially, the progenitor of tort, there is something to be said for the latter approach; but in a modern context it looks
out of date, since punishment is now a matter for the criminal law.

It has already been pointed out (above, p. 197) that in assessing damages in respect of claims for personal injuries account must be taken of social security and of industrial injury benefits received. And it must be added that in a claim for damages the amount of tax which a successful plaintiff would have had to pay on future earnings is taken into account by way of deduction from the damages he is to receive from the defendant who has deprived him of those earnings. This rule is applicable to claims based upon breach of contract as well as to claims in tort.

ii Injunctions – These are the creation of Equity, they are orders of the court commanding something to be done (*"mandatory"* injunction) or forbidding something (*"prohibitory"* injunction). As an alternative to claiming damages a plaintiff may, in the case of many torts, seek an injunction to restrain the commission or continuance of the tort. Applications for injunctions are most commonly made in order to restrain nuisances.

Injunctions, being equitable remedies, were originally granted only by the Court of Chancery, but they may now issue from any Division of the High Court. Like all other equitable remedies they are discretionary; the court is not bound to grant them, and it will usually refuse to do so if an award of damages will afford adequate compensation to the plaintiff. Since the Chancery Amendment Act 1858 (Lord Cairns' Act) the court has had power to award damages either in addition to, or in substitution for, an injunction. An injunction may be sought, not only where a wrong has already been committed, but also where there is a clear likelihood that it will be committed unless restrained (*Quia timet* injunction – "because he fears"). For example, if X threatens to build, and is about to build, a structure which will obscure the light to Y's windows (a form of nuisance) Y may sometimes obtain a *quia timet* injunction to prevent this infringement of his rights.

Finally, injunctions may be *"interlocutory"* or *"perpetual"*. An interlocutory injunction is one which is granted, if the court is satisfied that there is a serious case to be tried provisionally before the hearing of an action, to restrain the defendant's activities and maintain the *status quo* until the case has been heard. A perpetual injunction is one which is granted after the issue between the parties has been tried.

D LIMITATION

The Law on this matter is governed by the Limitation Act 1939, as amended by the Law Reform (Limitation of Actions &c.) Act 1954, the Limitation Act 1963 and the Limitation Act 1975. The 1939 Act prescribes a period of *six* years "from the date on which the cause of action accrued" as the normal period within which actions founded upon tort must be brought. Normally, therefore, where the tort consists of one simple act, such as converting a watch, the plaintiff's right of action runs from the date of the act which constitutes the tort. Sometimes, however, the injury does not become apparent until after the doing of the act which causes it; as, for example, where a man, by digging upon his own land, interferes with his neighbour's right of support. In this case the cause of action does not "accrue" until the damage occurs.

Where a tort consists of a continuing wrong, *e.g.* nuisance by continuing vibration, a new cause of action arises daily as long as the tort continues to be committed. Thus, if a tort of this sort continues for, say, seven years, and the plaintiff then brings an action for the first time, his right of action in respect of damage suffered in the first year, but in respect of that year only, will be barred.

In the case of actions for *negligence, nuisance* or *breach of duty* where the damages consist of or include damages in respect of *personal injuries* to any person the claim must (as in the case of a breach of contract) be brought within *three* years of accrual, and the provisions of the 1975 Act apply (see above, p. 264). The words "breach of duty" include trespasses.

The provisions of the Acts relating to disabilities and fraud apply to actions in tort as well as to actions for breaches of contract (see above, p. 265).

The Maritime Conventions Act 1911, fixes a *two* year period of limitation for actions in respect of collisions at sea.

Actions under the Fatal Accidents Acts must be commenced within *three years* from the date of *death* or from the date of *knowledge* of the injury on the part of the person for whose benefit the action is brought, whichever is the later: subject, in certain circumstances, to a discretion in the court to extend the period (Limitation Act 1975, s. 1). Further, by s. 4 of the same Act it is provided that in assessing damages payable to a widow under the Fatal Accidents Acts "there shall not be taken into account the remarriage of the widow or her prospects of remarriage."

CHAPTER 10

THE LAW OF PROPERTY

This chapter will be devoted to a discussion of the rights and interests which may be enjoyed in respect of property, and of the methods by which it may be transferred from one living person to another. The rules which govern devolution upon death will be treated separately in Chapter 13.

In any discussion of the Law of Property it is essential to deal with the land law separately. The reason for this is not far to seek. Land is, in the quaint phrase of Sir Edward Coke, "of all elements the most ponderous and immovable"; land endures, all other property perishes, alters or is lost in the course of time. It follows that the rights and interests which can be enjoyed in respect of land are necessarily more complex than those which can be enjoyed in respect of any other property. Moreover, as will be seen, this natural distinction between land and other forms of property was accentuated in England by the influence of feudalism.

THE LAND LAW

A INTRODUCTORY

The modern land law is largely founded upon certain statutes enacted in 1925. For our present purpose the most important of these are the Law of Property Act (L.P.A.), the Settled Land Act (S.L.A.), the Administration of Estates Act (A.E.A.), the Land Charges Act (L.C.A.) – now largely replaced by the L.C.A. 1972 – and the Land Registration Act (L.R.A.). These statutes will be referred to individually by the abbreviations indicated, collectively as the "Property Acts". They did not purport to introduce a self-sufficient code, but only to effect far-reaching changes in the land law and in the methods of conveying (transferring) land, and it is therefore still helpful to have some knowledge of the law prior to 1926 in order to understand the present law. Accordingly, by

way of introduction, it is proposed first to define the subject of inquiry
by explaining what is meant by "land", then to give a brief account
of the old land law, lastly to outline the purposes and general effect of
the Property Acts.

The Meaning of "Land"

The ordinary purchaser of land probably pictures himself as acquiring
a visible portion of the earth's surface. In fact the law entitles him to
something more than this, for, broadly speaking, in the eye of the law
"land" includes the surface of the land, everything beneath the surface,
and everything affixed to the land. Further, the right to land carries with
it rights of property over the air-space above the land.

And there is even more to it than this; for the word "land" in strict
law includes all "*hereditaments*" (Latin "*heres*" = heir), that is everything
which would at common law descend to the heir at law upon intestacy
(see below, p. 448). And such things included both "*corporeal*" and "*incorporeal*" hereditaments. The former are physical; the land itself and
things such as walls or houses adhering to it: the latter are non-physical
and include, *inter alia*, rights of way apurtenant to land (in the ordinary
sense of the word) and a number of legal notions such as *rent charges*
(sums of money charged upon lands). Thus, for historical reasons which
cannot here be mentioned, "land" in the legal sense embraces more than
a visible plot of soil.

Corporeal things attached to land are known as "fixtures" and the
term *fixture* is a term of art. *Prima facie* anything permanently attached
to the land, or to something else which is itself attached to the land,
is a fixture; hence it is a part of the land and will pass automatically
with the land upon a transfer. The fact of attachment, however, only
raises a *presumption* that the article concerned has lost its quality of being
a chattel (see below, p. 380) and has become technically part of the land.
This presumption may be rebutted by showing, for instance, that the
article is something in itself wholly unconnected with the use of land,
and that it has only been "annexed" (attached) for its better enjoyment
as a chattel. Thus, in *Leigh* v. *Taylor*, [1902] A.C. 157, it was held that
a valuable tapestry did not become a fixture by being battened to a wall.

There are, however, certain things which cannot be subject to private
ownership and however much they may be attached to the land they
cannot pass to a purchaser. Examples are unmined gold and silver and
(as a result of legislation) petroleum and coal.

The Old Land Law

The land law as it existed in 1925 was largely judge-made. It derived from two main sources. First, from principles which had been evolved by the courts of common law in mediaeval times. Secondly, from rules of equity which had been evolved by the Court of Chancery to adapt the mediaeval law to the needs of later ages.

Certain peculiarities were inherited from the mediaeval law. For the sake of clarity these may be enumerated –

i Tenure – The mediaeval law was designed to meet the requirements of *feudalism*. Feudalism was a system of government through the agency of landholders. In feudal theory no man could "own" land, save the king. All the land in England was divided among tenants (French, "*tenir*" = to hold) some of whom were *free* and others *unfree*.

The free tenants held their land either directly, or indirectly, by sub-grant from a superior tenant, *de rege*, "under the king". Every tenant, whether he were a tenant-in-chief holding directly of the king, or a sub-tenant holding of a mesne lord, owed duties to his overlord; these duties were manifold and were ultimately designed to supply the lack of a central government by ensuring certain basic *services*. For instance, there was *knight-service*, the duty of performing military service essential to the king; there was *sergeanty* which consisted of performing services – such as cup-bearer or mace bearer to the king ("grand" sergeanty) or performing lesser personal services ("petit" sergeanty); there was *socage* tenure, usually taking the form of fixed agricultural services, commuted by the fifteenth century to money payments ("quit rents"); there was *frankalmoign* (free alms), ecclesiastical tenure, by which the clergy might hold land in return for praying for the lord. Further, tenure carried with it certain "incidents", such as the lord's right to *wardship* and *marriage*, *i.e.* the right to enjoy the profits of the land during minority when a tenant died leaving an infant (21 boys, 14 girls) heir, and the right to dispose of infant tenants in marriage – which was valuable since an infant who refused the proferred marriage would forfeit the "value" of it to the lord. Every tenant who had sub-tenants had rights over them, such as the right to hold a court which they were bound to attend. By this means, with the king as ultimate overlord, the government of the country was carried on by a descending scale of landholders.

Beside free men, however, in mediaeval times there were serfs (or "villeins") who were unfree. Villeins originally held their land by unfree, or "villein" tenure. This was a form of bondage which obliged them to perform services for the lord of the manor in which they lived. They could not leave their holding; they were "bound to the soil". The status of villeinage, however, gradually became obsolete; villeins became free men, and the land which had once been held by villein tenure became subject to *copyhold* tenure. The term "copyhold" derived from the practice of recording tenancies of this type in the court roll of the manor in which the land was situated, the tenant being given a copy of the record as evidence of his title. The rules relating to copyhold differed in many respects from the rules relating to freehold tenure.

As a political system feudalism fell into decay within two hundred years of its introduction by the Normans. Though the Tenures Abolition Act 1660 converted all military tenures into free and common socage and most of the incidents appertaining to military tenures were then abolished, the idea of tenure remained long after the obligations incident to feudal land-holding had ceased to exist. And even today the theory of it remains in that "freehold" land (freehold being the basis upon which all land is now held) is historically no more than land held in free and common socage to which, of course, neither services nor incidents have for centuries attached.

ii   Estates – While the terms of the tenant's holding marked his tenure (*i.e.* knight-service, etc.), the extent (*i.e.* duration, *e.g.* life or fee simple) of the interest was known as his "*estate*" – the word is akin to the word "status". It survives in the terminology of the modern law.

iii   Freehold land, *i.e.* the land of a free tenant, called an "*estate of freehold*", was not devisable, that is to say it could not be disposed of by will. The reason for this was, probably, that the feudal overlord was entitled to certain rights upon the tenant's death. He was, for instance, sometimes entitled to a money payment called a "relief" from the heir. If the tenant were permitted to make a will the lord might be deprived of these rights.

During the mediaeval period another interest in land, beside the freehold estate, became common. This was the *term of years*, the forerunner of the modern leasehold interest. Terms of years were essentially different from freehold estates. The grant of a term was primarily looked upon as a commercial venture from which the grantor hoped to make a profit, and as such, it fell outside the feudal scheme of land tenure. This ostracism of the term of years had consequences which were important in the subsequent history of the law. These consequences were the following –

   a The tenant of freehold land who was dispossessed could recover the land by means of certain actions called *real* actions – "real" because they enabled him to recover the land itself *in rem* ("as a thing"). The termor (the holder of a term of years, corresponding to the modern "tenant") who was dispossessed was not entitled to the benefit of a real action. At first, indeed, his only remedy was an action for damages against his landlord.

b In the course of time the termor was granted a special form of action for the recovery of the land which was subject to his term. But it was not forgotten that he was denied the use of the real actions. This denial had lasting results. Chattels (goods) were, as we have seen (above, p. 304), never specifically recoverable; terms of years therefore appeared to have something in common with chattels. Hence terms of years came to be classified as *"chattels real"* in contradistinction to other interests in land, which were classified as *"real property"*; that is, property which could be recovered by real action.

c Chattels could be disposed of by will. It followed that terms of years, being in the nature of chattel interests, could also be disposed of by will. In this important respect they therefore differed from freehold estates.

d If a man died intestate, *i.e.* without making a will, the rules which governed the descent of land which he held for a term of years were similar to the rules which governed the descent of his chattels. Freehold land was subject to special rules of descent (see below, p. 380).

Such, then, were the chief peculiarities of the mediaeval land law.

Defects of the mediaeval law – The mediaeval land law suffered from two major defects. First, as has been explained, freehold land could not be disposed of by will. Secondly, the common law rules governing the limitation (grant) of freehold estates were severely restrictive.

Freehold estates had either to be *fee simple* estates, estates in *fee tail*, or *life estates*. A *fee simple* estate arose when land was limited (granted) to a man "and his heirs". This limitation gave the heirs nothing: the grantee acquired an interest as near to unrestricted ownership as it was possible to acquire under a system governed by the concept of tenure, and he could thus sell the land if he chose or give it away; but, of course, if he kept it till the time of his death, it would descend to his heirs.

Another form of disposition was a gift to "A and the heirs of his body" (or to A and certain designed lineal heirs, *e.g.* "To A and the heirs male of his body"). The object of this kind of disposition was to provide "family" land for a man (or woman) and his (or her) lineal descendants, with the intention that the land should revert to the donor or his successors if the line became extinct. Originally – probably in order to foster the policy of freedom of alienation, and to prevent the land from becoming "tied" in one line, a policy to which they have consistently adhered – just as they construed a disposition "To A and his heirs" as an out-and-out gift to A, so the courts construed this form of disposition as giving

A a fee simple *conditional* upon the birth of an heir of the designated class. Thus the claims both of the designated heirs and of the donor were frustrated. This somewhat perverse construction caused discontent which the *Statute De Donis Conditionalibus* (1285) was passed to allay. That Statute provided, in effect, that for the future dispositions of this nature should be strictly construed "*secundum formam in carta doni expressam*" (according to the true tenure of the deed of gift). A new form of estate was thus indirectly brought into being, which came to be known as a "*fee tail*" (French, *taillé* = "cut down") because, unlike a fee simple estate which *could* (although, if the fee simple tenant chose to dispose of the land, it need not) descend to the *general* heirs of the donee (lineal or collateral), the fee tail could only descend to the *limited* class of lineal heirs designated in the instrument of gift. Moreover, as a result of the provisions of the Statute, the fee tail differed from the fee simple in that the claims of the successive heirs and of the donor, upon the extinction of the designated line, were protected: when their turn came, they could claim the land, according to the terms of the original gift, whatever the original donee or their predecessors might have done – for example, if the donee sold it his successor in title could reclaim it – from the purchaser after the donee's death. But, from about 1472, even in the face of the provisions of the Statute, the courts reasserted their policy of fostering free alienation, and again frustrated the intentions of donors, by sanctioning the use of certain legal devices which enabled tenants in tail (*i.e.* the original donee and his successors) to bar the rights both of their successors in tail and of the person entitled to the reversion or remainder should the line become extinct; thus enabling the tenant in tail, if he wished, to sell the land free of the claims of the people entitled under the gift. As we shall see, the modern law governing entailed interests – the modern successors to estates in fee tail – has continued this policy (see below, p. 359).

A *life estate* arose when, for instance, land was granted to "A for life", or to "A during the life of B" (estate *pur autre vie* – "for the life of another").

Estates might be granted in *possession*, *i.e.* to take effect immediately, or they might be granted in *remainder*. In a grant, for instance, to "A for life and after A's death to B in fee simple", the grant to B was valid; it took effect "in remainder" because the land "remained away" from the grantor after the expiry of A's life estate. Further, estates in *reversion* were recognized. Thus if X, the tenant in fee simple, granted land to Y for life, X held the fee simple "in reversion" during Y's life; for after Y's death the land would "revert" to X.

For reasons which need not detain us, the mediaeval law hardly ventured to recognize any grants of freehold estates beyond these. In particular, it would not permit estates of freehold to be so limited that they would arise for the first time upon the happening of a *future* uncertain event.

Developments after the Middle Ages – From the early years of the fifteenth century, the Court of Chancery set to work to remedy these defects of the common law. The remedy was supplied through the instrumentality of the *use* (see below, Chapter 11). By means of this device it became possible to create *equitable* interests in freehold land which were capable of coming into being for the first time upon the death of the grantor. Thus the prohibition against the devise of freehold land was circumvented. Further, by means of the use, the Court of Chancery permitted *equitable interests*, different in nature from the old common law estates, to be created. In particular equitable *future interests* were allowed to be granted; these were capable of arising in ways which the common law had not permitted.

In respect of wills, the combined effect of the Statute of Wills (1540) and the Tenures Abolition Act (1660) rendered the assistance of equity unnecessary; for it made all land freely devisable. Moreover, as a result of the effect and interpretation of Henry VIII's famous Statute of Uses (1535) – which was not repealed until the Property Acts – a much wider range of *legal* estates became permissible than it had been possible to create in former times; for, under the provisions of this Statute, as a general rule, where one person became seised (possessed) of land to the *use* of another (see below, Chapter 11), then, in place of the equitable interest which the former would previously have held, he was for the future to be entitled to a *legal estate* to the extent of the interest granted. Nevertheless, by means of special conveyancing machinery, the Court of Chancery also, in the course of time, continued to enforce the *equitable interests* it had formerly created. And further, every new *legal* estate was permitted an *equitable* counterpart. Thus, for example, there could be equitable interests equivalent to estates in fee simple or in fee tail.

Hence, beside the older divisions of the law, a new division arose. Rights in land might either be *legal* or *equitable*. The nature of this distinction must be clearly understood. The man who has a legal right to property has a right which he can assert against all comers. The man who has an equitable interest in property has something more than the mere "personal" right which one party to a contract has against the other, for he has a right to the property itself. But the right of the equitable owner will, as has been explained, be lost if the property comes into the hands of one who is a *bona fide* purchaser of the *legal* estate in the property, provided that he is a purchaser for *value*, and that he has *no notice* of the equitable interest. "Notice" in this context may be either actual or "*constructive*". Constructive notice means such notice as the purchaser would have received of the equitable interest had he used reasonable diligence in making enquiries.

In respect of the land law, as will be seen below, the L.C.A. has made certain changes which affect the destructibility of equitable rights. Generally speaking, however, the doctrine of the *bona fide* purchaser still marks the boundary between legal and equitable ownership.

3 THE PURPOSES AND EFFECTS OF THE PROPERTY ACTS

Despite some reforms effected by nineteenth century statutes, the law in force immediately before the passing of the Property Acts was unsatisfactory for many reasons. In the first place, the distinction between "real property", "chattels real" and "personal property" produced unnecessary complexity and matters were by no means improved by the fact that real and personal property devolved upon intestacy by different rules. Secondly, the land law was highly artificial. Thirdly, owing to the multitude of interests which might encumber a given piece of land at one and the same time, the transfer of land was rendered, at the best a complicated matter, at the worst, well-nigh impossible.

The principal aims of the Property Acts were therefore –

(1) To minimize the distinction between real property and chattels real, and, as far as the natural distinction between movables and immovables permits, to assimilate the rules of law relating to land and other forms of property.

(2) To simplify the land law. This simplification was to be undertaken mainly with a view to the third object which was –

(3) To make transfers of land as easy as possible.

These aims were achieved in the following manner.

(*i*) The land law was assimilated to the law relating to personal property in two respects. (*a*) By the provisions of the A.E.A., the rules governing intestate succession to land and goods have been made uniform. Thus the main distinction which divided real property from chattels real ceased to exist. (*b*) Formerly when a man died intestate leaving no successors, his goods (*bona vacantia*) became the property of the Crown: his real estate fell to his immediate overlord, who took by right of "*escheat*" – one of the valuable "incidents" of tenure to which the feudal overlord was entitled. All property, whatever its nature, now lapses in these circumstances to the Crown.

(*ii*) The Law of Property Act 1922 completed the work of earlier statutes by abolishing copyhold tenure. All land is, therefore, now held by freehold or leasehold tenure. Since the feudal services incident to tenure have long since disappeared, the tenant in fee simple is today in practice, though not in strict theory, the "owner" of his land.

(*iii*) Conveyancing (*i.e.* the transfer of land) was simplified by the application of two principles. First, the categories of legal estates were reduced to a minimum. Second, certain devices were introduced which have made it possible, upon a transfer, to free land from equitable interests to which it is subjected.

The first principle was implemented by s. 1 (1) of the L.P.A. which provides that the only *estates* in land which are now capable of subsisting as *legal* estates are estates in fee simple absolute in possession and terms of years absolute. Apart from a limited number of *interests* which may still be *legal* (see below), all other interests are *equitable*. When it is recalled that legal rights over land are rights good against all and sundry, the importance of this provision will be understood.

The second principle was applied in two ways. On the one hand machinery was devised which now ensures that, wherever there are interests (which can now only be equitable) over land which are limited to be enjoyed by persons jointly or in succession, the land is either automatically subjected to a "trust for sale" (L.P.A.) or it becomes "settled land" (S.L.A.). In either case, as will be explained below, a purchaser may now acquire the land free from many equitable rights. On the other hand, certain rights of a less far-reaching nature than the above, have been made registrable at H.M. Land Registry under the provisions of the L.C.A. (below, p. 375). If they are not registered they are, as a general rule, void as against a subsequent purchaser of the legal estate whether he has notice of them or not. If they are registered, the fact of registration is deemed to constitute actual notice of their existence to all and sundry.

B ESTATES AND INTERESTS IN LAND

Legal Estates and Interests

"1 – (1) The only *estates* in land which are capable of subsisting or of being conveyed or created at law are – (*a*) An estate in fee simple absolute in possession; (*b*) A term of years absolute. (2) The only *interests* or charges in or over land which are capable of subsisting or of being conveyed or created at law are – (*a*) An easement, right, or privilege in or over land for an interest equivalent to an estate in fee simple absolute in possession or a term of years absolute. . . . ."

The italics are ours, but these are the words of part of s. 1 of the L.P.A. Although there are some other *interests* beside the estates and interests here mentioned, which are still capable of subsisting at law, we need not be concerned with them. For present purposes, it will suffice to examine the nature of fee simple estates, terms of years, and easements.

The words "*capable of subsisting at law*" are important, and the force of the word "*capable*", in particular, must be appreciated. The Act does not provide that the above classes of estates and interests *must* be legal in character: they may, and do, subsist as equitable interests, but what concerns us here is that they, and, as far as concerns our present purposes, they alone, are *capable* of being held as *legal* estates and interests.

1 THE FEE SIMPLE

(i) The nature of a fee simple – *The term "fee simple" survives from* mediaeval times. The word "fee" ("*feodum*") signified an estate of inheritance, that is an estate which would descend to the heir of a tenant who died intestate. Thus a life estate was not a fee. The word "simple" served to distinguish the fee simple from the estate in fee tail which, as has already been noted, descended, not to the heirs generally, but to a particular class of heirs designated in the instrument which created the entail.

It has already been stated that the modern holder of a fee simple estate is to all intents and purposes the owner of his land. He is still technically a *tenant* in fee simple, but his tenancy has no practical consequences. Ownership is, however, as has been remarked, a relative and not an absolute concept. An owner has greater rights than anyone else in respect of his property; but these rights are always subject to some restrictions imposed by the general law of the time and place in which he lives. Formerly the rights of landowners were great. An Englishman's home was his "castle". He could do much as he liked with his land provided that his user did not come within the prohibition of the law of torts that he should not injure his neighbour. Considerable limitations have, however, been imposed by modern legislation upon the rights attaching to land ownership. One series of statutes, in particular, culminating in the Town and Country Planning Act 1971 now place such restrictions upon land ownership that they must receive special notice and further drastic restrictions may well be imposed by the Community Land Bill which is before Parliament at the time of writing. [See Addendum: New Legislation.]

The Town and Country Planning Act limits the right of ownership by securing that any major change in the use of land must be approved; they also seek to impose a planned physical layout of land and building through Britain.

In order to achieve the first of these objects the Act provides that land (including buildings and structures) may normally only be "developed" by permission ("planning permission") of certain specified authorities. "Development" comprises the "carrying out of building, engineering, mining or other operations in, on, over or under land, or the making of any material change in the use of buildings or other land".

These words are wide and they embrace such activities as turning a house into flats or using an exterior wall, not previously so used, for advertising. Some types of development and change of use do not require planning permission: for example s. 22 of the Act specifies a number of things which are not to be treated as development and which therefore escape "control": for instance, improvements which do not affect the external appearance of a building. Section 23 of this Act also lists a number of kinds of "development" which are not to require planning permission; for example certain kinds of temporary use. Control is in the main exercised by local or area "planning authorities" such as county or borough authorities, and in certain cases the Secretary of State for the Environment has direct powers of control as well as having supervisory and appellate powers.

The second object of the Act is secured by provisions which impose upon local planning authorities the duty of submitting "development plans" of their districts for the consideration of the appropriate Minister. Their implementation will in many cases result in compulsory acquisition of private land, under powers conferred by the Act; where land is so acquired compensation will be payable.

(ii) The creation of an estate in fee simple – Words which define, or delimit, a right in land are known as "*words of limitation*". Originally the only words of limitation which would suffice in a conveyance *inter vivos* to pass a fee simple estate were the words "*To ... and his heirs*", although the Conveyancing Act 1881 permitted "*To ... in fee simple*" as an alternative. But by virtue of the L.P.A., s. 60, the necessity for words of limitation to create a fee simple was abolished in conveyances executed after 1925, and it is now the rule that the grantee will take "the fee simple or other the whole interest which the grantor had power to convey in such land, unless a contrary intention appears in the conveyance". Thus where A, the tenant in fee simple, conveys land "*To B*", B will acquire the whole fee simple unless a contrary intention appears. Wills were formerly treated more liberally than conveyances *inter vivos* and ever since the Wills Act 1837 the rule has been that a devise "*To B*" without words of limitation will pass the fee simple in the absence of a contrary intention shown in the will. The result today is that there is no difference between wills and conveyances in this matter.

It may be appropriate here to add that "words of limitation" must be distinguished from their even more tehnical counterpart, "*words of purchase*". The former define an estate or interest, the latter confer one; and they are nevertheless words of "purchase" even though the "purchaser" gives nothing in return for the benefit received. Thus in "To A and his heirs" the whole phrase *delimited* A's estate (*i.e.* marked it out as a fee simple in A) and also constituted words of "purchase" in A: but it was construed as conferring nothing upon the heirs. The words "and his heirs" were therefore *not* words of purchase *qua* the heirs. On the other hand, in "To X for life, remainder to Y" the words are words of purchase as regards both X and Y, since they mean what they say; X is to take for life and after death the estate will pass to Y.

(iii) The fee simple as a legal estate – It will have been observed that the L.P.A. defines the species of fee simple which is capable of subsisting as a *legal* estate as a *"fee simple absolute in possession"*. The expressions "absolute" and "in possession" require explanation.

"Absolute" signifies that the estate must be unqualified. The reason why only an unqualified fee simple is allowed to subsist as a *legal* estate is that it is a major object of the Act to make land freely alienable. The owner of a qualified legal fee simple does not have the whole interest in the land to convey to a purchaser. Hence, for example, in a grant to "X in fee simple until he shall marry" X's interest, not being absolute, cannot subsist as a legal estate; it can be equitable only, and this will have the desired effect of leaving the land freely transferable under the overreaching provisions (below, p. 356) of the 1925 legislation.

"In *possession*" signifies that the grantee must be entitled to immediate possession of the estate. Thus, suppose land to be limited "To A for life and after A's death to B in fee simple". In such a grant B's remainder is said to be "vested in interest" immediately the conveyance operates, for nothing remains to complete B's rights except the natural determination of the prior estate upon the death of A. This interest is not, however, at once "vested in possession", since B is not entitled to immediate enjoyment of the land. It is therefore an equitable interest only.

It must finally be noted that the L.P.A. takes account of the fact that land subject to a lease is in practice freely bought and sold. Thus a man who lets his land may still be "in possession" of a fee simple estate, for "possession" is for this purpose defined so as to include, beside actual physical enjoyment, "the receipt of rents and profits, or the right to receive the same".

2 LEASEHOLDS

(a) The nature of leasehold interests

The parties to a "term of years" or "leasehold interest" are today known as "landlord" and "tenant" (or as "lessor" and "lessee") respectively.

Some mention has already been made of the history of leaseholds. The principal feature which distinguishes this class of interest from freehold interests is that the landlord-tenant relationship is usually primarily a commercial one whereby the tenant obtains enjoyment of the land in return for a money consideration (rent). Freehold interests often arise as the result of inter-family dealings which are necessarily of a non-commercial nature, though, of course, the sale of a fee simple generally is.

The essence of a leasehold tenancy is a grant by the landlord to the tenant of *exclusive possession* of the property demised (let) coupled with an *intention* to create the relationship of landlord and tenant. Although there is a legal presumption that if the occupier is entitled to exclude the owner there is a tenancy, the second requirement is vital because it is the *intention* that matters, and not the parties' own description of their agreement; so that what is described as a "licence" may well in law be a tenancy and what appears on the face of it to be a tenancy may sometimes in law be a mere licence, or personal privilege, which (though it *may* amount to a *contract*) carries with it none of the rights or obligations of tenancy. An illustration may be helpful. In *Abbeyfield (Harpenden) Society, Ltd.* v. *Woods*, [1968] 1 All E.R. 352, the Society permitted the defendant to occupy a room, which he furnished, in an old peoples' home at a weekly rate: the Society provided a housekeeper, meals, heating and lighting. It was held that, despite the exclusive possession and the weekly "rent" the whole arrangement was too personal to amount to a tenancy: consequently the defendant was not within the protection of the Rent Acts (see below, p. 341) which apply principally to *tenancies*.

The expression "term of years", which is equivalent to the expression "leasehold interest", is perhaps misleading. Leases can exist for any *fixed* period (*e.g.* five years), but they may also take other forms. For example there are "periodic tenancies", such as quarterly or yearly tenancies, which are terms of years though they are determinable upon the giving of notice by either party. There are tenancies at *sufferance* arising where a tenant "holds over" after the expiry of his lease. And, as well as other forms, there are tenancies at *will* determinable by either party without notice which are really in essence bare licences, but which have the attribute that if rent is paid periodically they are converted into periodic tenancies.

Unlike fee simple estates, leasehold interests may subsist as legal estates even though the tenant is not to take *possession* at once. A term granted at a rent must, however, be limited *to take effect* within 21 years; any grant which purports to postpone the taking of effect of the term for a longer period is invalid (L.P.A. s. 149 (3)).

(b) The creation of leaseholds

In order to give rise to a *legal* estate a lease must *either* be created by deed *or* be one which takes effect in possession for a term not exceeding three years at the best rent obtainable. All kinds of informal leases other than the latter give rise to equitable interests only.

(c)   The relationship between landlord and tenant

The relationship of landlord and tenant is primarily governed by rules of the common law, but it has been to some extent modified by statute.

i   The relationship of landlord and tenant at common law – Tenancies are created by contract; consequently at common law their terms might be infinitely various. There are, however, certain obligations which are commonly implied, and certain covenants which commonly occur, in leases.

(a)   Implied obligations
Landlord's obligations – In the absence of express terms the landlord is under an obligation to ensure that neither he, nor anyone claiming under him, will disturb the tenant in his occupation of the premises. He impliedly covenants that the tenant shall remain in "quiet enjoyment". Further, where the premises are let furnished there is an implied warranty that they are reasonably fit for human habitation; for instance, a house infested with bugs has been held to be unfit for human habitation. This warranty does not, however, apply to houses which are let unfurnished, unless they are small dwelling-houses let at low rentals specified in s. 6 of the Housing Act 1957 which then imposes a statutory warranty to that effect: but even this has no application where the condition of the premises in question is such that they cannot be made fit at reasonable expense. The Housing Act 1961, by ss. 32 and 33, imposes implied covenants upon lessors of dwelling-houses for a term of less than seven years – (*a*) to keep in repair the structure and exterior of the house (including drains, gutters and external pipes); (*b*) to keep in repair and proper working order the installations in the dwelling-house – (*i*) for the supply of water, gas and electricity and for sanitation, and (*ii*) for space heating or heating water. These obligations can only be excluded or modified if both parties consent and an order of a county court is obtained. The obligation to repair only arises if the landlord knows, or reasonably ought to have known of the particular disrepair (*e.g.* a faulty floor) in question. Finally as a matter of practical importance, often not observed by landlords, there is a statutory requirement that the landlord must supply *weekly* tenants with a *rent book* in proper form. Failure to do this is an *offence*. Moreover, the Housing Act 1974 (ss. 121 and 122) provides that where a tenant makes a written request to a landlord's agent, the landlord's name and address must be supplied *in writing* to the tenant, and where the premises subject to the tenancy are assigned

to another landlord the latter must give the tenant *written* notice of his name and address.

Tenant's obligations – Generally speaking the tenant is liable for payment of rates and taxes, except such taxes as the landlord is under a legal obligation to pay. He is also under a duty to refrain from committing *waste*. This means that he is bound to refrain from damaging the property and that, quite apart from agreement, he must generally keep it in a reasonable state of repair.

(b) Express covenants

Two very common covenants beside the payment of rent, call for mention.

The covenant not to assign or underlet – In the absence of contrary agreement a tenant may assign his whole interest in the lease to a third person, or he may sub-let the premises for a term shorter than his own. In either event, if the tenant's interest amounts to a legal estate the third person will also acquire one. Landlords, however, very commonly exact a covenant against assigning or underletting. This may either be framed in the form of an absolute prohibition or as a prohibition against assigning or underletting without consent, and in the latter case the landlord is under a statutory duty not to withhold his consent unreasonably (Landlord and Tenant Act 1927, s. 19 (1) (a)). What is "unreasonable" is of course a question of fact but in some circumstances its nature is defined, *e.g.*, the Race Relations Act 1965, s. 5, provides that as a general rule consent withheld on the "ground of colour, race or ethnic or national origins" is to be treated as having been unreasonably withheld.

The covenant to repair – This may be either a landlord's or a tenant's covenant, though as a rule the landlord is responsible for the fabric of the house and the tenant for other repairs. The standard of "repair" required is the standard which a reasonable landowner would adopt in relation to his own premises and it is thus a variable standard; a house in Park Lane requires more attention than a house in Poplar. On the other hand, the standard is fixed as at the time of the letting in respect of the particular house and a decline in the neighbourhood will not affect the stringency of the duty.

It has been explained that as a general rule contractual obligations, being merely personal to the parties, are not assignable, but because of the enduring nature of land certain covenants between landlord and tenant form an exception to this rule. This exception is best described in the time-honoured words that "*covenants which touch and concern the land demised* (leased) *run with the land*"; they will bind the successors in title of either party. The principle is re-asserted in the L.P.A. (ss. 141 and 142). Whether any particular covenant falls within this category is largely a question of fact. Thus, in *Thomas* v. *Hayward* (1869), L.R. 4 Ex. 311, X who had let a public house to Y was held not to be bound as against Y's assignee by a covenant that he would not himself keep another public house within half a mile of the demised premises; for this covenant clearly had no direct reference to the land demised as opposed to the business conducted thereon. On the other hand where, upon the lease of a restaurant, the tenant covenanted that S should not be concerned in the business, it was held that this covenant directly concerned the use of the premises.

Where the covenant does "run" so as to bind successors, the original parties (*i.e.* the landlord and tenant) of course remain liable to one another according to the terms of their contract, but they are entitled to be indemnified by any successor who is in breach. It is of the greatest importance to note that these rules apply only where there is *privity of estate* between the party suing upon the covenant and the party in breach. This means that, in order for the covenant to be binding upon successors, they must take the same interest in the land as that originally created. Thus, covenants may run between landlord and assignee, but not between landlord and sub-tenant. If A leases land to B for a term of three years and B assigns the lease to X after 2 years, X may be bound by the covenants in favour of A contained in the lease. If, on the other hand, B sub-lets his term to Y for three years less one day, Y cannot be bound by these covenants but he will of course be bound by the covenants in the sub-lease.

ii Statutory provisions affecting the relationship between land-lord and tenant – Modern statutes have done much to restrict the freedom of the parties to a lease to make their own terms. The following examples may be given.

(a) Statutory provisions respecting improvements

Where a tenant increases the value of the premises by making improvements it is clearly unfair that he should lose the results of his industry upon the expiration of the tenancy. Thus even at common law he had a right to *emblements*, that is to say a right to enter, and to take artificially produced crops, such as wheat, when the tenancy had ceased unexpectedly before the harvest. Further a tenant may remove articles ("*tenants' fixtures*") used for trade or for ornamental or domestic purposes upon quitting the premises, even though they have been attached to the land, but he must not cause serious damage to the property by doing so. Thus, a tenant who keeps a garage may remove his petrol pumps as "trade fixtures". It will, of course, be realized that these rights in practice form an exception to the rule that things affixed to the land become the property of the owner (see above, p. 326).

Tenants' rights in respect of improvements are, moreover, greatly increased by the provisions of two statutes; namely the Agricultural Holdings Act 1948 and the Landlord and Tenant Act 1927 (as amended by the Landlord and Tenant Act 1954, Part III). The first Act entitles tenants of agricultural holdings upon the termination of the lease to receive compensation from their landlords for certain specified forms of improvements, such as the erection of farm buildings. The same Act also provides that certain classes of fixtures which have been attached to the land for agricultural purposes shall be removable by the tenant, either during the term or within two months of quitting. The landlord has, however, an option to purchase these fixtures at the end of the lease. The Agriculture (Miscellaneous Provisions) Act 1968 moreover, allows the tenant compensation on a prescribed basis to assist him in "reorganizing his affairs" at the termination of the lease.

The Act entitles a tenant who uses the premises for *business* purposes (an expression which includes "a trade, profession or employment") to compensation from the landlord, at the end of the tenancy, for any structural improvements he has made which increase the letting value of the premises. The amount of compensation must be approved by the landlord or, in case of dispute, by the court.

(b) The Rent Acts

It would be impossible to give an accurate account of this chaotic subject in the space available; yet some mention of it is called for. *Rent protection*, that is to say the control of rents and ensuring for the tenants security of tenure (*i.e.* making it difficult for the landlord to evict them) has been in force in one form or another since 1915; and it has been the subject of a series of enactments which almost defy explanation. The salient statutes now are the Rent Act 1968 (the principal Act) and the Rent Act 1974 – an abominable piece of drafting.

Shortly, the history of the subject is that from when the First World War caused housing shortage – which has of course been with us ever since – it became necessary to protect tenants. This has been sought to be achieved by no less than three different systems. The earliest was rent "control" which would have been phased out by now under the Housing Act 1969 and the Housing Finance Act 1972 had the relevant provisions of the latter Act not been repealed by the Housing Rents and Subsidies Act 1975 (an example of the political tergiversation which besets this subject). The Furnished Houses (Rent Control Act) 1946 introduced a special form of protection for *furnished* tenancies. And, finally, the Rent Act 1965 (*originally* only for *unfurnished* premises) introduced a system of "rent regulation" intended to replace the control system. We will consider the *control* system first, as first in point of time (though not of practical importance since many more tenancies are now subject to regulation than to control), then it will be best to take the *regulated* system, and, finally, what we will call the *"tribunal system"* originally created by the 1946 Act.

Controlled Tenancies – These originally arose under Acts of 1920–39 which brought *unfurnished* premises of stated rateable values, calculated at stated dates, within a system of "rent control". In order for premises to come within "control" various conditions must be satisfied. In the first place, as already mentioned, they must not exceed a certain rateable value. In the second place, there must be a "letting"; *tenants*, therefore, but not licensees or lodgers, are protected. In the third place, the accommodation let must be a "separate dwelling". This does not mean that only lettings of whole houses will fall within the Acts; it merely means that, generally speaking, the letting must be in respect of accommodation which affords a complete home in itself: flats, or even a single room, *may* therefore be subject to control, and so may accommodation shared with other tenants. In the fourth place, certain types of holding, whatever their rateable value, are specifically excluded from the operation of the Acts. The most important of these are all houses constructed after August 30th, 1954, and all separate and self-contained dwellings created by the conversion, after that date, of houses existing before that date (unless such conversion is effected with the assistance of a local authority grant). Crown property, all tenancies held of local authorities of new town development corporations, or of some kinds of housing associations, and of certain other bodies are also excluded.

Where a tenancy of unfurnished premises satisfies these conditions certain results follow –

(*i*) The premises become subject to a "rent limit" determined according to rules laid down in the Acts. Except in respect of certain "permitted increases" (in respect of *e.g.* rates, improvements, repairs, etc.) sanctioned by the Acts the landlord is not entitled to demand more than this amount, and the tenant can recover any payment made in excess of it. The tenant's claim must, however, be brought within two years of payment.

(*ii*) Beside fixing the rent, the Acts provide the tenant with security of tenure. Whatever the terms of his lease, he may *continue in occupation* after it has determined; he then becomes what is commonly called a *statutory tenant*. This means that he continues to hold over, not by virtue of any contract with the landlord, but under the authority of the Acts. The terms of the original lease, however, still continue to operate, except such terms (*e.g.* a contract by a tenant to pay less than the rent limit) as are incompatible with the Acts. This statutory tenancy is capable of subsisting until the death of the tenant, but he may neither assign it nor dispose of it by will. After the tenant's death, a member of his family may, in certain circumstances, step into his shoes and a widow or member of the family of that person may also, in succession become a "regulated" tenant (below). Only two transmissions of this kind, are, however, permitted; and once the interest of this second successor has determined the landlord may retake the premises.

(*iii*) Where premises are subject to a statutory tenancy the landlord cannot regain possession without an order from a county court. This order will only be made if (*a*) the court is satisfied that it is reasonable in the circumstances that it should be made, and (*b*) certain specified conditions exist, *e.g.* that the landlord requires the premises for his own occupation, or for that of certain other specified persons. The matter of eviction will receive further mention over page.

It should be stressed that the "control" system now applies only to premises of low rateable value.

Regulated Tenancies—These were originally the creation of the Rent Act 1965 (now replaced by the 1968 Act). The regulated scheme came into force on December 8th, 1965. It involves all tenancies of dwelling-houses (other than premises still within the "control" system) which had on March 23rd, 1965, a rateable value not exceeding £400 in London and of £200 elsewhere or if it had on April 1st, 1973 a rateable value, if in Greater London not exceeding £1,500 or £750 elsewhere—this of course embraces the vast majority of tenancies. Formerly only unfurnished tenancies were regulated, but the Rent Act 1974 brought furnished (other than resident landlord—below) tenancies into the system.

In respect of security of tenure the effect of regulation is, with minor modifications, the same as the effect of control (see (*ii*) and (*iii*) above) and the kinds of accommodation regulated are—except for difference in the rateable values selected—practically the same. The distinction between the two systems lies in the fact that regulated tenancies fall within a new kind of *registration*. Under the latter scheme "rent officers" are appointed locally and they have the duty of keeping a register of rents. The rent of regulated premises may be entered by the rent officer upon application of either landlord or tenant and he has to determine (subject to a right of appeal to a *"rent assessment committee"* composed of a legally qualified chairman, a valuer and a lay member) what he considers to be a *fair rent*. Once this is registered it will remain fixed (that is to say it must not be exceeded) save in exceptional circumstances, for a period of three years, after which time it may be reviewed. But where the registered rent represents an increase the landlord may not recover more than a proportion of the increase according to a scheme of "phasing". Until application is made the rent will normally, according to the case, either be a sum not above the rent limit, or, if the premises are outside control, the contractual rent. And it should be added that *rent allowances* are now payable from public funds in cases of hardship.

The tribunal system – This now applies to tenancies (within the same rateable values as those which apply to regulated lettings) which, in the main, are either (*i*) *furnished* lettings *where the landlord is resident at the commencement of the letting*; (*ii*) student lettings by educational institutions; (*iii*) lettings, whether furnished or unfurnished, where tenant and landlord *share* accommodation. "Furnished" here includes the supply of services as well as of furniture, and lodgers are embraced as well as tenants.

The determination of the rent (here "*reasonable*" rent) is in the hands of *rent tribunals*, which are composed of a chairman and members drawn from the same panels as rent assessment committees. The rent officer is not involved, and references are made direct to the tribunal; first references may only be made by a tenant or by a local authority. Tribunal decisions are registered in the offices of local authorities and, unless the tribunal confines it to the particular letting, the rent so registered becomes the lawful rent for the premises in future.

As regards *security*, the tenant has no such statutory security as has the tenant under the regulated system; but the tribunal has power to order that the tenant remain in possession for limited periods.

Two further points should be made. *First*, subject to minor exceptions, it is an offence to evict *any* residential *tenant* without a *court order*, and it is also an offence to deprive any residential *occupier* (even a licensee) of his occupation. It is also an offence for a landlord to cause "harassment" to his tenant (by *e.g.* making conditions unpleasant for him) with intent to cause him to quit. *Second*, it is generally illegal for anyone to receive a *premium* in respect of leases of any premises. This rule has been so strictly construed that it has been held to include a case where four guineas had been charged towards the cost of a tenancy agreement. It is also an offence to offer furniture or fittings at an excessive price in connexion with the granting of leases.

(c) *The Landlord and Tenant Act 1954, Part II*

Subject to certain exceptions (including, amongst other things most tenancies not exceeding six months, agricultural tenancies, and tenancies protected by the Rent Acts), tenants who occupy the demised premises wholly or in part for the purposes of *business* are, subject to certain conditions, granted security of tenure by this Part of this Act (as amended by the Law of Property Act 1969). These provisions are complicated, but their effect is that, in substance, such tenancies can only normally be terminated (even though the period for which they were originally granted has expired) by giving notice to quit. If the notice is served by the landlord the tenant may apply to the court (in most cases a county court) for the grant of a new lease. The landlord may oppose the tenant's application only on certain grounds and the court has power, if such grounds are not established by the landlord, and the parties cannot agree to the creation of a new lease, to order a new tenancy for a period not exceeding fourteen years; though, in certain circumstances, while ordering the tenant to quit, it must order the landlord to pay the tenant certain specified compensation. Subject to approval by the court, the L.P.A. 1969, s. 5 permits the parties to exclude the operation of Part II by agreement.

(d)   The Leasehold Reform Act 1967

This Act (as amended by the Housing Act 1974) for the first time brings into play the principle of leasehold enfranchisement. Politically this is by no means a new idea and it was mooted as far back as 1885. Basically the notion of the lease as an investment for the landlord, with the corollary that the tenant – however long he continues to pay – can never own the land, is something repugnant to much modern political thought; so enfranchisement (*i.e.* the compulsory converting of the tenant's lease into a freehold estate) was certain sooner or later to leave the realm of debate and become a reality.

The particular situation with which the Act is designed to deal is the case of the long lease at a low rental, which was thought by some to bear hardly upon the tenant. Thus, for example, in the latter part of the nineteenth century in certain mining areas long leases of land (usually 99 years' building leases) were granted by landowners to workers at a ground rent representing only the value of the *land* – for the workers to build upon. The effect of the transaction was thus that upon the expiry of the lease the house (being a part of the land) would revert to the owner, even though it had been built by the tenant and continuously inhabited by him or his successors. The Act is thus primarily designed to enable people of this kind, by giving a requisite notice to the landlord, to obtain compulsory enfranchisement. The right is, however, only exercisable within fixed limits. The lease must be one originally granted for more than 21 years; it must be one at a low rent, *i.e.*, an annual payment of less than two-thirds of the rateable value (usually the

assessment on April 1st, 1973); the property in question must be a house
(*e.g.*, flats are excluded); the rateable value of the premises must be not
more than £750 (£1,500 in Greater London) or, if the tenancy was
created after February 18th, 1966, the relevant values are £500 and
£1,000 respectively; and the time the tenant gives notice he must have
occupied the house for at least five years or for periods amounting in
the aggregate to five years out of the last ten. If all these requirements
are satisfied the tenant becomes the freehold owner of the house subject
to compensation payable to the landlord upon a somewhat complex
basis, this roughly amounts to the market value of the freehold (excluding buildings on the land), upon the hypothetical assumption that it
would continue to be let during the remainder of the current term, and
for a further 50 years thereafter, at a modern ground rent. It will be
realized that this is poor compensation to the landlord.

It must be added that as an alternative to purchasing the freehold, a
tenant has a right (upon giving notice) to demand that his lease shall
be extended for a further period of 50 years from the date of its expiry.
This is not, however, very useful to the tenant since if the extension
is granted the rent will be a modern ground rent (reviewable after 25
years) greater than the pre-existing one *and* the landlord will have an
over-riding right to claim occupation of the premises if he needs them
either for redevelopment or for occupation by himself or by an adult
member of his family. The extended lease provisions would therefore
seem to be as much weighted in the landlord's favour as the enfranchisement provisions are weighted against him.

(d)   The determination of leases

Leases for a fixed period – These leases normally expire automatically at
the end of the agreed term. But there are exceptions to this rule; they
include leases of *business premises* (see above, p. 344), leases for *more than
21 years* and *agricultural* leases. In order to provide farmers with security
of tenure the Agricultural Holdings Act 1948, enacts that agricultural
tenancies for a fixed period of two years and upwards shall only determine upon the agreed day if either party gives notice at least one year
in advance. If this notice is not given the statute operates to prolong
the tenancy into a tenancy from year to year, as from the original date
of expiry.

Periodic Leases – In the absence of special agreement (and apart from rent
protection) periodic leases (*i.e.* leases not expressed to expire on a fixed
date but created by reference to a period of determinability – *e.g.* from
week to week, quarter to quarter, etc.) normally expire when one full

period's notice is given by either party. Suppose, for example, A grants B a quarterly lease from Lady Day (March 25th) and suppose that, in April, A decides that he wants to determine the lease at Michaelmas (September 29th). A must give B notice on or before Midsummer Day (June 24th). Strictly speaking in this example, the notice should be served on the day *before* the quarter day and should be framed so as to require the tenant to quit at midnight on the day before the following quarter day. In practice, however, notices from quarter day to quarter day are allowed. Similar rules apply, *mutatis mutandis*, to all periodic tenancies except tenancies from year to year; but this is now subject to the important provision of the Rent Act 1957, s. 16, that in the case of *all* periodic tenancies (including, *e.g.*, weekly tenancies) premises "let as a dwelling-house" notice must be given "*not less* than *four* weeks before the date on which it is to take effect" (and this may exclude either the first or the last day of the period, but not both). In the case of yearly tenancies only six months' notice is required, but it must be calculated (like notice of all periodic tenancies) to expire upon one of the anniversaries of the date upon which the lease was granted. Yearly agricultural tenancies, however, require at least a full year's notice, which must expire at the end of a current year of the tenancy (Agricultural Holdings Act 1948). It has now been enacted by the Housing Act 1974, s. 123 that notices to quit must be in *writing* (in practice they always have been) and in due course they will be required to contain certain prescribed information.

3 RIGHTS IN ALIENO SOLO

It has been seen that one of the features of a lessee's interest is that it carries the right to exclusive enjoyment of the lessor's property. The three interests which now fall to be discussed, *Easements, Profits à Prendre*, and *Restrictive Convenants*, confer rights in respect of "other people's land" (*jura in alieno solo*) of a more limited nature than the lessee's right.

Easements and profits *may* subsist as *legal* interests. Restrictive covenants can only be *equitable*, but they are discussed at this place for the sake of convenience, since they bear a close resemblance to easements.

Before examining the nature of these three rights it must be stressed that they are all interests in land. As such they are not personal to the parties who create them, and they accordingly bind third parties and successors in title to the land. This characteristic formerly distinguished such interests from bare *contractual* rights or *licences*, which in strict theory were personal to the parties and did not bind the land; though some of them – such as the right of a theatre-goer to see the performance without arbitrary eviction by the proprietor – did afford some right to remain on the land. It must, however, now be admitted that there are forms of licences which are coming to acquire the status of at least something like equitable interests; as for instance where a person who has been permitted to dwell in a house by the owner has relied upon the permission sufficiently to expend money upon improvements. The law concerning rights of this kind has been described by a leading author on the land law as "highly controversial" and so it is; consequently it is unsuitable for examination here.

Easements and *profits* are limited rights in respect of the land of another person. The distinction between the two is that, whereas an easement is a bare right over or in respect of the land, a profit carries with it the right to remove something from the land; as, for example, the right of pasturage of cattle.

(a)   Easements

i   The nature of an easement – Examples of easements are rights of way, the right to have one's buildings supported by the land of one's neighbour, the right to discharge water over another's land, and the right to "light". The latter is a right to prevent adjoining owners from obstructing the flow of light to a particular window or windows of one's house.

Although there is no such thing as a "closed list" of easements, as a general rule, an interest can only be classified as an easement if the following requirements are satisfied –

(i) *An easement can only be enjoyed in respect of land* – This means two things. First, there must be a "*dominant tenement*" and a "*servient tenement*"; that is, there must be two parcels of land, one (the "dominant tenement") to which the benefit of the easement attaches (to which it is said to be "*appurtenant*"), and another (the "servient tenement") which bears the burden of the easement. Secondly, the easement must benefit the dominant tenement. Thus, although it is possible for X, in Sussex, to grant Y, who has land in Derbyshire, a right of way over X's Sussex land, this right cannot be an easement since it cannot benefit the use of Y's land.

(ii) *There must be a dominant and a servient owner* – Thus, suppose S to have two contiguous estates, and suppose that he habitually uses a footpath over the one to enable him to reach the other, this user does not constitute an easement.

(iii) *Easements must be capable of forming the subject-matter of a grant* – This rule arises from the fact that at common law the normal method of creating easements was by deed of grant. Thus it is possible to acquire an easement to the uninterrupted flow of air to a particular ventilator in a factory. It is not, however, possible to acquire an easement in respect of the flow of air over the whole of one's property; since it would not be possible to interrupt such flow, and therefore the right could not be ceded by grant. So also, it is impossible to acquire a right to protection of one's house from the weather through the instrumentality of one's neighbour's house.

ii The acquisition of easements – Easements usually come into existence in one of two ways: they are either acquired by grant, express or implied, or by prescription. *Express grants* require little notice. The rule is that they must usually be made by deed. An *implied grant* may arise where a man who owns two adjoining properties sells one of them. Suppose, for instance, X owns Blackacre *and* Whiteacre. It has been noted above that if he uses a path across Whiteacre in order to reach Blackacre his user cannot constitute an easement. Suppose, however, that he sells Blackacre to Y; then the law will sometimes presume, quite apart from anything that is contained in the deed of conveyance, that Y has been granted an easement of way over Whiteacre. Consequently such rights – which are capable of becoming easements – are sometimes called "quasi-easements". The readiness of the law to imply a grant in such circumstances was greatly strengthened by the L.P.A. (s. 62 (1)), which enacts that conveyances of land are to be deemed to include *by implication* "all liberties, privileges, easements, rights and advantages whatsoever, appertaining or reputed to appertain to the land". And it is to be noted that where it is sought to establish a grant in this way it is not necessarily, as is the case where it is sought to establish a right by prescription, a bar to its establishment that the exercise of the right was consented to by the owner. Further, "liberties, privileges and advantages" are things which defy precise definition; for instance a customary right to have a wall kept in repair by a neighbour has been held to come within the section.

A grant in *equity* may also be, in effect, conclusively presumed by the operation of the doctrine of *equitable estoppel*. The basis of this doctrine, it will be recalled, is that where B permits A to do some act in reliance upon B's acquiescence or where B, in return for a benefit received from A, permits A to do something (there being neither contract in the strict sense nor consideration) B will not be permitted to deny A's right. The principle may be illustrated by *Ives (E.R.) Investment, Ltd.* v. *High*, [1967] 2 Q.B. 379. In that case the plaintiffs and the defendant were adjoining landowners and the foundations of the plaintiffs' building ran under the defendant's land (technically a trespass to the land). The defendant objecting to this trespass, the plaintiffs' predecessor in title agreed that in return for the defendant condoning the trespass he would permit the defendant to have access for his car over the predecessor's land. Later the predecessor raised no objection when the defendant built a garage on his own land in such a way that access to it could only be gained by crossing the predecessor's land. The plaintiffs, having acquired the land from the predecessor with knowledge of the defendant's right of access, sought an injunction to restrain the defendant from using it. The Court of Appeal refused the injunction, declaring the plaintiffs estopped by the conduct of their predecessor both in agreeing to the access in return for consenting to their trespass and in acquiescing in the building of the garage.

In the case of prescription, as in the case of custom, the law permits long-continued practice to ground a claim of legal right. The reason rights can be acquired by prescription is that long and unchallenged user implies just as much acquiescence on the part of the servient owner as if he had made a grant. There are two forms of prescription, "*common law*" prescription and prescription *under the Prescription Act 1832*. In order to establish a claim to an easement by "*common law*" prescription the claimant must show that he, or his predecessors in title, have exercised the right which he seeks to establish, continuously for a very long period. The exercise must run from "time immemorial" and it must be "as of right". The limit of legal memory is fixed for this purpose at the year 1189; though all this means is that the right has to be proved to have been exercised for a considerable time and that there is no evidence that it has not been in existence from 1189. The expression "as of right" means that the exercise must be "*nec vi, nec clam, nec precario*", neither "forceful" nor "secret", nor dependent upon the "permission" of the servient owner. It is thus not easy to prescribe at common law. To take only one simple instance, it would be hard to acquire a right of support for one's house in this way, for few houses date from 1189. As a last resort, however, the difficulty may be avoided by reliance upon the fiction of the "*lost modern grant*". By this doctrine the court may *presume* after the right in question has been enjoyed for a reasonable length of time that a grant by deed was made at some time after 1189, and uphold the right by reference to this notional "deed" which it will conveniently presume to have been "lost". Moreover, the presumption will be made where 20 years' (the statutory period for the acquisition of an easement) uninterrupted enjoyment can be established. Though it will not be made if it be proved that a grant would actually have been *impossible*; nor will it be made if there is plain evidence that *no* grant *was* made; nor yet if there is no evidence of acquiescence on the part of the servient owner. The use of such a fiction may seem questionable; but the courts are rightly concerned to uphold established usage without being over particular as to any exact requirement as to the period of use.

Statutory prescription under the provisions of the Act of 1832 was introduced in order to remedy the defects of the older law. In order to establish a claim to an easement under the Act a claimant must show continuous user as of right for 20 years *immediately preceding* the bringing of an action in which his claim is called in question. Further, continuous use for 40 years will ground a claim even though the user has been subject to oral permission. If, however, the right is exercised by the written permission of the servient owner no claim can be established, and it makes no difference when the written permission was given. In the case of the easement of light, the Act provides that enjoyment for 20 years without interruption will suffice to ground the claim, even though it is not "as of right". The grant of written permission will, however, destroy the claim, even in this case. The words "immediately preceding" are important: statutory prescription can only – unlike prescription by lost modern grant – be involved if the user relied upon was in active exercise at the time of the claim: it would not be enough – under the Act – to show, say, 20 years' user twenty years ago. It may be of interest to add that the Court of Appeal have held that in the case of a right of way prescription will not be defeated by the fact that the actual alignment of the way is varied during the prescriptive period.

The Rights of Light Act 1959 provides that a servient owner may register a notice as a local land charge (below, p. 376) which will have the effect of an obstruction of the access of light known to and acquiesced in by all the parties concerned. This provision renders it unnecessary to erect screens or boards (which are in any case now subject to planning control) designed to interrupt the access of light.

(b) Profits

The essential difference between easements and profits has already been noted. There are certain minor differences. For instance, whereas, as we have seen, easements must be appurtenant to a dominant tenement, profits may be enjoyed "*in gross*" by an owner who has no such tenement. Moreover profits may be "*several*" (enjoyed by one person) or "*common*" (enjoyed by a number of people including the owner of the servient tenement). The prescription periods for profits are 30 and 60 years respectively, corresponding with the 20 and 40 year periods which apply in the case of easements.

These rules apart, the rules governing profits are very similar to the rules governing easements. Examples of profits are fishing rights, grazing rights and the right to enter land to cut turf.

(c) Restrictive covenants

We have seen that, in defiance of the rule that contractual obligations are personal to the contracting parties, certain covenants which touch and concern land "run with the land" and are valid not only between the parties, but against all other people too (see above, pp. 339–340). It will further be remembered that the power of these covenants to bind the land is subject to limitations. In particular, covenants do not bind people, such as sub-lessees, who have no "privity of estate" with their landlord; moreover the burden, as opposed to the benefit, of vendor and purchaser covenants do not bind the land at common law.

These limitations of the common law rules might well give rise to injustice. Consider the following case. T owned Leicester Square, London; T sold the garden in the centre of the square to E, and exacted a covenant from E to the effect that both E and his successors in title would keep it in its existing condition as an ornamental garden. T retained houses surrounding the square. E resold the garden, and after it had passed through the hands of a series of purchasers, M bought it, knowing of the covenant. M threatened to build upon it. T sought an injunction restraining M from this unconscionable action. The position at common law was that, since the covenant constituted a "burden" upon the land, it could not bind M. This position was clearly unjust, since T had a legitimate interest in preserving the amenities of the surrounding property which he had retained, and if M could snap his fingers at the covenant, he was in a position to buy "burdened" land cheap, and then to make a profit by disregarding the burden.

The facts which have just been set out are the facts of the leading case of *Tulk* v. *Moxhay* (1848), 2 Ph. 774. Impressed by the justice of T's claim, Lord Cottenham, L.C. cast about to find some reason for granting the injunction. He found himself able to do so by holding that since M had notice, his conscience was affected by the covenant. In other words, the decision in favour of T amounted simply to this, that he had an equitable interest in the enforcement of the covenant. Thus a new class of equitable interest was created in order to supply the deficiencies of the common law. This interest, as defined and modified by subsequent authorities, has now become the *Restrictive Covenant* of modern law.

Lord Cottenham based his decision in *Tulk* v. *Moxhay* solely upon the fact that M had notice of the covenant. Today, however, the fact of notice alone will not suffice to render a restrictive covenant enforceable. Such covenants will only "run with the land", so as to affect third party rights, if the following requirements are satisfied. (*i*) The obligation must be "restrictive", *i.e.* negative in *effect* (however expressed). Thus the covenant in *Tulk* v. *Moxhay* was restrictive. Although it was framed in positive terms ("To maintain ... uncovered with buildings"), it implied a substantially negative obligation, *i.e. not* to build: conversely, a covenant may be positive in effect even though framed in negative terms (*e.g.* a covenant not to allow a garden to fall into a bad state of cultivation *i.e.* to *keep* it tidy). (*ii*) The covenant must "touch and concern" an ascertainable area of land which is subjected to it. The meaning of this expression has already been discussed (above, p. 339); but it should be added that the covenant must in some way *benefit* the land in respect of which it is created. (*iii*) The land in respect of which the covenant is claimed must belong to the person who seeks to enforce it. In this respect restrictive covenants display some similarity to easements. The whole reason for their enforcement is that they form a valuable adjunct to what may loosely be termed the "dominant tenement". This requirement of "dominant" ownership does not, however, preclude an express assignment of the benefit of the covenant to a purchaser of part of the "dominant" land. (*iv*) If the claimant is anyone other than the original covenantee he must, as a general rule, either show that the benefit of the covenant has been expressly assigned to him, or that it was originally "annexed" to the land or that it relates to land the subject of a building scheme or scheme of development. A building scheme is a plan of development of land to be divided into plots for separate occupation and this presupposes, in the words of a famous judicial *dictum*, as between the purchasers of the plots "community of interest and reciprocity of obligation"; so that, for example, a restriction upon the height of trees or fences imposed upon plot A will be matched by a corresponding restriction upon all the other plots, and thus, though it is restrictive of A, it will inure to the benefit of the estate as a whole. A covenant will usually be held to be "*annexed*" if it indicates the land to be benefited and signifies an intention that the benefit shall inure to the land. It will not be "annexed" if it is expressed in terms which show an intention that it is to be *personal* to the parties or their successors. Thus there will be no annexation to the land where X covenants simply "for myself and my assigns", because "assigns" may include assignees of the covenant as well as assignees of the land.

Finally, the provisions of the L.C.A. removed the law relating to restrictive covenants further still from its origin in *Tulk* v. *Moxhay*. All restrictive covenants (unless between lessor and lessee) entered into since January 1st, 1926, are registrable as "*land charges*"; hence, as will later appear, if registered they are valid even against a *bona fide* purchaser for value without notice.

It must finally be noted that, by s. 84 of the L.P.A. (as amended by the Landlord and Tenant Act 1954, s. 52 and L.P.A. 1969, s. 28), restrictive covenants affecting freehold land and leasehold land where the lease was created for forty years or more, and not less than twenty-five have expired, can now, under certain circumstances, be modified or discharged by order of the Lands Tribunal (see above, p. 145).

Equitable Interests

Several matters require explanation in respect of this topic. In the first place, space will not permit of a discussion of all equitable interests, and only the more important of them will therefore be described. In the second place, the term "equitable interest" is here used to denote an interest which can *only* be equitable. In this respect, apart from restrictive covenants, the interests about to be described differ from the fee simple, terms of years, and easements and profits, since these are capable of subsisting as either legal or equitable interests. In the third place, all the equitable interests about to be described are "trust" interests. Trusts will be discussed in a separate chapter. All that need be explained here is that where land is conveyed to trustees "upon trust", the trustees may hold a legal estate in the land, but they hold it on behalf of other people (*beneficiaries*) who have equitable interests only. The nature and extent of these interests depend upon the instrument which creates the trust. Finally, it has already been stressed that one of the major objects of the Property Acts was to render land freely transferable. This object was partially achieved by employing settlements and trusts for sale to overreach equitable interests. The meaning of "*settlements*", "*trusts for sale*" and "*overreaching*" must therefore be considered before the modern equitable interest can be described in its proper perspective.

1   SETTLEMENTS AND TRUSTS FOR SALE

(a)   Settlements
i   Strict settlements – Much of the history of the land law can be epitomized in terms of a struggle between family pride and the law. Landowners consistently endeavoured, with the help of their legal allies, the conveyancers, to "tie up" the land in their families while the law has striven to keep it freely alienable.

We are first concerned with "strict", *i.e.* traditional, settlements. The strict settlement has been known since the seventeenth century. In its simplest form it arises in the following way. M, who owns land, is about to marry W. He hopes to found a family, and to preserve the land in the family for as long as the law will permit. We shall see later that the law, in pursuance of its policy of championing free alienation, will not permit the land to be "tied" for a very long period of time. It will, however, allow M to convey his land to trustees upon trust to hold it for him (M) for life, with remainder to his eldest son in tail and successive remainders (should this son die without issue) to M's younger sons in tail. This conveyance, which has the effect of earmarking the land as "family" land, creates a strict settlement. But it must be noted that (because estate duty on the whole capital value will today be payable on the death of each limited owner) the usual way of giving effect to the intentions of the parties in such a case would *not* today normally be by way of strict settlement; though since some such settlements still exist it is essential to deal briefly with this machinery.

The history of M must therefore be carried further. Suppose that the settlement is made, the marriage celebrated, and a son (X) is born. X attains his majority and desires to marry. At this stage it would be normal, for reasons which will be explained when entailed interests come to be discussed (below, p. 358), for X and M to agree to make a *re-settlement*. A re-settlement, at its simplest, will take the following form. The land is re-conveyed to the trustees upon trust to hold it for M for the rest of his life (subject to an annual sum of money charged upon the land in favour of X), remainder to X for life, remainder to X's eldest son in tail, etc. When M dies X may in due course make a similar re-settlement with his eldest son. So the process of settlement and re-settlement could continue from generation to generation and the land be retained in the family.

This ingenious method of "tying" the land was always satisfactory to the land-proud, but in practice, before the statutory modification which is about to be described, it often had disastrous consequences. The land was so effectively "tied" that there was never anyone at any given moment with power to dispose of it. Property which might have been sold at a good price often became nothing but a burden to an impoverished family. Further, since there was never anyone with the rights of an owner there was little incentive to make improvements. Consequently in the last century the Legislature intervened to strike the shackles from settled land. This branch of the law is now governed by the S.L.A. which made far-reaching changes with the object of facilitating sales of land subject to settlements, of safeguarding the interests of purchasers, and of encouraging improvements. The Act retained and enlarged powers previously conferred upon tenants for life (see below, p. 361). It further provided that future settlements must be made by two deeds. The one deed, called a *"trust instrument"*, declares the trusts upon which the land is to be held. The other deed, called a *"vesting deed"*, declares that the legal estate in the land is vested in the person who is for the time being entitled to the enjoyment of it as tenant for life (*i.e.* "M" and "X" successively in the above illustration). The names of the trustees of the settlement also appear in this deed but there is no mention of the trusts upon which they hold. A new vesting deed is, of course, executed from time to time as each new life tenant becomes entitled to the land.

Under this machinery a purchaser is normally only permitted to examine the vesting deed; thus, as far as he is concerned, the owner of the land is the tenant for life, not the trustees. He must, however, pay the purchase price to the named trustees. The trustees then hold the money in place of the land and they are bound to invest it, and to apply the income according to the trusts of the settlement. ·

In the ordinary case the effect of the Act is therefore this –

(*i*) The vesting deed makes the tenant for life *"estate owner"* with the result that he may sell the land and has general powers of administration and management, which include the power to lease or mortgage it.

(*ii*) A purchaser can and must (except as to the payment of purchase money – (*iii*) below) deal with the person declared in the vesting deed to be the tenant for life, as if he were the owner in fee simple.

(*iii*) The purchase money must be paid to the trustees: it takes the place of the land. ‚

(*iv*) A purchaser never knows the nature of the equitable interests affecting the land. He is thus not affected by notice of them. They lie behind the "curtain" of the vesting deed. They can therefore be *overreached* when the land passes to a purchaser, so that he acquires the entire fee simple free from the trusts.

It should generally be remarked that, though it is necessary to understand their history, *strict settlements are now seldom met in practice.*

ii   Implied settlements – We have seen that the S.L.A. freed land from the dead hand of family settlements. It did more than this, however. It applied the machinery just described to every case in which the free transfer of land is impeded by the absence of an adult owner who holds the fee simple absolute.

Subject to one important exception, to be noticed below, wherever the land is *so limited that there is no fee simple owner of full age entitled to dispose of it*, it automatically becomes "settled land" *by operation of law* under the provisions of s. 1 of the S.L.A. All major interests in land which are neither legal estates in fee simple, nor terms of years absolute, are now equitable interests and they can only exist *behind a trust. Trustees* must therefore be provided to hold this automatically "settled" land. Beside the trustees, as we have seen, in order for the machinery of the Act to operate, there must also be a *tenant for life* in whom the power of disposing of the land can be vested. The Act therefore provides that anyone of full age entitled to the possession of the land thus "settled" shall be endowed with this power. Where there is no such person, *e.g.* where the land is limited in fee simple in trust for an infant, the powers of a life tenant are conferred upon the trustees as *"statutory owners"*.

Thus the S.L.A. machinery makes it possible to overreach most equitable interests upon a transfer of land, whether or not these interests arise under a strict settlement. This statement must, however, be subjected to one important qualification. Land can never be "settled land" where it is held upon *trust for sale*.

(b) Trusts for sale

Settlements and trusts for sale are mutually exclusive.

Land becomes subject to an express trust for sale when it is conveyed to trustees under a trust which imposes upon them an *absolute duty to sell* it. Such a conveyance has the effect of involving the equitable doctrine of *conversion*. This doctrine is based upon the principle that equity "looks upon that as done which ought to be done". Thus, from the moment of the conveyance, whether there has been an actual sale or not, the land is regarded in equity *as if* it were the *purchase money* to be realized from the sale.

The implications of this doctrine will be obvious. If it is desired to make a complicated series of limitations in respect of land, and at the same time to leave the land freely alienable, this object can be achieved by means of a trust for sale. Immediately the conveyance takes effect the rights of the beneficiaries under the grant attach in theory, not to the land, but to the purchase money. The trustees have not only a power, but a binding *duty*, to sell the land itself and the equitable interests of the beneficiaries in no way adhere to it.

Upon this showing it might appear that a trust for sale constitutes a peculiarly perverse method of granting *land*, since the beneficiaries would seem not even to be entitled to equitable interests in the *land*, but only in the proceeds of sale. This, however, is not the case, since although the land is in theory "converted" from the time of the conveyance, the trustees are usually entitled to *postpone* the sale indefinitely. Hence in practice the beneficiaries may enjoy the land just as though they were entitled to it under a strict settlement. Thus the machinery of a trust for sale is similar to, and simpler than, the machinery of a strict settlement. Indeed, in some instances it may have the advantage of keeping the land in the family, as where the power is only exercisable with the consent of a particular person.

Some further points require elucidation. First, there is no need for a "tenant for life" where land is subject to a trust for sale: the *trustees* exercise the power of sale, since they are the legal owners. Second, by s. 28 (1) of the L.P.A., trustees for sale are given all the powers of a "tenant for life" under a settlement (below, p. 361). They may, however, revocably delegate their powers of leasing, accepting surrenders of leases and of management, at any time before sale, to any person of full age for the time being beneficially entitled in possession to the rents and profits of the land under the terms of the trust. This person, is, of course, in a position similar to that of a "tenant for life"; and he is clearly the proper person to exercise these powers. Third, since the rights which encumber the land are in theory rights only in respect of a share of the purchase money, notice of them will have no effect upon a purchaser: he pays the trustees, the distribution of the money is their business. He takes the land free. It follows that there is no need of machinery to conceal these rights and the trust may therefore be created by one deed, though, in practice, for simplicity, two deeds are generally used.

The trust for sale is thus a very straightforward device. It must, however, be stressed that no trust will be treated as a trust for sale unless the instrument which creates it imposes an "immediate binding" trust. This means that the trust must be intended to take effect at once upon the conveyance, and that the duty to sell (subject to the *power* of postponement) must be absolute. Where land is conveyed to trustees subject to a series of limitations, and the trustees are given only a *discretion* to sell, there is no conversion and no trust for sale; the land becomes "settled land". This is a fine distinction, and in practice it is often a matter of difficulty to determine whether the wording of (*e.g.*) a will makes the land "settled land" or subjects it to a trust for sale.

Finally, just as the S.L.A. created implied settlements in order to facilitate free alienation, so, for the same reason, it imposed "statutory" trusts for sale in certain circumstances; as where land is held by personal representatives upon an intestacy. Intestacy will be discussed in Chapter 13.

2 THE CLASSES OF EQUITABLE INTERESTS

(a) Entailed interests

(*i*) *The nature of entailed interests* – As a matter of history the idea of the entail derives, though somewhat remotely, from the ancient institution of the *maritagium*. The object of this was to convey land on the marriage of a daughter so that it should be held for at least three generations in the new family as a kind of starting inheritance. Should the family fail through lack of offspring the land reverted to the donor (father) or his heirs. The modern entail retains the notion, earmarking the property within the family and it is thus essentially connected with family settlements – which are now rare. There are two main classes of entails. Interests *in tail general* – these have the effect of limiting the property entailed in turn to the grantee and then to his heirs successively; including all heirs of any marriage that he may make. "*Heirs*" are the people designated as such by the common law rules of inheritance (below, p. 448). Interests *in tail special* – these have the effect of limiting the property to the grantee and then to the heirs successively who are descended from a *specified spouse* of the grantee. Both general and special entails may, however, be so limited as to descend to heirs of one *sex* to the exclusion of the other, being then either interests in *"tail male"* or in *"tail female"*.

Before January 1st, 1926, entailed interests were known as "estates in fee tail"; real property alone could be subjected to them, and they were capable, as we have seen, of subsisting as *legal* estates. Any property, whether land, goods or other personalty, can now be entailed (L.P.A. s. 130 (1)) but an entailed interest can only be an *equitable* interest and can only exist behind the curtain of a trust.

(*ii*) *The creation of entailed interests* – There are two main forms of words of limitation (*i.e.* words denoting the nature of the interest) for the creation of entailed interests. The first form is "To ... in tail (or 'in tail male' etc.)". The second form is "To ... and the heirs *of his body* (or 'the heirs male' etc.)"; or, in the case of a special entail, "To ... *and the heirs (or 'the heirs male' etc.) begotten by him on the body of* ... (the specified spouse)". The word "heirs", *must*, however, be used, since the essence of the entail is limitation to lineal *heirs*.

Either form of limitation will be permitted whether the grant be by deed or by will, but either the one or the other must be used.

(*iii*) *The barring of entails* – It will have become plain that the entail is the instrument, *par excellence*, of ancestral pride. Its essential purpose is to keep the property in the family by creating, in effect, an endless series of life interests. On principle, therefore, an entail fetters the property and makes it inalienable – except for the period of a particular life interest – until the family becomes extinct. The courts have, however, as we have seen, always striven to evade the achievement of this result. With the exception of a period during the Middle Ages (see above, p. 330), it has always been, and still is, possible for a tenant in tail to free the property of the interests of his remaindermen (the line of his successors) and, in certain cases, to give himself the fee simple by extinguishing the interest of the reversioner. The "reversioner" is the person to whom the land would revert should the family become extinct, *i.e.* normally the grantor or his successors.

Devious devices have been used in the past for "barring" entails. The position today is that a tenant in tail in *possession* may turn his interest into a fee simple estate by the easy method of executing a "disentailing assurance". This is merely a deed by which the tenant conveys the land to himself absolutely. A tenant in tail in *remainder* can only turn his interest into a fee simple (expectant upon the death of the tenant in possession) if he has the *consent* of the "protector of the settlement" who will usually, though not invariably, be the tenant in tail in possession. Without this consent, he can only bar his own successors in tail, not the reversioner. It should be added that at common law a tenant in tail could not devise the entail, and if he died without having disentailed, the estate descended to his heirs. This position was, however, altered by the L.P.A., s. 176 (1), which armed him with a statutory power – provided that specific reference is made to the property or to the instrument creating the entail, and that he is of full age and in *possession* of the property – to devise or bequeath it. And this testamentary disposition will bar the entail and pass the fee simple to the devisee.

The interest which arises where there is no such consent as we have described used to be called a "*base fee*" and is now technically an equitable interest equivalent to a base fee. Thus, if the land is limited "to A and the heirs of his body", A may, if in possession, by executing a disentailing assurance, obtain the fee simple for himself. If, however, A is not in possession, for example where his entail takes effect in remainder, then, a disentailing assurance by A without the consent of the protector of the settlement, will entitle A only to such an interest. This is clearly not a very valuable interest, since it is always threatened by the possibility that the family may become extinct, when the land will revert to the grantor or his successors. It was this unsatisfactory nature of the base fee that made the practice of re-settlement possible. A father who wished to keep the land in the family could always rely upon his eldest son to prefer the offer of an annual sum of money, and the expectancy of a future life interest, to a mere base fee. The base fee, being all that the son could acquire by his own efforts, was unattractive because it was not easily saleable. Like an entailed interest, an equitable interest equivalent to a base fee (L.P.A., s. 176 (3)) may now – subject to similar requirements, and especially that as to *possession* – be devised so as to pass a fee simple to the devisee.

(b)   Life interests

The normal life interest under the modern law is the interest of the tenant for life under a strict settlement. We have already seen how this interest arises; it therefore only remains to consider the rights and duties of the tenant.

The common law treats the tenant for life as if he were someone entitled to the income, but not to the capital, of a fund of money. He may enjoy the profits of his gift but he must pass on the bulk intact to his successors. Thus, generally speaking, he is entitled to the produce of the lands but he must not commit acts of "waste" which damage the inheritance. A tenant for life, for instance, who wantonly pulls down the mansion-house (*i.e.* the principal house of the estate) destroys something which belongs not to him but to his family.

Under the scheme of the S.L.A., as we have seen, the tenant for life now plays a dual rôle: he is both a beneficiary, who owns a part interest in the family property under the trusts of the settlement, and he is also at the same time an "estate owner" for the purpose of conveying the land upon a sale. Beside the *power of sale* (which can only be exercised for the best price reasonably obtainable) the S.L.A. confers further wide powers upon him. Amongst these powers are the following –

(*a*) *The power of exchange* – Instead of selling the land the tenant for life may exchange it for land of equal value.

(*b*) *The power to grant leases* – Subject to certain conditions, he may lease the land for a maximum period of 50 years. This maximum may be exceeded in the case of certain types of lease, such as building leases (999 years) and mining leases (100 years).

(*c*) *The power to grant mortgages* – In certain circumstances, as for instance when capital is required for making improvements, the tenant for life may raise this money by granting a legal mortgage over the land.

(*d*) *The power to make improvements* – It has been explained that the old law discouraged improvements. Few people will spend large sums out of their own pockets to benefit posterity primarily and themselves only secondarily. Under certain conditions the S.L.A. therefore permits a tenant for life to charge the cost of improvements upon "capital". Capital money under a settlement is any money subject to the trusts of the settlement: for instance, money arising from a sale of part of the land. This money will, of course, normally be in the hands of the trustees. The Act schedules various classes of improvements. Permanent improvements, such as irrigation, are entirely chargeable to capital, for they benefit posterity. Transitory improvements, such as the installation of oil heating, may be paid out of capital, but the tenant for life must refund the expenditure (usually within 25 years). Further, as a result of the amendment of the S.L.A. effected by the Agricultural Holdings Act 1948 a tenant for life of *agricultural* land can claim reimbursement of the cost of repairs out of capital money – this is, of course, very important in the case of large landed estates.

Before the tenant for life may exercise any of the above powers he must give notice to the trustees of the settlement. Some of the powers, moreover, can only be exercised with the consent of the trustees or by leave of the Court. In the exercise of all of them the tenant is acting not for himself alone, but on behalf of the "family", so that when he exercises them he is himself in the position of a trustee (S.L.A., s. 107) and he must not use them just to further his own interests. But, on the other hand, the Act (S.L.A., s. 106) secures for him an absolute right to exercise the powers, by enacting that any provision in any instrument that tends to fetter his right to exercise them shall be void.

(c) Future interests

The expression "future interests" is, perhaps, misleading. It has only been used in deference to tradition. It must not be supposed that we are about to discuss any fresh classes of estates and interests in this section. What we are now concerned to consider is the legal effect of creating any of the interests hitherto described in such a way that they shall arise, not immediately, at the time of the gift which creates them, but *at some time in the future.*

It need hardly be repeated that the only important estates and interests in land which are now capable of subsisting as *legal* estates are the fee simple absolute *in possession* and the term of years absolute. Generally speaking, all interests limited to arise in the future can now only be equitable interests, whatever their nature. The sole important exception to this rule, as we have seen, concerns *terms of years*. These may be legal estates, whether limited in possession *or in the future* (provided that they are to take effect within 21 years). As a general rule, in the absence of a trust for sale, the effect of conveying any other interest so that it shall arise at a future time is to subject the land concerned to an automatic settlement. Thus all future interests except terms of years are capable of being overreached.

It is necessary, however, to examine the effect of futurity a little further. Though future interests are thus subject to the "overreaching" machinery of the Property Acts, they are also only valid if they conform with the requirements of the *Rules against Perpetuities*. Since these rules only apply to *contingent*, as opposed to *vested* limitations, the difference between these two classes of limitation must be explained before they can be discribed.

"*Vested*" rights are of two kinds, they are either vested in "possession" or vested "in interest". A right which is vested in possession is one which usually carries with it the immediate right to the enjoyment of the land. Thus if A grants Whiteacre to B "in fee simple", B's title vests in *possession*. A right is vested in *interest* where it resides in an ascertained person whose right to possession merely awaits the natural determination of an existing estate. Thus where land is granted by X to Y for life, remainder to Z, in tail, whilst Y's interest is vested in possession, Z's remainder and X's reversion are both vested in interest. Z's remainder only awaits the natural event of Y's death. X's reversion resides in himself and his successors and only waits the failure of Z's successors. It must be noted that, whether vested in possession or in interest, a vested right actually exists in some holder; and this is nonetheless true if, though it will ultimately become ascertained, its exact extent is not known. Thus in *Beachway Management, Ltd.* v. *Wisewell*, [1971] 1 Ch. 610 it was held that a periodic payment imposed by way of rentcharge to meet the cost of road maintenance pending adoption of the road by a local authority – by an estate developer upon the purchaser of a house – was "vested" even though the periodic sums to be paid were to vary by reference to the rateable value of the land.

"*Contingent*" rights are rights which *do not come into existence* until some uncertain event takes place. Thus if A grants land to B, a minor, "if he reaches the age of 21", B has no real interest at all, he has a mere "contingency"; the hope of an interest which will only vest in him if he reaches the age of 21.

If it were possible to grant land contingently in such a way that the interest of the grantee could spring up at any time in the future, upon the occurrence of some uncertain event, it would become entirely "tied". No one would buy it. Suppose, for instance, that B were a bachelor and that A, the owner of Blackacre, were permitted to grant the fee simple to "any great-grandchild of B who shall have ten children at the age of forty". Clearly in such a case either the land or – if such a grant were possible under modern law – at any rate the proceeds of the sale of the land, would be "tied up" for a very long time indeed. The law, in its perennial anxiety to foster freedom of alienation, has therefore from time to time devised Rules against Perpetuities which aim at restricting future contingent grants within a reasonable period of time; some of these rules have been discarded and others modified. The subject is complex and it must not be supposed that the following outline is intended to provide anything more than a very general guide. Briefly, there are two main rules.

The *first rule* (common law) is time-honoured and it applies to all property, whether real or personal. It prescribes that where a future interest is created the limitation must be such that the interest must vest (if it is ever to vest at all: for a contingent interest may never vest if the contingency fails to occur) *within a life in being and 21 years thereafter*, adding, where appropriate, a period of gestation. "Life in being" means the life of a person extant at the time when the gift takes effect. In the case of a gift "*inter vivos*" (*i.e.* between a live donor and a live donee – as in the case of a conveyance by deed from A to B) the gift takes effect at the time of the *execution of the instrument* creating it; in the case of a gift by will it takes effect at the time of the *testator's death*. The period begins to run from one or other of these points of time, and upon the determination of the "life", only 21 further years are allowed. Moreover, at common law, at the relevant time the nature of the future gift had to be such that it could be predicted that it *must* vest (if it were ever to vest at all) within the period. Thus a gift to trustees to hold land in trust to convey it to X "20 years after the decease of the reigning Sovereign" was (and is) inevitably valid; since Sovereigns (here the "life in being") are mortal and X's interest (assuming only that X would be alive at the future date) must inevitably vest within the period. On the other hand a gift dependent upon a future uncertain contingency which *might* (or might not) fall outside the period when viewed at the relevant time was invalid at common law, since it could not be predicted that it *must* vest (if it were ever to vest at all) within the period. Thus at common law a gift "To A" (life in being), a bachelor, "for life, remainder to his first son to marry" was bad because A *might* have a son or sons none of whom would marry until after the period. Common law did not therefore allow the validity of the gift to lie in suspense to "wait and see" (as it has often been expressed) whether events would prove that the donee would *in fact* qualify within the period.

This position has now in the case of most (but not all) gifts depending upon some future uncertain contingency been altered by the Perpetuities and Accumulations Act 1964, s. 3. This provides that "where, apart from the provisions of this section ... a disposition would be void on the ground that the interest disposed of might not become vested until too remote a time, the disposition shall be treated, *until such time* (if any) as it becomes established that the vesting *must occur*, if at all, *after the end* of the perpetuity period, as if the disposition were not subject to the rule against perpetuities ...". This, in effect, means that now where the future interest in question depends upon an uncertain contingency the disposition will not be invalid simply because the predicted event *may* occur outside the period; it is permissible to await the determination of the period in order to discover whether the event has in fact occurred within it; if it has the gift will be good. On the other hand if during the period it becomes clear that the event *must* fall outside it, from that moment the gift fails. In the nature of things the former situation is likely to be the most common since an exact forecast of the time of occurrence of an uncertain future event is something which cannot often be made; but the latter situation may nevertheless arise in some cases. For instance, if one reverts to the last example one sees that it is a case of "wait and see" until the end of the period: then and only then can anyone be sure that A will *not* have a son who *will* marry within the period; if he does, of course, the gift will be saved by the section, if he does not it will *then* (and only then) become void. It is possible, however, to imagine a contingency which, as it were, clarifies its date of occurrence during the period and before it actually has occurred. Thus suppose a gift "To A for life, remainder to his eldest son when the comet White shall have appeared". Assume that the date of appearance is uncertain, though l'kely to occur after A's death: then assume that after the gift has taken effect the date of appearance is accurately predicted and that it will fall outside the period: the gift fails under s. 3 from the moment of this prediction.

So much for the common law rule as modified by the 1964 Act. Now as to the *second rule*, which is new, having been introduced by s. 1 of that Act. It introduces a period *alternative* to the first one and it is applicable to most (though not quite all) kinds of dispositions. To quote the section: "... where the instrument by which any disposition is made *so provides* ..." the alternative period shall be "... a duration equal to such number of years (*not exceeding eighty*) *as is specified ... in the instrument*". All that needs to be noted is that the duration chosen must be specified in the instrument; if it is, and is not in excess of *eighty* years, the gift is valid even though it would have been void under the "life in being" rule.

There is only enough space to add the following remarks. First, the time of *vesting* is all that matters; provided that this falls within one or other of the rules it does not matter that the interest in question will *endure* beyond that period. In the second place s. 4 of the Act provides that where a limitation would be avoided by the first rule because its date of vesting depends upon the attainment by someone of an age in excess of 21 the gift will be saved from invalidity by treating the specified age as if it were the age nearest to it which (had it been specified) would have complied with the rule. Thus in a gift "To A for life, remainder to his first son at 28" if we assume that at A's death there is a son aged 6 the prescribed age of 28 would take the gift out of the period (28 − 6 = 22); with the result that the figure 28 will be treated as if it were 27 (27 − 6 = 21); which accords with the rule. Finally, subject to exceptions, any limitations which offend the rules are void, though prior interests (such as "To A for life") upon which they depend remain valid.

Similar principles apply to "*accumulations*". Thus if X by will directs that the *income* accruing from his property shall be accumulated for a period of time, and then be given to a named beneficiary, X creates an accumulation. The permitted period of accumulation is governed by special rules in addition to the Perpetuity Rule. These rules are stricter than the Perpetuity Rule. They will be found set out in ss. 164–166 of the L.P.A., and s. 13 of the 1964 Act.

It should also be noted that the courts subject *any* gift which tends to make property inalienable to rules similar to the Perpetuity Rule. Thus a trust directing the income of a certain fund to be perpetually applied to furnishing a cup for yacht racing has been held to be bad. But there is some relaxation of this principle where gifts to charities are concerned (below, p. 399).

C MORTGAGES

A man who is in need of a loan may raise it in several ways. He may

have a rich friend who will lend it *gratis* or at so much per cent. If he
has no rich friend he will have to borrow from a stranger; but strangers
demand security. There are two principal forms of security, *"personal"*
security and *"real"* security. Personal security usually requires a friend
who will stand surety for the debt. Real security requires some form
of property; the borrower may, for instance, secure the loan by giving
the lender possession of his watch. If he is lucky, however, the borrower
may own land; in this case he will be able to secure the debt upon the
land. The best way of securing a debt upon land is by way of mortgage.
"Mortgage" is a strange word. It is said to derive from the ancient practice by which the borrower conveyed the land to the lender with a proviso for reconveyance should the loan be paid by a certain date: if the
loan was not repaid on that day the land became a "dead pledge" (*"mort
gage"*) for ever to the borrower, for it became the property of the lender.
The word survives, although mortgages are no longer created in this
way.

1   The Nature of Mortgages

The forms of mortgages recognized today are largely the creation of
the Property Acts. They fall into two main groups; legal mortgages and
equitable mortgages.

i   Legal mortgages – There are two forms of legal mortgage, the
mortgage by way of demise (lease), and the charge by way of legal mortgage. The *mortgage by demise* is effected in the following way. A, who
is fee simple owner of Whiteacre, wishes to borrow from B. He grants
B by deed, a legal term of years (usually for 3,000 years) of the land
with a proviso that if the principal loan and interest are paid by a certain
date, usually six months from the loan, the terms of years shall cease
to have effect. A further covenants in the deed to repay the loan and
interest upon the agreed date. The effect of this transaction is to give
certain rights both to A (mortgagor) and to B (mortgagee). These rights
will be described below. For the present it need only be noted that, under
the modern law, unlike the earlier law, B does not become absolutely
entitled to his 3,000-year term once the agreed date for repayment is
past: indeed, in the usual case it is never intended that the loan shall be
repaid on the agreed date, and the real purpose of this is to provide a
"redemption date", the significance of which will appear later. If A only
has a *lease* of Whiteacre he may achieve a similar result by sub-leasing
the property to B; the sub-demise will usually be for a period of ten
days shorter than A's own lease.

The *charge by way of legal mortgage* is the creation of s. 87 of the L.P.A. It is simply a short deed in which it is expressly stated that a charge is made by way of legal mortgage, though no term of years is thereby created. The important thing to note is that, once executed, it gives rise to the reciprocal rights to which we have referred.

Should A in the example given above, fall into further financial embarrassment, he may wish to execute a further mortgage to C over the same land. He may do this either by granting C a term of 3,000 years plus one day or, if he only holds a leasehold interest, by granting a second sub-demise nine days less in duration than his own lease. In either case he, of course, has the alternative of executing a second charge by way of legal mortgage. He can also grant further mortgages (3,000 years plus two days etc.) until he can no longer find a lender because his land is charged to its full value – mortgaged "to the hilt".

ii Equitable mortgages – (*a*) Mortgages of equitable interests can, themselves, only be equitable – by way of contrast with mortgages of legal interests, which may be either legal or equitable. They are made by way of an assignment of the equitable interest concerned, with a proviso for redemption upon payment by the mortgage of principal and interest. A deed is not required for the creation of these mortgages, but they must (in the absence of part performance – see above, p. 000) be made in writing.

(*b*) "*Equity looks on that as done which ought to be done.*" If, therefore, in consideration of money advanced, X agrees to grant Y a legal mortgage, but fails to do so, provided that this agreement is evidenced in writing or supported by a sufficient act of part performance, Y has a form of equitable mortgage, which the courts will uphold.

(*c*) An equitable mortgage also arises where title deeds are merely deposited with someone, other than the owner, as security for a debt, without any formal mortgage document. It is, however, advisable for the lender (mortgagee) to insist upon the execution of a memorandum under a seal (*i.e.* a deed), because, as we shall see, this gives him certain advantages in respect of the remedies which are open to him.

Finally, an equitable *charge* arises wherever there is a written agreement to treat property as security for a debt.

iii Mortgages of registered land – *Registered* land will be discussed below but it is convenient to mention mortgages in respect of it here. Where a holding is registered the two more important ways of mortgaging it are:

(*a*) By way of *registered charge*. This is a legal interest which can only be created by deed. It may take the form of a mortgage by demise (free-hold) or by sub-demise (leasehold) or by way of charge by way of legal mortgage. In the deed the land is usually described by reference to the register (see below). Such a charge will *only become* a legal estate by entry on the register. When it is so entered the mortgagee receives a "charge certificate" and the land certificate (below) is deposited at the Land Registry during the continuance of the mortgage; this machinery gives protection to the mortgagee.

(*b*) A registered proprietor may create a mortgage by depositing the *land certificate* with the mortgagee; this, provided that written notice is given to the Land Registry and an appropriate entry is made on the register, will give the mortgagee an effective lien (see below, p. 390) similar to an equitable mortgage.

2   The Rights of the Mortgagor

i   The right to redeem – It might appear from the foregoing that once the period fixed for the repayment of the loan has passed the mortgagee obtains an indefeasible right to his lease or to the property. This, indeed, was the way in which the common law looked at the matter. Equity, however, tracing its descent from general morality "looks to the *intent* rather than the form" and it has always insisted that a mortgage is, in essence, no more than a *form of security* as opposed to a conditional con-tract of sale. Hence equity disregarded the form of the contract and gave the mortgagor an equitable right to "*redeem*" (recover) the land at any time until the sale or foreclosure by the mortgagee. This right is called the "*Equity of Redemption*". The mortgagor can, of course, only exercise it if he repays the principal loan with interest to date.

So strictly did equity adhere to this principle that it did not, and does not, permit the right of redemption to be destroyed by expedients which hide what is in essence a mortgage transaction under the mask of some other form. Thus, in one case, B granted A a lease for twenty years, in return for a loan, and his right to terminate the lease was post-poned for nineteen years. It was held that the lease being no more than a cloak to cover a mortgage transaction, B could terminate it by repayment of the principal and interest at an earlier date. "*Once a mort-gage, always a mortgage*" – the equity of redemption is inviolable.

Further, equity insists that there must be "*no clog on the equity*". This means two things. (1) The court will not countenance any covenant in the contract which purports to postpone the repayment period for an unreasonable time. What will be regarded as "unreasonable" is a ques-tion of fact which must vary according to the relationship between the parties. Thus in *Knightsbridge Estates* v. *Byrne*, [1939] Ch. 441, it was held that where one company had lent another £310,000 at 5¼ per cent upon a mortgage of some very valuable property in London it was reasonable for the parties to agree to postpone the period for repayment for 40 years. The mortgagors fully realized that the mortgagees required a long term investment. This, however, was an exceptionally long period; it would not be regarded as "reasonable" as between private people in the case of a mortgage of property of little value in return for a small loan. If such a long period were agreed upon in a case of this sort the mortgagor would be entitled to disregard it, and to redeem long before it had expired. And he will also be entitled to disregard the contractual period of postponement and redeem where, although the time of postponement might not otherwise be objectionable, the transaction as a whole is illegal as being in unlawful restraint of trade. Thus in *Esso Petroleum Co., Ltd.* v. *Harper*, [1968] A.C. 269 (see above, p. 223), the agreement in respect of the M. Garage containing the illegal solus agreement, was a mortgage agreement expressed to be irredeemable for the 21-year period: hence, though (as the *Byrne Case* shows) 21 years might not normally have constituted an unreasonable clog on the equity, the plaintiff could redeem in disregard of the postponement clause because the whole transaction was invalid as being in restraint of trade. (2) Once the money has been repaid and the land "redeemed" the matter is at an end; the mortgagee must be satisfied with the return of his money together with the interest agreed. He must reap no other collateral advantage. This rule was evolved in by-gone days when mortgagors were usually necessitous people and mortgagees unscrupulous money-lenders who tried to secure more than their fair interest by imposing onerous stipulations upon the mortgagor, which would bind him beyond the mortgage period. Like the last rule, it has therefore become modified in modern times and stipulations of this sort will now sometimes be enforced even after the mortgage has been redeemed; but, once again, the collateral advantage secured must be reasonable. Thus where a loan of £2,900 in respect of the purchase of a house was secured by a charge on the property for the payment of £4,553 (the difference of £1,653 being by way of premium) it was held that, upon the mortgagor's default, the mortgagee could realize no more than the £2,900 at a rate of interest determined by the court.

ii The right to grant leases – Where, as will normally be the case, the mortgagor is in possession of the land, he has a limited right to lease it to third parties.

3 The Powers and Remedies of the Mortgagee

The mortgagee cannot "call in" (*i.e.* demand repayment of) the mortgage until the redemption date has passed, and in the case of certain mortgages of properties subject to the Rent Acts, not even then unless the mortgage payments are in arrears or there has been a breach of some other covenant – *e.g.* to repair – by the mortgagor. Subject to this, the principal powers and remedies of a *legal* mortgagee are the following:

    i   to take possession;
    ii to foreclose;
    iii to sell;
    iv to sue upon the personal covenant;
    v to appoint a receiver.

(*i*) *Entry into possession* – It should not be imagined that the mortgagee will normally take advantage of the lease which is granted to him. The usual position is that the mortgagor remains in possession of the premises throughout the duration of the mortgage. The term of years is granted merely as a security which the mortgagee may use if he wants to. If he does enter into possession the object of doing so is to keep down interest on the loan by paying himself out of the rents and profits arising from the land; but the court will exercise stringent supervision over him, and he is strictly accountable, not only for what he actually receives, but also for what, by the exercise of due diligence, he ought to have received.

(*ii*) *Foreclosure* – Equity, as we have seen, disregarded the *form* of a mortgage transaction and gave the mortgagor a right of redemption. Even equity, however, found it necessary to impose a limit upon the time for which this right could endure. The unpaid lender must sooner or later have a right to realize his security. Thus, if the debt be unpaid for an unreasonable time beyond the agreed repayment period, the mortgagee may "foreclose" by obtaining an order of the court that the land shall become his unless payment in full is made by a certain date. Once that date is past, the order may be made "absolute" unless the mortgagor has paid; he then loses all right to the land unless, as sometimes happens, he can persuade the court to "re-open" the order at a later date. Because of this, and certain other considerations, this right has a number of disadvantages and it is rarely exercised.

(*iii*) *Power of sale* – Under certain conditions, the mortgagee has a statutory power to sell the whole of the mortgagor's interest in the land. He may then recoup himself out of the purchase money, but he is not allowed to keep any *surplus* proceeds arising from the sale. The intervention of the court is not required for the exercise of this power; but although in its exercise the mortgagee does not act as a trustee for the mortgagor he nevertheless owes him a duty of care. For instance he must regard the latter's interests enough to take reasonable care to obtain a reasonable price. Sale is the most usual method of enforcing the security.

Where a mortgage is security for a regulated agreement (see above, p. 274) *the power of sale and the power of entry with possession* can, by the Consumer Credit Act 1974, s. 126, only be exercised by court order.

(iv) Action on the personal covenant – The repayment covenant is, of course – quite apart from the security over the land created by the rest of the mortgage – an ordinary contract. Hence the mortgagee may, at any time after the expiry of the repayment period, sue for the recovery of the loan.

(v) The appointment of a receiver – Under certain conditions, the mortgagee may exercise a statutory power of appointing a receiver to receive the rents and profits arising from the land on his behalf, with a view to ensuring payment of the interest. The receiver is deemed to be the agent of the mortgagor, and the mortgagee thus avoids the disadvantage of strict accountability to which, if he were to enter into possession, he would himself be subject.

The remedies of an *equitable* mortgagee whose mortgage is created by *deed* are much the same as the remedies of a legal mortgagee. The sole remedy of an *equitable* chargee is to have the land sold or a receiver appointed by the court.

D THE SALE OF THE LAND

There are always two elements in a sale, contract and delivery. In a cash transaction these two things may take place almost simultaneously, but this should not obscure the fact that they are distinct. Land is incapable of delivery, but *conveyance*, an outward symbol which evidences the passing of property, takes the place of delivery in sales of land. Due to the fact that two distinct types of conveyance are now in use we must treat them separately.

1 Conveyances of Unregistered Land

These will be discussed under five heads: (1) The Contract; (2) Between

Contract and Conveyance; (3) Conveyance; (4) Completion; (5) Land Charges.

1 THE CONTRACT

It will be remembered that by the provisions of s. 40 of the L.P.A., part performance aside, contracts for the sale of land must be evidenced in writing. This is not, however, the only way in which they differ from other contracts; the following are examples of the main differences.

In the first place, contracts for the sale of land fall into two classes, they are either "*open*" or "*formal*". An "open" contract is one which does not set out the terms of the sale: consequently certain conditions are implied by law. The most important of these conditions is that the vendor shall be obliged to show a good title (see below). A formal contract is one which contains specific conditions. It usually consists of *Particulars*, *Special Conditions* and *General Conditions*. The Particulars describe the property. The Special Conditions contain stipulations peculiar to the sale in question. The General Conditions are standardized: they are usually incorporated into the contract by reference to one or another of a number of set forms. Forms of General Conditions are put out by the Law Society and by local Law Societies and there is a commercial publication called the "National" Conditions of Sale. Where an open contract is concluded by *correspondence* certain Statutory Conditions of Sale, laid down by the Lord Chancellor under statutory authority (L.P.A., s. 46), apply, unless they are expressly excluded. It should be noted that although open contracts are theoretically of great importance they do not, as might be expected, often occur in practice.

In the second place, it is usual to provide for the payment of a deposit by the purchaser (usually 10 per cent), which he will forfeit if the sale fails to take place by his default.

In the third place, the vendor – who, upon conclusion of the contract becomes trustee of the land in favour of the purchaser, so that if he sells it to a third party he is accountable to the purchaser for the proceeds – acquires an "equitable lien" (see below, p. 390) over the property for the amount of the purchase price for the time being unpaid. The effect of this is that if the purchaser fails to pay the vendor may apply to the court to sanction a resale of the land in order to recoup his loss. The lien, arising as it does by implication in equity will terminate if the vendor secures his rights by some other means, such as the creation of an express charge.

In the fourth place, the risk of destruction by fire falls upon the purchaser from the time of the contract.

Finally, in most contracts for the sale of land, unlike most contracts for the sale of goods, both parties have a right to specific performance;

not merely to damages. Moreover, a peculiar rule was sanctioned by the House of Lords in *Bain* v. *Fothergill* (1874), L.R. 7 H.L. 158 in respect of damages: if the vendor finds that he is unable to effect the sale because of a defect in his title the purchaser will only be able to claim the return of his deposit (if any) and damages for his expenses in respect of the sale, not for the loss of his bargain. This rule is said to have been made because of the extreme difficulty of proving a good title to English land.

2 BETWEEN CONTRACT AND CONVEYANCE

Between the time of the completion of the contract and the conveyance the vendor has to satisfy the purchaser that he is in a position to make over to him a valid title. What constitutes a valid title depends either upon the express conditions of sale, or, if the contract is an open contract, upon the general rules of law. The rule is that in the case of an open contract the vendor must prove that he can trace his right to the fee simple back to a "good root of title" at least *fifteen* years old. This means that he must be able to produce a document, such as a conveyance upon sale, at least fifteen years old, which vests the whole fee simple in some person. He must then trace all dealings in the land from that time to the present, with the object of showing that he is the person entitled to sell. This means that he must produce all instruments which have disposed of the land during that period in historical sequence and show who has become entitled to it. Proof of the latter requires production of birth and death certificates, etc., where these affect the devolution of the title.

The first move in proof of title is for the vendor to prepare at his own expense an *abstract or an epitome of title*: the former sets out the history of the title to the property for the appropriate period, in narrative form, citing all material documents, the latter (now, perhaps, commoner procedure) consists of a schedule of documents back to the root of title with photostat copies of the documents listed. This must be delivered to the purchaser who is entitled to verify it by inspecting the original documents or authenticated abstracts of them. The purchaser is allowed a certain time (usually 14 days) in which to peruse the abstract. He will next deliver *requisitions on title* to the vendor. These are written questions designed to give the purchaser a complete picture of the property which he has agreed to buy, to satisfy him that it is in no way encumbered, and to clear up any doubts about matters concerning the title which he may have upon what is revealed by the abstract.

Before completion the purchaser will *search* the Land Registry (see below) in order to discover whether there are any registered land charges affecting the property. He should also make a search at the local land charges registry. If there are any registered charges and he fails to search, he will be forced to take the land subject to them.

Naturally in practice, all the above business is usually attended to by the parties' solicitors.

3 THE CONVEYANCE

When the purchaser is satisfied with the title the next step is the preparation of the conveyance (which must be effected by *deed* – L.P.A., s. 52 (1)). This is normally done by the purchaser's solicitor at the purchaser's expense. He first prepares a draft. When the draft has been approved it will usually be *engrossed*, *i.e.* copied out as a formal deed to be executed by the parties as a conveyance. The deed of conveyance usually contains the following :–

(*i*)   *The date.*

(*ii*)   *The names of the parties.*

(*iii*) *Recitals* – These begin "WHEREAS . . ." and contain a description of the vendor's interest (*e.g.* that he is "seised of an estate in fee simple free from encumbrances" in the land).

(*iv*) *Testatum* – This commences the operative part of the deed, and begins with the words "NOW THIS DEED WITNESSETH", or some such phrase. It contains a statement of the purchase price and an acknowledgement (the *receipt*) by the vendor that the price has been paid.

(*v*)   Where the vendor is the absolute owner of the land, the deed continues "THE VENDOR AS BENEFICIAL OWNER HEREBY CONVEYS". The words "*beneficial owner*" have a special signification, as explained below.

(*vi*) *Parcels* – A description of the property.

(*vii*) *Habendum* – This explains the extent of the interest conveyed. In the case of a conveyance of a fee simple estate it runs "To hold unto the purchaser in fee simple."

(*viii*) There now follow any express covenants, conditions, agreements and other special provisions peculiar to the particular conveyance, which have been agreed to in the contract or which are otherwise necessary.

(*ix*) *Testimonium* – This states that the signatories have signed and sealed the conveyance in witness of the foregoing contents.

The use of the words "*as beneficial owner*" in a conveyance of the fee simple gives rise, by operation of the L.P.A., to certain implied covenants on the part of the vendor. Shortly, these covenants ensure that the purchaser will be able to hold the vendor responsible if his title to, or his possession of, the land is in any way disturbed by the vendor or by anyone who claims title under him, or from whom he claims. The vendor will not, however, be held liable for the acts of strangers or of persons from whom he has purchased the land for value. These covenants will, of course, rarely need to be invoked because the purchaser

will, as we have seen, have satisfied himself that the title is good, and
the land free from encumbrances, before the conveyance is completed.
It should be added that this outline description of a conveyance gives
the main elements of what one may call a traditional conveyance; shorter
forms are now often used.

4 COMPLETION

When the engrossment has been checked, all that remains to be done
is to complete the conveyance by obtaining the signature of the vendor.
Completion will usually take place at the office of the vendor's solicitor.
The following points should be noted. First, there is no positive requirement that the deed should be witnessed by a third party. Second,
although a deed is a document "under seal" this does not mean today
that the parties append a private seal to it: a "seal" is a formal paper
wafer attached to the deed. Third, as a general rule the vendor must
hand over to the purchaser, with the deed of conveyance, all documents
of title relevant to the land.

5 LAND CHARGES

There are, as we have seen, certain equitable rights which the vendor
can and must clear off the title by means of the overreaching machinery
of the Acts; but there are some rights to which this machinery does not
apply. Some of these are obvious and the purchaser must usually become
aware of them: he should know, for instance, if there is a lessee in occupation, or if a mortgagee has the title deeds. The existence of some others –
which do not come within the overreaching machinery – is not, however, so easy to discover. The L.C.A. (now largely replaced by the
L.C.A. 1972 which consolidated the law on this matter) completed the
work of previous legislation by setting up a system of registration of
rights of this kind which makes it possible for purchasers and other interested parties to get to know of their existence. It is not thought that,
especially since *unregistered land alone is here concerned*, it is necessary to
examine these land charges in detail. *Inter alia*, they consist of such in-
visible things as puisne mortgages (*i.e.* any legal mortgage except one
which is protected by deposit of documents), estate contracts (*i.e.* contracts to convey or create a legal estate in land), restrictive covenants
and the spouse's right of occupation of the matrimonial home (see
below, p. 412). They are registrable in the *Land Charges Register*,
which is under the ultimate control of the Chief Land Registrar and is
now situated at Plymouth. Registration of such charges constitutes
notice to all the world and a purchaser cannot complain if he fails to
discover their existence by omitting to consult the Register, which he
is at liberty to do; though by s. 24 of the L.P.A. 1969 he may, as against

his *vendor*, rescind the contract where he discovers that there was, at the time that it was made, a land charge (other than a local land charge) in existence of which he did not *actually know*. The reason for the latter relaxation of the general rule that registration constitutes notice to all the world is that in the case of unregistered land search does not normally take place until after conclusion of the *contract*, and that it would thus be wrong to penalize a purchaser (as against his vendor) for failure to search at that stage. This relaxation does not, however, apply to charges upon *registered* land (below) entered in the Land Register. By s. 15 (1) of the 1972 Act purchasers are in general entitled to *compensation* in respect of loss suffered by reason of the existence of a registered land charge of which they did not *actually know* provided that it was registered more than 15 years before the purchase or (where the contract provides for a longer period than the statutory 15 years) before the root of the title.

It should also be noted that s. 15 of the L.C.A. requires local authorities to keep registers of *local land charges*. These charges arise as the result of the provisions of various statutes, such as the Private Streets Works Acts which empower local authorities to recover the cost of street works from neighbouring owners, and the all-important Town and Country Planning Acts by which many plans and orders have to be registered. Failure to register such charges renders them void as against a purchaser for value of the legal estate.

2 Conveyances of Registered Land

Registered land is land the title to which is registered at H.M. Land Registry which is in London, though for convenience registers are kept at a number of *district* land registries. Transfers of it are simpler than the conveyances just described. The chief difference between the two systems of conveyancing is that whereas, as we have seen, in the case of conveyances of unregistered land it is for the *parties* respectively to prove and ascertain the validity of the title, in the case of registered land the title is *officially* examined and officially guaranteed. The system of registration of title is now being rapidly expanded by successive extension of areas of compulsory registration and it is anticipated that all land will be subject to it by 1980. Thus the traditional method of conveyancing which has been outlined above will eventually disappear.

Land registration is governed by the L.R.A. and the principle of it is that, once the title has been subjected to official verification, the holding concerned is registered. This means that it is given an individual card entry consisting of three parts (confusingly also called "registers"). These are (*i*) a *property* register, (*ii*) a *proprietorship* register, (*iii*) a *charges* register. The first contains a description of the land with plan annexed, and of the title registered (usually, in the case of a fee simple, an "*absolute*" title). The second identifies the proprietor. The third gives notice of any land charges which affect the holding (this, in the case of registered land, removes the need to search the Land Charges Register). The latter, as we have just seen, concerns charges on *unregistered* land.

The registered proprietor is given a *land certificate*: this corresponds to title deeds, and it evidences his ownership. If therefore a registered proprietor wishes to convey his land, all that he has to do is to execute a very short and simple deed of transfer, and to have the purchaser's name substituted for his own on the Register. The purchaser will then receive the certificate back duly endorsed. Purchasers are fully protected because all subsisting encumbrances over the land are entered in the register (see (3) and (4) above) and the mere fact of registration constitutes notice of these. As an exception to this rule, there are, however, certain "*overriding*" interests, *e.g.* leases for 21 years or less and easements (such as rights of way) which bind a purchaser whether they are noted in the register or not. The purchaser must therefore ascertain the existence of these for himself. It should be stressed that the land certificate, though valuable evidence of title, *is* only *evidence* of it: the proof lies in the entry in the Register. Thus, for instance, the certificate may be out of date if entries have been made in the Register after the certificate was last deposited with the Registry for comparison. It may also be of interest that as a general rule no one may inspect the register (not even a purchaser) without written authority from the registered proprietor.

If the Registrar is satisfied that the title of the proprietor is flawless, it may be entered as "*absolute*", and a purchaser who suffers by reason of a subsequent discovery that this absolute title is invalid will have a right to compensation from the State. There are also other, less effective, forms of entry which need no mention here.

Perhaps it should finally be noted that the Land Registration and Land Charges Act 1971 (s. 4) exempts "souvenir" land from registration. This is, in effect, defined as land "being of inconsiderable size and little or no practical utility" which "is unlikely to be wanted in isolation except for the sake of pure ownership or for sentimental reasons or commemorative purposes".

E LIMITATION

It will be recalled that one of the methods of acquiring easements and profits is by means of prescription. The essence of prescription is that long, open and unchallenged user founds a claim of right. It might be expected that not only the right to easements and profits, but the title to land itself might be acquired in this way. English law, however, has confined the principle of acquisition by prescription to "incorporeal" rights such as easements, which do not carry with them the right to *possession* of the land. Where a man is in possession of something "corporeal", a physical object, such as land, the law grants protection to his *possession as such*. Thus a possessor has no need to rely upon prescription to constitute a title: the law will protect him against anyone except a person with a better right to possession than his. Thus if "squatter" A is evicted by "squatter" B, A may bring an action to oust B, though naturally A may himself be evicted by the rightful owner of the land. Though, since possession is protected, as such, the possessor will acquire a complete defence to a claim *even by the latter* after the requisite period of *limitation* has run in respect of an action by him: so that then the possessor's possession will have become ("ripened" by lapse of time into) ownership.

The general rule laid down by the Limitation Act 1939, s. 4 is that anyone, including the owner, who is ousted from the possession of land must bring his action to recover it within 12 years from the time when the cause of action first accrued. Once this "limitation period" is past, the plaintiff's right to sue is lost, and his title itself is destroyed. Thus if X ousts Y, a tenant in fee simple, and after 13 years Y ousts X, X may bring an action to eject Y. Y will not be able to rely upon his former title; he will have lost it through his own inertia. But in order for the limitation period to *start* to run against Y the latter must have discontinued his possession; or, to put the reverse, he must be "ousted" by X. Thus it has been held that the mere fact that a person makes use of another's land (as by ploughing it – a trespass) will not, even though it continue for 12 years, confer upon the former a title by reason of limitation if the reason that the owner raised no objection was that he was only leasing the land alone because he was waiting to build upon it when a projected road should be made. A border-line decision, two to one with powerful dissent: which illustrates the difficulty of deciding what is an "ouster".

The period (which, by the provisions of s. 7 (1), applies to claims by owners of equitable interests as well as to owners of legal estates) runs from the time when the cause of action *accrues*. In the simplest case where B evicts A, who is in possession, this will be from the moment of eviction. Often, however, people are entitled not to immediate, but only to ultimate, possession (as for instance in the case of a fee simple owner whose land is subject to a term of years). The Act provides that those who are in this position must bring their claim either within 12 years of the actual entry of the wrongful possessor or within six years of the time when they themselves become entitled to possession, whichever of these two periods is the longer. Thus suppose that B is the remainder-man under a grant to "A for life, with remainder to B in fee simple" and that X ousts A: B's right to recovery will be barred either 12 years after X's entry or six years after A's death. Landlords form an exception to this rule; their rights of action normally only "accrue" against someone who evicts their tenants on the date when the tenancy is due to determine. They are permitted the full 12-year period from that time.

Minors and people of unsound mind are exempted from the ordinary rules. They may claim at any time up to six years from the cessation of the minority or disability (subject in the latter case to an overriding period of 30 years). Actions *by* the Crown are also subject to a 30-year period.

The provisions of the Act which govern fraud and mistake have already been considered (above, p. 265).

PERSONAL PROPERTY

A THE NATURE OF PERSONAL PROPERTY

Property is any object which a man may own or possess. Under the modern law "*personal*" property is any property other than land, except that for the purposes of descent leaseholds are treated as personal property (see below, p. 449). The main difference, as we have seen, between land and personal property, is that the former, being indestructible, may be subjected to interests of a more complex nature than the latter. Moreover, personal property, unlike land, escaped the hand of feudalism. Hence the doctrine of tenure never applied to it. Personal property may be owned in theory, as well as in fact.

Leaseholds (terms of years) have already been discussed. We have seen (above, p. 329) that they came to be classified technically as "chattels real" because of their assimilation in many ways to land. But it should be borne in mind that, strictly speaking, they still form an anomalous species of personal property.

Personal property is divided into two main categories; *choses in possession* and *choses in action*. These must be considered separately.

1 Choses in Possession

Choses (i.e. things) in possession ("chattels") are the familiar tangible movables, such as books, cars or furniture, of everyday life. They are property which can actually be possessed and transferred by physical delivery. Like other forms of property, they may be the subject of a contract or of a gift (below, p. 391). The owner's or the possessor's rights to them are protected by the law of torts and by the criminal law.

2 Choses in Action

There are many forms of property which are not tangible physical objects. Debts, for instance, and shares in a company, are "property", but they cannot be touched or seen. Property of this kind is known as a *"chose in action"*; the owner's right to it cannot be asserted by taking possession, but only by means of an action. There are many such things: among the more important are negotiable instruments, patents and designs, copyright and trade marks and trade names. For the sake of brevity the first alone will be examined here.

NEGOTIABLE INSTRUMENTS

It is possible that in the dawn of history men lived in family groups, and that there was no such thing as commerce. Today, however, even the most backward peoples engage in some form of commerce, even if it only takes the form of barter.

From early times coined money came to be used by all progressive peoples as a medium of exchange, and the coinage circumvented the obvious defects of barter. Money itself, however, is not always a very convenient medium of exchange; it is, for example, both difficult and dangerous to transport from place to place. This inconvenience, moreover, as the "Great Train Robbery" demonstrated, affects large sums of money in the form of notes almost as much as it affects coined money. Hence, at least by the Middle Ages, the merchants of Europe had invented *negotiable instruments* as a substitute for money in business transactions.

A negotiable instrument is a written document embodying a promise, usually (not invariably), to pay money. Three requirements have to be satisfied before the courts will recognize an instrument as "negotiable". It must be freely transferable, like cash, by delivery so that it can be passed from hand to hand in such a way as to entitle the holder of it to enforce the original promise. Either it must have been made negotiable by statute, or it must be a document which is treated as negotiable by commercial custom. It follows that there is no "closed list" of negotiable instruments, for statute and custom may approve appropriate new classes of documents from time to time. Custom, however, is never easy to prove, and it should not, therefore, be imagined that new classes of negotiable instruments are constantly being recognized in modern times.

When an instrument has thus acquired "negotiability" it will be treated as representing money, and it therefore acquires a basic characteristic of money. If I steal your bicycle and sell it to X it will normally remain yours and you can recover it, or the value of it, from X. If I steal your money and buy a bicycle with it from Y the money ceases to be yours from the moment of the sale. In other words, money is not subject to the rule *nemo dat quod non habet* ("no one can give a better title than he himself has"). The same rule applies to negotiable instruments. Provided that a person who acquires a negotiable instrument takes it in good faith, and provided that he can prove that value has been given for it, he obtains a good title to it, even though he acquired it from a thief.

Three of the more common classes of negotiable instruments must now be considered: bills of exchange, cheques and promisory notes.

(a) Bills of exchange

The law governing bills of exchange, and the other negotiable instruments about to be discussed, is now for the most part codified in the Bills of Exchange Act 1882 (here abbreviated "B.E.A.").

The Act (s. 3 (1)) defines a bill of exchange as "*an unconditional order in writing, addressed by one person to another, signed by the person giving it, requiring the person to whom it is addressed to pay on demand, or at a fixed or determinable future time, a sum certain in money to, or to the order of, a specified person, or to bearer*".

The meaning of this definition may be illustrated. A, a London merchant, is going to Paris. He will need money to buy goods when he is there and he cannot, or does not wish to, take currency with him. He has a friend, B, in London who has a debtor, C, in Paris. A pays B, say, £1000. B then writes out an order for an equivalent amount of money in francs "drawn" on C, expressed to be payable to "A or order". This document is a bill of exchange. A takes it with him to France. When he arrives he can either demand the money from C, or "negotiate" the bill by indorsing it to D, a third party. D will, of course, pay A; and, since the bill is "negotiable", he will be entitled to recover from C the sum appearing on the bill. Should C, for some reason, refuse to pay, D will be entitled to recover from either B or A; but, on the other hand, he may "negotiate" the bill to E; E to F and so on.

The following is a common form for a bill of exchange –

£1,000   London, November 7th, 1976
  Three months after date pay to Mr. Thomas Smith or order
One Thousand pounds for value received.
                                            John Johnston
To Mr. Peter Roberts

John Johnston is the *drawer*, Thomas Smith is the *payee*, Peter Roberts
is the *drawee*. Once Peter Roberts accepts he becomes the *acceptor*. When
the bill is delivered to Thomas Smith he becomes the *holder*. If Thomas
Smith "indorses" the bill and transfers it to X, Thomas Smith becomes
the *indorser*, X, the *holder*. And every holder to whom the bill is *negotiated*
by further indorsement may, as may X himself – provided all the requirements about to be discussed are satisfied – claim against the drawer
or, failing him, the drawer on some prior holder.
    Various points require to be considered –

Bearer bills – The bill in the above example was made payable to
Thomas Smith "or order". The effect of this is that if Thomas Smith
wishes to transfer the bill to Timothy Transfer he must indorse it. It
might, however, have been made payable to Thomas Smith "or bearer".
In that case Thomas Smith could transfer it without indorsement. Bills
may also be made payable simply "to bearer", and anyone who holds
them may then sue upon them (unless of course it can be *proved* that
he is a thief). On the other hand, since s. 3 (1) of the B.E.A. requires
that in order to be a bill of exchange the document must demand
payment to a "specified person" or order, or to "bearer", an instrument
requiring payment to "cash or order" cannot be a bill of exchange; nor
(since a cheque is a special form of bill of exchange) a cheque.

Delivery – "Delivery" means transfer. No one may claim rights upon
a bill until it comes into his possession by delivery. Thus, until delivery
to the payee or acceptance, the bill is ineffectual, and the drawer can
incur no liability upon it. The first delivery (*i.e.* to the payee) is known
as the "*issue*" of the bill.

Indorsement – Indorsement is effected by signing the bill; usually on
the back. It may be "*in blank*" or "*special*". An indorsement is in blank
where the indorser simply signs his own name, *e.g.* "Thomas Smith".
An indorsement is special where the indorser signs his own name, then

adds the name of a new payee, *e.g.* "Thomas Smith – pay Timothy Transfer or order". The effect of an indorsement in blank is that the bill becomes payable to any bearer who may obtain it. The effect of a special indorsement is that the person named ("Timothy Transfer") can only make a new transfer by indorsement.

Acceptance – A bill is "*accepted*" when it is signed (usually across the face of it) by the drawee. He may do this at any time, even before the drawer himself has signed. Acceptance may be "*general*" or "*qualified*". A general acceptance is an unconditional acceptance; a qualified acceptance is one which is subject to condition, *e.g.* that the acceptor undertakes to pay only a part of the amount of the bill. A bill may be payable "on demand" (or "at sight") or it may be payable upon a fixed date (as in the example). This date is known as the date of "*maturity*". Bills of the latter type need not actually be paid on the due date; for the acceptor is allowed three statutory "*days of grace*" running from that date (B.E.A., s. 14).

Holder – Any payee or indorsee in possession of a bill, or any bearer of a bill, is called a "*holder*" (B.E.A., s. 2).

Holder for value – Any holder of a bill, for which *at any time* value has been given, is deemed to be a "*holder for value*" as regards all parties to the bill prior to himself (B.E.A., s. 27 (2)). Moreover, provided that valuable consideration is given *for the bill* the holder is nevertheless a "holder for value" if he has given such consideration to a person who is not a party to it, or if the person sued upon it has received it from such a person. Thus if A sues B upon a bill drawn by B it is no defence to B that A's consideration for it was supplied by X, nor is it a defence that B received consideration from X rather than from A.

Holder in due course – A "*holder in due course*" is any holder of a bill, complete and regular on the face of it, who takes *in good faith and for value* (see below) before the bill is overdue, and who has no notice that it has previously been dishonoured (should that in fact have been the case), or of any defect (should there be such) in the title of the person who negotiated it to him. A bill will not be "complete and regular on the face of it" if the payee, when indorsing it, does not make it apparent by his signature that he really is the intended payee. Thus, though the designation used by the drawer need not always be adopted by the indorser, yet, if the bill is to be "complete and regular on the face of it", he must be careful to avoid a patent discrepancy between the designation he uses and that used by the drawer. For example, a bill drawn in favour of "Colonel John Brown", and simply indorsed by the person in question "John Brown", will be "regular"; but it has been held that where promissory notes drawn in favour of "X & Y Co. or order" (a foreign partnership firm) were indorsed by one of the partners simply "X and Y", the notes were not "regular", so as to entitle a subsequent holder to claim the rights of a "holder in due course" (though he *could* claim to be a "holder for value"). The reason for this was that the indorsement ought to have led to a reasonable doubt in the mind of the holder whether "X & Y *Co.*" and "X & Y" represented two different entities (see *Arab Bank, Ltd.* v. *Ross*, [1952] 2 Q.B. 216).

"*Value*" has a special meaning in the present context. By way of exception to the ordinary rules as to consideration (see above, p. 215), for the purposes of this branch of the law, "consideration" may include an "antecedent debt or liability" (B.E.A., s. 27 (1) (b)). This point should be stressed, for, as has been explained, normally "past" consideration is no consideration.

Presumption of good faith and value – Every *holder* of a bill is *prima facie presumed* to be a *holder in due course* (B.E.A., s. 30 (2)). This is a most important rule; but it must be realized that it only imports a *presumption*, and that presumption may be rebutted (so as to render his claim invalid) if it is proved that the holder lacked good faith, *i.e.* took the bill knowing of a defect in title *or* knowing that the acceptance, issue, or subsequent negotiation was affected by fraud, duress or illegality. The burden of proving such knowledge in respect of defective *title* lies upon the acceptor or other person who seeks to establish that the plaintiff is not a holder in due course, but where fraud, etc. is alleged the holder *himself* must *prove affirmatively* that at some time subsequent to the wrongdoing in question, and before the bill came into his hands, *value* was in fact given for it by *someone* (not necessarily himself) who took in good faith, without knowledge of the wrongful act.

Presentment – There are two forms of presentment: "presentment for acceptance" and "presentment for payment".

(*a*) *Presentment for acceptance* – Strictly speaking this is only necessary (and even so, subject to exceptions) in three cases. First, where the bill is payable "after sight" (*i.e.* is expressed to be payable within a certain time after it has been brought to the notice of the drawee) – clearly here it *must* be "presented" because, until it is, its maturity date remains unascertained. Second, where the bill itself expressly stipulates that it shall be presented for acceptance. Third, where the bill is drawn payable elsewhere than at the place of residence or business of the drawee. Of course these categories do not include cheques.

Where a bill of these kinds comes into the hands of a holder he must either present it to the drawee for acceptance, or negotiate it within a reasonable time. Upon presentment, the drawee must accept the bill within 24 hours. If the drawee fails to accept within this time, or if he repudiates liability, he will have "dishonoured" the bill. If this happens, the holder must give notice of dishonour to the drawer, or to the person who indorsed the bill to him. Notice of dishonour must not be given prematurely before dishonour. It is effective from time of *receipt* and must be given within a reasonable time of dishonour or in the case of written notice sent by post it must normally be despatched on the day of dishonour or, at least, by the following day.

The effect of giving notice is to fix the drawer, or the previous indorser, with liability for payment. All parties who have signed the bill prior to the holder are sureties for the payment of it. Thus an indorser who receives notice of dishonour will give notice to the person who indorsed it to him, and so forth, until the drawer receives notice. After the acceptor, the drawer is, of course, primarily liable. Moreover, failure to present for acceptance (where this is required) will discharge the drawer and previous indorsers.

Unless a bill is payable on demand it need not normally be presented for acceptance; moreover, if it is so payable, we have already seen that a holder need not present it if he transfers it to another person within a reasonable time.

(*b*) *Presentment for payment* – All bills must be presented for payment at the proper time. A bill payable on demand must be presented by the holder within a reasonable time of receiving it (unless he indorses it to someone else). A bill payable upon a fixed date must be presented for payment upon that date. If the acceptor refuses to pay, his refusal constitutes "*dishonour*" and the holder must give notice to prior holders, as in the case of dishonour by non-acceptance.

Dishonour – The effect of dishonour is, as we have seen, that the acceptor, and all parties who are prior in order of time to the present holder, are liable upon the bill. Any one of these parties who pays has rights against parties prior to him. Thus, suppose that W is drawer, X acceptor, Y indorser and Z holder; X dishonours the bill by non-payment, and Z is paid by Y. Y may claim against W or X. If W pays Y, he may still sue X.

Discharge of bills – Bills may be discharged in five ways –
(1) By payment. This is the normal method of discharge.

(2) By renunciation. Any holder may renounce his rights. In order to be effectual, however, the renunciation must be evidenced in writing.

(3) By delivery up of the bill.

(4) By cancellation, *i.e.* written cancellation upon the bill itself.

(5) By "material alteration". If, for instance, a holder alters the date of payment appearing on the bill, all parties liable up to the time when the alteration was made will be discharged. If, however, the holder later transfers the bill he will be liable upon it himself, as altered.

(b) Cheques

A cheque is defined by the B.E.A. as a "*bill of exchange drawn on a banker payable on demand*" (s. 73). The rules governing cheques are in most respects similar to the rules governing other bills payable on demand, except that, since the Cheques Act 1957, s. 1, it is usually unnecessary for the payee to indorse the cheque unless he wishes to negotiate it. There are, however, certain other special rules which govern cheques alone. Some of these rules must be noted.

In the first place, as everyone knows, cheques may be "*crossed*". Crossing may be "*general*" or "*special*". General crossing is effected by drawing two parallel transverse lines across the face of the cheque. The words "and company" (or some abbreviation thereof) may also be added, though this is not strictly necessary. A cheque which has been crossed generally can only be cashed through a banker. Special crossing is effected by placing the name of a *particular* banker across the face of the cheque; in this case, though they are often also added, lines are not strictly necessary; and the effect of this is that the cheque can only be paid through *that* banker. The purpose of crossing is the avoidance of fraud. No banker may pay a crossed cheque over the counter; he must credit the amount paid by the bank which has "accepted" the cheque to his customer's account. Should a banker pay a crossed cheque over the counter, and should it turn out that he made the payment to a thief, he will be liable to the true owner for the amount paid.

In the second place, if cheques are marked "not negotiable", although they can still be transferred by the payee, they cease to be negotiable. This means that if I pay you with a cheque so marked, and the cheque is stolen from you and then transferred by the thief to X, X, even though he gave value and took it in good faith, may be liable to you for the amount of the cheque. Other negotiable instruments cease to be *transferable* altogether when marked "not negotiable".

In the third place, cheques are governed by certain rules which arise by reason of the special relationship which a banker bears to his customer. For instance a *banker* must use, in *all* his dealings with his customer, such reasonable care to protect the customer's interests as conforms with the ordinary practice of bankers of repute; though more than this is not expected of him. Thus, for instance, in *Schioler v. Westminster Bank, Ltd*, [1970] 2 Q.B. 719 it was held that the Bank was not in breach of duty in forwarding a dividend warrant from its Guernsey branch to England with the result that the customer who owned it had to pay tax on it; a result which could have been avoided by, for example, forwarding the warrant to Cork; for, without special agreement, banks are not expected to act as their customers' tax advisers. As regards *cheques* a banker is, however, expected to know his customer's signature. If, therefore, he has reason to suppose that the signature on a cheque presented to him for payment is not authentic he should withhold payment until he has made inquiries; but, though he must take reasonable care to guard against forgery, he will not be expected to have such skill as a hand-writing expert might be expected to have in detecting it. Moreover the banker must, within reason, warn the customer of any suspicious circumstances relating to any dealing which might suggest the presence of fraud or suchlike which might be detrimental to the customer's interests. On the other hand in *Hedley Byrne & Co., Ltd. v. Heller & Partners, Ltd*, (above, p. 292) the House of Lords made it reasonably clear that a banker who gives a reference to *others* about his customers' credit is not under a duty not to be negligent but is merely obliged to make an *honest* statement. The *customer* also owes special duties. He must, for example, exercise due care in keeping cheques, and he must also be careful how he draws them. Suppose, for instance, that A signs a bearer cheque and negligently hands it to a creditor to fill in the amount of his debt (say, £10). The creditor writes "£100" and presents it to a banker, who pays him. This means that A's banker will wrongfully debit A's account to the amount of £90. A, nevertheless, cannot complain, since the wrongful payment has been induced by his own breach of the duty of care which he owes to his banker, and he must accordingly submit to having his account debited with the £100. He of course has a right of action against the creditor; though rights of action against knaves are not usually satisfactory forms of property.

Attention must also be drawn to the Cheques Act 1957, s. 4, which enacts that "where a banker *in good faith and without negligence* receives payment for a customer of a cheque crossed generally or specially to himself, and the customer has no title . . . thereto, the banker *shall not incur any liability* to the true owner of the cheque by reason only of having received such payment". Thus suppose Smith to have drawn a cheque in favour of White and suppose Black to have obtained this cheque; suppose Black to have represented himself to the Z bank as White and to have opened an account with them (as White) and then to have drawn out the money for himself and absconded with it. The bank will be protected by s. 4 against a claim by Smith *if they can establish* that, in all the circumstances, they took reasonable steps – by obtaining references or otherwise – to assure themselves that Black was White.

Finally, it should be noted that the relationship of banker and customer, at any rate in respect of a current account, is a relationship of debtor and creditor. But, even in this respect, the relationship is a special one because, although it is normally the duty of a debtor to seek out and pay his creditor, it is in the nature of the banker-customer relationship that the banker shall only have to pay such sum or sums as the customer may happen to require when he is asked to make the payment, and, even then, only at a particular office; hence, before any legal right of action can accrue in favour of the customer, he must, by cheque, or in some other way, make a demand for payment.

(c) Promissory notes

A promissory note is defined as "*an unconditional promise in writing made by one person to another signed by the maker, engaging to pay, on demand or at a fixed or determinable future time, a sum certain money to, or to the order of, a specified person or to bearer*" (B.E.A., s. 83 (1)).

Promissory notes were made negotiable by eighteenth century statutes. They are very similar to bills of exchange and most of the rules governing bills also govern notes. Notes, however, differ from bills in one important respect. From the above definition, it will be appreciated that there is no *drawer* of a note; though the *maker* corresponds to the acceptor of a bill; and so it follows that, since the maker must necessarily have signed the note from the start, the rules relating to presentment for acceptance cannot apply to notes. The whole object of this form of presentment is to make sure that a drawee who has not already accepted is going to do so. By definition a promissory note must be an engagement to pay at "a determinable future time": an undertaking to pay "on or *before*" a certain date cannot therefore be a promissory note.

It should be explained that an "I.O.U." is not a promissory note: it is only evidence of a debt. The border-line between the two classes of document is, however, a narrow one, because any addition to an I.O.U. which brings it within the terms of the above definition will turn it into a promissory note.

Bank notes are promissory notes.

The following are possible forms for a promissory note and an I.O.U.

£50   London, August 8th, 1976
  One month after date I promise to pay to John Brown or order
fifty pounds.
                                                 Thomas Atkins.

                                       London, August 8th, 1976
Hugh Dix
  I.O.U. £20
                                                    Peter Hicks.

N o t e – In relation to a "regulated agreement" (see above, p. 274), at least
in respect of transactions confined to the United Kingdom, a creditor or
owner is forbidden by the Consumer Credit Act 1974, s. 123 (1) to "take
a negotiable instrument *other than a bank note or cheque* in discharge of any
sum payable". And by s. 123 (2) he can only validly negotiate such cheque
to a banker. Should he negotiate it to someone else there will be a defect
in title (s. 125 (2)) with the result that if the debtor can establish that the
holder knew the circumstances the latter's claim will be invalidated. By
s. 123 (3) a creditor is forbidden to take *any* negotiable instrument as *security*
for a sum payable under a regulated agreement. Section 124 provides that
contravention of s. 123 (1) or of s. 123 (2) renders the debt or, as the case
may be, the security unenforceable save by *court order.*

B   SECURITY UPON PERSONAL PROPERTY

Personal property, like land, may be used as a means of securing debts.
There are various forms of security upon personal property; but we can
make no more than a bare reference to three of them.

First, personal property may be mortgaged. In the case of a mortgage
of goods (other than ships) if the terms of the mortgage are such that
the debtor is to retain possession of the goods, while the creditor acquires
the ownership, and if the transaction is effected by a *written document*,
the document will be a "security *bill of sale*". As such, it must be
registered at the Central Office of the Supreme Court under the provisions of the Bills of Sale Act 1882. It must also contain certain prescribed particulars, such as the consideration paid by the creditor; and
it should be made according to a prescribed form. The particulars and
the form are required in order to protect the debtor against usury, while
registration is required in order to give the public notice of the transaction. If the document were not registered the debtor would be in a
position to hold himself out to the world as a more affluent man than he

really is, and thus he might obtain credit on the strength of property apparently, but not really, his own. A bill is void where the amount of the loan is less than £30.

Secondly, goods may be *"pledged"* (or "pawned"). In this case the pledgee (pawnee) acquires *possession* of them. There is thus no danger that the pledgor will acquire false credit. Further, the pledgee, being in possession, is entitled to bring actions of conversion or detinue if the goods are taken from him. When ss. 114–121 of the Consumer Credit Act 1974 come into operation pledges relating to *regulated agreements* (above, p. 274) will be subject to special rules contained in those sections (similar in many respects to the rules previously pertaining under the Pawnbrokers Acts 1872 to 1960), but it must be noted that since chattel mortgages and pledges are consumer credit agreements the provisions of ss. 60–64 of the 1974 Act also apply: these relate, it will be remembered, to the form of agreement, the giving of statutory copies and of notice as to cancellation rights. In the case of *pledge* agreements it is an *offence* (s. 115) for the pawnee (pawnbroker) to fail to supply the relevant copies and notice as to supply a "pawn receipt" (formerly "pawn ticket").

In the third place, personal property (and in some cases real property; as in the case of a purchaser of land–who has a lien over the land in respect of his deposit) may be subject to *liens* which arise by *implication of law*. Liens (if we omit maritime liens, which bind ships in respect of such claims as those of masters and seamen in respect of their pay) are of two main kinds: *"possessory"* (or "common law") liens and *equitable* liens. The essence of the possessory lien is the right to *retain* the property *until payment*, as in the case of the unpaid seller of goods (see above, p. 273), the *innkeeper* – who may thus retain most property which a guest brings to the inn – the *repairer*, such as the tailor or the motor repairer in respect of goods actually repaired, the carrier in respect of his freight money, and the auctioneer over the goods in respect of payment of the purchase price. All these are examples of "particular" liens. But possessory liens may also be *"general"*: here the lien is not in respect of a particular matter, but may cover all claims arising during a course of business: thus a *solicitor* has a lien for his charges upon his clients' property entrusted to his possession, and a *banker* in respect of his clients' money or securities at the bank.

The suitable lien differs from the common law lien in that it may attach by law *irrespective of possession*: the purchaser's lien, already mentioned, is an example – it attaches before the land is conveyed; and the vendor has a similar right in respect of purchase money which is unpaid. Upon dissolution of a partnership a partner also has a lien over the partnership property for payment of partnership debts.

Possessory liens carry their own sanction; the right to *retain* against payment: generally the lienor has no right of sale to satisfy his debt. Equitable liens (since they do not rest upon retention) may be enforced by sale if their existence is confirmed by a declaration of the court. By way of exception, however, certain statutes do confer special rights of sale in certain cases. For instance, the unpaid seller has a statutory power of resale under the S.G.A. s. 48 (3). The innkeeper also has a similar power in respect of the guest's property under the Innkeepers Act 1878; though only if the property has been six weeks on the premises and the sale has been advertised for at least a month. The repairer may also sell under the Disposal of Uncollected Goods Act 1952; but only if he has complied with certain strict conditions, such as displaying notices indicating that his acceptance of the customer's goods is subject to the provisions of the Act and also stating that the Act does, after twelve months from the date of redelivery, empower him to sell.

C GIFTS

There are two classes of gifts: gifts *inter vivos* (between living people) and *donationes mortis causa* (gifts conditional upon death).

1 GIFTS "INTER VIVOS"

In order for an effective gift of personal property to be made there must be an *intention* on the part of the donor (giver) *to give* and *delivery* of the gift to the donee (recipient) or to a trustee on his behalf.

The intention to give may sometimes be paramount. For example, in *Dewar* v. *Dewar*, [1975] 2 All E.R. 728 it was held that where a mother gave, and intended to give, her son a sum of money to buy a house the transaction was nevertheless a gift though the *son* intended to treat it as a loan and, in due course, to return the money: a common situation in family affairs.

What will amount to "delivery", varies according to the nature of the property. A physical object, such as a fountain pen, may be delivered by actual transfer. Choses in action, such as shares in a company, are delivered when the donor does all that is necessary to make the donee owner in place of himself. In the case of shares, for instance, he must execute a valid transfer of the shares; mere transfer of the share certificates will not suffice. But even in the case of a physical object it may be a sufficient delivery if the donor indicates his intention to give and informs the donee of the whereabouts of the thing to be given so that the latter can collect it for himself. Thus in *Thomas* v. *Times Book Co., Ltd.*, [1966] 2 All E.R. 241, the gift of the manuscript of "Under Milk

Wood" to a B.B.C. producer was held to be valid when Dylan Thomas, the poet, having indicated his intention to make the gift, and being about to fly to America, told the donee that he had left the manuscript in a Soho public house where the latter then found and collected it.

Some forms of property, however, cannot be easily transferred, even though they are physical objects. Thus, it may be inconvenient to transfer hay which is stored in a barn. In cases of this sort the law recognizes the transfer of the means of control – as by handing over the key of the barn – as a valid delivery. Further, in certain special cases, where the goods are of a cumbersome nature, the law permits a document of title to "represent" them. So the right to a ship's cargo may be transferred by delivery of a document called a "bill of lading".

Unless delivery is effected in one way or another there can be no gift. Hence, if I promise to give you my morning suit and I say that I will deliver it at your house, I may change my mind up to the very moment that I hand it to you; even on the very door-step.

A mere promise to give is not actionable. This is the hall-mark which distinguishes contracts from gifts.

The above rules are subject to two exceptions. First, a promise to give is, as we have seen (above, p. 211), enforceable if it is made by *deed*. In the second place, a gift may be perfected without delivery if the donor declares himself *trustee* for the donee. This does not, however, mean that an attempted, but uncompleted, gift will be construed as a declaration of trust. Moreover, except where a donor declares himself trustee of his property for the donee, equity also insists upon delivery for the creation of a trust.

Lastly, intending donors should, perhaps, be warned that if there is some inherently dangerous quality in the article given they may sometimes be held legally responsible for any damage it causes; but this rule will only apply if the article is not obviously dangerous (for example, it would not apply in the case of a gift of a gun with a patently fractured barrel) and the donor, knowing of the hidden danger at the time he makes the gift, omits to warn the recipient.

2 DONATIONES MORTIS CAUSA

A *donatio mortis causa* is a gift of personal property made by a donor in contemplation of his own death. These *donationes* differ from gifts *inter vivos* in this respect, that, whereas a gift *inter vivos* takes full effect upon delivery, a transaction will only amount to a "*donatio*" if it can be inferred from the words of the donor, or from all the circumstances of the case, that he intended the gift to take effect only in the actual event of his death; and that if he should recover, he should be entitled to resume full ownership of the property. A *"donatio"* is not, therefore, an informal way of making a will.

Most of the rules which apply to gifts *inter vivos* also apply to *donationes mortis causa* and, in particular, *"donationes"*, like gifts, must be effected by delivery. A valid *donatio* may, however, sometimes be effected by the transfer of documents of title to a chose in action even though the documents do not fully "represent" the chose. For instance, provided that the donor shows a present intention to give, a valid *donatio* of money in a Post Office Savings Bank may be made by transfer of the savings book.

If the donor does die, the *donatio* is similar to a legacy; it is liable, like other legacies, to be taken in satisfaction of the donor's debts (see below, p. 462).

CHAPTER 11

TRUSTS

We have already had occasion to refer to *uses*. The word "use" is said to derive from the Latin *opus* ("help" or "need"). A "use" arose in mediaeval times where a person conveyed property of any sort to another (*feoffee to uses*) upon the understanding that that other was to become seised of (*i.e.* hold) it on behalf of himself (the donor) or on behalf of some third party (*cestui que use*). Clearly the feoffee to uses was in a position of confidence which he might abuse. Consequently the rights of the *cestui que use* required protection. The common law courts refused to recognize uses, and therefore failed to afford this protection; but at an early date the Court of Chancery, acting as a court of "conscience", intervened to force the feoffee to uses to administer the property for the benefit of the *cestui que use* according to the terms of the grant. In the course of time the *cestui que use* thus came to have a special interest in the property enforced only in the Court of Chancery. This interest became an *equitable interest*, since the Chancellor administered equity. The nature of equitable interests has been explained (above, p. 25).

For our purposes we may treat the ancient use as the exact counterpart of the modern trust: the *cestui que use* has now become a *cestui que trust* (or "*beneficiary*"), the feoffee to uses has become a *trustee*. Thus, to borrow the late Sir Arthur Underhill's definition (*Law of Trusts and Trustees*) a trust is "an equitable obligation, binding a person (who is called a trustee) to deal with property over which he has control (which is called the trust property), for the benefit of persons (who are called the beneficiaries or *cestuis que trust*), of whom he himself may be one, and any one of whom may enforce the obligation".

It is impossible to enumerate all the purposes for which trusts are used. Broadly speaking, they enable people to enjoy the benefit of property, who are, for one reason or another, unable to hold the legal ownership in it themselves. Thus, as we have seen, the rights of beneficiaries under a settlement of land are always held for them in trust: the reason for this is that it has been found impracticable for the *legal* ownership of land to be split between a number of people. Moreover, groups of

394

people, such as unincorporated associations, can enjoy the benefit of property held in trust even though the law does not accord legal "personality" to their group. The "trust and confidence" imposed in the trustee by the creator of the trust is the core and essence of the matter. Equity will not permit the trustee to depart from his undertaking. The right of the beneficiary arose only as a sidewind of this principle.

Any form of property may be held in trust.

Trusts may be classified in many ways. The classification here used is not the only possible one – it has only been adopted because it is thought to be the simplest.

THE VARIETIES OF TRUSTS

Trusts may be divided into two main classes: *private* and *charitable*. Private trusts are enforceable at the instance of beneficiaries, while charitable trusts are "public" in the sense that they are generally enforced at the suit of the Attorney-General acting on behalf of the Crown, and that it is generally held that in order to be valid they must always be of benefit to the public or to a section of it, as opposed to individuals.

1 Private Trusts

i **Express private trusts** – An express trust is a trust which is expressly imposed. It may be created in any manner: by deed, by writing, by will, or (except in certain cases) merely orally. Whatever the method of creation, however, the creator must make his intention absolutely plain. It has thus been laid down that in order for a trust to arise there must be three "*certainties*". There must be certainty of *words*, certainty of *subject-matter* and certainty of *objects*.

(*a*) *There must be certainty of words.* This means that the words used must show a clear intention that a *trust* shall arise. Thus if X gives Y a ring and says, "I charge you to hold this ring in trust for Z", X has plainly imposed a trust. On the other hand, when "*precatory*" (praying) words are used, it is sometimes difficult for the courts to determine whether the donor has intended to impose a trust or merely to express a wish. In one case, for instance, a man gave property to his wife by his will and added that he did so "in full confidence" that she would do what was right as to the disposal of this property among the children of the marriage. It was held that although precatory words of this sort may sometimes give rise to a trust, these particular words in their particular context did not show an intention to create one, since the giving of the property to the wife "in full confidence" was merely the *motive* for the husband's gift. The wife therefore took the property absolutely, and the children were not entitled to be treated as beneficiaries under a trust. It must be added that *intention* is paramount, so that facts as well as words may furnish evidence of it – as, for example, where intending to create a trust of money a special account is opened in respect of it.

(*b*) *There must be certainty of subject-matter.* This requirement speaks for itself: if the subject-matter to be held in trust is indeterminate the courts cannot enforce the trust. Thus if A, by his will, were to direct his executor to hold "some portion of my property" in trust for B the trust would fail.

(*c*) *There must be certainty of objects.* Thus if a man were to give a picture to another upon the understanding that it should be held in trust for someone who should be subsequently named, and if the donor were to die without disclosing a name, there would be no express trust and the picture would "revert" to the donor's estate by operation of law. On the other hand, as the result of a series of recent decisions, which yet await final elucidation by the House of Lords, the objects need not fail merely because the wording of the trust is not such that it is possible to compile a complete list of all the beneficiaries. For example a trust empowering the trustees to make grants at discretion "to or for the benefit of any of the officers or employees or ex-officers or ex-employees of (a certain company) or to any relatives or dependants of any such persons" is probably not void for uncertainty simply because who the *relatives are* cannot be known until, by proof, they establish the fact of their relationship. For the rule appears to be that, as the House of Lords decided (in a slightly different context) in *Wishaw* v. *Stephens*, [1970] A.C. 508, "the trust is valid if it can be said with certainty that any given individual is or is not a member of the class (selected for the benefaction)". He who is *in fact* a relative can certainly bring himself within the class.

Beside being "certain" the trust must be "*completely constituted*". This may be brought about in three ways. The creator of the trust may declare himself trustee, he may impose the trust in his will, or he may convey the trust property to trustees.

Where the last of the above methods is adopted the trust will not be "completely constituted" until an out and out transfer to the trustees has been effected. An attempted transfer will not suffice (see above, p. 392), for "*there is no equity to perfect an imperfect gift*". Thus, if the property concerned is land there must be a deed of conveyance: if it consists of shares there must be a valid transfer. Until the trust is thus "completely constituted" by transfer it will normally be ineffectual.

There is, however, one important exception to the rule as to out and out transfer. If the creator of the trust has agreed to convey the property for *valuable consideration*. Equity, which *"looks upon that as done which ought to be done"*, will enforce the transfer of the property in due course, and thus render the trust "completely constituted". "Valuable consideration" in this sense means not merely money consideration, but includes "marriage consideration". Thus if John, who is about to marry Joan, settles property upon trustees in favour of Joan and any issue of the marriage, Joan *and the issue* come within the "marriage consideration". If therefore the transfer to the trustees is incomplete – as it will always be where the property within the trust comprises property which the settlor may acquire after the marriage ("after-acquired" property) – this will be no bar to the "complete constitution" of the trust. Joan and the issue are regarded as "purchasers", just as if they had given value in return for the benefits they are to receive. It should, however, be noted that only those persons, who are within the "marriage consideration" will benefit: thus an unascertained class of next of kin are mere "volunteers", not furnishers of consideration.

ii Implied trusts – Implied trusts arise either from presumed intention (*"resulting trusts"*) or by the operation of rules of law or equity (*"constructive trusts"*). (Implied trusts are sometimes called "constructive trusts", and then divided into *"resulting"* and *"non-resulting"* trusts.)

(a) *Resulting trusts* – Without expressly creating a trust, people sometimes act in a way which shows that they presumably intended to do so. Human activities being infinitely various, obviously no exhaustive list can be given of trusts which arise in this way, and random illustrations must suffice.

In the first place, where a man settles property upon trustees in a way which makes no provision for the exhaustion of the entire interest in the property, the unexhausted interest will "revert" to him. Thus if Robinson settles property upon Jones in trust to pay the income to Smith for life, and makes no further disposition, after Smith's death the property will be held by Jones in trust for him (Robinson), or if he is dead, for the persons entitled under his will or upon his intestacy. It is clear that Jones himself is not intended to take since he is designated "trustee".

In the second place, where A (otherwise than by way of loan) supplies money for B to purchase property, B will, in the absence of evidence of a contrary intention, be presumed to hold the property upon a resulting trust in favour of A. This presumption may, however, sometimes be counterbalanced by a contrary presumption called the *presumption of advancement*. This arises where a husband or a father advances money for a purchase by his wife or child. In this case it is presumed that the advance is intended as a gift, so that no resulting trust in favour of the donor arises. The presumption of advancement, like the presumption of a resulting trust, may, of course, be rebutted by evidence of a contrary intention. It should be noted that the presumption extends to cover the case of a person in the place of a parent (*in loco parentis*) who supplies money for someone whom he treats as his child. Grandparents or godparents, for instance, may often be in this position. Similarly where matrimonial property stands in the name of one spouse only, but the other has contributed to its acquisition, the courts will, in case of dispute between them about the property, imply a trust in favour of the other (or even in favour of a mistress where the couple have lived together) to the extent of his or her contributions, including not only money payments but also the fruits of labour: as where the wife (or mistress) has helped to build the (matrimonial) home. The underlying principle was well expressed by Lord Denning, M.R. (*Hussey* v. *Palmer*, [1972] 3 All E.R. 744): "By whatever name it is described (*i.e.* 'resulting' or 'constructive' trust) it is a trust imposed by law whenever justice and good conscience require. It is a liberal process founded on large principles of equity, to be applied in cases where the defendant cannot conscientiously keep the property for himself alone, but ought to allow the other to have the property or a share of it."

In the third place, when a trust is declared which the law will not permit to be carried out, *e.g.* because it infringes the perpetuity rule, there may be a resulting trust in favour of the donor.

(*b*) *Constructive trusts* – Constructive trusts are imposed by law independently of anyone's intention. A stock example of a case in which a trust of this type arises is where property held in trust is conveyed by trustees to someone who has notice of the trust: here equity protects the rights of the beneficiaries and treats the stranger as a constructive trustee, whether or not he consents to act as such.

A further example of a constructive trust is provided by the rule in *Keech* v. *Sandford* (1726), Cha. Ca. 61. In that case a trustee held a lease of Romford Market on behalf of a minor. He attempted to renew the lease in the same capacity. The lessor only condescended to grant renewal on the terms that the trustee was to hold the lease for his own personal benefit. It was held that, despite the attitude of the lessor, the renewed lease must be held in trust for the minor. Equity will not permit a trustee to acquire a benefit for himself by reason of his fiduciary position; if he does acquire such a benefit he holds whatever he acquires in trust for the beneficiaries. *Keech* v. *Sandford* therefore illustrates the general principle that a constructive trust in favour of the beneficiaries will always arise where if it were not implied the trustee would benefit from his position. Further, a person who is not a trustee may, where he obtains information which enables him to make a personal profit – which information he would not have had had he not been acting for the trust –, be forced to account for such profits to the beneficiaries as being held by him constructively in trust for them. This may be illustrated by *Board-man v. Phipps*, [1967] 2 A.C. 46: in that case a solicitor was requested by trustees to advise on the affairs of a certain private company in which the trust had a substantial minority holding. In the course of so advising the solicitor acquired information which enabled him on the one hand to play a positive role in making the trust holding more valuable, and on the other had to acquire for himself a considerable number of the outstanding shares and the office of managing director. In an action by one of the beneficiaries it was held that the solicitor held the shares – the capital value of which was now far in excess of what it was originally – as a constructive trustee for the beneficiaries and was furthermore accountable for the profits received by him by way of dividend declared on these shares. The court was not, however, wholly unappreciative of the solicitor's efforts and directed that he be paid a substantial sum by way of remuneration for his services.

2 Charitable (Public) Trusts

No comprehensive definition of a legal "charity" has been provided either by statute or by the courts. The meaning is, however, not the same as the popular meaning and it has to be determined by reference to the relevant case law. The *classification* of charitable purposes which is most often quoted is the one made by Lord MacNaghten in *Income Tax Special Purposes Commissioners* v. *Pemsel* [1891] A.C. 531. According to this classification charitable trusts comprise trusts (1) for the relief of poverty; (2) for the advancement of education: and this means education, not propaganda. Thus where there was a trust for the advancement of "socialized medicine" by means of lectures to promote that aim and socialism generally, rather than to educate the public by stimulating thought on the subject, the object was held not to be charitable; (3) for the advancement of religion; (4) for other purposes beneficial to the community. This last category is usually said to be overriding, so that all trusts, if they are to be charitable, must conform with the requirement that they are for the *public benefit*: though it is established that, in the case of relief of poverty, trusts in favour of poor relations or of employees (even of a particular firm) as a class are charitable, though clearly they benefit only a fraction of the public. Trusts in favour of needy individuals are, however, private trusts. "Benefit to the community" is a very indeterminate object and the cases conflict – though recently an ill-advised parliamentary group suggested it as the *sole* criterion – but it may be of interest to remark that the Court of Appeal in *The Incorporated Council of Law Reporting for England and Wales* v. *A.-G.*, [1972] Ch. 73, held that the Council is a charity because reports of judicial decisions serve the community by disseminating knowledge of the law; and it was also suggested that the objects of the Council might fall within Lord Mac-Naghten's second category.

Any object which falls outside the *Pemsel* rule is not charitable – and cannot obtain the advantages of that status – so that where the students of the Sussex University Union which was constituted as a charity with the object of advancement of learning sought to change its constitution so as to make it possible for it to devote funds to political ends this change was held invalid.

It must be added that the Recreational Charities Act 1958 settled doubts by enacting that – as long as they are for the public benefit – trusts for providing facilities in the interests of social welfare for recreation or other leisure-time occupation are to be deemed "charitable", although the meaning of "social welfare" is carefully defined. The same Act makes trusts for "social welfare activities", as defined in the Miners' Welfare Act 1952, "charitable".

The difficulties of definition apart, once it is clear that a particular "object" is a "charity" any trust in favour of it will be subject to special rules, some of which were modified and clarified by the Charities Act 1960 (hereafter "C.A."): for example –

a Most charities have to be registered in registers kept by the Charity Commissioners and, where appropriate, by the Secretary of State for Education and Science. Both the Commissioners – whose office is in effect a sub-department of the Home Office – and the Secretary of State (the latter within the field of charities for educational purposes) have general supervisory powers over trusteeships of charities, and in particular they share with the courts the power of sanctioning "schemes" for the administration of charitable trusts.

b Legal proceedings in respect of charitable trusts could formerly only be taken by the Attorney-General, either acting *ex officio* or by relation of interested parties. The C.A. has now also empowered the trustees and certain other parties to take such proceedings, but only when the authority of the Charity Commissioners has been obtained.

c Charitable trusts are to some extent *exempted* from the *perpetuity rules* (above, p. 363): although gifts to charities must in the first instance vest within the required periods, a "gift over" from one *charity* to *another* may lawfully be limited to vest at any future time. This is perhaps a corollary of the further rule that trusts for the benefit of charities, unlike other trusts, may be perpetual.

d Charities are to a large extent exempt from *taxation* and premises occupied by charities and "wholly or mainly" used for charitable purposes have some exemption from rates. But in order to qualify for exemption they must be so used: thus in *Oxfam* v. *City of Birmingham District Council*, [1975] 2 All E.R. 289 the House of Lords held that "Oxfam" *shops* which are directly used for raising funds, and only indirectly for the charitable purpose of relief of poverty which Oxfam espouses, are not exempt for rating purposes. It is the carrot of tax exemption which causes many institutions to seek charitable status: and it is also this crucial attribute of charities that leads to an overwhelming, confusing and conflicting case law of the subject.

A trust with exclusively charitable objects will never fail for "uncertainty of objects". Once property has been conveyed upon trust in circumstances which show that the settlor had a general charitable intention (as opposed to an intention merely to benefit some particular charity) the trustees must apply it for the benefit of *some* charity or charities, and if necessary obtain sanction for a "scheme" ((*a*) above) to that end.

Where in certain ways defined in the C.A. s. 13 – as for instance that the original purposes "cannot be carried out, or not according to the directions given and to the spirit of the gift" – the objects of the trust have become impossible of fulfilment a charitable trust, unlike a private trust, need not necessarily fail so as to create a resulting trust in favour of the donor or his representatives. For the *cy-près* ("as near as can be") doctrine may apply. This means that sanction may be obtained for a scheme to devote the trust funds to some other charitable object as nearly as possible similar to the object which has failed.

But the doctrine only operates in the case of a trust which is *initially* impossible where it can be established that the donor has a general charitable intention or (under C.A. s. 14) where the donor cannot be identified – as for example where the fund consists of a cash collection from multifarious donations deposited in collecting boxes, or where the donor cannot be found, or where the donor has made a written disclaimer of his right to the return of the gift. Failing these possibilities the property will revert to the donor in the usual way.

On the other hand where the impossibility arises *after the trust has come into operation* the *cy-près* doctrine applies without restriction unless the settlor or testator has provided for the contingency of impossibility by stipulating a gift over to some other charity or person, or by declaring a resulting trust to himself or his estate. Even here – except in the case of a gift over to some other charity – the perpetuity rules (above, pp. 363–365) will apply so as to limit the ability of the disponor to do this.

TRUSTEES

The law governing trusteeship was originally evolved in the Court of Chancery. Much of it is now contained in the Trustee Act 1925 (here abbreviated T.A.).

Their appointment and discharge – Trustees are normally appointed in the instrument which creates the trust. There is no general rule as to the number to be appointed, though it is unusual to appoint a single individual as a sole trustee. Where, however, *land* is settled, or held upon trust for sale, there may not normally be more than four trustees (T.A., s. 34 (2)). Further, it is laid down (s. 14) that not less than two trustees are required to give a valid receipt to a purchaser of such land. (See also Law of Property Act 1925, s. 27 (2), and Settled Land Act 1925, s. 94 (1)). This rule is, however, subject to a further exception, namely that a *trust corporation* acting as a sole trustee can give a valid receipt.

"Trust corporations" are corporate bodies empowered by the T.A., s. 68 (18), to act as trustees. They include any corporation appointed by the court in a particular matter to be a trustee, and bodies, such as banks and the larger insurance companies, which, as is generally known, conduct trustee business.

The mere fact of appointment does not oblige a trustee to take office. He may refuse to do so, either expressly or by implication, as by refraining from entering upon his duties. If all the trustees appointed under a particular instrument refuse to act their duties devolve upon the person who created the trust, or upon his *personal representatives* (below, Chapter 14).

Where one out of a number of trustees dies his duties devolve upon the rest. Where a sole surviving trustee dies his personal representatives can exercise his powers.

The court has special powers of discharging trustees and of sanctioning the appointment of new ones to replace them (T.A., s. 41). These powers are not, however, normally invoked, because certain provisions of ss. 36 and 39 of the Act usually render such an application unnecessary. Under the provisions of s. 36 a trustee may be replaced by a new trustee in certain circumstances, *e.g.* if he remains abroad for over a year. The section provides that this replacement may be effected by the people (if any) nominated in the instrument creating the trust to appoint new trustees. Where there are no such people the power of replacement falls upon the other trustees. Section 39 provides that a trustee who wishes to retire may obtain his discharge (without need for replacement) provided that two conditions are satisfied: (*i*) He must obtain the consent of his co-trustees and of any person who is empowered to appoint trustees. (*ii*) Upon the discharge of the retiring trustee there must remain either at least two trustees or a trust corporation to perform the duties of the trust.

In either of the above cases, though under s. 36 this is not essential, the retirement will normally be effected by deed. The reason for this is that when a retirement occurs the trust property must be divested from the retiring, and revested in the remaining, trustees. Section 40 of the T.A. provides that if the transaction is effected by deed this divesting and revesting will be deemed to have taken place automatically in respect of any interest in land and certain choses in action (though in the case of *stocks and shares* deeds of transfer are still necessary).

Their duties – Trustees have two main duties. First, they must administer the trust property prudently. Secondly, they must strictly comply with all the terms of the trust.

For instance, trustees are entitled to invest trust funds only in investments either authorized by statute or by the express terms of their trust instrument. Before the coming into force of the Trustee Investments Act 1961 (T.I.A.) the investments authorized by statute comprised only the limited range prescribed by the T.A., s. 1. Generally speaking, these were restricted to stocks issued by the British Government and by Commonwealth countries and Colonies, stocks and mortgages issued by British local authorities, stocks guaranteed by the British Government, and mortgages of land in Great Britain. The list did not include "equities", *i.e.* the ordinary shares and stock of limited liability companies. Most of the authorized investments were repayable at par and it was felt that this provided no safeguard against inflation or against the continuing fall in the value of the pound. The effect of the T.I.A. is that, subject to detailed conditions, trustees may now invest a proportion of the trust funds in what are described as "wider-range" investments, including "equities".

It must, however, be stressed that the statutory powers (under the T.A. and the T.I.A.) are *additional* to powers conferred by the trust instrument. This instrument may, and in the case of most modern trusts does, extend the statutory powers or, indeed, confer unrestricted powers of investment upon the trustees.

If all possible beneficiaries (both present and future) are of full age and capacity they can together authorize the trustees to deal with the trust property in any manner desired. Otherwise, the trustees have no power to vary the trusts, whatever the circumstances, though on behalf of certain specified classes of beneficiaries (mostly persons under incapacity, such as minority or unsoundness of mind) the court has jurisdiction under the general law and by statute (principally the Variation of Trusts Act 1958) to sanction the variation or revocation of trust dispositions where it is satisfied that such variation or revocation is of benefit to the person or persons concerned.

As a general rule trustees may not delegate their duties. Section 23 of the Act, however, sets out a list of exceptions to this rule. These exceptions include, for instance, the right to employ a solicitor, a banker, or a stockbroker to effect transactions in connexion with the trust property. The charges of these agents are paid out of the trust estate.

Their liabilities – In the absence of express authorization in the instrument, if any, which creates the trust or by the court, trustees have no right to be paid for their services. They are, however, entitled to be reimbursed out of the trust funds for any expenses properly incurred in the performance of their duties.

Any action by the trustees which is in excess of their powers – as where trust funds are misappropriated – or which contravenes the terms of the trust instrument constitutes a breach of trust, and a trustee will be personally liable to the full extent of any resulting loss. A frequent example is where trust moneys are invested in unauthorized securities and a loss results – if more than one such investment has been made the trustee cannot set off any profits against the losses, but must make good each individual loss.

A trustee who has been held liable for breach of trust has a right to be indemnified by any beneficiary who has directly instigated the breach to the extent to which he has benefited therefrom, and in suitable circumstances the trustee also has a right of contribution from his co-trustees (if any). By s. 61 of the T.A. the court has power to relieve a trustee from personal liability for breach of trust when he has acted honestly and reasonably and ought fairly to be excused for the breach: the scope of this statutory protection is, however, uncertain (in particular, it is problematical how far it will avail a professional trustee).

Actions by the beneficiaries against a trustee are statute-barred after six years (Limitation Act 1939, s. 19). This time begins to run either from the time of the breach or, where the beneficiary suing is not at that time entitled to possession of his interest, then from the time that he becomes entitled. There is, however, no limit to the time in which an action may be brought where a trustee has been guilty of fraud, or where the action is an action to recover the trust property itself or its proceeds and it is either in the trustee's possession or has been converted by him to his own use.

BENEFICIARIES

The principal right of beneficiaries is their right to the enjoyment of the interest in the trust property to which they are entitled under the terms of the trust.

In the case of a private trust the beneficiaries have, as we have seen, a right to force the trustees, by action if necessary, to administer the property according to the terms of the trust.

In the case of a breach of trust the following rights may be open to beneficiaries –

a They may bring a personal action against the trustees;
b They may be able to follow the trust property itself or to claim anything into which it has been converted;
c They may be able to institute criminal proceedings against the trustees.

The personal action requires no comment. Being an action against the trustees in person it has the disadvantage that if they are men of straw, or are already seriously in debt, the beneficiaries may get little or nothing from them. Beneficiaries have, however, one advantage over ordinary creditors, for should a defaulting trustee become bankrupt, their right to repayment of their claim in full survives his discharge (Bankruptcy Act 1914, s. 28).

Equity has always permitted beneficiaries to "follow the trust property". In this respect they are unlike people whose rights are based upon the common law, who can usually only, as we have seen, claim damages for their infringement. Thus, suppose that X holds a valuable picture in trust for Y, and that X, in breach of trust, gives the picture to Z. Y may, of course, sue X. This, as we have seen, may be fruitless. But Y has a better remedy: he may claim the return of the picture from Z, who is in the eyes of equity a constructive trustee. This right to the property is defeated, like all equitable rights, once a *bonâ fide* purchaser for value without notice obtains the picture. Thus if Z sells to T, who has no notice of the trust, Y cannot recover the picture from T (but can recover the proceeds of sale from Z).

Equity, however, favours the beneficiary further than this; for it will force a trustee to return not only the trust property, but also anything into which it has been *converted*. For instance, if A holds £50 in trust for B and, in breach of trust, spends the money on a carpet for his house, B will be entitled to the carpet. This claim is not merely personal but a claim to the *carpet* or its full value: thus if A is insolvent B's claim will not be diminished by the rights of other creditors; his right is something like a right of ownership. This rule, however, only applies where there is a direct substitution of one form of property for another. It would not apply, for instance, if A bought an £80 carpet, supplying £30 of his own. In this case B's claim would still be to £50 only – secured, if necessary, by the sale of the carpet: but it would yet be a claim to the full £50 as against other creditors.

There are certain complex rules governing the rights of beneficiaries to trust monies paid into a trustee's personal bank account, but they are not suitable for consideration in an introductory work.

CHAPTER 12

FAMILY LAW

In this chapter we will consider certain aspects of the law relating to marriage and to children and the family.

A MARRIAGE

It may be appropriate to discuss this subject under five heads –
  (1) Engagements to marry;
  (2) The formation of marriage;
  (3) Nullity of marriage;
  (4) The effects of marriage;
  (5) Dissolution of marriage.

Much of the law relating to it will now be found in the Matrimonial Causes Act 1973 which consolidated previous legislation, including in particular the Matrimonial Causes Act 1965 and 1967, the Divorce Reform Act 1969, the Matrimonial Proceedings and Property Act 1970 and the Nullity of Marriage Act 1971.

1 Engagements to Marry

Traditionally the common law looked upon an engagement, as upon marriage, as a contract, and it had the legal effect that a man who broke his engagement could be sued by his ex-fiancée for breach of promise of marriage – a type of action which was, not unnaturally, discouraged and for which there were special evidentiary requirements. This form of action was, however, abolished by the Law Reform (Miscellaneous Provisions) Act 1970 which (s. 1) enacted that "An agreement between two persons to marry one another shall not under the law of England and Wales have effect as a contract giving rise to legal rights...." Thus the jilted lass can no longer vent her spleen in a court of law. This provision, however, could not stand alone because broken engagements sometimes leave not only injured feelings but also, like broken marriages, tangled property relationships: hence, by s. 2, the Act applies the provisions of s. 37 of the Matrimonial Proceedings and Property Act 1970 (below) and of s. 17 of the Married Women's Property Act 1882 (below) to broken engagements: so that, for example where there have been contributions by the engaged couple towards the proposed matrimonial home the parties' interests may be safeguarded after the engagement has been broken off. Moreover, s. 3 of the 1970 Law Reform Act settled disputes about the engagement *ring* by ruling that it shall be presumed to be an *absolute gift*; though this presumption may be rebutted (*i.e.* proved unfounded) by evidence showing a contrary intent.

2 Formation of Marriage

The formalities required for the celebration of a valid marriage are now in general prescribed by the Marriage Acts 1949 to 1970. In broad terms all marriages celebrated in England under English law must either be solemnized according to the rites of the Church of England in the presence of two witnesses, or they must be solemnized – whatever other religious ceremony there may be – upon the authority of the certificate of a superintendent registrar. Further, Church of England marriages will only be valid if either there has been publication of banns, or a common licence has been obtained from the Archbishop of Canterbury, or the certificate of a superintendent registrar has been obtained. Normally civil marriages unaccompanied by a religious ceremony must be celebrated either in a registered building or in the office of a superintendent registrar; but the Marriage (Registrar General's Licence) Act 1970 permits such marriages elsewhere, under licence of the Registrar General, in cases of very serious illness where one of the parties is not expected to recover and cannot be moved to one of the normal places of marriage.

3 Nullity

Although obviously one of a very special nature, marriage remains in essence a contract; and, in particular, it is like one in that what seems upon the face of it to be a valid marriage may, like a void or voidable contract, turn out not to be so. Marriages may thus either be *void* or *voidable*. The law on this matter is now governed by the Matrimonial Causes Act 1973 (consolidating the provisions of the Nullity of Marriage Act 1971).

Under s. 11 of the 1973 Act (hereafter "M.C.A.") marriages will be void (*i*) If the parties are *within the prohibited degrees* of relationship (these are set out in the Marriage Act 1949 Schedule 1, as subsequently amended); (*ii*) If either party is *under the age of sixteen*; (*iii*) If the parties have inter-married in disregard of certain requirements as to the *formation* of marriage – such as wilful neglect to obtain a marriage certificate – contained in the Marriage Act 1949, s. 49; (*iv*) If at the time of the marriage either party was already *lawfully married*; (*v*) If the parties are *not respectively male and female*. This last ground alone requires comment: it concerns trans-sexualism which has posed a problem for the courts in recent years: what, in this penumbral situation, can be defined as "male" or "female" is perhaps near insoluble, and the judgment of Ormrod J. in *Corbett* v. *Corbett* [1971] P. 110 is instructive; it is probably the biological make-up of the subject that must determine the matter. Marriages falling within the above categories, being void, have no effect since no marriage has ever existed at all; consequently there is theoretically no need for either party who wishes to impugn them to petition the court to declare them null, but such petitions will be entertained, and it may often be desirable to seek them.

Section 12 of the M.C.A. sets out the grounds upon which a marriage is *voidable*. These are – (*i*) That it has *not been consummated* due to the incapacity of either party; (*ii*) That is has not been consummated due to the *wilful refusal* of the respondent to consummate it; (*iii*) That either party did *not consent* to it, whether in consequence of *duress, mistake, unsoundness of mind* or otherwise; (*iv*) That at the time of the marriage either party, though capable of giving a valid consent, was suffering (whether continuously or intermittently) from *mental disorder* ... of such a kind or to such an extent as to be unfitted for marriage: (*v*) That at the time of the marriage the respondent was suffering from *venereal disease* in a communicable form; (*vi*) That at the time of the marriage the petitioner was *pregnant* by some person other than the petitioner.

Of these various grounds of voidability there is only space to comment upon the third. This illustrates the consensual and contractual nature of marriage. Like any ordinary contract its basis lies in free consent; consequently some essential *mistake* as to identity, or some deceit which vitiates the consent, will render the union voidable: indeed, prior to the Nullity of Marriage Act 1971 it rendered it void. It is the same with *duress*, some factor which draws a person into marriage by force or fear: for instance, a marriage contracted (note the significance of the colloquial use of the word "contracted") in order solely to escape some oppressive political régime which poses a threat to the life, limb or liberty of the person involved may be annulled. Yet it must not be thought that fear of a merely unpleasant consequence will have so drastic an effect: so if a girl, according to the custom of her people, consents to a marriage arranged by her parents, she cannot treat the custom as a form of duress so as to enable her to escape the marriage if she discovers that the charms of her partner fall short of her expectations. It must be added that where grounds (*iii*)–(*vi*) are in issue the M.C.A., s. 13 (2) provides that no decree may be granted unless the court is satisfied that proceedings were instituted within *three* years from the date of marriage. Further, where grounds (*v*) and (*vi*) are involved (M.C.A., s. 13 (3)) the court must be satisfied that the petitioner was at the time of the marriage ignorant of the facts alleged. And finally by s. 13 (1) *no* decree upon the ground that the marriage is voidable may be granted if the respondent satisfies the court that "the petitioner ... so conducted himself ... as to lead the respondent reasonably to believe that he would not seek" to avoid the marriage *and* that it would be unjust to grant the decree.

A marriage which is voidable (as opposed to void) is one which (M.C.A., s. 16) is to be "treated as if it had existed" up to the time of decree absolute, and the latter now operates "to annul the marriage only as respects any time after" it. This serves to underline the fact that where a voidable marriage is in issue a *decree of nullity* is not merely advisable, but essential, if the petitioner wishes to terminate the matrimonial state.

4 The Effects of Marriage

At common law the effect of marriage was to make husband and wife "one"; chiefly to the former's advantage. For instance most of the wife's property, at least during the subsistence of the marriage, became her husband's; she lost contractual capacity but the husband, who took so much by way of benefit, incurred the burden of becoming liable for her torts. Now after a long and piecemeal process of change, effected by equity and various statutes, married women have become emancipated from their husbands, and they are treated in law for most purposes as if they were single.

Yet invariably, marriage being a union of the parties, their legal status is affected by it. There is only space here to mention a few of its more important effects; and these may be considered from three aspects – first, as to court proceedings, second, as to mutual duties, third, as to the effect of marriage upon the property of the parties.

As to *court proceedings*. Though husbands and wives may now sue each other in contract or in tort, in the case of the latter the Law Reform (Husband and Wife) Act 1962 gives the court power to stay the action if it appears that it is likely to afford no benefit to either party or that the question is one which may more conveniently be settled under s. 17

of the Married Women's Property Act 1882 (below). As regards theft; though since the Theft Act 1968 spouses may be prosecuted for stealing from each other, prosecution will normally require the leave of the Director of Public Prosecutions. Moreover, in certain classes of proceedings (mostly criminal) husbands and wives are not *compellable* as witnesses against each other, though they are competent to give such evidence if they wish. Nor, in a criminal (as opposed to a civil) case, can one spouse be *compelled* to disclose any communications (such as a confession of crime) made between them.

As to the *mutual duties* of husband and wife. A husband is normally under a duty to maintain his wife and any children of the marriage according to his ability, and under certain circumstances he may be ordered to do so by the court. Thus under the M.C.A., s. 27 such an order may be made against a husband upon the application of the wife in the case of wilful neglect to maintain either the wife or the children; but it must also be noted that – in accordance with the modern policy which seeks to place the sexes upon an equal footing – the *husband* may also now apply for a similar order against the *wife* where through age, illness or disability, and having regard to the respective resources of the parties, it is reasonable to expect the wife to provide such maintenance. Where a husband and wife are cohabiting there is a *presumption* (but no more) that the wife has authority to pledge the husband's credit for necessaries supplied for the common household, according to the particular standard of life of the particular couple concerned.

The *property* of married couples presents difficulties. It has been remarked that originally the common law of England, in the absence of agreement to the contrary, like the ancient law of Rome, endowed the husband with all the wife's worldly goods by very reason of the marriage. This was in keeping with the needs of ancient societies in which the family group, under the protection of the male, needed to face the world as an entity. As society became more cohesive, both in Rome and in England this male supremacy broke down; and, as has been remarked, by the end of the nineteenth century the English wife's property had in general come to belong to her as her own. This separation of property during marriage is, however, a fact more observed in law than in the reality of a stable marriage where "his" and "hers" is often meaningless, and both parties treat the contents of their homes as something joint which gives outward expression to the marital unity. There is thus something to be said for systems of law which neither treat the husband as sole manager nor the property as separate, but see the situation as one of "community of goods". This legal solution, again, however, is not entirely realistic since, let a quarrel arise and "he" and "she" will at once bethink them of their "own". It is thus not surprising that modern legislation in this field rests upon no one principle. Thus though, in law, property which clearly belongs to the wife is her "separate" property, the Married Women's Property Act 1964 makes special provision in respect of money or other property derived from a housekeeping allowance provided by the husband to the wife: it is enacted that this is *prima facie* (*i.e.* in the absence of evidence to the contrary) to be treated as belonging to the parties in *equal shares*. Moreover, in *equity* property which is jointly acquired belongs to the parties respectively in proportion to the amount of the contribution of each; or where – as will often be so – the amount of the contribution is not determinable, the ownership is divided according to such proportions as the court may consider just. Further, by the Matrimonial Proceedings and Property Act 1970, s. 37 where one spouse makes a substantial contribution to the *improvement* of property in which either or both have a beneficial interest he or she will be entitled to such a share in the value of the improvement as may be agreed between the two or, in default of agreement, as the court may deem just. Now, too, since the Matrimonial Homes Act 1967 (as amended) where one of the spouses has no interest (whether legal or equitable) in the matrimonial home he or she is accorded "rights of occupation" in it: thus during the subsistence of the marriage one of the parties deserted by the other cannot be evicted from the house without a court order. This is, of course, a right of particular importance to a deserted wife: and the expectations of third parties, such as purchasers of the property, are protected by the fact that the "rights of occupation" are registrable as a land charge (above, p. 375), which means that the third party has a means of knowing about the occupancy. It should be noted, however, that this only affects the "home", and not the furniture.

Mention must also be made of the Married Women's Property Act 1882, s. 17 (as amended). This provides that in any question between husband and wife as to the title to, or the possession of, property either party – and certain other people – may apply in a *summary way* to a judge of the High Court or to a circuit judge who may make such order as to the property in dispute as he thinks fit. The judge also has power to order payment by the defendant spouse to the aggrieved one of the value of any property to which the latter was entitled if, at the time of the application, it is no longer in the possession or control of the former. Moreover, the judge may when necessary order the sale of property to satisfy the aggrieved party's claim. The Matrimonial Proceedings and Property Act 1970, s. 39 extends these provisions to cover a period of three years after the determination of the marriage by divorce or annulment (but not by death). The effect of marriage in relation to wills and intestacy will be considered in Chapter 13.

5 Dissolution of Marriage

Attitudes to marriage have varied in the course of history – looking back, they seem to swing from one extreme to another. Thus in ancient Rome divorce was originally rare, but by the early Empire it became both easy and common: indeed one party could repudiate the marriage by unilateral act; after Constantine (and the advent of Christianity) the pendulum swung back, and divorce came under the ban of the text which prescribes that "those whom God hath joined together let no man put asunder". In the main this ostracism of divorce was inherited by the common law and it continued until the nineteenth century when judicial divorce (as opposed to divorce by Act of Parliament) became possible. Judicial divorce, however – though the grounds for it were extended by various statutes – was in general beset by the notion of the "matrimonial offence": the success of a petition depended upon the "guilt" of the respondent, upon the respondent having done something "wrong", *e.g.* adultery. In the course of this century public opinion came to two conclusions. First, that, whatever the will of Divine Providence, there can be no point in tying people to what Sir Alan Herbert once called "holy deadlock"; second, that to base the right to divorce upon the commission of a "matrimonial offence" was a senseless approach. This change of attitude eventually came to be reflected in the Report of a Group appointed by the Archbishop of Canterbury which published the pamphlet "Putting Asunder" (1966), and in the Law Commission's Report "Reform of the Grounds of Divorce. The Field of Choice" (1966) Cmnd. 3123; and as a result of the suggestions contained in these documents the Divorce Reform Act 1969 was passed, and (as re-enacted in the M.C.A.) is now in operation.

This Act was a compromise between the view of the Church of England Group that divorce should depend upon "irretrievable breakdown" of the marriage and the view of the Law Commission that divorce must depend upon specific grounds. Thus by s. 1 (now s. 1 of the M.C.A.) it enacted that "the sole ground on which a petition for divorce may be presented . . . shall be that the marriage has *broken down irretrievably*". But it is to be noted that what the State here gives to Peter it takes back from Paul; for s. 2 (3) (now s. 1 (4) of the M.C.A.) provided that "if the court is satisfied on the evidence of any such fact as is mentioned in subsection (1) of this section" (which will shortly be examined), then, "unless it is satisfied on all the evidence that the marriage has not broken down irretrievably, it shall – grant a decree". In other words, prove the grounds (called by the Law Commission "guidelines" for determining the question of "breakdown") and the issue of "breakdown", which appears superficially to be the main one, becomes in practice academic.

This is inelegant legislation, but the fact is that if the main issue were one solely of "breakdown" it would be very difficult to establish, and trials would become unduly protracted by the need to examine all kinds of evidence.

The essence of the D.R.A. therefore lay in s. 2 (1) (now s. 1 (2) of the M.C.A.) – "The court hearing a petition for divorce shall not hold the marriage to have broken down irretrievably *unless the petitioner satisfies the court* of one or more of the following facts. . . ." These facts are – (*a*) That the respondent has committed *adultery* and that the petitioner finds it intolerable to live with him (or her) – *both* these things must be proved: the intolerability may be something independent of the adultery and is not *necessarily* something which springs from it. (*b*) That the respondent has behaved in such a way that the petitioner cannot *reasonably* be expected to live with him (or her) – this does not mean that divorce can now be obtained simply because the petitioner alleges that the respondent is an incompatible partner; it means that the court must be satisfied that for the petitioner the situation is such that the marriage has become, through the behaviour of the respondent, really unendurable. (*c*) That the respondent has *deserted* the petitioner for a continuous period of *at least two years* immediately preceding the presentation of the petition. (*d*) That the parties *have lived apart* for a continuous period of at least *two* years immediately preceding the presentation of the petition *and* the respondent *consents to a decree* being granted – This, for the first time, was a recognition by our law of a right of divorce by mutual *consent*, and it is now the commonest ground of divorce. It must be noted that there are two safeguards in this case: for (s. 5 – now s. 10 (1) of the M.C.A.) where the court finds, between the time of decree *nisi* and decree absolute, that the petitioner *misled* the respondent into giving consent the decree may be rescinded; moreover, the provisions of s. 6 (below) apply. Both in this case and in case (*c*) (above), and (*e*) (below), in order to encourage reconciliation it is provided that in determining whether the prescribed period is "continuous" no account shall be taken of any consecutive period or non-consecutive periods not exceeding six months during which the parties have cohabited. (*e*) That the parties to the marriage have *lived apart for a continuous period of at least five years* immediately preceding the presentation of the petition. Here the petitioner may succeed even though the respondent does *not consent*. But there are also safeguards in this case. First (s. 4 – now s. 2 (4) of the M.C.A.), the petition may be opposed upon the ground that dissolution of the marriage "will result in grave financial hardship to the respondent and that it would *in all the circumstances* be wrong to dissolve the marriage": "all the circumstances" include such matters as the interests of children of the marriage, and are not confined to financial circumstances.

Second (s. 6 – now s. 10 (2)–(4) of the M.C.A.), after grant of a decree *nisi* under either (*d*) or (*e*) the court may take into consideration such circumstances as the age and health of the parties and the financial position of the respondent, and refuse to make the decree absolute unless it is satisfied that the petitioner (husband or wife) has, where appropriate, made reasonable provision for the respondent, or has given an undertaking so to do.

It remains to be added that, generally speaking, no petition for divorce will be entertained during the *first three years* of marriage, and that by long practice there is a waiting period (now of three months) between decree *nisi* ("unless") and decree "absolute" in order to allow time for the revealing of any cause why the divorce should not be permitted – which corresponds in the twilight of marriage with the Church's banns which may herald its dawn. The Queen's Proctor is the official charged with the duty of intervening if such a cause should appear, the court in granting the decree *nisi* order that it may be made absolute in a shorter period than three months if grounds for this are shown, *e.g.* to enable a woman to remarry before the birth of an expected child.

On granting a decree of dissolution of marriage, nullity, or judicial separation it has for some time been the practice for the court to make incidental orders concerning the property of the parties and the welfare of any children of the marriage. The M.C.A., ss. 21–25 contains important provisions to this end. By reason of these the court may make "financial provision" and "property adjustment" orders. The former may require periodical payments or (and this is new) the payment of a lump sum, and these may be payable to the spouse of the person ordered to pay or for the benefit of the children of the family. The latter consist (*inter alia*) of orders for the *transfer* of property to the other spouse or for the benefit of the children (this, also, is new). In making such orders s. 25 sets out a number of important considerations which must guide the discretion of the court: it must take into account (*a*) the income, earning capacity, property and other financial *resources* which each of the parties to the marriage *has* or *is likely to have* in the foreseeable future: (*b*) similar financial *obligations*: (*c*) the standard of living enjoyed by the family before the breakdown of the marriage ... (*f*) the contributions made by each of the parties to the welfare of the family, *including any contribution made by looking after the home* ...: (*g*) the value to either of the parties ... of any benefit (for example, a pension) which ... that party will lose the chance of acquiring. And s. 25 (1) terminates with the crucial words "and so to exercise those powers as to *place the parties, so far as it is practicable* and, having regard to their *conduct, just to do so,* in the financial position in *which they would have been if the marriage had not broken down* ..." (Very like a breach of contract?)

There is already a massive case law on these sections, though since all is here discretion few cases can give general guidance. Two points must suffice. First, following the ancient practice of the ecclesiastical courts, and of the Divorce Court, the *general* guide in cases where the husband is ordered to compensate the wife was provided in *Wachtel* v. *Wachtel*, [1973] Fam. 72; [1973] 1 All E.R. 829 namely that, as formerly in relation to payments from income, so now in relation to payments in respect of either income or capital, or in relation to division of property, the *normal* rule is that the wife's share should be ⅓ of the husband's resources. This is, of course, *not* modelled on "community of goods" (which entails *half* shares). In the second place, although it is true that s. 25 enjoins the court to take into account the "conduct of the parties" this does not mean that, as under the old law (based as it was upon the concept of the 'matrimonial offence') adultery or other forms of *matrimonial* misconduct will necessarily reduce the amount to be awarded. Finally, the cases constantly stress the essentially discretionary form of this jurisdiction in describing the policy of the Act as arriving at an *equitable re-distribution* of the assets of the family following upon the breakdown. It should be added that there are a number of provisions aimed at encouraging reconciliation.

If the M.C.A. and the preceding Acts are far from perfect they should be an improvement on the previous law – though one may wonder whether divorce really is a suitable sphere of activity for courts of *law*.

Dissolution of marriage (divorce) must be distinguished from *judicial separation* (separation). Divorce ends marriage, leaving the parties free to re-marry; judicial separation only has the effect of sanctioning a state of affairs in which they live apart. It is now (D.R.A., s. 8 – now M.C.A., s. 17) granted upon the same grounds as divorce, *except* that there is no need of proof of "irretrievable breakdown". Magistrates' courts have power to make orders for separation having the same effect as orders for judicial separation, whereas they have no divorce jurisdiction.

B CHILDREN AND THE FAMILY

The subjects now to be discussed are legitimacy, legitimation, adoption and guardianship.

1 Legitimacy

A child whose parents are lawfully married at the time it is begotten or born, or at any time between those two events, is legitimate. Moreover the issue of voidable marriages born during the subsistence of the marriage are legitimate; and it was provided by the Legitimacy Act 1959 that the issue of void marriages are also legitimate provided that at the time of the act of intercourse resulting in their birth (or at the time of the celebration of the marriage, if later) both or either of the parties to the marriage believed that it was valid.

2 Legitimation

Any child which is not thus born in lawful wedlock or of a void or voidable marriage under the conditions just considered is initially illegitimate. Before the passing of the Legitimacy Act 1926 people so born could not be legitimated (*i.e.* made legitimate) unless a special Act of Parliament were passed to render them so. By the provisions of the 1926 Act people may become legitimated by the subsequent marriage of their parents and under the 1959 Act it is no longer a bar to such legitimation that either of the parents was married to a third party at the time of the birth of the child thus legitimated. The effect of legitimation is that, from the date of the marriage, the legitimated person is treated in most respects as though he had been born in lawful wedlock; he may thus, for example, succeed to the property of his parents should they die intestate.

Formerly, on the other hand, an illegitimate person had no rights of succession to property. But this position was altered by the Family Law Reform Act 1969 and the Children Act 1975, with the result that illegitimate people have normal succession rights. Unlike a legitimate, or a legitimated, child, an illegitimate child has no common law right to be maintained by his father; though his mother is under a duty to maintain him until he is sixteen. By statute, however, an "affiliation" order may be made by a magistrates' court ordering his father to pay for his maintenance until that age; and under the 1959 Act the court may also, upon the application of either parent, make such orders as it may think fit regarding the custody of the child and the parents' right of access to it. Moreover, for the purposes of social security a husband is liable to maintain his wife and children and a wife her husband and children, and in this context "children" includes illegitimate children. Further, under the provisions of certain statutes, illegitimate children are entitled to receive benefits as "dependants" of their parents; for example, under the provisions of the Law Reform (Miscellaneous Provisions) Act 1934 respecting claims under the Fatal Accidents Acts (see above, p. 289).

3 Adoption

The effect of adoption is to vest the rights and duties which a parent has in respect of his child in some other person. Adoption was not a recognized legal institution in England until the passing of the Adoption of Children Act 1926. But the law on this subject is now fully regulated by the Adoption Acts 1958 to 1964 (as amended by the Adoption Act 1968 and the Children Act 1975).

Adoption of children (people under *eighteen* and *unmarried*) may be effected by court order, and particulars of the adoption must be entered in the Adopted Children Register kept at the General Register Office. In making an *adoption order* the court must have regard to the welfare of the child and (as far as possible) it must consult its wishes. Generally speaking, the order cannot be made unless the child has had his home with the adopter(s) for at least twelve months.

Adoption orders may be made in favour of the following: (*i*) married couples both of whom must have attained the age of *twenty-one*, one of whom, at least must be domiciled in the United Kingdom; (*ii*) one person alone who has attained th age of *twenty-one* and who is *unmarried*; though a married person may be sole adopter in certain circumstances: *e.g.* that he or she is permanently separated. A sole adopter, also, must be resident in the United Kingdom. Where natural parents adopt (as, for instance, in the case of an illegitimate child) an order can only be made in favour of *one* of them if there is some reason (*e.g.* the death of the person in question) for excluding the other.

No order may be made unless the child's parent or guardian gives unconditional agreement to the adoption. Once the order is made the child will be treated in law for all purposes as though he were the natural legitimate child of the adopter(s). Adoptions are arranged by adoption societies and by local authorities which are now, by statute, bound to work in co-operation; and the former are enjoined to provide "adoption services" designed to meet the needs of adopted children, their parents or guardians and adopters or would-be adopters.

The Adoption Act 1968 (subject to special rules) permits adoptions under the Hague Convention 1965 where all parties to the adoption are habitually resident in the United Kingdom and one of them is a national of some *other country* which is a party to the Convention.

Adoption orders must be distinguished from *custodianship orders*. The object of these orders is not to bring the child into the family of the custodian, but only, in certain circumstances and subject to certain rules, to give *legal custody* of the child to some person; this means that the custodian will have vested in him (or her) so much of the parental rights and duties – but *only* so much – as relate to the *person* of the child. But, unless the legal custodian is the child's parent or guardian he will not be entitled to arrange for the emigration of the child from the United Kingdom.

It should be added that an *adopted* minor is not the same thing as a *foster* child. By general definition foster children are children below the upper limit of compulsory school attendance who are placed, for reward, for a period exceeding one month under the care of someone other than a relative or guardian. By the provisions of the Children Act 1958 the foster parent is obliged to notify the appropriate local authority which has wide supervisory powers, including a power to inspect the premises where the child is kept and to impose conditions as to the way in which it is to be housed and cared for.

Jurisdiction in matters of adoption is usually exercised by magistrates' courts but the Family Division of the High Court also has jurisdiction. There is a right of appeal from the magistrates' courts to a Divisional Court of the Family Division.

4 Guardianship

In the broad sense of the term, "guardianship" denotes a relationship between guardian and ward whereby the guardian has the right to the custody of the ward and to the control of his upbringing, education, welfare, maintenance and property. The law concerning it is now to a large extent regulated by the Guardianship of Minors Act 1971 as amended by the Guardianship Act 1973.

There are three classes of guardians. First, the *parents*. Formerly the father, to the exclusion of the mother, had the legal right of guardianship but as regards legitimate children the 1973 Act, s. 1 (1), gave a concurrent right to the latter and provided that in case of disagreement as to the course to be taken in respect of the child either parent (or both) may apply to the court for directions. After the death of one parent the other will normally succeed to the sole guardianship. In the second place, either or both parents may by deed or by will appoint a "*testamentary*" guardian or guardians to act after their death. Finally, the *court* may, upon application, as it thinks fit, having regard to the welfare of the minor and to the conduct and wishes of the mother and father, appoint *any person* (whether or not one of the parents) as sole guardian, and may order a parent thus excluded from the guardianship to pay for the maintenance of the minor. The court may also make a *supervision order* to ensure supervision of a guardian by an independent person of a local authority or a probation officer; and in exceptional circumstances it may commit the minor to local authority care. Although the age of majority is now eighteen, court awards for maintencance of persons under guardianship may be made up to the age of twenty-one.

The court itself becomes responsible for the minor's custody, whether or no he has other guardians, when he or she becomes a "ward of court". This will now only occur where the court makes an order to that effect (Law Reform (Miscellaneous Provisions) Act 1949, s. 9). When a minor becomes a ward of court he or she may not, amongst other things, leave the jurisdiction without leave of the court, and may not marry without the court's permission.

Guardians may assert their right to custody in various ways: in particular by means of the writ of *Habeas Corpus* or by making application to the Chancery Division which, as we have seen, has special jurisdiction in matters of guardianship.

CHAPTER 13

SUCCESSION

Wherever one man transfers property to another the transferee may be said to "succeed" to the title of the transferor. For the purposes of this Chapter, however, the word "succession" will be used in a special sense. The type of succession about to be discussed is "universal" succession. This takes place where, for one reason or another, the whole, or substantially the whole, of one person's estate (property) passes to another or to others. This may happen in a number of ways, but we can only discuss succession upon death and succession upon bankruptcy.

1 SUCCESSION UPON DEATH

When people die their property does not die with them. It follows that in every legal system there must be rules governing the distribution of property after death. These rules must be designed to solve two main problems. First, "Who is to receive the property"? Second, "How is the distribution to be effected"? The first problem is answered by the rules relating to Testate and Intestate Succession. The second problem is answered by the rules governing the Administration of Estates. These two sets of rules require separate treatment.

Testate and Intestate Succession

A TESTATE SUCCESSION

Testate succession (Latin, *testamentum* = a will) arises where the deceased person has expressed his wishes concerning the devolution of his property during his life-time, in the form of a *will*. Intestate succession arises where there has been no will or where, for one reason or another, a will has failed to take effect, and consequently the people who are entitled to the property have to be designated by rules of law. We have seen that, for special reasons, wills of freehold land were not permitted at common law (above, p. 328). The law, however, had no reason to frown upon wills of personal property or of leaseholds; they were permitted, but they were regarded as being within the province of the Church. Death, like birth and marriage, was the Church's concern. Hence, until the Court of Probate Act 1857, wills were a matter for the ecclesiastical courts. They now fall within the jurisdiction of the ordinary civil courts, but many of the rules concerning them derive from the ecclesiastical and the (Roman) civil law.

i   The nature of a will – A will is a declaration made by a person in his life-time of his intentions concerning the devolution of his property after his death. Unless there is a clear intention to the contrary it *takes effect from the time of death*, not from the time it is made; it is said to be "*ambulatory*" until death. Thus, if X leaves "All my property" to Y, Y will be entitled to receive not only such property (undisposed of before death) as X had at the time he made the will, but also any other property X may have acquired between that time and his death. The will "*speaks from*" the death.

ii   Testamentary capacity – The general rule is that anyone (except a minor or a person of unsound mind) may make a will. If it is desired to show that a testator (the deceased person) was not capable, through unsoundness of mind or from any other cause, of forming a proper intention to make his will the fact of his incapacity must be clearly proved.

iii   Formalities – A will is not normally a mere informal declaration of intention. The Wills Act 1837 prescribes the following formalities –
  a   A will must be made in the form of a written document. Any written document, however, will suffice; even a letter.
  b   It must either be signed by the testator or by someone else in his presence and by his direction; though the "signature" need not necessarily be in writing but may consist of a mark or of some other form of identification which is unmistakably ascribable to him.
  c   The signature must be "attested" by at least two witnesses *after* the testator has completed his signature, who must themselves sign the will in the testator's presence. Since the purpose of attestation is to authenticate the testator's signature it follows that the witnesses *need* not be present at the time of the signing of the will by the testator: they must, however, both be present *together* either at this time or at some later time when the testator himself acknowledges the signature. Thus, for instance, there will be no valid attestation if the testator calls first Jack and then Joe into a room separately and each acknowledges the signature in the testator's presence, but not in each other's.

The testator's signature must appear at the foot of the will. Nothing should be added to the will after signature. If the signature appears, say, in the middle of the will, everything below it becomes invalid (Wills Act Amendment Act 1852, s. 1). This does *not*, however, mean that once a will is made it is unalterable: additions may be made in the body of it *provided that* they are initialled by the testator and the witnesses, and they may also be made even below the signature *if* they are signed and attested in the same way as the will itself. The will may also be supplemented by *codicils* signed and attested in the same manner as the will.

If anyone to whom, or to whose husband or wife, the testator has left property acts as a witness he will not be entitled to take under the will; but the Wills Act 1968 provides that if the will is duly executed without the attestation of such a person that attestation must be disregarded. In other words, provided that there are two qualified witnesses the attestation of any other witness or witnesses must be disregarded and they thus become entitled to take under the will. (The rule which disqualifies beneficiaries from taking under the will is, of course, designed to prevent frauds). Similarly no one who kills the testator by murder or manslaughter may benefit; and this rule has been held to apply even where on a charge of murder, reduced to manslaughter on account of diminished responsibility, the claimant was committed to detention for hospital treatment. By parity of reasoning, the killer is, of course, also debarred from inheriting from an intestate victim.

iv Soldiers' wills – It was a rule of Roman Law that soldiers in the field might make informal wills; for a soldier may often be in imminent fear of death and far from legal advice. This rule has passed into our law. Soldiers, sailors, and airmen while in *actual military service* and seamen at sea (under any conditions) have special privileges. (*a*) They may make wills even though they are not of age, provided that they have attained the age of fourteen years. (*b*) They may make informal wills. Even an oral declaration will suffice provided that it is a serious statement of intention; thus a soldier about to embark for France upon active service during the Second World War, took out his pay book, tapped it, and remarked, "If anything happens to me, everything is to be for R". This was held to be a valid will. A witness to a "soldier's" will *may* receive benefits under it.

The construction of the words "actual military service" (Wills Act 1837, s. 11) has often given rise to difficulty and they have been liberally construed. For example, it was held by the Court of Appeal that an airman on an instructional course in Canada during the war came within the privilege afforded by the rule. And further, seamen have been held to be technically "at sea" for this purpose while actually ashore between voyages.

v   The classes of testamentary disposition – Testamentary dispositions of freehold land are, as we have seen, technically called "devises". Dispositions of personal property (including leaseholds) are called "*bequests*" or "*legacies*".

A gift may be general, specific, demonstrative or residuary. A *general* gift is a bequest of some money or thing not distinguished from all others of the same kind, *e.g.* a bequest of "£100" or of "*a* horse". A *specific* gift is a gift of a specified thing which can be distinguished by the description in the will from all other things, *e.g.* "I bequeath to X my mare, Daisy". A *demonstrative* gift is one of a sum of money to be paid out of a particular fund, *e.g.* "£500 out of my 2½% War Stock". A *residuary* gift is a gift of the residue of the estate, or part of it, left over after all other gifts have been made and debts paid.

These distinctions are important because the nature of the gifts will determine whether they are liable to ademption or abatement. *Ademption* occurs when something which is subject to a specific bequest perishes between the time the will is executed and the death. If, for instance, A bequeaths a specified picture to B and this picture is destroyed by fire before A's death, B is clearly entitled to nothing. The gift is "adeemed". This doctrine obviously could not apply to general legacies and it is established that it does not apply to a demonstrative gift, for it is deemed to be the intention of the testator to give effect to such a gift even though the fund from which it is to come has ceased to exist at the time of the death. *Abatement* occurs when there is not enough property to satisfy all beneficiaries after the creditors of the deceased have been paid. In this case clearly some of the beneficiaries must lose their rights, and they "abate" in a specified order. "Residuary" gifts abate first and "specific" gifts last. If the residue is exhausted, general gifts are resorted to next: they abate proportionately, according to the value of each. Demonstrative gifts will not abate unless the fund out of which they are payable is itself exhausted: if that happens they will be treated for the purposes of abatement as if they were general gifts.

vi   Revocation – A will may be revoked either expressly or by implication.

Express revocation can only be effected if the instrument by which the testator purports to revoke is properly executed according to the formalities the Act requires for the making of a will. The same rule applies to alterations or interlineations in the will: they must be signed and witnessed.

Implied revocation arises in three ways. (*i*) By the making of a subsequent inconsistent formal testamentary document which disposes of the whole property embraced by the original will. Thus, though it is usual for solicitors to insert in wills a clause, "I hereby REVOKE all other Wills and Testamentary dispositions heretofore made by me", this is not strictly necessary; for provided that the second will does dispose of the *whole property* it automatically revokes the first. If there is only a *partial* inconsistency the parts of the former will not inconsistent with the latter will remain effective. (*ii*) By "Burning, tearing, or otherwise destroying" the will (Wills Act 1837, s. 20). This, however, only effects a revocation if there is both physical destruction and an intention to revoke by such destruction. Further, the destruction must be effected either by the testator or by someone *in his presence* who acts with his authority. Thus, if you accidentally throw your will into a waste paper basket, and it is taken away and destroyed, it is not revoked. (This recalls to the writer a memorable and unfortunate occasion when a zealous cleaner consigned a batch of examination scripts to the dustbin. Upon the maxim *omnia praesumuntur recte et solemniter acta* all the candidates had to pass.) Evidence of the contents of such a will may be given (if it can be obtained) after your death. (*iii*) By marriage. Whether a will be made by a man, or by a woman, subsequent marriage will revoke it automatically for most purposes. This rule does not, however, apply where the will is expressed to be made "in contemplation" of a marriage, provided that it was made after 1925 (L.P.A., s. 177): where, therefore, a man made a will leaving everything "unto my fiancée, M.E.B.", and then married M.E.B., the will was not revoked; for the form of disposition clearly contemplated marriage with M.E.B. whom the testator did, in fact, marry.

B   INTESTATE SUCCESSION

i   The Law before 1926 – Before January 1st, 1926, there were two separate sets of rules governing intestacy. *Freeholds* descended to the *heir-at-law*, *leaseholds* and *personal property* descended to the *next-of kin*.

The practitioner may still need to consult these rules. On the one hand he still has to understand them when examining titles acquired under intestacies prior to 1926; on the other hand, the "heir" to an entailed interest is still ascertained by reference to them. It is not, however, necessary to examine them in detail here.

The rules for ascertaining the "heir" were complex and essentially feudal. They aimed primarily at vesting freehold land in a single male tenant who would be capable, originally, of performing the feudal duties of a tenant (see above, p. 327). Primogeniture therefore applied: the eldest son always took the entire interest in the land, to the exclusion of the younger children, and males were preferred to females of equal degree. Thus, suppose A were fee simple owner, and that he died intestate leaving a daughter aged 35, a son aged 30, and another son aged 28. The elder son took the entire fee simple. Suppose, however, that A left one child only, a daughter, and that he was also survived by a brother. Then the daughter took all, for her relationship was closer in degree to A than her uncle's. Detailed rules for ascertaining the heir were evolved by the common law courts. They were eventually incorporated in, and to some extent amended by, the Inheritance Act 1833.

Descent of property *other than freehold land* was governed by rules originally adapted by the ecclesiastical courts from the Roman Law. Feudalism had no concern with property of this nature. Hence there was no rule of primogeniture, and next-of-kin of equal degree, whether male or female, were entitled to take equally. These rules were placed upon a statutory footing by the Statutes of Distribution 1670 and 1685.

ii Intestacy since January 1st, 1926 – The Administration of Estates Act 1925 (A.E.A.) – as now amended by various statutes, including the Intestates' Estates Act 1952 and the A.E.A. 1971, swept away the old law governing intestacy and replaced it by simpler rules which apply uniformly to all kinds of property.

Before the rules relating to distribution can be set out the machinery adopted by the Act for effecting it must be explained. Wherever there is an intestacy it is provided that all the deceased's property, other than money, is to vest in his *"personal representatives"* (see below, p. 433), upon trust for sale. It must be realized at once that this trust for sale is no more than a practical device which makes distribution possible where there are a large number of beneficiaries. Its imposition does not mean that the property *must* be sold. There is a power to postpone sale indefinitely. Thus the trust may never operate to produce an actual sale; the property *may* remain "unconverted" right up to the time when the personal representatives hand it over in its original form to a person entitled to it.

This point may be illustrated by an example. Suppose X dies intestate. His estate consists of a farmhouse, a farm and some cash at the bank. The house and the farm at once become subject to a trust for sale in the hands of the personal representatives. If, however, the case is a very simple one and X's sole surviving relation is his wife, the personal representatives need not sell; they only have to vest the entire estate (after payment of debts, etc.) in the wife. The administration is then completed. If, however, there were a large number of people entitled to take a share in the property (say, for instance, X had five children), then clearly the trust for sale may come into play. The reason for this is that, although it would not be easy to split up the entire property into many different parts, it is comparatively simple to divide up the money realized from the sale. This does not, however, mean that, even in a complicated case, the property need always be sold if it is possible to distribute it (as by distributing shares comprised in the estate among the beneficiaries) without turning it into money.

For the present that is all that needs to be understood about the machinery of administration. We may now consider the problem of distribution.

The statutory rules governing the distribution of intestates' estates are based upon the assumption that people who die intestate would, if they had made a will, have wished to make provision for certain classes of near relations; preferring some of these relations to others if they happen to be alive at the time of the intestates' death. Thus, the primary assumption is that people usually wish to provide for their children equally, and also to make provision for their widows or widowers during the remainder of their lives. Failing surviving children or a surviving spouse, or both, they usually wish to benefit their nearer relations, and only wish to leave their property to remoter relations if there are no nearer ones surviving. It is equally true that after divorce or judicial separation people do *not* usually wish to benefit the divorced or separated spouse, and the law takes this also into account (see below, p. 431). The actual rules are complicated; but if the reader will bear the principles in mind, their effect should be fairly easy to understand.

Five main groups of people have to be considered –

    (1) A surviving husband or wife;
    (2) Surviving children;
    (3) Surviving parents;
    (4) Surviving brothers and sisters of the whole blood;
    (5) Surviving relations of remoter degree.

(1) *A surviving husband or wife* – (a) If the intestate leaves *no children and no parent or brother or sister of the whole blood* (categories (2)–(4) above), then (subject to what will appear under (2) (*b*) (*i*) below), the surviving husband or wife will be entitled to the whole residuary estate absolutely.

"*Residuary estate*" here means the entire property of the deceased, less the funeral and administration expenses, and any debts or other liabilities incurred by the deceased during his or her life.

Further, it must be understood that sometimes even though children or brothers and sisters *do* survive the intestate, the spouse may still become absolutely entitled. The reason for this is that the survival of these classes of people will ultimately only affect the rights of the surviving spouse if they attain a "vested interest" in the property; this will only happen if they attain the age of eighteen years or marry before that age. The surviving spouse will therefore become absolutely entitled to the estate if all children and brothers and sisters alive at the time of the intestate's death in fact die minors and unmarried; though unless (and *until*) *these events occur*, the income of the estate will be distributed upon the assumption that they will become entitled according to the rules set out below, and the rights of the surviving spouse are provisionally curtailed accordingly.

(*b*) If the intestate *leaves children* as well as the surviving spouse, then (subject to what has just been explained about the attainment of vested interests), he or she has an absolute right to receive *the sum of* £15,000 (duty free and bearing interest until payment) from the estate, or from the proceeds of its sale. Of course the payment of this sum, or indeed, of only a part of it, will often exhaust the entire estate; and there will then be nothing for the children. Further, in all circumstances the surviving spouse is absolutely entitled to the *"personal chattels"* of the deceased. These include all articles of a personal nature, such as jewellery, motor cars, furniture, pictures, collections of stamps acquired by way of hobby, etc., but exclude chattels used at the death of the intestate for business purposes, money and securities for money. Thus in *Re Crispin's Will Trusts*, [1974] 3 All E.R. 772 it was held that for this purpose a clock is a clock: so that even a collection of clocks may be a collection – provided, at least, that it has not been bought by way of commercial speculation for resale – of personal chattels. Moreover, the surviving spouse has a right to have the matrimonial home appropriated as part of his or her share of the residue. Apart from the absolute right to what has sometimes been called the "statutory legacy" of £15,000 (this figure may, however, be altered by statutory instrument), and the other rights mentioned, the surviving spouse is also entitled to the *income produced by half the remainder* of the residuary estate during his or her life-time. The capital of this half of the remainder of the residuary estate, and the *other* half of it are, as we shall see, held on the *"statutory trusts"* (below) for the children. By s. 2 of the Intestates' Estates Act 1952 a surviving spouse may, upon giving notice to the personal representatives, have the life interest converted to a lump sum: exercise of this right often, as it will be appreciated, enables rapid winding up of the estate.

It must be realized that where there are surviving children, as well as the surviving spouse, the above provisions operate in favour of this, his immediate family, to the *complete exclusion of all other relatives*.

(*c*) If the intestate leaves *no children*, but leaves a surviving spouse and a *surviving parent or parents or surviving brothers or sisters*, then the surviving spouse is at present entitled to receive *the sum of* £40,000 (free of duty and bearing interest until payment) and the *personal chattels*. Once more, of course, a far smaller sum than this will normally exhaust most estates; but if there is any residue after these deductions have been made, then the spouse is entitled to *one half* of it *absolutely* (not merely to the *income* of this half, as in (1) (*b*) above). As to the remaining half, see (3) (*b*), below.

(2) *Surviving children* – The term "children" here includes adopted and legitimated children, but not illegitimate children. Their rights may be summarized under the following heads –

(*a*) *Where there is a surviving spouse as well as a surviving child or children.* The spouse will, as we have seen, be entitled to a "statutory legacy" of £8,750, to the personal chattels, and also to a life interest in the income of one half of the remaining residue (if any). The other half of the remaining residue (if any) will be held on the "statutory trusts" for the children. After the death of the surviving spouse the whole of the remaining residue will be held on the "statutory trusts" for the surviving child or children; in the case of a child who survives the intestate but dies before the surviving spouse his share will pass to his estate.

(*b*) *Where there is a child or children, but no surviving spouse.* The residuary estate is held on the "statutory trusts" for the child or children. Here "residuary estate" means the entire residuary estate as above defined. All children, of either sex, are entitled to equal shares in it.

The following further points must be noted –

(*i*) Where a child dies *before the intestate*, leaving children of his own who survive the intestate, those children are entitled to "represent" him, *i.e.* his share of the estate is divided between them. Thus, suppose that A dies intestate. He leaves children B and C. He had another child D, who predeceased him. D had two children D^1 and D^2, living at the death of A. A's estate will ultimately be divided (subject to deductions in favour of a surviving spouse, if any) in the proportions, B$=\frac{1}{3}$, C$=\frac{1}{3}$, D^1 and $D^2=\frac{1}{6}$ each.

(*ii*) Wherever anyone who is entitled to take upon intestacy is under the age of 18, the A.E.A. provides that the statutory powers of "maintenance" and "advancement" conferred by the T.A. shall apply to his share. This means that the income of his share can either be spent on his upkeep or else accumulated and added to the capital of the share, and that up to one half of this capital can be applied for his "advancement or benefit"; a phrase which by judicial interpretation may now be said to extend to practically any provision which can be considered to be for the long-term benefit of the child.

(*iii*) It sometimes happens that, during his life-time, an intestate who has more than one child has made an "*advancement*" to one or more of his children, or has paid him or her money for the purpose of marriage. These payments have to be taken into account in assessing the share, if any, to which the favoured child will be entitled upon the intestacy, unless the circumstances show that the intestate did not intend this result. In the technical phrase, the payments must be brought into *hotchpot*. Although an advancement will usually consist of some substantial payment for the purpose of establishing a young person in life – *e.g.* in practice at the Bar – it need not necessarily be of that nature: any substantial payment to a "child" – even though later in life – which supplies some need (as where shares in a company are given in order to give him a controlling interest) may be construed as an advancement.

The effect of bringing a payment into hotchpot is that the value of it will be deducted from the particular child's share, and may of course exhaust it entirely; the value of the shares of his or her brothers and sisters will therefore be proportionately increased.

(3) *Surviving parents* – (*a*) *Where there are surviving children* the parents will receive nothing.

(*b*) *Where there is a surviving spouse,* he or she will, as we have seen, be entitled to £40,000 and the personal chattels and to one half of any outstanding residue absolutely. The surviving parents will be entitled to share the other half of this residue; or if only one parent survives, he or she will be absolutely entitled to all of it.

(*c*) *Where there is no surviving spouse and there are no surviving children,* then the *entire* residuary estate will be divided equally between the surviving parents; or, if only one parent survives, he or she will be absolutely entitled to the whole.

Where there are surviving parents, brothers and sisters therefore have no claim.

(4) *Brothers and sisters of the whole blood* –

(*a*) *Where there are surviving children,* the surviving brothers and sisters will receive nothing.

(*b*) *Where there is a surviving spouse and a surviving parent,* the surviving brothers and sisters will receive nothing.

(*c*) *Where there is a surviving spouse, but no surviving children and no surviving parents,* subject to the right of the spouse to £40,000, the personal chattels, and half of the residue, the remaining half of the residue will be held on the statutory trusts for the surviving brothers and sisters.

(*d*) *Where there is no surviving spouse, and there are no surviving children, and no surviving parents,* then, the surviving brothers and sisters will be entitled (upon the statutory trusts) to the entire residuary estate.

Provided that at least one of these brothers or sisters of the whole blood acquires a vested interest all other relatives will be excluded.

Nephews and nieces "represent" brothers and sisters who predecease the intestate, in the same way that grandchildren represent children ((2) (*b*) (*i*) above).

(5) *Surviving relations of remoter degree* – If any relatives included in categories (1)–(4), above, survive the deceased, provided that at least one of them takes a vested interest, he or they entirely exclude all relations of remoter degree. But failing the survival of relatives included in categories (1)–(4), then such relations are entitled to take according to their classes in the following order of priority (each class excluding other classes, according to that order) –

(*i*) Brothers and sisters of the half blood, upon the statutory trusts.

(*ii*) Grandparents.

(*iii*) Uncles and aunts who are brothers or sisters of the whole blood of a parent of the intestate.

(*iv*) Uncles and aunts who are brothers or sisters of the half blood of a parent of the intestate.

In the case of class (*i*) nephews and nieces "represent" the brothers and sisters, and in the case of classes (*iii*) and (*iv*) cousins "represent" uncles and aunts in cases where the brother, sister, uncle or aunt predeceases the intestate.

No one can be entitled to benefit upon an intestacy unless he either falls directly within classes (1)–(5) above, or "represents" some person who would have done so had he or she lived.

The rules apply in cases of partial intestacy as well as in cases of total intestacy. Partial intestacy may arise where, for instance, a testator only disposes of part of his estate in his will, thus dying intestate as to the other part.

Where a person dies leaving no relatives within the prescribed categories *the estate passes to the Crown*; but, "in accordance with the existing practice ... the Crown ... may ... provide for dependants, whether kindred or not, of the intestate, and other persons for whom the intestate might reasonably have been expected to make provision ... out of the property" (A.E.A., s. 46 (1) (*vi*)).

It must be added that in cases of divorce or judicial separation (provided in the latter case that the parties have not resumed cohabitation) where one spouse dies intestate the property will devolve as if the other party had been dead at the time of the intestate's decease (see the Matrimonial Causes Act 1973, s. 18 (2), Sched. 1, para. 13): this accords with the general policy of the A.E.A. to give effect to presumed intention (see above, p. 427). This does not, however, mean that the Inheritance (Provision for Family and Dependants) Act 1975 may not be invoked.

C FAMILY PROVISION

Unlike Scots law and the civil law of the Continent, before the passing of the Inheritance (Family Provision) Act 1938 English law had no rules to ensure that testators should not leave all their property "away" from their families. People were therefore free to cut off their children without a penny. That Act remedied this situation to a large extent by permitting certain "dependants" of deceased people to apply for an order of the court to make reasonable provision for them from the "deceased's" estate where he, by his will, had failed to provide it.

The law on this matter is now governed by the Inheritance (Provision for Family and Dependants) Act 1975, and now (s. 1 (1) "where ... a person dies domiciled in England and Wales and is survived by ... (a) a wife or husband ... (b) a former (spouse) who has not remarried ... (c) a child ... (d) any person who was treated by the deceased as a child of the family (in relation to any marriage of his) ... (e) any person ... who immediately before the death of the deceased was being maintained ... by the deceased ... may apply to the court for an order ... on the ground that the disposition of the deceased's estate effected by his *will* or the law relating to *intestacy* ... is *not such as to make reasonable financial provision* for (that person). "Reasonable financial provision" means (s. 1 (2)), in the case of an application by a surviving *spouse* (whether or no, being not remarried, be as she was divorced or separated from the deceased at the time of death) such provision as is "reasonable in all the circumstances", in the case of any other applicant only such provision as is required for his maintenance. The court may, *inter alia*, make an order for periodical or lump sum payments from the estate (s. 2); and (s. 3) in making the order must have regard to a number of specified matters: *e.g.* the applicant's resources, the size of the estate and the applicant's conduct. By s. 4 a time-limit of *six months* from the date of taking out of representation of the estate is (normally) imposed upon the making of applications. There are stringent provisions (including – s. 11 – the avoidance of colourable contracts ot leave property to others by will) designed to prevent the deceased from defeating the objects of the Act.

The Administration of Estates

Having considered who is entitled to succeed to property on death we will now consider the practical problem of how the estate is administered. First, as to personal representatives.

A   PERSONAL REPRESENTATIVES

i   The nature and purpose of representation – Hitherto we have considered the estates of deceased persons only from the point-of-view of possible beneficiaries. Few of us, however, are without creditors in our life-time and few of us die without leaving some outstanding debts. Hence our estates are usually subject to two principal classes of claims; the claims of creditors on the one hand and of beneficiaries on the other. These claims often conflict and yet they have, somehow or other, to be met. They might be met by permitting the property to pass direct to the beneficiaries and allowing the creditors to claim against them. This is what is actually done under some systems of law. English law, however, adopting its procedure ultimately from the ecclesiastical courts, interposes the *personal representatives* between the competing claimants. It is their duty to administer the estate by paying creditors, collecting debts and distributing the assets to the people entitled to take under the will or intestacy.

The general rule is that, since the A.E.A., all the property which the deceased owned at his death vests in these representatives. There is, however, an important exception to this rule. Sections 22–24 of the Act contain provisions designed to ensure that, on the death of a tenant for life under a settlement, the settled land (where the land remains settled) shall vest in the trustees of the settlement as "*special*" personal representatives. The settled land alone vests in them; the rest of the life tenant's property is administered by his ordinary or "general" representatives. The duty of the trustees is to pass the legal estate in the land to the next tenant for life.

ii The duties of personal representatives – The law which governs the duties of personal representatives, who are in a fiduciary position in many ways similar to trustees, is to be found partly in the T.A. but the essentials are now set out in the A.E.A. 1971, s. 9 – "The personal representative of a deceased person shall be under a duty to – (*a*) collect and get in the ... estate of the deceased and administer it according to law; (*b*) when required to do so ... exhibit on oath in the court a full inventory of the estate and when so required render an account of the administration to the court; (*c*) when required to do so by the High Court, deliver up the grant of probate or administration to that court." Like trustees, personal representatives may take advantage of s. 23 of the T.A. (see above, p. 404), and if they administer the estate properly they will incur no liability, and the expenses of administration will be borne by the estate.

iii The classes of personal representatives – Personal representatives who are appointed by a *testator in his will* are called *executors*. They are usually appointed expressly; but sometimes an appointment may be implied, as where a testator nominates a particular person to pay his debts. In the latter event the executor is known technically as an executor *according to the tenor*.

The personal representatives of an *intestate* are called *administrators*: they derive their powers, as we shall see, from the grant of *letters of administration*.

The matter is, however, somewhat more complicated than this, because even though there is a will, administrators may sometimes have to be appointed. Some examples of this situation may be given. In the first place, where there is a will but for some reason there are no executors, or the people named as such decline to act, someone must be appointed to act as personal representative. These people, when appointed, are known as *administrators cum testamento annexo* ("with the will annexed"). In the second place, minors cannot act as representatives, and it follows that if a minor is appointed by will there must be someone to act for him: such a person is known as an administrator *durante minore actate* ("during minority"). In the third place, if there is a dispute concerning the validity of a will clearly an executor appointed in the will cannot take office. In this case an *administrator pendente lite* ("during the litigation") has to be appointed. An administrator of this latter class may proceed with the administration of the estate, but he must not distribute the property.

Where an executor dies in the course of administration his own executor will take his place. If, however, he does without appointing an executor there is no one to succeed him, and an administrator *de bonis non administratis* ("of the unadministered estate") must therefore be appointed. It should be noted that executors, and executors alone, are "succeeded" in this way. Where an administrator of the estate of an intestate dies a new administrator must be specifically appointed.

A person who intermeddles in the estate (*i.e.* does some act, such as collecting the assets, normally done by a personal representative) is liable to account as personal representative even though he has never had any intention of becoming formally appointed as such; such a person is called an "*executor de son tort*".

iv   Probate and letters of administration – Although an executor can enter upon his duties immediately after the death of the testator, his right to dispose of the estate is not fully established until he has obtained a grant of *probate* of the will. "Probate" is official acceptance of the authenticity of the will and official sanction of the executor's right to act. It may be obtained in two ways; in "*common form*" or in "*solemn form*". The former method is the more usual. The procedure is for the executor to apply either to the principal registry of the Family Division of the High Court at Somerset House or to a District Registry. He must produce the will, an affidavit called the "executor's oath", and an Inland Revenue affidavit. The "oath" is in effect a promise by the executor to administer the estate according to law. The affidavit contains particulars of the property comprised in the estate, which enable the Inland Revenue Commissioners to assess the estate duty payable. If these documents are in order, and payment on account of estate duty is made, "probate" will then be granted and a copy of the will will be handed to the executor; the original is retained at the Registry.

"Probate" in "common form" is granted very much as a matter of course. If, however, there is any serious dispute, for instance as to the validity of the will, probate in "solemn form" will have to be obtained. This entails the hearing of evidence, and amounts in effect to an action, normally heard before a judge of the Chancery Division in London.

Letters of administration are granted in much the same way as probate. There is, however, one substantial difference in the procedure. An executor is a person in whom the testator has reposed confidence, an administrator is not. Formerly, therefore, administrators were normally required to enter into an "administration bond" by which they undertook to pay the Principal Registrar double the gross value of the estate if they failed to administer it according to law and also they usually had to produce sureties against default. This has now, however, been altered by the A.E.A. 1971, s. 8 which only provides that the High Court may require one or more sureties (in practice usually insurance companies) to make good, within any limit imposed by the court, any loss which any person interested may suffer in consequence of a breach of his duties by the administrator. No action may be brought against the surety without leave of the court and in a number of cases a surety will not be required.

v **Who may be appointed** – Executors are appointed by the will. Nothing therefore need be mentioned about them under this head, beyond pointing out that probate will not be granted either to a minor or to more than four executors. It is usual, however, to appoint more than one, for it is open to an executor to refuse to act.

The appointment of administrators is within the discretion of the court, and Rules of Court prescribe an order of priority of choice. This order roughly follows the order of priority of persons entitled to take upon an intestacy; though sometimes – where for instance the estate is insolvent – a creditor may be appointed.

The maximum number of administrators is four. In certain cases, as where there is a minor beneficiary, there must normally be at least two; though, even in these cases a trust corporation (above, p. 402) may act alone.

iv   The powers and liabilities of personal representatives – Personal representatives are endowed with absolute powers of disposing of the property for the purpose of administration. We have seen that in the case of a total intestacy an automatic trust for sale is imposed. By s. 39 of the A.E.A. the *powers* of trustees for sale are also conferred upon executors. This, of course, means that personal representatives have all the powers of a life tenant under the S.L.A.; in particular the power of selling land comprised in the estate. Even before the Act they had the power to sell or pledge personal property comprised in the estate. All these powers, of course, come to an end when the administration is complete, the debts paid and the property vested in the beneficiaries.

By law personal representatives are officially allowed one year from the death in which to wind up the estate (A.E.A., s. 44), but the courts will not tie them strictly to this period. Thus if any creditor or beneficiary complains that he has suffered as the result of a delay in distribution beyond the "executor's year", he will have to prove that this delay was the result of some neglect on the part of the personal representatives.

The liability of personal representatives is in general limited by the value of the estate they administer. They are, however, in a similar position to trustees, and if they do anything unlawful, *e.g.* distribute the assets of an insolvent estate to beneficiaries instead of to creditors, they may be personally liable. A personal representative is then said to have committed a *devastavit* ("he was wasted"). He can, however, take advantage of s. 61 of the T.A. (above, p. 404).

B   ADMINISTRATION OF ASSETS

Having described the nature of personal representatives we are now in a position to consider their duties.

They normally administer the estate themselves (usually through a solicitor) without interference. If, however, someone interested in the estate – such as a beneficiary or a creditor – is dissatisfied with the administration he may, by an "administration action", apply for administration by the court. If the estate is "solvent" it will then be administered in the Chancery Division of the High Court. If it is "insolvent" it may be administered either in the Chancery Division or in the Bankruptcy Court. Small estates, however, may sometimes be administered in a county court.

The four main duties of personal representatives are –

(*a*) To collect all debts due to the estate;

(*b*) To pay all the debts and satisfy all the liabilities of the estate;

(*c*) To convert unauthorized investments into authorized ones (above,

p. 403); though they almost invariably have power to postpone doing this.

(*d*) To distribute the remainder of the property according to the will, or to the rules of intestacy.

Where personal representatives are in the happy position of administering an estate sufficiently large to satisfy all creditors and all beneficiaries their duties are comparatively simple. This is, however, often not the case. On the one hand, the estate may be "*insolvent*", *i.e.* not large enough to satisfy all creditors in full. in this case, of course the beneficiaries can hope for nothing. On the other hand, though it is "solvent" (*i.e.* the creditors can all be satisfied) it may be insufficient to meet the claims of all beneficiaries in full. In either case rules of law have had to be provided to govern the conflicting rights of claimants, so as to determine who will be paid and who will not. We will first consider the rules concerning "insolvent" estates.

i Insolvent estates – Where the estate is insufficient to meet the claims of *creditors* in full the following rules apply (A.E.A., s. 34 (1) and First Schedule, Part 1) –

(*i*) *Funeral expenses, testamentary expenses* and the *costs* of administration have first priority. They must, if possible, be paid in full.

(*ii*) *Debts* have next priority. They have to be paid in the order pre-scribed by the Bankruptcy Act 1914 (as amended by later Acts). This order is the following:

a *Preferred* debts rank first. Examples of these are arrears of rates and taxes for any one year and the wages of clerks, servants, and workmen (up to £200) due for a period of four months prior to the death.

b *Ordinary* debts. These are any debts which are neither "preferred" nor "deferred".

c *Deferred* debts. Examples of these are claims by the husband or wife of the deceased for money lent to the deceased for the purposes of business, and claims for money lent to him upon a stipulation that it is to bear interest at a rate varying with the profits of the deceased's business.

Secured creditors are also entitled to special rights.

If the estate is insufficient to satisfy the claims of all creditors in any one class, these claims must usually be cut down proportionately, according to their respective amounts. Thus suppose that when classes (*i*) and (*ii*) (*a*) claims have been satisfied, only £100 remains; then if A and B are ordinary creditors owed £1,500 and £500 respectively, they will receive £75 and £25 each.

By section 10 of the A.E.A. 1971 a personal representative who, in good faith and at a time when he has *no reason to believe that the estate is insolvent*, pays the debt of any person (*including himself*) who is a creditor of the estate is not to be liable to account to an unpaid creditor *of the same degree*. This rule does not, however, apply to a creditor who has been granted letters of administration solely because he is a creditor in respect of debts *due to himself*.

ii   Solvent estates—Even though an estate is "*solvent*" (*i.e.* there are sufficient funds available to meet all the claims of creditors) sufficient funds may not be available to pay the beneficiaries in full. The creditors must of course be paid somehow. It is therefore essential to know the order in which the beneficiaries are to lose their rights so that the creditors may be satisfied.

This order is laid down in s. 34 (3) and Part II of the First Schedule to the A.E.A. The funeral, testamentary and administration expenses and the debts are to be paid out of the following funds in the following order—

a   First, resort is to be had to any property in the estate which is undisposed of by will, subject to the retention of a fund to meet pecuniary legacies.

b   Next, to any property included in a "residuary" gift, subject to the retention of a fund to meet the balance of the pecuniary legacies. A "residuary" gift is a gift of anything that may remain of a testator's property after specific devises and bequests have been set aside.

c   Next, to property specifically appropriated by the testator for the payment of debts.

d   Next, to property left by the testator subject to a charge for the payment of debts.

e   Next, to the fund, if any, retained to meet pecuniary legacies.

f   Next, to property specifically devised or bequeathed, rateably, according to value.

g   Finally, to property appointed by will under a general power (including the statutory power to dispose of entailed interests), rateably, according to value. This class of property comes last on the list because, in a sense, it is not really the testator's "own" to dispose of; though he is free to dispose of it, it comes to him from elsewhere.

It is provided that this order of application may be varied by the will of the deceased. Thus if a testator shows a clear intention that a special fund of £x shall be set aside for payment of debts *in exoneration* of all other funds, this fund will be liable first, even before property in category (*a*). The intention to exonerate must, however, appear clearly from the will: otherwise a fund which is merely set aside for the payment of debts will fall within category (*c*).

Such then, is the order in which beneficiaries are liable to lose their interests. It only remains to be noticed that it may sometimes happen that an interest of a lower category (say, (*e*)) is disposed of in favour of creditors before an interest of a higher category (say, (*b*)). At one time this often occurred, since creditors were permitted, in certain circumstances, to proceed to satisfy their claims by direct resort to real property comprised in the estate. In this event the creditor would not concern himself with the "priority" of the beneficiary entitled to the property attacked, so that a "lower" beneficiary might lose his interest while "higher" beneficiaries retained theirs. This cannot occur today, since creditors may no longer proceed against the land directly. It is possible, however, that a personal representative may delve unnecessarily "low" on the list in order to discharge liabilities. He may, for instance, dispose of property comprised in category (*e*) in favour of a creditor, intending to dispose of all the property in the "higher" categories later. He may then discover that the estate is richer than he supposed, or that the liabilities are less than he supposed, so that he need never have attacked category (*e*) at all.

In such a situation the doctrine of *marshalling of assets* comes into play. This means that a beneficiary who loses property of a "lower" category to which he is entitled may recoup his loss by claiming to be indemnified out of undisposed property to which someone else "higher" on the list is entitled. The doctrine of marshalling is thus no more than an application of the principle that, whatever the method of distribution, the prescribed order will in fact always be observed. This principle is obviously elementary. Suppose, for example, all property comprised in the estate, down to and including category (*d*) is actually disposed of in favour of creditors. Suppose that it is then discovered that the deceased had concealed certain property. Clearly category (*d*) beneficiaries will have first claim on this "new" property.

C   TRANSFER OF PROPERTY TO BENEFICIARIES

When all testamentary and other expenses have been paid and all liabilities discharged, the final duty of the personal representatives is to transfer the appropriate property to the appropriate beneficiaries.

The rule is that the representatives must *assent* to the transfer. In respect of any property other than land the assent requires no special formality. Representatives may signify their intention to divest themselves of the property in favour of beneficiaries by any legally recognized method. Thus, a beneficiary may remove books which have been bequeathed to him with the consent, express or implied, of the executors. This will amount to an "assent". Shares may be transferred by executing a transfer to the beneficiary.

Where, however, it is desired to transfer the legal estate in land it is enacted by s. 36 (4) of the A.E.A. that the *assent "shall be in writing, signed by the personal representative, and shall name the person in whose favour it is given"*, and that *"an assent not in writing . . . shall not be effectual to pass a legal estate"*. This requirement must therefore always be satisfied; and it is, moreover, of cardinal importance in conveyancing. The reason for this is that s. 36 (7) provides that a written assent shall be taken, by a purchaser of the land for money or money's worth, to be sufficient evidence that the person in whose favour the assent is given is entitled to the legal estate. This means that a purchaser from the beneficiary who has obtained such an assent need not, and must not, examine the will in order to assure himself that the vendor is entitled to convey. All he needs to see is the assent. In two cases, however, he must not accept the bare evidence of the assent (the Act only provides that it is to be "sufficient" evidence). First, if there is a memorandum of a previous assent endorsed upon the probate or letters of administration: this naturally renders the later assent suspect. Second, if, without examining the will, the purchaser actually has notice of a defect in the vendor's title, despite the assent. This might happen, for instance, where it appears from a recital in the assent itself that the vendor is not the person entitled to convey – that he is, for example, a beneficiary under a trust for sale – for it will be recalled that in this case it is the duty of the trustees, not of the beneficiary, to make the conveyance.

This may be the proper place to remark that an apparent problem in the law of succession, testate or intestate, may sometimes arise where two or more people die or appear to have died simultaneously. Suppose, for example, that by his will X leaves Y a legacy and X and Y are both drowned in the same shipwreck, there being no evidence as to which of them died first. Can Y's representatives claim the legacy upon the assumption that X died first and that his will therefore operated in favour of Y, or is it to be assumed that Y died first so that the legacy "lapsed" (Y being presumed dead before X died) and fell into residue so as to pass to X's intestate successors? This problem of *"commorientes"* (people dying together) is solved by L.P.A. s. 184 which provides that such deaths shall, subject to court order, be presumed to have occurred in order of *seniority*: thus, in the problem, Y's representatives would take if he were younger than X and X's intestate successors if X were younger than Y.

2 BANKRUPTCY

Bankruptcy is a form of universal succession by which the property of an insolvent debtor is made available for his creditors. The purpose of the law of bankruptcy is twofold. First, to ensure that the distribution among the creditors of what property there is, is fair and that it is proportionate to the amount of their claims. Secondly, to give the debtor a chance of making a clean start, discharged of his liabilities.

Bankruptcy law is now principally governed by the Bankruptcy Act 1914 (here abbreviated B.A.), the Bankruptcy (Amendment) Act 1926, and statutory Bankruptcy Rules. Briefly, the position is this. Where a man who has contracted debts which he cannot pay commits an "*act of bankruptcy*", his property may be vested in a trustee in bankruptcy. It is the duty of the trustee to distribute the property proportionately among the bankrupt's creditors; and after the creditors have thus succeeded to the property the bankrupt may be "*discharged*" and freed from further liability. The law may be considered under four heads.

A BANKRUPTCY PROCEEDINGS

Bankruptcy proceedings start with the filing of a written bankruptcy *petition*. Either the debtor himself or any creditor may petition. The latter, however, can only do so if a debt of more than £50 is owed, the debt is for a liquidated sum (*i.e.* an ascertained money sum, not, *e.g.*, a personal claim in tort), the act of bankruptcy upon which the petition is founded occurred within three months of the presentation of the petition and, generally speaking, only if the debtor is domiciled in England. It should be added that the £50 limitation is an aggregate amount: so that a debtor who owes, say, £20 to X, £20 to Y and £10 to Z may be made bankrupt provided that X, Y and Z petition jointly.

The court hears the petition and may either accept or dismiss it; and in the case of acceptance, a *receiving order* will be made. This means that an "*official receiver*" is appointed to control the debtor's financial affairs. An official receiver is a public officer who acts on behalf of the court and of the Department of Trade. The latter has a special interest in bankruptcy proceedings.

Within seven days of the order (or within three if the debtor is himself the petitioner) the debtor must submit a written *statement of affairs* to the official receiver. This sets out his exact financial position.

A *public examination* follows. The debtor is examined before the court, being subjected to questions by the creditors (or their legal representatives) and others. The debtor must appear in person and the statement of affairs forms the basis of the examination. The examination may be adjourned. It often lasts for a considerable time.

The making of the receiving order is advertised and the official receiver must, normally within 14 days of the order, summon a *"first meeting"* of creditors. No creditor may attend this, or any other, meeting unless he has "proved" his debt by affidavit. The debtor himself attends the meeting. The purpose of the meeting is to give the creditors an opportunity of deciding whether to accept a "composition" (see below) or whether to make the debtor bankrupt. If they decide to adopt the latter course the court will duly adjudge the debtor bankrupt.

The effect of a bankruptcy order is to vest such of the debtor's property as is by law liable in the official receiver who holds it until a *trustee in bankruptcy* is appointed. The trustee will normally be either one of the creditors or, exceptionally, the official receiver himself. In the latter case the effect of adjudication is simply to alter the receiver's position from that of supervisor to that of trustee.

A *committee of inspection* may also be appointed by the first or any subsequent meeting of the creditors. This consists of from three to five people who may exercise supervision over the trustee.

The trustee must then distribute the property among the creditors according to the rules of bankruptcy. For this purpose he, of course, has full powers over the property, including the power of sale. He also has a right to "disclaim" onerous property within a limited time. For instance, if the bankrupt held partly paid shares in a company the trustee may disclaim them.

The court concerned with bankruptcy proceedings is either the Chancery Division of the High Court or a County Court. Jurisdiction in any particular case depends upon the place of residence of the debtor during the six months preceding the presentation of the petition. Not all County Courts have bankruptcy jurisdiction.

B ACTS OF BANKRUPTCY

Bankruptcy proceedings can only be started if the debtor has committed an "act of bankruptcy". The following are recognized "acts" (B.A., s. 1 (1) (*a*) to (*h*)).

(i) Certain *personal* acts done with intent to defeat or delay creditors. Examples are leaving England, remaining away from England, departing from a dwelling-house, or absence in any form, with intent to deprive creditors of their rights.

(ii) Certain dealings with *property*. (*a*) Making a conveyance of the whole of his property, or of substantially the whole of it, to a trustee for the benefit of creditors generally. Of course only such creditors as have not assented to this conveyance may generally rely upon it as an act of bankruptcy; these creditors clearly *may* because the act deprives part of his property. There need not be an actual intent to defraud in this case. Thus if a man, who has already been lent money, conveys a large part of his property as security for the *existing* debt to the same lender, this will be a fraudulent conveyance. It would not, however, be fraudulent if it were made in good faith to secure a present or future advance. (*c*) Doing any act which would amount to a *"fraudulent preference"* if he were adjudged bankrupt (see below). (*d*) Doing certain acts showing *insolvency*. E.g. himself filing a bankruptcy petition, or giving notice to his creditors that he intends to suspend payment of his debts.

(iii) Failure to comply with a *bankruptcy notice*. Shortly, this means that he has failed to comply with a notice, served on him by the creditor, to pay a judgment debt. It is the commonest act of bankruptcy.

C THE EFFECTS OF BANKRUPTCY

The general effect of *adjudication* in bankruptcy is that the bankrupt's property becomes vested in the trustee, for proportionate distribution among the creditors. We must therefore explain what property is available to the trustee in bankruptcy and then consider how it must be distributed.

(a) The property available

This comprises everything which the bankrupt has at the *commencement* of the bankruptcy and everything acquired between commencement and discharge. The "commencement" is not the date of adjudication, which for this purpose *"relates back"* to the date of the *act of bankruptcy* upon which the petition is based. Where more than one act has been proved the bankruptcy commences on the date of the *first* of the acts of bankruptcy proved to have been committed within *three months* preceding the presentation of the petition.

To this general rule there are certain exceptions: for on the one hand some kinds of property are *exempt* from the bankruptcy, and on the other hand some kinds of property are included which are not strictly the bankrupt's.

Exempted property. (i) The B.A. contains provisions designed to validate transactions prior to the receiving order. For instance, where, between the date of the act of bankruptcy and of the receiving order, the bankrupt pays a creditor or conveys property for value to a third party, the transactions will – provided that the person who dealt with the bankrupt acts in good faith and has no notice that an act of bankruptcy has been committed – be valid: and the property concerned cannot be claimed by the trustee. (ii) The Act provides that the bankrupt shall be permitted to retain personal effects, such as clothes for himself or his family to the value of £20; and he is also entitled to retain so much of his earnings as are necessary for his support and theirs. (iii) No property held by the bankrupt as a trustee is available. (iv) Nor are certain benefits under the National Insurance Acts. (v) Government and service pay are exempt unless the court orders otherwise. (vi) Claims for damages relating to personal torts do not pass.

Property specially included. Two matters must be mentioned under this head, the doctrine of *"reputed ownerhsip"* and voidable transactions.

(i) *Reputed Ownership.* By s. 38 of the B.A. the trustee is entitled to any goods which the bankrupt has in his "possession, order or disposition" at the commencement of the bankruptcy, provided that they are goods which he uses for the purposes of his *trade or business*. This rule usually applies to the goods of other people who have consented to leave them with the bankrupt for the above purposes. The reason is that the true owner, by his act, "holds out" the bankrupt as a man of greater substance than he really is, thus encouraging other people to give him unwarranted credit as "reputed owner".

(ii) *Voidable transactions.* Various classes of transactions effected by a debtor, even before he commits an act of bankruptcy, are voidable by the trustee. The transactions in question are, broadly speaking, of two classes: transactions, such as voluntary conveyances, which tend to defraud creditors generally, and *fraudulent preferences*. The law relating to transactions of the former class is somewhat complicated and is not suitable for discussion here: fraudulent preferences must, however, be mentioned.

A person commits a fraudulent preference when, being unable to pay his debts in full, he transfers property to one of his creditors with a view to giving such creditor a preference over other creditors. For example, A has property worth £2,000. He owes £3,000 in all. He pays B, a creditor friend, £700 which he owes him. He does this in order to ensure that B will get his full £700 and will not have to have his share abated, with those of the other creditors, should he (A) be made bankrupt. This is a fraudulent preference. The effect of it will be that, provided that the payment was made within six months of the presentation of a bankruptcy petition against A, A's trustee in bankruptcy may avoid the transaction and claim the money for the benefit of the creditors generally.

(b) The distribution

The main function of the trustee, after paying certain costs and expenses – such as his own and the official receiver's remuneration – is to distribute the bankrupt's property among all the creditors who prove their debts, if need be proportionately according to the size of their claims; though there are certain *"preferred"* and certain *"deferred"* classes of debts. Any kind of debt may in general be *provable*; but there are exceptions such as claims (like tort claims) for unliquidated damages, debts contracted by the debtor after the creditor knows of the act of bankruptcy, debts contracted after the receiving order, and debts the value of which cannot be estimated.

Preferred Debts. One debt is preferred to all others and is payable in full without regard to other claims: that is the right of a personal representative of a deceased debtor to reimbursement of the debtor's funeral and testamentary expenses paid by him. Other preferred debts must be paid in full in priority to other debts of the bankrupt unless the assets are insufficient to meet them: in which case they must abate proportionately among themselves. Preferred debts include rates and taxes, salaries or wages of any clerk, servant or workman in respect of services rendered to the bankrupt during four months preceding the receiving order and insurance contributions (whether private or national) payable by the bankrupt during twelve months before the date of the receiving order. It may also be of interest that the trustee has a discretion to return to an apprentice or articled clerk who has been serving with the bankrupt so much of his fee or premium (if in these days any) as the trustee may deem reasonable.

Deferred debts. At the other end of the scale there are certain *deferred* debts which are postponed by statute until *all* other creditors have been fully satisfied (*i.e.* paid in *full*)). These are, amongst others, loans between husband and wife made for business purposes and claims to interest *in excess* of 5 per cent (*i.e.* up to 5 per cent is provable as an ordinary unpreferred debt). It may be added that logically enough, one partner cannot in general prove in with the other creditors against another partner – for the other partner's debt is his own partnership debt.

Secured Creditors. It must also be added that secured creditors (*i.e.* creditors who hold a mortgage, charge or lien on the debtor's property as security for a debt due from the debtor) are in a peculiar position because, to the extent of their security, they have an advantage over the other creditors. They need not, of course, "prove" and may simply rely upon their security; but if they do prove, then the fact that they have the security must be taken into account. This means that the secured creditor will then have a choice *either* to *surrender* his security and prove for his debt, *or* to *realize* the security and prove for any surplus deficiency after realization; *or* he may (subject to the trustee's right to redeem it) *assess the value* of the security and prove for any deficit.

D DISCHARGE

Once the public examination has been concluded a bankrupt may at any time apply to the court for his "discharge". The court may grant or refuse the application. If a discharge is granted it may be unconditional or conditional. Unconditional discharge frees the bankrupt from all provable debts and liabilities; but not from unprovable liabilities, such as claims for unliquidated damages; nor from certain other specified liabilities, such as debts incurred by fraud. The bankrupt is thus given, more or less, a clean start.

The court may, however, suspend discharge, and may, and in some cases must, grant a merely conditional discharge. For instance, where a bankruptcy offence has been committed the discharge must be suspended until certain specified conditions are fulfilled, *e.g.* that the bankrupt has paid a dividend of not less than 50p in the pound to the creditors. There are numerous "bankruptcy offences". The most important offence is that it is a misdemeanour for an undischarged bankrupt to obtain credit for any sum exceeding £10 unless he discloses to the lender the fact that he is an undischarged bankrupt.

As a general rule bankrupts are prohibited from sitting in either House of Parliament within five years of adjudication. They may not, moreover, be *elected* to the House of Commons within this period. They are also prohibited from holding certain public offices, *e.g.* from acting as justices of the peace.

E COMPOSITIONS AND DEEDS OF ARRANGEMENT

It is always open to a debtor who wishes to avoid bankruptcy to make a "composition" or "scheme of arrangement" with his creditors, *i.e.* to obtain their agreement to accept so much in the pound. If a debtor wishes to propose a composition during bankruptcy proceedings he must submit a scheme to the official receiver within four days of submitting his statement of affairs. A majority of the creditors (representing three-fourths in value) who have proved in the bankruptcy must then approve the scheme. The approval of the court must also be obtained; though this cannot be granted until after the close of the public examination. It is also possible for the debtor to submit a scheme, subject to similar approvals, after adjudication. An approved scheme binds all creditors who have provable debts.

Compositions, and various other forms of arrangement, may also be made quite apart from bankruptcy proceedings. In this case, however, if the scheme is in writing and is for the benefit of creditors generally (or, where the debtor is insolvent, is for the benefit of three or more creditors), the document containing the scheme will form a "deed of arrangement". The Deeds of Arrangement Act 1914 provides that deeds of arrangement will be void unless they are registered with the Department of Trade within seven days of execution. The Act also prescribes certain other rules in respect of deeds of arrangement which are not suitable for discussion in a work of this nature.

of attempt to settle the controversy. It is for equity to act with the Prayer...
...it is clear that even the old remedies. The Act also prescribes...
...everything relating to the ... in which ... ... in its own...
... ... decisions in favour of the ...

PART IV
REVENUE LAW

SUMMARY OF PART IV

CHAPTER 14

REVENUE LAW

In Britain there are many taxes each with its own rules. Some have out-lived their usefulness and others have complexities which seem to be no longer necessary. Nevertheless, even if a new system were to be designed, it would need many branches, as taxes exist for a variety of reasons and there must be a compromise between conflicting objectives.

The primary purpose of taxation is to finance government expendi-ture, that is to divide the national income between the public and private sectors. This requires taxation of the whole community, whether rich or poor, because there must be a transfer of real income from the indivi-dual to the state. It is not enough to consider this transfer in money terms alone. If it were, then there would be no need for taxation since a govern-ment can create money. It is the taking away of spending power from private individuals and companies that is important. Moreover, these must include those who would have used this power to spend. It has become more difficult to achieve this objective in recent years. As tax rates have increased so have individuals tended to look at their take-home pay and to demand rises which take taxation into account. This trend is inflationary for there are no resources for the state to use if the private citizen succeeds in passing on the burden of his taxation.

A second purpose of taxation is to regulate the general state of the economy. Thus in times of industrial depression a government may reduce taxation so as to release additional consumer demand and stimu-late the economy. If there is too much demand then an increase in taxa-tion should help to restore equilibrium. Taxes with this objective must also extend to the whole population and cannot be confined to the wealthy, although the tax rates may take account of ability to pay. In this area taxation is also one of the factors which affect the balance of trade with other countries.

Social objectives provide a third purpose for taxation which may be introduced to encourage investment or to discourage some supposed evil such as smoking. Commonly an object is to secure a more equal distribu-tion of wealth throughout the community and taxing the wealthy also

451

makes the burden of the poorer sectors of the population fairer and more acceptable to them. Taxes of this kind will be progressive, that is the tax rate will increase for the wealthier taxpayer. Other taxes may be proportional, without any change of rate, or may even be regressive. For example, with a tax such as that on tobacco a poor man who smokes spends a greater proportion of his income on tobacco tax than does a wealthy smoker.

Taxes may be on expenditure, on income or on capital. Those on expenditure are known as "indirect" because they are not assessed directly on the ultimate taxpayer. The taxes on capital and income are known as "direct" taxes since they are directly assessed although indirect means may be used for their collection.

The legal framework of taxation in Britain is statutory. The general terms of a tax are set out in a permanent act, often supplemented by statutory instruments. The authority to collect the tax and the tax rates are, however, commonly not in the general act but authorized by Parliament in annual Finance Acts. The Provisional Collection of Taxes Act 1968 then gives legal effect to tax rates fixed by the House of Commons in a budget resolution provided that a finance bill is introduced and passed within certain time limits.

Tax legislation consists first of *charging* provisions. It is the duty of the tax authority to establish that a particular transaction falls within the terms of an appropriate charging provision to claim payment at all. There are then *computation* provisions to show how the amount of the tax is calculated and when and how it is to be paid. Finally, there may be *exemptions* or other provisions favourable to the taxpayer. *He* has the burden of proving that his circumstances fall within these.

There is no equity in a taxing statute. This means that a judge has no discretion to mitigate hardship which is unforeseen by the legislature. His task is to interpret the statute and normally the wording is applied strictly in its literal sense.

The law permits a taxpayer so to arrange his affairs as to reduce his tax liability. If there is a choice between two ways of arranging a transaction frequently they will receive different tax treatment. Sometimes this permits a taxpayer to choose between two taxes and, occasionally, he may avoid tax altogether. Such action is known as "tax planning" and this is encouraged by the existence of anti-avoidance legislation which can set up tax traps. An ethical problem arises where artificial transactions are created simply for tax avoidance reasons. They are not illegal unless they conceal the true facts or furnish the revenue authority with false information. Illegal activity of this kind is known as "tax evasion".

The rigidity of the tax legislation is mitigated to some extent by "extra-statutory concessions". The Commissioners of Inland Revenue publish a list of such concessions where, as a matter of policy, they do not enforce the law to its fullest extent.

TAXES ON EXPENDITURE

Nearly half of British tax revenue is from the indirect taxes on expenditure administered by the Commissioners of Customs and Excise. In terms of yield the taxes on alcoholic beverages, on petroleum products and on tobacco stand out. A tax with a more interesting legal background is Value Added Tax (VAT), and this provides a good example of a tax of this type.

VAT was selected by the members of the European Economic Community as their standard expenditure tax and Britain would have been obliged to adopt it if it had not already done so. The tax has also proved attractive to many countries outside the EEC. It is claimed to be neutral in its economic effect. It does not favour any particular way of organizing industry and it does not distort free competition. A full tax refund is given on exports and a full tax charge is made on imports and they are consequently placed on the same basis as home production. As a tax with a broad base on a large number of transactions and with relatively low rates it is a good economic regulator and efficient as a revenue producer. It has a "self-policing" element in that businessmen can frequently secure an advantage to themselves by ensuring that their suppliers have paid tax. On the other hand it is administratively cumbersome and it may be regressive because the poorer sections of the community are likely to spend a larger proportion of their resources on taxable transactions. In Britain this latter effect is mitigated by the existence of a "zero-rate" of tax on food and some other essentials and by the existence of a higher rate of tax on some luxuries. Britain is the only member state of the EEC whose VAT system incorporates a zero-rate and this may cause problems since there is a long term policy to harmonize VAT within the EEC so as to remove tax frontiers. It is also intended to provide the EEC with financial resources of its own and as part of this policy ultimately the first 1% rate of this tax will be paid direct to the EEC.

The charge to VAT is found in s. 2 of the Finance Act 1972. The tax is payable –

(1) *On the supply of goods and services in the U.K. where –*
  (a) *The supply is a taxable supply: and*
  (b) *The goods or services are supplied by a taxable person in the course of a business carried on by him.*

(2) *On the importation of goods (but not services) where the tax shall be charged and payable as if it were a customs duty.*

The tax is paid by the person supplying the goods or services and the Act gives him no right to reclaim the tax from his customer. This must be a matter for the contract between the supplier and the customer. If the tax rate is increased then a right is given for the supplier to recover the increase from the customer. If the supplier gives goods away he must still pay the tax on them but services may be supplied free without incurring any tax liability.

Many of the words and phrases in the charging section are defined in the Act and do not bear their ordinary meaning. For example, a "business" includes any trade, profession or vocation and also the charging of fees for admission to any premises, subscriptions to any club or organization except a trade union and the charging for facilities by clubs and associations. A "taxable person", who has to register with the Commissioners of Customs and Excise, is a trader with an annual turnover exceeding £5,000 (or proportionate quarterly turnover) unless the particular trade is exempt.

If an activity comes within the charge to tax it is necessary to examine the computation provisions to discover how the tax is to be calculated and paid. Usually a trader must every three months make a return showing the total tax on his sales turnover. This is his "output" tax. He also shows the total tax paid on his purchases. This is his "input" tax. If the output tax on his sales exceeds the input tax on his purchases he pays the excess to the VAT office. If purchases exceed sales a refund may be claimed or the excess may be carried forward. The effect is that over a period a trader will pay VAT at the appropriate rates on his gross profit or the value added by him to his product. The input tax cannot be reclaimed in respect of expenditure on business entertainment. The ultimate consumer of goods or services will bear the tax in full, for he is not in a position to reclaim anything. The price he pays will include tax at the appropriate rate. This will not have been paid to the VAT office in a lump sum but by each of the suppliers through whose hands the product has passed paying the tax on his mark-up.

The time of supply will decide when the tax has to be included by a trader in his return and the Act has detailed rules to determine this.

A supply of goods or services cannot be cancelled because the customer does not pay; and thus a trader who is not paid will lose not only the amount of the bad debt itself but also the tax on it.

The rate of VAT is fixed in the annual Finance Acts. At present there is the zero-rate on essentials, a standard rate and a higher rate on luxuries. There is authority for the Chancellor to vary these rates by up to 25% as an economic regulator. A trader who deals in supplies which carry tax at different rates must choose one from a number of schemes to ensure that the full amount of tax is paid at the appropriate rates. For example, a trader may have separate departments each restricted to goods in one tax group, or he may have a separate till for each tax rate. As a third alternative he may apportion his total turnover in proportion to his purchases of goods in each tax category.

The most favourable category is to be zero-rated and Schedule 4 of the Act lists the goods which are given this treatment. Not only is there no tax payable on the supply but any input tax paid on purchases may be reclaimed. This applies (*inter alia*) to food, books, newspapers, fuel, the construction but not the repair of buildings, the transport of passengers and goods and the supply of medicines on prescription. The zero-rate for food does not extend to food supplied in the course of catering nor to certain categories such as chocolates, sweets, ice cream and manufactured beverages.

Schedule 5 lists supplies which are exempt from tax. This is less favourable than a zero-rate. The supply itself bears no tax but the input tax paid on purchases related to the exempt supplies cannot be reclaimed. Exempt transactions include sales and leases of land, insurance, postal services, finance and banking, education in schools and universities, health services and burial and cremation. A trader in exempt supplies may avoid tax by supplying himself. For example, a bank pays tax on a solicitors' bill if it employs outside solicitors but not on the salaries of its own legal department. Since this could lead to abuse orders can be made which make such self-supplies subject to tax. Such an order has been made for stationery and printing. If a trader's business is partially exempt then the proportion of his exempt turnover must be calculated and the same proportion of his input tax on purchases will be disallowed as a deduction.

Public authorities, but not charities, are put in the same position as if they had been zero-rated for their non-business activities such as welfare and education. Although charitable bodies generally receive no special treatment there is a zero-rating for charity shops run by charities established primarily for the relief of distress and also a zero-rating for the export of any goods by a charity. This puts them in the same position as traders who can generally reclaim VAT paid on goods which they export.

There are special rules for a dealer who sells second-hand cars, motor cycles, caravans, works of art, antiques or scientific collections. If he buys such items from a private person there will be no input tax on his purchase which he can reclaim and VAT would be payable when he sells on the full price. The special scheme for these items consequently provides that the dealer only has to charge VAT on his mark-up and not on the full sale price. In the case of other second-hand goods there is no such concession and here the United Kingdom provisions are more severe than EEC proposals. In Britain there is an element of double taxation because VAT may well have been paid on the goods when new, but no credit is available for this.

For imported goods there is a system of bonded warehouses, which also applies to customs duties. The goods may be stored under the supervision of the Commissioners of Customs and Excise and tax need only be paid when the goods are removed from the warehouse.

The administration of VAT is through a central office and local offices throughout the country. The Commissioners have wide powers which they exercise through these offices. They can call for returns and for the production of records and other documents. They have the power to enter and to search premises and to take samples. If returns appear to be incomplete or incorrect the Commissioners may make estimated assessments. They can require a trader to give security as a condition of his supplying goods and services.

Any tax due may be recovered by the Commissioners as a civil debt and they also have a power to levy distress on the goods and chattels of any person refusing or neglecting to pay tax.

There are many criminal offences created to support the tax authority. For example, it is a crime to be knowingly concerned in the fraudulent evasion of tax or to supply false information to the Commissioners.

Local VAT tribunals have been set up to resolve disputes relating to the tax. There is an appeal to the High Court from such tribunals but only on points of law. An examination of some of the reported decisions will indicate the legal problems which arise. Perhaps the most common type of case concerns the classification of goods. A typical decision was that in *Customs and Excise Commissioners* v. *Blackpool Pleasure Beach Co.*, [1974] 1 All E.R. 1011 that a ride on a coaster train was not a zero-rated supply of transport because that must involve the moving of persons or goods from one place to another. In *Carlton Lodge Club* v. *Commissioners of Customs and Excise*, [1974] 3 All E.R. 798 there was an unsuccessful attempt to escape the charge to tax altogether. It was decided that a supply of drinks in the bar of an unincorporated members' club is a taxable supply within the charging section notwithstanding the fact that such goods are legally the property of the members already. *Customs and Excise Commissioners* v. *Automobile Association*, [1974] 1 All E.R. 1257 decided that the AA members' subscription gives the right to a number of specific benefits. Some of these, such as the supply of publications, are zero-rated and the subscription must be apportioned. Tax is only due in respect of the part attributable to taxable supplies. A more difficult problem, not yet finally settled, is the position when a trader includes on his bill disbursements which would normally be exempt or zero-rated if supplied direct to the customer. It was decided in *Rowe and Maw* v. *Customs and Excise Commissioners*, [1975] 2 All E.R. 444 that a solicitor's travelling expenses included in his bill of costs was an expense to be included in the total bill to which VAT should be added as it was expenditure on a service supplied to the solicitor rather than the client. On the other hand it appears that a disbursement for stamp duty or for a rail ticket to be used by the client is made as agent and is not a supply by the solicitor to the client, so that no VAT is payable. The border-line between these two types of case is not yet clear. What is the position regarding postages? The Commissioners argue that these are a supply which should carry tax. If there is a postage and packing charge in one item then this interpretation could well be sustained. On the other hand if the disbursement is for postages alone is the supply not by the Post Office and still within the exemption?

TAXES ON CAPITAL AND INCOME

These, the direct taxes, are normally administered by the Commissioners of Inland Revenue, although some taxes on the development value of land have, in the past, been separately administered. The Inland Revenue has some central departments but most of its work is decentralized into local offices of the Inspectors of Taxes and the Collectors of Taxes. This separation, between *inspectors* who assess the taxes and *collectors* who receive the cash, is of long standing and was originally introduced as a precaution against dishonesty. More recently it has been suggested that physical separation is no longer necessary with modern methods of accounting and audit. The statutory authority for most of the administration of the Inland Revenue is consolidated in the Taxes Management Act 1970. This also provides for the General Commissioners and the Special Commissioners of Income Tax, to whom appeals lie from the decisions of the Inspectors of Taxes. There is an appeal on points of law only from the General and Special Commissioners to the High Court.

The Inland Revenue Commissioners have powers in many ways similar to those of the Commissioners of Customs and Excise, although in some instances the VAT legislation gives wider powers than does the Taxes Management Act. A taxpayer liable to pay income tax, capital gains tax or corporation tax has a duty to give notice that he is so liable. The Inland Revenue has a power to call for returns, make assessments, including estimated assessments, call for documents and accounts and there are provisions for the payment of interest on unpaid tax and for various penalties and criminal offences.

1 Income Tax

Introduced originally as a temporary tax to provide additional finance required during the Napoleonic Wars, income tax is now the largest revenue yielder of all the British taxes and is a permanent feature of the system. It was originally designed to be collected at low rates but has been modified over the years to incorporate high and progressive rates. This, with legislation to counter the efforts of the tax avoider, has led to greater complexity. Recently there have been successful attempts to modernize and simplify the system. The "unified" system, introduced by the Finance Act 1971, abolished surtax as a separate tax administered by a separate central surtax office, and there is now one income tax, incorporating the higher rates and investment income surcharge which replace surtax. This is administered by the local Inspectors of Taxes. There is room for further simplification in some areas.

The general legislation is consolidated in the Income and Corporation Taxes Act 1970, more commonly referred to as the Taxes Act. An attempt has been made to keep this up to date. Legislative changes are made, so far as possible, by amending the Taxes Act or by inserting additional or substituted sections in it. This method has not always proved possible and it is still necessary to look to the various annual finance acts. It is also necessary to look to the latest finance act to discover the rates of tax as parliamentary authority is only given for the collection of income tax on an annual basis.

The name income tax would indicate that this is a tax on income. Judicial recognition has been given to this fact and it is generally true, but there are instances where income tax is charged on a capital receipt and others where income may escape. To illustrate the difference between *capital* and *income* it is usual to apply the analogy of an orchard, where the trees represent the capital and the fruit the income. There is no statutory definition of income and no attempt to charge income tax on income generally. The system adopted is to charge particular types of income to tax under six "schedules". Liability to tax depends on whether or not a particular receipt falls within the wording of one of the charging sections creating these schedules. The reasons for this are historical. Originally the tax was only made to apply to some forms of income. Others have been added until it is difficult to discover income which falls outside any schedule. There is still development in this area. One of the basic forms of tax planning is to arrange one's affairs so that a cash receipt will be treated as capital and any profit charged to capital gains tax rather than income tax. The attraction is a lower tax rate. When the Commissioners of Inland Revenue find that some particular method is leading to a serious loss of tax they arrange for the introduction of anti-avoidance legislation and thereafter capital receipts of the particular type are brought within the charge to income tax. There will then be another tax trap for the unwary. An innocent taxpayer who has no desire to engage in tax avoidance may find that a perfectly normal capital receipt is caught and made subject to income tax at a high rate.

The income tax schedules are mutually exclusive and there is one schedule only appropriate to any receipt. Neither the Inland Revenue nor the taxpayer has any discretion as to which schedule shall apply, although the taxpayer may be able to arrange his affairs so that a receipt falls within the ambit of one schedule rather than another. For example, if commencing to trade he may form a company and be employed by it so as to be taxed under Schedule "E" or he may form a partnership so as to be taxed under Schedule "D". The appropriate schedule is discovered by tracing a receipt to its source and examining the nature of the source.

Each of the tax schedules has its own rules for the computation of the tax and for the time of payment. Sometimes, where the profit cannot be known until the financial year-end, the tax is not assessed until the following tax year. This means that the Inland Revenue is this year collecting tax on last year's profits and they refer to this situation as a "preceding year basis". More commonly there is a "current year basis" where tax is paid in the same year as the taxpayer makes his profit or receives the taxable payment.

It was decided in *Mitchell and Edon* v. *Ross*, [1962] A.C. 814; [1961] 3 All E.R. 49 that a taxpayer with income falling into more than one schedule must keep separate his expenses relating to the various sources of income. The expenses attach to the income to which they relate and, for income tax purposes, may only be deducted if the rules of the appropriate income tax schedule allow this.

THE INCOME TAX SCHEDULES

Schedule A: income from land
Rents and other income from land are charged under this schedule on a current year basis. This may seem strange because there may be repairs and other expenses to be deducted which cannot be ascertained until the end of the year. Formerly Schedule A depended on a valuation of the land rather than the calculation of a profit so that there was no reason why a current year basis was not appropriate. When the present system was adopted special arrangements were necessary to avoid the loss of

one year's tax to the Treasury. The legislation provides for a provisional assessment to be made at the beginning of the calendar year based on the previous tax year's figures. This is then adjusted at the end of the year if necessary. In practice current delays often mean that the initial assessment is not prepared until the true figures are available.

The charge is specifically extended to premiums payable by leases for terms not exceeding fifty years. This is an instance of a capital payment which is made subject to income tax. The charging section also provides that the tax shall be calculated by reference to the receipts to which the taxpayer is entitled and not those he actually receives. If rent is not received he can claim relief from tax only if all reasonable steps have been taken to secure payment or if the payment has been waived without consideration and the waiver was made reasonably to avoid hardship. There is no attempt nowadays to tax owner-occupiers under Schedule A. Income from furnished lettings is not normally charged under this Schedule but the taxpayer can elect that this shall be done.

There are quite complicated rules to determine which expenses may be deducted from rent and when expenses for one property may be deducted from the rent received for another. These are set out in ss. 72 to 74 of the Taxes Act.

Schedule B: income from woodlands

At one time this Schedule applied to all farming activities. Now it applies to the occupation of woodlands managed on a commercial basis and with a view to the realization of profits.

The effect is to give a favourable treatment to woodlands which would otherwise be unattractive as an investment due to the long period when they have to be kept up without any income return. The tax under this Schedule is on a notional value which is favourable when income is coming in. Taxpayers may elect to be taxed under Schedule D Case I when they are in a position to set-off the cost of the woodland against other income and so secure tax relief.

Schedule C: income from government securities

This Schedule extends to securities of foreign governments and public authorities as well as British ones, if the payment is made through an agent resident in the U.K. The charge does not extend to foreign stocks held by non-residents and British securities may be exempted if held by foreign residents. Some British investments such as $3\frac{1}{2}\%$ War Stock, National Savings Certificates and Defence Bonds, are excluded even if held by British residents. If they are liable to pay income tax it is then collected under Schedule D, Case III, but the exclusion provides a convenient investment for charities and those with low incomes who are not liable to tax at all.

Under Schedule C the paying agent is required to deduct income tax at the basic rate from the dividend at the time of payment. The tax deducted is then paid to the Inland Revenue. There are no provisions for the deduction of expenses under this Schedule. If a holder of securities is not liable to pay the tax he has to reclaim it from his own Inspector of Taxes.

Schedule D:

Schedule D is divided into six cases. If there is an overlap the Inland Revenue can choose which case to apply.

Cases I and II: income from a trade, profession or vocation.

Case I charges to tax the income of a United Kingdom resident in respect of any trade carried on anywhere in the world, including farming and market gardening. Case II applies to the income from any profession or vocation not contained in any other schedule. The same principles apply to both except that although "profession" and "vocation" have their ordinary meaning "trade" is defined to include "any adventure in the nature of trade". This means that Case I applies to a single isolated transaction. Whether a particular activity amounts to trading or to the exercise of a profession or vocation is a question of fact, although the application of the facts and the appreciation of their nature is a question of law. There have been many tax appeals on this topic. The subject is complex but one can say that a number of factors, such as profit motive and the skill of the person concerned, are regarded as "badges of trade". The more badges of trade there are present the more likely there is to be a finding of trading.

Trading and professional income is charged to tax on a preceding year basis so that the tax in any fiscal year is calculated on the profits in the previous fiscal year. There are special arrangements to calculate the tax for the opening and closing years of any trading activity.

A number of restrictions apply to the deduction of expenses from profits charged under Cases I and II.

Firstly, the taxpayer must show that the expense is of a revenue and not a capital nature. A recurrent payment is likely to be deductible whilst a once for all payment is more likely to be classified as of a capital nature, particularly if some permanent asset remains as a result of the expenditure.

Secondly, the expense must not be disallowed by section 130 of the Taxes Act. This section excludes a number of specific items but also establishes a general test that to be tax deductible any expenditure must be *wholly and exclusively* laid out for the purpose of the trade, profession or vocation. If there is a private benefit then that particular expense will be disallowed because it fails this test. The cost of travelling to work is an example of expenditure which is excluded, unless it can be established that the work commenced at home.

Finally, the expense must not be the cost of business entertainment unless it falls within certain minor exceptions of which the only important one is that the reasonable cost of entertaining an overseas customer is permitted as a tax deduction.

No deduction is allowed for the depreciation of machinery or other capital assets. Instead the taxpayer may deduct for tax purposes capital allowances when he buys new items. These are calculated in accordance with rules set out in the Capital Allowances Act 1968. The actual taxable income is calculated by first taking away from the gross profit the allowable deductions. Generally an "earnings basis" is employed and this means that further adjustments have to be made to allow for the value of "work in progress" and outstanding accounts. There must also be adjustments to allow for changes over the year in the amount or value of the trading stock.

Case III: "pure income".

This case charges to tax interest, whether yearly or otherwise, and also annuities and other annual payments. A Case III assessment is most commonly made for loan interest or for dividends from those government stocks specifically excluded from Schedule C.

An assessment is not usually necessary for annuities and annual payments as here the income tax is usually collected at source. The person making the payment has to deduct tax at the basic rate from it. If the payment is being made out of income which has already paid income tax the payer is entitled to a tax refund and this is given by allowing him to retain the tax he deducts. If the payment is not made out of taxed income no tax refund is due and the tax deducted must be paid to the Inland Revenue. This system no longer applies to payments of interest unless the payment is being made by a company or local authority, except in a fiduciary capacity, or where the payment is made by or on behalf of a partnership of which a company is a member or where the payment is made to a person resident outside the U.K. The Inspector of Taxes needs to verify claims for the deduction of interest by a taxpayer as this is now restricted. In the case of the first two exceptions the system of deduction is applied as it fits in with the system of Corporation Tax. Deduction is necessary when money is being sent abroad to prevent a loss of revenue. One country does not enforce the fiscal claims of another so that tax is lost if money is allowed to leave the country without the tax being collected first.

Payments made under *Deeds of Covenant* are annual payments within the scope of Case III. A Deed of Covenant is a transfer of income from a donor to a donee which has legal effect, even though there is no consideration, due to the form of the deed. Such a transfer means that the donor's income is reduced and the donee's income is increased by the gross amount transferred. Tax is deducted from the payment and so long as this is made from taxed income may be retained to obtain the tax refund which is due to the donor. For the transfer to be of benefit the donee must be a charity or other non-taxpayer. A non-taxpayer may claim a refund of the tax from the Inland Revenue. The tax refunded is the original tax paid by the donor.

Deeds of Covenant were misused and anti-avoidance provisions now apply. The deed can only operate in respect of tax at the basic rate and the income is not transferred from the donor for the purposes of tax at higher rate or for investment income surcharge. A deed cannot operate in favour of the children of the donor and it must not be revocable, nor must the donor receive any benefit in exchange for the payment. The deed must also be for a period which may exceed six years. The usual period is for seven years although the deed may provide for termination on the death of either the donor or the donee.

A life annuity purchased by a taxpayer for his own benefit is another example of an annuity within Case III. These are usually bought on retirement and they receive favourable treatment. Each payment of the annuity really consists of part interest and part a refund of the original capital, the proportion of the two parts depending on the age of the purchaser at the date of purchase. Relief from income tax is given on the capital element as determined by the legislature. Tax is paid on the income element. This treatment is not given to annuities paid under a superannuation scheme as tax relief will already have been given in that case.

Cases IV and V: income from foreign property.

Case IV applies to income from foreign securities not already taxed under Schedule C. Case V applies to income from foreign possessions. For both cases the assessment is on the basis of the income preceding the year of assessment. British residents are liable to pay tax on the whole of their income under both cases. Persons not domiciled nor ordinarily resident here are only taxed on their remittances of such income to the U.K.

Emoluments of foreign offices and employments were formerly assessed under Case V but are now taxed under Schedule E instead.

Case VI: other income.

This charges to tax any annual profits or gains not falling within the scope of any other Case of Schedule D. Casual earnings are subject to this charge as are the rents from furnished lettings unless the landlord elects for these to be taxed under Schedule A within two years of the end of the year of assessment.

Case VI is frequently the method of charging tax under anti-avoidance provisions.

The tax is normally charged on income for the current year but the Inspector of Taxes may direct that some other basis is used. There are no express provisions relating to the deductions which may be permitted. Generally expenses of an income nature incurred in making the profit will be allowed. Losses arising in respect of income which would be charged under Case VI can only be allowed as a deduction from Case VI profits and not from any other income.

At the time of writing profits on development gains of land are charged under Case VI. This charge seems likely to be replaced for an interim period by a new separate development land tax. Ultimately it is intended that there will be no tax for such gains as land will always be purchased for development by local authorities at a price which yields no development gain to the seller.

Schedule E: income from offices, employments and pensions.

This charge applies to emoluments arising from offices and employments and to pensions. There are three "cases" which relate not to the type of income but to the foreign element involved.

Case I covers the ordinary taxpayer who is both resident and ordinarily resident in the U.K. All his earnings are taxable except that for work performed wholly out of the U.K. during a continuous period of absence, a proportion is tax free. This proportion depends on the length of the period abroad and on other conditions in Schedule 2 of the Finance Act 1974.

Case II applies to emoluments of those either not resident or not ordinarily resident in the U.K. Their earnings are subject to deductions set out in the same Schedule 2.

Case III brings into charge earnings remitted to Britain by British residents which have escaped tax under the other two Cases.

An "office" includes judicial appointments, company directorships, company registrarships and the like. An "employment" involves a contract of service and there is the same distinction as occurs in other branches of the law between an employee and a self-employed person.

An "emolument" includes anything of money value, whether in cash or kind, so long as it flows from the office or employment.

There are strict rules to govern the expenses which may be deducted from emoluments for tax purposes. These are similar to those for Schedule D, Cases I and II but expenditure must not only be *wholly and exclusively* but must also be *necessarily* incurred. This cuts out any claim for an item which is desirable but not essential. There are, however, some concessions which permit, for certain industries, claims for protective clothing and tools provided by the employee. The subscriptions to certain professional bodies and institutions may also be deducted.

By concession some receipts are not treated as emoluments. The two best known are luncheon vouchers and the "concessionary" coal received by a coal miner. The benefit of an approved superannuation scheme is also not taxed as an emolument, although the pension which ultimately arises under such a scheme is Schedule E income.

A "golden handshake" given to an employee on leaving, or damages for wrongful dismissal are tax-free up to the first £5,000 but any excess over this sum is taxed under a complicated formula. This provision also applies to damages received in connection with the termination of an office or employment from a person other than the employer and this causes some difficulties. The provision does not apply to damages for personal injuries. It is clear from the decision in *British Transport Commission* v. *Gourley*, [1956] A.C. 185; [1955] 3 All E.R. 796 that a judge must take tax liability into account when assessing damages. It is far from clear how this principle is to be applied to the benefit of the £5,000 tax free payment.

Income subject to Schedule E is assessed in the year in which it is received. The tax is collected by the employer under the "Pay As You Earn" scheme and he pays it to the Collector of Taxes.

Schedule F: some company dividends.

Prior to the introduction of the imputation system of Corporation Tax in 1973, Schedule F was the usual method for collecting the income tax on company dividends. Now dividends are not normally subject to income tax and the Schedule has lost much of its importance. It now applies only to special kinds of company distribution where there is still a liability to income tax.

THE INCOME TAX COMPUTATION

An income tax computation is made on an annual basis for the fiscal year ending on April 5th. First it is necessary to add together the income assessable under each Schedule. In each case the appropriate deductions will have been made. The result is the "total income" for the tax year. From this "charges on income" are deducted. The charges include loan interest, within the restrictions for such interest, contributions to approved superannuation and retirement annuity schemes and some trading losses. The next stage is to deduct the lump sums for reliefs and allowances to which the individual taxpayer is entitled and what remains is the taxable income. At present loan interest, apart from loans for appropriate business purposes which comply with the rules applicable to them, is only a tax deduction if the loan is made for the purchase or improvement of a house which is the taxpayer's only or main residence up to a maximum of £25,000, or, within the same maximum for a dependent relative. There are still some transitional provisions in force for loans incurred before March 26th, 1974.

The reliefs given in the form of a lump sum include a personal relief, increased for a married man, and reliefs for children, dependent relatives and blind persons and an age allowance for those aged 65 or more. If the taxpayer is in receipt of family allowances the total of reliefs is reduced by a "claw-back" for every family allowance. This provides a means test for the receipt of family allowances. There is a different method for life assurance relief so as to give this relief at the basic rate of tax only. The other reliefs give benefit from tax at all rates. Life assurance premiums, which meet various restrictions, secure tax relief by deducting from the final tax bill a proportion of the premium at the basic rate of tax.

The tax is calculated on the taxable income first at the basic rate. This is at present 35%. Income exceeding £4,500 per annum is taxed at higher rates ranging from 40% to 83%. Unearned income is subject to an investment income surcharge if it exceeds £1,000 per annum or £1,500 per annum for taxpayers aged 65 or more. The rates are 10% and 15% making a maximum tax rate for unearned income of 98%. In calculating the amount of investment income surcharge any allowable loan interest may be set-off first against the unearned income. The personal allowances have to be set-off first against any earned income, only the balance being available to reduce the investment income surcharge.

INCOME TAX OF MARRIED WOMEN

Normally a wife's income is added to that of her husband and he is assessed on the total. He receives an increased personal allowance and, if the wife is working, there is an additional allowance for her earnings. They are free of tax up to the amount of this allowance. There is a provision where a wife's income may be "separately assessed" to tax. This does not alter the total of income tax paid but the Inspector of Taxes divides the tax liability between the husband and wife. Another provision allows a husband and wife to be taxed as single persons as regards their earned income. The wife's unearned income is still added to that of the husband. He loses the additional personal relief for a married man and the additional allowance for the wife's earned income is also lost.

Instead husband and wife each receives the personal relief for a single person and for the calculation of income tax at the higher rates the earned income of husband and wife is not added together.

WEALTH TAX PROPOSALS

There are proposals to introduce an annual wealth tax which would be calculated at a percentage on total net wealth. There is a case for such a tax to prevent the avoidance of tax by investing in such a way that the investment produces no income but only an ultimate capital gain. Investments of this kind escape income tax at present. It would be possible to devise a wealth tax which achieved this object and which replaced the investment income surcharge. Present proposals are not in this form and the suggestion is for a tax additional to income tax. This would appear to introduce further unnecessary complications. The proposals are also controversial in so far as they would apply to the value of such assets as works of art.

2 Capital Gains Tax

This tax was introduced by the Finance Act 1965 which has been amended by subsequent finance acts. There has been no consolidation of the legislation. An earlier tax on "short-term" capital gains was abolished although traces of it still remain, notably in the provision that government securities are exempt from capital gains tax unless held for less than a year.

The tax is charged on the disposal of a chargeable asset. This may be an actual disposal by sale or gift or a "deemed" disposal. There are deemed disposals on the ending of a trust, when a capital sum, such as an insurance payment, is derived from an asset, and on the first letting of non-residential property. Transfers between husband and wife are not treated as disposals. At present there is generally no capital gains tax payable on the death of the owner of property. The beneficiaries who receive his property acquire it for capital gains tax purposes at the value it had at the date of death. The disposal of a part of property is treated as a disposal of the whole although special computation provisions apply. In a transaction where there is a contract followed later by a transfer or conveyance the date of the contract is normally the date of the disposal. A conditional contract operates when the condition is met.

Assessment is on an annual basis for the fiscal year ending on April 5th. For each transaction the chargeable gain or allowable loss is found by deducting the acquisition cost from the disposal price. The expenses of acquisition and disposal and any capital expenditure "wholly and exclusively" referable to the asset during the period of ownership are also deducted. If for any year the gains exceed the losses then tax is payable on the net gain. If the losses exceed the gains the net loss is carried forward and may be set off against gains in subsequent years. Tax already paid cannot be reclaimed except on the death of a taxpayer. Then losses in the year of death may be set off against gains in the previous three years and an appropriate repayment is made.

The rate of capital gains tax is normally 30% although there is an alternative lower rate for individuals but not for trusts. This applies when the total gains in any tax year do not exceed £5,000 and is calculated on one half of the gains at the taxpayer's highest rate of income tax for that year. For a taxpayer paying only basic rate income tax this means that the capital gains tax rate is effectively one half of the basic income tax rate. There are also special arrangements to tax gains realized by unit trusts and investment trusts, so as to avoid double taxation. They pay tax at half the basic rate of income tax and a credit is available at the same rate when the holder disposes of his holding. This means that the basic rate taxpayer will have his own tax liability met by the tax paid by the trust.

Capital gains are normally calculated by using the actual consideration of a transaction. The market value is applied, however, for gifts, in cases where the consideration cannot be valued and for transactions between "connected persons". Persons are connected if they are close relations and they may also be connected for this purpose through a trust, a company or a partnership.

When the tax was introduced on April 6th, 1965 it was not made retrospective in its operation. No tax is charged on gains arising prior to the date of introduction nor may losses be claimed. There are detailed rules to govern the operation of the tax in these situations.

Not all transactions are subject to capital gains tax. There is an annual exemption if the aggregate consideration for all the disposals of a taxpayer in one tax year does not exceed £500. There is "marginal relief" if this figure is exceeded by a small margin. There is a separate exemption for gifts if their total value does not exceed £100 in any tax year. Here there is no marginal relief.

Some types of property are excluded from taxation. These include motor cars, most government securities if held for one year or more, cash, including foreign exchange required for the taxpayer's personal use abroad, gambling wins and losses, life assurance policies unless they have been sold by the original owner, damages or compensation for personal loss or injury and decorations for valour unless acquired for valuable consideration.

A taxpayer is given exemption from capital gains tax for one private dwelling-house, including grounds of appropriate size, occupied by him as his only or main residence. There is also relief for one house provided for a dependent relative. If the taxpayer has more than one house for his own use then he can choose which is to have the benefit of the tax exemption within two years of owning more than one house. If he does not elect within that time limit the choice becomes that of the Inspector of Taxes. Although the exemption only applies during occupation by the taxpayer himself certain periods of absence are ignored. If a house is used partly for business purposes then this part will not have the benefit of the tax exemption.

If chattels are disposed of for £1,000 or less then the transaction is exempt from capital gains tax. Any number of separate items may be sold in any tax year except that if a number of items constitute a "set" they are treated as a single item if disposed of to one person or to connected persons. There is marginal relief for disposals just over £1,000. If there is a loss on the disposal of chattels for less than £1,000 then the tax loss is restricted to what it would be if the sale price had been £1,000.

There is exemption for disposals of works of art in certain circumstances, for gifts to the National Trust and other similar bodies and disposals by charities are exempt if the gain is applicable and is applied for charitable purposes.

A relief, known as "roll-over relief", is available when a business asset is sold and the proceeds used to buy another. Any capital gains tax due in respect of a profit on the sale of the first asset is postponed until the replacement asset is sold.

There is a retirement relief for the owner of a business or of shares in a family trading company. If he disposes of his interest when he has been the owner for at least the previous ten years and he is over the age of sixty then gains on the disposal are exempt to the extent of £4,000 for every year by which his age exceeds sixty up to a maximum of £20,000.

3 Corporation Tax

Corporation Tax was introduced by the Finance Act 1965 but the legislation is now consolidated into the Income and Corporation Taxes Act 1970 which has been amended by subsequent finance acts. The system was biased in favour of the retention of profits within a company but, since 1973, a new "imputation system" has removed this bias, and it is claimed that the tax is now neutral as regards encouraging or discouraging the distribution of profits.

Although the main application of the tax is to companies it also applies to any body corporate or unincorporated association as the definition of company is extended to include bodies of these kinds.

The rules of income tax are used to ascertain the taxable profit of a company and those of capital gains tax are applied to find the chargeable capital gains, but the tax is for the accounting year of the company and not for the fiscal year ending on April 5th. The tax rate is fixed by the budget at the end of the tax year for a tax year ending on March 31st and a company pays tax on its profits and gains at the rate or rates appropriate for the proportions of its accounting year falling in each tax year. A preferential rate of tax is charged to smaller companies.

If a company makes a profit it may make a distribution to its shareholders, a dividend. If it does so it must pay to the Collector of Taxes a payment equivalent to the basic rate of income tax on this distribution. This payment serves two purposes. Firstly it is a payment on account by the company of "Advance Corporation Tax". Secondly it is available to the shareholder as a credit against his own income tax. This "imputation" of the company's tax to the shareholder prevents, to the extent of tax at the basic income tax rate, the double taxation of the same profits both as profits of the company and as income of the shareholder. If the income of any shareholder exceeds the appropriate figures for any tax year he will pay "investment income surcharge" and "higher rate" income tax on the excess, as the imputation system only covers income tax at the basic rate. The company pays the remainder of its corporation tax at the end of the year.

The imputation system does not apply to chargeable capital gains and here there is still an element of double taxation. A company pays corporation tax on its gains (though at a reduced rate) and there is no provision for this to be available as a credit to shareholders. Consequently, a shareholder will either pay income tax on the gain if it is distributed or capital gains tax if he sells his shares and makes a profit on them.

There are special provisions applying to "close" companies. These are generally the family type of private company. There is a definition which refers to companies under the control of five or fewer "participators" or under the control of participators who are directors. Participators means not only shareholders but also loan creditors, including debenture holders other than banks. Directors include managers if they or their families own 20% or more of the voting capital of the company. There are complex provisions for such close companies but these only apply where there are shareholders who are liable to pay income tax at above the basic rate. If such a company does not distribute sufficient of its "relevant income" in any year of account the excess may be apportioned amongst its participators so that tax at the higher rates and investment income surcharge is payable as if a distribution had actually been made. The relevant income for this purpose is normally the whole of any investment income plus one half of any other income, but the level of distribution required may be reduced below this level by the Inspector of Taxes if he is satisfied that there is a good commercial reason for the company to retain a larger amount.

When a company pays a dividend to another company and has paid the appropriate advance corporation tax on this dividend so that a tax credit is available to the recipient, this is said to be "franked investment income" of the receiving company. It may be set-off against its own advance corporation tax due.

There are complicated provisions relating to the corporation tax of groups of companies, and also for the foreign income of companies.

4 Capital Transfer Tax

This is a combined gifts tax and death duty applying to lifetime gifts made after March 26th, 1975, to transfers on death occurring after March 12th, 1975 and also to some capital distributions made out of settled property and some special cases such as gifts made by close companies after March 26th, 1975. The legislation is found in the Finance Act 1975. The tax replaces estate duty after the commencement dates although some of the features of estate duty are retained.

There are two progressive scales of tax rates, a lower scale for lifetime gifts and a higher one which operates in the event of death. If the donor dies within three years of making a chargeable transfer then additional tax is payable to make up the difference between the two scales.

The donor is primarily liable for the tax on lifetime gifts. If he pays the tax the value of the gift is "grossed up", that is the tax is added to the value of the gift. The effect will often be to raise the tax into a higher band or bands in the scale. If the donee pays the tax then there is no grossing up and this can result in a saving of tax. It will for this reason be advantageous for the donee to pay the tax on a gift if he is in a position to do so.

The executors are generally liable for the payment of tax arising on death. The principle of grossing up does not apply here, as the duty is paid on the value of the whole estate at the date of death.

The progressive rates of tax are applied on a cumulative principle. From the commencement date of the tax there is first a tax free band of £15,000. When gifts have been made which aggregate to this sum further transfers are charged to tax at increasing rates.

The tax applies to the whole of the property, anywhere in the world, of a person domiciled or deemed to be domiciled in the U.K. The Act has provisions to deem certain persons who acquire a domicile in the Channel Islands or the Isle of Man as retaining a former British domicile for this purpose.

The value of a lifetime transfer is not the separate value of the property given but the loss to the donor's estate. This can be materially different if, for example, shares of little value in themselves are transferred and the result is that the donor ceases to have control of a company. The transfer would be charged on the value of the loss of control because the donor's estate would have lost this value as a result of the transfer. On death the position will be similar to that applying in the case of estate duty. The whole estate is valued, including the value of settled property passing on the death, and tax is paid on the whole amount.

Transfers between husband and wife are ignored completely for the purposes of capital transfer tax unless one of them is domiciled abroad.

There are a number of exemptions from the tax. The initial amount of £15,000 has been mentioned. In addition and not reducing the initial amount there is an exemption for transfers of up to £1,000 in value for each tax year ending April 5th. Also up to £100 may be given to any one person for each tax year. Gifts may also be made out of taxed income if made in the way of normal expenditure. The capital element of a purchased life annuity is not taxed income for this purpose. For expenditure to be normal there must be an element of regularity about it. Finally, gifts made in consideration of the marriage of the donee or to be settled on the spouses and their issue are exempt up to £5,000 in the event of a gift by a parent of those married, £2,500 for a gift by a grand-parent or great-grandparent or £1,000 in any other case.

Gifts to charities up to £100,000 are exempt if made on death or within a year of death. Gifts made more than a year before the death are exempt without limit. Gifts to political parties have the same treatment as those to charities. There is also exemption for some gifts for national purposes given to various national institutions or approved by the Treasury.

Special treatment is given to transfers of agricultural property by "working farmers".

Settled property is specially provided for and some of the provisions are difficult to understand. Generally, capital transfer tax will be payable when a settlement is created, on the loss to the donor's estate in making the gift, and again when a beneficiary obtains an absolute interest, on the value of his interest. If an interest in a settlement comes to an end the person concerned is treated as having made a chargeable transfer of the interest coming to an end. In the case of discretionary trusts and other trusts where there is no beneficiary with an interest in possession tax will be paid both on capital distributions to beneficiaries and periodically on the whole capital value of the trust. This is usually every ten years. There is an exemption in the case of Accumulation and Maintenance Settlements for beneficiaries not exceeding twenty-five years of age even though there is no beneficiary with an interest in possession.

There are various anti-avoidance provisions. For example, several transactions may be treated as "associated operations" and become for the purposes of the tax one single transaction.

A loan free of interest is to be treated as a chargeable transfer of the interest at the market rate after April 5th, 1976.

It must by now be all too obvious that taxation is a highly complex subject! This chapter has been confined to broad principles with a consequent omission of much detail leading to oversimplification. Taxation is a subject which of necessity concerns each individual and has the additional complication of economic and political involvement. This leads to constant change in both the principles and practice of tax law so that each situation must be individually studied.

INDEX

475

Printed in Great Britain by
Butler & Tanner Ltd, Frome and London